10 – Rudolf Hess flies to Scotland on personal peace mission
20 – Germany launches airborne assault against British-held Crete
24 – British battlecruiser *Hood* sunk by Germany's *Bismarck*
27 – *Bismarck* sunk; Roosevelt proclaims national emergency because of events in Europe and Africa

MAY
31 – Crete falls

JUNE
8 – British and Free French troops attack Syria
14 – Vichy French forces in Syria overcome by British
15 – British counteroffensive into Libya defeated
22 – Germany, Italy and Rumania declare war on Soviet Union; Germany invades Soviet Union
26 – Finland declares war on Soviet Union, followed by Hungary next day

JULY
12 – Britain and Soviet Union sign treaty assuring British aid to Soviets
14 – British complete occupation of Syria and Lebanon
24 – Japan occupies French Indochina
26 – U.S. halts trade with Japan

AUGUST
12 – Roosevelt and Churchill meet off Newfoundland and draw up Atlantic Charter
25 – British and Soviet troops enter Iran to secure oilfields

SEPTEMBER
8 – Germans lay siege to Leningrad
19 – Germans capture Kiev

OCTOBER
17 – Hideki Tojo becomes Prime Minister of Japan

NOVEMBER
8 – Germans move into Crimea
18 – British launch offensive in Libya

DECEMBER
5 – German drive on Moscow halted
7 – Japan bombs Pearl Harbor
8 – Japan declares war on U.S. and Britain; bombs Philippines, Wake Islands and Guam; invades Thailand, Malaya and Hong Kong
9 – Japan invades Gilbert Islands
10 – British relieve besieged garrison at Tobruk
11 – Germany and Italy declare war on U.S.; Japan invades Burma
16 – Japan invades Borneo
22 – Japan launches major offensive in Philippines
23 – Japan captures Wake Island
25 – Hong Kong surrenders

31 – Japan occupies Manila, capital of Philippines

1942

JANUARY
1 – Declaration of the United Nations signed by 26 nations in Washington, D.C.
11 – Japan invades Dutch East Indies
20 – Japan starts major offensive in Burma
21 – Rommel's Afrika Korps launches counteroffensive in Libya

FEBRUARY
1 – U.S. planes bomb Japanese bases in Marshall and Gilbert islands
15 – Singapore surrenders

MARCH
7 – Japanese enter Rangoon, capital of Burma
9 – Java surrenders
13 – Japanese land on Solomon Islands
17 – General MacArthur arrives in Australia from Philippines

APRIL
5 – Japanese aircraft raid Ceylon
9 – U.S. troops surrender on Bataan Peninsula, Philippines
18 – Doolittle air raid on Tokyo

MAY
7-8 – Battle of Coral Sea; Japanese fleet suffers first setback
6 – U.S. fortress of Corregidor falls; all U.S. forces in Philippines surrender
20 – Japanese complete conquest of Burma
26 – Afrika Korps goes on offensive in Libya
30 – RAF bombs Cologne, Germany

JUNE
4-6 – Battle of Midway; Japan's eastward thrust decisively halted
21 – Rommel captures Tobruk
24 – Eisenhower assumes command of all U.S. troops in Europe
25 – German troops victorious at Kharkov on Eastern Front

JULY
1 – Germans secure Sevastopol in the Crimea
23 – Rostov-on-Don, U.S.S.R. falls to German forces

AUGUST
7 – U.S. Marines land at Guadalcanal in Solomon Islands
9 – Germans capture oilfields in the Caucasus
12 – Churchill and Stalin meet with U.S. and Free French Representatives in Moscow to discuss Second Front
13 – General Montgomery takes command of British forces in Egypt
19 – Allied cross-channel raid on

Dieppe
23 – Battle f

SEPTEMBER
22 – Germans
but Soviet troops cling to part of city
26 – Australians repulse Japanese near Port Moresby, New Guinea

OCTOBER
23 – Montgomery's forces attack at El Alamein, Egypt

NOVEMBER
4 – Rommel withdraws from El Alamein
8 – First major Allied invasion takes place in Morocco and Algeria
11 – Axis forces occupy Vichy France
13 – Tobruk retaken by British
16 – U.S. and Australian forces attack Japanese in Buna-Gona area, New Guinea
19 – Soviets launch counteroffensive at Stalingrad
27 – French scuttle their warships in Toulon Harbor
30 – Germans repulse Allies in Tunisia

DECEMBER
16 – German attempt to relieve Stalingrad fails

1943

JANUARY
2 – U.S. and Australian forces take Buna, New Guinea
14-24 – Roosevelt and Churchill meet at Casablanca to plan Allied war strategy
23 – British occupy Tripoli, Libya
27 – U.S. bombs Wilhelmshaven in first attack on Germany
30 – Admiral Karl Dönitz takes command of German Navy
31 – General Paulus surrenders German Sixth Army at Stalingrad

FEBRUARY
9 – U.S. troops secure Guadalcanal
16 – Soviets regain Kharkov
22 – Rommel withdraws through Kasserine Pass, Tunisia

MARCH
2-4 – Japanese suffer heavy losses in Battle of Bismarck Sea
5 – Allied bombing of Ruhr begins
14 – Germans recapture Kharkov

APRIL
18 – Admiral Isoroku Yamamoto, commander-in-chief of Japan's navy, shot down and killed in U.S. aerial ambush
23 – Anglo-U.S. HQ set up in Britain to plan invasion of Europe

MAY
11 – U.S. troops attack Japanese at Attu in Aleutian Islands

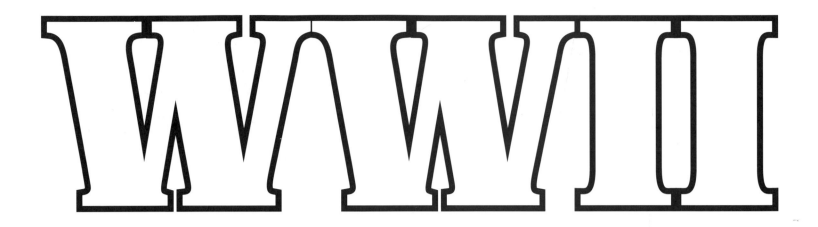

WWII

Time-Life History of the Second World War

BARNES
&NOBLE
BOOKS
NEW YORK

Time-Life Books History of the Second World War
was produced by
ST. REMY PRESS

MANAGING EDITOR	Kenneth Winchester
MANAGING ART DIRECTOR	Pierre Léveillé

Editor	Dianne Stine Thomas
Art Directors	Philippe Arnoldi, Francine Lemieux
Senior Art Director	Diane Denoncourt
Contributing Editor	Elizabeth W. Lewis
Research Editor	Nancy D. Kingsbury
Editorial Assistant	Daniel McBain
Art Assistant	Julie Léger
Electronic Designer	Jean-Luc Roy
Chronology	Christine M. Jacobs
Index	Hazel Blumberg-McKee

Administrator	Denise Rainville
Coordinator	Michelle Turbide
Systems Analysts	Simon Lapierre, Daniel Bazinet
Proofreaders	Gilles Humbert, Joseph Marchetti

*Time-Life Books History of the
Second World War* was adapted from
the *World War II*, produced by
TIME-LIFE BOOKS INC.

EDITOR	George Constable
Executive Editor	Ellen Phillips
Director of Design	Louis Klein
Director of Editorial Resources	Phyllis K. Wise
Editorial Board	Russell B. Adams Jr., Dale M. Brown, Roberta Conlan, Thomas H. Flaherty, Lee Hassig, Donia Ann Steele, Rosalind Stubenberg
Director of Photography and Research	John Conrad Weiser
Asst. Director of Editorial Resources	Elise Ritter Gibson

PRESIDENT	John M. Fahey Jr.
Senior Vice Presidents	Robert M. DeSena, James L. Mercer, Paul R. Stewart, Joseph J. Ward
Vice Presidents	Stephen L. Bair, Stephen L. Goldstein, Juanita T. James, Andrew P. Caplan, Carol Kaplan, Susan J. Maruyama, Robert H. Smith
Production Manager	Prudence G. Harris
Publisher	Joseph J. Ward

THE CONSULTANTS

George Daniels, Consulting Editor, is a writer, editor and editorial consultant who has served as Senior Editor of Time Magazine and Executive Editor of Time-Life Books.

Col. John Elting (Ret.) is a former associate professor at West Point and has written or edited some 20 books on military history.

THE WRITERS

Rosa Harris-Adler is a journalism instructor at Concordia University in Montreal and past national president of the Periodical Writers Association of Canada.

Champ Clark teaches newsmagazine writing at the University of Virginia, and is a former Senior Editor of Time Magazine.

Valerie Moolman is a freelance writer who began her career in the documentary film business. She subsequently worked as a text editor for Time-Life Books.

George Ronald, who served during World War II as a lieutenant in the Royal Canadian Navy, is former Managing Editor of Reader's Digest Books (Canada).

Charles Smith served during World War II as a Royal Tank Regiment officer in North Africa, and is former Executive Editor of *Reader's Digest* magazine's Canadian edition.

David Thomson has taught literature at Harvard and Columbia universities and Williams College, and is a former Time-Life Books editor and writer.

Bryce S. Walker, a war correspondent for *Stars and Stripes* during the Korean War, is a former editor of Time-Life Books.

Brendan Walsh is a freelance fiction and non-fiction writer, and the author of several books.

This edition published by Barnes & Noble, Inc.,
by arrangement with Time-Life Books Inc.

1995 Barnes & Noble Books

ISBN 1-56619-984-0

Printed and bound in the United States of America

M 9 8 7 6 5 4 3 2

HITLER'S ARTFUL SPECTACLES

all International Brigades and tried vainly to get the League of Nations to intervene with Franco for something other than unconditional surrender. Franco refused.

In January Barcelona fell to the Nationalists. With the Republic near ruin, the Loyalists began fleeing for France. On February 27, London and Paris recognized Franco's government; in March he began his final assault on Madrid.

Even before the attack was fairly under way, the Republican armies simply broke up, with exhausted men abandoning the front for home. At midday on March 28, the Nationalists entered the heart of the capital. Abruptly the streets filled with members of the Fifth Column, the city's clandestine Nationalist supporters. For years, they had heard the cry: "¡No pasaran!—They shall not pass!" As Franco's troops paraded through the city, the Fifth Column shouted: "¡Han pasado!—They have passed!"

The Spanish Civil War had caused over 600,000 deaths, cost more than $15 billion, and produced still another totalitarian regime in Europe. The war had served Russia, Italy and Germany, providing not only military field experience but also treasure—$315 million in gold for Stalin, and access to Spain's iron ore and magnesium deposits for Hitler's munition manufacturers. Among the Western leaders doubts grew about the wisdom of neutral policies toward the war.

In Berlin on June 5, 1939, the Germans of the Condor Legion returned home to a triumphal parade. British author George Orwell, who had fought for the Republic, returned home to London, and found no acknowledgment that there had even been a war at all: "Here it was, still the England I had known in my childhood: the railway cuttings smothered in wild flowers . . . The men in bowler hats, the pigeons in Trafalgar Square, the red buses, the blue policemen—all sleeping the deep, deep sleep of England, from which I fear that we shall never wake till we are jerked out of it by the roar of bombs."

Adolf Hitler, arriving at the annual Harvest Day festival in 1937, whips one million people into a frenzy of cheers and Nazi salutes.

REKINDLING PRIDE WITH PAGEANTRY

"I'm beginning to comprehend some of the reasons for Hitler's astounding success," wrote American journalist William L. Shirer from Berlin in September 1934. "He is restoring pageantry and color and mysticism to the drab lives of twentieth-century Germans." Indeed he was. Hitler's Nazi Party, empowered in 1933 to lead the nation, had made a fine art of staging enormous spectacles that inspired a new sense of national pride.

In Nuremberg each September hundreds of thousands of Germans cheered as battalions of storm troopers goose-stepped through the streets to the martial music of brass bands. At the 1937 rural Harvest Day festival, a great mass of farmers thrilled to the sight of a mock tank battle that attested to the Wehrmacht's increasing strength. At night the spectacles were crowned by the surrealistic splendor of 100 or more searchlights sending their beams 20,000 feet into the air. "The effect," wrote the British Ambassador, "both solemn and beautiful, was like being in a cathedral of ice."

At each grandiose festival, the main attraction was Hitler, the man who made the Nazi magic work. He presided over the exhibitions and parades, and took the adoring salutes of the marchers. Then, invariably, he excited the crowds and the nation with variations on the speech that had swept him to power—a vigorous attack on the Bolsheviks, the Jews, and the nations that had imposed the humiliating Versailles Treaty on Germany at the close of World War I.

Above all, Hitler pledged a greater, stronger Germany—and the extravagant spectacles were intended to prove to the people that he was making the promise come true. Under his leadership, he was saying, Germany had recovered from the political chaos and economic ruin of the '20s, and was regaining its rightful place among the great powers.

While they inspired the Germans, the Nazi spectacles stunned the rest of the world. Many correspondents sent home stories that spoke apprehensively of Germany's growing armed forces. "All the talk here has been of peace," wrote *The New York Times* reporter as early as 1933, "yet the atmosphere has been far from peace-loving."

Deputy Führer Rudolf Hess (left) and architect Albert Speer (second from left) listen as Hitler outlines plans for the 1934 Nuremberg rally.

The Führer dedicates the Volkswagen factory in June of 1938 with a promise to manufacture a "people's car" for every German citizen. It was rumored that Hitler himself had helped to design the prototype (foreground) and that the vehicle could easily be converted to a light tank.

In a display of precision marching, a Nazi Party band leads a regiment of Brownshirts into the city of Nuremberg during the 1938 rally. The tent city seen in the background provided shelter for thousands of participants throughout the one-week-long festival.

Saluting stiffly from his Mercedes touring car, Hitler reviews columns of parading Brownshirts during the Nazi Party rally in Nuremberg in 1938. In the foreground at left stand Deputy Führer Rudolf Hess and Victor Lutze, chief of staff of the Brownshirts.

Units of Brownshirts wait their turn to join the procession through the banner-decked streets of medieval Nuremberg. The storm troopers are fitted out with field packs, blanket rolls, black metal mess kits and canteens.

Linking arms across an immense athletic field, thousands of members of the League of German Girls dance in celebration of "faith and beauty" during the Nazi Party rally at Nuremberg in 1939. This particular performance required long and meticulous advance preparation: The women who participated had been selected from local chapters months ahead of time and had spent almost every evening thereafter in rehearsal.

Performing at the Nuremberg rally, young men demonstrate their strength and skill in a precision drill with heavy poles. The colossal stadium, designed in 1934 by Hitler's leading architect, Albert Speer, had two adjoining grandstands, one a quarter of a mile long, and seats for 124,000 spectators.

At left, the many medals and awards won by
Adolf Hühnlein, head of the National Socialist
Motor Corps, are displayed at his funeral on
June 21, 1942, by a pair of Brownshirts standing
in front of an elaborate display of shrubbery
and flowers. The Nazi Party usually saluted its
departed leaders with floral arrangements,
music by Wagner, and lengthy eulogies that
were specially written for the occasion
by Joseph Goebbels' Ministry of Propaganda.

Nazi representatives turn out in full regalia
on April 17, 1944 (right), to mark the passing of
Adolf Wagner, Gauleiter of Munich-Upper
Bavaria. The funeral, held in the cavernous
Kongresssaal of Munich's Deutsches Museum,
featured the trappings and symbols of the
party: the swastika draped over the coffin, the
standards emblazoned with ''Deutschland
Erwache'' (''Germany, Awake!''), the Nazi eagle.

Trucks filled with Wehrmacht infantrymen assemble in the Tiergarten, Berlin's sprawling central park, for a parade honoring Hitler on his 50th birthday, April 20, 1939. The trucks, along with columns of tanks and artillery, rumbled past the Führer's reviewing stand, while great formations of Luftwaffe warplanes droned overhead. This intimidating show of German power was witnessed by two million Berliners and many representatives of foreign nations. After the parade, the visiting dignitaries—including the American Chargé d'Affaires—signed their names in Hitler's birthday register as a matter of course.

45

As three soldiers on bicycles entered Cologne's Cathedral Square, approving murmurs rippled through the crowd. Then the sounds swelled to an ecstatic roar. Into the square marched line after line of German infantrymen, goose-stepping in perfect unison.

It was March 7, 1936, and two other towns along the west bank of the Rhine were rejoicing as German troops streamed across bridges from the river's east bank. The significance of their arrival was clear to Rhineland residents: Hitler was moving to remilitarize the region, bringing Germany's rapidly reviving armed power to the doorstep of its once and future foe, France.

The French protested to the League of Nations, and the League pronounced Germany guilty of violating the Locarno Pact. But the League had long since been recognized as powerless, and in the end, a rationale was found for Hitler's coup: after all, the *London Times* noted, Hitler was "only going into his own back garden."

Although the Führer's well-drilled troops and Luftwaffe—Germany's new air force—appeared combat-ready, they were an ill-equipped token force with little more to back them up than their leader's boldness. Had France moved in, the Führer later admitted, "we would have had to withdraw with our tails between our legs."

Instead, the Rhineland provided Hitler with a successful formula for future action elsewhere: an avowal of peaceful intentions followed by a lightning-swift military move. Over the next three years, he was to use this formula to expand into Austria, Czechoslovakia and Poland.

Despite the Rhineland move, many officials in London, Paris and other capitals were slow to recognize Hitler as a war monger. They believed he wanted only to undo the humiliating damage inflicted upon Germany at Versailles—a

3

Few parts of the Versailles Treaty had galled the Germans as much as the sections concerning the Rhineland. All 9,450 square miles of the Rhineland west of the Rhine, and a 30-mile-wide zone east of the river, were to be permanently demilitarized to form a buffer between Germany and France. By mid-1930, the Allied forces were gone and the Germans had voluntarily renewed their pledge to keep the Rhineland demilitarized under the terms of the 1925 Locarno Pact. In fact, as recently as May 1935, Hitler had publicly hailed an unarmed Rhineland as Germany's "contribution" to European peace.

THE OPENING GAMBITS

feeling some of them had come to share. In fact, any of them could have known otherwise had they troubled to read Hitler's 1924 book, *Mein Kampf*, in which he had blueprinted Germany's elevation to "lord of the earth."

The march into the Rhineland was not the first step in Hitler's master plan. Three years before, within a few months of coming to power, he had launched a campaign to absorb Austria into Germany—an objective recorded on the first page of *Mein Kampf*.

The Austrian move had begun with an undercover operation: Hitler dispatched secret agents south to stir up the hundreds of thousands of Austrian Nazis who passionately wanted what they called *Anschluss*—political union with Germany. The operation culminated in the assassination of Austria's Chancellor, Engelbert Dollfuss. To the surprise of the Nazis, the assassination did not lead immediately to the fall of the Austrian government; instead, within hours of the murder, the leaders of the abortive coup were arrested by troops loyal to the Dollfuss regime.

Officially, Britain and France had declared themselves ready to preserve Austria's independence. They made it clear that it was up to Austria's best friend, Italy, to take action. Mussolini, in fact, had felt personally affronted by the assassination: Dollfuss had been killed while his young wife and two children were house guests of the Mussolini family. The Duce's eyes brimmed with tears as he put the widow aboard a plane for Vienna. He then ordered 50,000 troops to the Brenner Pass, on Italy's Austrian frontier.

The ploy worked. Germany issued a denial of any connection with the Dollfuss murder and the Führer himself professed an earnest desire to restore friendly relations with Austria. *Anschluss* was postponed, and there was no confrontation with Mussolini's troops. For his decisive action

in the crisis, the Duce was to earn an ironic sort of credit from history. He proved to be the only one among Europe's leaders to have faced Hitler down in the stormy era preceding World War II.

Hitler's embarrassment over the fiasco soon vanished, and the Führer's moves became more blatant. In 1935, he announced the reintroduction of compulsory military service and the formation of a new air force. He would begin to build a new German war machine, including powerful airplanes and tanks. Now Hitler was dropping all pretense, and the implications were staggering.

Britain and every country on the continent stood in potential jeopardy. This prospect prompted a conference on the highest levels. A month after Hitler's announcement, Prime Minister Ramsay MacDonald of Britain and Premier Flandin of France met with Mussolini in Stresa, Italy, for intensive talks. They agreed to use all suitable means to oppose any aggression by Germany.

Yet, within nine weeks, their plans lay in ruins—wrecked by Hitler's political chicanery. Blandly ignoring the Stresa talks, the Führer sent a private message assuring the British of his deep desire for them to retain supremacy over the seas. The British were seduced by this appeal to their heart of hearts. Without consulting their Stresa partners, they agreed to sign the Anglo-German pact, fixing Germany's naval strength at one third the strength of Britain's. What was presumably intended as a restraint on German naval expansion was in fact a green light. At the time of signing Germany had no navy to speak of; in order to reach the limit of 35 per cent, the Reich's shipyards would be kept humming for years. Moreover, the pact recognized Germany's right to have submarines—a right expressly denied them by the Versailles Treaty.

Ten months later, Hitler's troops marched into the "demilitarized" Rhineland, tramping the remaining tatters of the treaty beneath their boots.

Sharing Germany's southeastern border, Austria soon felt compelled to seek accommodation with Germany; the two countries signed a nonaggression treaty. Germany promised not to interfere with Austria's internal affairs, while Austria pledged to conduct itself as a "German state" in foreign matters. But Austria also agreed to release imprisoned Nazis, and to make room for Nazi sympathizers in the government—two concessions that made a mockery of the treaty. Hitler had scored again.

Mussolini, meanwhile, appeared unperturbed by these events. He had accepted Hitler's assurance of Austria's sovereignty and was even beginning to show tacit approval of the Führer. The Duce was also beginning to view Britain and France as weak allies, particularly in light of the Anglo-

On March 7, 1936, German troops march across the Hohenzollern Bridge over the Rhine. Clearly, Hitler was moving to remilitarize the region, putting his guns and his men directly on the French border. As viewed by statesmen around the world, Hitler had torn up the Treaty of Versailles.

German pact and their inaction concerning the Rhineland. Furthermore, if the Führer was on his way to upsetting the old balance of power in Europe, it would benefit Italy to be on the winning side.

Hitler encouraged this kind of reasoning by Mussolini, and began to feed the Duce's vanity by lauding him as a great leader. By the autumn of 1936, the two leaders agreed to synchronize their foreign policies. Speaking to a Milan audience, Mussolini coined the historic phrase, "Rome-Berlin Axis" to describe the two countries' relationship.

The following year the Duce paid a state visit to Germany, his first trip abroad in 14 years. Upon Mussolini's return to Italy, he radiated satisfaction over his journey. Hitler shared the feeling; Mussolini was now under his control, and the Führer could turn his attention elsewhere.

Five weeks later Hitler called a top-secret meeting in his Chancellery to reveal a plan for making the rest of *Mein Kampf* come true. He summoned six men to that historic meeting on November 5, 1937: Field Marshal Werner von Blomberg, Minister of War and commander-in-chief of all Germany's armed forces; General Werner von Fritsch, Chief Admiral Erich Raeder and General Hermann Göring,

respectively commanders-in-chief of the army, navy and air force; Baron Konstantin von Neurath, the Foreign Minister; and Colonel Friedrich Hossbach, Hitler's military adjutant.

As his select audience settled at a big round table, Hitler launched into a four-hour discourse. Germany's future, he declared, entirely depended on meeting its need for more *Lebensraum*—living space; the German nation had a right to a larger share of land "in immediate proximity to the Reich."

The "first objectives" were Austria and Czechoslovakia which—when joined with Germany—would provide better strategic frontiers for a Greater Germany and free the Fatherland's military forces for other purposes. The annexed countries would also be a source of food for Germans—once "compulsory emigration" had rid these countries of three million racially unsuitable persons.

Although Hitler conceded that "a strong German colossus in the center of Europe would be intolerable" to France, Britain and other countries of Europe, he accepted both the risk and the consequences. Blomberg, Fritsch and Neurath were stunned to hear that Hitler was willing, in fact, to wage a war on two fronts, east and west, a nightmare any sensible German military planner hoped to avoid. They objected to

THE VENGEFUL VANDALISM OF KRISTALLNACHT

On November 7, 1938, a young Polish Jew named Herschel Grynszpan *(inset)*, an unemployed 17-year-old, shot and killed the third secretary of the Reich's embassy in Paris. He did it, Grynszpan declared, to avenge Nazi treatment of his fellow Jews. On hearing the news, Hitler flew into a rage and prepared to exact vengeance in the form of the worst pogrom that had ever taken place in modern Germany.

On Hitler's instructions, all German Jews were to be punished, and German non-Jews responded with terrible enthusiasm. Within 60 hours of Grynszpan's confession a wave of lethal vandalism swept through Jewish synagogues, homes and stores. In the course of their thuggish orgy, which came to be called *Kristallnacht* for the shards of glass that littered German streets, the Nazis by their own estimates killed 35 Jews, arrested many thousands, and levied against all German Jews fines that totaled one billion marks. They also wrecked a total of 7,500 shops and 119 synagogues.

Curious Germans peer at the gutted interior of a Jewish shop—one of hundreds the Nazis wrecked in retaliation for a political murder committed by a Jew. The destruction sped up a process that eliminated Jews from Germany's economic, social and political life.

the plan, and all three were replaced within three months.

The following February, Hitler announced to the nation that he personally was taking "over command of all the armed forces." Thenceforth Hitler was to direct Germany's military adventures by intuition, accepting less and less advice from professional soldiers.

In just five years, Hitler had made significant progress in achieving the goals of *Mein Kampf*. He had broken the old aristocracy's hold on the Army and the Foreign Office and intimidated other ideological enemies into submission. Jews were deprived of their livelihoods. The German Evangelical Church was brought under state control. In Catholic Bavaria, anti-Nazi Catholic priests were imprisoned on immorality charges. Germany's labor forces were also firmly in hand. And, while Britain and France still floundered under the impact of the depression, fewer than 200,000 Germans out of a total work force of 25 million were idle.

Internationally, Britain and France continued to be thorns in Hitler's side, but he was also becoming increasingly aware of the rising power on another front. In Russia, Stalin's Great Purge was disposing of every last vestige of dissent. As many as eight million Soviet citizens were executed, and tens of millions more condemned to forced labor camps. Two thirds of the Central Committee of the Communist Party and 35,000 Army officers were among the hapless victims.

Even so, Stalin's political machinations did not prevent a steady buildup of Russia's war machine until, by 1938 he had 1.6 million men under arms, and his Army and Navy budget was 20 times larger than in 1933.

France, too, had begun to reorganize its defenses. But, while most Frenchmen were united in their dread of Germany, they were not so on other issues. France's splintered party system spawned much quarreling, frequent changes of government and recurring internal crises. In fact, during the period 1936 to 1937, the old revolving-door pattern of French politics reappeared: three governments were in and out of power.

Britain too was enmeshed in its own difficulties. It was now obviously a small nation plagued by a faltering economy. With its strength sapped by World War I debts and loss of foreign markets, a drastic cutback in military spending was necessary. A new war was clearly something for which Britain was neither ready nor willing. Furthermore, its leaders were determined not to make a commitment that would place the decision for war or peace for their people in the hands of another nation.

When Neville Chamberlain became British Prime Minister in 1937, he could see no reason why differences between nations could not be solved by rational men in calm deliberation. In this spirit he was determined to approach Hitler. The Führer, however, was occupied with his long-standing plan for *Anschluss*, and the final takeover of Austria. His next step involved what was to become another well-known Hitler tactic, a confrontation designed to bully and soften up the adversary.

In February, 1938, the Führer summoned Austrian Chancellor Schuschnigg to his mountain retreat at Berchtesgaden. He launched into a two-hour tirade against Schuschnigg and his government. Nervous and browbeaten, the Chancellor signed an ultimatum: the legalization of the Austrian Nazi party was guaranteed, with Nazis appointed to key cabinet posts.

But on his return to Vienna, Schuschnigg did a complete about-face. He called for a nationwide plebiscite to determine whether Austrians wanted a "free, independent, social, Christian and united Austria." The newly-appointed pro-Nazi Austrian Minister of the Interior—a Hitler protégé—threatened Schuschnigg with a German invasion if he did not postpone the plebiscite. On March 11, 1938, Schuschnigg gave in. But by then it was too late. The general unrest in Austria gave Hitler the excuse he needed for invasion—the pretext of restoring order.

German troops, with the blessing of Mussolini, crossed into Austria on March 12, and were welcomed with flowers and Nazi flags. Hitler was given a rapturous reception when he arrived later that day. Indeed, as his big black Mercedes-Benz passed, adoring onlookers knelt to scoop up bits of earth the tires had touched.

Less well disposed Austrians, however, soon learned what *Anschluss* held in store for them. Known Socialists and Communists were stripped to the waist and flogged; Jews were forced to scrub streets and public latrines. Schuschnigg was eventually sent to a concentration camp.

When Britain and France protested Hitler's new coup, the response was icily insolent: German-Austrian relations were the sole concern of the German people. Understandably, the Czechoslovakians were also becoming concerned. Yet even as German troops advanced on the Austrian border, Luftwaffe Commander-in-Chief Hermann Göring earnestly reassured the Czechoslovakian envoy in Berlin. "I give you my word of honor," Göring pledged. "Czechoslovakia has nothing to fear from the Reich."

Czechoslovakia's position appeared strong, with a well-equipped military and treaties of alliance with France and the Soviet Union. Its weakness, however, lay in the multiplicity of its ethnic groups. One of these groups, the Sudetenland Germans, began to fall for the siren song of Nazism, which had affirmed their German roots. In addition,

the leader of the Sudeten German party, Konrad Henlein, was on the Nazi payroll.

Scarcely two weeks after Austria was annexed, Hitler had begun laying plans to swallow Czechoslovakia. He summoned Henlein to Germany and told him that on no account was he to propose any settlement of Sudeten grievances that the government in Prague could conceivably accept. The demands Henlein subsequently presented to Prague called, in effect, for the creation of a German state within the Czechoslovakian Republic. Prague reported the proposals to its ally, France, and asked if they would be willing to come to Czechoslovakia's aid if its security were threatened.

France's newly-appointed premier, Edouard Daladier, was determined not to involve France in another war. He flew to London with a proposal for joint action: Britain and France would urge Prague to make maximum concessions in the Sudetenland and would immediately inform Berlin of their intent to support Czechoslovakian independence. Chamberlain, however, would participate in only the mildest of warnings to Berlin; he was not convinced that Hitler intended to destroy Czechoslovakia.

Through the spring and summer of 1938, Hitler's propagandists stoked the fires of unrest in the Sudetenland. They accused Prague of deliberate brutality to its German minority and manufactured rumors of Czech troop movements along the common frontier.

Czechoslovakia's beleaguered president, Eduard Beneš, was under pressure not only from his enemies; his allies in Paris and London kept hammering at the need for concessions to the Sudeten Germans. In early September Beneš agreed to accept Sudeten demands for a German state. Nevertheless, Sudeten Germans continued to promote unrest, and a week later Beneš placed the Sudetenland under martial law.

War between Czechoslovakia and Germany now seemed inevitable. Although France and Russia had agreed to protect Czechoslovakia against Germany, indecision and inaction again engulfed the French cabinet. The British Prime Minister, however, was still clinging desperately to the possibility of appeasement, and went to Germany on September 15, 1937, to meet Hitler for the first time. The Führer told Chamberlain that if the British agreed to self-determination of the Sudeten Germans, he would consider the Czechoslovakian matter settled.

With great relief, Britain and France urged Prague to cede to Germany all areas in which the Sudeten Germans comprised at least half the population; and President Beneš finally conceded. His country, he said, had become totally isolated by its allies. "We had no choice," he told his colleagues. "We have been basely betrayed."

The next day, September 22, Chamberlain presented the new proposals to Hitler in Germany. Hitler responded that they were "no longer of any use" for a number of reasons: the transfer of power would be too slow, said Hitler, and other areas of Czechoslovakia must be allowed to decide their own future. In addition, Germany would not guarantee Czechoslovakia's future boundaries. Chamberlain refused to accept the new conditions and left in shock.

That evening Chamberlain met with Hitler again and discovered that the Nazi leader had added yet another demand: a deadline. The Czechs would have to evacuate the Sudetenland by September 28. When Chamberlain

We, the German Führer and Chancellor and the British Prime Minister, have had a further meeting today and are agreed in recognising that the question of Anglo-German relations is of the first importance for the two countries and for Europe.

We regard the agreement signed last night and the Anglo-German Naval Agreement as symbolic of the desire of our two peoples never to go to war with one another again.

We are resolved that the method of consultation shall be the method adopted to deal with any other questions that may concern our two countries, and we are determined to continue our efforts to remove possible sources of difference and thus to contribute to assure the peace of Europe.

The crowning irony of prewar efforts to appease Hitler was Prime Minister Neville Chamberlain's "triumphal" return from his negotiating mission with Hitler in Munich. At right, he stands before a welcoming British crowd and waves the so-called Anglo-German peace declaration (above) that Hitler had signed with Chamberlain that morning. The document was useless.

protested, the Führer agreed to extend the deadline to October 1, which had long been the date fixed in his mind for the start of *Case Green*, the invasion of Czechoslovakia.

Prague rejected the proposals on September 25, and Britain and France began preparing for war. Several developments, however, gave Hitler pause. According to his military attaché in Prague, combined Czech and French troops outnumbered German forces two to one. In addition, the German Ambassador in Washington reported that, in the event of a war between Germany and Britain, the United States would support Britain.

On September 27, Chamberlain was overjoyed to receive a telegram from the Führer, encouraging further appeasement efforts. The following afternoon, Hitler invited Chamberlain to meet with him, Mussolini and Daladier in Munich; the Czechs were not permitted to attend.

The conference at the Führerhaus in Munich validated the surrender of the Sudetenland to Germany. Only after the agreement was reached were the participants handed maps of the areas to be ceded, and the occupation timetable. It was to begin October 1. Hitler's *Case Green* was right on schedule—and without a single shot being fired.

Chamberlain was elated by the "victory" at Munich, and addressed a cheering crowd in London: "My friends . . . there has come back from Germany peace with honor. I believe it is peace for our time." This sentiment was shared by both the British and French people. Daladier, on the other hand, was deeply depressed at having gone back on old pledges made to the Czechs. As for Hitler, publicly he was delighted; privately he was annoyed at Chamberlain for helping him procure an unwarlike victory.

The Munich pact had spelled Czechoslovakia's doom. Loss of the Sudetenland not only stripped the country of its principal line of fortifications against Germany, but also whetted the appetite of Czechoslovakia's other enemies. Poland and Hungary simply walked in and took possession of some 8,000 square miles of Czech territory. The previously independent provinces of Slovakia and Ruthenia demanded and got a large degree of autonomy.

Meanwhile President Beneš resigned and went into exile in England. His aging successor, Emil Hácha, tried to halt his country's further disintegration by dismissing the fractious governments of Slovakia and Ruthenia in March 1939. On Hitler's orders, Slovakia again proclaimed its independence; Hungary, posing as the protector of Ruthenia, demanded the evacuation of the Czech army from that province.

Hácha reacted by seeking an audience with Hitler. The Führer received him at one in the morning, an hour deliberately chosen with the thought that Hácha, who suffered from a weak heart, would be at his lowest ebb. Hitler announced he intended to impose "German protectorates" on Czechoslovakia's two remaining provinces. If Hácha did not sign by 5 a.m., German bombers would strike Prague that morning. At 4 a.m., near collapse, Hácha signed away his country's independence. Later that day Hitler announced to the world that "Czechoslovakia had ceased to exist."

Despite this latest act of blatant aggression by Hitler, Britain and France failed to act—and Hitler moved again. Before March was out he had forced Lithuania to cede the city of Memel, once a part of German East Prussia. Then he fixed his eyes on Poland and the city of Danzig.

The Treaty of Versailles had carved a corridor out of Germany giving Poland an outlet to the sea; it had also given the former German seaport of Danzig the status of a free city. An overwhelming majority of Danzig's residents were Germans, clamoring for reunion with the Reich. But the city lay within the corridor at its very tip. Hitler ordered Foreign Minister von Ribbentrop to discuss settlement of the corridor and Danzig with Poland's Foreign Minister, Colonel Joseph Beck.

Chamberlain also approached Beck, asking him to join with the British, Russians and French in a guarantee of Polish independence. But Beck declared that his country's interests were best served by keeping both Germany and Russia at arm's length.

On March 31, Chamberlain made an uncharacteristic

Three Sudetenlanders, one overcome with emotion as she raises up a Nazi salute, pay homage as the Wehrmacht (German armed forces) enters the border town of Cheb in 1938. To greet the occupying troops, whom the Czech forces had been ordered not to resist, huge Nazi flags—smuggled in earlier by party agents—sprouted from buildings.

Obeying German orders, a Czech policeman gets ready to change a street sign in the city of Brno from "Freedom Avenue" to Adolf Hitler Place. After Czechoslovakia capitulated, German administration began rearranging various aspects of Czech life, and the silence of despair descended.

move that was to stun even his own countrymen. He offered Beck a unilateral British guarantee of Poland's security. Beck accepted, and France soon joined in. The unilateral guarantee was a complete reversal of a policy England had maintained since World War I: Chamberlain had, in effect, placed the decision for war or peace in the hands of another nation. He had done so on the preposterous assumption that Poland was in no immediate danger and that it was militarily strong. But, despite the pledge, Britain was in no position to provide effective aid to its new ally if it were suddenly attacked.

"I'll cook them a stew they'll choke on!" Hitler said of the British; he was no happier with the Poles, who had rebuffed a proposal to settle the questions of Danzig and the corridor. He alerted the German army to prepare a new plan of operation: *Case White*, an armed invasion of Poland. The date was set for September 1, 1939.

Meanwhile Chamberlain was encouraging Russia to give its own guarantee to Poland, but the talks were stalled. The Russians preferred an Anglo-French-Soviet Alliance that would also guarantee the security of Baltic states against German aggression.

In May, Stalin appointed Vyacheslav Molotov as his new Foreign Minister. In his first speech, Molotov said he believed that continuing to negotiate with the Western Democracies in no way precluded strengthening Russia's trade relations with Germany and Italy. Prodded by Molotov's position and fear of a German attack on Poland, the British and French tried to resume the dialogue with the Russians. Again the talks failed.

The Germans watched Molotov with interest, and read his speech with great care. When they asked Molotov to clarify his position of improving trade relations, he replied that Stalin wanted to improve "political relations" as well. To Hitler, this was a signal that Russia might be neutralized in the coming war with Poland.

On August 23, Ribbentrop, Stalin and Molotov hammered out a mutual nonaggression pact. It freed Hitler to invade Poland, and allowed Stalin to make whatever moves he chose into Finland, Estonia, Latvia (Lithuania was annexed later), the Rumanian province of Bessarabia, and the eastern half of Poland. Only the nonaggression pact would be announced; the rest was kept in secret protocol.

News of the Nazi-Soviet treaty burst over Europe like a clap of thunder before the deluge. On September 1, exactly as Hitler had planned all along, the German army invaded Poland. Two days later, the French and British declared war on Germany.

The prelude to war had ended.

Shocked and angry Czechs, some waving fists, watch German troops enter Prague on March 15, 1939, after Czech President Hácha surrendered.

II

A TIME OF CALAMITY AND COURAGE

On September 1, 1939, the first day of the invasion of Poland, German infantrymen symbolically break a wooden barricade on the Polish border.

It was a curious request to make of the German Army, and Chief of Staff General Franz Halder noted the fact in his diary. Heinrich Himmler, head of Hitler's *Schutzstaffeln (SS)*, the Nazi Party's own armed forces, wanted a supply of Polish military uniforms. Puzzling or not, Himmler's appeal was honored by the Army with its usual efficiency; the uniforms were swiftly procured and delivered.

Very probably, neither Halder nor any other Wehrmacht officer was aware of the reason for the clothing. But they understood it all too well before very long. Sometime during the last two weeks of August 1939, thirteen German convicts were taken from a concentration camp in eastern Germany and installed in a nearby schoolhouse. On the last day of that month, all but one of the prisoners were ordered to dress themselves in Polish uniforms; then they were injected with a fatal drug, taken to a small forest near the German-Polish border and shot. Their bodies were arranged as though they were Polish soldiers who had died while advancing into Germany.

Later that day, the thirteenth convict was hustled off to the nearby town of Gleiwitz. Wearing Polish civilian clothes, he and other similarly disguised SS security men took over the local radio station and broadcast an inflammatory statement announcing that Poland was attacking Germany and urging all Poles to join the colors. Whereupon a simulated scuffle with station personnel ensued before an open microphone, leaving the convict who had impersonated the firebrand "Polish" broadcaster lying dead of gunshot wounds on the studio floor.

4

After six years of spectacular bloodless triumphs, Adolf Hitler was now ready to prove himself the warlord supreme. His chief weapon, complementing his grasp of such political stratagems as secrecy, bluff and deception, was a unique form of swift, mechanized, mobile warfare. The total concept was called blitzkrieg, or lightning war, in which coordinated forces of armored divisions, high-level bombers, dive bombers and motorized infantry divisions would smash through enemy defenses in a sudden, massive assault.

THE CONQUEST OF EUROPE

The next day, September 1, at 10 a.m., Hitler stood before the Reichstag in Berlin and cited the charade at Gleiwitz as an instance of Polish aggression on German soil. By then the first phase of his military campaign against the Poles had already begun. In the darkness before dawn, an assault by land, sea and air had been launched and every sign pointed to a quick German victory.

Thus Hitler commenced World War II.

The plans for the invasion of Poland, although meticulously detailed, were basically quite simple. Poland formed a rounded salient projecting westward—a plump victim trapped between the two steely arms of a massive German pincer; one arm threatened from Pomerania and East Prussia in the north, the other from Silesia and occupied Slovakia in the south. The plan called for those German arms to snap together in a single bloody crunch across Poland's waist. A total of more than 1.5 million men were positioned to strike from the west, north and south, to be supported by almost 2,000 warplanes and 1,700 tanks. When the pincers met, the bulk of the Polish Army would be destroyed.

For such a devastatingly simple plan to work however, there were at least two conditions that had to be met: the first was a guarantee that the Soviets would not oppose the assault; the second was an assurance that Poland's western allies would fail to come to its aid. The signing of the crucial Nazi-Soviet nonaggression pact on August 23 fulfilled the first condition; only Hitler's intuition promised that the second condition would be met.

Just hours before Hitler's speech in the Reichstag, the first shots of the war were fired—at Danzig in the Polish corridor, which cut East Prussia off from the Reich. Two days earlier, the *Schleswig-Holstein*, a German Navy training battleship, had steamed into harbor there, on a so-called courtesy visit. Then, on the morning of September 1, the battleship turned its 11-inch guns against the Polish naval installation of Westerplatte overlooking Danzig's harbor, and submitted the garrison to a murderous point-blank bombardment.

Meanwhile, as day broke on the land frontier, squadrons of German planes appeared like flocks of cranes, droning south in the direction of Warsaw. These were Hitler's high-level bombers. In the course of a few hours they reduced much of the Polish rear to a shambles, and destroyed the bulk of the Polish Air Force on the ground.

Against the Polish defenders in the front lines near the border, the attack opened with waves of Junkers-87 dive bombers—the deadly Stukas. After the dive bombers came the motorcycles, the armored cars, the tanks—and after them the armored infantry and artillery of the armored panzer divisions. When they found such weaknesses, they plunged through and fanned out in the rear, disrupting communications, bursting among formations of troops and spreading confusion that easily turned to panic.

Driving across open country, German mobile forces soon split the Polish armies into fragments. Each of these broken pieces faced an impossible situation: the harder they fought, the worse off they were. If isolated units stood their ground and beat back frontal attacks, they would soon be

Londoners read the grim news on Friday, September 1: Germany had invaded Poland before dawn; Parliament would convene at 6 p.m.

A superbly self-assured Hitler receives the salutes of Nazi faithful in the Reichstag moments after announcing that German troops and tanks had invaded Poland. Out of 821 deputies, more than 100, who had been drafted into the military for the Polish campaign, could not be on hand for the Führer's announcement; they were replaced by hastily assembled party hacks who had not been legally elected, but who were nonetheless empowered to vote. They promptly rubber-stamped the incorporation of Danzig—the first city captured by the German invaders—into the Reich.

GRAND DESIGN FOR A WARRIOR'S DREAM

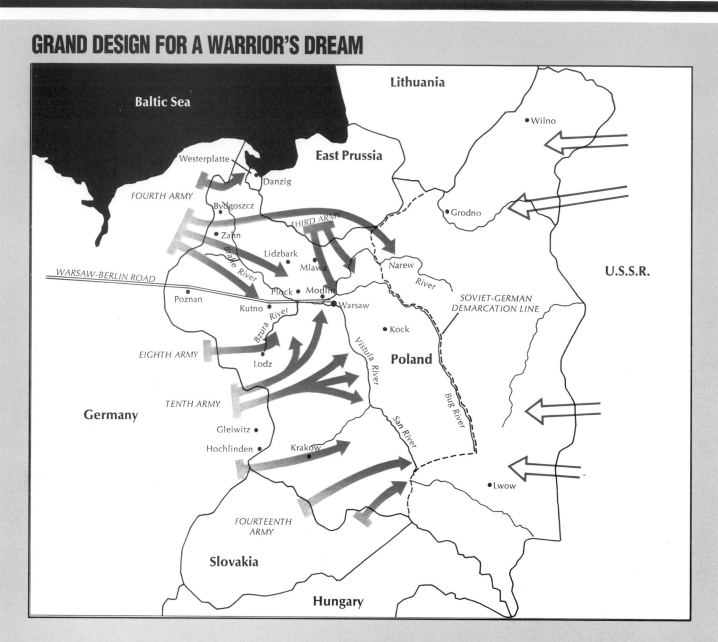

Every military man has dreamed of directing a classic battle in which his armies slash the enemy with the deadly precision prescribed by the arrows on this map. Hitler's blitzkrieg in Poland offers a rare picture of such a dream come true—though when Wehrmacht troops met Soviet forces *(lined arrows)* coming from the east, the triumphant panzers teetered momentarily on the nightmarish edge of the wrong war.

During the main battle against the Poles, the Germans surged forward in set-piece order. After thrusting across the Polish border on September 1, one corps of the Third Army swept in on Warsaw, while another trapped the fleeing Polish troops west of the city.

In the south, the Fourteenth Army roared through the city of Krakow, the Tenth Army shoved in between Lodz and Krakow, and German units from Slovakia cut into the Polish rear and turned toward the Bug River. In the north, part of the Fourth Army raced through the Polish Corridor and entered Danzig; other Fourth Army units fanned out toward East Prussia, Warsaw and Kutno— where they linked with the Eighth Army to capture 170,000 Poles by mid-September.

As the near-perfect battle was ending, stunned German troops deep in Poland looked up to see Russian soldiers advancing. The High Command had not passed down word of a secret, high-level agreement calling for the Russian advance that began on September 17. In the melee when the powers met, sporadic gunfire killed and wounded a few German and Soviet soldiers before the two forces separated across a previously negotiated demarcation line along the Bug.

surrounded by troops pouring through the gaps the panzers had made. If they retreated, they faced the hell that the blitzkrieg was generating in the rear.

The Poles struggled against enormous handicaps from the start. The country's weak industrial base left the army undersupplied, and its loyalties divided along ethnic lines. Moreover, the army was far from full strength on September 1, and of the 935 aircraft and 500 tanks at their disposal, many were obsolete. Furthermore, the Poles were faced with the awesome task of defending a meandering 1,750-mile border with no natural river or mountain frontiers. Their thin defense system of barbed wire, trenches and gun emplacements at key points was not much of a bulwark against the onslaught of German tanks.

Equally defenseless was the Polish cavalry. At one point, the crack Pomorske Cavalry Brigade spearheaded an attempt to break out of a German encirclement and rejoin their main forces in the southeast. As the Germans looked on in disbelief, the troopers came riding splendid horses; white-gloved officers signaled the charge, trumpets sounded, pennons waved, sabers flashed in the sun. Like an animated page out of an old history book, the brigade galloped, lances

at the ready—straight into the fire of German tanks. In a few minutes the cavalry lay in a smoking, screaming mass of dismembered men and horses.

On the fifth day of the campaign, Hitler visited the battlefield. General Heinz Guderian, commander of the XIX Armored Corps, pointed out traces of Polish defeat everywhere: hundreds of guns destroyed or taken, hundreds of square miles safely conquered, thousands of prisoners—all at the minuscule cost to his four divisions of 150 dead and 700 wounded. Clearly blitzkrieg was working.

And it had nonmilitary benefits as well. Since "lightning war" made for short, decisive campaigns, fewer burdens were placed on the German economy and population. Politically, such quick results would justify Hitler's aggressive foreign policy to his people, and help identify them ever more closely with him and the Nazi party. Furthermore, by exploiting the speed and efficiency of his disciplined troops, Hitler felt prepared to take the kind of gamble that had paid off in the past: to make war with a force that was far from full strength.

Indeed, the Wehrmacht's weaknesses were considerable. Massive propaganda efforts after the Polish campaign

Stuka dive bombers skim the trees ahead of a German armored car in an attack on Polish troop concentrations and supply depots down the road. Many of these planes were fitted with sirens on their undercarriages, which produced an unnerving, ear-shattering racket as the Stukas came plummeting down.

General Heinz Guderian, the principal architect of Germany's devastating blitzkrieg strategy, uses a periscope to observe his tanks. Guderian and his associates conceived the idea of "panzer divisions." These were self-contained organizations, which consisted typically of two tank regiments and a regiment each of infantry and artillery.

During an infantry assault, a German soldier, supported by two of his comrades, cocks his arm to throw a "potato masher" hand grenade.

showed the German Army as a ruthless, sophisticated fighting machine. But the reality was far different. Of the 44 divisions the Germans loosed on Poland, only six were real panzer divisions by Guderian's standards. The bulk of the fighting in Poland was done by old-style infantry divisions. In addition, the armored formations themselves were not as powerful as originally intended; most of the tanks used were thin-skinned models armed only with machine guns.

To make matters worse, since Hitler had to throw most of Germany's military strength against the Poles, only limited forces garrisoned the Siegfried line—the complex of fortifications along the German-French border. What if, Hitler's generals wondered, the French were to strike Germany in force? But Hitler gambled that France would not attack on the ground, and Luftwaffe chief Hermann Göring assured him that France's air force was no match for the Luftwaffe. Events were to prove both men correct.

The tank-led blitzkrieg forces slammed persistently through the countryside. Every night the Poles prayed for one substantial rain that would turn Poland's primitive dirt road system into quagmires, and bog down German tanks, trucks and foot soldiers. But every day the sun came up relentlessly bright and red, baking the land to parade-ground hardness. People began to call it "Hitler Weather."

Among civilians, the sudden descent of the planes and tanks spread disquieting news, then alarming rumors, then blind fear upon the peaceful hinterland. Householders packed a few prized possessions and took to the roads—the very roads over which the Polish forces had to maneuver if they were to halt the onrushing German tides.

Clearly, the Poles barely stood a chance. The goal was to hold the invaders off long enough for the British and French to come to their aid. But the Allies were unprepared; no help came. The Poles' last thin hope of reprieve was shattered on September 17. On that fateful day, with no more declaration

Smoke rises from the Warsaw gasworks during one of the Luftwaffe attacks that reduced vital urban services to mounds of smoldering rubble.

Bombed-out survivors wander down a littered street among the shells of Warsaw buildings. Even after it was clear that Poland had lost the war, Warsaw struggled grimly on. When crowds of refugees tried to flee the battered city, the Germans drove them back so that the Poles could be more easily starved into surrender. And the threat of starvation was a major factor in forcing the Warsaw garrison to capitulate at last on September 28.

of war than Hitler had made—and based on his pact with Hitler—Stalin sent an immense concentration of troops across the undefended eastern frontier of Poland. Shortly thereafter, the world reeled at photographs of German and Russian officers shaking hands at the border of their respective occupation zones. For all practical purposes, Poland had ceased to exist. The war was over.

Although some Polish resistance continued, the Germans and Russians did not wait to carve up their victim. The original pact signed by foreign ministers Vyacheslav Molotov and Joachim von Ribbentrop provided for a partition line between spheres of influence running through the center of Poland. Stalin now proposed to leave central Poland to the Germans, retaining only the eastern regions where a majority of the population was of Ukrainian or Belorussian stock. In return, he demanded a free hand in Lithuania—although the pact had originally allocated Lithuania to Germany—and possession of all the oil fields in southeast Poland, from which he promised to send 30,000 tons of crude oil yearly to Germany.

Hitler was not happy with the change in plans. Nonetheless, he agreed; the new partition line along the Bug, San and Narew rivers was duly ratified. The eastern

provinces were incorporated into the Soviet Union. The western provinces, inhabited by many ethnic Germans, were annexed by the Reich. For the ethnically Polish population of the central portions, Hitler was about to provide an object lesson in how Germany would treat conquered territory. These lands would become a Nazi fief called the Government General, and its function was stated very succinctly by Hans Frank, who would be its ruler for the next four years: "The Poles will be the slaves of the Greater German World Reich." The means to achieve this end would be naked brutality and terror. The Jews were to be "housecleaned"; so were the Polish intellectuals, clergy, nobility—any group that might provide leaders for a potential resistance.

For Hitler, all was glory. He had annihilated the enemy at minimum cost; he had a quiescent frontier on the eastern flank. Now he could turn all his powers as a strategist, his thoroughly vindicated intuition, and the full-armed might of Germany against his enemies in the West. But for all his confidence, Hitler's plans were nearly ruined by the ineptitude of two ambitious Luftwaffe majors.

On January 9, 1940, Major Hellmuth Reinberger and Major Erich Hoenmanns struck up an acquaintance over convivial rounds of beer in the German Officers Club at a Münster air base, and hatched a plan for their mutual benefit. Reinberger was due in Cologne for an important meeting the next day. An ambitious man with hopes of rising high in the Luftwaffe command, he dreaded the idea of arriving late and unpresentable after an uncomfortable overnight train ride. Hoenmanns, for his part, was delighted to be of service. As a former World War I flyer, he hoped to get back to active duty by clocking in more flying time; flying Reinberger to Cologne would also allow him to visit his wife, who lived nearby.

Next morning the two officers were on their way in a new-model Messerschmitt Taifun scout plane, heading west from Münster toward the Rhine through a clear blue sky. But the air did not stay clear for long. Hoenmanns was not prepared for the fog that built into a thick cover. Nor was he equipped to deal with the plane—a far faster model than he was used to. As the minutes ticked by, the panic grew: where the devil was the Rhine?

All Hoenmanns could see below was solid white. He had never thought of asking Major Reinberger if he had any maps. And Major Reinberger had never thought of telling him that his briefcase contained maps, all right—and much more. Reinberger was carrying a copy of sections of the secret operational plan for the German invasion of Holland and Belgium, which was due to start in exactly one

A day after the surrender, Polish Jews wait nervously in a railroad station after being rounded up by Hitler's SS, the elite Nazi security corps. The SS was under orders to segregate and deport or shoot Jews and any other Poles judged to be intellectually dissident or otherwise undesirable.

EASY LIFE IN A SUPERTRENCH

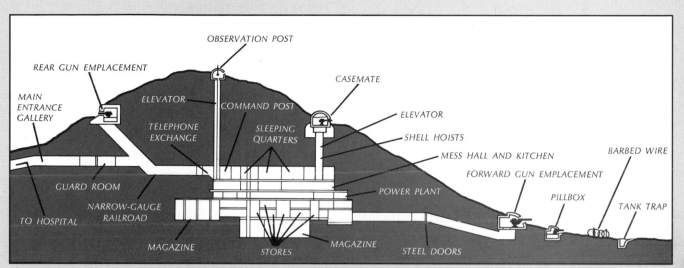

This cutaway profile of an immense Maginot fort shows its main elements: multilevel areas connected by tunnels to gun and observation posts.

After almost losing to the Germans in World War I, the French were determined to make their land impregnable. Beginning in 1930, at a cost of over $200 million and seven years' labor, they built an 87-mile-long string of underground forts facing Germany.

Named after André Maginot, the Defense Minister when work began, the Line was a masterpiece of static defense. At its forward edge were tank traps; behind lay barbed wire and pillboxes. Next came rows of gun emplacements walled in concrete that was 10 feet thick and armed with machine guns and antitank weapons ranging from 37mm to 155mm. Located at three-to-five-mile intervals were fortresses *(above)*, buried as deep as 100 feet underground.

Within these forts, up to 1,200 men lived for three-month tours. They had sun lamps and went topside to plant roses; still, their most deadly enemy was boredom.

But when the Wehrmacht began its attack in earnest, the French realized that the age of static warfare was over. Even the strongest fortress would prove no match for the maneuverability of German panzers.

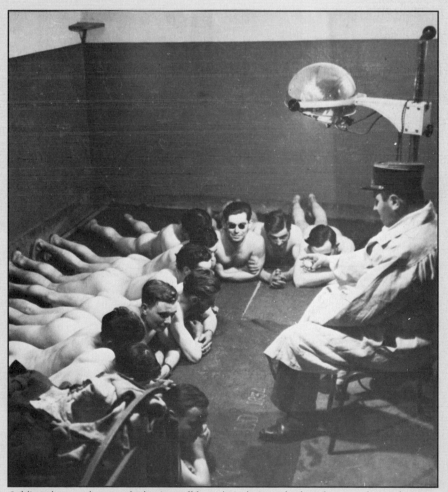

Soldiers deep underground take time off from their duties to bask in the rays of a sun lamp.

week—documents he had been specifically ordered never to take up in an airplane. Out of control and lost, Hoenmanns crash-landed in a field of hedges—in Belgium—confirming the Luftwaffe's doubts about his flying abilities. Reinberger tried to set fire to his papers, but Belgian border guards quickly put out the flames and escorted the two officers to the nearby town of Mechelen-sur-Meuse for questioning.

It quickly became clear to Belgian authorities that they had stumbled onto something extraordinary. So extraordinary, in fact, that at first they thought the papers might be a plant—a false alarm to induce Belgium and the Western allies to rush to arms. Unfortunately, once they were convinced of the plans' authenticity, they declined Allied intelligence officers access to them—only a précis was shared. Soon after, ambiguous and garbled information about the captured German plans circulated between Brussels, Paris and London.

There had been an eight-month pause in fighting since the Polish defeat and, as subsequent events unfolded, the crash at Mechelen-sur-Meuse and its aftermath became the perfect symbol of the mood on both sides. Indecision, ineptitude and lassitude enveloped nearly all decision-makers. For example, fearful of giving Hitler an excuse to strike, the Belgians—and the Dutch—not only refused to allow French and British troops on their soil but also refused to let the Allies make systematic analyses of Belgian and Dutch defenses. United only in the fear of a repeat of the bloodbath that was World War I, their mutual mistrust aborted any effort at concerted action.

The Allied High Command, in particular, was mired in a profound intellectual lethargy. And it did not help matters that General Maurice Gamelin—described by one observer as "A nice old man, not remotely equal to his enormous job"—was named Supreme Commander of the Allied ground forces in Europe. Nevertheless, the British generals were determined not to repeat the organizational errors of the First World War, when it took four years to get a unified command of the French and British under Marshal Foch. Despite their misgivings, they accepted Gamelin's orders.

The end result was that, in the months following the September declaration of war, the Allies wasted one opportunity after another to seize the initiative from the Germans. In actual fact, they were enjoying a mood of self-congratulation. The French had mobilized five million men and moved them to their battle stations along the Maginot line. The British had sent four divisions across the Channel and set up a Royal Navy blockade designed to lead to the economic strangulation of Germany. These moves added up, in the Allied view, to a spectacular feat of arms—at a meager price. At the outset, so few casualties occurred and so

cautious were the Allies, that the French called it a "*drôle de guerre*," an "odd war"; Neville Chamberlain called it a "twilight war"; the Americans called it a "phony war."

Only at sea did anybody really fight and die. German submarines had sunk the British liner *Athenia* at the very start of the war, and a few days later a German U-boat had slipped into the main anchorage of the British fleet at Scapa Flow in the Orkneys and had sunk the British battleship *Royal Oak*. For lack of land action of any sort, events such as these made big headlines, but they were only minor incidents in the developing conflict.

The prevailing opinion among Allied leaders, as expressed by the British Foreign Office, was that "if Germany cannot win a quick success, she cannot hope to win a long-drawn war." The only chance of a quick success for the Germans—so Allied leaders believed—would have been to smash into France before the French and British armies were ready to take the blow. Now that they were in place behind their fortifications, the Allies reasoned, that hope was gone.

While the Allied High Command was taking false comfort in the unexpected hiatus in the war, Hitler and his top generals wrangled about how to defeat the Allies. Shortly after Poland had been taken, the bulk of the German Army was moved west to positions along the French frontier, and waited for the Führer to make up his mind. At first the lack of a satisfactory plan held up Hitler's ambition to occupy the Low Countries. Later, bad weather set in; the beginning of

British, French and Polish soldiers on a hillside overlooking the Norwegian port of Harstad watch smoke rising from a fuel dump hit by Luftwaffe bombs. From start to finish, the Norwegian campaign lasted less than two months at the relatively minor cost of 5,000 German casualties. The Germans had surprised and humiliated their enemies by mounting a successful amphibious operation in the face of Allied navies many times more powerful than their own. And what they had lacked in strength, they made up for with bluff and imagination.

the severest European winter in decades caused further postponement. Finally, at the end of the year, Hitler decided to augment his projected campaign in western Europe, and protect his northern flank with an attack on Scandinavia.

Then in January came the plane crash in Belgium. When the news reached Hitler, he literally foamed at the mouth, according to accounts. Now, the Germans had to decide whether to abandon their plans for the Western Front. The Führer and his generals worked furiously, and by February the revised plan was in final shape. The attack on Belgium, Holland and Luxembourg was set for May 10—and a second German force was already embarked to invade Scandinavia.

While Hitler and his High Command were refining their strategy for conquering Europe, the Allied Supreme Command cemented plans for a preemptive invasion of two neutral nations—Norway and Sweden. The decisive meeting, on February 5, 1940, was attended by the top military and civilian brass of Britain and France, and was marked by unusual accord. "Everyone was purring," noted one British participant.

It was First Lord of the Admiralty Winston Churchill who had originally come up with the plan in 1939. Almost half of the iron Germany needed to make steel for its guns came from the mines in northern Sweden, and about 80 per cent of the ore was shipped through Narvik. By cutting off this Narvik traffic, the British could strike a blow against the Nazi war industry.

Then in November of that year, while the value of this

plan was still being debated, Russia attacked its small neighbor, Finland. It was the climax of a series of moves by Stalin to consolidate his sphere of influence under the Nazi-Soviet treaty. The world was at first shocked by the Soviet attack, then amazed at the Finns' resistance. Contrary to all expectations, the Finns had the Russians staggering—if not on their knees. A tough winter and poor leadership, coupled with gross overconfidence, had resulted in Russian units being annihilated group by group.

Russia's move on Finland offered the Allies the perfect pretext for launching Churchill's Scandinavian campaign. Obviously, the only thing to do was come to the defense of the hapless Finns, and the most practical route was through northern Norway and Sweden. The Allies would land at Narvik, moving one brigade into Finland and holding two in the Narvik area. Among its numerous flaws, the proposed action underestimated the enormous administrative difficulties involved, and failed to take into account the possibility of turning Finland into a battleground for the great powers. But the campaign, as such, never took place. The weight of overwhelming Russian numbers finally crushed the valiant Finns; by early March it was all over and a humiliated Finnish peace delegation to Moscow was forced to give Stalin more land than he had originally demanded.

Finland's defeat was a devastating surprise for the Allies. All the ambitious plans of the Supreme Command now added up to zero. The Finnish capitulation even brought about the downfall of the Daladier government in France; Daladier was succeeded by Paul Reynaud, who was installed with a mandate to take action.

The Allies hastily devised a new plan: during the first week of April, a British fleet would lay minefields in Norwegian coastal waters to prevent ore ships from getting down from Narvik to Germany. If the Germans retaliated heavily, British and French forces would land and seize not only Narvik but also harbors to the south   and then they would advance to the Swedish frontier. The total force allocated to this grand design would be one division, which was to operate without air support.

As it turned out, here as elsewhere in Europe thus far, Hitler was two steps ahead. He was already convinced of the importance of the Norwegian coast—not only as a route for ore ships, but also as a base for surface raiders and submarines then blockaded in the Baltic. Furthermore, he had been receiving dire warnings of "the dangers to Germany arising from a British occupation" of Norway from an ambitious Nazi-oriented Norwegian politician named Vidkun Quisling. The warnings were confirmed by a minor naval scuffle in Norwegian waters involving a German

Finnish ski troopers, their supplies carried on reindeer-drawn wooden sleds, patrol against invading Russians in a forest north of the Arctic Circle.

BITTER HARVEST IN THE ARCTIC

When the Soviet Army High Command attacked Finland in November of 1939, there seemed little reason to expect anything but a swift and complete victory. The hugely outnumbered Finns had no more than a few tanks and an air force of obsolete biplanes to put up against the latest mechanized units of the Soviet Army. And since the Russians believed they would crush Finland in 12 days at the most, they saw little reason to worry about Finland's snow and arctic cold.

They were dead wrong. It took the Soviets more than half the winter, which turned out to be the coldest in a century, to subdue the tough, weather-wise Finns. Soviet tanks, stuck in deep-drifted snow and paralyzed by temperatures of 40 to 50 degrees below zero, were easily destroyed by artillery, grenades and hand-thrown gasoline bombs. Thousands of Russian infantrymen, hurled into the attack without proper cold-weather clothing, were crippled by frostbite. Red soldiers learned that a man who touched the bare metal of his rifle with ungloved hands risked stripping off skin. Severely wounded men often froze to death in grotesque contortions, while others who might have been saved perished for want of blood plasma, which the weather turned to ice.

By contrast, the Finns were well prepared for the winter war. For the field, they wore warm, snow-camouflaged clothes, and in the fortifications of the Mannerheim Line, named for the Finnish Commander-in-Chief, they stayed fit and relatively snug in quarters that shielded them from both shells and cold, and that included such amenities as saunas.

Underground shelters protected Finnish civilians, as well, against the Soviet air attacks that swept over from Russia whenever the weather was clear. But the most efficient shelters were located in such cities as Helsinki and Viipuri; in rural areas, the bombs fell on relatively unprotected villages and towns. Many country-dwelling civilians, their homes destroyed, were cast out onto snowy roads, or forced to take miserable refuge in forests. In March of 1940, when the Russians finally overwhelmed the defenders with irresistible masses of men and steel, 400,000 Finns fled the territories of eastern Finland that were ceded to the Soviets.

A Finnish soldier (above) guards the camouflaged entrance to a bunker on the Mannerheim Line, which was so well constructed that during one dawn-to-dusk shelling by the Russians no soldier inside was killed.

A snow-masked sign in the village of Suvilahti locates Finnish towns near the Soviet border; the burning buildings have been hit by Russian bombs.

supply ship and two British destroyers; the outcome convinced the Führer that Norway would not physically oppose Allied infringement of its neutrality. He put an urgent priority on the conquest of Norway, adding Denmark almost as an afterthought.

Germany's plan at this time was to seize simultaneously every major port and airfield in the whole thousand-mile length of Norway. The date agreed upon was April 9, one day after the Allies themselves were scheduled to go ashore.

Again, Hitler weather prevailed. Fog and storms concealed the movements of German ships as they sailed out on April 7. Nevertheless, that night, a group of German ships was sighted by British reconnaissance. But the British Admiralty blundered. They assumed that it was the German war fleet putting to sea to interfere with the British landing in Norway. Britain's expeditionary forces had already been embarked on cruisers in the port of Rosyth in the Firth of Forth. They were abruptly put ashore, leaving all their equipment on board; the cruisers went off to look for the German fleet. Soon the cruisers were joined by all available British warships. And, once the mining operation of Narvik's harbor was completed in the early morning of April 8, the ships of the mining force joined in. In the meantime, the German invasion fleet slipped past them in the fog.

It was not until later that day that the government in Oslo realized that two mighty, contending powers were about to sweep down on Norway. The government reacted by ordering partial mobilization—by mail. The letters were barely in the Oslo post office when the Germans landed in Scandinavia an hour before dawn on April 9.

The Norwegians and Danes had no chance. Denmark was conquered in four hours—with a total of 56 casualties. The Norwegians, however, managed to delay the German ships off the ancient fortress of Oscarsborg long enough to allow the Royal Family to escape.

But in Oslo no one thought to place obstacles on the runways of Fornebu airfield; when the German transport planes came in with their loads of heavily armed infantry, the antiaircraft defense merely slowed their landing and inflicted minor casualties. The entire invading force, however, amounted only to a few hundred fighting men accompanied by a military band, and could have been wiped out by a determined counterattack. But the German commander was a man of nerve. Instead of fretting about hostile action, he snapped his men into formation behind the oompah-ing band and brazenly marched them down Oslo's boulevards unopposed. The city of 250,000 people was captured without another shot being fired.

Meanwhile, as the Royal Navy was still searching in the fog for the phantom grand fleet, the troop-laden German ships pulled boldly into Norwegian seaports. By the time the British reboarded the troops originally assembled for the Narvik expedition and organized reinforcements, it was too late to keep the main Norwegian airfield and ports from falling into German hands. After that, it was impossible for the Allies to land enough troops to prevent the conquest of the entire country.

Only in the far north did there seem a possibility of salvaging something from the wreckage of the campaign. At Narvik, the German forces were unsupported by aircraft and short of supplies; to Allied planners looking for a way to recoup, this force looked like the easiest target. Indeed, the force's only advantage was a first-rate commander, General Eduard Dietl. First a British destroyer flotilla surprised and

Britain's brand new Prime Minister, Winston Churchill, emerges from Number 10 Downing Street. Churchill, who from 1932 on had vainly urged British preparedness—and a stronger line against Adolf Hitler—had been called to power on May 10, 1940, exactly five days before Holland would fall and as both Belgium and France were being threatened.

HITLER'S STRATEGY FOR SEIZING WESTERN EUROPE

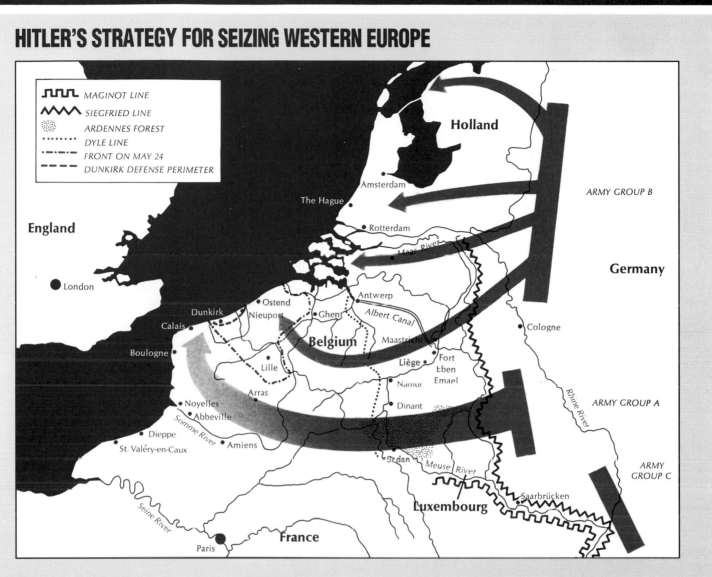

Hitler's bold design for conquering Western Europe relied on speed, surprise, deception—and power. Arrayed along a 200-mile front facing Holland and Belgium, 30 Wehrmacht divisions (Army Group B) were scheduled to swoop through the Low Countries in a four-pronged attack.

Hitler hoped the Allies would regard that attack as the major threat and rush the best and readiest French and British troops north to help the Dutch and the Belgians hold their key defenses along Belgium's Dyle River.

The real thrust would come farther south through the forest of Ardennes. Army Group A, whose 45 divisions included most of the Germans' armor and motorized infantry, would squeeze between the Maginot and the Dyle lines, race across France to the Channel, then swing north to help Group B encircle and annihilate the nearly one million Allied troops that Hitler hoped to entrap.

The Germans could then devour the remainder of France at leisure—including the Maginot Line, whose enormous garrison was meant to be kept occupied by feints made by the 19 divisions of Army Group C.

From the start on May 10, 1940, both Germans and Allies enacted Hitler's scenario to perfection. At the first sign of attack Allied troops sped north to take on Army Group B, which nevertheless overran Holland in five days. In Belgium, other Group B units pushed back Allied forces after swiftly reducing Belgium's vaunted fortress, Fort Eben Emael.

With the Allies busy and the Maginot garrison pinned down, Group A panzers raced through the Ardennes Forest and on to the French coast in 10 days.

After turning north, Army Group A joined B to drive the cornered Allies into a pocket around Lille by May 24. The whole left flank of this salient dissolved four days later when its battered Belgian defenders surrendered on orders from King Léopold, and by May 30 the surviving Allied troops had withdrawn behind a seven-mile-wide, last-ditch perimeter around the port of Dunkirk.

seriously damaged the German squadron at anchor in Narvik harbor. Then a British battleship wiped out the remaining German naval forces protecting Dietl's position. With only 4,600 to hold Narvik, half of whom were sailors with no infantry training, Dietl's plight was desperate.

But again the Germans were decisive while the Allies fumbled. Long-range Luftwaffe planes made artillery drops and the Swedes allowed food and medical supplies to reach the Germans. Meanwhile, the British were bogged down in contradictory orders and interservice wrangling. When at last French and Norwegian troops entered Narvik on May 28, Dietl had abandoned the town and had consolidated his position to the north, where he held 100 square miles of territory. By then the Allies were faced by greater disasters closer to home, and withdrew their troops from the area. The entire country was under German control.

In Britain, the Norwegian campaign had a political consequence that was resoundingly decisive. By early May it was clear that the Allied effort had been an abysmal failure. On May 7, Conservative M.P. Leopold Amery rose in British Parliament to give a pitiless analysis of the fearful shortcomings of the British government, as led by Neville Chamberlain. In his peroration, Amery borrowed a 1653 line from Oliver Cromwell; turning toward Chamberlain, Amery said: "Depart, I say, and let us have done with you. In the name of God, go!"

It was exactly what the British people had been saying in their hearts for a long time. Chamberlain was swept out of office and Churchill was called upon to form a government of genuine national unity. And none too soon. For on the very day—May 10, 1940—that Churchill presented his new government to Parliament, the long-delayed storm of German assault broke on the Western front.

Precisely at dawn, hundreds of German planes swept in over Allied air bases and communications centers in the north of France. Simultaneously a wave of tanks and infantry—the vanguard of an army of two million men—broke over the borders of Holland, Belgium and Luxembourg. The battle that was to decide the fate of the West had begun.

Aimed at Holland was the German Eighteenth Army, comprised of armored, airborne and cavalry divisions, a motorized SS infantry division, and seven other infantry divisions. In addition, two regiments of paratroopers, about 4,000 men, suddenly materialized over Holland. Four paratroop groups headed for the big highway and railroad bridges and one other unit headed for the Dutch capital at The Hague.

The Dutch had assumed all along that they would be hit by armored forces on the frontier and by parachute troops dropped into their rear. They hoped to cut off and neutralize the latter before they could do fatal damage, and to slow down the former by slowly retreating, blowing up bridges and flooding the countryside as they went. If all went well, the attacking forces would be stalled on one side of a huge lake, while on the other—in "Fortress Holland," the populous stretch of coast between Rotterdam and Amsterdam—the defenders could settle down for a siege.

But before the Dutch could do more than destroy bridges over the Ijssel River and some of those over the Maas River, the Germans were upon them. While the defenders were still trying to collect their wits, the Germans captured the bridges and held them against counterattacks as their armor came rumbling up from the frontier.

Dark rumors and hints of treachery followed the parachute drops. It was said that some of the German prisoners were found to be carrying instructions for making contact with certain citizens of The Hague. This rumor gave rise to fears that the capital city was riddled with Fifth Columnists and Nazi sympathizers. As reports of parachutists began coming in from far and near, soldiers and civilians fell prey to ever wilder delusions: the parachutists were disguised as policemen, as farm laborers, even as priests and nuns, and they were misdirecting traffic,

A German motor column churns through a field in Holland, passing to one side of a roadblock of dynamited trees. Overwhelmed by the suddenness of the German strike, the Dutch abandoned carefully laid defense plans but still made attempts to slow the panzers with makeshift barricades—which included old trucks and buses dumped across the highway.

THE WORKHORSE OF THE WEHRMACHT'S STABLE

The fast, maneuverable medium tank shown here was the cutting edge of the German sword that sliced through the Low Countries and France in May 1940. With its 75 mm gun, the Panzer IV could easily stand off and destroy more lightly armed Allied tanks. Against the better Allied tanks, such as the French Char B—which also carried a 75 mm gun—and the more heavily armored but slower British Matilda, the Panzer IV's speed was a distinct advantage.

The Panzer IV, with a large fuel tank, could go 125 miles without filling up. The driver and a radio operator, who was also a machine-gunner, sat in the hull up front. The turret housed the commander, the gunner for the 75, and a loader.

However, the Panzer IV's were in scarce supply at the start of the war. Because of production problems, there were only 278 of the new tanks available for the Western campaign, which forced tank commanders to use the versatile weapons sparingly. The record for applying this stinginess probably belongs to General Erwin Rommel, a brilliant tactician and Germany's greatest tankman. When one of his columns was stalled in a village by a detachment of heavier French tanks, he ordered just one Panzer IV to attack the French rear. Firing at a furious rate, the Panzer knocked out 14 of the French machines, which were too ponderous to maneuver in the narrow village streets.

Not even Rommel could make the Panzer IVs invincible, however. When caught by surprise—as they were near Arras when the British and French armor fell on the flank of Rommel's advancing column —they showed a streak of vulnerability. French shells, which were fired from close range, penetrated the Panzer's armor, knocking out three of them. Soon after, the Germans modified the Panzer IV, giving it thicker armor and a more powerful gun. Thus improved, it became the workhorse tank, better than a match for most Allied armored fighting vehicles throughout the War.

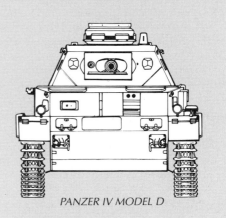

PANZER IV MODEL D

Weight: 20 tons
Length: 19 feet
Width: 9 feet
Height: 8 feet
Maximum speed on roads: 25 mph
Maximum speed cross country: 12 mph
Maximum radius on roads: 125 miles
Maximum radius cross country:
     80 miles
Fuel supply: 120 gallons
Trench-crossing capacity: 7 feet
Gradient-climbing capacity: 30 degrees
Fording depth: 3 feet
Crew: 5
Armament: one 75mm gun, two
     7.92mm machine guns
Front armor thickness: 1.2 inch
Side and rear armors: .8 inch
Roof armor: .4 inch

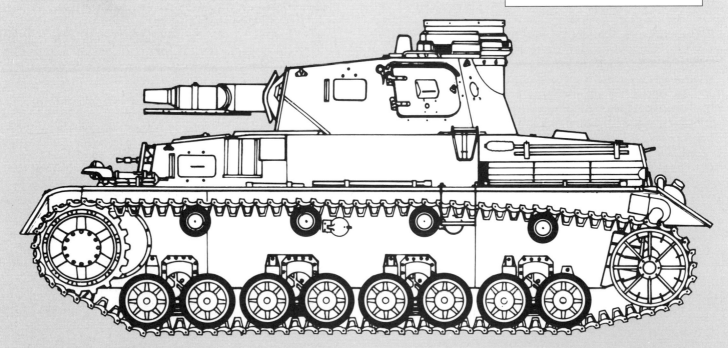

The original Panzer IV hull, designed in 1934, was used for all subsequent models, allowing mass production of more than 8,000 of these tanks.

poisoning wells, planting alarmist lies. It was just the touch the Germans needed to turn confusion into chaos.

Yet for all that, "Fortress Holland" remained initially intact. Though German troops held the bridges leading to Rotterdam, Dutch defenders had sealed off the bridgeheads at the northern ends so enemy tanks could not cross. If Allied reinforcements arrived on time, there was still a chance. The Dutch fought on, and waited and hoped.

They might have waited forever. Allied plans to meet the expected attack on the Low Countries, and France did not include provision for a major thrust in Holland; the Allies planned to meet the enemy in Belgium. Only the French Seventh Army was to advance to southern Holland, where it could join up with the Dutch forces and close the gap between Antwerp and the Channel.

But these and other Allied plans for the Low Countries began too late. The Nazis pounced on Belgium; the Seventh Army was driven back. The Germans moved on Rotterdam. On May 13, as Dutch defenses crumbled, Queen Wilhelmina and the government fled The Hague for London.

Only at Rotterdam did the German onslaught stall, unable to break through the Dutch bridgeheads. Hitler lost patience, and he ordered the Luftwaffe to bomb the city into submission. On May 14 a massive air attack hit Rotterdam. More than 800 died; 25,000 houses were completely gutted and 78,000 civilians were left homeless. Later that evening the Commander-in-Chief of the Dutch forces ordered a ceasefire. In five days, 2,100 Dutch troops had been killed and 2,700 wounded.

The bombing of the Netherlands' second largest city produced a highly unwelcome consequence for Hitler: the next day, British bombers that were based in France began hitting back at the important industrial cities in Germany's Ruhr Valley. But the attack on Rotterdam paid the Führer an unexpected dividend as well: a wave of panic engulfed the Western World. It was believed that 35,000 people were killed and the city destroyed. During the coming campaign in Belgium and France, thousands of civilians, fearing another Rotterdam, would seriously clog the roads, interfering with Allied military movements.

The German offensive in Belgium began at 4:30 a.m. on May 10, when 42 Junkers transport planes, each hauling a glider carrying a team of airborne troops trained in the use of special assault equipment, took off from Cologne for Fort Eben Emael and the Albert Canal bridges. At five minutes before dawn and the start of the main offensive, the 42 silent craft came skimming down on the gateway to the Belgian plain—which the Allies were convinced could be held for days, perhaps weeks.

One group of gliders swooped directly onto the roof of the fort. In a maneuver rehearsed repeatedly in the preceding months, they sabotaged the fort's massive armaments. Within an hour, the fortress was a helpless giant, incapable of holding up the sweep of the invading armies. But the garrison somehow managed to fight on until May 11 before capitulating.

Meanwhile, the primary force of the gliders—300 assault troops—landed on the west bank of Belgium's Albert Canal. Soon reinforced by 500 paratroopers, they secured two of the three main bridges. To make this small force look larger, dummy parachutists with explosive charges were also dropped. These blew up, adding to the confusion, while the Stukas and panzers of Army Group B swept behind the assault troops onto the Belgian plain.

To meet this expected thrust, the Allied units in northern France began their advance to form a continuous front with the Belgian army along the Dyle and Meuse rivers. But the Germans unexpectedly dealt a deathblow to the Allies by smashing through the wooded ravines of the Ardennes in less than half the time predicted by the French. By May 13, three German armored divisions were crossing the Meuse—the French guns covering the river having been pounded into silence by the Luftwaffe. Once across the river in force, the German armor fanned out as it sliced westward, spreading terror in the rear of the French forces.

Colonel Charles de Gaulle, leading the 4th Armored Division to strike the southern side of Guderian's rapidly growing salient ran into a sight for which nothing in his life had prepared him: droves of French troops shuffling southward, disarmed and dispirited. They had been overrun by the panzers, and the Germans had shouted to them contemptuosly from their tanks: "Drop your rifles and get the hell out of here—we don't have time to take you prisoner."

Twice de Gaulle attempted counterattacks against Guderian's troops; twice he failed. By May 16, the French defense line was breached with a gaping hole. The impact was so sudden and so great that even the Germans found it hard to believe.

Instead of capitalizing immediately on their sudden advantage, the Germans waited for the infantry. But they soon realized they had the chance of a lifetime. Every tank was packed into the bulge—and tens of thousands of refugees trailed down the roads away from them. "They fled," said one observer, "accelerating their cars, pushing their handcarts. In their scattered houses they had enjoyed relative safety. They preferred to congregate in long columns exposed to the enemy's fire. Their flight was suicide."

By May 20, Guderian's forward units were in Amiens and Abbeville; they had gone farther in 10 days than the Kaiser's

Tommies watch as a line of their comrades, some chest-deep in the sea, wade out toward a transport anchored well off the shallow beach at Dunkirk.

Motorboats, requisitioned by the British Admiralty, are towed down the Thames to join other small craft bound across the Channel for Dunkirk.

World War I armies had been able to get in four years. Hitler was beside himself with joy. Nearly a million men were rapidly becoming cut off in the north by the rush of the panzers to the sea—including the entire Belgian Army, all but one of the divisions of the British Expeditionary Force (BEF) and the two best French armies. Unless this combined Allied force could manage to break out quickly and to link up with the rest of the French armies south of the Somme, they would be hopelessly boxed up in northern France and western Belgium.

On the 28th of May, after 18 shattering days of seeing his small, tough forces torn to shreds, Léopold of Belgium, acting not as King but as Commander-in-Chief of the Belgian armed forces, capitulated to the Germans. The battle in the Low Countries was at an end.

No one was more aware of how close to the end the Low Countries were than General Lord Gort, commander of the BEF. As early as May 19, in a message to London, he had raised the possibility of withdrawing the BEF to Dunkirk. The top brass in London, believing optimistic reports from the French, sternly ordered Gort to forget about retreat.

But Gort could not forget. On the morning of May 23rd, after a breakfast of hard biscuits and marmalade at BEF headquarters at Premesques, near Lille, Gort confided to an aide: "You know, the day I joined up, I never thought I'd lead the British Army to its biggest defeat in history." He then spent most of the afternoon sitting alone, going over his options, or lack of them, in his mind. He knew that a decision to retreat would be contrary to orders not only from London but also from his French superior, General Maxime Weygand, who was Allied Commander-in-Chief. But Gort was convinced that if he were to save any of the BEF from annihilation, he must retreat. By 6:00 that evening his mind was made up. The BEF would not fight its way south, but would head north and east to Dunkirk, to the Channel and—God willing—to England.

The great question was: Could the BEF make it? At the time of Gort's decision the Germans were much closer to Dunkirk than the BEF were. But what made Gort's decision the right one—though of course he could not have known it—was the fact that the Germans were making strategic blunders. The chief error was made by Hitler himself. On May 24, he ordered Guderian's panzers stopped at the Aa Canal, a scant 12 miles from Dunkirk.

Historians have puzzled over that decision ever since; one more day of advance could have brought the German tanks sweeping down on Dunkirk to close off the last exit for the BEF. Most likely, Hitler halted the tanks simply to conserve them. The Führer felt that victory was certain if he took his time to make sure of it, step by step; the tanks

should be husbanded for greater battles to come. After all, the rest of France remained to be conquered and the goal was Paris, not an unimpressive port city such as Dunkirk.

The retreat to Dunkirk, finally sanctioned by London, saw hundreds of thousands of British, remnants of the Belgian Army and half of the French First Army on the roads to the port—all in the line of fire. Each day the strafing increased. The agile bombers would come in at a shallow, shrieking dive, spray the road, make a tight climbing turn, and come back from the opposite direction.

Meanwhile, as early as May 20, the British Navy was planning the rescue from the shores of Dunkirk. With only 41 British destroyers and escorts available, the Navy conscripted every other type of vessel: pleasure craft, fishing trawlers, fireboats, Thames river barges, and even ancient paddle-wheelers. French, Dutch and Belgian vessels also raced to the scene. The armada that set forth on May 26 presented an unbelievable sight. Stacked three deep along the Dover quays like people in a pub were motor launches and sloops, fishing boats and schooners.

The Channel crossing was as much an ordeal as the corridor through which the soldiers were fleeing France. In

A German soldier snapped this grim tableau of a Dunkirk beach littered with casualties, wrecked vehicles, artillery pieces and ammunition boxes, shortly after panzer units finally succeeded in smashing through Allied lines. Ironically, the scenes became grim for German commanders, too, when they discovered that while most of the British and French forces' equipment had been captured, the bulk of the troops had escaped by sea.

the open Channel, the lighted buoys and lightships were blacked out and the waters were heavily mined. In addition, the Germans had already moved big guns against Calais and swept enormous areas of the Channel with shellfire. And the dive bombers were worst of all. The ships creeping between the shoals off Dunkirk were like sitting ducks. They could not speed up; there was not enough sea room in the narrow approaches to Dunkirk for evasive action. Skippers who tried to make it ran aground.

Yet somehow, hundreds of vessels did get through—not only to the harbor and its beach, but to outlying beaches north and south of the town. Most of the quays had already been destroyed; the only harborside structure where the big transports could dock was one of the two breakwaters enclosing the harbor itself. This jetty was a mole constructed of rock, with thick pilings alongside it; the swells of the open Channel rushed against it and sucked and swirled through the rocks. The tides rose and fell 15 feet; at high tide men walked across makeshift bridges onto ships' decks. At low tide they had to jump from the mole.

From the vessels making fast, the sight of the men waiting along the top of the mole was never to be forgotten by

anyone. The line stretched the length of the mole and back along the beach in one endless serpentine mass. The troops were in every state of disarray. Their gaunt, unshaven faces were expressionless with exhaustion. Some were supporting others too tired to stand any longer.

When German planes came in over the town, there was no place to take cover; men could only lie flat and watch the line of bullets splatter across the harbor toward them—"crackling like frying fat," as one man remembered.

Bombs churned the harbor and smashed into the ships. During one raid, the paddle-wheel steamer *Fenella* had just loaded 600 troops; many were killed instantly. The crew evacuated the remaining troops off the stern—some were able to jump and run for it, some were carried on stretchers—while enemy fighters machine-gunned them. Most made it to the *Crested Eagle*, another paddler steamer alongside the jetty. Later as the *Crested Eagle* chugged past the smoldering wreckage, another dive bomber swung down on her. The *Crested Eagle* burst into flame and drifted onto the beach; most of the troops died in the fire.

As this and other vessels burned and sank, the harbor became an obstacle course. But the ships still came, and the troops still shuffled down the mole. Aboard some ships, there were so many men on deck that the guns could not even be worked. One of the smaller ships took on so many troops that the vessel slowly sank to the bottom.

Despite the planes and the artillery, the mines and the shoals, nearly 900 ships kept going back and forth across the Channel and they brought more than 200,000 troops of the BEF home to England. By the end of May, Dover was overflowing with them; yet for some reason it never occurred to the Germans to bomb that city.

Among the thousands of troops heading down to the beaches on June 3 to board whatever rescue craft they could find was Private Peter Anderson of the Royal Army Service Corps unit attached to the British 48th division. Anderson, whose job it had been to convoy supplies, had just completed his final run from the outskirts of the city into Dunkirk with food for the last of the waiting troops. After stripping the gears of his truck and smashing the engine as he had been ordered to do, he cast aside his rifle and tin hat, substituted a pair of abandoned riding boots for his scuffed army boots and strolled down through the dunes.

There were still lines of men on this beach. Offshore destroyers were running back and forth. To Anderson, it looked as if all he had to do was be patient and he would be taken off. There was no sign of the enemy. He met friends and spent a pleasant, mildly alcoholic afternoon and evening drinking behind a secluded dune. Next morning, however, the shooting war was on again.

As Anderson and his companions watched from behind their dune, the Stukas and Messerschmitts shrieked over the beach and scattered waiting men. Other planes dive-bombed the destroyers, which went into evasive action and opened up with their deck guns. Anderson remembers gasping as he saw a plane dive at a destroyer. There was a blinding flash and then nothing but churning water where the destroyer had been.

By dawn of June 5, there were still a great many men remaining on the beach. And the rescue boats had gone. Anderson's group ran out of liquid sustenance, but found some barely edible chocolate bars and settled down patiently to wait and hope. Perhaps the night would bring the rescue ships back.

Shortly they noticed a group of men engaged in trying to reach one of the lifeboats that had been stranded on the sand bars. Anderson and his friends joined the operation and brought back one ship's lifeboat, big enough to carry about 40 men. They readied it for use and retired to the dunes to await darkness before setting out to sea.

Later that afternoon, a shout went up as a big paddle steamer hove into view and stood right off their beach. Anderson's group raced for the lifeboat, pushed it into the water and clambered in. When they reached the looming side of the paddle steamer, there was a rope netting for the men to climb up over the side. The boat then went back and forth until the beach was empty and the steamer was full. She was the *Margate Belle*; and when her huge paddles churned up the sea as she headed for England, Anderson went below and collapsed. He slept all the way across the Channel waking only when the steamer creaked into her regular berth at Margate, just as if she had completed an uneventful peacetime crossing.

Meanwhile, the pocket around Dunkirk had shrunk to nothing. The rear guard headquarters staff had come out on the mole to ships that had slipped in to evacuate them; the last staff members departed at 2 a.m. on June 4. Later that day the Germans entered the city.

They found the jetty still packed with French troops. As the Germans were taking prisoners, a French Navy doctor, near the end of the jetty, noticed what looked like a perfectly good lifeboat aboard a ship that had sunk before his eyes.

Accompanied by 12 other daredevils, he leaped aboard the ship, launched the lifeboat and paddled furiously away under a rain of German machine gun bullets. Hours later, they were picked up by a naval vessel and brought safely to England, the last of 338,226 British, French, Belgian and Dutch troops to escape Dunkirk.

While the final stages of the battle of Dunkirk were taking place, French Commander-in-Chief General Maxime Weygand set about organizing a new defensive position in northern France. He was faced with a desperate situation: there was little help for France now. The Belgians and the Dutch had been defeated, and the British, but for a few divisions, had been driven from the Continent. The French Army, on which the country's fate depended, had been badly mauled in the fighting in Belgium and northern France, with 370,000 dead, wounded or captured. It had also lost three quarters of its medium tanks and most of its motor transport.

Moreover, the morale of the army and of the French nation itself was at rock bottom. The supposedly invincible Maginot Line, which had been counted upon to keep the Germans out of France, had proved irrelevant in the fighting so far. The Germans had simply outflanked the costly fortifications by attacking through Holland and Belgium. Nothing had availed against the surging panzers, and now they were threatening to swoop down from the north and overrun all of France.

As Hitler massed his forces for the decisive blow against France, he was acutely aware that the principal threat to his domination of Europe lay not here, but across the Channel. "Our most dangerous enemy is Britain," Hitler had declared after the blitzkrieg in Poland, "but we must first beat her continental soldier, France."

Thus, in the early days of June, the Germans turned their full offensive resources against the hapless French—an operation that would call upon approximately 143 divisions. Against this confident, finely honed and battle-tested fighting force, General Weygand was able to muster 71 French divisions, including the 17 that were still defending the Maginot Line. In addition, he had available two British divisions that had been stranded in France after the

German infantrymen, under shellfire during the blitzkrieg, dash through a village whose road sign shows they have just entered France. Fast-moving foot soldiers like these were part of the new concept of war in which mobile infantry exploited gains made by tanks and aircraft.

evacuation of Dunkirk, plus another two divisions already committed to coming ashore from England.

Weygand chose to make his stand behind the line of the Somme and Aisne rivers, stretching southwestward a distance of 225 miles from the English Channel to the northern end of the Maginot Line at Longuyon. General Charles de Gaulle urged him to mass the remaining 1,200 tanks in two concentrations in the rear in order to attack the German columns when they broke through. That way, said de Gaulle, they might have "a battle instead of a debacle." But Weygand was old and no more suited to the task at hand than General Gamelin had been. Though he had served as Chief of Staff to the revered Marshall Foch in World War I, he had not commanded troops in combat since 1914, nor made any effort to absorb the new concepts of mobile, armored warfare. De Gaulle's plea went unheeded.

In addition, the Germans had gained a crucial advantage during their encirclement of Allied forces at Dunkirk by seizing five bridgeheads across the lower Somme. When the final battle began, these advanced German positions were poised like daggers against the heart of France.

Yet all was not yet lost for the French. Resistance to the onslaught of the German armies was heavy. As one of the groups from General Fedor von Bock's Army Group B moved against the French on the plain of Picardy in the early morning of June 5, it found itself under fire from all quarters. In his diary, General Bock noted in an understated fashion, "it seems we are in trouble."

His gloom was soon dispelled: Erwin Rommel, commander of the 7th Panzer Division and one of the War's most daring and resourceful commanders, achieved a spectacular coup on the Somme. In full view of French troops on an escarpment that overlooked the south bank of the Somme, Rommel's panzer units seized the bridges and tore up the rails. Then the tanks and motor transport crossed the narrow rights-of-way under shellfire, an operation that Rommel himself compared to a combination of walking a tightrope and running the gauntlet. In this way they hammered a fatal wedge into the French front: by nightfall they were eight miles beyond the Somme; by the next morning they were 12 miles farther still, and on the following day they were driving hard for the Seine. The French front had been torn wide open, and was never to be sealed again.

Rommel next trapped part of the British 51st Division and a sizable French force at the seaport of St-Valéry-en-Caux. For a time, a miniature Dunkirk appeared to be in the making but a thick fog enveloped the port and the rescue fleet could not get in. On June 12, the Allied forces surrendered there, yielding more than 40,000 prisoners, including 12 generals, to the Germans.

Devastating though this was, this German drive was not the main punch. That had been launched farther east on June 9 by General Rundstedt's Army Group A over Belleau Wood and Château-Thierry. Again, French resistance was stubborn, and it even looked as though the Aisne line might hold. But the German tide rose again and swept over the defenders. On the evening of June 10, Guderian's tanks crossed the Aisne near Rethel. Three days later, they broke through the line at Châlons-sur-Marne; then they drove steadily southward approximately 200 miles to Pontarlier on the Swiss border, cutting off the 17 divisions still locked in the great concrete fortress of the Maginot Line.

The breakthrough quickly turned into a gigantic rout, with whole armies and mobs of panic-stricken civilians fleeing together. Hans Habe, a Hungarian journalist who had volunteered for service with the French, described the scene: "Your eyes turned back to the flood of limping soldiers," he recalled, "trying in vain to look like men in the presence of the fleeing women. You saw children screaming desperately or still as death; officers' cars blowing their strident horns; bright cavalry uniforms on nervous, weary horses; cannon without ammunition; the whole disordered funeral procession of a disintegrated army."

All that remained for the French was to either surrender or salvage what they could of their forces and ship them to French colonies in North Africa to continue the war there. Premier Paul Reynaud's cabinet was deeply divided. For de Gaulle and others in the diehard faction, capitulation was unthinkable. For Weygand and Marshal Pétain, the 84-year-

A smiling Parisian shopkeeper sells models of the Eiffel Tower to a German soldier. The invading troops were under strict orders to behave themselves, and they did. Wir sind keine Barbaren, we are not barbarians, they told civilians in the places they overran. They smiled, they helped old ladies cross the streets. They did no looting—they had no need to; they had plenty of paper marks, which the French had to accept as legal tender and which could be used for buying anything available.

In the Franco-German armistice, Hitler did not insist on the occupation of all French soil; he kept approximately the regions his armies had conquered (red stripes on map) plus a coastal strip running down to Spain. He made no demands, for that moment, on the French overseas empire. Vichy became the capital of a nominally independent state headed by Marshal Pétain who, on accepting the leadership of Vichy France, said: "I make to France the gift of my person, to mitigate her suffering."

Hitler pauses during his tour of occupied Paris for a snapshot with architect Albert Speer (left) and sculptor Arno Breker near the Eiffel Tower.

old "hero of Verdun" and now Vice Premier, there could be no possibility of continued resistance; the entire Allied cause was doomed. The English had scuttled for home, abandoning their commitments, and would not last more than a couple of weeks once France had fallen. "England will have its neck wrung like a chicken," said Weygand. ("Some chicken. Some neck," said Prime Minister Churchill later, after the Battle of Britain had been won.)

Even as Premier Paul Reynaud was deciding which course of action to take, the tide of disaster swept ever closer to Paris. Paris had already had a bitter taste of war: waves of German bombers had flown over the city on June 3 and 4, dropping an estimated 1,000 bombs on industrial districts. Yet in spite of this, there was no panic, only outrage and a sense of unreality. Theatergoers jammed the Comédie Française and the Bouffes to see the new production of *Cyrano de Bergerac* or the latest Cocteau play. Cafés were full and the bookstalls on the Left Bank were doing their usual trade.

Then, on Sunday, June 9, author André Maurois recalled, "We began to read in the papers and to hear on the radio quite unexpected names of places: Mantes, Pontoise. Was it possible the Germans were only half an hour from us by car, while we're living and working just as usual?"

One of Maurois' friends, brain surgeon Thierry de Martel, declared that he would kill himself the moment the Germans entered the city. "My only son was killed in the last war. Until now I have tried to believe that he died to save France. And now here is France, lost in her turn. I cannot go on."

As further news of the German offensive filtered into the city, the sad exodus began. Steady files of cars, taxis and trucks loaded hastily with provisions and homely treasures, made for the few highways to the south that were still open. The next day, Paris was declared an open city. And by June 13, it was almost empty; four fifths of its population had fled.

Not one shot greeted the enemy as they approached the French capital. On the morning of June 14, German soldiers goose-stepped down the Champs Elysées and gigantic swastika banners were hoisted at the Arc de Triomphe and atop the Eiffel Tower. Maurois' friend, Thierry de Martel, plunged strychnine into his veins, and died.

On June 14, the day Paris fell, the French government fled to Bordeaux. General Alan Brooke, in command of the remaining British troops in France, went to see General Weygand for orders. Weygand ordered Brooke to organize and hold a 150-kilometer line to defend Brittany. Brook felt that in the prevailing chaos this idea was pure Alice in Wonderland, and the only way to save the British troops was to get them out of France at once. He was explaining this to London on a very bad telephone connection when suddenly he found Churchill on the line. "You are there to make the French feel that we are supporting them," said the Prime Minister. "You can't make a corpse feel," said the general bluntly. After much persuasion Churchill finally agreed to permit another evacuation in a series of Dunkirk-style operations just in time to avoid capture.

On the other side of France, in an anticlimax of pathetic proportions, the much-vaunted Maginot Line was pierced within a few hours of an attack by General Wilhelm Ritter von Leeb's Army Group C. Millions of francs had been spent on sinking tons of concrete into the earth to build the well-equipped, well-ventilated fortresses of the line—all in vain. On June 17 the dazed people of France learned that their government, now headed by Marshal Pétain, was ready to surrender, as Pétain announced, "It is with a heavy heart that I tell you today that we must stop fighting."

Four days later, in a sleeping car at Compiègne where Marshal Foch had dictated his armistice terms to the Germans in November 1918, the French accepted the German terms of surrender. Although harsh, the terms were not harsh enough to drive them to reject the proposal and continue fighting. And so, with France vanquished, Hitler could now turn his attention to the conquest of the island kingdom across the Channel.

"To all Frenchmen. France has lost a battle but France has not lost the war" proclaims this poster, which was excerpted from a speech made by Charles de Gaulle on June 18, 1940, a few days after the fall of France. From a newly set up London headquarters, to which de Gaulle had fled from Bordeaux, he was presiding over a government-in-exile and striving to build an army made up of French troops evacuated from Dunkirk, colonial forces, and French civilians who managed to slip out of France. With these men, who were to be supplied and armed by the British, de Gaulle hoped to reverse the tide of defeat and reconquer France.

5

In one of history's great ironies, the last battle of the French campaign was fought between the Allies. To prevent the French fleet from falling into German hands following the armistice, the British Admiralty decided to secure or sink every French warship afloat. On July 3, 1940, after an appalling mixup in negotiations, the Royal Navy opened fire on the base at Mers-el-Kebir in Algeria, destroying three battleships and killing 1,267 Frenchmen. Outraged, Marshal Pétain's Vichy government broke off diplomatic relations. It was an act without much military consequence; France was largely finished with the war. But it symbolized Britain's melancholy position—an island-nation utterly alone and under siege, facing the full weight of Adolf Hitler's confident legions.

The two German generals climbed down from their staff cars and walked out on the beaches of Dunkirk. Only hours before, the last destroyers and small ships had carried off the remnants of the British Expeditionary Force, and the sands were littered with the flotsam and jetsam of defeat: thousands of boots discarded by soldiers wading out to the rescue boats, long lines of trucks and heavy guns, piles of rifles. At one point, the two officers came to a mound of empty wine and whisky bottles. One of them, Luftwaffe General Hoffmann von Waldau, waved an arm across the landscape. "Here is the grave of British hopes in this war," he said. Then, contemptuously indicating the bottles: "And these are the grave stones!"

His companion, Erhard Milch, Inspector-General of the Luftwaffe, shook his head. "They are not buried yet," he said. Then, almost to himself: "We have no time to waste."

Later that day—June 5, 1940—Milch attended a meeting of the Luftwaffe High Command called by its chief, Field Marshal Hermann Göring. Resplendent in a new silk uniform, the Field Marshal looked unusually fit. He had cut down his intake of addictive paracodeine to 30 pills a day and his masseur had pounded off some of his fat. He was jubilant with the outcome at Dunkirk—after all, more than 200 ships of the armada fleet had been destroyed by German bombers. But when Milch pointed out that the British, having evacuated 224,000 of their troops and 114,000 French, "had gotten practically the whole of their army back across the Channel," Göring's glee waned. Asked what the next move should be, Milch was emphatic: "I strongly advise the immediate transfer to the Channel coast of all available Luftwaffe forces. The invasion of Great Britain should begin *without delay.*"

Göring's initial reaction was a terse "It can't be done." But gradually a plan for the Battle of Britain took shape. It envisioned an airborne invasion, starting with a massive bomber attack on England's south coast. Under this cover, paratroops would drop and seize an airfield. In their wake would come a shuttle service of troop transports carrying five crack divisions that would fan out like a brushfire across the English countryside. To bring the British to their knees, their planes would have to be shot out of the sky, their ports put out of action and the seaways closed to shipping.

After outlining the plan to Hitler the next day, Göring concluded by stressing the one prerequisite for success: the operation must be carried out immediately—within days.

"I await your orders, mein Führer," said Göring expectantly.

The order he got dismayed him: "Do nothing," Hitler told the Field Marshal. Convinced that the British were a reasonable people who would soon recognize the

BRITAIN AT BAY

hopelessness of their position, Hitler did not wish "to rub their noses in the mud of defeat," as he put it.

Germany's armed service chiefs, on the other hand, had no such qualms. Though Hitler's shackling order barred any full-scale attack on England at present, it did not preclude preparing for the eventuality that he might suddenly change his mind. Consequently, the Luftwaffe began shifting its fighter and bomber squadrons to French airfields along the Channel coast facing England. At the same time invasion barges and small craft were moved through a network of canals to assembly points on the Channel and on the North Sea coast.

By the end of June, German peace-feelers were reaching London through neutral sources. Officially, Churchill stood adamant against these overtures. But unofficially, according to some evidence unearthed after the war, he encouraged both appeasers in Parliament and intermediaries in neutral countries. His government, he suggested, would not be unwilling to come to an arrangement with the Nazis, provided the Führer meant sincerely what he said about preserving the British Empire "as a factor in world equilibrium."

The truth was that Churchill was playing for time. The Home Guard—composed of farmhands, retired World War I Army majors and other local defense volunteers—was patrolling Britain's roads and 5,000 miles of coastline with ineffectual hunting weapons, obsolete rifles, even pitchforks and golf clubs. Until they could be furnished with the proper equipment, until the veterans of Dunkirk and other

A few days after the fall of France, Reich Marshal Hermann Göring (fifth from right) and members of his Luftwaffe staff gaze across a low-lying haze over the English Channel toward the white cliffs of Dover 20 miles away. In a fateful stab at personal glory, Göring was about to launch an air offensive that he—and Hitler—believed could bring Britain to its knees.

The job of defending Britain's 5,000-mile coastline required ingenuity and hard work. In one spectacular example, the British installed pipes beneath the surf through which oil could be pumped to spread over the surface of the water. When ignited by flare pistols, the oil would blaze into a wall of flame designed to incinerate troops approaching in landing craft.

regular army troops could be supplied with fresh weapons, until more Royal Air Force (RAF) planes could be built and more pilots could be trained, every day now was precious.

Churchill's sense of urgency was shared by many. At the end of June the Germans occupied the Channel Islands, and their power seemed to grow daily. Few Britons doubted a bleak prediction by the Imperial Defense Committee: in a German air attack, 600,000 would die, more than a million would be injured; no one even guessed at what the casualties might be if the Germans invaded. Still, unswayed by grim predictions, Britons did prepare, although few had any idea what to do. Concerns varied widely: zoo officials wondered how to keep animals from escaping if their cages were bombed; local road signs were removed to baffle potential invaders. In order to better "stand up to the Nazis without worrying what will happen to our tots," as one father put it, many parents sent their children to safety in the countryside.

By early July, Hitler's belief that the British would come to their senses had faded. Their obstinacy not only baffled him but threatened to upset his plan to invade and destroy his present ally, the U.S.S.R. Scheduled for sometime in 1941, the conquest of Russia would be infinitely more complicated if a hostile Britain still opposed him.

On July 16, Hitler issued a top-secret directive to prepare for an invasion. Operation *Sea Lion*—as this new strategy was called—lacked the melodrama of the abortive Milch-

In Winston Leonard Spencer Churchill, the British were blessed to have a Prime Minister whose style, temperament and background made him the ideal wartime leader. His unerring ability to focus the national spirit was summed up in a speech he made to Parliament, even as the last British soldiers were escaping from the debacle at Dunkirk: "We shall fight on the beaches, we shall fight on the landing grounds, we shall fight in the fields and in the streets . . . we shall never surrender."

A soldier gives a farewell kiss to his son, one of the two million children to be evacuated into the countryside during 1939 and 1940. Equipped with a parcel of belongings and a gas mask in a box slung over his shoulder, he bears an identification tag around his neck.

Göring plan, but it was far more grandiose in concept. Once the Luftwaffe had defeated the RAF and gained command of the air, as many as 250,000 German soldiers would land along a 200-mile front of England's south coast. Arriving in three waves, they would secure their beachheads, then push inland to cut off London from the rest of the country.

Three days after issuing his top-secret directive, Hitler made a rousing speech at the Kroll Opera House in Berlin. The boxes were packed with foreign diplomats as the Führer gave Britain one more chance to be reasonable. The only obstacle in the way of peace, he charged, was an unscrupulous "criminal warmonger" and megalomaniac named Winston Churchill. His voice rose in an angry crescendo: "Mr. Churchill ought, perhaps, for once, to believe me when I prophesy that a great Empire will be destroyed—an Empire which it was never my intention to destroy or even to harm."

Within an hour a reply came over the BBC—defiant and wholly spontaneous. The broadcaster, journalist Sefton Delmer, addressed Hitler directly in German: "Let me tell you what we here in Britain think of this appeal to what you are pleased to call our reason and common sense. Herr Führer and Reich Chancellor, we hurl it right back at you—right back into your evil-smelling teeth."

The legend has grown that the Battle of Britain was a David-and-Goliath confrontation between a brave but weakly defended island kingdom and the mightiest air power the world had yet known. This impression of an invincible Luftwaffe was, initially, the work of Nazi propagandists and was enhanced in September 1939, when the Luftwaffe completely wiped out the Polish Air Force.

Although the Luftwaffe was far bigger than the RAF—with an estimated 4,500 first-line aircraft to the RAF's 2,900—the protagonists in the Battle of Britain were much more closely matched than was generally realized. In the quality if not the quantity of its planes, Britain could compete favorably with the Luftwaffe. Moreover, with each day that Hitler delayed his all-out air attack, Britain's furiously working aircraft factories were narrowing the gap in numbers of planes. The British also possessed the incalculable advantage of fighting on their own home ground. And finally, Britain had outstripped its foe in developing the all-seeing eye of radar.

In 1940, this remarkable device was still relatively new, but it had already proved its ability to analyze the ultra-high-frequency radio waves reflected from the surfaces of distant objects. The result was an ability not only to detect approaching aircraft, but also to determine their location and speed. The plotting room at Bentley Priory was the top-secret hub of Britain's defensive air operations. There, members of the Women's Auxiliary Air Force (WAAFs) moved aircraft symbols across a giant chart of the area under radar surveillance, according to reports coming in from coastal radar stations. From a balcony in the plotting room, Air Chief Marshal Sir Hugh Dowding and air-controllers would watch the chart below them. The moment a flight of German planes took to the skies over France and began to climb, the WAAFs would begin to move the symbols across the chart, and RAF battle dispositions would be made.

In deciding how to allocate these dispositions, Dowding had another aid besides radar—an aid so secret that not even his subordinate commanders knew about it. The British had acquired a machine that could break the German military code. Thus Dowding could estimate from transcripts of German radio traffic the Luftwaffe's targets and numbers of aircraft involved even before the planes left the ground.

In preparation of Operation *Sea Lion*, the Luftwaffe organized its plan of attack into three phases. The first phase was designed to lure the RAF into the skies by attacking

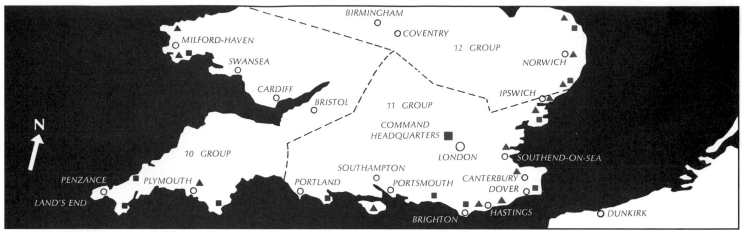

Concentrated on England's southern and eastern coasts, Britain's radar network was a crucial factor in Britain's survival of the Blitz. The system included 240-foot-high long-range antennae (squares on map) for picking up planes 150 miles away at altitudes of 30,000 feet and low-level antennae (triangles) for detecting planes flying barely above the waves as they came in from offshore.

British naval bases and merchant ships. In Phase Two—code-named Operation *Eagle Attack*—a massive onslaught of bombers and fighters would destroy RAF airfields, defenses and aircraft factories. In the third and final phase the Luftwaffe would provide cover for invasion.

By mid-July both sides were primed for the great test to come. The RAF had built up its strength to 640 combat ready front-line fighters. The Luftwaffe could count on 824 fighters—thus, in a contest of fighter versus fighter, the odds were not so long. But in the intensifying clashes over the Channel, there was no doubt which side at first had the preponderance of expert fliers. Scores of Luftwaffe pilots had flown with the German Condor Legion in the Spanish Civil War. They were trained in battle to make the best use of sky, sun and their enemy's weaknesses.

British pilots were soon aware that something was badly wrong with their tactics in the air. The RAF flew in tight formations wingtip to wingtip—a spectacular sight at air shows but not much good in a fight. They were so busy keeping in formation, they had little time to look around for the enemy, and no room to maneuver when he came at them. The German fighters, on the other hand, flew in loose formations. Units patrolled and stalked the enemy at different heights, each pilot keeping a sharp lookout for attackers instead of worrying about the proximity of his neighbor's wingtip. He had freedom to initiate attacks on his own, and a much greater range of vision.

It is not surprising that in its opening encounters with the Germans, the RAF was hurt. In ten days of clashes, it lost 50

fighters—a critical drain in view of the pace at which the action was mounting. But the pilots learned and adapted quickly. They abandoned tight formations and began flying the so-called Finger Four formation—each plane at the tip of a finger of an imaginary outstretched hand. The odds on survival improved.

As the days passed with no end to the so-called Battle of the Channel in sight, the Luftwaffe stepped up its attempts to inveigle more and more RAF planes into the air. In addition to routine operations, so-called decoy-duck tactics were used to tempt RAF fighters into chasing German planes back to the French coast where Me-109s waited to pounce. Major Adolf Galland, one of the Luftwaffe's best junior commanders and long since an ace, had a favorite ploy for luring RAF pilots into foolhardy maneuvers. He would fly out across the Channel alone; when he saw an RAF patrol, he would meander around just out of range, until one of them broke to take him on. Then he would turn for France, keeping just ahead of his pursuers, while radioing to two of his pilots waiting over the French coast.

It was in this fashion that one of Dowding's most brilliant pilots, Flight Lieutenant Alan Deere, lost his Spitfire—and almost his life. As he chased a 109 across the Channel, he saw the enemy pilot "stand his aircraft practically on its nose and dive vertically toward the airfield, which I now recognized as Calais/Marck," a Luftwaffe base. He realized he had been tricked. Two other 109s turned to cut Deere off "as, with throttle wide open, I headed for home at sea level, muttering to myself: 'You bloody fool.' "

Coatless and in civilian clothes, German air commander Hermann Göring (far left) discusses the air assault on England with aides summoned to his estate near Berlin. In addition to leading the air force, Göring, as Reich Marshal of Germany, ranked second only to Hitler in the Nazi hierarchy. A swashbuckling flying ace in World War I, by 1940 he was an overweight morphine addict nicknamed Der Dicke (fatty) by Berlin wags.

FIGHTERS OVER BRITAIN

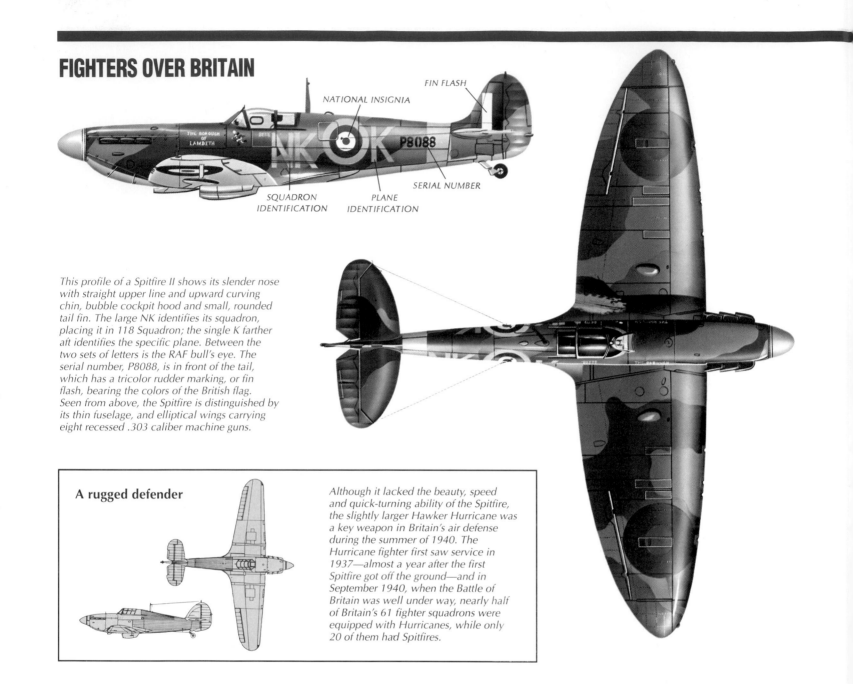

This profile of a Spitfire II shows its slender nose with straight upper line and upward curving chin, bubble cockpit hood and small, rounded tail fin. The large NK identifies its squadron, placing it in 118 Squadron; the single K farther aft identifies the specific plane. Between the two sets of letters is the RAF bull's eye. The serial number, P8088, is in front of the tail, which has a tricolor rudder marking, or fin flash, bearing the colors of the British flag. Seen from above, the Spitfire is distinguished by its thin fuselage, and elliptical wings carrying eight recessed .303 caliber machine guns.

A rugged defender

Although it lacked the beauty, speed and quick-turning ability of the Spitfire, the slightly larger Hawker Hurricane was a key weapon in Britain's air defense during the summer of 1940. The Hurricane fighter first saw service in 1937—almost a year after the first Spitfire got off the ground—and in September 1940, when the Battle of Britain was well under way, nearly half of Britain's 61 fighter squadrons were equipped with Hurricanes, while only 20 of them had Spitfires.

The survival of Britain in the great air battle of the summer and the fall of 1940 was made possible in large measure by a superb pair of fighter planes, each with its own particular strengths: the Spitfire *(color illustration above)* and the Hurricane *(box above)*.

The sturdy Hawker Hurricane was a flying gun-platform armed with eight machine guns, and later by four 20mm cannons. Although the Hurricane's top speed was almost 30 mph less than that of the Messerschmitt, its superior range—600 miles—enabled it to remain in the air longer than the German fighter. Because the heavily armored Hurricanes were less maneuverable and slower—its maximum speed was 325 mph versus 370 mph for the Spitfire—the British developed the tactic of letting them take on the vulnerable German bombers while the Spitfires went after the fighters.

Adapted from the design of a sleek racing seaplane, the first Spitfire fighter plane rolled off the assembly line at the Supermarine Division of Vickers-Armstrong before the outbreak of World War II, in 1938. Its streamlined design enabled it to carry a pilot, a 1,175-hp Rolls-Royce engine and eight machine guns, yet it still managed to achieve such a high degree of maneuverability that it was able to turn in a tighter radius than any other front-line fighter—a vital advantage in a dogfight. The quickness and agility of the Spitfire prompted one aircraft expert to describe this airplane as "the best conventional defense fighter of the War." Although it could not match the climbing rate of its chief adversary, the Messerschmitt-109, the Spitfire was swift enough to outrun the German plane—a feat that the Hurricane was not able to match.

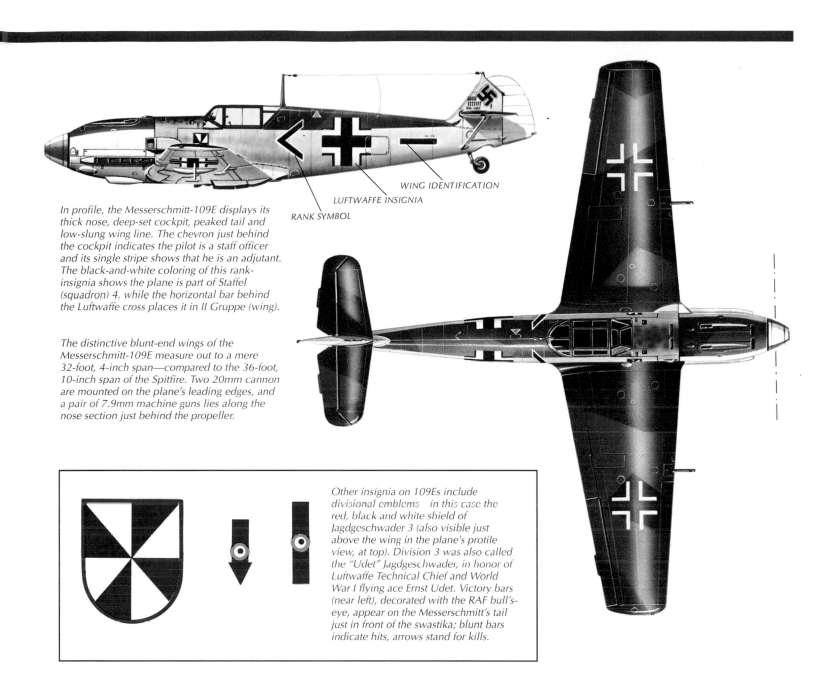

In profile, the Messerschmitt-109E displays its thick nose, deep-set cockpit, peaked tail and low-slung wing line. The chevron just behind the cockpit indicates the pilot is a staff officer and its single stripe shows that he is an adjutant. The black-and-white coloring of this rank-insignia shows the plane is part of Staffel (squadron) 4, while the horizontal bar behind the Luftwaffe cross places it in II Gruppe (wing).

The distinctive blunt-end wings of the Messerschmitt-109E measure out to a mere 32-foot, 4-inch span—compared to the 36-foot, 10-inch span of the Spitfire. Two 20mm cannon are mounted on the plane's leading edges, and a pair of 7.9mm machine guns lies along the nose section just behind the propeller.

WING IDENTIFICATION

LUFTWAFFE INSIGNIA

RANK SYMBOL

Other insignia on 109Es include divisional emblems in this case the red, black and white shield of Jagdgeschwader 3 (also visible just above the wing in the plane's profile view, at top). Division 3 was also called the "Udet" Jagdgeschwader, in honor of Luftwaffe Technical Chief and World War I flying ace Ernst Udet. Victory bars (near left), decorated with the RAF bull's-eye, appear on the Messerschmitt's tail just in front of the swastika; blunt bars indicate hits, arrows stand for kills.

On the German side, perhaps the deadliest weapon in the Luftwaffe's arsenal during the Battle of Britain was the stub-winged Messerschmitt Bf-109E fighter. Called the "Emil" by German airmen (and often referred to simply as the Me-109), the plane had an initial climbing rate of 3,100 feet per minute—against the Spitfire's 2,530. Though its top speed of 354 mph was 16 mph slower than the Spitfire's maximum, the 109's ceiling of 36,000 feet gave it a 2,000-foot advantage over the Spitfire. This, plus a fuel-injection system which kept its 1,150-hp Daimler-Benz engine going

in the pressure of steep, sudden dives, made it possible for skilled Luftwaffe pilots to maneuver their 109s above and behind opponents, and then dive down for the kill.

Although some German fliers candidly considered the Spitfire more maneuverable, British pilots who handled captured 109s tended to disagree, rating the two a close match. All pilots agreed that only an expert could successfully operate the 109. Extremely sensitive to the touch, it was hard to hold steady and was cursed with a barely controllable tendency to veer to the left on takeoff

and to the right or left on landing. To achieve maximum speed and maneuverability, its designers had sacrificed some structural strength, which sometimes caused its wings or landing gear to collapse under stress. For the Battle of Britain in which the 109's principal function was to fly escort, its most serious defect was its very modest 410-mile maximum cruising distance, which allowed only 20 minutes of fighting time over enemy terrain. Of twelve 109s returning from one mission, five barely pancaked on the French shore, while seven others went down in the Channel.

Combat experience with a heavy dose of luck had saved him. As he fled for home, the two 109s formed up on either side and alternately attacked him. He forced them to break off by making a vicious turn in the direction of first one attacker, then the other, resuming his retreat as they reformed. He was in sight of Dover when one 109 shot up his instrument panel, canopy and gas tank. His Spitfire in flames, he turned it over and parachuted out.

Though Deere lived to fight again, many others did not. Dowding ordered his pilots not to take on the foe beyond gliding distance of the English shore. "I want live fliers, not dead heroes," he said.

Toward the end of July, the figures of RAF casualties that Luftwaffe intelligence officers produced convinced Göring—and Hitler—that Phase One of the Battle of Britain had been won. Accordingly, on August 1, the Führer gave the go-ahead to launch Phase Two—the destruction of RAF airfields, radar stations and British aircraft factories. There was, however, one proviso: The Luftwaffe must not execute any "terror raids" against British civilian populations. London, in particular, was off-limits to German bombers.

On August 8, having been warned by Churchill that the Luftwaffe's supreme effort was imminent, Dowding issued an Order of the Day to Fighter Command: "The Battle of Britain is about to begin. Members of the Royal Air Force, the fate of generations lies in your hands."

In fact, due to bad weather, Göring delayed the assault by several days. On August 13, German bomber squadrons and fighter escorts attacked targets from Southampton to the Thames estuary—a distance of 150 miles. The Luftwaffe crews came back with reports of successful attacks on six RAF airfields and other installations, the destruction of dozens of planes on the ground, the wiping out of several factories and the paralysis of the port of Southampton. It had flown an unprecedented number of sorties—1,485 compared to 700 by the RAF.

What pleased Göring most was the number of RAF planes his pilots claimed to have shot down—88 fighters against 12 planes lost by his Luftwaffe. However, his intelligence reports were, once again, overoptimistic. The day's real losses were 13 RAF fighters destroyed against 23 Luftwaffe bombers and 11 fighters.

The Luftwaffe intelligence officers interrogated pilots and crews to try to evaluate the lessons learned on Eagle Day—the opening day of Phase Two, *Eagle Attack*. One fact about the day's combat had made a particularly painful impression on the bomber forces: the British always seemed to know where the enemy aircraft were. The accuracy of Britain's radar system was now being reported from every Luftwaffe base in the war zone.

Fortunately for the British, the reports do not appear to have convinced Göring and his High Command that radar was by far the most dangerous threat to their enterprise. Although they had discussed radar and its capabilities, none of them had suggested assigning top priority to its destruction. All they had done was to agree that preliminary attacks upon the system should be made before Eagle Day proper began.

The first of these assaults had taken place one day earlier on the 12th of August. Six RAF radar stations were bombed and one of them, Ventnor on the Isle of Wight, was completely destroyed. Since Ventnor was the station that screened the approaches to the port of Southampton, its leveling was a great triumph for the Germans. But they did not know it. Evidently they were unaware that a 10-mile gap had been blown in the coastal radar chain. Through this hole their bombers could have struck without warning, en masse, to sow death and panic.

The British radar system, in fact, was vulnerable in a special way: its personnel was largely unprotected. The operators of this invaluable defensive cordon were members of the WAAF who worked near the radar towers in flimsy wooden huts. Well-placed bombs—or cannon shells from fighters—could have reduced the huts and their vital equipment to splinters. But this happened on only two occasions, and then it seems, by accident. Instead, when bombing a radar station, German dive bombers targeted the narrow radar towers; direct hits on them were as difficult as dropping peas on pinheads.

Convinced that attacks on radar stations were fruitless, Göring issued a memorandum saying: "It is doubtful whether there is any point in continuing attacks on radar sites, in view of the fact that none of those attacked has been put out of action." It was one of his worst mistakes.

RAF fighter pilots at an airdrome in southern England scramble for their airplanes after being alerted to the approach of German attackers. At the height of the Battle of Britain, in August 1940, Britain's overworked pilots flew up to seven sorties per day, and were often on call around the clock in the bone-wearying struggle to fend off the numerically superior Luftwaffe.

Back at home base after battling Luftwaffe bombers and fighters, tired RAF fliers recount the day's action—including the tally of enemy kills and their own losses.

On August 15, the Luftwaffe flew 1,780 sorties. Stukas, Heinkels, Dorniers and Ju-88s methodically shuttled back and forth across the Channel, bombing RAF airfields. Hangars were set afire and runways pocked with bomb holes. There was hardly an empty patch of sky anywhere over the 200 miles of coastline. Aircraft were dueling everywhere. Not only were vapor trails visible, but watchers below could see smoke from damaged planes. Though the dogfights were fought thousands of feet up, the noise of battle reached the ground—the scream of propellers and engines as planes went into impossible dives; the rattle of machine guns; the thunderclap of a Spitfire or Me-109 as it blew up in the air.

By the third week of August, true summer weather prevailed; the sun was bright, the sky unclouded. Conditions for daily combat—for killing or getting killed in the air—were ideal. The pilots of both sides were living a strange life. From dawn onward they hung around the airfield, listening for the bell that would signal them to scramble. After hastily relieving themselves beside their planes, they were off for an encounter with the enemy that rarely lasted more than 15 minutes. But these were 15 minutes in which a man lived or died, got his arm or leg blown away, ended up in the Channel, walked home from a wreck, or swooped down in triumph to report a victory.

Göring's experts calculated at this time that the RAF had fewer than 150 front-line aircraft left. The truth was that it still had 750 fighters. Nevertheless, Fighter Command was now reaching the point of exhaustion. Far too many pilots had been killed or wounded. Their surviving comrades, though still physically intact, were bone-tired, and their morale was waning. Fighter Command was now 200 pilots short. Although newly trained fliers were arriving, what Dowding needed was a flock of veterans who could shoot down bombers, dodge enemy fighters and come back whole and ready to fight again. The growing scarcity of seasoned men was affecting Fighter Command's strength.

On August 31, the RAF suffered its worst day. Wave after wave of German bombers put most of southeastern England's bases out of action. Landing grounds became bomb-pocked moonscapes; hangars and operational buildings were razed, power cables cut, planes blown up and ground personnel killed. In all, the attackers dropped more than 4,400 tons of bombs and Fighter Command lost 39 planes and 14 pilots. After only one week, Phase Two of the Luftwaffe's operation seemed to be succeeding beyond Göring's wildest expectations. Buoyed by success, Hitler scheduled the start of Phase Three, operation *Sea Lion*, for September 21.

Dowding was a religious man who had never faltered in his belief that God was on Britain's side. At this point however, he wanted some encouraging sign from the Almighty. "What we need now," he confessed, "is a miracle." What he did not realize was that he had already

been handed one—a navigational error by two night-flying Luftwaffe pilots whose blunder was to change the whole course of the Battle of Britain.

Throughout Phase Two, the Luftwaffe had carefully observed Hitler's ban on the bombing of London. But on the night of August 24, a number of German bombers were assigned to attack the aircaft factories of Rochester and Kingston and the huge oil-storage tanks at Thameshaven, 15 miles downriver from London. The lead planes, which were flying on directional radio beams, were followed by others not so equipped. On the run-in to the targets, two bombers lost visual touch with their pathfinders. A fountain of flak rose to meet them, and realizing they were lost, the pilots jettisoned their bombs and raced for home. As it happened, they were over London when they unloaded. Two bombs fell on the heart of the city, the rest crashed down on several London boroughs, killing customers as they came out of the pubs at closing time and audiences on the way home from movie houses.

There is little doubt that the August 24 bombing was unintentional. But Churchill, who believed that nothing would better gain American sympathy—and aid—than the spectacle of London laid waste, was delighted to believe otherwise, and he acted accordingly. A wing of RAF bombers was ordered to carry out a reprisal raid on Berlin. While the raid did little damage, Göring's prestige was hurt. He had assured the German people that no enemy bomber would ever reach the capital. The bombs had hardly stopped falling when he promised Hitler there would be no more such attacks. But there were. Churchill had given the RAF instructions to keep hitting Berlin until the Germans reacted.

After three more quick strikes by the British, Hitler was aroused sufficiently to call in Göring and order him to prepare his bomber forces for a major riposte. On September 4, Hitler addressed a massive meeting in Berlin's Sportspalast: "Mr. Churchill," he shouted, "is carrying out these raids not because they promise to be highly effective, but because his air force cannot fly over German soil in daylight." But the Führer went on: "We will stop the handiwork of these night pirates, so help us God! When the British air force drops 3,000 or 4,000 kilograms of bombs, then we will, in one raid, drop 300,000 or 400,000 kilograms. In England they are filled with curiosity and keep asking: 'Why doesn't he come?' Be calm. Be calm. He is coming! He is coming!"

Three days later, in the late afternoon, Dowding was in his office at Fighter Command when his aide came in. "It looks like a big one, sir," he reported. "Operations Room says several formations of 20-plus are boiling up over Calais."

Outside the day was lovely and soft, but Dowding's office was chill with the air of impending disaster. The Luftwaffe's attacks had forced him to abandon his coastal bases. But that morning the Air Ministry had issued a curt warning: Invasion Alert No. 1—signaling that invasion was expected within 24 hours. To throw back the Germans as they approached the beaches, Dowding needed the forward airfields he now no longer had.

He went to the operations room and looked down on the great map. The raid being charted was indeed a big one. Already 250 bombers and 500 fighters were moving across the Channel, while more were assembling behind Calais. He was relieved to see No. 11 Group's fighters were airborne, hovering around 20,000 feet waiting for the raiders to split up and head for their various targets. Once the Germans split, the RAF squadrons would hurtle down to take on the foe, section by section.

As he watched the chart, Dowding had a sudden premonition, as he recalled later, "like a stab in the heart." *What if, this time, the raiders did not split up but came on instead en masse?* No preparations had been made for that contingency. And the city of London was wide open. As he contemplated this prospect, his aide said: "That's funny, they don't seem to be splitting up, do they, sir?"

The bombers were flying higher than usual, around 16,000 feet. They were escorted by twin-engined Me-110 fighters and above them patrolled steplike formations of weaving 109s. Watchers far below could see the occasional glint of a wing in the sun as the enemy raiders swept in. But there were no British fighters to intercept them, except where a few dogfights developed on the fringes of the raiders' flight path.

As news of the developing massive attack was flashed to Britain's ground defenses, antiaircraft fire opened up along the banks of the Thames and steadily increased in intensity. But the planes were too high, and the white puffballs of smoke as the ack-ack shell bursts proved to be more of a

A German bomber makes its run over a curve in the Thames River that encloses many of the city's vital East End shipping docks and warehouses.

salute to the raiders than a threat. The German planes came in like a neat and inexorable procession. At fixed points on their routes, a signal was given by the leaders and the bombs were released.

Soon the docks and streets of London's East End were ablaze. Caught off balance, the RAF tried desperately to recover. But their effort came too late. Some 400 Londoners were already dead, thousands injured. As night approached, watchers on the high ground around London remarked at the glorious red glow of the setting sun. Then they slowly realized that it was setting in the wrong place. The glow was the reflection in the sky of the East End in flames. And these same fires served as beacons for waves of night bombers, come to punish the city even more. As they rolled in, Churchill and his Chiefs of Staff compounded the mess that Fighter Command had made of the day.

At 8 that evening, Britain's war leaders emerged from a daylong meeting in the Hole in the Ground—the government's underground headquarters in Whitehall—and sent an urgent message to all Home Forces in the United Kingdom. The message was a single code word: *Cromwell*.

There has been some argument ever since as to whether the signal *Cromwell* meant "Invasion Begun" or "Invasion Imminent." At any event, on September 7, 1940, there was no doubt about the way it was interpreted: "The German Invasion of Britain has begun."

Although meant for Army eyes only, soon everybody knew about it. Church bells tolled to sound the invasion alarm. Road blocks were set up. Bridges were blown. Mines were sown on roads and fields. In London's battered East End, firemen—dodging new bombs raining down—were ordered to keep a lookout for parachutists and infiltrators.

"Ow the 'ell d'you tell friend from foe," growled a disgruntled Cockney fireman, "when we're all covered in the same s---?"

In round-the-clock raids over the next seven days, another 2,000 Londoners died and more than 10,000 were injured or entombed. But for those trying to save Britain, there were certain compensations. The Germans' concentration on the capital had taken the pressure off Fighter Command's airfields. Britain now knew where the Luftwaffe was focussing its attacks, and the RAF could hit back hard.

On September 15, Göring ordered a maximum effort from his bomber and fighter forces. The leaders of both units were concerned about mounting losses. Bombers were being hit by RAF fighter squadrons that, Luftwaffe intelligence reports had asserted, no longer existed. Fighters were being shot down because they lacked the fuel for more than a few minutes of dogfighting; others had to crash land on the Calais beaches with empty tanks. One last big daylight raid, Göring assured his officers, and it would be all over; the RAF would be eliminated by the *coup de grâce* and London hit so hard that Churchill would scream for mercy.

Sunday, September 15—henceforth to be known in RAF annals as Battle of Britain Day—was again sunny, with only a faint haze blurring an otherwise clear autumnal sky. At about mid-morning, masses of blips began to appear on British radar screens, and soon waves of Luftwaffe bombers were on their way. About 400 bombers and 700 fighters swept in thickening numbers toward London.

But this time the raiders were attacked from the moment they hit the English coast. Fighter Command sent up its own maximum force and nearly 300 planes were soon dogfighting with Me-109s or inflicting mayhem on the bombers. The clashes continued all day, until the sky was crisscrossed in every direction with vapor trails.

Next morning a London newspaper triumphantly headlined "185 ALL OUT." The true figures were more modest: 56 German aircraft shot down, 26 RAF planes lost. Still, several dozen more Luftwaffe bombers limped home

A Royal Engineers' bomb-disposal squad gingerly defuses a 1,200-pound delayed-action bomb that has gouged a crater near a North London hospital. Disarming such missiles called for high courage and iron nerves since the bomb's timing device could trigger an explosion at any moment. This particular bomb was safely defused and later detonated in Hackney Marshes, far from populated areas.

with some crew members dead, engines ablaze and undercarriages shot away. And at least 20 Me-109s, their tanks dry, had ditched in the sea.

Göring was chastened. He had told Hitler to expect a turning point in the battle as a result of the September 15 onslaught. The turning point had been reached, but not in the direction the Germans had anticipated. On September 17, the Führer postponed *Sea Lion* indefinitely, and instructed his strategists to bring about Britain's demise by other means.

A second legend about the Battle of Britain—almost as widespread as the myth of the totally outmanned RAF—had Britons unfailingly united and staunch amid the terror and the hardships. They shook their fists at the sky and never wavered in their determination to see the war through.

The truth was far more complex and human than that. Many of them indeed showed great courage, while others were terrified; some were excited by the bombings and some were depressed. While the balance of the battle swayed to and fro, British attitudes were also fluctuating. Class feelings intensified, with bitter resentments that the burdens of the war were not—at least at this stage—being fairly and equally shared.

The most restive and disaffected were the Cockneys of London's East End. Nazi bombs they had to accept, but they could not tolerate what they saw as the callousness of British officialdom. In their view, there was a heartless efficiency in government preparations for the Luftwaffe's big offensive: for example, the London County Council stored thousands of papier-mâché coffins; and on the city's outskirts, great pits were dug and supplies of lime assembled, ready for the mass burials of the numerous people expected to die under the rain of German bombs.

East Enders, like most people, were more concerned with surviving than with being properly buried. And they were furiously aware that their government, which might now be stockpiling resting places for the dead, had historically failed to provide adequate shelters for the living.

Behind their plight was a simple fact of geography. The East End was next door to some of England's most important targets: the London docks and armament works; car, tank and truck plants; miles of warehouses; textile factories. So when the bombs began falling, it was the East Enders' squalid homes that caught fire like matchwood. In the better parts of town it was possible to stand in the blacked-out streets, see the glow in the sky and hear the thud of explosions across the city. But it all seemed far away.

To make matters worse there were too few street shelters; those that did exist were too fragile. And there were no deep underground shelters—or none that were officially sanctioned. At first makeshift shelters of all kinds were used. As the raids continued, a spontaneous evacuation began. Whole families, dragging what was left of their belongings on bicycles or wheelbarrows, set out to find a place to hide. One such group settled into an abandoned railway tunnel.

"The first thing I heard," reported police superintendent Reginald Smith who visited the tunnel, "was a great hollow hubbub, a sort of soughing and wailing, as if there were animals down there moaning and crying. And then, this terrible stench hit me. It was worse than dead bodies, hot and thick and so fetid that I vomited. About 50 yards in, I stopped. Ahead of me I could see faces peering towards me lit by candles and lanterns. It was like a painting of hell."

Not suprisingly, the East Enders felt abandoned and isolated. So long as it was they who were taking a beating they told one another, the folks up West in Mayfair and Knightsbridge weren't worrying. "We feel as if we've been put in bloody quarantine," snapped one docker.

On September 10 the King and Queen and the two little Princesses had a narrow escape when a bomb fell on Buckingham Palace. The censors banned the story. When Churchill heard this, he erupted. "Stupid fools!" he shouted. "Spread the news at once! Let the humble people of London know that the King and Queen are sharing their perils with them!" Later the Queen said, "I'm glad we've been bombed. It makes me feel I can look the East End in the face."

Gradually as the weeks passed, the bombs spread, hit or miss all across London. A debutante in Park Lane was as much in danger as a docker in Bermondsey. With the whole population facing the same dangers, just about everyone felt better. Since the government still had not constructed the large, deep shelters that were needed, more and more people decided to take over the Tubes—the subway whose tracks ran deep beneath the city and the River Thames. Every night as dusk fell and the sirens sounded the approach of the raiders, people would arrive in the Tubes with food, drink, blankets and babies, and settle in for the night.

Since the start of the Battle of Britain, the Luftwaffe had lost some 1,600 planes. By October, it was becoming clear that daylight raids were too costly. Following orders from Göring, German bomber fleets abandoned round-the-clock attacks and concentrated on night-bombing instead. By flying at night, the Luftwaffe would cut its losses in the air, while continuing to inflict grave damage on the ground.

At the start of this phase of the Luftwaffe's offensive, the RAF had only eight night fighter squadrons—two of Defiants and six of Blenheims. Both types had been assigned night duty because neither plane had proved effective by day; the Defiant was heavily armed but fatally slow, while the

At a station underneath the Elephant and Castle section, just south of the Thames, Londoners attempt to catch some sleep on the subway platform. Not all Underground station platforms were havens. One such station was Balham. On October 14, a bomb fell close to where some 600 people were sheltering on the platforms. The bomb smashed the gas, water and sewer pipes and electric cables just above. The lights went out; water and sewage poured down and gas began to pump in. In the darkness, panic erupted. Eventually station officials with flashlights led 350 people through the shoulder-high water to the street. But 250 others drowned.

Blenheim was in fact a modified light bomber. And the newer, faster Beaufighter, specifically designed for night fighting, was only beginning to come off the assembly line. To make matters worse, radar was of little help against night bombers that penetrated deep inland, since the stations covered only the coastal areas.

The immediate effect of the Luftwaffe's new offensive was to swing the course of the Battle of Britain back in Germany's favor. All over England the night raids intensified. Large sections of the biggest cities were demolished. On a moonlit night in mid-November, it was the turn of the medieval cathedral city of Coventry—also one of the biggest concentrations of armaments factories in the United Kingdom. Pathfinder aircraft blanketed Coventry with incendiaries, transforming the hapless city into a mammoth beacon on which 437 Heinkel-111s dropped 450 tons of high-explosive and incendiary bombs. By dawn the heart of Coventry had been all but wiped out. The cathedral was devastated. More than 50,000 structures were damaged or destroyed, 380 people killed, 865 citizens seriously hurt.

In London on the night of December 29, most of those who firewatched in the area and manned the stirrup pumps and fire hose had taken a chance and gone home to their families. The Luftwaffe unleashed one of its heaviest raids, with 224 bombers dropping showers of incendiary bombs on the ancient churches and historic landmarks in the old heart of the capital known as The City. The autumn season had been dry; the Thames was so low that the fire engines soon drained the river down to its bed and only a trickle of water came out. Hundreds of venerable buildings burned to the ground.

The year 1941 began on a deceptive note. Just after the terrible bombing on December 29, the weather went sour and the Luftwaffe was forced to slacken its attacks. Throughout the months of January and February the raids were more widely spaced, providing a respite for the British people. The letup had a strange effect: instead of reviving people's spirits, it made morales sag even further. People began to fret about the increasing scarcity of food; the shortage of tea in particular was distressing.

At the end of February, the weather began to improve and the heavy attacks began again, with the Germans concentrating now on cutting Britain's vital marine supply links. Bristol, Cardiff, Portsmouth, Plymouth were blitzed repeatedly. On March 19, London suffered its worst raid so far: 750 civilians were killed.

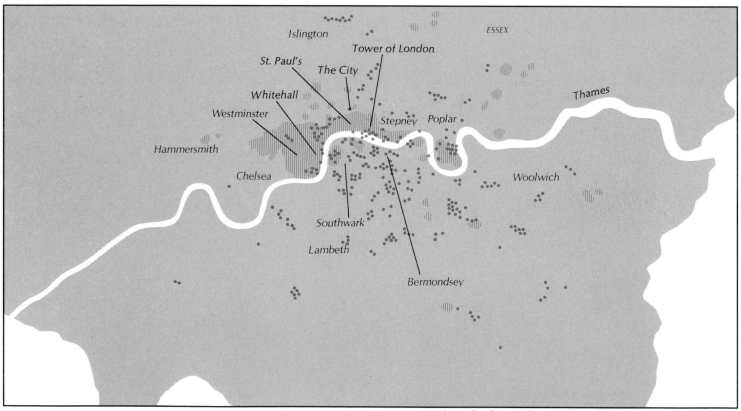

On the night of December 29, 1940, a total of 224 German bombers bombarded London. Their pattern of destruction is shown on the map above. Striking incendiary bomb attacks (shaded areas) started 1,500 separate fires, especially in Westminster and The City, the capital's administrative and financial areas. The highly explosive bombs (each dot represents a cluster) were concentrated along the Thames, with particular damage to the riverside boroughs of Southwark, Bermondsey and Poplar, which were crowded with offices, factories and docks. Despite the intensity of this attack, St. Paul's Cathedral (right) escaped virtually unscathed. A dedicated volunteer firewatch snuffed out every fire bomb that hit the cathedral before serious damage was done.

Then in April, bomb-weary Britons were hit with more bad news. First Yugoslavia and then Greece fell to the Germans. Was this a rehearsal, the British wondered, for the invasion? Their suspicions seemed confirmed when the attacks reached a new peak in the second half of April. London was hit twice; more than 2,000 people were killed and 148,000 houses damaged or destroyed.

These massive raids were indeed a prelude to invasion, but not of Britain. Their real purpose was to distract attention from Hitler's latest grand scheme: Operation *Barbarossa*, an all-out attack by land and air on Russia. By early May, secret orders instructed most German bomber and fighter fleets to prepare to move into Czechoslovakia and Poland in readiness for the invasion. Before packing up they were given orders for one last, massive attack on London for Saturday, May 10.

The raid began at 11:30 p.m. and lasted until 5:37 a.m. on Sunday. Antiaircraft fire kept the raiders so high that they could not pinpoint their targets. But they simply dropped their cargo somewhere over the capital, inflicting the worst damage of the entire war to date. Every section of the capital fell prey to showers of incendiary bombs. The Tower of London was hit; high explosives ripped through the House of Commons; the magnificent oak roof of Westminster Hall was pierced by bombs; incendiaries gutted the British Museum's Library; and one of London's oldest churches,

Winston Churchill inspects the damage inflicted by incendiaries to the Debating Chamber of the House of Commons, the scene of some of his greatest triumphs. Though not positively identifiable, the man in the foreground is believed to be Sir William Stephenson, also known as "Intrepid," a British master spy in World War II, and Churchill's friend.

St. Clement Danes, was reduced to a ruin. The great bells, which had long rung out the melody of the old nursery rhyme, "Oranges and lemons say the bells of St. Clement's," cracked asunder when they crashed to the ground.

By a final count, 1,436 Londoners had been killed in the May 10th raid, 1,800 seriously injured; for the survivors, it seemed almost more than they could bear. The wreckage of their beloved capital, the crumbled buildings and blackened monuments they saw all around them aroused a terrible despair. For days afterward, many Londoners walked around in a semi-daze, dreading new trials to come.

When four weeks passed with no big raids, a headline in the *Daily Express* asked "WHAT'S HITLER UP TO?" A select circle around Churchill, armed with decoded information, was well aware that there would be no more major raids: the Luftwaffe was on its way out of Western Europe. But no one told the British people. Two more weeks of uneasy nights passed. Then, on June 22, 1941, the German armies jumped off against Russia.

"IT'S MOSCOW'S TURN NOW," said a headline in the *Evening News*. To the British people, it became an undreamed-of reprieve. As July gave way to August and still no raiders came, Churchill confirmed that the Blitz was over. "We won," the British began to tell each other, in tones mingling surprise with pride.

There were Germans who would not agree with them, who would say, in fact, that there never was anything called the Battle of Britain. General Adolf Galland of the Luftwaffe, for instance, said later: "All that happened was that we made a number of attacks against England between 1940 and 1941. Then we discovered that we were not achieving the desired effect, and so we retired. There was no battle, and we did not lose it." To which, much later, an RAF pilot who had fought against him in 1940 replied: "General Galland, do you know what happens in the tenth round of a boxing match, when one fighter is groggy on his feet, and his trainer throws in the towel, shouting: 'My fighter retires!'? Who has won the fight and who has lost it?"

The British people had no doubt whatsoever. They bore many bruises, but they knew who had thrown in the towel.

Seen from the north transept of St. Paul's Cathedral, London's core lies in blackened ruins. The dome of Old Bailey—the city's ancient prison—is at left; to the right of it are the four spires of the Church of the Holy Sepulcher. Despite the visible destruction, very few people lost their lives in the devastation of this primarily commercial area of London.

THE BATTLE OF THE ATLANTIC

Cargo-laden Victory ships in a Europe-bound convoy plow through stormy seas after a gale in the North Atlantic, a favorite stalking ground for U-boats.

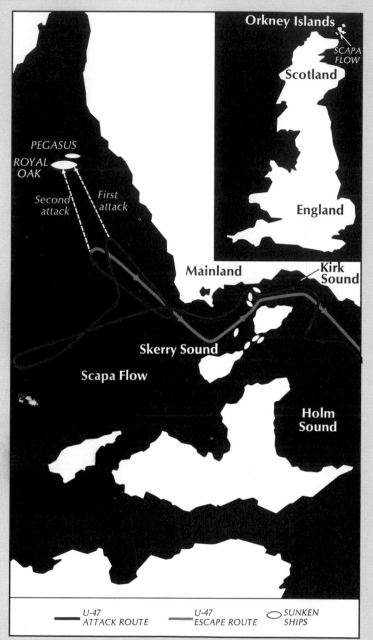

PEGASUS
ROYAL OAK
Second attack
First attack
Orkney Islands
SCAPA FLOW
Scotland
England
Kirk Sound
Mainland
Skerry Sound
Scapa Flow
Holm Sound

U-47 ATTACK ROUTE   U-47 ESCAPE ROUTE   SUNKEN SHIPS

The British battleship Royal Oak was sunk on October 14, 1939, with the loss of 833 aboard. The daring raid by German submarine U-47 on the British Home Fleet's base at Scapa Flow—located in Scotland's Orkney Islands (inset map above)—began (red line, large map) when the U-boat entered the protected anchorage of Kirk Sound, and spotted the battleship. The U-47 scored one inconclusive hit on the Royal Oak, and turned to escape. When no alarm was raised, the submarine circled, and this time sank the battleship. The U-47 escaped (gray line) through Kirk Sound.

UNLEASHING THE SEA WOLVES

Not 10 hours after Britain declared war on Germany, a U-boat torpedoed the British liner *Athenia*. Of the 1,400 passengers aboard (many of whom were fleeing the war in Europe), 112 lost their lives. In the weeks that followed, Hitler's sea wolves—as his submarine force was called—struck time and time again.

One of the first big casualties took place at Scapa Flow, the British Home Fleet base which held a special bitter significance for the Germans: the main units of the German fleet had been scuttled there by their defiant crews after World War I. Now the Germans were returning—with a submarine, *U-47*, under the command of Lieutenant Günther Prien.

Commodore Karl Dönitz, head of the German Navy's submarine arm, had planned the operation, studying aerial photographs to find the best route into the anchorage; he personally picked Prien to lead the attack. Although Dönitz had argued repeatedly that the only weapon that could throttle Britain was a large submarine fleet, he had been ignored in favor of the German Army and the Luftwaffe.

But the Scapa Flow exploit would be a catalyst for change. At 12:30 the morning of October 14, 1939, Prien carried out an audacious attack on the British fleet right in the middle of its home base. The raid resulted in the sinking of the British battleship *Royal Oak* and, two days later, a fateful memorandum went out under the name of Grand Admiral Erich Raeder, the commander in chief of the German Navy. Among other war orders, he directed that "All merchant ships definitely recognized as enemy (British or French) can be torpedoed without warning." Passenger ships still were supposed to be warned. But by the middle of November, even that rule had been dropped.

In the months that followed, the German subs missed no opportunity to attack the merchant shipping so vital to Britain's economic survival. The British, for their part, fought back desperately. The resulting Battle of the Atlantic was one of the fiercest—and in many ways the most crucial—of all the armed confrontations of World War II. So deadly was it, and so close did the German submarines come to severing Britain's lifeline, that Winston Churchill, Prime Minister through all but a few months of the War, would later recall: "The only thing that ever really frightened me during the war was the U-boat peril."

New U-boats get final fittings at the Germania Shipyard in Kiel. Krupp, Germany's biggest armament and munitions maker, launched the U-1, the first post-World War I submarine, in secrecy from this yard in 1935. By 1942, the Krupp shipyard was building 20 submarines a year; by the end of the War, it had built 168 of Germany's 1,099 U-boats.

Skipper of the U-47 that sank the Royal Oak, Günther Prien (right) received a hero's welcome back in Germany from Commodore Dönitz. Prien was awarded the Knight's Cross at the Kriegsmarine base in Wilhelmshaven. Dönitz was promoted to rear admiral for conceiving the attack.

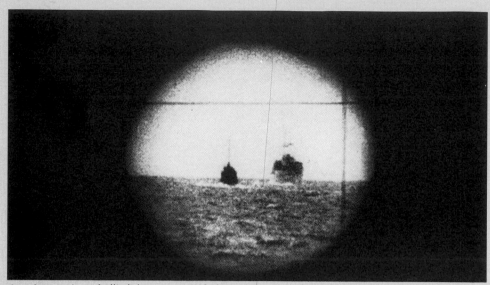

A periscope view of Allied ships moments before a U-boat attack demonstrates the vulnerability of unsuspecting surface vessels to subs lying in wait just below the waves. A favorite tactic of U-boat captains was to race their surfaced vessels ahead of a convoy, then submerge in its path and wait for the ships to sail into the cross hairs of the periscope.

With his cap reversed to keep the peak from obstructing his view, U-boat commander Kurt Diggins studies a convoy through the periscope. When France fell to the Germans in June of 1940, British ships faced an increased threat. The U-boats could now operate in the Atlantic for greatly lengthened periods of time, receiving more support from squadrons of long-range, land-based planes operating out of Occupied France and Norway.

MISJUDGING THE U-BOAT MENACE

Commodore Dönitz and his staff had always known that their chief hope of blockading Britain lay in the U-boats, which could sink the ships that were bringing supplies and troops across the Atlantic. Britain however—albeit the world's foremost sea power—was ill-equipped to fight such a battle. The reasons stemmed from a variety of misjudgments.

First there was the belief that the Germans would never again resort to the kind of unrestricted submarine warfare that had been waged in World War I. Naively, the British expected the Germans to honor their signature on the London Submarine Protocol of 1936, which outlawed the sinking of any unescorted merchant ship without warning. In fact, however, the German Navy's battle instructions directed: "Fighting methods will never fail to be employed merely because some international regulations are opposed to them."

In addition, Britain's naval building program in the late 1930s had been tailored to classic above-surface battleship warfare, not hunting and killing U-boats. Still another reason the Admiralty did not take the submarine threat more seriously was an undue reliance on a newly developed weapon. The device, named asdic for the Allied Submarine Detection Investigation Committee that developed it (the American version was called sonar), gave the British false confidence in their ability to battle the U-boats. Unfortunately, the device could be used only underwater; it could not locate U-boats on the surface. Dönitz simply ordered his boats to attack at night, from the surface, where they could almost double their speed.

From the conning tower, a U-boat crewman watches a British freighter sink. Split in two by a torpedo, the ship was finished off by the submarine's deck guns.

Battered by high seas and a northwesterly gale, two German U-boats on patrol in mid-Atlantic meet unexpectedly in the winter of 1941. The chance encounter

surprised both boats, which had been fighting the storm for over a week.

RUNNING THE GAUNTLET

Even in perfect weather, herding a compact formation of 30 to 40 ships across the Atlantic Ocean without a collision or some other major mishap would have been a feat. But in winter the undertaking demanded a superhuman effort. The main convoy route cut through a region of the North Atlantic where some of the world's foulest winter weather prevails. Ships that were jacketed with ice or blinded by snow struggled to keep their places in the formation. Seas up to 60 feet high could break the backs of ships and smash lifeboats to splinters. Men who were blown or washed overboard often froze to death in seconds.

Even in the most difficult circumstances, peak alertness had to be maintained. At night, crews kept bone-aching vigils, searching the white wave caps for a conning tower. By day, they hunted periscopes with binoculars in tedious but methodical patterns, each man searching a small quadrant of sea again and again.

Always, the strain and the exhaustion were mingled with fear. Round-the-clock vigilance was no guarantee that a torpedo would not strike at any moment. Emboldened by success, U-boats might even surface in the middle of a convoy to slaughter ships all around.

In October 1940, a year after the War began, Convoy SC-7 lost 16 ships out of 35 in one attack. As the War progressed, shipping losses mounted. In May of 1942, U-boats sank 120 Allied ships, and in June they accounted for another 119. Before the Battle of the Atlantic would end, Great Britain would lose more than 32,000 of its merchant seamen, almost one fourth of the total number who served during all of World War II.

Torpedoed amidships, a tanker becomes an inferno of fuel oil. Tankers carried the convoy's most valuable cargo and received the best protection.

A tanker crew plays a hose on a blaze. Their quick action saved this ship, which was then towed to an American port for repairs.

MARAUDERS PROWLING THE SURFACE

"The surface forces can do no more than show that they know how to die gallantly," wrote the German Navy's commander in chief, Grand Admiral Erich Raeder, on September 3, 1939.

At the beginning of the War, Germany's surface fleet was not numerically large enough to risk direct combat with the Royal Navy. Realizing that his ships would have to depend on stealth, power and speed, Raeder resurrected a weapon that had been used successfully during World War I: armed merchant raiders. Disguised as cargo vessels, these deadly marauders would exploit the element of surprise, prowling the seas like pirates of old, swooping down on solitary, unsuspecting ships. Starting in 1939 and continuing for the next three and a half years, the marauders would sink 130 ships, totalling 850,000 tons—almost three times the tonnage sunk by Germany's conventional warships.

By late fall 1940, Raeder was ready to send battleships after bigger game: the Atlantic convoys. The following year, Germany's most powerful battleship, the *Bismarck*, was prepared to join the action. On May 18, 1941, the *Bismarck*, along with the heavy cruiser *Prinz Eugen* left Gotenhafen on the Baltic Sea, to attempt a breakout into the Atlantic. Reports of the ships' movements reached London by radio and, three days later in a fjord off Norway, a British reconnaissance plane spotted them.

On May 23, the *Bismarck* and the *Prinz Eugen* were discovered by a patrolling British cruiser in the Denmark Strait. The British battleships *Hood* and *Prince of Wales* raced through the night, headed for

By dispersing his forces, German naval commander in chief Raeder hoped to keep the Royal Navy tied up searching the oceans for raiders. Above, oil-soaked crew members of the British destroyer Glowworm, just sunk by the German heavy cruiser Admiral Hipper, wallow on a nearly swamped lifeboat while being hoisted aboard by the raider's crew. The Glowworm was caught alone off the Norwegian coast by the Admiral Hipper and four destroyers on April 8, 1940.

confrontation. On May 24, the British and German battleships exchanged fire. The *Bismarck's* final salvo hit the *Hood's* magazine and she was blown to pieces; of the 1,419 men aboard, only three survived. The *Prince of Wales* was hit several times in succession, and withdrew out of range of fire.

Bismarck Captain Ernst Lindemann urged his commander to bring both German ships home. Instead, the *Bismarck* was ordered to head to the French port of Saint-Nazaire for repairs. Steaming toward France with one ruptured fuel tank, the *Bismarck* fended off attacks by torpedo-carrying Swordfish planes from British carriers. Before darkness fell on May 26, planes from the British carrier *Ark Royal* made a final attack.

While the *Bismarck* blazed away at the incoming Swordfish with 56 antiaircraft guns, two torpedoes struck and one jammed the mighty battleship's rudders. By morning the British were closing in rapidly and, although the *Bismarck* returned their fire, she was barely maneuverable. Shell after shell smashed into the *Bismarck* and, by 10:00 a.m. she was still afloat and under way, but her guns were silent. Finally, as one surviving crew member recalled, the great battleship "slid down to the bottom."

Of the more than 2,000 men aboard, only 110 were rescued.

As the *Bismarck* disappeared, the major effort of Germany's surface navy in the Battle of the Atlantic died with her. Within a month the Royal Navy located and destroyed half a dozen supply ships that were vital to sustained German operations in the Atlantic. A few disguised merchant raiders remained at large until the end of 1943, but for the most part they limited their clandestine work to the Indian and Pacific oceans.

Swordfish torpedo bombers on the carrier Victorious are readied for a May 25, 1941 foray against the Bismarck. The canvas-covered biplanes flew more than 100 miles to hit the massive battleship. "It was incredible," said one German officer, "to see such obsolete-looking planes having the nerve to attack a fire-spitting mountain like the Bismarck." Equally remarkable, none of the slow-moving Swordfish were shot down and all of them managed to return safely to the Victorious.

An aerial photograph taken from a British Spitfire flying over Norway's Grimstad fjord on May 21, 1941, betrays the powerful new German battleship Bismarck (lower left). The picture was so important that the pilot who took it returned to Scotland, had prints developed there, and then took off for London. When his plane ran short of fuel, he landed about 120 miles away from the city, managed to borrow a car, and drove the rest of the way—through a blackout, at 50 mph.

THE SINKING OF A U-BOAT

The terror that U-boats spread was matched by the terror that the men on the U-boats faced. For being a U-boat captain or crew member was one of World War II's most hazardous occupations. An attack on one U-boat, the *U-175*, is shown at right.

The episode began when Captain Gerhardt Muntz, while searching from his conning tower for Allied ships in the North Atlantic 600 miles west of England, spotted an approaching convoy. At the same time, Muntz's submarine, the *U-175*, was seen by the U.S. Coast Guard cutter *Spencer* in the vanguard of the convoy. Hastily, the *U-175* dived, and for a short time successfully evaded detection. But trailing the *Spencer* in 11 parallel columns were the 19 tankers and 38 freighters of Convoy HX-233, an irresistible target. Muntz decided to chance an attack—a fateful decision. As the *U-175* eased up from the ocean depths, the *Spencer* passed over her, and the cutter's sonar detection device picked up the sub.

Commander Harold S. Berdine, aboard the *Spencer*, ordered an immediate depth-charge barrage: 11 of the lethal drums, set to explode underwater at 50 and 100 feet, then he released 11 more depth charges. The furious assault worked: the *U-175*'s air pumps and diving controls were damaged, and Muntz had no choice but to surface.

As the *U-175*'s conning tower rose into view, the convoy ships and the *Spencer*'s sister cutter, the *Duane*, opened fire. It was all over in moments. Captain Muntz and six of his crew died on the *U-175*'s deck. The remaining crew members jumped overboard; while they were still bobbing in the seas, the *U-175* sank to the bottom.

Exploding depth charges produce a mountainous geyser from the deep as the U.S. Coast Guard cutter Spencer attacks the German submarine U-175. During World War II, Germany lost 28,542 of its 41,300 submariners and 753 of its 863 operational U-boats.

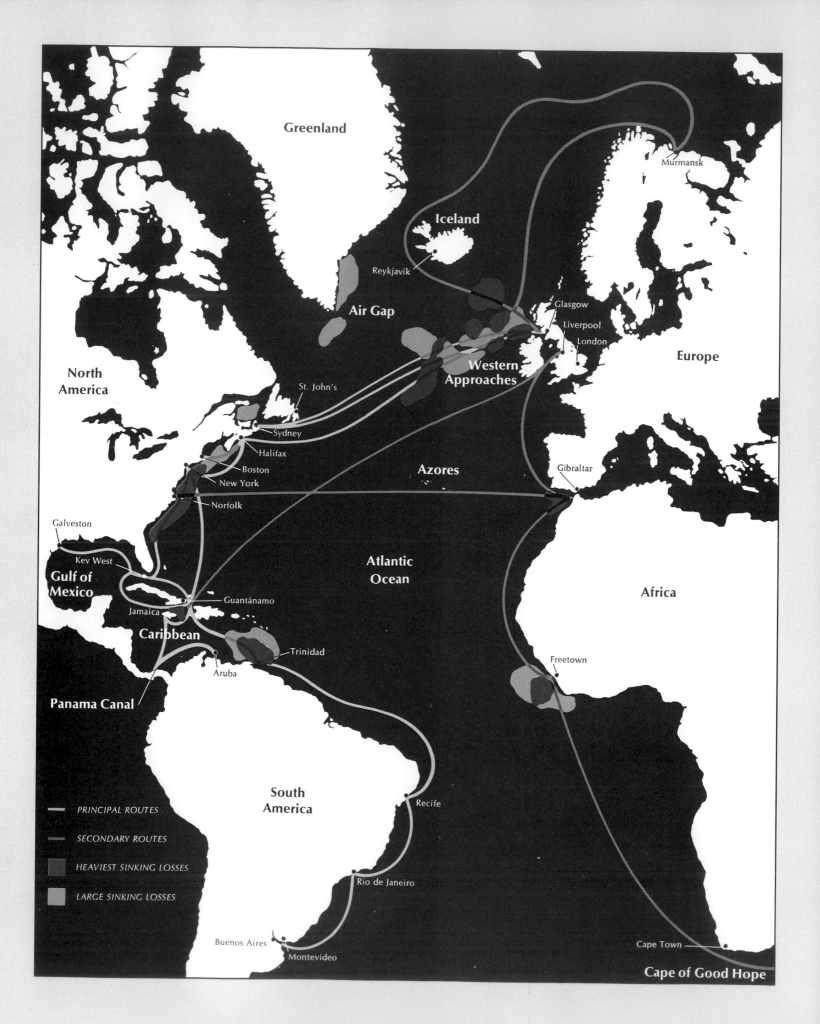

Greenland

Iceland

Reykjavik

Air Gap

Murmansk

North
America

St. John's

Western
Approaches

Glasgow
Liverpool
London

Europe

Sydney

Halifax

Boston

New York

Norfolk

Azores

Gibraltar

Galveston

Key West

Gulf of
Mexico

Atlantic
Ocean

Africa

Jamaica

Guantánamo

Caribbean

Aruba

Trinidad

Freetown

Panama Canal

South
America

Recife

PRINCIPAL ROUTES

SECONDARY ROUTES

HEAVIEST SINKING LOSSES

LARGE SINKING LOSSES

Rio de Janeiro

Buenos Aires

Montevideo

Cape Town

Cape of Good Hope

VITAL ARMADAS

The first British convoys were makeshift fleets, comprised of 35 to 45 freighters and tankers; many were so decrepit and unseaworthy that only the urgent demands of wartime could justify their use.

The conditions of the ships, the inexperience of their crew members and the lack of up-to-date equipment made the duty of the escort vessels an especially onerous one: they had to accompany these motley armadas, shepherd them through dangerous waters, protect them from submarine attack and bring them safely to port. The task was awesome; yet the very outcome of the War depended upon its being carried out successfully.

By 1940, the convoy concept was being transformed. In July, a new sea training base began individualistic training, producing teams with confidence in themselves and pride in their ships. A year later, entire escort groups were training and remaining together for bigger periods of time. With time, more destroyers were released for escort duty, while radar technicians ashore worked night and day to develop sets for fleet ships, aircraft and escort vessels.

In the end it was the better-trained crews on better-equipped ships sailing in larger, more vital convoys, that swung the Battle of the Atlantic in the Allies' favor.

In March 1941, despite the frightening toll of Allied merchant shipping losses, the convoy-escort system was beginning to prove itself. British Captain Donald G.F. Macintyre, escort leader of Convoy HX-112, was instrumental in bagging two of the three top German U-boat aces killed or captured that month.

Broad-beamed and solid, corvettes like the one at left were the ideal, most common convoy escorts. Inexpensively produced and able to maneuver in the worst kinds of weather, the 925-ton vessels stood up to the North Atlantic battering far better than destroyers did. But they were notoriously uncomfortable, making even the hardiest skipper queasy.

The Battle of the Atlantic centered around the shipping routes shown at left. The U-boats began their attacks in the Western Approaches, near Britain, and later divided their effort between the area around Greenland and the coast of Africa. Next the East Coast of the United States became the main target region. Then the subs moved down to the Caribbean, before returning to the area west of Britain.

THE TRIUMPH OF TECHNOLOGY

Within the short space of 10 days in March 1941, three of Germany's top U-boat aces were eliminated from the War, and a deep sense of satisfaction flowed through the embattled Royal Navy. What few of the rank and file realized at the time was that a new device had helped knock out the wiliest of enemies. That device was radar, and it was only the first of several advances in antisubmarine warfare that began to give the British reason to think that the advantage was at last shifting their way.

In the years before World War II, scientists in Germany, Britain, France and the United States had been working on radar; the British effort dated from the winter of 1934-35. Although RAF fighters could use radar effectively by 1940, shipboard radar was longer in coming about. The first shipboard sets reached units of the Royal Navy in 1941.

Until the appearance of radar, U-boats had been able to rise to the surface at night and attack Allied shipping with impunity. Once on the surface, they could not be located by asdic—or sonar—but only by the human eye. And in the concealing darkness, they were frequently able to steal up on convoys without being noticed, fire their torpedoes and guns, and then sneak away.

But once radar was installed on the escort vessels that accompanied the convoys, the U-boats could no longer count on such easy pickings—or on so easy an escape. Radar could see in the dark, and in foul weather as well. Asdic and radar working in tandem could track submarines both above and below the surface, enabling the escort ships to move in on them.

A less complicated electronic detection device was also in use among Britain's antisubmarine forces. This was the ship-borne high-frequency direction finder—British sailors called it "Huff-Duff" from its initials. Except for radar, no single invention would prove more telling in the struggle against the U-boats.

By mid-1941 the British were making use of the content of German

radio transmissions as well as the signals themselves. The submarine *U-110* had been captured, yielding intact a German electronic coding machine. British cryptanalysts used the captured machine to break the Germans' U-boat code. When the ship-borne version of Huff-Duff appeared, it enabled two ships of an escort to get their own fix on a submarine, and to close in together for a well-targeted depth-charge attack.

Other advances in antisubmarine warfare came not from new inventions, but simply by improving old detection devices and visual aids. "Snowflake," for example, was a rocket that could be fired into the air with minimal flash. The resultant explosion left a strong white light lingering in the sky for several minutes. When all of the ships in a convoy fired snowflakes in unison, the combined fire could light up the sea for miles around, revealing U-boats lurking in the area.

As 1941 got under way, the planners began to recognize the importance of air power in the antisubmarine campaign. Planes fitted with radar, carrying depth-charges, bombs, and machine guns could locate the U-boats, and then move in for the kill. The value of air cover was soon appreciated in terms both of U-boats sunk and of ships saved.

When a wolf pack chose to tackle a convoy head on, its torpedoes could still take a heavy toll. But the risk was now greater, for the U-boats had to penetrate rings of escort ships that were faster and better armed, and fight off more, and more deadly, attacks from above.

As 1941 drew to a close, the U-boats were suffering heavy losses; they needed easier hunting grounds than what they were encountering in the North Atlantic. On December 7, Japan had bombed Pearl Harbor and America was in the scrap at last. The vast flow of unprotected shipping from the Gulf of Mexico up the Eastern Seaboard of North America, was now fair game for the submarines. In 1942 they turned to it with a vengeance.

In their war against the U-boats, the Allies developed an ungainly looking, multiple-barreled weapon called the Hedgehog that fired a barrage of 24 small bombs in an oval pattern over a wide area. Before the development of this weapon, submarine-killers employing depth-charges had to pass directly over a submerged U-boat. Hedgehogs could be fired up to 250 yards ahead of the ship. Because their bombs were equipped with contact fuses, the missiles exploded only when a hit was scored—and were almost always fatal.

Among three of Britain's most effective aerial weapons in the Battle of the Atlantic were the Sunderland flying boat (left), which carried bombs and depth charges and bristled with machine guns, and was dubbed the "flying porcupine" by the Germans. Another surprisingly effective innovation was the catapult-equipped merchant ship, which carried a Hurricane fighter that strafed U-boats and ships and attacked German aircraft, but could not return to deck once launched. The third weapon—the ancient-looking Swordfish biplane used to attack the battleship Bismarck—laid mines, dropped flares and attacked submarines and surface raiders with torpedoes.

AMERICA'S ICY CITADEL

"Whoever possesses Iceland," wrote the German geopolitician Karl Haushofer in the 1930s, "holds a gun pointed permanently at England, America and Canada." It was a pistol that Great Britain was quick to seize. In May 1940, with the fall of Denmark, the island's former ruler, Britain raced to take control of this subarctic outpost that lay within easy reach of vital shipping routes, putting ashore more than 24,000 men. But a little more than a year later, when the British troops there were needed for duty in Africa, all but a few were gradually pulled out and American Marines took over—a full five months before the United States formally became involved in the War. Eventually as many as 50,000 Americans were stationed there.

U.S. Navy pilots based in Iceland provided air support for the convoys bringing vital supplies to Britain. Air coverage of the convoys started 600 miles out, with patrol planes taking turns at escorting the vessels in four-hour shifts. Amphibious PBY Catalina planes bucked gales and rain squalls to comb the waters for U-boats and deadly ice. They also conducted searches for planes downed in the sea and for survivors of ship sinkings.

The American defenders of Iceland found themselves in a bleak realm. At the height of winter in the far northern latitudes, daylight lasted only four hours. Gale force winds buffeted men and machines. Heavy rains could transform camps into quagmires. With the weather in mind, the Army issued every GI skis and snowshoes—and an unheard-of five pairs of shoes.

Monotony was the No. 1 enemy, more real to most servicemen than the Germans. Some men flew routine air patrols or patched up ships damaged by ice, but the chief excitement available to most of them was training, building roads, erecting huts or hauling supplies. There were few diversions afterhours, except for letters home, card games or reading. The local girls were none too friendly, the beer was weak and Scotch cost a dollar a shot—a lot of money in the days when a buck private got only $30 a month.

The Americans made the most of their surroundings. They did their laundry in natural hot springs that bubbled up out of Iceland's volcanic terrain, and paved the streets around camp with crushed lava to combat the mud. And as an indication that they had not lost their sense of humor, they fashioned trees out of empty cans and discarded pipes to decorate the barren landscape, built wooden fireplugs and put up street signs bearing familiar hometown names.

British and American warships assemble in Iceland's sprawling Hvalfjordur harbor before starting out with a convoy for the Russian port of Archangel.

AN OUTPOURING OF SHIPS

One reason why the Allies were able to win the Battle of the Atlantic was that the United States could build ships faster than Germany could sink them. In 1939-1940 only 102 sea-going ships were constructed in the U.S. But in September 1941, the nation launched a crash program, mustering all its industrial skills to produce a doughty vessel called the Liberty ship. By the end of 1942, 646 freighters had been completed, 597 of them Liberties. Launchings outnumbered sinkings in the Atlantic for the first time since the war began. By 1943, 140 Liberty ships were being launched each month.

At yards all over the country, 1.5 million workers learned to rivet and weld prefabricated components. Every effort was made to get the job done as quickly as possible. Yards competed to find ways to cut corners; awards and bonuses were given to workers for time-saving ideas.

The 441-foot ships—homely adaptations of a British tramp steamer—were built working without letup and at the surprisingly low cost of two million dollars per hull. Such a ship could travel 17,000 miles at 11 knots, using old-fashioned steam engines. She was not pretty or fast, but her straight lines and flat planes made her simple and quick to build, and she could carry 10,800 tons of badly needed cargo.

The genius behind this miracle of manufacture was bald and portly Henry J. Kaiser, a 60-year-old California contractor, who had completed the mammoth Boulder, Bonneville and Grand Coulee dams ahead of schedule. The secret to rapid ship construction, Kaiser realized, was to build as much as possible on dry land. Components were assembled all over the country. Freight cars carried them to shipyards, where they were stacked in a "filing system" along the ways where hulls were being built. When a hull was ready, cranes lifted bulkheads, fuel tanks, decks and superstructures into place. Special cranes—the largest ever built—were needed for the job. Once the hulls were launched, tugs towed them to finishing areas, where engines were installed and all the equipment a ship would need at sea was put aboard.

At the peak of the wartime effort, workers were able to construct one ship in 80 hours and 30 minutes. So fast were the shipbuilders that a joke was told of a woman who stepped up with a champagne bottle to christen a new ship. The keel had not been laid. "What shall I do now?" she asked Kaiser. "Just start swinging," he said.

Shipbuilding wizard Henry J. Kaiser assembles a prefab model Liberty ship in seven and a half minutes to show how yards could do it in 10 days.

A massive bulkhead is lowered by a crane into the ribbed hull of a new Liberty ship while welders wait in the bilges, ready to secure it in place.

Rows of Liberty ships, nicknamed "Ugly Ducklings," await final outfitting in California before sailing through the Panama Canal for duty in the Atlantic.

6

The 1939 nonaggression pact with Stalin had served Hitler well. The agreement enabled him to take what he wished of Poland and to pursue the conquest of Western Europe without having to worry about his neighbor to the east. But now Hitler's eyes had turned eastward to Russia's immense natural resources and rich agricultural land. In addition, he said, the country's Slavic population comprised "a mass of born slaves" for the Germans to exploit. In July 1940, the Führer ordered his commanders to launch an invasion no later than spring of the following year. The plans were ready within five months and on December 18 Hitler set them in motion with an order labeled Directive No. 21. "The German Army," it declared, "must be prepared to crush Soviet Russia in a quick campaign."

At 3 a.m. on Sunday, June 22, 1941, the summer calm of the Russo-German frontier was shattered by the thunderous roar of artillery. From staging points in East Prussia and Poland, three million German soldiers began swarming into the Soviet Union in a grandiose scheme of conquest called Operation *Barbarossa*. It was the largest attack in history—and it would be the last of Adolf Hitler's blitzkriegs.

Barbarossa called for a plunge into Russia along three major axes. Army Group North would strike northeastward to Leningrad, thereby securing the Baltic Sea flank. Army Group South would move across the Ukraine toward Kiev to gain control of the Soviet breadbasket, and then head southeastward to seize the industrial basin of the Donets River. But the major effort would be undertaken by Army Group Center, which would smash the Russian lines in two wedges and drive toward Minsk and Smolensk to encircle large elements of the Russian army. Beyond Smolensk—700 miles from the frontier—lay Moscow.

To seal the fate of the Soviet lands and peoples, power in the conquered territory was assigned to Heinrich Himmler, overlord of the SS, which would follow the regular army into Russia. Since Nazi planners intended that Russian agriculture would feed all of the German armed forces, millions of Soviet citizens would necessarily have to starve. That suited Himmler, who cooly estimated that as many as 30 million racially unacceptable Slavs would have to be liquidated anyhow. As for the Russian armed forces, Hitler declared that "This is a war of extermination."

The buildup for *Barbarossa* was massive. As doomsday approached, 186 divisions stood poised on the Russian border, 19 of them panzer units, ready to strike into the Soviet Union with more than 3,000 tanks. Along the frontier, 6,000 German guns began zeroing in while a fleet of more than 2,000 Luftwaffe warplanes was assembled in the rear.

All along, the Russians had received ample warning. In March, the United States gave the Soviet ambassador in Washington a copy of German invasion plans that had been acquired by the American commercial attaché in Berlin. On May 15, Richard Sorge, a brilliant Soviet spy in Tokyo, informed Moscow that some 150 German divisions would invade Russia on June 22. Even as late as June 18, Moscow received a message from a Soviet agent in Switzerland, saying: "General attack on territories occupied by Russians dawn of Sunday 22 June 3:15 a.m."

The warnings were not only dismissed but derided. Less than a week before the invasion, the official Soviet news agency, TASS, stated unequivocally that rumors of an imminent German attack were "completely without foundation." According to Soviet Foreign Minister Vyacheslav Molotov, "Only a fool would attack us."

ASSAULT ON RUSSIA

Arctic Ocean

• Murmansk

Norway

Finland

Union of Soviet
Socialist Republics

• Archangel

Sweden

Lake
Ladoga

Karelian
Isthmus

Baltic Sea

• Leningrad

Estonia

• Luga

Latvia

• Demyansk

• Kalinin

Volga *River*

BALTIC MILITARY
DISTRICT

Dvina *River*

Rzhev •

• Mozhaisk

MOSCOW
MILITARY DISTRICT

Oka River

Lithuania

• Moscow

**ARMY GROUP
NORTH**

• Vitebsk

• Vyazma

East Prussia

WESTERN
MILITARY
DISTRICT

Smolensk •
Orsha •

Ugra
River

• Tula

**ARMY GROUP
CENTER**

Belorussia

• Roslavl

Berlin •

• Bialystok

• Minsk

• Bryansk

• Orel

Dor
River

**ARMY GROUP
SOUTH**

Bug
River

• Brest

Pripyat Marshes

• Kursk

Germany

Desna River

• Kharkov

Poland

• Lvov

KIEV MILITARY
DISTRICT

• Kiev

• Lokhvitsa

Donets River

Dnieper River

• Stalingrad

Czechoslovakia

Ukraine

• Uman

• Rostov

Bukovina

Hungary

Bessarabia

• Odessa

Sea
of Azov

Yugoslavia

Rumania

Crimea

• Sevastopol

Caucasus

Caspian Sea

Adriatic Sea

Albania

Bulgaria

Black Sea

Turkey

Greece

Iran

| 0 | 100 | 200 | 300 | 400 | 500 |

Scale of miles

On June 22, 1941, Operation Barbarossa sent the German Army into Russia in four main drives along a front that stretched from the Arctic to the Black Sea.

Such attitudes clearly reflected those of the Kremlin's master, Josef Stalin. As the buildup of German troops on his border progressed, Stalin may have been convinced that it was a feint to cover the real Nazi plan: an invasion of Great Britain. More likely, he was simply borrowing a few precious months. By one account, Stalin recognized that war with Germany was inevitable, and even acknowledged that the Soviet Union itself might initiate a conflict in 1942. Yet at the moment, he said, the Red Army was poorly equipped and trained; a delay would allow him to build up its strength.

Stalin was right about one thing: seldom has a major power been so feebly prepared. Although the Soviet Union possessed the world's largest army, with some five million men, it was hopelessly anachronistic. In an age of tank warfare, the U.S.S.R. was the only big nation that still had a large traditional cavalry force, a full 30 divisions numbering some 210,000 horsemen. Of the Red Army's 24,000 tanks, all but 1,500 were obsolescent. Equally primitive was the Red Air Force: 80 per cent of its 12,000 planes were obsolete, and its old fighters, many of them biplanes, had top speeds of less than 300 miles an hour.

Worst of all, Stalin's Great Purge—beginning in 1937 and lasting a year and a half—had left the Red Army demoralized and deprived of 35,000 of the Army's most talented commanders. The bulk of those who escaped the Purge felt that survival depended upon servility. "The Boss knows best," became the watchword of even the highest-ranking officers.

Confronted by those circumstances, Stalin staked Russia's future on the gamble that he could buy Hitler off with acts of appeasement. He insisted that German planes violating Soviet airspace were not to be fired upon. He urged his trade commissars to rush deliveries to Germany of oil and other supplies. Most regrettably, he forbade any defense preparations that Germany might construe as hostile.

Stalin's obduracy endured until the very end. On the evening of June 21, he relented to the extent of authorizing commanders in border regions to bring their troops to combat readiness. But even then, a Stalin directive warned that "no other measures are to be taken without special orders." It was sent out at 12:30 a.m., Sunday, June 22—less than three hours before the invasion began.

Even as the German artillery bombardment began, assault

German engineers hastily construct a bridge over the Berezina River for their onrushing army.

parties darted across bridges on the River Bug, surprising Russian defenders before they could detonate demolition charges. Along the 500-mile length of the river the Germans successfully seized every bridge essential to their strategy, and the tanks started rolling across. The Red Army was thrown into chaos, and German radio operators gleefully monitored desperate Russian messages: "Staff Third Army wiped out" and "We are fired upon. What do we do?" To one such plea, the uncomprehending answer from Russian headquarters was: "You must be insane. And why isn't your message in code?"

Meanwhile, Luftwaffe aircraft filled the sky. By midday they had knocked out 1,200 Russian warplanes—800 of them on the ground—while losing only 10 of their own. German bombers were virtually unopposed. "The blasts rent the air and made our ears ring," recalled a Soviet officer caught in a bombing raid. "Thick black pillars of smoke billowed up. Somewhere a high-pitched hysterical female voice was crying out a desperate, inconsolable 'aaaaaa!'"

In Moscow, confusion was mixed with disbelief. On learning of the attack, Defense Commissar Semyon K. Timoshenko conferred with Stalin, then called Western Military District headquarters in Minsk, where he reached the region's deputy commander, General Ivan V. Boldin. "No actions can be taken without our consent," said Timoshenko. "Comrade Stalin has forbidden our artillery to open fire."

"It's not possible," Boldin shouted. "Our troops are retreating. Whole towns are in flames. Everywhere people are being killed." The order stood, Timoshenko replied.

Not until the afternoon of June 22 did Soviet Air Force Lieutenant General I.I. Kopets receive orders to retaliate by bombing the enemy. Kopets did as he was told, although by then his fighters had been destroyed and the bombers had no escorts. The lumbering Russian Ilyushin and Tupolev bombers flew off to be chewed up by the German Messerschmitts; shooting them down, said Luftwaffe Field Marshal Albert Kesselring, was as easy as "infanticide." By the second day of the war, Kopets had lost all his undefended bombers, and subsequently killed himself.

In the first days of the invasion, Field Marshal Wilhelm Ritter von Leeb's Army Group North sped along Lithuania's forest tracks toward the Dvina River, the only major obstacle before Leningrad. By morning on June 26, the leading tanks of General Erich von Manstein's LVI Panzer Corps were 190 miles inside Russia and only four miles from the bridges that led across the 250-yard-wide river to Dvinsk.

Fearing an attack would cause the Russians to blow up the bridges, the Germans stopped there and began the most

A group of panzer grenadiers, leaving the safety of their armored half-tracks, rush forward to clean out Soviet sharpshooters who had taken refuge in a farmhouse during the Germans' advance.

daring and successful ruse of the invasion. A 30-man engineering platoon piled into captured Russian trucks that were driven by Germans in Russian uniforms. Nearing the road bridge at Dvinsk, they were waved on by a Russian rear guard of about 50 men. Then, racing across the bridge, they jumped out, dismantled its demolitions, and sustained 20 minutes of intense fire that killed five of them before a heavier German force arrived to secure the bridge—intact. The war was only four days old and already the Germans were threatening Leningrad, about 300 miles away.

On the southern flank, resistance in the Kiev Military District under Colonel General M.P. Kirponos was stronger. Yet Field Marshal Gerd von Rundstedt's Army Group South pushed steadily into the Ukraine just south of the vast Pripet Marshes, and Kirponos' deputy chief of staff was bewildered by a message from Moscow ordering Kirponos to "surround and destroy the enemy group." There was never the remotest chance of the order being obeyed.

Instead, all the Russians could do was dig in, fight until almost overrun, fall back, dig in and fight again. Without even the simplest of implements. "Occasionally trenches had to be dug with helmets," wrote an infantry corps commander. Even so, whether from patriotism or fear, Soviet soldiers acquired a reputation for courage. As the Russians persisted in counterattack, stories of their fanaticism circulated widely among the Germans: how a single Soviet tank, punctured by antitank missiles and ablaze, charged on against a German position, firing wildly, until its crew burned to death; how the pilot of a damaged Soviet fighter, instead of bailing out, plunged his machine into a convoy of German fuel trucks. It was said that Russian women and children were fighting in the front line and stories abounded of teenaged girls found dead on the battlefield, still clutching automatic weapons.

Even in the Ukraine, some who had at first welcomed the Germans were later fighting valiantly alongside other Russians. The Germans paid with lives for every mile they advanced. "Our ranks got thinner every day," said a German infantry commander. But even where the Russians fought most vigorously and effectively, they could not halt the invading juggernaut. By July 8 German tanks were only 100 miles from Kiev, the ancient capital of the Ukraine, and the Soviet Union's third largest city. Although some German generals urged a lightning panzer attack to seize Kiev, Hitler said no, ordering that the advance be continued to the southeast. Russian efforts were to no avail against the force of the German onslaught. In the Uman region in early August, the Germans trapped 20 Russian divisions, between Kleist's panzers and the infantry closing in from Rumania, capturing 103,000 prisoners, 300 tanks and 800 guns. At the

end of August, the Red Army withdrew all its forces from the Ukraine west of the Dneiper except for Kiev and an isolated garrison that was to try to hold the Black Sea port of Odessa. *Barbarossa* had scored another big success.

Perhaps most dramatic were the achievements of Army Group Center's 2nd and 3rd Panzer Groups, commanded by Colonel General Heinz Guderian and Colonel General Hermann Hoth respectively. The two armored columns rapidly penetrated weak Soviet defenses and moved east like a giant pair of claws designed to envelop three Russian armies in the Bialystok salient, a piece of Soviet territory that jutted westward into Poland.

Guderian, a master of armored warfare, moved at a breakneck pace. By June 26, his panzers were 75 miles inside Russia and 60 miles south of Minsk, while Hoth's tanks circled to the north. At that point the commander of Russia's Western Military District, General Dmitry Pavlov, made an ill-considered and fateful decision: he moved his reserves westward to attack the infantry of two German armies that were in the process of surrounding Russian forces within the larger panzer pincers. Left almost undefended, Minsk was easily taken by the Germans, and on June 27 the panzers' trap snapped shut.

For the Germans, the catch was magnificent: some 300,000 prisoners, 2,500 tanks and 1,500 guns. Five Soviet armies had been knocked out of the war in little more than a week. Among those who escaped was General Pavlov—only to be summoned to Moscow and shot.

After more than a week in the Minsk area, a fretful Guderian finally determined that he would no longer await orders to cross the Dnieper River and head for Smolensk. The impetuous operation, as recorded in the diary of Colonel General Franz Halder, Chief of the Army General Staff, paid off splendidly: July 11: "Guderian has crossed to the eastern bank of the Dnieper." July 14: "Guderian's attack has made astonishing progress." July 15: "Smolensk was

Guderian (left) halts briefly in Roslavl in August of 1941 to discuss the next phase of his Russian push with one of his subordinate commanders, as motorized artillery pieces move out in the background.

reached as early as 10 o'clock this morning." The capture of Smolensk involved another double envelopment in cooperation with Hoth, and within the Smolensk pocket the Germans took a further 138,000 prisoners, 2,000 tanks and 2,000 guns.

Yet in spite of their rapid and stunning victories, the Germans had already begun to face an increasing number of problems. Their intelligence was bad, and their maps were grossly inadequate. "The roads that were marked nice and red and thick on the map turned out to be tracks," complained Rundstedt. And though some Soviet forces took to their heels at first sight of the advancing Germans, others put up a desperate fight—a fact for which Hitler's barbarous decrees could be partly blamed.

Stories of German atrocities had spread through the Red Army. Special SS units were working full time slaughtering

prisoners of war and Russian civilians in accordance with the Führer's policies. Otto Ohlendorf, commander of one such outfit, later testified that his team of 500 men killed 90,000 Russians in the war's first year. Even by Nazi standards, murders were indiscriminate: one day in Minsk, SS men pulled 280 prisoners from jail, lined them up by a ditch and shot them. Then, simply because the ditch was not yet full, they took 30 more from the jail and shot them too.

Russia's soldiers were also driven by fear of their own masters. One political commissar, for example, encouraged a corps commander with these alternatives: "If you occupy Dubno by this evening, we will give you a medal. If you don't, we'll shoot you." Russians taken prisoner by the Germans were declared traitors by the government; their families had their food rations taken away—or worse. When Stalin's eldest son, Yakov, was captured, the dictator imprisoned Yakov's wife, Yulia. She was held until 1943, when reports of Yakov's honorable conduct convinced Stalin that no treason had been involved.

Rising above fear was patriotism, which Stalin tapped with a speech broadcast to the nation on July 3—his first public utterance since the invasion began. Russia, he declared, was fighting "a war for the freedom of our Motherland." Declaring a scorched-earth policy, he insisted that the enemy "must not be left a single engine, a single railway car, a single pound of grain, a single gallon of fuel."

The product of fear and fervor was often fanatical courage of a kind witnessed by General Aleksandr V. Gorbatov, who commanded a Russian infantry corps. Touring his sector one day, he saw a wounded Russian, his cheeks wet with tears, being tended by a medical corpsman. "When he heard us talking," Gorbatov recalled, "he opened his big grey eyes and said, as though justifying himself: 'I am not crying from pain. I am crying because I promised myself not to die until I had killed five Fascists.'" Assured that he had doubtless killed well over that quota, the wounded soldier stopped crying and died peacefully.

Despite the stiffening Soviet resistance, the Germans had every reason to feel satisfied with their work of the first two months. They controlled, roughly speaking, the westernmost 500 miles of the Soviet Union. In the vital center, Guderian, Hoth, and other German commanders believed that total victory was within their reach if they would only grasp it immediately by advancing along the concrete highway that led to Russia's heart—Moscow—little more than 200 miles away.

But Hitler had other ideas. Although he did authorize infantry to march toward Moscow, he weakened the move by ordering Hoth to turn his tanks north to assist in the seizure of Leningrad; Guderian would head south toward

The western Ukrainians detested the Communist regime, and rejoiced when the German conquerers arrived. But disenchantment came all too soon.

VENGEFUL KOBA'S PATH TO GLORY

In the summer of 1923, when Josef Stalin was locked in a struggle for the control of the Communist Party, he revealed to a comrade, in a rare moment of candor, his preferred method for dealing with his foes: "To choose one's victim, to prepare one's plan minutely, to slake an implacable vengeance, and then to go to bed—there is nothing sweeter in the world."

If that was the case, life must have been truly sweet to the swarthy, saturnine man who became the most powerful and successful dictator of his time; in the three decades of his brutal rule, he chose his victims with stony ruthlessness, eliminating millions of enemies, both real and imagined.

Born in 1879 to peasant parents in czarist Georgia, Josef Vissarionovich Djugashvili made up his mind to become a priest, but was expelled at age 20 from a theological seminary for reading radical literature. In 1901 he went underground and spent the next 16 years in the shadowy substrata of the revolutionary movement, agitating for strikes, organizing terrorist banditry, signing socialist broadsides with the by-line "Koba" (The Indomitable). He was jailed frequently and exiled six times to Siberia. During one stint of freedom, while organizing the oil-field workers of Baku on the Caspian seacoast, he chose the pseudonym Stalin, or Man of Steel.

Few of his revolutionary peers warmed to the enigmatic, sardonic Stalin. V.I. Lenin, outraged at his cruel suppression of a Georgian uprising in 1921, called him a "coarse, brutish bully." His archrival, Leon Trotsky, in a devastating misjudgment, thought him "the most eminent mediocrity in the Party." Through cunning and deceit Stalin manipulated his adversaries, and on the death of Lenin in 1924 he seized the helm of state. A reign of terror followed as Stalin liquidated peasants who resisted collectivization, crushed party contemporaries who displayed any vestige of independence and purged the Red Army of many of its most brilliant officers. "When are you going to stop killing people?" Lady Nancy Astor once asked him on a visit to Moscow. "When it is no longer necessary," Stalin replied.

In his spacious Kremlin office, seated beneath a picture of Communist philosopher Karl Marx, the dictator looks up from his work for a benign portrait.

A despairing woman watches her house burn. Though the advancing Germans often set fire to captured villages, fleeing peasants sometimes burned their own houses in compliance with Stalin's "scorched earth" orders: Leave nothing behind the enemy could use.

the Ukraine. In response to anguished protests from the field commanders, Halder replied: "The Führer right now is not interested in Moscow; all he cares about is Leningrad."

Formerly St. Petersburg, the beautiful old imperial capital built by Peter the Great, Leningrad seemed especially vulnerable, with the Baltic on one side and Lake Ladoga on the other. Germans closing from the west and Hitler's Finnish allies coming from the northeast could easily block its land approaches.

By September 8, Leningrad was cut off on all sides, surrounded either by enemy forces or by water. Against the coming onslaught, Leningrad's citizens had prepared with frenzied activity for stubborn resistance. Many elderly persons and children had been evacuated, although not without some bureaucratic foul-ups: trainloads of children, for example, had been shipped off to cities in the southwest—squarely in the path of German attacks.

With most of Leningrad's able-bodied men already mobilized, hundreds of thousands of women were pressed into building bunkers, digging antitank ditches and felling trees across the roads leading into the city. By August, they had prepared air-raid shelters for 918,000 people and had dug enough slit trenches to hold 672,000 more. On August 20, Andrei A. Zhdanov, the city's Communist Party leader, announced that the whole population would be given elementary training in grenade throwing and street fighting.

"Either the workers of Leningrad will be turned into slaves, with the best of them exterminated," he proclaimed, "or we shall turn the city into the fascists' graveyard."

Leningrad, in short, was girded for a last-ditch defense against assault, but was totally unprepared for a siege—which was exactly what Hitler had in mind. His reasoning was coldly logical. A winter siege would mean at least one million deaths by starvation—and that would damage Soviet morale even more than the city's surrender. It would also save the German Army from potentially heavy casualties. Even though food rationing had begun in July, it was not until the end of August that Leningrad authorities discovered they had only a month's supply of food on hand.

Beginning on September 4, German artillery bombardments—272 of them, over a total of 430 hours by the end of November—had become a regular affair. German bombers launched massive air assaults, and as early as September 8 they dealt Leningrad a crippling blow. Now, incendiaries dropped by German Junkers set fire to the warehouses, where much of the city's food was stored. Flour and fats burned furiously, and Leningrad's entire sugar supply—2,500 tons of it—melted and flowed into the cellars.

To protect the remaining stocks of food, the Leningrad Military Council made any offense involving a ration card a capital crime. One woman who worked in a ration-card

DIARY OF DEATH

The poignant story of one family's tragic experience during the two-and-a-half-year siege of the city of Leningrad is recorded in the school notebook of Tanya Savicheva. As food supplies dwindled and German shelling intensified, Tanya's family members died one by one. "Zhenya died 28 December, 12:30 in the morning, 1941. Babushka died 25 January, 3 o'clock, 1942. Leka died 17 March, 5 o'clock, 1942. Dedya Vasya died 13 April, 2 o'clock at night, 1942. Dedya Lesha, 10 May, 4 o'clock in the afternoon, 1942. Mama, 13 May, 7:30 a.m., 1942. All died. Only Tanya remains."

Tanya was evacuated from the city in mid-1942, and sent to a children's home, where she died in the summer of 1943 as the result of chronic dysentery that she had contracted during the siege.

Tanya Savicheva, whose notebook (left) recorded the deaths of six members of her family, was survived by an older brother and sister who were not in Leningrad during the seige. In 1944 the sister returned to the family's apartment in the heart of the city and found 11-year-old Tanya's notebook lying in a box with their mother's wedding dress.

The 900-day siege of Leningrad began after German and Finnish troops fought their way to the city's outskirts and occupied the shaded areas on the map by autumn 1941. The Germans cut rail lines south to Luga and east to Tikhvin and Moscow. During the siege, most of Leningrad's meager supplies were brought to the city via the Zaborye Road to Novaya Ladoga and across frozen Lake Ladoga to Osinovets. Another route ran from Kabona to Kokkorevo on the Leningrad side of the lake.

printing shop was found in possession of 100 cards and was immediately shot. On November 20, rations were reduced to 250 grams of bread a day for manual workers—about a third of what was normally needed by adults.

As hunger grew, cattle and horse feed were issued to humans; the countryside was scoured for stinging nettles, which made a nourishing soup. People laid traps for dogs and cats, crows and rats. One woman's diary recorded that she was existing on bread, salt water and cooked glue. Another's described the nightmare of starvation: "It was so horrible and—above all—disgusting: to die...Not from a shell fragment, not from a bomb, but from hunger." As conditions worsened, there were reports of cannibalism, of murder to provide food. Finally, after rumors of children disappearing, parents kept their youngsters off the streets.

Leningrad's death toll soared—from 11,000 in November to 53,000 in December, according to official figures that were certainly too low. A resident's diary recorded the dirge: "Death...death...Everywhere death...Leningrad is dying."

With winter, bitter weather intensified the suffering. Yet the cold was Leningrad's ally as well as its enemy: the only thing that could save the city was ice over Lake Ladoga, providing a solid highway to the rest of Russia. Eight inches would be needed to support a truck with a one-ton load. By mid-November, ice had begun to form on the lake, and by November 22, it had thickened sufficiently for 60 trucks to cross, bringing 33 tons of flour to Leningrad. With increased activity, as many as 400 three-ton trucks journeyed across the ice road every day. On January 24, the daily bread ration for workers was increased to 400 grams.

Nobody knows how many people perished that winter in Leningrad. The official total is 264,000—a figure reported during the Stalinist years, when Leningrad's sufferings were minimized. However, most Western scholars believe that the number of deaths from starvation during the entire siege exceeded one million, and that several hundred thousand more were killed by bombs, shells or gunfire. By contrast, the United States and Britain together suffered fewer than 800,000 deaths during all of World War II.

Although Leningrad's ordeal was far from over, its supply

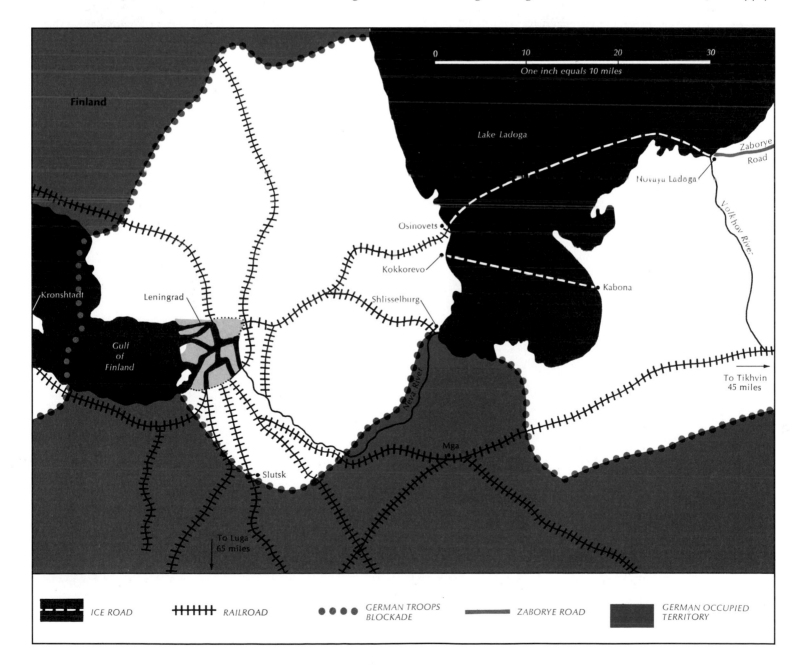

▬▬▬ ICE ROAD	╫╫╫╫ RAILROAD	●●●● GERMAN TROOPS BLOCKADE	▬▬ ZABORYE ROAD	GERMAN OCCUPIED TERRITORY

129

corridor was now open. By March, food was no longer a major problem, and the death rate slowly returned to normal. With the arrival of spring, life in the besieged city returned to some semblance of normalcy. By then, the war's focus had long since shifted to other cities—Moscow, Stalingrad. Only when the Soviet Army launched its massive counterattack would the Germans retreat from their siege lines around Leningrad. And not until January 27, 1944 would fireworks arc over the city, to mark the end of Leningrad's 900-day agony.

The previous August, when Hitler had ordered troop diversions to the north and south, panzer leader Heinz Guderian spoke on behalf of field commanders who believed the Führer's orders to be a mistake. He flew to Hitler's headquarters to plead for a drive directly on Moscow. After listening silently to Guderian's impassioned plea, Hitler sprang to a wall map, gestured toward the Ukraine, and spoke in his high-pitched earnest voice. He said that the region's raw materials and agriculture were vital for the prosecution of the war, as was the industrial area of the Donets River basin; that the Soviet Union must be denied the oil supplies of the Caucasus, and that Germany required control of the Crimea, which the U.S.S.R. was using as an "aircraft carrier" against Rumania's all-important oil fields. "My generals," Hitler exclaimed, "know nothing about the economic aspects of war."

Later, Guderian explained to his senior staff officers, "There was nothing I could do, gentlemen. I was faced by a solid front of the High Command. All those present nodded at every sentence the Führer said."

With that, Guderian threw his panzer group into the drive for the Ukraine. The first objective was Kiev, previously ignored by Hitler, and the tactic would again be a pincer movement. A northern prong would consist of Guderian's 2nd Panzer Group and the Second Army; a southern thrust would be made by Colonel General Ewald von Kleist's 1st Panzer Group and the Sixth and Seventeenth Armies.

The drive got under way on August 25—a blistering day. As tanks, trucks, wagons and boots threw up clouds of dust as thick and soft as flour, the Germans made spectacular progress. In two weeks' time, Guderian's tanks covered a distance of 250 miles, getting as far as Romny, east of Kiev. Meanwhile, Kleist crossed the Dnieper at Kremenchug, 170 miles southeast of Kiev, and pushed northward.

The Russians, once again misjudging German intentions, still expected an attack on Moscow; it was not until September 11 that Marshal Semyon Budenny, commander of the Southwest Theater, finally perceived that the Germans were coming his way. He asked Stalin for permission to withdraw from Kiev, but the dictator angrily refused. "Not one step," he ordered. "Hold out and, if necessary, die." He replaced Budenny with Colonel General M.P. Kirponos.

On September 16, Guderian and Kleist forged the last link in a giant ring 130 miles wide around Kiev. Next day, the Russian defenders finally received Moscow's permission to pull out. It was, of course, too late. Kirponos was killed defending the city, and Germany's General Halder noted in his diary that "the encircled enemy units are ricocheting like billiard balls within the ring around Kiev."

The Russian toll was appalling. Four Soviet armies were annihilated, and two more were almost destroyed. One million men were killed, wounded, taken prisoner or unaccounted for. Perhaps more important, Hitler's armies had torn a 200-mile gap in the Russian defenses. The whole of the Ukraine now lay open to the Germans, and beyond lay the oil deposits of the Caucasus. In Moscow, Stalin gloomily told British Ambassador Sir Stafford Cripps, "All that Lenin created—we have lost forever."

Field Marshal von Rundstedt's Army Group South wasted no time going after the prizes. On October 24, his Sixth Army captured the great industrial city of Kharkov. Five days later, the Eleventh Army smashed into the Crimea; by mid-November it had occupied the entire peninsula except for the city of Sevastopol. On November 20, Kleist's 1st Panzers took Rostov, a major port on the Don.

Meanwhile, the shooting had hardly ended in Kiev before Guderian got orders to head northward and join with Army Group Center in the thrust toward Moscow that he had so strongly urged. The operation was called Typhoon, and Hitler expected a swift knockout. "Today," said his directive, "begins the last, the great, battle of this year."

What has come to be known as the Battle of Moscow actually consisted of several battles. The action extended over a period of months, across a front 250 miles wide and 180 miles deep, and involved dozens of cities and villages that were strung in two broad concentric semicircles lying to the west of Moscow.

Advancing from the Ukraine, Guderian covered 50 miles in one October day, and nearly 100 more during the next three. As he rolled along, the only ominous note was Halder's October 7 diary entry that Guderian's force had been "hampered in its movements by bad weather"—rain mixed with melting snow.

However, there seemed every reason to believe that Operation Typhoon would end before winter. Colonel General Erich Hoepner's 4th Panzer Group quickly tore open the Russian line between the strongholds of Vyazma, situated between Smolensk and Moscow, and Bryansk,

Overcome with exhaustion, a gaunt rifleman collapses against a tree as the German campaign reels under the Russian winter. "Our people are kaputt," wrote Wilhelm Prüller, an ardent Nazi who became a first lieutenant. "You've got to say it; and see why: one hour outside, one hour in the hut, watch, alarm, sentry duty...one thing after another. It wouldn't surprise me to see some of them break down."

roughly halfway between Kiev and the capital. On October 14, Colonel General Hermann Hoth's 3rd Panzers, back by now from their expedition to Leningrad, crossed the Volga at Kalinin, cutting the all-important Leningrad-Moscow railway, and took a position 70 miles northwest of Moscow.

In Moscow, Stalin summoned one of his toughest commanders, Marshal Georgy K. Zhukov, who, during a brief stay in Leningrad, had successfully strengthened the city's defenses. Stalin's orders to Zhukov were blunt: "Organize the Western Front quickly and act!" Zhukov did just that: he assembled 90,000 new reserves and deployed them along the 150-mile Mozhaisk line, named after a strong point 60 miles west of Moscow.

At the same time, the government-controlled press began for the first time to let the Russian people in on the nation's desperate plight. On October 10, *Pravda* somberly stated that "the land of the Soviets, our people and their great achievements are in danger." On the 16th, *Pravda* reported that "the mad fascist beast is threatening Moscow."

Since Muscovites were accustomed to hearing almost nothing but glowing reports, the bad news threw them into a mass panic and they started to flee, jamming the roads to the east, and looting abandoned households and shops. On October 19, Stalin stemmed the panic by imposing martial law, along with a curfew from midnight to 5 a.m. Anyone caught inciting disorder was to be executed.

In fact, Moscow's citizens had less to fear than they thought. The early October rains were the beginning of a downpour that lasted for days and turned roads into quagmires. German trucks and wagons sank to their axles, horses to their bellies. Supplies became mired: for want of fuel the tanks stalled; for want of ammunition the guns fell silent; for want of food the troops went hungry.

The Germans also ran into trouble of another kind. On the road to Tula, Guderian had his first disturbing encounter with the T-34, a lethal new Russian tank with sloping armor plates that deflected German shells, wide tracks that nimbly rolled over the roughest terrain, and a powerful 76mm gun that could cripple a German panzer with a single shot. Wrote one of Guderian's men: "When they hit one of our panzers there is often a deep long explosion, a roar as the fuel burns, a roar too loud, thank God, to let us hear the cries of the crew."

Yet for all their difficulties, the invading armies kept slogging ahead, spurred by an adamant Hitler. Hungry, cold, ridden with lice and sick with fatigue, men of one German battalion reached Lobnya, only 10 miles from Moscow. Field Marshal Fedor von Bock, commander of Army Group Center and riding in its vanguard, could see the spires of the Kremlin through his field glasses.

That was the closest the Germans got to the Soviet nerve center. In the worsening weather, the troops could take no more, and the commanders one by one suspended their attacks despite decrees from headquarters. By then, Soviet

troops were already preparing to move—toward the west.

Toward nightfall on November 6, wet snow began to fall. By morning, Moscow was in the throes of a classic Russian snowstorm. It was the anniversary of the outbreak of the 1917 Revolution—traditionally the occasion for a triumphant military parade in Moscow's Red Square—but, with Germans only miles from the capital, 1941 hardly seemed a time for celebration. Yet Stalin, in one of his boldest and most imaginative acts, buoyed the morale of civilians and soldiers alike by holding the parade as usual.

On that day and the next, he also made two remarkable speeches that went straight to the hearts of the Soviet people. "The German invaders want a war of extermination against the peoples of the Soviet Union," he said emotionally in one speech. "Very well then! If they want a war of extermination they shall have it!" He closed with the rousing words: "Our cause is just. Victory will be ours!"

In addition to inspiring words, Stalin had in reserve a solid military resource: his army in the Soviet East. Since the war had begun, nearly three-quarters of a million troops—plus strong cavalry, tank and air support—had been held in Siberia as a hedge against a possible Japanese attack. By now, however, it was apparent that Japan had no such present intention. Stalin dipped into his precious hoard: half the strength of the Far Eastern Command—18 divisions—was rushed by rail to the defense of Moscow. With the help of such acquisitions, the Soviets slowly—and briefly—gained the initiative.

Far more accustomed than the Germans to bitter winter weather, the Russians also had the advantage of being much closer to their supply sources. The Germans were weakened by frostbite and other casualties, as well as frozen machine guns that would not fire. On December 5, hopeful of little more than relieving the immediate pressure on Moscow, the Russians launched a series of local counterattacks. To their surprise, Soviet commanders found that in many places the Germans were prepared to yield ground without a fight. To the great satisfaction of the Russians, the temperature continued to fall.

Finding it impossible to hold their positions against what soon became a major counteroffensive, German generals urged Hitler to permit an organized retreat. He refused. Later, when Guderian flew to the Führer's headquarters at Rastenburg to renew the plea, Hitler met him with "a hard unfriendly expression in his eyes." The German armies, Hitler insisted, "must dig into the ground where they are and hold every square yard of land!"

On December 23, after returning to the front, Guderian was forced to pull one of his divisions to Belov, 135 miles southwest of Moscow. The following day, another division lost Chern, 150 miles south of the capital. With similar reverses occurring elsewhere, Hitler vented his fury by relieving more than 30 generals of their commands —including Guderian, Bock and Rundstedt.

Enormously encouraged by this success, the Russians planned for the encirclement of the German Army Group Center in the Mozhaisk-Vyazma area west of Moscow. But, as Zhukov later confessed, the enemy "proved to be a harder nut to crack than we believed." Indeed, the encirclers became the encircled: extricating themselves from the trap, the German Fourth Panzer Army and the German Ninth Army attacked the Russian flanks. Meanwhile, the Soviet Twenty-ninth Army, which had been converging with the Thirty-ninth Army on Vyazma, was cut off and encircled by the German Ninth Army. Only 5,000 men managed to escape.

Still, the Russian counteroffensive continued throughout February. In perhaps the most promising Soviet effort, two armies attacked toward Demyansk, northwest of Moscow, surrounding about 100,000 troops of the German 2nd Corps within a 20-by-40-mile stronghold. The Germans were finally rescued, but only after holding out for 72 days while living and fighting on 65,000 tons of supplies flown in to them by Junkers transports. Given the enormous scale of the war in Russia, Demyansk was a relatively insignificant affair.

Panzer troops use picks and shovels to dig out a camouflaged tank from the 5th Panzer Division, bogged down in the snow despite its cleated tracks.

Yet because it gave Hitler a vastly inflated notion of airlift capabilities, it carried the seeds of future German disaster.

By late February, it was the Germans who occupied sheltered, fortified positions close to their supply lines. And it was the Russians who were out in the cold, their supply lines growing longer and more vulnerable. By March, the Germans had established a firm defensive line that ran 300 miles from Rzhev through Vyazma and Bryansk to Orel—and the front settled into stalemate.

Moscow, however, had been saved, and the Red Army's effort had a tremendous effect on Soviet morale. A more remote benefit was that Great Britain and the United States, whose military experts only months before had almost unanimously predicted a swift Russian collapse, were now impressed by the Soviets' staying power.

From the first moments of the German invasion of the Soviet Union, both Prime Minister Churchill, who had once denounced Bolshevism as a plague-bearing infection, and President Roosevelt had made it clear that they would do anything within their practical power to support the Russians. That resolve was reaffirmed in August, 1941, at the Atlantic Charter meeting held by the two Western leaders at Placentia Bay in Newfoundland. Later that month, British and Soviet forces even joined in the military occupation of oil-rich Iran, whose ruler was suspected of sympathizing with the Germans.

Stalin, however, wanted more—much more. As his first priority, he insisted that Great Britain relieve the pressure on his own armies by opening a second front in western Europe. The British, of course, were utterly unable to comply. Time and again, Stalin submitted lengthy shopping lists for all manner of war supplies. When the Western powers offered little more than flowery promises, the Soviet dictator responded with surly distrust.

Now, with Russia's demonstrated willingness to fight for its life, assistance became even more imperative, and the West would eventually contribute in full measure: by the end of the Russo-German conflict, more than $11 billion in supplies would come from the United States. At the end of 1941, however, the dribs and drabs of materiel being shipped to the Soviet Union actually fell off—if only because the U.S. was by then at war with Japan.

Hands upraised and clutching white flags of surrender, four German soldiers cautiously approach a Russian trench that is manned by camouflaged troops.

133

THE HOLOCAUST

On a bleak plain in the Nazi-occupied East, an SS trooper takes aim at a Jewish mother and child while frightened peasants prepare a grave for them.

135

THE DEATH OF A PEOPLE

In April 1933, scarcely three months after Adolf Hitler took power in Germany, the Nazis issued a decree ordering the compulsory retirement of "non-Aryans," from the civil service. This edict, petty in itself, was the first spark in what was to become the Holocaust, one of the most ghastly episodes in the modern history of mankind. Before the campaign against the Jews was halted by the defeat of Germany, some 11 million people had been slaughtered in the name of Nazi racial purity.

The Jews were not the only victims of the Holocaust. Millions of Russians, Poles, gypsies and other "subhumans" were also murdered. But Jews were the favored targets—first and foremost.

It took the Nazis some time to work up to the full fury of their endeavor. In the years following 1933, the Jews were systematically deprived by law of their civil rights, of their jobs and property. Violence and brutality became a part of their everyday lives. Their places of worship were defiled, their windows smashed, their stores ransacked. Old men—and young—were pummeled and clubbed and stomped to death by Nazi jackboots. Jewish women were accosted and ravaged, in broad daylight, on main thoroughfares.

Some Jews fled Germany. But most, with a kind of stubborn belief in God and Fatherland, sought to weather the Nazi terror. It was a forlorn hope. In 1939, after Hitler's conquest of Poland, the Nazis cast aside all restraint. Jews in the millions were now herded into concentration camps, there to starve and perish as slave laborers. Other millions were driven into dismal ghettos, which served as holding pens until the Nazis got around to disposing of them.

The mass killings began in 1941, with the German invasion of the Soviet Union. Nazi murder squads followed behind the Wehrmacht enthusiastically slaying Jews and other conquered peoples. Month by month, the horrors escalated. First tens of thousands, then hundreds of thousands of people were led off to remote fields and forests to be slaughtered by SS guns. Assembly-line death camps were established in Poland and trainloads of Jews were collected from all over occupied Europe and sent to their doom.

At some of the camps, the Nazis took great pains to disguise their intentions until the last moment. At others, the arriving Jews saw scenes beyond their comprehension. "Corpses were strewn all over the road," recalled one survivor. "Starving human skeletons stumbled towards us. They fell right down in front of our eyes and lay there gasping out their last breath." What had begun as a mean edict against Jewish civil servants was ending in the death of a people.

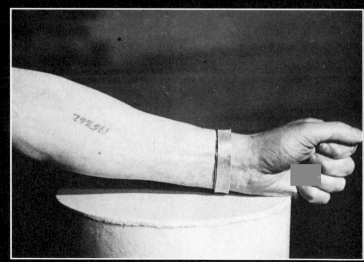

Symbols of the "Final Solution" are a human-skull hood ornament on an SS vehicle (left) and a number tattooed on the arm to identify a camp inmate (right).

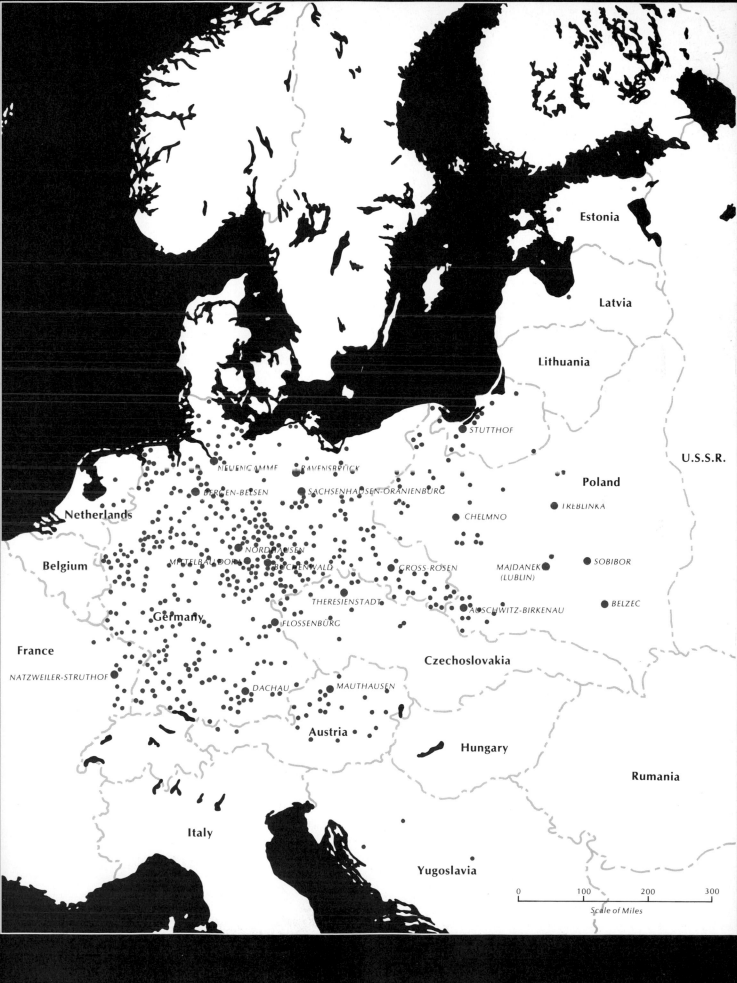

Estonia

Latvia

Lithuania

U.S.S.R.

STUTTHOF

NEUENGAMME   *RAVENSBRÜCK*

Poland

BERGEN-BELSEN   *SACHSENHAUSEN-ORANIENBURG*

TREBLINKA

Netherlands

CHELMNO

Belgium

NORDHAUSEN

MITTELBAU-DORA   *BUCHENWALD*

CROSS-ROSEN   *MAJDANEK*   *SOBIBOR*
(LUBLIN)

THERESIENSTADT

Germany

AUSCHWITZ-BIRKENAU   *BELZEC*

FLOSSENBÜRG

France

Czechoslovakia

NATZWEILER-STRUTHOF

DACHAU   *MAUTHAUSEN*

Austria

Hungary

Rumania

Italy

| 0 | 100 | 200 | 300 |

Scale of Miles

Yugoslavia

137

Ghetto residents in Cracow, Poland, clamber into a boxcar. Their likely destination was a concentration camp or death camp.

Preparing for a hasty departure, Jews drag bundles of belongings to an assembly point.

UPROOTED, INTERNED AND DEPORTED

In Germany, and later in the conquered countries as well, Jews were uprooted and subjected to bewildering evacuations and relocations. They were forced from their homes into crowded ghettos or local holding camps. They were packed onto trains and moved to labor camps, where many were worked to death.

In the constant upheaval, families were forever separated. One 19-year-old man was ordered from his Polish town to a labor camp. "I barely managed to say goodbye to my sister," he said. "She gave me her picture with this inscription: 'If you survive, remember, you live to take revenge.'" He never saw her again.

Jewish victims of an execution line a square in Cracow, while other Jews wait for deportation.

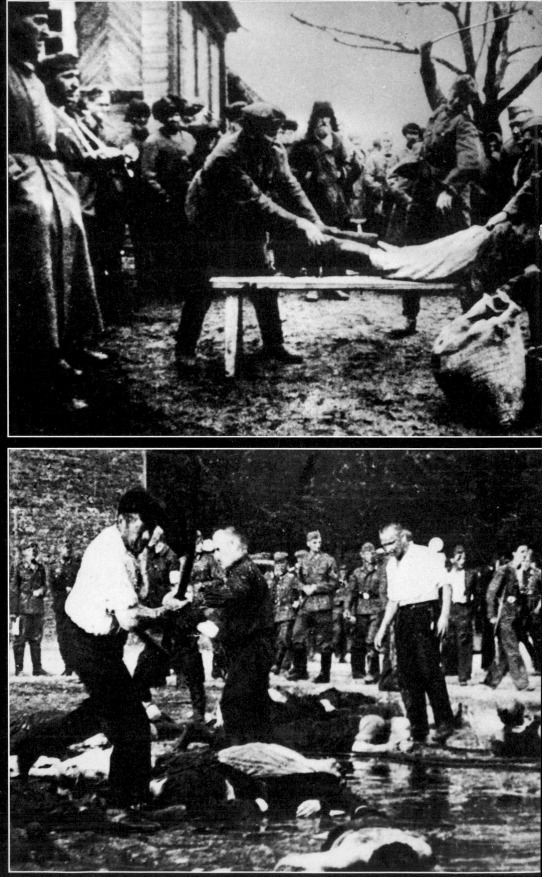

THE FIRST ATROCITIES AFTER THE CONQUEST

All the unfortunates on the Nazis' long list of enemies and "subhuman" *Untermenschen* were stunned by the violence that erupted with the arrival of the victorious German armies in Eastern Europe. But the Jews suffered the worst horrors. They were beaten and humiliated by German soldiers, by local anti-Semites and—most often and most viciously—by the SS.

SS men ripped clumps of hair from the Jews' beards and sometimes set the beards on fire. Terrified Jews in the Polish town of Turck were driven into their synagogue by the SS men; they were forced to drop their pants and were lashed with horsewhips.

At times, the Jews' Gentile neighbors of only a short time before bade fair to outdo the Nazis in savagery toward the Jews. Under the prod of the SS, latent anti-Semitism exploded into the pogroms in which Jews were robbed and beaten and murdered in the most barbaric fashion.

In an occupied town in the Ukraine, a mob of Gentiles tied a Jewish woman's hair to the tail of a horse and drove the animal off. The horse dragged the woman until—in the words of a Jew who watched horrified the scene from a distance—"her whole face was completely disfigured and there wasn't the slightest sign of life from her body. Most of the crowd was hysterical with laughter."

A convict released by the Germans uses a lead pipe on a Jewish pogrom victim in Lithuania. The pogrom took place on June 28, 1941, just days after the invasion of the Soviet Union.

A rape victim in the city of Lvov cries out in rage and anguish as an older woman comforts her. Anti-Semitic citizens rounded up 1,000 Jews and turned them over to the Germans.

"SO MANY BODIES WERE LYING ALL OVER"

In the wake of the German armies, the communities of Polish and Russian Jews were wiped out by the journeymen killers of the SS *Einsatzgruppen*. In most of the massacres the procedure was the same. The Jews were marched to a remote execution site. They were ordered to undress; they did not understand why. It was partly to facilitate the use of their clothes, and partly because naked people rarely resisted.

"Our father did not want to undress," said Rivka Yosselevska, who survived a massacre of Russian Jews at Zagrodski in spite of a bullet wound in her head. He did not want to stand naked. They tore the clothing off the old man and he was shot."

Immobilized by horror, Rivka watched as her mother was shot. Then the 80-year-old grandmother was shot along with the two children she held.

Rivka's younger sister was the next to die. She went up to the Germans with one of her friends—and she asked to be spared standing there naked. A German looked into her eyes and shot the two of them."

The Germans then shot Rivka's second sister, and finally it was Rivka's turn. "I felt the German take the child off my arms. The child cried out and was shot immediately. And then he aimed at me. He aimed the revolver at me and ordered me to watch and then turned my head around and shot me. Then I fell to the ground into the pit among the bodies."

After the Germans left, "I rose, and with my last strength I came up on top of the grave, and when I did, I did not know the place, so many bodies were lying all over. Not all of them dead, but in their last sufferings; naked; shot, but not dead."

A Polish Jew kneels before his SS executioner while other Germans watch. The executed man fell into the common grave below.

Wearing blindfolds and with their arms linked, apprehensive Jews are guided by an SS man to a barren execution site in Poland.

Near the Latvian town of Lijepaja, women and girls huddle together, waiting in fear. Their clothes are scattered about on the ground.

Forced to strip, four Jewish men and a young boy from a town in Poland are brought forward by members of a killing squad.

Barbed-wire fences surrounded the 15 square miles of the Auschwitz-Birkenau death camp. An estimated two million people from German-occupied countries were killed there in less than three years.

THE FINAL TRAIN TRIP TO POLAND

In the spring of 1942, Jewish leaders in the ghettos of Poland and nearby Slovakia were directed by Nazi authorities to prepare a specified percentage of their population for "resettlement." Unaware of the horror that lay ahead, the Jewish communities yielded thousands of deportees. These people would become the first victims of the new death camps in Poland.

Most Jews traveled to their places of death by train. They were marched to the nearest station and packed into boxcars that lacked sanitary facilities,

seats and often ventilation. For some the trip took weeks.

In the cramped quarters, people slept in relays or in layers. There was little food or water. Many passengers fell sick. The stench of vomit and excrement was overpowering.

On his arrival at a death camp, one Jew later recalled: "The doors were torn ajar. SS men with whips and half-wild Alsatian dogs swarmed all over the place. Parents screamed for lost children."

At the death camps where laborers were needed, the Jews were lined up and prodded past an SS officer. The officer separated out the strongest ones. They would work until they died; the rest would die immediately.

A carload of captives from the Jewish ghetto of Lublin, Poland rumbles towards the Belzec death camp. The German authorities began liquidating the Lublin Jews on March 17, 1942. By May 9, some 30,000 of them had been deported; only 4,000 were still left in Lublin.

Jews from Hungary, newly arrived at Auschwitz, pass a camp office whose task it was to determine their fate. About 10 per cent, mostly men, were sent to the work camp. The crippled, the ill, the elderly, and women and young children were automatically sent to the gas chambers.

Prisoners peer out from rows of numbered bunks in a men's barracks at Sachsenhausen concentration camp in Germany.

Granted a few minutes of rest, weary inmates at Bergen-Belsen camp in Germany wander the small yard in front of their barracks.

The long wooden death-camp barracks each held up to 1,000 people. The buildings were infested with millions of fleas and hordes of rats.

A shrill of whistles in the dawn announced line-up for the rag-clad inmates, followed by a day of slave labor. Food consisted of thin broth, a piece of bread and a scrap of potato. The hunger was so intense, a survivor recalled, "that if a bit of soup spilled over, prisoners would converge on the spot, dig their spoons into the mud and stuff the mess in their mouths."

Diarrhea and dysentery were epidemic, but prisoners were denied free access to latrines. Clothing, bunks and floors were fouled, spreading disease. "They had condemned us to die in our own filth," wrote a survivor. "They wished to destroy our human dignity, to fill us with horror and contempt for ourselves and our fellows."

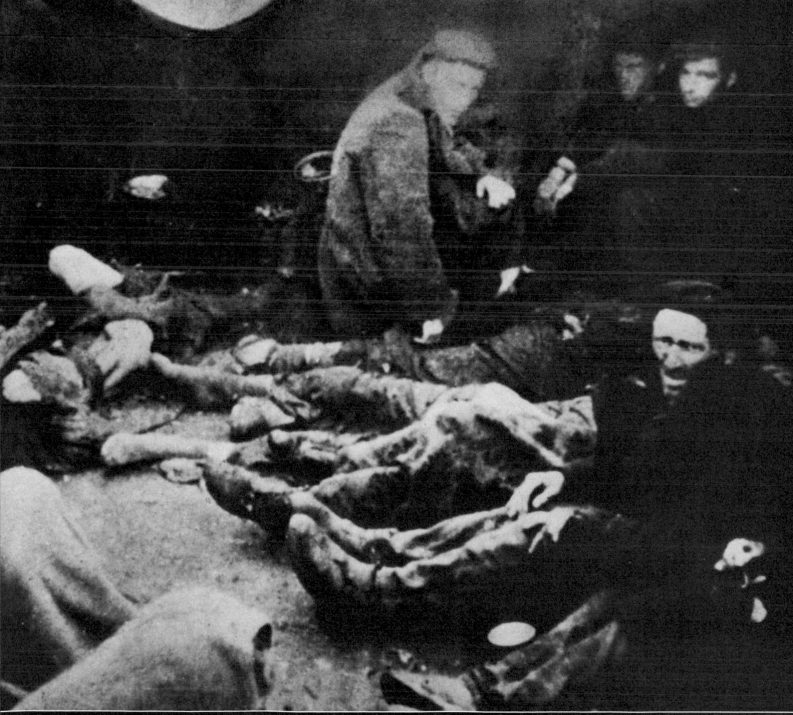

Weakened by hunger and illness, prisoners in Sachsenhausen sprawl in their filthy quarters among the bodies of fellow inmates.

His hands clenched in a death grip, a Mauthausen prisoner who committed suicide hangs from the electrified barbed-wire fence surrounding the compound.

A guard keeps watch on Mauthausen's main square, where inmates were often forced to stand naked for a day and night. This was common treatment for new prisoners.

VICTIMS OF CASUAL BRUTALITY

Every day, Jews and other prisoners were subjected to torture or random cruelty at the whim of the guards. At Auschwitz, women inmates were brutalized by Irma Grese, a guard who liked to pick out buxom ones and flay their breasts with a whip. Kurt Franz, the camp commandant at Treblinka, periodically hung prisoners upside down from gallows and turned his fierce dog loose to savage them. At every camp, inmates were crippled or beaten to death with cudgels, rifle butts or shovels.

In some cases, beatings and worse were meted out as punishment for imagined breaches in discipline. At Auschwitz, a guard stopped a young girl who seemed to be trying to avoid him, as if she were smuggling something. He aimed his rifle at her but assured her he had no intention of killing her for her "crime." Instead he shot her once in each foot. Her wounds festered and her feet were amputated.

Slave laborers at Auschwitz were frequent victims of large-scale sadism. After the day's work was done, they were forced by SS guards to exercise for hours—to run, fall down in the mud, crawl, get up and run again. Many prisoners died of heart failure during the drill. Others crept away to their barracks and perished there.

Suspended by their wrists, two tortured inmates dangle from trees near Buchenwald. An SS guard stands over a fallen victim.

Carrying great chunks of granite, prisoners climb steep steps in a quarry near the Mauthausen camp in Austria. They were often whipped into an agonizing run.

DESPERATE TOIL TO STAY ALIVE

The incoming Jews and other prisoners at concentration and death camps served as a pool of slave labor for SS enterprises and private German companies. The condemned prisoners drained swamps, built roads, toiled in nearby factories manufacturing benzene or synthetic rubber or munitions. Some prisoners labored to construct or expand the very camps where they would perish.

Prisoners who weakened or sickened to the point where they could no longer work were swiftly sent to the gas chambers. The meager fare fed to the prisoners guaranteed that they would not have the strength to work for more than a few months. Accidents and brutality by SS guards reduced the prisoners' life expectancy still further.

In desperation, sick and crippled prisoners somehow managed to work on and on. One prisoner at a Mauthausen satellite camp, building an airplane-assembly plant, was beaten by his overseer with a shovel, "until he broke both the shovel and my arm." But the man stayed on the job without medical attention. "If they took me to the infirmary," he said, "I'd lose the work and my life."

Emaciated workers at Dachau show the effects of a starvation diet: watery soup, sawdust-filled bread and an occasional putrid sausage.

Labor-camp inmates toil at an airfield near Hamburg. Jews fueled the German war effort on the Eastern Front as well, building bases and repairing equipment.

GUINEA PIGS FOR GRUESOME EXPERIMENTS

Uncounted thousands of Jews and other concentration-camp inmates were used as guinea pigs in a wide range of medical and scientific experiments, most of them of little value.

Victims were infected with typhus to see how different geographical groups reacted; to no one's surprise, all groups perished swiftly. Fluids from diseased animals were injected into humans to observe the effect. Prisoners were forced to exist on sea water to see how long castaways might survive. Gynecology was an area of great interest. Various methods of sterilization were practiced—by massive X-ray, by irritants and drugs, by surgery without benefit of anesthetic. As techniques were perfected, it was determined that a doctor with 10 assistants could sterilize 1,000 women per day.

The "experimental people" were also used by Nazi doctors who needed practice performing various operations. One doctor at Auschwitz perfected his amputation technique on live prisoners; after he had finished, his maimed patients were sent off to the gas chamber.

A few Jews who had studied medicine were allowed to live if they assisted the SS doctors. "I cut the flesh of healthy young girls," recalled a Jewish physician who survived at a terrible cost. "I immersed the bodies of dwarfs and cripples in calcium chloride (to preserve them), or had them boiled so the carefully prepared skeleton might safely reach the Third Reich's museum to justify, for future generations, the destruction of an entire race. I could never erase these memories from my mind."

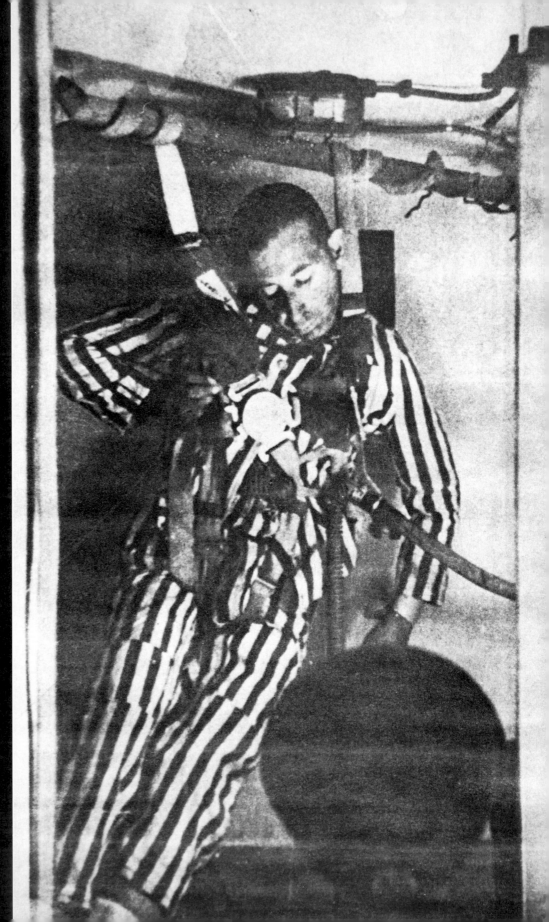

In a pressure chamber at Dachau, a victim of a low-pressure experiment hangs from a pipe. He died when his lungs burst in the thin air. Of 200 test subjects, 70 died this way.

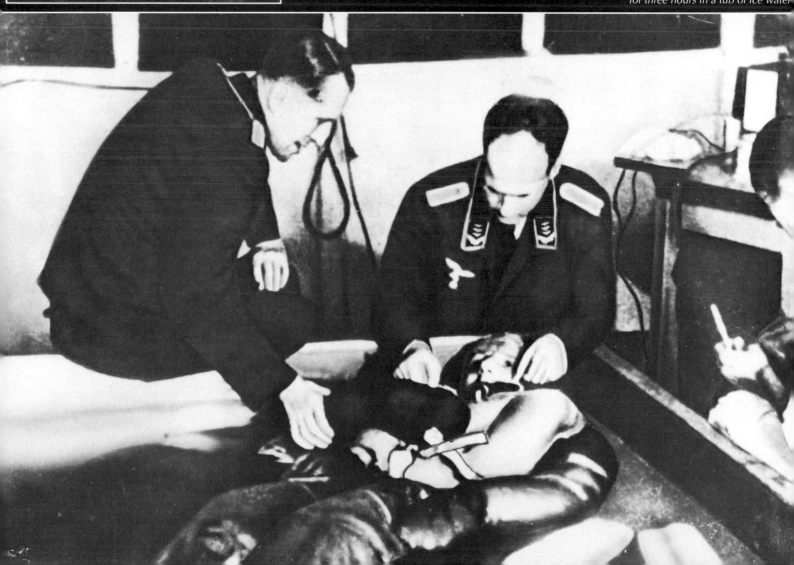

A Nazi medical team irrigates the brain of a prisoner through an incision in his skull. The purpose of the experiment is unknown.

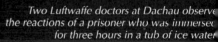

Two Luftwaffe doctors at Dachau observe the reactions of a prisoner who was immersed for three hours in a tub of ice water.

Cavernous in extent, this gas chamber was one of the seven installed at the Majdanek camp in Poland, where an estimated 1.3 million prisoners were put to death. The Majdanek camp was in operation for slightly more than two years, from 1942 to 1944; only Auschwitz claimed more lives.

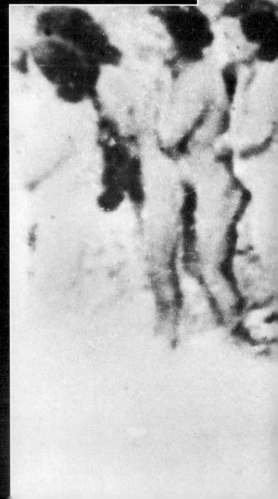

THE "SHOWER BATHS" OF DEATH

After their arrival at a death camp, the Jews who had been chosen to die at once were told that they were to have a shower. Filthied by their long, miserable journey, they sometimes applauded the announcement. Countless Jews and other victims went peacefully to the shower rooms—which were gas chambers in disguise.

In the anterooms to the gas chambers, many of the doomed people found nothing amiss. At Auschwitz, signs in several languages said, "Bath and Disinfectant," and inside the gas chambers other signs admonished, "Don't forget your soap and towel." Unsuspecting victims cooperated willingly. "They got

out of their clothes so routinely," said a Sobibor survivor. "What could be more natural?"

In time, rumors about the death camps spread, and underground newspapers in the Warsaw ghetto even ran reports that told of the gas chambers and the crematoriums. But many people did not believe the stories, and those who did were helpless in any case. Facing the guns of the SS guards, they could only hope and pray to survive. As one Jewish leader put it, "We must be patient and a miracle will occur."

There were no miracles. The victims, naked and bewildered, were shoved into a line. Their guards ordered them forward, and flogged those who hung back. The doors to the gas chambers were locked behind them. It was all over quickly.

Naked women clutching their children queue up outside the gas chambers at the Treblinka death camp, where about 900,000 Jews were killed. Because women and children were not strong enough to do heavy labor, they were among the first of any group to be gassed.

A hand rests on the sill of an oven door in an unknown Nazi death camp. The photograph may have been taken by an SS officer to record the operation of the

156

camp, or by an Allied soldier who, after the camp had been liberated, wanted to document the horrors that he found there.

7

The 1930s in Japan were later remembered as *kurai tanima*, the "dark valley." They were years of economic distress, of plots, abortive coups and assassinations, a time when the Imperial Army hatched plans of conquest. By mid-1937, Japan was at war with China. In December of that year, Japanese planes bombed an American gunboat, the *Panay*, in the Yangtze River. Although the United States had no desire to fight, measures were taken to initiate a two-ocean navy—and to tighten the economic screws on Japan. Finally, in October 1939, President Roosevelt took his first military step toward Japan: he ordered the U.S. Pacific Fleet from its base of San Diego to Pearl Harbor, on the Hawaiian island of Oahu.

At 6 a.m. on November 26, 1941, a Japanese force of five aircraft carriers and 25 support vessels weighed anchor in remote Hitokappu Bay in the Kurile Islands. As it slid out into the chill waters of the North Pacific, a patrol boat at the harbor mouth flashed a message: "Good luck on your mission." The dark gray flagship carrier *Akagi* signaled "Thank you." Down on the *Akagi*'s flight deck, crewmen roared a lusty "*Banzai!*" Captain Mitsuo Fuchida, the fleet's air-strike commander, was profoundly moved. "I realized my duty as a warrior," he wrote later. "I thought at the time, `Who could be luckier than I?'"

Twelve days later, just before dawn on December 7, the carriers reached their launch point north of Oahu. In the darkness, the big ships heaved in heavy seas as aircraft engines started turning over. A green light flashed for takeoff and Fuchida yelled to his crew chief: "Kick out the blocks!"

His single-engine bomber lurched forward, gathered speed and lifted off. Heading due south, Fuchida was accompanied by 48 Nakajima-97 bombers like his own, each carrying a 1,760-pound armor piercing bomb. Other formations held 40 torpedo bombers, whose projectiles were designed for shallow harbor waters, and 51 stubby Aichi dive bombers. Flying escort high above were 43 Mitsubishi Type-O fighters—the fast, deadly "Zeroes" soon to dominate Asia's skies.

Their destination: the great U.S. naval base at Pearl Harbor, 230 miles away.

Behind the fateful flight lay more than a decade of rising tensions between Japan and the United States. What began as economic conflicts were nurtured by cultural misunderstandings, then inflamed by a superpatriotic generation of Japanese army officers who had thrown off the bonds of civilian control. Ahead lay nearly four years of remorseless fighting in eastern skies and seas, in fetid jungles, on volcanic islands and coral atolls.

In the war's opening phase, the Japanese would have everything their way—everything, that is, except the swift and final triumph upon which they had so desperately wagered their empire's future. "In the first six to twelve months of a war with the United States and Britain, I will run wild and win victory after victory," Admiral Isoroku Yamamoto, commander of the Combined Imperial Fleet, had said. "After that, I have no expectation of success."

Seldom has anyone been more prescient.

Yamamoto, like a number of other senior Japanese officers, had served overseas and was well aware of the West's awesome might; the United States alone, by Tokyo's own estimate, had ten times the industrial capacity of Japan. Yamamoto himself had studied briefly at Harvard and had served two years as naval attaché in Washington. "Japan

Crack Imperial Marines march proudly behind a Rising Sun standard-bearer at Yokosuka Naval Station on January 19, 1937, to celebrate Japan's termination of the Washington Conference treaty that had limited the size of the Japanese Navy. Freed of all restraints, Japan quickly built a fleet powerful enough to challenge the might of United States and British forces in the Pacific.

RISING SUN IN THE PACIFIC

Throughout that peevish autumn, Japan perfected its war plans. The 25th Army under Lieut. General Tomoyuki Yamashita was to slice southward down the 600-mile Malay Peninsula and take the fortress of Singapore, with its key naval base. The 14th Army under Lieut. General Masaharu Homma was to invade the American-owned Philippines—a potential thorn in the eastern flank of Japan's push south. The 15th Army under Lieut. General Shojiro Iida was to step from Thailand into Burma and close the Burma Road, the last overland supply route from India to China. In addition, the Japanese Navy and the 16th Army, under Lieut. General Hitoshi Imamura, would seize the oil-rich Dutch East Indies.

The assaults would be massive and simultaneous, catching the Americans and their allies totally by surprise. Then—and before the U.S. war machine rolled into high gear—Japan would wage a war of attrition from behind a barrier of western Pacific bases. Accordingly, the U.S. would be forced to sue for peace and leave Asia in Japanese hands.

The man responsible for the Japanese Navy's role in the grand strategy was Admiral Yamamoto. Though he had played no part in Japan's decision to go to war with the United States—and in fact had opposed it—this loyal and professional officer threw himself into the planning with a fierce intensity. His foremost concern was the destruction of the U.S. Pacific Fleet at Pearl Harbor. He was adamant about it. The American fleet, Yamamoto insisted, was "a dagger pointed at our throat."

His proposal provoked a storm of controversy on the Navy General Staff, whose members thought the plan was too risky. Only when Yamamoto threatened to resign his commission if the plan was not approved, did the General Staff concede. "If he has that much confidence," said the Navy Chief of Staff, "it is better to let Yamamoto go ahead."

In fact, at Kagoshima, a small southern city topographically similar to Honolulu, squadrons of Navy pilots had been practicing pinpoint bombing and torpedo attacks since late summer. So incessant was the din of aircraft engines that the hens in one seaside village quit laying eggs. At night, the flyers studied a seven-foot-square model of Oahu, and silhouettes of the U.S. ships at Pearl Harbor until they could call out their names at a glance. Meanwhile, the Japanese Consul General in Honolulu cabled coded reports on U.S. fleet movements and harbor berthing positions. Studying those dispatches, Yamamoto noted that the U.S. fleet was in port at Pearl Harbor every weekend; Sunday, December 7 (December 8, in Tokyo) would be a fine time to attack. Then it would be up to the Japanese fleet—and its flyers.

At 7 o'clock on that historic December morning, the airborne Mitsuo Fuchida switched on his radio. Hawaiian

TOJO

YAMAMOTO   IIDA   HOMMA   IMAMURA   YAMASHITA

Few soldiers ever entered upon a war with less enthusiasm than General Hideki Tojo (foreground), Japan's Prime Minister and Minister of War. His misgivings about taking on the Western Allies were shared by the Commander of the Combined Imperial Fleet, Isoroku Yamamoto, as well as the four lieutenant generals entrusted with Japan's conquest of Southeast Asia: Shojiro Iida in Burma, Masaharu Homma in the Philippines, Hitoshi Imamura in the Dutch East Indies and Tomoyuki Yamashita in Malaya. All five men had spent time abroad and all respected their opponents' potential strength. But once the decision for war was made, they threw themselves behind the effort and in six months the Japanese had overrun more territory than any conquerer since Napoleon.

By 1941 the Japanese had outgrown their home islands. Between the turn of the century and 1931 Japan acquired all of the territory shown on the map in solid red. Starting in 1937, it extended its sway to the shaded areas. Then in September 1941, its rulers decided upon an audacious gamble—to seize control of the riches of Asia by expanding their empire to the limits indicated by the dashed line. Within six months Japan had achieved most of its objectives. Then, an ill-considered reach for Midway Island and the Aleutians encountered resurgent Allied resistance that checked—and finally reversed—the tidal wave of Japanese conquest.

music filtered faintly through his earphones. He twisted his antenna until the music was loudest. Bearing on it, he made a 5-degree course correction, then turned the dial again. Over the engine roar he heard what he had been hoping for. "Partly cloudy," said a Honolulu announcer. "Clouds mostly over the mountains. Visibility good. Wind north at ten knots." Fuchida rejoiced: "What a windfall for us!"

The Japanese planes came in over Kahuku Point, Oahu's northern tip, banked to the right and flew down the island's west coast. As they approached the target area, Fuchida peered through binoculars and counted the ships lying at anchor. "They're there, all right," he thought exultantly.

Seven towering vessels were lined up on "Battleship Row" on the eastern edge of Ford Island in the center of Pearl Harbor. At the southwestern end, from which Japan's torpedo bombers would make their run, was the *California*. Then, moored together in pairs, were the *Maryland* and the *Oklahoma*, the *Tennessee* and the *West Virginia*, the *Arizona* and the repair ship *Vestal*. Alone at the northeastern end was the *Nevada*. An eighth battlewagon, the flagship *Pennsylvania*, lay in drydock with the destroyers *Cassin* and *Downes*, at the Navy Yard across the channel from Battleship Row. In all, 94 vessels—including nine cruisers and 31 destroyers—were clustered in an area not three miles square. "Never, even in the deepest peace," Fuchida later recalled, had he seen a target so thoroughly unprotected.

He glanced at his watch. It was 7:49. With an order to his radioman, the signal went out to the rest of his air armada: "To-, to-, to-," the first syllable of *Totsugeki*—"Charge!" That done, he flashed to his carrier force and to Tokyo a code word signifying that the attack was a complete surprise: "*Tora, tora, tora*"—"Tiger, tiger, tiger."

Beneath him, Oahu lay peacefully in the morning sun—even though authorities had had plenty of warning. Because the U.S. could decipher Japan's top-priority code, Washington had been advising its Pacific outposts for months that Japan was preparing for war. In fact, on November 27, 1941, Admiral H.R. Stark, Chief of Naval Operations, sent an urgent message to the Pacific admirals: "This dispatch is to be considered a war warning. An aggressive move by Japan is expected in the next few days." But, he added, evidence "indicates an amphibious expedition against either the Philippines, Thai or Kra Peninsula or possibly Borneo." There was no mention of Hawaii.

Despite all the indications of trouble brewing, no one was overly concerned. Warnings of every sort—reports of Japanese destroying their codes, false submarine sightings, tales of spying throughout the islands—had poured into Pearl Harbor's intelligence offices for months. Even as late as that morning of December 7, there were two warnings that

might have saved the day. Both were discounted by people who should have acted.

The first occurred in the early morning when the destroyer *Ward*, having spotted a submarine conning tower, attacked and scored a bull's eye. When the news reached headquarters, it was decided that the *Ward's* sub sighting was probably false. In fact, the midget submarine, which was sunk, had come from the Japanese Advance Expeditionary Force—27 submarines that were intended to distract U.S. attention from the air attack and cause what damage they could.

Meanwhile two Army privates operating a radar unit at Opana, on the northern tip of Oahu, reported first one suspicious blip on the oscilloscope and then, a few minutes later, a larger blip. The reaction at Army Aircraft Warning Center at Fort Shafter, east of Pearl Harbor, was dismissive. When the privates argued that the screen seemed full of planes, all headed directly for Oahu, the officer in charge, Lieutenant Kermit Tyler, replied with one of the more memorable phrases of the war, "Well, don't worry about it."

Aboard the *Oklahoma*, the forenoon watch had just been piped to breakfast. On the ship's bridge, men were readying the Blue Peter signal flag, which was hoisted as a preliminary to raising the Stars and Stripes. From across the water, men could hear church bells for 8:00 mass. Suddenly, the quiet harbor was bedlam. Explosions erupted; horns blared everywhere. The *Oklahoma's* loudspeakers crackled and shouted: "AIR RAID! NO DRILL!"

The first torpedoes hit the *Oklahoma* with a crump and a boom. One sailor later remembered a phonograph playing the popular song, "Let Me Off Uptown." The battleship's lights went out; emergency lights flickered on, went out, came on again. The big ship started to list. Within 20 minutes, it began to roll over.

Forward of the *Oklahoma*, the *California* was struck by two torpedoes. Oil spewed like blood from its sides, but its guns opened fire and continued throughout the raid.

Aft of the *Oklahoma*, the *West Virginia* began to sink with its decks afire. The harbor's encroaching waters put out the flames, but the battleship settled into the mud while its men swarmed into the surrounding oil slicks.

At the northeastern end of Battleship Row, the *Nevada* was hit in the bow by a torpedo, but its skipper closed off the forward compartments and got under way. As dive bombers swarmed over it like hornets, the big ship almost disappeared in the smoke of its own withering antiaircraft fire. Two Japanese planes were shot down. A bomb blasted through a starboard gun battery; another detonated a terrific blast below decks, spewing sheets of flame into the air. Despite its frightful wounds, the *Nevada* came on, bow

THE NIMBLE NEMESIS OF ALLIED FIGHTERS

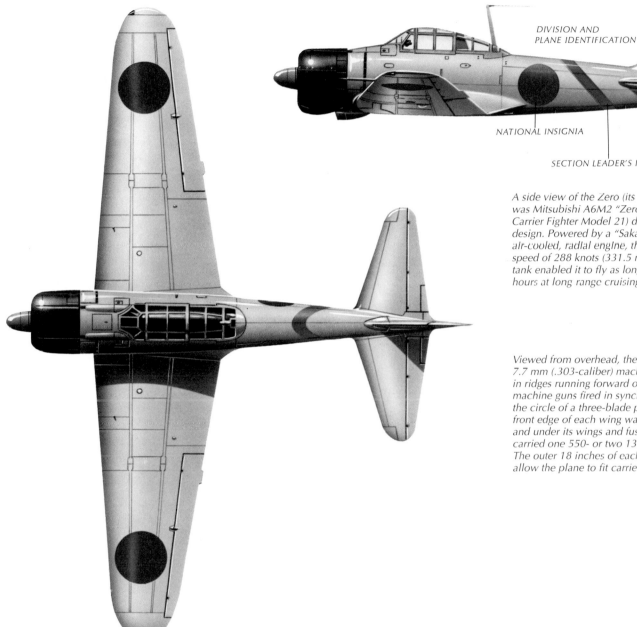

DIVISION AND
PLANE IDENTIFICATION — V-103

NATIONAL INSIGNIA

SECTION LEADER'S INSIGNIA

A side view of the Zero (its full official name was Mitsubishi A6M2 "Zero-Sen" Navy Type O Carrier Fighter Model 21) displays its clean design. Powered by a "Sakae 12" 14-cylinder, air-cooled, radial engine, the Zero had a top speed of 288 knots (331.5 mph). A reserve fuel tank enabled it to fly as long as six to eight hours at long range cruising speeds.

Viewed from overhead, the Zero reveals its twin 7.7 mm (.303-caliber) machine guns protruding in ridges running forward of the cockpit. The machine guns fired in synchronization through the circle of a three-blade propeller. On the front edge of each wing was a 20mm cannon, and under its wings and fuselage the fighter carried one 550- or two 130-pound bombs. The outer 18 inches of each wing folded to allow the plane to fit carrier elevators.

In the first few months of the war in the Pacific, an aura of invincibility developed around the Japanese Navy's single-seat Zero fighter. The frisky little plane chewed up Allied fighter opposition with contemptuous ease at Pearl Harbor. Effortlessly, it brushed aside air opposition in the conquests of the Philippines, Malaya and the Dutch East Indies, causing havoc on the ground and scoring lopsided victories in the air.

The remarkably agile Japanese fighter was built of a light new aluminum alloy. Armor plating to protect the pilot and self-sealing gas tanks were sacrificed to give the Zero maximum speed and maneuverability. Powered by an engine that delivered only 950 hp, the light Zero could still outspeed and outdistance most other fighters early in the war. It could also outclimb any Allied plane then available in the Pacific.

But by 1943 the Zeroes were encountering new breeds of American fighter aircraft: P-38 Lightnings, F4U Corsairs and F6F Hellcats. Though less maneuverable at close range than the Zero, they could fly faster, were more durable and were more heavily armed. In addition, the new U.S. fighters were equipped with self-sealing tanks and with armor plating that afforded protection to the pilots. As a result, the new planes could close in on the Zero and slug it out at short range, where their superior firepower was fatally effective.

down, still fighting fiercely, the Stars and Stripes fluttering from its fantail.

Finally, someone ashore realized that if the *Nevada* went down in the channel—and it looked as if it might—its hulk would bottle up the entire fleet. Accordingly, signal flags went up on the Naval District water tower: stay clear of the channel. The *Nevada's* quartermaster nosed the ship toward shore and grounded it at Waipo Point.

Then came the most thunderous explosion of all as the battleship *Arizona*, which had already taken several torpedoes, suffered a direct hit from a bomb that smashed through the deck and detonated in a forward magazine. In one huge convulsion, the *Arizona's* ammunition went up and the battlewagon seemed to lurch from the water. In an instant, the *Arizona* became a towering flame 500 feet high. Three more bombs found the blazing battleship. Booming and crackling, it sank so fast it had no time to turn over. More than 1,000 men, almost four fifths of the crew, went down in the inferno.

At Schofield Barracks, north of Pearl Harbor, soldiers of America's peacetime army had just settled in at the mess tables for their Sunday pancakes and extra half-pint of milk when they heard explosions in the distance. Suddenly a plane roared low overhead, its guns blazing. Soldiers, many of them still carrying their milk, ran out to see what was happening. Private James Jones, for one, saw a plane that "came up the boulevard, preceded by two lines of holes that kept popping up 80 yards in front on the asphalt." As the plane swooped past, the Japanese pilot grinned and waved. After the war, Jones would describe the scene in his best-selling novel, *From Here to Eternity*.

The men breakfasting at Hickham Field did not even have time to run out and watch. One of the first dive bombers hit the mess hall. In the shower of crockery and cutlery, 35 men died and many were wounded. Nearby, a Navy chaplain, who had been setting up his altar for an outdoor mass, rushed for a machine gun. He set it up on the altar and began firing—an act that would later be memorialized in a popular song, "Praise the Lord and Pass the Ammunition."

From his command post in the sky, Mitsuo Fuchida saw that the American defenders were firing back, and he was astonished at the speed of their response. "Were it the Japanese Navy," he said later, "the reaction would not have been so quick." A Zero exploded in midair; one torpedo plane pinwheeled into the water and another, in flames, flew flat out into a United States ship. Fuchida's wingman was hit and then the commander's own plane bounced "as if struck by a huge club." But the Nakajima-97 kept flying, and soon it was time for Fuchida to run the gauntlet of antiaircraft fire. His target was the *Maryland*, just in front of the smoldering

The destroyers Cassin (right) and Downes lie partially submerged in Drydock No. 1, while smoke billows from Battleship Row and Ford Island in the distance. Three bombs passed through Cassin and exploded in the bottom of the drydock, starting intense fires and damaging the hulls of both destroyers. As the drydock was flooded to extinguish the fires, the Cassin's hull lifted from her keel blocks and rolled over against the Downes. The flagship Pennsylvania, behind the two destroyers, got off with relatively light damage.

A TERRIBLE TOLL IN SHIPS AND MEN

Rarely has the advantage of surprise in major warfare produced such dramatic and devastating losses. When the Japanese finally ceased their attack on Pearl Harbor, the toll for the United States was:

CASUALTIES

Navy	2,008 killed	710 wounded
Marines	109 killed	69 wounded
Army	218 killed	364 wounded
Civilian	68 killed	35 wounded

SHIPS

Lost: battleships *Arizona*, *Oklahoma*, target ship *Utah*; destroyers *Cassin*, *Downes*

Sunk or beached but salvageable: battleships *West Virginia*, *California*, *Nevada*; minelayer *Oglala*

Damaged: battleships *Tennessee*, *Maryland*, *Pennsylvania*; cruisers *Helena*, *Honolulu*, *Raleigh*; destroyer *Shaw*: seaplane tender *Curtiss*; repair ship *Vestal*

AIRCRAFT

ARMY

96 planes destroyed, 128 planes damaged

NAVY

92 planes destroyed, 31 planes damaged

By contrast, out of a strike force of 31 ships and 353 raiding planes, the Japanese lost only 29 planes. In addition, one large submarine, and five midget two-man subs, which had arrived in the Hawaii area earlier, were lost. Total deaths were 64 men, plus an unknown number of crew members aboard the large submarine.

Tennessee. As his bombs fell, Fuchida peered through a peephole in the floor of his plane. "Four bombs in perfect pattern plummeted like devils of doom," he recalled. "They became small as poppy seeds, and finally disappeared as tiny white flashes of smoke appeared on and near the ship." Aloud, Fuchida cried: "Two hits!"

Even then, his work was not yet done. At precisely 8:54, a second wave swept in around Diamond Head. Fifty-four were bombers, targeting Hickham and the Naval Air Station at Kaneohe; 81 dive bombers continued the assault on the American fleet; 36 Zeroes supported them with cannon and machine-gun fire. Then, as suddenly as they had appeared, the attackers vanished. Fuchida made a final pass to photograph the stricken harbor, but even he did not grasp the full extent of the destruction carried out by his raiders in the hour and 45 minutes of their attack. Back on the *Akagi,* Vice-Admiral Chuichi Nagumo, in charge of the carrier fleet, contentedly received the reports on the damage done at Pearl Harbor. "We may conclude," he said, "that the results we anticipated have been achieved."

Japan's surprise assault on Pearl Harbor was part of a coordinated series of blows against United States possessions that stretched across the Pacific to Wake Island, Guam and—most important by far—the Philippines, where the Americans would make their last stand within the tunnels of a natural island fortress nicknamed "The Rock."

The first to fall was Guam—1,500 miles east of Manila in the Mariana Islands. After midnight on December 10, 5,400 Japanese Marines and infantrymen splashed ashore on the little island that was hardly more than a Pan American Clipper stop. Since isolationists in the United States Congress had refused to allow the island to be fortified, Guam was defended by a token garrison of 427 Marines and Navy men, plus native troops numbering 247. By dawn, the invaders reached the Governor's Palace, where a brief firefight took place. At 5:45 a.m., three toots on an auto horn announced an American cease-fire. Navy Captain George McMillin surrendered Guam to a Japanese officer, who immediately ordered him to strip to his undershorts as a further gesture of submission.

The next to go was Wake—a three-islet atoll 2,300 miles west of Hawaii. Previously distinguished for little more than its roaring surf and terns and frigate birds screaming overhead, Wake had recently been transformed: as war clouds gathered in 1941, the U.S. Navy belatedly began turning Wake into an air station that would command the approaches to the southwestern Pacific.

The initial attack came just before noon on Pearl Harbor Day, as 36 enemy planes winged in under squall clouds from the Japanese-held atoll of Kwajalein. Of the eight U.S. planes on the ground, seven were destroyed and one was damaged. However, four American fighters in the air at the time—albeit slow, clumsy Grumman Wildcats—remained.

They later shot down half a dozen of the Japanese bombers that began making daily visits.

Wake was defended by 447 Marines under Major James Devereux, along with 75 Army Signal Corps and Navy personnel. Shortly after midnight on December 11, lookouts saw blinking lights on the horizon. By dawn, a Japanese invasion force—three light cruisers, six destroyers, two patrol boats and two transports—was headed for the island's coral reefs. At four miles offshore, the Japanese ships opened fire; still the Marines' guns were silent. Not until four of the warships were within 4,500 yards did the Americans open with their six five-inch guns.

The ensuing 45-minute battle resulted in what a Japanese naval authority later called "one of the most humiliating defeats our Navy ever suffered." Before the firing faded away, the guns had sunk or damaged at least four Japanese destroyers, two cruisers, and a troop transport. Moreover, Captain Henry Elrod's Grumman scored a direct bomb hit on the destroyer *Kisaragi*, which blew up and sank with no survivors. At that, the Japanese commander turned his force around and sailed away. Yet despite the Americans' elation, Wake's defenders knew the Japanese would return.

They did—at 2 a.m. on December 23. This time the invasion force included about 2,000 elite Japanese Marines and was supported by six heavy cruisers plus two of the aircraft carriers that had attacked Hawaii. The fighting was savage: on one of the atoll's three islands, 70 American Marines all but wiped out a landing force of about 100 Japanese. Even so, by 7:30 a.m., it was clear that Wake was doomed, and that continued resistance might lead to a massacre of the island's 1,000 civilians. Major Devereux, accompanied by a noncom who carried a white rag lashed to a mop handle, surrendered Wake Island to the Japanese.

Although the ordeal on Wake was over, another was underway—this time in the Philippines.

Within hours of the attack on Hawaii, Japanese planes sent from Formosa had assailed Clark Field, northwest of Manila on Luzon—the Philippines' largest and northernmost island. Expecting to find an American hornet's nest stirred up by the news of Pearl Harbor, one Japanese pilot later recalled, "we looked down and saw some sixty enemy bombers and fighters neatly parked along the airfield runway. They squatted there like sitting ducks." By the time the Japanese airmen departed, they had blown to bits 18 B-17s, 53 P-40s and about 30 other aircraft. In the first hours of the war, General Douglas MacArthur, commander of U.S. Army Forces in the Far East, had lost half his air force.

Although small groups of Japanese troops landed on southeastern and northern Luzon in the week following the

Deep inside Malinta Tunnel (above), an elaborate network of bombproof underground passages on Corregidor, the U.S. Army headquarters staff directs Bataan's defense. Corregidor fell at the climax of a campaign launched with an attack on Clark Field (below). Landing on northern Luzon, the Japanese fought their way down through Bataan. The capture of Corregidor completed the five-month campaign.

The commander of U.S. Army Forces in the Far East, General Douglas MacArthur, confers with President Manuel Quezon of the Philippines on Corregidor as the Philippine campaign approaches its climax. Shortly before his nation was occupied, Quezon left by submarine for Australia, and later went to the United States to set up a government in exile. MacArthur departed by PT boat for Mindanao, then flew to Australia, where he established a new headquarters.

devastating raid on Clark Field, it was not until just before Christmas that the Japanese launched their main attack. On December 22, at dawn, 43,000 troops of Lieut. General Masaharu Homma's 14th Army waded onto the beaches of Lingayen Gulf, 120 miles north of Manila. Hardly were Homma's men ashore before another Japanese amphibious force struck Luzon's Lamon Bay, about 70 miles southeast of Manila. The two enemy columns thus formed a pair of pincers closing in on the capital city.

As commander of the combined U.S. and Philippine Army forces, General MacArthur could field almost three times as many troops as Homma. However, unlike Homma's veterans of the Japanese war in China, MacArthur's men included 100,000 raw Philippine reservists; in all, he could count on no more than 30,000 reliable regulars. MacArthur's strategy, as it developed, was to pull all his Luzon forces back into the defense of Bataan, a 30-mile peninsula of wooded mountains and dense jungle separating Manila Bay from the South China Sea. The move would sacrifice Manila to Homma and his Japanese. But a strong garrison under MacArthur's personal command would also remain on the island fortress of Corregidor. And from there the Americans could still deny Homma the use of Manila harbor. "He may have the bottle," said MacArthur before leaving for Corregidor, "but I have the cork."

On January 2, the invaders occupied Manila; a Japanese sergeant hauled down the Stars and Stripes and ground it under his heel. Meanwhile, 15,000 American and 65,000 Filipino troops were digging in on Bataan. The peninsula, jammed with 80,000 troops and 26,000 civilian refugees, had only enough rations to feed 100,000 people for a month. Ammunition and quinine—the only malaria remedy—were in short supply.

MacArthur's troops were deployed in a 20-mile line across the peninsula's upper neck. One corps, under Major General Jonathan Wainwright, held the precipitous western coast. Another, commanded by Major General George Parker, stretched to the swampy eastern shore. The two corps were separated and prevented from establishing effective contact by the 4,200-foot Mount Natib.

After a fortnight of hard fighting, two Japanese regiments advanced along the slopes of Mount Natib and turned the flanks of the two American corps. MacArthur ordered a withdrawal to a new line halfway down the peninsula. Although the troops were exhausted—one officer said they looked "like walking dead men"—by the time they got there, they nonetheless braced and defended their positions so fiercely that Homma suspended the offensive. By the second week of February Homma's time was up: Tokyo had given him only 50 days to conquer Luzon. His forces had lost more than 7,000 dead and wounded, while 11,000 more were down with a variety of tropical diseases.

At the same time, sickness and malnutrition were gradually paralyzing MacArthur's army and morale was descending toward despair. Resentment was building against MacArthur, who, in relative safety on fortified Corregidor, became derisively known as Dugout Doug. His popularity was hardly enhanced when, on March 10, he was summarily ordered by President Roosevelt to Australia to assume command of American forces scheduled to assemble there. Leaving Wainwright in command, a reluctant MacArthur departed, accompanied by his family. The MacArthurs were taken by motor-torpedo boat on a perilous 500-mile journey through enemy-infested waters to Mindanao, thence by B-17 to Australia. There the general made his renowned pledge. "I came through," he said, "and I shall return."

Back in the Philippines, the stalemate ended on the morning of April 3, when the self-named Battling Bastards of Bataan were assailed by a five-hour Japanese bombardment followed by a massive armor and infantry attack. By Easter Sunday, the Japanese had stormed their first objective, the upper slopes of 1,900-foot Mount Samat. The next day, Major General Edward King, who had replaced Wainwright as field commander on Bataan, threw most of his reserve into a desperate counterattack. But by nightfall the trails and crude roads to the south were clogged with thousands of fleeing Americans and Filipinos.

From Corregidor, under explicit orders from MacArthur, Wainwright ordered another counterattack. But King, in the field, decided it was impossible. At 11 a.m. on April 9 he faced Homma's operations officer, Colonel Motoo Nakayama across a field table. The American general asked for a 12-hour stay to collect his wounded. Nakayama coldly refused. "Will our troops be well treated?" asked King. Replied Nakayama: "We are not barbarians." Wearily, King unstrapped his sidearm, laid it on the table, and surrendered the remaining 76,000 men on Bataan.

Holed up in Malinta Tunnel on Corregidor, General Wainwright still held the cork to Manila Bay. Now the Japanese turned all their power against The Rock, and its three nearby fortified islands. For nearly a month, 13,000 Americans and Filipinos were subjected to day-and-night pounding from more than 100 Japanese guns. Fires raged on the surface of the island until it was little more than a cinder. The fissures in Malinta Tunnel's concrete walls widened under the bombardment. Dust, dirt and the stench of death were everywhere, while fatigue, hunger and the terror of the endless cannonade exacted their toll on the defenders. Wrote one survivor, "We asked only to live from day to day."

Filipino and American troops give up outside Corregidor's 1,400-foot Malinta Tunnel, in which their garrison withstood 27 days of artillery bombardment.

On May 2, Corregidor's last big gun emplacement took a direct hit in its magazine. Three nights later, Homma's troops and tanks came ashore; within four hours, they were only a mile away from the mouth of Malinta Tunnel. Finally, on May 6, 1942, Jonathan Wainwright radioed MacArthur in Australia: "I have fought for you to the best of my ability from Lingayen Gulf to Bataan to Corregidor. Goodbye, General." The last message from Corregidor was tapped out by a young operator, Corporal Irving Strobing: "Everyone is bawling like a baby. They are piling dead and wounded in our tunnel. The jig is up." Under a white flag, General Jonathan Wainwright surrendered not only Corregidor but, at Homma's demand, the entire Philippines.

The United States was by no means the only victim of Japan's Imperial ambitions in Southeast Asia. One after another, the possessions of the British and Dutch came under the glare of the Rising Sun. Even as the carrier-borne strike force swept down on Pearl Harbor, the Japanese were preparing to strike three small fishing ports on the east shore of the Kra Peninsula where southern Thailand bordered British-held northern Malaya. Around midnight on December 7, transports offloaded the first contingents of

Lieut. General Tomoyuki Yamashita's 25th Army. Pattani fell without a fight, and Singora put up only token resistance. Kota Bharu was slightly tougher, but within 24 hours the town and its air base were in Japanese hands.

These landings belatedly attracted a flotilla of British warships, which on December 8 pulled out of mighty Singapore's naval base and steamed north with orders to sink the invasion fleet. Four of the six British ships were destroyers, pygmies in the company of a pair of giants: the spanking new 35,000-ton battleship *Prince of Wales* and the 32,000-ton battle cruiser *Repulse*—a veteran rebuilt so extensively that wags called it H.M.S. Repair.

Aboard the *Prince of Wales* was Admiral Sir Tom Phillips, the new commander-in-chief of Britain's Far Eastern Fleet, a 5-foot 4-inch dynamo inevitably nicknamed "Tom Thumb." En route, Phillips was informed that the Japanese had knocked out northern Malaya's air fields and his ships would have no fighter cover. Later, three planes were spotted in the distance, and Phillips assumed—wrongly—that they had discovered his flotilla and that his mission was imperiled. He turned back for Singapore.

Sailing south, Phillips now received a report that the enemy had also landed at Kuantan, a port halfway between the Kra Peninsula and Singapore. A destroyer was sent to investigate, and soon signaled back: "All's as quiet as a wet Sunday afternoon." It was later learned that the supposed invaders had been a few water buffalo that had wandered into a field planted with mines. But the delay was fatal.

Japan's conquest of Malaya was launched December 8, 1941, when Lieut. General Tomoyuki Yamashita's 25th Army landed at Singora, Pattani, and Kota Bharu, near the border between Malaya and Thailand. (Thailand was called Siam until 1939, when the name was changed. It switched back to Siam in 1945 and again to Thailand in 1949.) Yamashita's troops advanced west to cut off Malaya at the Kra Isthmus, then swept south along both coasts to Johore, where the British made a desperate stand before withdrawing to Singapore. The island fortress fell 70 days after the campaign began, a month earlier than Yamashita had predicted.

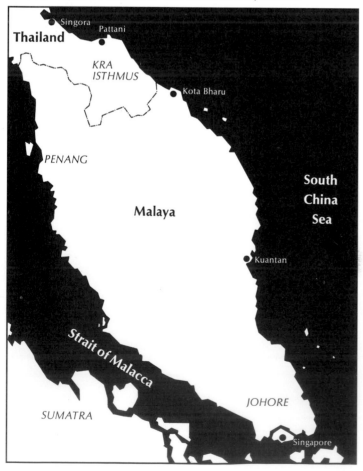

At 10:20 a.m. on December 10, a shadowing aircraft was spotted and battle stations were manned. The men did not have long to wait. Forty minutes later, Japanese bombers appeared, followed by torpedo planes. Struck simultaneously by two torpedoes, the *Prince of Wales* flashed a message to the *Repulse*: "Not under control." Rushing to the injured battleship's assistance, the *Repulse* was smashed by five torpedoes; it too went out of control. "Good luck and God be with you," said Captain William Tennant as his men scrambled over the side. Several officers seized Tennant and forced him to come along. At 12:33 p.m., the *Repulse* rolled over and slid into the sea.

New waves of bombers now concentrated on the *Prince of Wales*. At 1:15, already stricken, the battleship was hit by a bomb that rocked it like a giant sledge. On the bridge, Admiral Phillips and the battlewagon's skipper, Captain John Leach, stood side by side, ramrod straight, as the *Prince of Wales* heeled over and sank.

In all, 820 British seamen were lost, while 2,081 were picked up by the flotilla's destroyers. Of 88 Japanese planes, only four were shot down. The next morning in London, Winston Churchill was still abed when he received the dire tidings. "As I turned over and twisted in bed," he later recalled, "the full horror of the news sank in on me. Over all this vast expanse of waters Japan was supreme, and we everywhere were weak and naked."

Back on shore, Yamashita's warriors were already heading south in two columns, one on Malaya's west coast and one on the east. Although the 60,000 Japanese who would undertake the conquest of Malaya were badly outnumbered by 88,000 British, Australian, Indian and native troops, the Allied superiority was misleading. Unlike the British, who, as one critic put it, were "laden like Christmas trees" with packs, haversacks, blankets, gas masks and bulky canned rations, the Japanese soldier's clothing and weapons were lightweight and he could manage on a few handfuls of rice, with some pickles and preserved seaweed to flavor it.

Led by hard-pedaling bicyclists who reconnoitered ahead, Japan's troops were skilled jungle fighters. When they came upon a British roadblock, their tanks would rush it, followed by infantry in trucks. If the tanks were stopped, foot soldiers melted away into the jungle undergrowth or mangrove swamps alongside. In small groups they moved out around the enemy's flanks, padding along the narrow tracks used by native hunters or poling down the sluggish swamp waterways on crude rafts. Coming up behind the enemy position, they set up a cacophony of fireworks and other noisemakers, convincing the defenders that they were surrounded by superior forces. The tanks then took advantage of the resulting confusion by attacking.

Employing these tactics time and again, the Japanese made steady progress, and by mid-January Yamashita controlled two thirds of the peninsula. At that point General Sir Archibald Wavell, supreme head of the joint Allied command in the Far East, flew to Malaya. There he ordered a retreat all the way to Johore, Malaya's southernmost state, separated from Singapore by only a shallow channel.

The fighting in Johore raged for two weeks. Finally, the Japanese breached one end of the 90-mile front, exposing the defenders to the threat of encirclement; orders came to withdraw. On the morning of January 31, remnants of the last British battalion on the mainland—90 Argyll and Sutherland Highlanders with pipers skirling "Hielan' Laddie"—came over the 1,100-yard causeway into Singapore. British engineers then blew up the causeway, and the waters of Johore Strait poured through a 60-yard gap.

Singapore was now isolated, the smoldering symbol of a dying empire. Yet, for the next month and a half, it remained a stronghold, enduring constant bombardment from Yamashita's 400 guns and attacks through the mangrove swamps to the northwest. By February 15, Singapore's water supply was running out and looters roamed the city's streets. British and Australian commanders conferred in a bombproof underground briefing room. "Silently and sadly," one recalled, "we decided to surrender."

At 8:30 p.m. the guns ceased firing. Japanese soldiers began singing *Kimigayo*, their slow, stately national anthem. At his headquarters, Yamashita—ever after to be known as

Marching to the surrender of Singapore, Lieut. General A.E. Percival (far right) the British ground commander in Malaya, is accompanied by his aides, one of them bearing the Union Jack, and another (far left) carrying a white flag. The Japanese officer at center escorted them to the Ford Motor Company's assembly plant on the outskirts of Singapore Town. There, at a bare wooden table, Percival yielded Britain's proud bastion of the Orient to Lieut. General Tomoyuki Yamashita.

the Tiger of Malaya—and his staff held the traditional victory celebration of dried cuttlefish, chestnuts and *sake*. Silently lifting the cups of wine, the officers faced northeast toward Tokyo in a solemn toast.

Indeed, it was cause for celebration: Yamashita had estimated that it would require 100 days to capture Singapore; instead, it took 70. The Japanese had inflicted 138,708 casualties on the British while suffering only 9,824 of their own.

It was, in fact, a day of double victory for the Japanese, who also took Palembang, on Sumatra, and with it half the oil reserves of the Dutch East Indies. Next they would turn their attention to the neighboring island of Java—another major source of oil and the center of Allied operations in southeastern Asia.

The climactic battle for Java began at sea on February 27 when an already battered Allied fleet left Surabaya to stop an approaching invasion force. Under the overall command of the Dutch Navy's Rear Admiral Karel Doorman were nine destroyers and five cruisers: two Dutch, one British, one Australian and one American—the U.S.S. *Houston*, which had been reported sunk so many times that crewmen had nicknamed it the "Galloping Ghost of the Java Coast."

The following afternoon, about 90 miles north of Surabaya, the fleet encountered two enemy convoys protected by three cruisers and 14 destroyers. Two of the Japanese cruisers immediately swung all 20 of their 8-inch guns westward and let go at extreme range—28,000 yards—while a *Houston* officer grimly noted in his diary: "Sheets of copper-colored flame lick across their battle line."

During the melee, two Allied destroyers sank and a cruiser on each side limped out of the battle. As night fell, the Japanese force broke contact to escort its transports to less dangerous waters. Doorman's fleet pursued, its course illuminated by flares dropped from Japanese planes. Lurking in the darkness, the Japanese warships fired new superpowered torpedoes: a tremendous explosion rent the Dutch cruiser *Java*, and it plunged to the bottom. Seconds later, Doorman's flagship *DeRuyter* erupted in a pillar of flame and went down, taking Doorman and 366 of his men.

Making a run for it, the *Houston* and the Australian cruiser *Perth* tried to escape into the Indian Ocean through the Sunda Strait, between Java and Sumatra. As they rounded a headland west of Batavia, they came upon the Japanese transports and sank two of them. But minutes later three Japanese cruisers and nine destroyers appeared. Four torpedoes sank the *Perth*. The *Houston* took a salvo of gunfire, torpedoes tore open its hull—and the Galloping Ghost disappeared beneath the surface of the oily sea.

Thereafter, the Japanese conquest of Java was but a formality. On March 9, the Dutch surrendered their holdings in the Indies. The last word came from a commercial radio station in Java. "We are shutting down now," said a voice. "Goodbye till better times. Long live the Queen!"

As important as the natural resources of the Dutch East Indies was the strategic location of Burma. A British preserve since the late 19th Century, Burma was wedged between China and India and was the key to both neighboring giants. Perhaps most importantly, the 681-mile Burma Road, hacked at heartbreaking human cost through the mountains, was virtually the only land route by which embattled China could receive supplies. If Burma could be taken, Japan might at last strangle and subdue China, once and for all.

Japan's campaign in Burma had begun on December 23, 1941, with a massive bombing raid on Rangoon—the nation's capital and one of the most active ports on the Indian Ocean. By the third week of January, Lieut. General Shojiro Iida's 15th Army moved in from Japanese-held Thailand, taking the strategic port of Moulmein, only 90 miles southeast of Rangoon.

Among the Allies a conflict arose over where to make a stand. Major General John Smyth, whose 17th Indian Division was responsible for the defense of southern Burma, wanted to concentrate his troops on the west bank of the swift-flowing Sittang River. His plan, however, was vetoed by General Wavell, who hoped to gain time by ordering that the fight be waged "as far forward as possible."

Accordingly, on February 14, Smyth tried to make his stand behind the Bilin River, 30 miles east of the Sittang. But after sustaining serious casualties, his force was compelled to fall back to the Sittang anyhow. Smyth, his staff and part of a thinned-out brigade managed to cross to the west side of the river on a single-lane railroad trestle. There, at about 4 a.m. on February 22, a truck slipped off the planking laid

With their bayonets flashing, troops of Lieut. General Shojiro Iida's 15th Army present arms in a mass salute shortly before crossing the border between Thailand and Burma. Four months later Burma fell, completing a six-month sweep of Southeast Asia that put more than one million square miles and 150 million people under Tokyo's rule.

Lieut. Colonel James H. Doolittle piloted the B-25 that led the historic surprise raid on Japan.

BOMBERS THAT BLASTED JAPANESE CONFIDENCE

Ever since the 13th Century, when a typhoon demolished an invading Mongol armada, the Japanese people had believed that a *Kamikaze*, or Divine Wind, made their island nation invulnerable. In 1942 that belief was buttressed by a modern confidence in naval air and sea patrols. But on April 18 of that year, both beliefs were shattered when 16 U.S. Army bombers, led by Lieut. Colonel James H. Doolittle, swept in from the sea to bomb Tokyo and four other major Japanese cities, then vanished westward as swiftly as they came.

Planning for this bold thrust began soon after the United States debacle at Pearl Harbor, with the dual aim of denting Japanese confidence and boosting American morale. But Japan was beyond the reach of any land-based U.S. bombers, and an attack by regular carrier-based planes with their limited 300-mile range would be suicidal; Japanese air and sea forces would blow the U.S. carriers out of the water before they could get close enough to launch their aircraft.

The solution was unique: to launch land-based B-25 bombers from a carrier cruising beyond the normal radius of Japanese patrols. Amid tight security, a Navy pilot taught short-takeoff techniques to hand-picked Army airmen. They learned their destination only after they were aboard the carrier *Hornet*, whose decks were packed with lashed-down B-25s. After 18 days at sea, laden with bombs and extra fuel tanks, the B-25s staggered into the air from the *Hornet*'s pitching flight deck some 700 miles from Tokyo. Picket boats had spotted the carrier, but while the Japanese waited for her to come within normal launching range, the bombers zoomed in to drop their loads on the soil of Japan. Then, unscathed by disorganized ground and air attacks, the B-25s flew toward sanctuaries in Russia and China.

Though the brief foray did no great damage, it did help to change the course of the war. Haunted by the fear of another attack, the Japanese rashly accelerated plans for extending their defense perimeter, a decision that led within weeks to a costly defeat in the Battle of Midway. The raid also affected ordinary citizens. "We started to doubt," one of them later recalled, "that we were invincible."

As the lead plane dissolves into a speck in the distance, the second Japan-bound B-25 lifts off from the spray-swept deck of the U.S.S. Hornet.

on the tracks and got stuck between the ties. All traffic on the Sittang's east side came to a complete halt, with thousands of British and Indian soldiers backed up for six miles. When the Japanese attacked, the bridgehead commander, Brigadier Noel Hugh-Jones, faced a cruel dilemma: if the bridge continued to stand, the Japanese could cross it and march on Rangoon; if the bridge were blown up, the Allied troops across the river would be lost.

Hugh-Jones gave the order to blow the bridge. At 5:30 next morning, one soldier recalled, "there was a series of deafening explosions followed by a blinding flash of light and a blast of red-hot air." Of the 8,500 men who had been involved in the battle from the beginning, only about 3,500 had made it across the swirling waters of the Sittang. They were jammed into trains headed for Rangoon. The city was now in its death throes, under relentless attack by enemy planes.

On February 27, Burma's Governor cabled London: "I can see nothing in sight which can save Rangoon." A week later, a new British field commander, General Harold Alexander, ordered the demolition of the Burmah Oil Company's storage tanks, outside Rangoon. In 70 minutes, 150 million gallons of oil were destroyed, sending up a column of smoke that aircraft pilots estimated to be 23,000 feet high. While the detonations thundered, Alexander moved out his troops and headed north to assist in the defense of the Burma Road. Despite the debacle suffered so far by the Allies, the struggle for Burma and its lifeline to China had, in fact, scarcely begun.

In less than six months, the Japanese had seized what the old colonial powers had taken several centuries to acquire. More than a million square miles of land in Southeast Asia—and practically the entire western half of the Pacific Ocean—had come under Japan's domain. More than 150 million people had been added to Emperor Hirohito's subjects. In addition, more than half a million European and American civilians and close to 150,000 military prisoners were in Japanese hands.

Yet by the very size and swiftness of the conquest, Japan had exceeded its capacity to digest what it had gorged. Distances between the Japanese homelands and the conquered territories were staggering, cultural differences were vast, and there was a critical shortage of trained Japanese colonial administrators. As an expedient, absolute authority was given to the army's field commanders.

The excesses of which the Japanese military was capable became clear within days after the fall of Singapore. All of the island's Chinese residents were rounded up and screened, and those who were judged to be anti-Japanese

were summarily killed. Among them were hundreds who were selected for extinction merely because they wore tattoo marks—which, although they were simply popular Chinese adornments, the Japanese believed to signify membership in a secret society. By Tokyo's own later admission, the victims of the so-called Chinese Massacres numbered at least 5,000.

The slaughter at Singapore was Japan's way of venting its fury and frustration over the continuing stalemate in its war with China. With the surrender of the Dutch East Indies, the Japanese settled another sort of score.

Enraged at finding many of the area's coveted oil fields set afire, they took out their wrath on the government officials and oil-company officials deemed responsible. At Balikpapan, in Dutch Borneo, the entire white population was dispatched: some had their arms and legs lopped off with swords, while others were driven into the sea and shot.

Although Japan had refused to ratify the Geneva Convention of 1929, it had been widely assumed that the treaty's humanitarian terms would apply to military

174

prisoners. Instead, the Japanese chose to deal with prisoners according to their own centuries-old code of *Bushido*—literally, "the way of the warrior"—in which surrender to the enemy was strictly forbidden. The Japanese soldier was required to commit suicide rather than allow himself to be captured. By corollary, Allied prisoners who fell into Japanese hands merited utter contempt, hence every sort of abuse.

An early indication of what might be expected came with the surrender of the 13,000 defenders of Corregidor, who were given no food for a week, then hauled ashore in freighters and driven like cattle through the Manila streets to celebrate the Japanese triumph. Finally they were shipped by train to an improvised prison camp at Cabanatuan.

The fate of Bataan's 76,000 survivors was even worse. Food, water and medicine quickly ran short. Far too few trucks and trains had been allotted to haul the prisoners 65 miles north to Camp O'Donnell. For most captives, the trip became a foot-slogging endurance test in which the Japanese clubbed, stabbed and shot helpless stragglers; in one bloody two-hour orgy, they bayoneted and beheaded 350 Filipino soldiers. Some guards forced captives to bury stricken companions alive, even as they struggled feebly to escape from their newly-dug graves. A soldier-poet who would later die in captivity wrote of Bataan's benumbed marchers: "The suffering column moves. I leave behind/ Only another corpse, beside the road."

In a 41-nation pact made at The Hague in 1907, Japan had agreed not to use military prisoners for work that was either excessive or connected with war. In fact, however, 46,000 Allied prisoners of war were transported to the torrid jungle of the Thai-Burmese border, along a river known as the Kwai Noi. There, they laid tracks for a railroad that was to link Bangkok and Rangoon.

"Except for our G-strings, we worked naked and barefoot in heat which reached one hundred and twenty degrees," recalled Ernest Gordon, who had served as a company commander in the Argyll and Sutherland Highlanders. "Our bodies were stung by gnats and insects, our feet cut and bruised by sharp stones. Somewhere the guards had picked up the word 'Speedo.' They stood over us with their nasty staves of bamboo yelling 'Speedo! Speedo!' until 'Speedo' rang in our ears and haunted our sleep. When we did not move fast enough to suit them—which was most of the time—they beat us."

When the eventual toll of brutality and disease was finally known, it was estimated that each of the railway's 250 miles had cost 64 Allied lives and those of 240 native workers in the ordeal that would subsequently be described in the fictional *Bridge over the River Kwai*.

With their slogan of "Asia for the Asians" and by painting a rosy picture of an economically self-sufficient "Greater East Asia Co-Prosperity Sphere," the Japanese had ingratiated themselves to large numbers of the native populations in the lands they intended to conquer.

However once they took over, the Japanese banned all political parties, public assembly, and the spreading of "fabulous wild rumors." Schools were closed pending the completion of a new curriculum that included the compulsory study of Japanese. Like the civilian internees, natives were slapped in the face for failure to bow to all Japanese. And under pain of arrest, Southeast Asians had to carry identification cards. It was not long before many of those who had joyfully welcomed the lifting of the white man's yoke—were soon beginning to wonder if they had merely exchanged it for another.

Women internees at a concentration camp at Singapore, assembled for roll call, bow before their captors in a ritual required by the Japanese. Prisoners were made to stand at attention first, then bend at the waist to a 15 degree angle and remain silent in that position to a count of five. On the whole, civilians incarcerated by the Japanese were spared the mistreatment visited upon military prisoners. Theirs was a subtler form of torment: the Japanese simply dumped them behind the guarded gates of internment camps and left them there to fend for themselves.

THE FIRST CARRIER CLASH

The world's first battle between aircraft carriers—and the first major sea engagement between fleets far out of sight of each other—was joined in the spring of 1942 in the Coral Sea. It began on May 4 when a Japanese force shielded by three carriers threatened to occupy the crucial Allied air base at Port Moresby on the southeastern tip of New Guinea. Hurrying to counterattack came U.S. Task Force 17, including the carriers *Lexington* and *Yorktown*.

For the first 24 hours, Task Force 17 and the Japanese groped for each other like blindfolded wrestlers. Then search planes of both sides found targets. Carrier-based Japanese pilots sank the U.S. destroyer *Sims* and mortally wounded the tanker *Neosho*. The American pilots had even greater success. "Scratch one flattop!" a U.S. squadron leader radioed back to the *Lexington* as the 12,000-ton *Shoho* (below) went down.

The next morning both fleets, almost simultaneously, launched their fighters, dive bombers and torpedo planes. The aerial armadas—some 70 Japanese planes versus 83 American aircraft—passed without sighting each other and at 11 a.m. swarmed down on their enemies' nests for 45 furious minutes. The box score favored Japan: both Task Force 17's carriers were hit, the *Lexington* fatally.

But in overall effect, the Coral Sea battle was to prove the war's first decisive check to Japan's southward expansion. The Port Moresby invasion was scotched—for good, as it turned out. Moreover, the two big Japanese carriers, the *Shokaku* and the *Zaikaku*, were so badly damaged that they had to limp home for refitting. They were still there, and sorely missed, during the decisive Battle of Midway only a month later.

The target of 93 American planes, the light carrier Shoho burns and founders in the Coral Sea, marking the first Allied success against a Japanese carrier.

Sinuous white slashes upon the Coral Sea are the wakes of a Japanese carrier force twisting at top speed to avoid U.S. torpedoes and bombs. Had the Japanese succeeded in occupying Port Moresby, their air superiority over the Coral Sea would have been facilitated and their domination of the South Pacific all the way to the coast of Australia assured.

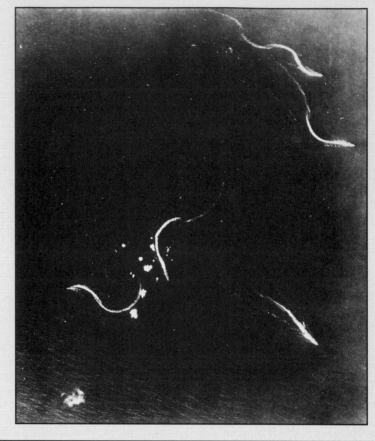

A tremendous mushroom cloud billows up from the carrier the U.S.S. Lexington (below), after Japanese torpedoes set off the ship's own torpedoes. By late afternoon the crew had to abandon ship; their departure was as disciplined as a routine drill. Although 216 men died as a result of the battle, 2,735 other men and a dog (the captain's cocker spaniel) went over the side and were rescued without one drowning.

Led by the carrier Enterprise (foreground), the arrival of Task Force 16 at the battle's end temporarily thwarted a Japanese plan to extend the invasion to the east.

III

TURNING OF THE TIDE

Soviet snipers hunt Wehrmacht opponents in the ruins of Stalingrad. With the battle's end in February 1943, the tide of the war began to turn in Russia's favor.

8

Little more than a series of desperate attacks that fell far short of their objectives, Stalin's winter offensive finally ground to a halt in late February 1942. The Red Army had won back isolated chunks of relatively unimportant terrain and had been gravely weakened in the process. Yet the winter campaign had not been much of a victory for the Germans either. Against his generals' advice, Hitler had insisted that the troops not yield an inch. German casualties amounted to nearly 200,000 men, and only by dint of skillful and courageous fighting had the Wehrmacht been able to hold—in roughly the same position that the generals had planned to occupy in the strategic withdrawal forbidden by the Führer.

In Russia, the *rasputitsa*—spring thaw—of 1942 came as a godsend to both sides. As it worked its way north, turning the steppes into seas of mud and mercifully curtailing large-scale operations, the Wehrmacht and the Red Army prepared for the cataclysmic fighting of the summer campaigns.

Although Hitler gave his plan a modest name, Operation *Blau* (Blue), it was in fact a stupendous scheme. Its main feature was an overwhelming strike into the oil-rich Caucasus. Ultimately, Hitler envisioned this as the left prong of a gigantic pincers movement. The right prong would be General Erwin Rommel's Afrika Korps, which would capture Tobruk and eliminate the British in Egypt. Rommel would then take the Arabian oil fields and lance through the Middle East to link up with Wehrmacht forces slashing south through the Caucasus Mountains to the Turkish border. At this point, Hitler expected the Turks to enter the war on the Axis side.

When all was in order, the Führer planned to construct an East Wall—a giant line of defense—that would seal off his immense conquests for leisurely exploitation. Once the Soviet Union had lost the Caucasus, he believed, the Russians would drop out of the war and a peace could be negotiated with the Western Allies.

Hitler took charge of planning *Blau* in every detail, from logistics down to tactical operations at the division level. His work progressed rapidly in March—although not, of course, without the usual irksome sounds from cautious generals who found fault with his imaginative schemes. Hitler listened, but only from time to time.

Before *Blau* could be properly launched, however, some housekeeping chores were required. On the Leningrad front, Army Group North would wipe out a Soviet pocket in the Volkhov swamps and later take Leningrad itself. In the southern sector, German forces would nip off a big Soviet salient, created during the winter fighting, at Izyum. And, not least, the Kerch Peninsula in the Crimea would be swept clean, and besieged Sevastopol would at last be captured.

Simultaneously, in Moscow, Stalin was laying his own ambitious springtime plans, and for that purpose he convened a meeting in the last week of March. The belligerence of his intent was denoted by a recent change in the decor of his Kremlin office: gone from their customary places on the wall were portraits of the Communist political idols Marx and Engels; in their stead were pictures of Suvorov and Kutuzov, military heroes who had fought in long-ago wars against the Turks and French.

Among those present at the meeting were Marshal Boris M. Shaposhnikov, Chief of the Soviet General Staff, a capable officer who was by now toilworn and ready to retire; Lieut. General Aleksandr M. Vasilevsky, who would soon succeed Shaposhnikov; General Georgy K. Zhukov, the sav-

Red Army units parade through Red Square in the November 7 anniversary review in 1941. Minutes later they marched to the front to defend Moscow. A searing speech delivered the night before by Josef Stalin had tapped the wellsprings of his people's national and ethnic pride. Now the struggle against the invader took on the character of a holy war. "The Russian people felt the insult of the German invasion," reported one journalist. "It was something more deeply insulting than anything they had known before."

RED ARMY RESURGENT

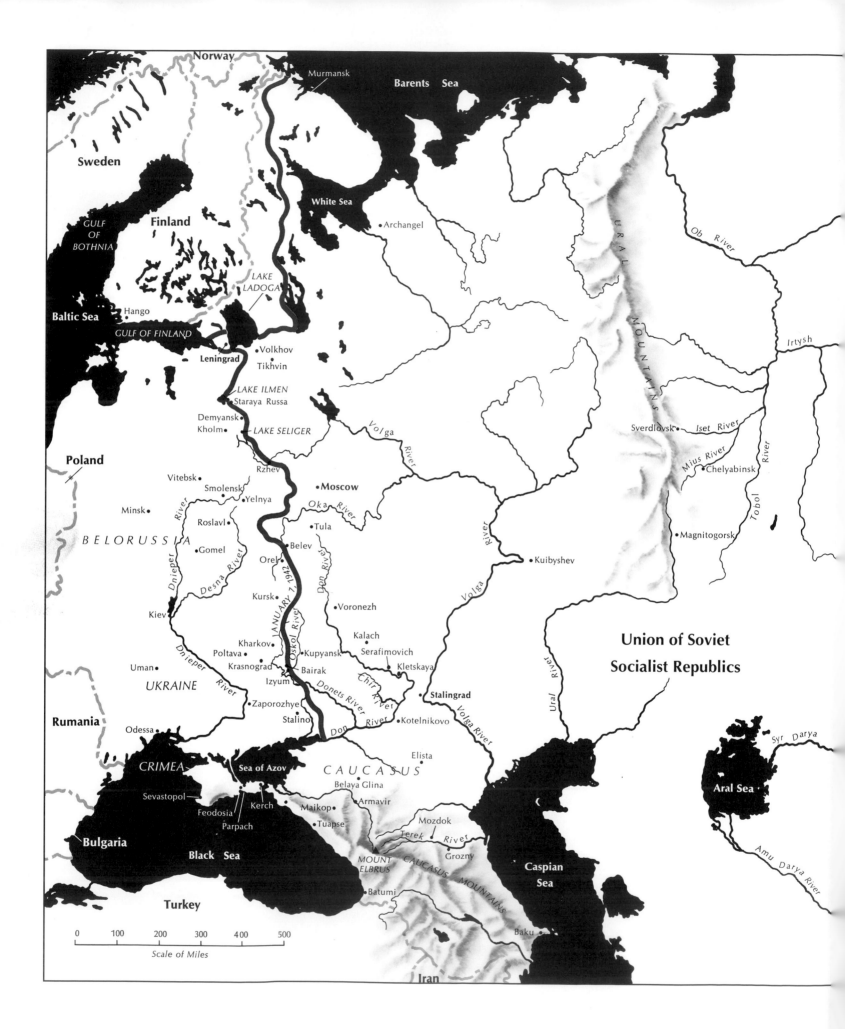

Norway

Murmansk

Barents Sea

Sweden

White Sea

Archangel

GULF
OF
BOTHNIA

Finland

URAL MOUNTAINS

Ob River

Baltic Sea

Hango

LAKE
LADOGA

GULF OF FINLAND

Leningrad

Volkhov

Tikhvin

Irtysh

LAKE ILMEN
Staraya Russa

Volga

River

Sverdlovsk

Iset River

Demyansk

Kholm

LAKE SELIGER

Mius River

Chelyabinsk

Poland

Rzhev

Tobol River

Vitebsk

Smolensk

Yelnya

Moscow

Minsk

Roslavl

Oka River

Tula

Magnitogorsk

BELORUSSIA

Gomel

Belev

Kuibyshev

Orel

Dnieper River

Desna River

Volga River

Kiev

Kursk

Don River

Voronezh

JANUARY 7, 1942

Oskol River

Kalach

Union of Soviet

Kharkov

Kupyansk

Serafimovich

Socialist Republics

Poltava

Krasnograd

Bairak

Kletskaya

Uman

Dnieper River

Izyum

Donets River

Chir River

UKRAINE

Zaporozhye

Stalingrad

Rumania

Stalino

Don River

Kotelnikovo

Ural River

Volga River

Odessa

Elista

CRIMEA

Sea of Azov

CAUCASUS

Belaya Glina

Aral Sea

Sevastopol

Kerch

Armavir

Syr Darya

Feodosia

Maikop

Mozdok

Parpach

Tuapse

Terek River

Caspian
Sea

Bulgaria

Black Sea

MOUNT
ELBRUS

CAUCASUS MOUNTAINS

Grozny

Baku

Turkey

Batumi

Amu Darya River

0   100   200   300   400   500

Scale of Miles

Iran

ior of Moscow; Marshal Kliment E. Voroshilov, a mediocre commander but an old drinking companion of Stalin's; and Marshal Semyon K. Timoshenko, who in 1940 had barely managed—using more than one million Red Army troops—to defeat the 200,000-man army of Finland.

Stalin began by casually dropping a large piece of bad news: the Western Allies were not going to relieve German pressure on Russia by opening a second front in Europe in 1942. In fact, he said, there was no reasonable expectation of large-scale landings in France until the spring of 1943.

Then, having deepened his generals' gloom, Stalin gave the floor to Shaposhnikov, who outlined plans for the Red Army to undertake major assaults at no fewer than seven points along the 1,500-mile-long front. At that point, Zhukov, who typically had strong opinions, spoke up. Arguing that the multiple offensives would stretch Soviet resources too thin to be effective anywhere, Zhukov urged that he be allowed to attack west of Moscow, while Russian forces elsewhere put up an active defense.

Stalin exploded: "We cannot remain on the defensive and sit on our hands until the Germans strike first! We must strike on a broad front and probe the enemy's intentions." The dictator called Zhukov's proposals "half-measures."

Yet when Stalin made the final decision, he was surprisingly willing to modify the overblown plans that Shaposhnikov had worked up. In the end, the Soviets would mount only three offensives—all of which, as it happened, would place them on direct collision courses with the assaults being planned by the Germans. According to Stalin's plan, the Soviets would attack to lift the siege of Leningrad in the north. To the south, Timoshenko would burst out of the Izyum salient, then drive northwest and recapture Kharkov, the fourth largest Soviet city and a prime strategic target. In the Crimea, the Germans would be thrown out and Sevastopol would be saved. However, based on the erroneous assumption that the main German attack would be directed toward Moscow, Stalin ordered the bulk of the Red Army reserve to be stacked up in a blocking position around Voronezh, south of the Moscow front.

Thus, the plans perfected during the *rasputitsa* would set the warring mastodons on marches in which millions of men would maneuver and fight and die. And yet, in classic irony, it would be at a modest industrial city on the Volga River, now 300 miles behind the battle front and immediately vital to nobody's blueprint for victory, that a gargantuan battle would be waged—a battle that Winston Churchill grandly called "the hinge of fate." The place was Stalingrad, and its rubbled streets were to become the crucible of the Russo-German war.

At last, the armies began to stir. At Leningrad, neither side had succeeded in its designs for the isolated city, and the stalemate continued. The Germans could not crack the stubborn Soviet defenses and the Russians could not break through to relieve the defenders. Their efforts to advance were all but doomed by the plight of the Second Shock Army, which had been cut off in the nearby Volkhov swamps. To extricate the army, Lieut. General Andrei Vlasov, a brilliant leader and popular hero, was flown in to assume command. But even Vlasov could work no miracles. In April, when the frozen swamps melted, his men and tanks were immobilized by mud. By June, the men were sick, starving, almost out of ammunition and under constant fire. Vlasov radioed for help repeatedly; headquarters invariably told him to attack. Finally, in late June, the trapped army made its last attempt to escape. It too failed, and only 32,000 Russians survived to surrender. All the rest lay dead or dying in the putrid swamp. The debacle cost the Red Army nearly 100,000 men.

In the Izyum sector, while Vlasov's army in the north still nursed a hope of surviving, more opposing armies were poised to spring at each other's throats. Marshal Timoshenko's units jumped first, launching a drive on May 12 that in five days took him to within 12 miles of Kharkov. In Berlin, a radio analyst viewed the situation with such concern that he prefaced a broadcast with the phrase, "Even if the Russians succeed in capturing Kharkov . . ."

But the Soviet commanders were equally concerned, and with better cause. They were way out on a limb; vanguard units had outrun their supply lines and, to make matters worse, German panzers were reported assembling on the southern flank. Among those who claimed to have scented trouble was Timoshenko's political commissar, a bouncy, bellicose man named Nikita S. Khrushchev. "We had broken through the enemy's front line of defense easily—too easily," Khrushchev recalled. "We seemed to have a clear road ahead, deep into enemy territory. This was unsettling. It meant we had stumbled into a trap."

It did indeed, and on May 18 the jaws began to close. Forces led by General Ewald von Kleist entered the Soviet corridor from the south. When the Russians scrambled to face that threat, the Sixth Army under Lieut. General Friedrich von Paulus attacked the northern Soviet flank.

To prevent Paulus and Kleist from linking up, the Soviet commanders threw everything they had into the battle: men, tanks, guns, mines, felled trees, and hundreds of dogs. Huge packs of dogs, most of them Alsatians and Doberman pinschers, had been trained to run beneath enemy vehicles. On their backs the dogs carried explosive charges with trigger-rods that detonated on contact and blew up everything in

By January 7, 1942, the Wehrmacht had conquered more than 500,000 square miles of the Soviet Union and confronted the Red Army along an immense front (red line) extending from the Barents Sea in the north to the Black Sea in the south. Moscow was still being threatened by German forces less than 100 miles to the west; Leningrad remained surrounded, and Sevastopol, in the Crimea, was under siege. Hitler had decided that his primary target would be the rich oil fields of the Caucasus. But, as the year began, neither side guessed that the great battle on which the war would hinge would be fought at Stalingrad, a modest industrial city on a bend of the Volga River 300 miles behind the present front lines.

the vicinity—including, of course, the dogs. German infantrymen soon learned to shoot every dog in sight, and the bomb-carrying canines did little damage.

It seemed that nothing the Soviets could throw against the Germans had much effect. On the afternoon of May 22, Kleist and Paulus joined hands at the Donets, trapping the Russians in a circle of steel.

In their crazed efforts to break out, the Soviet soldiers stampeded. Primed by vodka and shouting "Ura! Ura!" ("Hurrah! Hurrah!"), they fell against the German lines with fists, bayonets and clubbed rifles. To no avail. The Soviet command admitted to 5,000 men killed, 70,000 missing and 300 tanks destroyed. In fact, the losses were far higher, almost a quarter of a million men—and with the Izyum salient now his, Hitler could crowd it with troops and tanks for Operation *Blau.*

As for Stalin's Crimean offensive to relieve besieged Sevastopol, it was another recipe for disaster. Beefed up with five armored brigades, Soviet forces on the Kerch Peninsula attacked General Erich von Manstein's Eleventh Army in April and learned that it, too, had been reinforced—by the fresh 22nd Panzer Division, the newly arrived Rumanian 7th Corps and the whole of the 8th Air Corps, with 21 fighter groups and plenty of Stuka dive bombers. After three days, the Soviet assault was stopped dead.

Now Manstein could proceed with his own offensive, as assigned by the Führer. For some reason he had called the assault Operation *Bustard Hunt* and in spite of the formidable Soviet defenses, the game-bird name would turn out to be quite felicitous. The operation called for an eastward attack that would clear the Kerch Peninsula, allowing

Manstein to conclude his lengthy siege of Sevastopol without interference from an enemy to his rear. Once that was done, he would be free to take part in *Blau* operations in the Caucacus, just across the Black Sea from Sevastopol.

Manstein himself had found the key to the assault. On May 6, while visiting a forward observation post, he had peered through binoculars at a great, water-filled antitank ditch—16 feet deep, 11 yards wide—that ran from one side of the Kerch Peninsula to the other and barred the way to the town of Kerch. "That's where we've got to drive through," he told aides.

On the day of *Bustard Hunt*, conspicuously deployed decoy units led the Russians to believe that Manstein was attacking from his northern flank. Then, while the attention of the defenders was riveted in the wrong direction, German troops rode assault boats from the Black Sea right into the antitank ditch from the south.

The Russians were soon in rout. By May 17, more than 170,000 Soviet troops had been captured, plus 250 tanks and 1,100 artillery pieces. "There was something unforgettable about the tempestuous chase," wrote Manstein. "All the roads were littered with enemy vehicles, tanks and guns, and one kept passing long lines of prisoners."

The Black Sea fortress of Sevastopol came next. As he shifted his forces toward the city, Manstein knew from long experience that Operation *Sturgeon*—the final assault on Sevastopol—would be much more difficult than *Bustard Hunt.* The defenders had the Black Sea at their backs, along with the guns of the Russian fleet. Between the Germans attacking from the north and east were three heavily fortified

A MODERN-DAY IVAN THE TERRIBLE

In training, Soviet infantrymen edge across a log.

The Red Army possessed only one secret weapon: the Soviet infantryman. The Germans, lulled by the success of their early blitzkriegs, were not prepared for the tenacity and ferocity with which the "Ivans" fought at Moscow and all during the winter of 1941-1942. Indeed, as the War went on, many a Wehrmacht trooper found himself struggling with an almost superstitious fear of his counterpart.

"In the evenings," wrote one German, "we used to talk of the end. Some slit-eyed Mongol was waiting for each of us. Sometimes all that mattered was that our bodies should get back to the Reich, so that our children could visit the graves."

Certainly there was little in the appearance of the Red Army infantryman to inspire such terror. He wore a shapeless tunic belted over his trousers; his winter boots were more often made of felt than leather. He wore a forage cap in summer and one with ear flaps

in winter, and it was only later in the War that he enjoyed a steel helmet.

Ivan suffered for weeks on end without hot food, subsisting on cold cooked grain, salt fish and hardtack. When the field kitchens did catch up with him, they had little more to dispense than cabbage soup and tea.

But his peasant background made him at home on the land, he took easily to military training and, perhaps most importantly, he was possessed of a terrible determination to beat back the invaders. The Germans found him to be a master of entrenchment. "When the Russian has dug himself into his native soil he is a doubly dangerous opponent," said a German officer. He called the Soviet infantry "brave and endowed with a self-sacrificing devotion to duty." The ultimate compliment came from German Field Marshal Ewald von Kleist: "The men were first-rate fighters from the start. They became first-rate soldiers with experience."

lines. It was a battle, Berlin admitted, in which advances would be measured "not by miles but by yards."

During the winter Sevastopol had become a bedlam of death. Ceaseless German artillery barrages and bombing raids had sent the city's citizens into underground shelters and caves. There they set up factories that continued turning out arms and ammunitions for the defenders.

Now, the Germans brought up their heaviest artillery, and the awful bombardment began. For the next five days, a deadly rain of incendiary and explosive shells fell on the city. Soldiers and civilians died by the thousands. By June 7, Manstein decided that he had sufficiently softened Sevastopol's defenses to take the city by storm. A wave of seven German and two Rumanian divisions attacked the first line of defense: it was a zigzag, one to two miles deep, of trenches, tank obstacles and mines, and it took the Germans two days to break through.

With that preliminary success under their belts, the Germans faced the formidable, mile-deep second line, with a string of heavy fortifications concentrated north of the city, and a section to the south known as the Zapun Line. German gunners nicknamed the forts Stalin, Maxim Gorky I, Molotov, Volga, Cheka and Siberia.

Fort Stalin was captured on June 13 by Manstein's 22nd Infantry Division. Only four Russian prisoners were taken, and they surrendered only after their political commissar had killed himself. "This," wrote the 22nd Division historian, "was probably the toughest enemy we ever encountered."

To take Maxim Gorky I, whose guns controlled the Belbek Valley north of Sevastopol to the Black Sea, the Germans used Röchling "bombs"—one-ton shells that burrowed through rock and concrete before they detonated. Yet even

after two barrages of Röchlings had cracked open Gorky's gun emplacements, German sappers and infantrymen had to fight for every foot of the fort's labyrinthine passages before they secured it. Gorky fell on June 17.

With the capture by June 20 of all the remaining northern fortresses, Manstein held Sevastopol's entire second defense line—except for the southern Zapun fortifications. Manstein's plan was to outflank the heavily defended Zapun heights by breaking through at the line's northernmost point, the old Inkerman fortress. From an observation post, Manstein took stock of the situation. "To the right was the city of Sevastopol," he later recalled, "and straight ahead a wall of cliff honeycombed with enemy positions." Inside the cliff was an arms factory—and a haven for thousands of wounded and refugees.

On June 28, a German assault force crossed the Chernaya River east of Severnaya Bay and successfully assailed the Inkerman. Just as they were entering the fortress, Manstein recalled, "the whole cliff behind it shuddered under the impact of a tremendous detonation, and the 90-foot wall of rock fell over a length of 900 yards, burying thousands of people beneath it." Rather than surrender, the Russians had blown themselves up.

When the Inkerman heights and valley had been taken, German assault boats swept across Severnaya Bay under an umbrella of artillery and air support. On June 29 the Germans breached the Zapun line, took a cemetery for the British dead in the 1854-56 Crimean War, and silenced the Soviet artillery batteries stationed among the shattered marble monuments. Then, south of the Zapun line, they took "Windmill Hill," and the main road into Sevastopol.

On July 1, the Germans began bombarding the inner city.

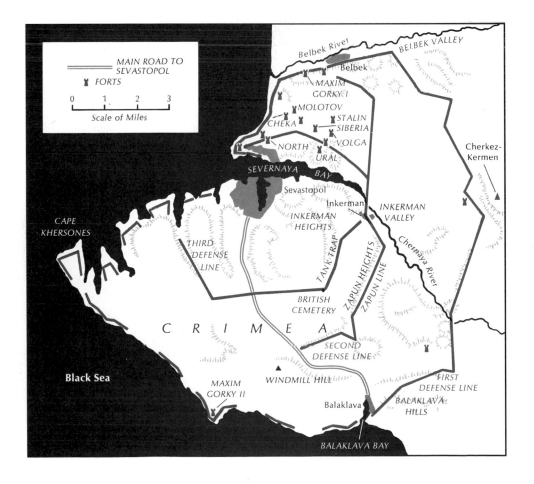

Sevastopol was protected from attacking German forces by three formidable lines of defense. The outermost line, some six to eight miles from the port, was a belt of strong points and minefields. Just to the rear, the second line was studded with machine gun nests and was anchored on steel-and-concrete fortifications that guarded the northern approaches to Sevastopol. The last defense line, ringing the outskirts of the town, featured a wide antitank ditch and numerous pillboxes.

187

The Russians were gradually forced back into a tight perimeter along Sevastopol harbor. Submarines evacuated top military leaders and as many of the wounded as they could carry. Those who remained were entrusted with a hopeless holding action. "We trust you to die here," one officer was told. "You will do this job and you will not get back alive."

The Russians continued to fight valiantly. "Whole masses of them rushed at our lines," recalled Manstein, "their arms linked to prevent anyone from hanging back." But the effort was useless. On July 3, the siege of Sevastopol ended, 247 days after it had begun. The Germans claimed 100,000 prisoners and "booty," said Manstein, "so vast that it could not immediately be calculated."

Afterward, Soviet propagandists portrayed Sevastopol as a heroic sacrifice—and so, in some ways, it was. Among other things, the struggle for the Crimea had occupied the German Eleventh Army for eight months when it could have been used more profitably on the war's main fronts.

Yet by no stretch of the Soviet imagination could the fall of Sevastopol, the failure to relieve Leningrad, and the fiasco that followed the breakout from the Izyum pocket be construed as hopeful signs for the summer, when the year's major German offensive would strike. Instead, Stalin's campaigns had only added enormously to the string of Red Army disasters. Uncounted thousands of Soviet troops had perished so far in 1942, and approximately 500,000 more had been taken prisoner. It was hardly surprising that Hitler

could contemplate the carnage and gloat: "Der Russe ist tot!" ("The Russian is dead!").

In fact, the Russian was far from dead. To be sure, 1942 would continue to see a stupefying succession of German triumphs and Soviet calamities. Yet in ways that few could have grasped, the conflict had already begun to change.

Even as the spring campaigns were scheduled to commence, Lieut. General Walter Warlimont, chief of the German high command's National Defense Section, had recognized the precarious nature of his country's situation. "Our war potential," he said, "is lower than in the spring of 1941." Warlimont backed his judgment with figures. Of the 162 German divisions on the Russian front in March, only 58 were deemed capable of conducting offensive operations in the near future. Furthermore, the heavy winter losses could not be replaced since Hitler had assigned all available reinforcements to other fronts. Altogether, the Army was short 625,000 troops.

In the matter of weaponry and equipment, Hitler had been so confident of a quick victory over Russia that he had ordered cutbacks for the Wehrmacht in favor of production of U-boats and planes for an attack against Great Britain. As one result, German forces began the springtime fighting in Russia with only 7,500 new trucks, personnel carriers and other vehicles to replace the 75,000 that had been lost during the winter campaign. Furthermore, to bolster Operation *Blau* in the south, armored divisions on the north and central fronts were required to give up all but 40 or 50 of their normal complement of 150 panzers.

The Luftwaffe was also far below its best fighting strength, with only about half its usual number of serviceable aircraft. Because of poor administration and obsolete methods of

A tremendous explosion destroys a Soviet arms factory and munitions dump at Sevastopol on June 28, 1942, as the German Eleventh Army begins its final assault on the port city. The ammunition, stored in a fortified cave 90 feet high, had been blown up by fanatic defenders to make sure it would not fall into enemy hands; the blast killed thousands of homeless or wounded civilians who had taken refuge in chambers underneath the cave.

General Erich von Manstein, seen here overseeing his great artillery offensive, was concerned about the enemy's "advantage of terrain and tenacity." As early as 1939, Manstein was regarded by fellow officers as the most promising staff officer among Germany's younger generals.

production, German factories had produced only 10,000 combat planes in 1941 and would produce only 4,000 more in 1942—not nearly enough to keep pace with losses. For this, Hitler could blame Reich Marshal Hermann Göring, who doubled as commander of the Luftwaffe and chief of its aircraft industry. The industry, said one high-ranking German, was "like its boss, fat and incompetent."

Despite such woes, however, the German fighting forces were still clearly superior to those of the Soviet Union. Yet even in the face of continued adversity, the Russians were gaining strength—thanks largely to a monumental migration.

During the German onslaughts of 1941, the Russians had lost about two thirds of their industrial facilities. The 1,500 factories that had survived were ordered—in the Soviet government's most important wartime edict—to pack up and move thousands of miles eastward, out of reach of German panzers and Luftwaffe bombers. The enormous undertaking was comparable to moving all the industries of Pittsburgh and Detroit to California, and it was supposed to be accomplished in six months. It almost was.

By Christmas of 1941, more than 1,300 large plants manufacturing tanks, planes, artillery and ammunition had been shipped eastward; 200 of them were sent to the Volga River region; 500 went to the Ural Mountains and the remainder were moved to Central Asia and Siberia.

With the plants went the workers, 210,000 from the Moscow area alone. All told, about 20 million went east—the greatest and swiftest mass migration in history. Their destinations were the burgeoning Ural cities of Magnitogorsk, Chelyabinsk and Sverdlovsk, and the mushrooming Siberian towns of Omsk and Tomsk, as well as Tashkent and Alma-Ata in Central Asia, as close to Peking as to Moscow.

For the workers, the journey was a nightmare. Since most passenger trains had been consigned to military traffic, the civilians traveled on freight cars, with as many as 50 people crammed into a boxcar too small to accommodate half that number comfortably. "At night it was so crowded," recalled one worker, "people took turns sleeping, often atop one another." Even the best facilities were primitive: perhaps a wood-burning stove in a corner of the car and a hole chopped in the floor for a latrine.

In winter, the journey killed. In cars without stoves, uncounted thousands froze to death or were crippled by frostbite. Even a stove was a mixed blessing; often it was not vented and travelers choked on the acrid wood smoke.

Not all the travel scenes were grim ones. Transiting soldiers often pulled aboard women who were waiting for civilian transport. The novelist Alexander Solzhenitsyn, who was a young army officer at the time, later recalled such a scene. "The only shy one of the girls," he wrote, "sat by the stove

A German gun crew swarms over a 24-inch Karl-type mortar, one of two such immense weapons that hurled 4,800-pound shells into Sevastopol's defenses.

like a little ruffled owl. In the heat, the other girls had long since thrown off their overcoats and quilted jackets and even their blouses. One girl, wearing only her red shift and flushed all over, was washing shirts for the lads."

The workers' destinations were singularly cheerless places. Magnitogorsk, just beyond the Urals, was typical. It sprawled across a barren steppe toward a 27-square-mile open-pit iron mine in the distant hills. The center of the city was its reason for being: vast, grimy steel mills with huge blast furnaces, open-hearth furnaces and satellite factories that turned the steel into artillery shells, heavy machinery and a dozen other finished products. The steel mills alone employed 45,000 people.

Peering through the murk of a Magnitogorsk mill, one Western journalist at first thought the male workers looked "like black dwarfs"; they were, he discovered, mostly boys, aged 14 to 16 and undersized from inadequate wartime diets. Laboring in filthy, hazardous conditions, the workers put in 10-, 12- and even 14-hour shifts, often outstripping their government-set production quotas.

The transported industrial system was everywhere as crude as at Magnitogorsk—but it worked. War production of all kinds had dropped sharply in 1941. But it began edging up early in 1942, and then it soared. By the end of the year, tank production exceeded 2,000 units a month, more than eight times the previous high rate in 1940.

Back in the German-occupied Russian areas whence the factories had fled, a growing number of civilians began forming small guerrilla bands with the Red Army men left behind. The German invaders claimed they had come to free the Russians from the chains of Bolshevik tyranny, and some citizens—especially those in the fiercely separatist Ukraine—had listened hopefully at first. But people of every ethnic background were quickly alienated by the Nazi orders for the ruthless exploitation of the land and its *Untermenschen*—subhuman inhabitants. Most of the food produced in the occupied territories was shipped to Germany. "The feeding of the civilian population," said a German overseer, "is a matter of utter indifference."

Still, it was in the great mass of the Soviet people who remained in their homes and went about their daily wartime business that lay the salvation of Mother Russia. "All for the front! All for victory!" was the ringing slogan, and those citizens lived it to the letter.

Children gathered medicinal herbs and scrap metal: in a single day, an official Soviet history reported, the youth of a Moscow district collected enough metal for 14,000 artillery shells. When necessary, factory workers labored around the clock, while farmers struggled to meet crop quotas with an inadequate supply of labor and equipment. Soldiers went off to war with bouquets of flowers from the womenfolk, and a patriotic female, young or old, offered her seat on the bus, train or trolley to a man on leave.

It was a time of stringent rationing, yet civilians sent food

Three orphaned children weep beside the ruins of their home after German troops swept through their village in the Caucasus Mountains in 1942. According to the Soviet government, the Wehrmacht ravaged more than 1,700 towns and 70,000 villages in its invasion of the U.S.S.R.

190

packages—as well as millions of sheepskin coats, felt boots and wool socks—to the troops. "We were poor," recalled a worker who donated some clothes, "but to the front—we gave what we had."

The Red Army never lacked manpower, but civilians of all ages and both sexes continually sought to volunteer. When one graybeard was refused because of his age, he protested: "If I'm too old to fight, I can drive a truck. I'll go with the soldiers, I'll help up ahead and they'll follow on foot." Soviet propagandists told the story, possibly apocryphal, of Ivan Boiko and his wife Aleksandra, who were determined to go to the front. But Ivan was a truck driver and Aleksandra a factory secretary, and they were told that they were too valuable to be released from their jobs. Undaunted, the couple saved enough money to donate a tank, then got permission from Stalin to enroll in tank school and, upon graduation, to drive their tank into battle.

The Kremlin was continually exhorting the population to greater and greater effort. But the people did not really need to be rallied, for as one citizen later put it, "The best time of our lives was the War because we all felt closer to our government than at any other time in our lives. It was not *they* who wanted this or that to be done, but *we* who wanted to do it. It was not *their* war, but *our* war. It was *our* country we were defending, *our* war effort."

On June 28, two mighty German forces—the Second Army and the Fourth Panzer Army—exploded out of the Kursk area, 90 miles north of Kharkov, and roared east toward Voronezh, about 100 miles away. The town, on the Don River at its junction with the smaller Voronezh River, was at the center of all north-south Russian rail, road and river communications between Moscow and the Black and Caspian seas. Two days later, with its crack 40th Panzer Corps clearing the way, a third army, the powerful Sixth, under General Friedrich von Paulus, kicked off from Kharkov and slashed northeast toward Voronezh.

These three armies—later designated Army Group B and commanded by Field Marshal Fedor von Bock—were assigned to trap the Soviet forces between the Oskol and Don rivers, then wheel down the Don, execute another pincers, seal off the Volga River city of Stalingrad, and surge into the Caucasus.

The plan looked perfect on paper. And during the first few days, it seemed to be working equally well in practice. However, the men of the Sixth Army began feeling uneasy—they were meeting virtually no resistance. Their edginess was explained by a German war correspondent: "The Russians, who up to this time had fought stubbornly over each kilometer, withdrew without firing a shot. It was quite disquieting to plunge into this vast area without finding a trace of the enemy." The troops grew even edgier when one of Paulus' panzer divisions, recently arrived from Paris, was greeted with an air-dropped leaflet. "Men of the 23rd Panzer

Supporting the Red Army, citizens in the Far Eastern town of Khabarovsk sort the scrap metal that they collected for munitions factories.

Maria Shirmanov, her son Andrei and Andrei's comrades sit upon the tank purchased with Shirmanov family savings as a gift to their country.

Division," read this chilling missive. "We welcome you to the Soviet Union. The gay Parisian life is over now. Your comrades will have told you what things are like here, but you will soon find out for yourselves."

The strange Soviet withdrawal that so bemused the Germans was by no means uncalculated. The Soviet front had been ordered by Stalin to fall back in an orderly fashion in the direction of Stalingrad. There the Red Army was to make its stand; if all went well, the Germans would batter themselves into exhaustion against the Volga bastion.

The Russians' precipitous retreat jeopardized the whole first phase of Operation *Blau*, by making it impossible to trap and destroy the enemy. And now Hitler muddied the plans even further. Realizing that Paulus was wasting time and fuel in his attempt to trap the Russians near Voronezh, Hitler flew into Field Marshal Bock's field headquarters on July 3. There, the Führer grandly informed Bock of a brand-new plan for Voronezh: "I no longer insist on the capture of the town. You are free, if you wish, to drive southward at once."

The discretionary instructions confused Bock, who at first thought he might bypass Voronezh. But then a number of his leading units hit the town on the run, and captured it on May 6 after some brisk fighting. At that moment, Hitler made perhaps the most disastrous decision in a career liberally sprinkled with bad decisions. Overconfident at the quick victories, the Führer abandoned his carefully worked-out plan to settle matters in the north before opening the campaign in the south. Instead, he now resolved to seal off Stalingrad with one arm and, simultaneously, with the other arm, to unlock the gateway to the Caucasus by capturing the city of Rostov.

Toward that end, Hitler unleashed Army Group A, which had been charged with the Caucasus and had been assembling to the south under Field Marshal List. The components dedicated to the assault were the 17th Army and the First Panzer Army. According to the plan, General Ewald von Kleist's First Panzer Army had been meant to serve initially as the southern prong in a pincers movement against Stalingrad. Only later was it to strike for the Caucasus. But now the impatient Führer sent Kleist roaring directly toward Rostov with the 17th advancing on his flank. To assist this great thrust, veteran Hermann Hoth's Fourth Panzer Army, which had been slated to stiffen the Sixth Army's march toward Stalingrad, was also ordered southward.

The diversion of forces required a diversion of supplies, and since the armies attacking Rostov had the greater distance to travel, they received the larger share of ammunition and fuel. Stalingrad, Kleist wrote later, could have been taken "without a fight at the end of July." But the Sixth Army, deprived of fuel by Hitler's decision, failed to meet that deadline. And with each day of delay, the Soviet defenses of Stalingrad were strengthened.

Meanwhile, the Soviet defenses deep in the Caucasus were also being improved while the Red Army defenders fought a delaying action at Rostov. "The defenders would not allow themselves to be taken alive," recalled a German colonel. "They fought to their last breath; and when they had been bypassed unnoticed, or wounded, they would still fire from behind cover until they were themselves killed." The conclusion, however, was foregone: Rostov fell on July 24 and the Germans crossed the Don. Ahead of them lay 300 miles of open steppe—and the Caucasus.

At the same time, on the Don to the north, a small Russian contingent was worriedly awaiting the approach of Paulus' Sixth Army at Kalach, where a key bridge offered the Germans the best place to cross on the way to Stalingrad. But the Sixth Army failed to arrive. The officer in command at Kalach signaled Marshal Timoshenko: "The Germans are not following up."

"What does it mean?" Timoshenko asked his chief of staff. "Have the Germans changed their plans?" In fact, the fuel tanks of Paulus' panzers had run dry and the Sixth Army had come to a dead stop about 150 miles short of Kalach. There it remained for 18 days.

Taking what he thought was advantage of the situation, Timoshenko committed his worst blunder thus far: into the great bend of the Don around Kalach he crammed elements of four armies and two tank armies. There they remained without room to maneuver until the Sixth Army, its fuel replenished, engulfed them in a pincers movement. More than 35,000 Red Army troops, along with about 270 tanks and armored vehicles, and 600 guns, were trapped within the Kalach pocket.

The way was now clear for the German advance on Stalingrad. Yet after that furious burst of energy, Paulus spent nearly two weeks tidying up. Only on August 21 did Sixth Army units at last cross the Don and gather for the lunge toward the Volga. The Red Army had been granted just enough time to regroup again and gird for its fight for survival at Stalingrad.

Stalingrad, a provincial center of 500,000 inhabitants, was the Soviet Union's third largest industrial city, producing more than a quarter of the Red Army's tanks and other mechanized vehicles. It was an inviting target. A narrow ribbon of a city, stretching more than 30 miles along the precipitous west bank of the Volga, it could be snipped with ease at almost any point—or so the Germans believed.

Remarkably, Stalingrad at first held only a place of tangential importance in the plans of the warring dictators.

"THE BEST TANK IN THE WORLD"

When the U.S.S.R. was invaded in June 1941, the Red Army had four times more tanks than the Wehrmacht, but most of them were light, obsolete or out of commission for some reason. Besides ordering an all-out maintenance drive, the government doubled and redoubled the production of modern tanks. Cutting corners as ordered, factories sent many tanks to the front roughly finished and unpainted.

Almost half of the new tanks in 1942 were 27-ton T-34s—improved versions of a model that had been introduced in 1940. As more and more T-34s rumbled into battle, panzer pioneer Heinz Guderian conceded that it was "the best tank in the world." The tank was faster and more maneuverable than its German opponents: its 76.2mm cannon and two machine guns gave it more firepower, and its thick, sloped armor gave it better protection against shells. Although the T-34 was outclassed by the German Panther in 1943, the Germans were unable to match the Soviets' output of improved T-34s.

A worker toils on a Ural T-34 assembly line. Some plants reportedly reduced the tank's production time from 110 hours to less than 40.

T-34/76C MEDIUM TANK
A radical advance in engineering, the T-34 had a top speed of 32 mph and, thanks to its light diesel engine and 120-gallon fuel tank, it was able to cover 150 miles without refueling. Wide tracks kept the tank going through mud and snow that stalled German panzers.

Factory workers consign a newly completed tank to a Soviet Army official. Sometimes, the Russians said, soldiers helped to finish a tank—and then drove it off to the front line.

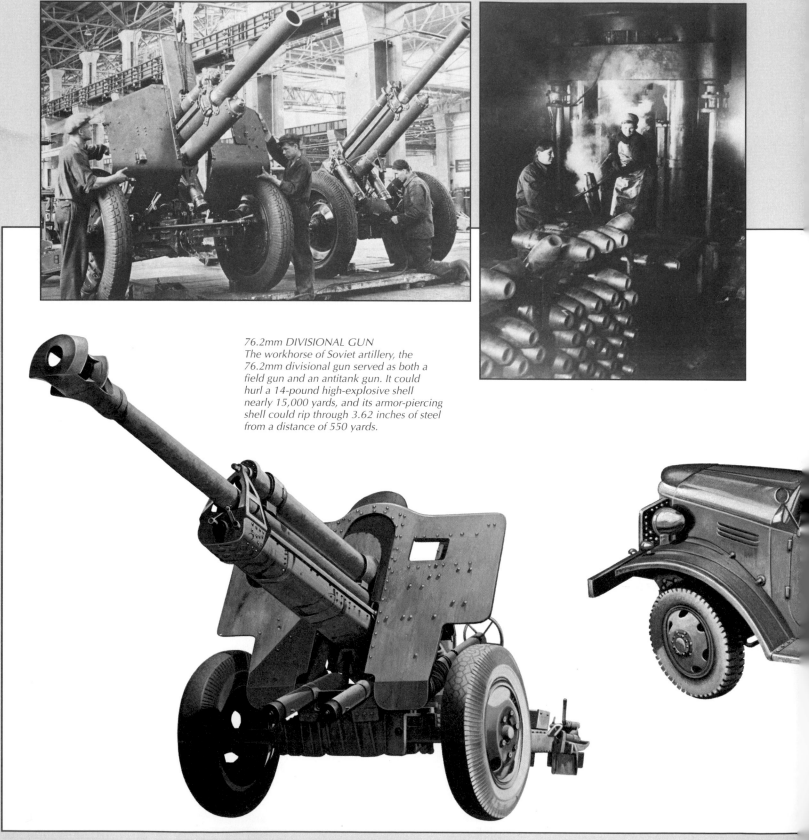

76.2mm DIVISIONAL GUN
The workhorse of Soviet artillery, the 76.2mm divisional gun served as both a field gun and an antitank gun. It could hurl a 14-pound high-explosive shell nearly 15,000 yards, and its armor-piercing shell could rip through 3.62 inches of steel from a distance of 550 yards.

ENORMOUS OFFERINGS TO STALIN'S "GOD OF WAR"

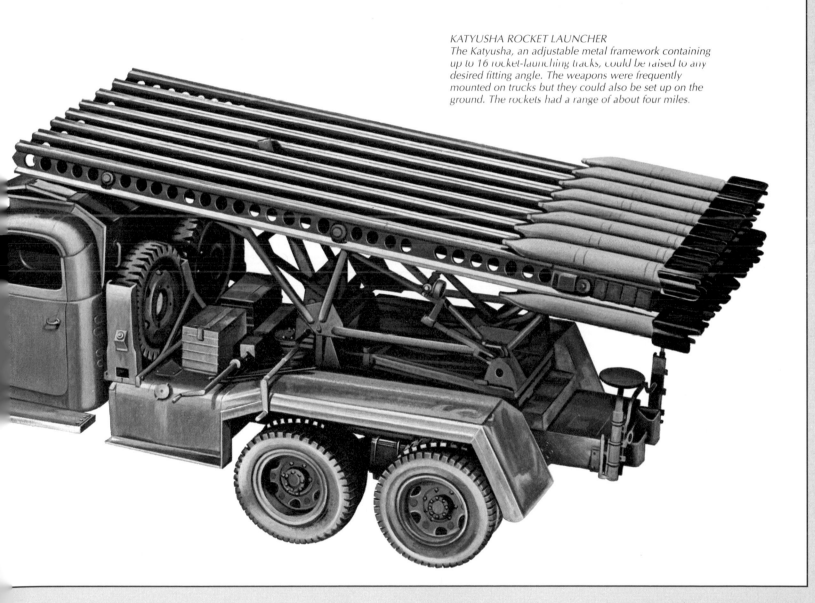

KATYUSHA ROCKET LAUNCHER
The Katyusha, an adjustable metal framework containing up to 16 rocket-launching tracks, could be raised to any desired fitting angle. The weapons were frequently mounted on trucks but they could also be set up on the ground. The rockets had a range of about four miles.

Josef Stalin called artillery the "god of war," and he saw to it that his ground forces had more field guns than the German Army. The Soviet artillery pieces were also more appropriate to the terrain. Formidable weapons such as the 76.2mm divisional gun were light enough to be hauled by horses through mud or snow that bogged down the heavier German artillery.

One of the Soviets' most successful artillery weapons was the simple, inexpensive "Katyusha," the first effective multiple-rocket launcher. When the Katyusha was introduced to combat in 1941, the rockets' screaming launches so terrified German invaders that some men fled the battlefield.

197

Hitler had viewed it as secondary to his thrust into the Caucasus, while Stalin had been so certain the enemy would strike elsewhere that he held his reserves far to the north.

Stalin, however, had nourished a special affection for the city ever since the Russian civil war, when its name was Tsaritsyn. As a visiting People's Commissar in 1918, he had assisted in Tsaritsyn's defense against White Army forces—a defense that, he forever after insisted, was the turning point of the Bolshevik Revolution. By 1925, he was powerful enough to honor the city by naming it after himself. Now he had no intention of letting his namesake fall into Adolf Hitler's hands. As soon as the direction of the German advance became clear, he issued a grim directive to Stalingrad's defenders: "Not one step backward. The Volga has now only one bank."

As for Hitler, once he had set his mind on seizing Stalingrad, the city became an obsession. "You may rest assured," he boasted to the German people, "that nobody will ever drive us out of Stalingrad."

Thus, the struggle for Stalingrad would become a titanic contest of wills that exacted a colossal toll. More than one million soldiers and civilians—men, women and children—would die at the lowest level of the human condition. The Germans called it *Rattenkrieg*—the War of the Rats.

So baleful a future was far from the minds of the soldiers in 16th Panzer Division, led by Lieut. General Hans Hube, that August in 1942. They, like the rest of the Sixth Army, were confident of victory at Stalingrad. At dawn's first light on August 23, the tanks began to roll as the striking tip of the Sixth Army's 40-mile march from the Don to the Volga. Survivors of the outfit would long remember the wild beauty of that morning—the predawn gray pierced first by bolts of orange, violet and red light and then suffused with the unbroken ruddy brilliance of the sun. Behind the panzers, the main body of Paulus' Sixth Army lurched forward. But it soon lagged far behind, slowed down by fuel shortages and its own dawdling in the expectation of an easy victory.

Ahead of the panzers, the steppe bristled with Soviet forces—but only on maps. In fact, the Russian Sixty-second Army had been severely mauled while fighting west of the Don; now, most of its shattered units were fleeing in confusion toward what they supposed was the safety of Stalingrad. In the absence of significant opposition, Hube's tanks maintained a crackling pace. Early that afternoon, the leading panzer commander announced on his radio, in tour-guide fashion, "Over on the right, the skyline of Stalingrad."

Nearing Rynok, Stalingrad's northernmost suburb, the German tanks came under heavy artillery fire from their right. The tanks briskly turned to deal with it, knocking out

37 gun emplacements. Later, the Germans found the twisted corpses of the gunners strewn about the barriers. They were factory workers—and they were women.

That night, camped amid vineyards and chestnut trees on the Volga's west bank, men of the 16th Panzer Division witnessed a spectacular display of fireworks as Lieut. General Wolfram von Richthofen used every available plane of his 8th Air Corps in a terror raid against Stalingrad. More than half the bombs were incendiaries, and they threw up a wall of flames by whose light a newspaper could be read halfway back to the Don. Later, Richthofen contentedly wrote in his diary: "We simply paralyzed the Russians."

Next morning, Hube confidently launched his panzers south against a huge tractor factory—and was stopped cold by Soviet metal from a nearby hill. Overnight, the Soviets had established a defense line of militiamen, women and units of the Sixty-second Army. Brand-new T-34 tanks rolled straight into battle from the factory's assembly lines, many driven by the very workers who had made them.

For five days, with Soviet forces now closing in behind him and cutting his supply lines, Hube fought a brutal battle, sustaining heavy losses. By August 29, he was penned up along a three-mile stretch of the Volga. The division had received no supplies, no reinforcements. Looking for a way out, Hube said, "Our only chance is to break through to the west"—away from the Volga and Stalingrad. But Hitler was inflexible. "The 16th Panzer," he signaled, "will hold its position in all circumstances." Thus, Hube had to cling to the ground he held, and wait for the rest of his corps to break through the Soviet line between them.

Meanwhile, back from its detour to Rostov, Hoth's Fourth Panzer Army was moving toward Stalingrad from the south—and also having a hard time. On August 20, still 20 miles short, Hoth found himself confronted by some of the worst tank country he had ever seen: deep ravines guarding the approaches to a line of hills that commanded the bend

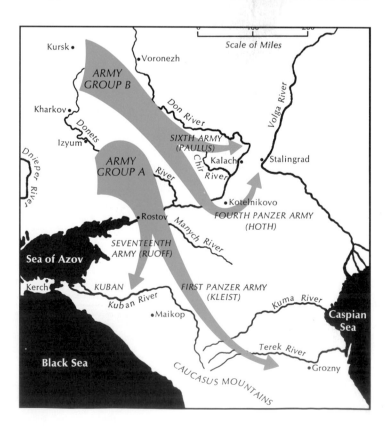

Operation Blau—Hitler's grandiose military scheme for the summer of 1942—envisioned an offensive on two major fronts. In the north, Army Group B—comprising General Paulus' Sixth Army and General Hoth's Fourth Panzer Army—was to clamp an iron vise on the city of Stalingrad from the north and south by advancing across the Don River and by curling up from the Kotelnikovo area. While the northern flank was being secured, Army Group A—General Kleist's First Panzer Army and General Richard Ruoff's Seventeenth Army—was to sweep southward and capture the critical Caucasus oil fields at Grozny and Maikop.

of the Volga. Again and again, Hoth drove for the hills and was thrown back by divisions of the Soviet Sixty-fourth Army. "We've got to tackle this thing differently," Hoth finally told his chief of staff. "We are merely bleeding ourselves white in front of those damned hills."

Masking his intentions with consummate skill by shifting infantry to the front, Hoth pulled out his tanks and swung them 30 miles to the south and west. Then, on August 29, he struck northward with devastating effect. Within two days, his troops and tanks had ripped through the inner ring of Stalingrad's fortifications and threatened to drive a wedge into the Soviet Sixty-second and Sixty-fourth armies.

Hoth's situation presented a glorious opportunity for the main body of Paulus' Sixth Army to swing south, join the Fourth Panzer Army, and cut off huge Soviet concentrations. Unfortunately, Paulus was not the man to seize the chance.

Friedrich von Paulus was a picture-book general, a handsome man who took pains to bathe and change his uniform twice a day. Although passionately interested in war games, he lacked decisiveness when it came to the crunch. Furthermore, before taking command of the Sixth Army on January 12, 1942, Paulus had never led a soldier into battle.

After his success at Kalach on the Don, Paulus' progress toward the Volga had been dilatory. Now, even after Hoth had urged his cooperation, he hesitated for three days, fretting about his northern flank. By the time he finally moved to join Hoth, the Russians had retreated into Stalingrad, where the Soviet commander had been given priceless time to prepare his defenses.

That commander was Lieut. General Andrei Ivanovich Yeremenko, a thickset combat veteran with shoulders like slabs of beef. Although still limping from a leg wound suffered on the central front, Yeremenko had been hurried by Stalin to Stalingrad. There he was joined by Nikita Khrushchev, who was still in Stalin's doghouse for his involvement in the Soviet disaster at Kharkov.

In their frantic efforts to organize Stalingrad's defenses, Yeremenko and Khrushchev were hampered by ruinous Luftwaffe bombing raids. On the day and night of August 23, for example, the municipal waterworks were smashed, the

Pravda building went down, switchboard operators in the telephone exchange were buried by rubble, and more than 100 downtown blocks were set afire. Next morning, mental patients who had walked out of their asylum during the confusion were found wandering naked along a dry streambed at the bottom of a ravine.

Such horrors sapped the morale of some Soviet defenders, including the raw troops of the 64th Infantry Division, who began deserting in droves. To remedy the situation, the division commander called out his men and made a speech extolling the virtues of patriotism and denouncing the evils of cowardice. Then, pistol drawn, he began walking down the front row of troops, counting as he went: "One, two, three, four . . ." He shot the tenth man through the head, then repeated the gruesome process five times. After that, there were no complaints about the division's courage.

Not only raw Soviet troops but ranking officers were unmanned by the terrors of Stalingrad. When Lieut. General Aleksandr I. Lopatin, commander of the Sixty-second Army, announced his intention to abandon Stalingrad, Yeremenko immediately relieved him of command. In his place, he named a previously obscure general named Vasily Ivanovich Chuikov—who, almost upon the instant of his accession, became the central figure of the battle of Stalingrad.

Chuikov was a peasant's son and, with his rumpled uniform, unkempt black hair and rows of gold-capped teeth, he looked the part. But he was also abrasive and ruthless, and it was no mere bombast when, upon accepting command of the Sixty-second Army on September 12, he told Yeremenko: "We shall hold the city or die there."

Dying seemed the more likely alternative. To hold a 20-mile line, Chuikov had an army of six divisions, most of them sadly depleted from previous fighting: a 10,000-man division, for example, now numbered 1,500, while a tank brigade, normally possessing 80 tanks, was down to a lone tank. In all, Chuikov could count 55,000 men.

Against those ravaged forces, the Germans could throw 100,000 men, 1,800 guns and 500 tanks, backed by more than 1,000 aircraft. Having acted too late to take advantage of Hoth's masterful maneuver, Paulus by now had drawn up

Cloaked against the chill, Commissar Nikita S. Khrushchev (second from right) surveys an October 1942 battle with the overall commander at Stalingrad, Lieut. General Andrei I. Yeremenko (second from left) and two aides. Khrushchev, the Communist Party's top representative at Stalingrad, held Yeremenko in high regard; at one gloomy point in the fighting, he talked Stalin out of firing the general.

the main body of his Sixth Army on a broad front along Stalingrad's western outskirts, whence he would simply try to butt his way through the city.

The attempt began on September 13, when three infantry divisions from the Sixth Army's main force attacked from the west and four of Hoth's divisions struck from the south. Paulus' primary objective was the central city, including the 330-foot Mamayev Hill, which would soon become known and feared as the "Iron Heights," and Railroad Station No. 1, whose occupants could control the nearby main ferry landing for traffic across the Volga.

As their forces broke into the city's center, many German soldiers were convinced that victory was in their grasp. Chuikov later recalled that Russian soldiers, concealed in houses, cellars and other firing points, "could watch the drunken Nazis jumping off the trucks, playing mouth organs, bellowing and dancing on the pavements."

The celebration was entirely premature. With good reason, Hitler had never before permitted his Wehrmacht to fight street by street, building by building. Now, panzers

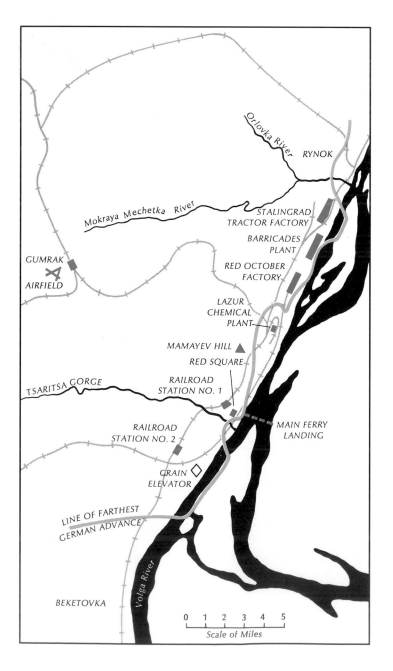

often found their way barred by the debris of the shattered city. In street fighting, superior German training and teamwork were canceled out by the raw strength and cunning of the Russian soldier.

Despite their difficulties, the Germans inched toward the ferry landing, which Chuikov had to hold at all costs. Reinforcements in the form of 10,000 men belonging to the elite 13th Guards Division were about to be ferried across from the east bank, and if they were prevented from landing, Stalingrad was doomed. At one point, the commander of a brigade that was blocking the approaches to the landing came to Chuikov with a despairing report. "If you don't hold out," Chuikov said, "I'll have you shot."

The ferry landing was saved, and the 13th Guards Division was transported across the Volga just in time to help stop Paulus' head-down frontal assault. But Stalingrad was still menaced on its southern flank by Hoth's Fourth Panzer Army, which had smashed through all but one of the Soviet defensive lines. The only unbroken line was anchored to a huge grain elevator, still filled with wheat; by September 16 it had become the focal point of a vicious fight.

A German soldier named Wilhelm Hoffmann described the struggle: "Our battalion, plus tanks, is attacking the elevator, from which smoke is pouring—the grain in it is burning, the Russians seem to have set light to it themselves. The battalion is suffering heavy losses. There are not more than 60 men left in each company."

Two days later, Hoffmann noted: "Fighting is going on inside the elevator. The Russians inside are condemned men. The battalion commander says, 'The commissars have ordered these men to die in the elevator.' If all the buildings of Stalingrad are defended like this, then none of our soldiers will get back to Germany."

September 20: "The battle for the elevator is still going on. The Russians are firing on all sides. We stay in our cellar; you can't go out in the street. Sergeant Major Nuschke was killed today running across a street. Poor fellow, he's got three children." Not until September 22 was Hoffmann able to write: "Russian resistance in the elevator has been broken. Our troops are advancing toward the Volga."

In fact, however, the Soviet defense of the elevator had blunted Hoth's drive, and the battle of Stalingrad slowly settled into an agonizing standoff, with scores of savage fights raging day after day and night after night throughout the smoldering city.

Though every building, every barricaded street corner and square, every hill and ravine in Stalingrad became a fortress, the main defenses were concentrated on Mamayev Hill in the center of the city and on the line of industrial plants and railroad stations running north and south of the hill. At the climax of the German advance, the Russians were driven from virtually all their strong points, and they clung precariously to only a few footholds on the banks of the Volga. The most critical of these was the main ferry landing, where supplies and reinforcements came from across the river; without this the defenders would have been doomed.

Soviet commanders expected their troops to turn every house into a fortress. Gutted buildings proved ideal (right and far right); there was nothing left to burn, so defenders could not be smoked out. The men seeded the surrounding area with mines and dug long trenches that enabled them to scurry safely from one building to the next. Each deadly little maze of strong points created a barrier that was all but indestructible. Protected by interlocking fields of fire, small bands of resolute Russians could—and did—hold off much larger German forces almost indefinitely.

By now, the generals on both sides showed physical signs of the unrelenting battle pressure. Paulus, whose forces had suffered losses of 7,700 dead and 31,000 wounded, developed an uncontrollable tic in his left eye. For his part, Chuikov was afflicted by an eczema that forced him to wear bandages to cover the open sores on his hands. The disorder was caused by nerves, and small wonder: so far, Stalingrad's defenders had suffered 80,000 casualties.

On October 2, Paulus launched a major attack on the factory district just south of where Hans Hube's 16th Panzer Division had bogged down in the first days of the fighting. "It was an uncanny, enervating battle," wrote a German major, "above and below ground, in the ruins, the cellars and the sewers. Tanks clambering over mountains of debris and scrap, crunching through chaotically destroyed workshops, firing at point-blank range into rubble-filled streets and narrow factory courtyards."

In that nightmare world, strange things happened to men's minds. A Russian named Aleksei Petrov was set off on a wild killing spree by the sight of a friend lying pinned to the ground with a bayonet through his stomach. Shrieking madly, Petrov rushed to a nearby house, followed by some comrades. Several Germans tried to surrender. Petrov killed them all with his submachine gun. In a hallway, he heard a German moaning, "Oh God, let me live." Petrov shot the man in the face. Racing from floor to floor, he killed three more Germans. Then, calm at last, he left the house.

In early November, Paulus possessed 90 per cent of an utterly desolated city. By day, wrote a German officer, Stalingrad was "an enormous cloud of burning, blinding smoke. And when night arrives, one of those scorching, bleeding nights, the dogs plunge into the Volga and swim desperately to gain the other bank. The nights of Stalingrad are a terror for them."

The ruins were the natural habitat of snipers, and each army had its recognized champions. For the Russians, Vasily Zaitsev was a onetime shepherd who had perfected his marksmanship hunting deer in the Ural foothills. In one ten-day period, he had killed no fewer than 40 Germans and his fame had spread into enemy lines. The Germans retaliated by flying to the scene SS Colonel Heinz Thorwald, head of their snipers' school near Berlin. Zaitsev soon heard talk of the deadly Thorwald, and he set down a tense account of their dual to the death.

"The arrival of the Nazi sniper set us a new task," wrote Zaitsev. "We had to find him, study his habits and methods, and patiently await the moment for one, and only one, well-aimed shot."

For two days, Zaitsev stalked his rival, trying to locate his precise whereabouts. On the third day, Zaitsev was accompanied in his search by a political instructor named Danilov. As the two lay hidden, peering intently through their telescopic sights, Danilov suddenly said: "There he is! I'll point him out to you!" Recalled Zaitsev: "He barely, literally for one second, but carelessly, raised himself above the parapet, but that was enough for the German to hit and wound him.

"For a long time I examined the enemy positions, but could not detect his hiding place. To the left was a tank, out of action, and on the right was a pillbox. Where was he? In the tank? No, an experienced sniper would not take up position there. In the pillbox, perhaps? Not there, either—the embrasure was closed. Between the tank and the pillbox, on a stretch of level ground, lay a sheet of iron and a small pile of broken bricks. It had been lying there a long time and we had grown accustomed to its being there. I put myself in the enemy's position and thought—where better for a sniper? One had only to make a firing slit under the sheet of metal, and then creep up to it during the night."

To test his theory, Zaitsev raised a small plank with a mitten attached to its end. A shot rang out and a bullet smashed

into the plank. "Now," wrote Zaitsev, "came the question of luring even a part of his head into my sights." Before that could be done, however, Zaitsev would have to change his own position, which had clearly been marked by the German. Zaitsev and a fellow sniper, Nikolai Kulikov, spent much of the night working their way to a new vantage point. By dawn they were ready.

"The sun rose," Zaitsev recalled. "We had decided to spend the morning waiting, as we might have been given away by the sun on our telescopic sights. After lunch our rifles were in the shade and the sun was shining directly on the German's position. At the edge of the sheet of metal something was glittering: an odd bit of glass—or telescopic sights? Kulikov carefully, as only the most experienced can do, began to raise his helmet. The German fired. For a fraction of a second Kulikov rose and screamed. The German believed he had finally got the Soviet sniper he had been hunting for four days, and half raised his head from beneath the sheet of metal. That was what I had been banking on.

"I took careful aim. The German's head fell back, and the telescopic sights of his rifle lay motionless, glistening in the sun until night fell." Russian sources credited Vasily Zaitsev with killing 242 Germans before the end of the battle of Stalingrad. Then he was blinded by a detonating land mine.

As the awful autumn of 1942 neared its end, General Chuikov began casting worried looks at the Volga: sludge ice was beginning to drift down the river and soon it would form into floes and stop river traffic—cutting him off from supplies and reinforcements. Against that contingency, he had stored 12 tons of chocolate for his troops—enough chocolate to feed each man in his army half a bar a day.

By mid-November, it had happened, and Chuikov sent an angry, despairing message across the ice-choked river: "No ships arrived at all. Deliveries of supplies have fallen through for three days running. Reinforcements have not been ferried across, and our units are feeling the acute shortage of ammunition and rations." When he got no relief, he began to suspect that something big was up. He was right about that: at dawn on November 19, Chuikov, Paulus, and all their weary men in the ruins, heard the boom of big guns far to the northwest. Those guns meant that a Russian counteroffensive had begun.

The big push, which mustered more men and matériel than any previous battle on the Eastern Front, had been in the works since the night of September 12. That evening, Stalin had met with General Zhukov, who had recently been assigned to devise an overall strategy for Stalingrad, and General Vasilevsky, the new Red Army Chief of Staff.

At one point during the session, Stalin moved away to study his maps, and the generals, in low, confidential tones, discussed the possibility of saving Stalingrad by means other than a last-man defense. They had not meant Stalin to hear, but the dictator had sharp ears.

"What other way out?" Stalin demanded. Taken aback, Zhukov and Vasilevsky had no ready answer.

"Look," said Stalin, "you better get back to General Staff and give some thought to what can be done at Stalingrad and how many reserves we will need to reinforce Stalingrad. We will meet again tomorrow evening at nine."

The two generals who had been handed this ticklish assignment were unlikely collaborators. Zhukov, who had clearly become the star of the Red Army, was beloved by few, feared by many, professionally respected by nearly all. Although he was coarse, profane and a bully, he was also a serious military scholar, steeped in the works of great commanders and theorists from Caesar to Clausewitz. Vasilevsky, on the other hand, was the son of a priest and, like Stalin, had once attended a theological seminary. Now, as Stalin's military adviser, he displayed the quiet patience of someone long accustomed to awaiting conversion.

Yet despite the differences in their personalities, Zhukov and Vasilevsky worked well together. When they appeared before Stalin at the appointed time on September 13, the dictator abruptly asked: "Well, what did you come up with? Who's making the report?" Replied Vasilevsky: "Either of us. We are of the same opinion."

What the generals presented was a plan that encompassed not merely the relief of tormented Stalingrad but a giant pincers movement that would ensnare the entire German Sixth Army. The scheme would require ruthlessness, which the Soviet leaders possessed in ample measure, and a delicacy of touch, which they had never before displayed.

The offensive would await freezing weather, to give the tanks firm footing, and also the planned November invasion of North Africa by Anglo-American forces, which would pin down German reserves. Meanwhile, Chuikov and his Stalingrad forces would serve as bait, luring more and more Germans into Paulus' assault on the city. To accomplish that purpose, Zhukov would stingily feed in just enough reinforcements to enable Chuikov to hold out. Meanwhile, Zhukov would gather up all other available Red Army units, deploying them on the Germans' northern and southern flanks, opposite the weak and overextended fronts of the German-allied Rumanian Third and Fourth armies. When the time came, the Soviet armies would smash through the Rumanians and swing toward a junction at Kalach on the Don, enclosing Paulus and his men in a fist of steel.

So secret was the plan that not even the beleaguered Chuikov was told of it. Refusing to permit written orders to

During a Luftwaffe bombing raid on Stalingrad, citizens and Red Army troops man an antiaircraft gun in the flaming central city. From late August of 1942 to February 1943, the Luftwaffe flew more than 100,000 sorties over Stalingrad and dropped about 100,000 tons of bombs. This fierce bombardment, together with almost as many tons of artillery and mortar shells, left scarcely a building standing in the city.

be drafted, Zhukov and Vasilevsky used verbal commands, issued in bits and pieces, to assemble in the staging areas a gigantic stockpile of men and matériel from all parts of the Soviet Union—more than one million men, 13,451 cannon, 900 tanks and 1,115 aircraft. Obviously, congregations of that size could not be completely concealed from the Germans, but when Paulus received reports of the buildup he merely issued a morale-boosting proclamation that advised his units, "It is unlikely that the Russians will fight with the same strength as last summer."

Hitler, on the other hand, was fretful about the Rumanians' ability to withstand attack, and on November 9 he allowed himself a rare expression of anxiety: "If only this front were held by German formations, I would not lose a moment's sleep over it. But this is different." Next day, he ordered the 22nd Panzer Division, which had been in reserve, to drive 150 miles north to support the Rumanians. Of the unit's 104 tanks, only 42 arrived in operational condition. In their reserve bivouac, the men had covered the tanks with straw against the cold; mice had nested in the straw and the rodents infested the tanks, nibbling away the rubber insulation of the wiring and causing short circuits.

On November 19, the Soviet onslaught was set into motion by a coded radio signal from Moscow: SEND A MESSENGER TO PICK UP FUR GLOVES. At daybreak, 3,500 guns began pounding the Rumanian positions. Then, at 8:50 a.m., the Russian forces attacked from a bridgehead at Serafimovich, on the west side of the Don about 75 miles north of Kalach. Hordes of infantrymen plodded through swirling snow, all but invisible in their white winter-combat garb. The Rumanians fought for several hours, but their formations dissolved when Soviet T-34 tanks broke through their lines and the cry went up: "Enemy tanks in the rear!" By nightfall, a 50-mile-wide gap had been ripped in the Rumanian lines.

Next morning, from a launching point south of Stalingrad, came an attack by two fresh Soviet armies under General Yeremenko. The Rumanians on his front fled in panic, and within a few hours Yeremenko took 10,000 prisoners. By darkness, his armies had broken through on a 30-mile front and were swinging northwest toward Kalach.

At that town, an implausible fluke opened the door for the Soviet forces. Near a crucial bridge across the Don was a German training school that had been using captured Russian tanks for gunnery demonstrations. German guards were accustomed to seeing these tanks lumber back and forth across the bridge. And so, on the morning of November 22, a German sergeant named Wiedemann casually waved on five tanks when they approached the span. Only when one of them got across and started firing did Wiedemann take a closer look. "Those damn tanks are Russian!" he cried—too late to save the bridge.

Next day, beneath green signal flares that reflected eerily on the snow, the Russians from the north and the south joined hands 30 miles below Kalach. The steel fingers around Paulus' Sixth Army had clamped shut.

Within the deadly ring, Paulus was fully aware of his predicament, and on that same day he pleaded for "the immediate withdrawal of all divisions from Stalingrad" as a preliminary to a breakout toward the southwest. The appeal

In this painting by aviation artist, R. G. Smith, a formation of Soviet Il-2 Shturmoviks sweeps down from a snowy sky to batter a German column

with bombs, rockets and 37mm cannon fire. Perhaps the most devastating of Soviet aircraft, these planes were known as "the Plague."

drew a reply in the form of a *Führerbefehl* (Führer's Decree), the highest and sternest of all German commands. "Present Volga front and present northern front to be held at all costs," Hitler ordered. "Supplies coming by air."

By air? The mere idea caused consternation among German commanders. The Luftwaffe's General Richthofen even placed a call to Göring's chief of staff. "You've got to stop it," he demanded. "In the filthy weather we have here, there's not a hope of supplying an army of 250,000 men from the air. It's stark-staring madness."

The sorry fact was that Hitler—his mind doubtless on the airlift at Demyansk the previous winter—had so far not even discussed the problem seriously. When, on November 24, he did broach the question, he found Göring willing and eager. "My Führer," Göring said grandly, "I announce that the Luftwaffe will supply the Sixth Army from the air."

Because of foul weather, a shortage of Luftwaffe transports and an awful administrative mess (at one point the suffering soldiers of the Sixth Army were supplied with millions of contraceptives), the airlift was a debacle from the start. By

December 9, when the Luftwaffe was bringing in an average of 84.4 tons a day—less than one fifth the minimal need—two Sixth Army soldiers had died of starvation.

Obviously, the Sixth Army would have to look beyond the Luftwaffe for its salvation, and help was already at hand in the person of Field Marshal Erich von Manstein, the silver-haired, hawk-nosed victor of Sevastopol. On November 20, Manstein had been named to command the newly created Army Group Don, comprising the Sixth Army, the Rumanian Third and Fourth armies, and Hermann Hoth's Fourth Panzer Army, which, although outside the Soviet encirclement, was still tending the wounds inflicted in its September attempts to roll up the Soviet flank.

Of the units now theoretically under Manstein's aegis, the Sixth Army was the largest and most powerful. But its nearly 250,000 miserable men—Hitler called them "the troops of Fortress Stalingrad"—were huddled within a hedgehog perimeter defending about 450 square miles of open steppe and most of Stalingrad, where they were still locked in battle with General Chuikov's Sixty-second Army.

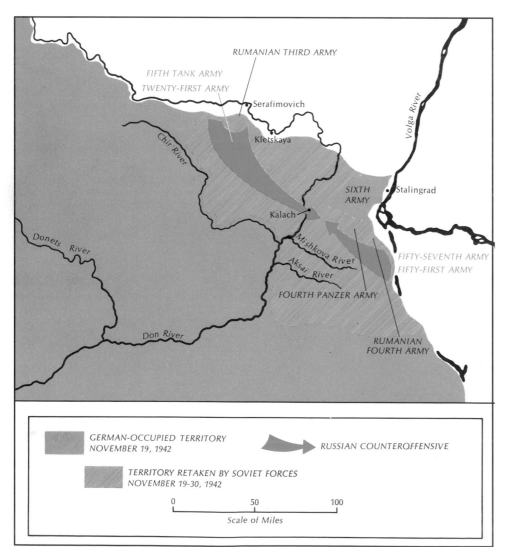

On November 19, 1942, a million Soviet troops launched a two-pronged assault (arrows) to break the siege of Stalingrad. Attacking from the northwest, the Fifth Tank and Twenty-first armies pushed past the Rumanian Third Army and closed in on Kalach. From the southeast, the Fifty-first and Fifty-seventh armies punched through the Rumanian Fourth Army and the German Fourth Panzer Army, and then linked up with the northern forces near Kalach. By November 30, the Russians had retaken almost 10,000 square miles (striped area) and had squeezed 250,000 Germans into a tiny pocket (gray) west of Stalingrad.

Promoted during and just after Stalingrad, Aleksandr Vasilevsky (top) and Georgy Zhukov appear in the bemedaled and braided uniforms of Marshal of the Soviet Union. The generals were elevated to the Red Army's highest rank in recognition of their roles as chief architects of the stunning Soviet victory.

Manstein set about planning to remedy that lamentable situation. In an operation called *Winter Storm*, he would launch one of Hoth's corps from Kotelnikovo, southwest of Stalingrad, toward Paulus' perimeter, 73 miles to the northeast. The panzer corps would try to blast open and hold a corridor through the Soviet lines around Paulus. If it succeeded, then Paulus, upon receiving the radio signal "*Donnerschlag*," or "Thunderclap," would attempt to join the relief column and fight his way to freedom.

Hoth's corps kicked off on December 12 and a week later fought its way across the Mishkova River, the last natural obstacle on the way to Paulus' pocket. The next morning, Hoth informed Manstein that he was ready to make his final lunge toward the Sixth Army. All that remained was for Paulus to undertake his part of the operation.

There lay the rub. Hitler had not yet given the Thunderclap command, and Friedrich von Paulus was no man to chance his Führer's wrath. On December 19, Paulus pronounced the rescue effort "a sheer impossibility"; his chief of staff noted that "withdrawal would be a catastrophic solution." Instead, Paulus demanded supplies to sustain him in Stalingrad until a proper relief could be mounted. Manstein ordered Hoth to withdraw from the Mishkova. As the movement started, one officer stood at attention in his tank turret and saluted to the north in final farewell to the doomed Sixth Army.

On a dismal Christmas, 1,280 Sixth Army soldiers died within the surrounded pocket, fewer from wounds than from frostbite, typhus, dysentery and starvation. There were a few pathetic attempts at celebration. At an outpost designated Hill 135, a tiny pine tree was hung with paper ornaments. To the east, in the besieged ruins of a Stalingrad factory, a single candle, lighted by some unknown mourner, shone over the graves of four German soldiers. From across the battlegrounds came solemn voices raised in "*Stille Nacht, heilige Nacht.*"

So far the Russians had been content to contain the Sixth Army within a ring nearly 40 miles deep in places. But that required seven Soviet armies, which Stalin needed elsewhere. The time had come to erase the Sixth Army.

On the morning of January 10, some 7,000 guns of the Red Army artillery began to boom. Above the barrage swarmed Soviet planes, and surging through deep snow came tides of tanks and infantry, red flags flapping. Huge holes were ripped in the German lines, but the Germans closed the gaps and doggedly fought a controlled retreat, maintaining a solid perimeter for nearly a week.

At his Gumrak airport headquarters just outside Stalingrad, Paulus was in a pitiable state; the tic that had afflicted one eye now extended from brow to jaw. When Gumrak fell, Paulus was driven back to the place where his troubles began: Stalingrad. He set up headquarters in a basement warehouse, sharing with his troops the onslaught of an old enemy, Chuikov, and a new one: hordes of lice that left angry red welts on the Germans' emaciated bodies.

Still, Hitler was pitiless, and as late as January 25 he ordered: "Surrender is forbidden. Sixth Army will hold their position to the last man and last round, and by their heroic endurance will make an unforgettable contribution toward the establishment of a defensive front and the salvation of the Western World." On January 30, the Führer made Paulus a field marshal for reasons both transparent and macabre: never in any war had a German field marshal surrendered his command, and Hitler hoped Paulus would measure up to that proud tradition either by dying in battle or by suicide.

Paulus did neither. At 5:45 a.m. on January 31, 1943, an operator at Sixth Army headquarters sent a final message: "The Russians stand at the door of our bunker. We are destroying our equipment. This station will no longer transmit." Minutes later, a young Soviet tank lieutenant named Fyodor Yelchenko entered Paulus' headquarters with two other soldiers. Paulus stepped from a side room to be taken captive. "Well," said Yelchenko, "that finishes it."

It did indeed. On February 3, three days after Paulus surrendered, a lone Luftwaffe Heinkel-111 flew low over the snow-covered steppe between the Volga and the Don, seeking Sixth Army survivors to whom it might drop supplies. Finally, the pilot looked to his radio operator, who shook his head and said: "Nothing anywhere."

Haggard and unshaven, German Sixth Army commander Friedrich von Paulus (left) and two of his staff officers are taken prisoner on January 31, 1943, at a Soviet headquarters in Stalingrad.

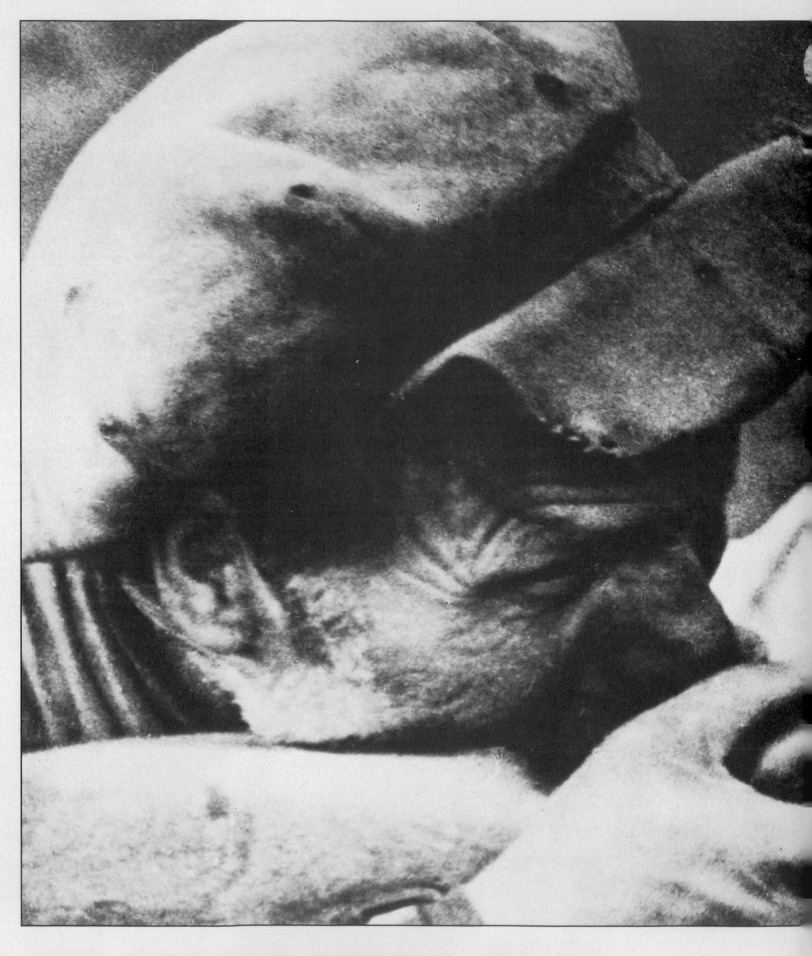

THE PEOPLE STRIKE BACK

Between raids, a partisan soldier practices shooting at a target with a Moisin 7.62mm, the basic Russian rifle, while a kerchiefed comrade-in-arms looks on.

THE IMPLACABLE WAR BEHIND ENEMY LINES

On July 3, 1941, Stalin addressed the nation by radio. "In the occupied regions," he said, "the enemy and all his accomplices must be hounded and annihilated at every step and all their measures frustrated." At the end of the year there were 30,000 partisans; by the following summer their number had grown to 150,000. Although some Russians joined partisan units to escape the German labor draft, most did so out of patriotism or hatred for the invaders. Said one partisan of the members of his detachment, "There was not one person in whose family blood had not been shed. These people were fired with one desire—to kill Germans."

The partisans were concentrated mainly in the forests of Belorussia, bordering on Poland and the Ukraine. From their hideouts, they made forays against the German rear lines, gathering intelligence of troop movements, blowing up bridges, derailing trains, slashing telephone and telegraph lines, pouncing upon small enemy forces and setting fire to supply depots. At first their activities were limited by the lack of arms and radios, and by hostile villagers who betrayed them. But their operations soon expanded, as the Soviet High Command started airlifting supplies to them and peasants began giving them food and concealing them from the invaders.

Lacking the strength to engage major units in battle, the partisans nevertheless proved to be an ever-present threat to the Wehrmacht. A warning had to be issued to the troops: "We Germans make the mistake of thinking that if neither offensive nor defensive operations are in progress then there is no war at all. But the war is going on . . . when we are cooking potatoes, when we lie down to sleep. A soldier must carry his weapons always and everywhere."

The majority of the pictures on these pages come from Russian sources. It is impossible to tell whether all are legitimate action shots: Russian war photographers were not above setting up photographs to suit their purposes, and it may be that a few of those that follow were staged. Most, however, are clearly authentic.

One of the most famous partisan leaders was Sidor A. Kovpak, a minor Soviet official who led a regiment near the Ukraine's northern border.

With their rifles stacked carefully off to one side, partisan soldiers receive their instructions prior to splitting up into demolition and reserve groups for a raid.

HIT-AND-RUN TACTICS TO CRIPPLE THE ENEMY

The partisans fought with whatever weapons they could lay hands on. They hurled handmade Molotov cocktails—bottles of gasoline—at trucks. They raided German convoys and supply dumps, and scavenged weapons from battlefields.

Stealth, deception and surprise were the hallmarks of their operations. Many an enemy motorcyclist was toppled by a wire strung across the road. German tanks hiding in the

A partisan adds a fuse to explosives fastened under the supports of a bridge. Blowing up bridges to disrupt supply lines was one of the partisans' most effective tactics.

A partisan uses a knife to hollow out a space underneath a railroad track, where a companion will place the packet of explosives that he is holding.

woods sometimes found themselves ringed with flames when partisans set fire to the trees. And on at least one occasion, as enemy vehicles rumbled over a bridge, it collapsed; the partisans had sawed through the beams below.

The Germans reserved a special hatred for the partisans, and for these bold comrades, capture was tantamount to death—or worse. Public hanging was merciful compared to the torture accorded some captives. The Germans broke their fingers, burned the soles of their feet, and even amputated women's breasts, before finishing off the maimed and dying with a bullet or noose.

Anyone suspected of aiding a partisan also stood in danger of a horrible death. In one pro-partisan town the Germans set every house on fire and kept every window and door under gunfire to guarantee the deaths of the inhabitants. Often the Germans accused innocent civilians of being partisans or partisan-supporters and ruthlessly slaughtered them. Hitler approved. "This partisan war has its advantages," he told his associates. "It gives us a chance to exterminate whoever opposes us."

A captured Belorussian is hanged in a village square while his executioners coldly look on. The Germans built gallows in each village for such public avengement.

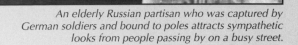

An elderly Russian partisan who was captured by German soldiers and bound to poles attracts sympathetic looks from people passing by on a busy street.

As the seasoned men in Britain's Western Desert Force already knew by September of 1940, and the soldiers in Italy's North African army were about to discover, war in the desert was a different kind of war. In fact, in many ways it was not unlike a war at sea.

"Each truck or tank was as individual as a destroyer, and each squadron of tanks or guns made great sweeps across the desert as a battle-squadron at sea will vanish over the horizon," wrote Australian writer Alan Moorehead, then a correspondent in Egypt for the London *Daily Express*. "When you made contact with the enemy you maneuvered about him for a place to strike much as two fleets will steam into position for action. There was no front line. Always the essential governing principle was that desert forces must be mobile. We hunted men, not land, as a warship will hunt another warship, and care nothing for the sea on which the action is fought."

From a military standpoint, the worst aspect of the Western Desert was its lack of distinctive landmarks. Traversing it, except along the coastal road, was like sailing an uncharted sea, navigable only by sun, stars and compass. Furthermore, something intangible was required to prevail in that parched and desolate land: a "desert sense" that told a man never to tamper with this formidable environment but

9

Since the start of World War II, Benito Mussolini had enviously watched his Axis partner, Adolf Hitler, achieve one conquest after another across Europe. Now, in the late summer of 1940, final victory in the West appeared within Hitler's grasp. Unless Mussolini put on his own show of military might while there was still time, he could hardly make a case for sharing the fruits of Axis victory. To be able to attend a peace conference "as a belligerent," he once told a member of his staff, "I need a few thousand dead." And so he sent his North African troops out from eastern Libya across the Western Desert to invade British-controlled Egypt.

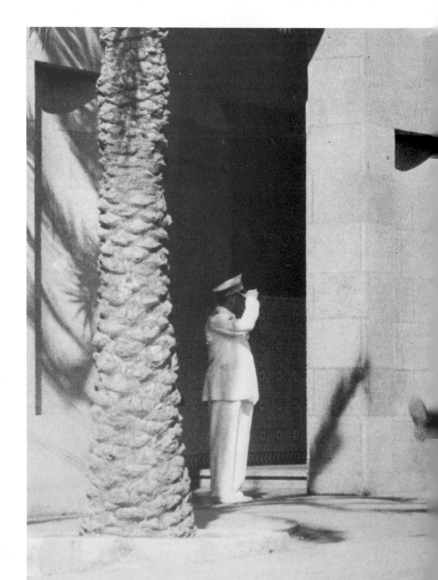

NORTH AFRICA AND ITALY

to use or circumvent it as best he could. "We did not try to make the desert livable," wrote Moorehead, "nor did we seek to subdue it. We found the life in the desert primitive and nomadic, and primitively and nomadically the army lived and went to war."

Italy's North African forces lacked this basic understanding, and much more—even the tangible requirements for waging war were often absent. Some of their weapons were better suited to a war-surplus dump. Their planes, tanks, antitank and antiaircraft guns, and even their mines were often outdated and in short supply. At places along the Egyptian border, Italian soldiers on night patrols were forced to steal British mines to sow their own minefields.

Much of this was apparent to Marshal Rodolfo Graziani, the army's commander. But in the late summer of 1940, when he had tried to convince his leader, Benito Mussolini, that Italy's forces were no match for the British, he failed utterly. It was Mussolini's ardent dream to wrest Egypt from Britain's control, and nothing would dissuade him. And so, at dawn on September 13, the men under Graziani's command set out from Fort Capuzzo, just inside Libya's border with Egypt, and headed east.

At first Graziani's pessimism seemed unfounded. Within a week his troops were 60 miles inside Egypt and digging in along a 50-mile front from the coast south to Sidi Barrani. Although the village was little more than a collection of mud huts, Rome Radio boosted the victory to improbable heights. "Thanks to the skill of Italian engineers," it announced, "the tramcars are again running in Sidi Barrani." The Italian troops, expecting a static war, settled in comfortably.

Meanwhile, the forward units of Britain's Western Desert Force, led by General Richard Nugent O'Connor, had fallen back 80 miles and dug in at Mersa Matruh. There, the British would bide their time until they were prepared to take the offensive. All that fall, General Sir Archibald Wavell, commander-in-chief of the British forces in the Middle East, resisted pressure from Prime Minister Churchill, who wanted to teach the Italians a lesson. A methodical man who detested politicians meddling in military matters, Wavell planned to counterattack only when he was good and ready.

During that period two events occurred elsewhere—events that would directly affect the North African campaign. Mussolini invaded Greece, compelling Britain to honor a 1939 pledge of aid when needed. The only source of such aid at that time was Britain's limited reservoir of strength in the Middle East. From then on, Wavell worked in a race against time, amid renewed Churchill demands for action to save Greece. The second event took

Trim and cocky, goose-stepping Italian Blackshirts pass a saluting Marshal Rodolfo Graziani in Benghazi on August 14, 1940, on their way to the Libyan front.

place a few days later: on November 11, British torpedo bombers swooped in on the naval base at Taranto in southern Italy. The attack left three battleships crippled, substantially reducing a major Italian threat to British supply lines and enabling the Royal Navy to step up its own harassment of Italian convoys.

By December, Wavell's preparations were complete. The Italians had left a 15-mile gap between two of the seven fortified camps shielding Sidi Barrani, and Wavell intended to punch through the gap, then wheel about and fall upon the Italians from the rear.

The British sweep to Sidi Barrani began on December 6, and achieved total surprise. By December 12, almost 40,000 Italians had been captured; the British had expected 3,000 at most. One tank commander radioed: "I am stopped in the middle of 200—no, 500—men with their hands up. For heaven's sake, send up the bloody infantry." A battalion commander estimated his prisoners as "five acres of officers, 200 acres of other ranks." Lines of Italians in dusty green uniforms choked the road to Mersa Matruh. There, astonished officers furnished the arrivals with wood and barbed wire and set them to building their own stockade.

In Cairo, Wavell realized that his "five-day raid" had acquired the momentum of a major campaign. The sweep continued for the next two months; moving into Libya, the British took Fort Capuzzo, Sidi Omar and other strong points near Bardia. Bardia itself fell on January 4, 1941, then Tobruk, followed by Derna a few weeks later.

On February 4, O'Connor sent his army racing across the interior wasteland to cut off the retreating Italians south of Benghazi. For 30 hours, striving to cover 150 miles, his men jounced in tanks and trucks over rocky, bone-jarring ground, blinded by sand squalls and vomiting from sheer fatigue. At midday on February 5 they met up with the Italian force, and for a day and a half a raging battle ensued. Time and again, the Italian tanks charged in a desperate attempt to break through; but with only one wireless set for every 30 tanks, coordinated action was impossible.

An endless stream of Italian captives reflecting the demoralization of defeat, marches toward a detention area after the fall of Bardia in early January 1941.

216

By February 6, with one British brigade down to 15 cruiser tanks, bluff counted as much as armor. When a noncom complained that his tank gun barrel was bent, his commander suggested that he stay put and simply look dangerous.

At first light on February 7, O'Connor received word that Graziani had abandoned his army and decamped to Tripoli, and that the force left behind was now surrendering. All through the day in the battlefield mess tent and at O'Connor's headquarters near Beda Fomm, there was a strange sense of anticlimax. Some men wondered whether the fighting was really over. And yet at the moment victory did seem complete.

Sipping a celebratory drink, O'Connor commented that not since 1911, when he had attended a resplendent international gathering in India, had he seen so many Italian generals in one place. In two months, the British had advanced 500 miles and taken 130,000 prisoners, 400 tanks and more than 1,000 guns. But they had defeated the Italians too quickly. Four months later, all of Hitler's resources would have been irrevocably committed to Operation *Barbarossa*, his attack on Russia, and other military ventures would have been out of the question. But now the Führer had the means to come to the rescue of his Italian allies.

It was a spectacle of twofold design: to awe Tripoli's Italian population, and to impress any British spies present. Across the city's main piazza rumbled a seemingly endless column of formidable 25-ton Panzer III and Panzer IV tanks, painted in the desert-camouflage shade of sand yellow. The tank commanders, wearing tropical uniforms much the same color as their vehicles, stood at attention in their turrets, as impassive as the death's-head badges adorning their lapels. Taking the salute on the reviewing stand was the man who had ordered this parade of armored power, a short and muscular German lieutenant general dedicated to the twin concepts of speed and surprise: Erwin Rommel, commander of the newly formed Afrika Korps.

As the continuous line of tanks clattered through the square and out a side street, a young lieutenant named Heinz-Werner Schmidt watched with growing amazement. After 15 minutes, he noticed a Panzer IV with a distinctive faulty track, and realized that he had seen it earlier in the procession. Schmidt chuckled; Rommel was running the tanks in circles to stretch a panzer regiment to the proportions of an armored corps.

The date was March 12, 1941. Rommel, who had arrived in North Africa only four weeks earlier, was already demonstrating his mastery of audacity and deception, qualities that were to play as great a part as armored power in the next phase of the desert war. As commander of the 7th Panzer Division in May 1940, Rommel had time and again outsmarted the British retreating across France. But now this fervent exponent of wide-open offense had been sent to North Africa with distinctly distasteful orders.

While Hitler meant to save his Axis partner, he did not yet have enough force to drive the British back to Egypt. For the time being, Rommel would limit his actions to defense.

Meanwhile, on March 4, the British had launched their own expedition to Greece. This move stripped their defenses in eastern Libya, and while Rommel waited for the British to resume their westward thrust, what remained of the British forces struggled to pull itself together.

When Rommel learned of the "momentary British weakness," he decided—against direct orders from the German High Command—to take the offensive. On March 24, the 5th Panzer Regiment attacked, and Rommel's tactic of deception was put to a test. Many of the tanks were incapable of firing a shot; they were Volkswagen-mounted dummies, now known as "the Cardboard Division." But their outlines in the swirling dust suggested a formidable fighting force. The British garrison of El Agheila swiftly withdrew, falling back on Mersa Brega.

Lieut. General Erwin Rommel arrived in Tripoli on February 12, 1941. Almost immediately he took control of the desert front from the sluggish Italian command. Soon to become known as the "Desert Fox," Rommel applied blitzkrieg tactics to warfare in the desert with a mastery that awed the British. His maxim was "Sturm, Swung, Wucht": attack, impetus, weight.

Seven days later Rommel struck at Mersa Brega, touching off a week-long, 500-mile British retreat. With gallows humor, some British Tommies later dubbed their hurried withdrawal "The Tobruk Derby" or "The Benghazi Handicap." More typical perhaps was the reaction of one soldier who described that week as seven of the most inglorious days in the British Army's history. Lacking instructions to stand and fight, the British fell back in disorder—packed ignominiously 30 to a truck, with nerves at breaking point and faces thick with yellow dust that made them look like jaundice victims.

On April 8, in a waterfront hotel in Tobruk, Wavell announced a crucial decision: Tobruk must be held. As long as the city was in British hands, Rommel could not go far. Tobruk was the only suitable port in Cyrenaica east of Benghazi and, without it, Rommel's supplies had to be carried across the desert from Benghazi or Tripoli.

No one was more acutely aware of this than Rommel. Intent on conquering Egypt and Suez, he realized that it was futile to continue his swing east along the coast as long as the British still posed a threat to his flank and rear. Tobruk was to become a thorn in his flesh, an obsession that was to dog him for seven months.

Tobruk was manned by 35,000 soldiers: Britons, Indians and Anzacs—as the Australians and New Zealanders were known. Their commander, Australian Major-General Leslie James Morshead, told his staff: "There'll be no Dunkirk here. If we have to get out we shall fight our way out. There is to be no surrender and no retreat."

On April 14, and again two days later, the Germans attacked. But the garrison stood firm, and Rommel, convinced that he would be able to take Tobruk once reinforcements arrived, decided to wait before trying again.

Since to move about during the day was to court snipers, the men guarding Tobruk's perimeter turned their routines upside down. They breakfasted at 9:30 p.m., ate lunch at midnight and dinner at dawn. Concealment was the key to life. Men entering camouflaged dugouts smoothed their footprints behind them with camel's-thorn switches so enemy bombers would not be led to the dugouts by the tracks. They had to fight not only the enemy, but also boredom, sunburn, lice, sand fleas and dysentery.

The Luftwaffe kept up its attacks on supply vessels. The harbor was soon littered with rusting wrecks of ships destroyed by German Stukas. It was with good reason that the Western Desert Lighter Flotilla, which brought food and

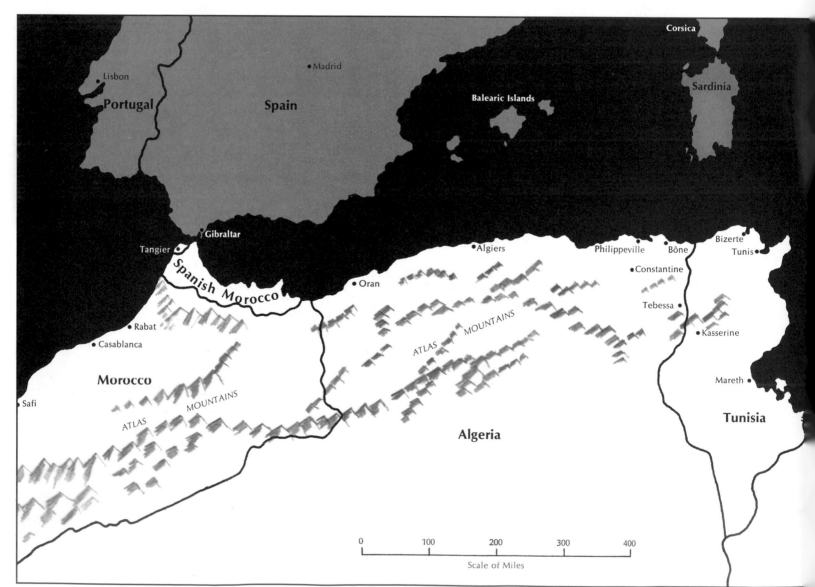

The North African theater stretched across more than 2,000 miles from El Alamein in Egypt to south of Casablanca in Morocco. The war seesawed in the Western

equipment from Alexandria, contended that its initials stood for "We Die Like Flies."

On the perimeter, a consciousness of hardships shared bred a wry camaraderie between besiegers and besieged. Both endured the same desert privations—water that "looked like coffee and tasted like sulphur," and canned meat that the Germans called "Mussolini's ass." Each night at 9:57, Britons and Germans alike tuned in to Radio Belgrade, to hear Lale Andersen sing—in German—the sensuous lament about the girl who waited underneath the lamplight by the barracks gate. "Lili Marlene" became the unofficial anthem of all the desert warriors.

On April 30, the lull ended with Rommel's most furious attack on Tobruk to date. Thrust and counterthrust went on for days, with dust storms making tactical control difficult for both sides. In the frenzied chaos, few could grasp with certainty who was winning—or for how long. It was Rommel's most costly engagement so far. Still, even though he had lost more than 1,000 men in battle, he remained undeterred. Then an ultimatum arrived from Berlin: Rommel was forbidden to attack Tobruk again. He must hold his position and conserve his forces.

Although bitter about having to take a defensive stance, Rommel was soon to prove as consummate a practitioner of the defense as of the offense. At Churchill's insistence, the British were about to launch their own Cyrenaican offensive—code-named Operation *Battleaxe*.

On June 15, in one of several costly and ultimately futile engagements with Rommel's army, the British came up against one of the great weapons of the war: the dual-purpose 88mm cannon. Originally designed as an antiaircraft gun, the high-velocity 88 proved equally effective against enemy armor; its 22-pound shells could punch a basketball-sized hole in a British tank a mile distant. Some 88 crews took to painting their gun barrels with white rings—like notches on a gunslinger's six-shooter—to tally the British tanks they had destroyed. "It could go through all our tanks like butter," one awed Englishman later attested.

Besides costing the British more tanks, aircraft and men than they could afford, *Battleaxe* lost the chance to restore morale with a desert victory. London was angry, and on June 22, Churchill replaced Wavell with Lieut. General Sir Claude Auchinleck.

Auchinleck immediately went to work reorganizing the newly named Eighth Army and planning the next British offensive—which he launched on November 18. But opera-

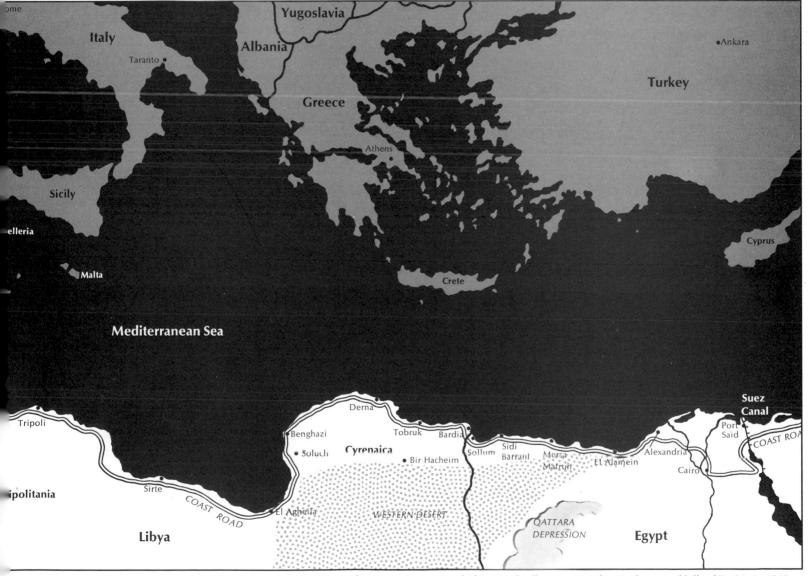

Desert until late 1942, and then focused upon the beaches and towns of Morocco and Algeria. It finally came to a close in the rugged hills of Tunisia in 1943.

tion *Crusader*, as this offensive was called, also began to unravel. Again and again, Rommel succeeded by brilliant maneuvers in achieving effective numerical advantage over the British with a smaller force. Then on November 24, Rommel brazenly led his troops straight through British lines, seeking to threaten the enemy rear and perhaps force the Eighth Army to withdraw.

The thrust was so unexpected and swift that British rear echelons panicked and fled. It was like a replay of Rommel's first offensive in Cyrenaica. Units of both sides raced east for six hours and found themselves hopelessly confused, many with no idea of where they were. At dusk a British military policeman directing traffic suddenly realized that the vehicles he was now controlling were German. Rommel himself, and another general, spent much of the night in the midst of British troops; they were in a big, enclosed command vehicle captured from the British, and its new German markings were not discernible in the dark.

Having penetrated 15 miles inside Egypt within two days, Rommel's panzers now outran their supply line and had to retire to Bardia to refuel. Taking advantage of Rommel's temporary supply problems, the British took the offensive again, sending a division to relieve Tobruk and, over the next month or so, forcing the Axis to retreat all the way back to El Agheila. By mid-January 1942, they had regained Cyrenaica—and driven Rommel back to the very point at which he had started in the desert in March 1941. "Here then we reached a moment of relief," wrote Churchill, "and indeed of rejoicing, about the Desert war."

The moment was all too brief. Events thousands of miles away were beginning to work in favor of the Axis forces in North Africa. Japan's attack on British territories in the Far East forced London to divert men and matériel earmarked for the desert war. Then, at the end of the year, two factors worsened British supply problems, while easing those of the Axis: the Luftwaffe intensified its bombing of the strategic

island of Malta, and German submarines arrived in the Mediterranean.

By the end of January, Rommel's forces were bolstered by the arrival of fresh equipment and supplies, and were now strong enough to launch an attack on the British forward positions. What had begun as a spoiling action to forestall any new British advance soon grew into a full-scale offensive. And once again Rommel was pushing the British to Gazala, halfway back across Cyrenaica.

There, Eighth Army commander, Major General Neil M. Ritchie, organized his forces along a 60-mile-long chain of defenses called the Gazala Line. From Gazala on the coast, the line ran a jagged course southeast for about 40 miles, then elbowed to the northeast for another 20 miles. The line was densely sown with mines, and defended by a series of strongholds, each a mile or two square, called "boxes" by the soldiers who manned them. There were six boxes in all. Some, like the one at Bir Hacheim, were known by Arabic place-names; others were dubbed "Knightsbridge" and "Commonwealth Keep" by British soldiers.

Each box was defended by artillery, mines, barbed wire, slit trenches and pillboxes, and each had stores enough to withstand a week-long siege. Between the boxes, British tanks roamed freely, with a double mandate: to intercept German armor and also to aid any box that might be attacked.

On May 27, after a winter lull, Rommel resumed his offensive. At first his forces met with success, but then they ran into an unwelcome surprise. The British were armed with a shipment of U.S. tanks—31-ton Grants equipped with 75mm guns that could pierce the German armor. Rommel lost a third of his tanks and was stopped outside a box 10 miles behind the Gazala Line. Now was the time for Ritchie to attack Rommel.

But Ritchie was not ready. For two days he deliberated, while Rommel regrouped, and on June 1 German panzers smashed through the Gazala Line. Then, after a particularly

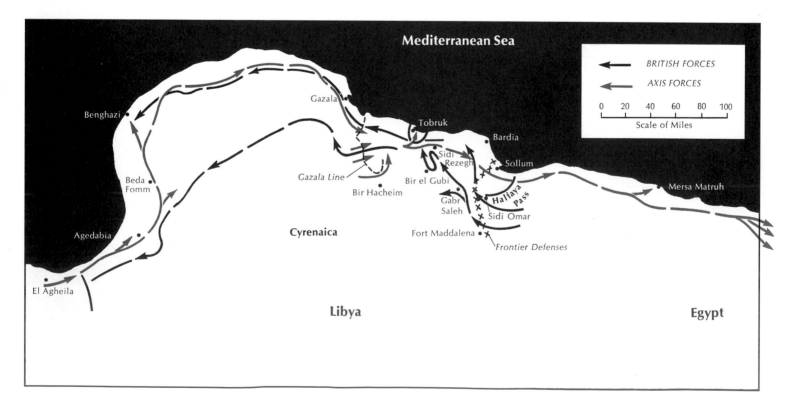

grueling week-long battle against the Free French holed up in the Bir Hacheim box, Rommel took on the remaining boxes, and knocked them out one by one.

Now Rommel turned to Tobruk, which he had promised himself since the beginning of the offensive. "To every man of us," he wrote later, "Tobruk was a symbol of British resistance, and we were now going to finish with it for good."

In the calamitous days of early June, the troops at Tobruk made some frantic last-minute efforts to reinforce their defenses. But even as they did so, they did not know whether they should make plans to hold the fort at all costs or to evacuate it. No word came from Ritchie to guide them.

On June 20, the Afrika Korps and the XX Italian Corps attacked, with the crucial assistance of the Luftwaffe. As soon as a path was cleared through the mines, infantry swarmed in, engaging the British in hand-to-hand combat. Then the tanks rolled. At 9:40 the next morning Tobruk surrendered. In scarcely 24 hours, Rommel had finally won his rich prize. Smiling broadly, he told a group of captured British officers, "Gentlemen, you have fought like lions and been led by donkeys." The next day he learned that Hitler had made him a field marshal. Later, he told his wife, Lu: "I would much rather he had given me one more division."

The fall of Tobruk was a heavy blow to the Allies. Churchill later called it a "shattering and grievous loss." Auchinleck had to shoulder the blame for the Eighth Army's failure and for Ritchie's command in particular. In August therefore, two new figures arrived on the desert stage. General Sir Harold L.R. Alexander would replace Auchinleck. A veteran of Dunkirk, Alexander had been the last commander off the beach. And, replacing Ritchie as commander of the Eighth Army, was Lieut. General Bernard Law Montgomery—eager, prickly, ruthless and unconventional. The two new leaders met over tea at Shepheard's Hotel in Cairo. Alexander issued only one order: "Go down to the desert and defeat Rommel."

Montgomery, "Monty" to his men, quickly instilled a new mood of confidence. To all ranks he issued a blunt ultimatum: "From now on the Eighth Army will not yield a yard of ground to the enemy. Troops will fight and die where they stand." Although a stern disciplinarian, Montgomery scored resoundingly with the lower ranks. Their job was to kill Germans, he told them, "Even the padres, one per weekday and two on Sundays."

Sixty miles from Alexandria, El Alamein stood on a neck of land, between the Mediterranean and the hills that formed the lip of the impassable Qattara Depression. The Axis forces were dug in only a few thousand yards from British lines in a position—the so-called Alamein Line—that could not be outflanked. If the British were to overrun it, they would have to do so by a massed frontal attack.

From August to October, British reinforcements streamed to El Alamein: 41,000 men, 800 guns and more than 1,000 tanks, including 300 of the new 36-ton Shermans whose 75mm guns could outshoot most Axis tanks.

Montgomery planned to strike in the north, at the Alamein line's most heavily defended sector. To ensure complete surprise, an elaborate bit of fakery was contrived. Monty would dupe Axis air reconnaissance into believing the British intended to attack in the south. Taking a page from Rommel's own book, Monty had dummy regiments of heavy artillery constructed from timber and canvas and manned by dummy gunners. Dummy soldiers even squatted on dummy latrines. A dummy water pipeline of empty gasoline cans ran 20 miles south to an area dotted with stacks of dummy supplies. Everything suggested that no attack would come until the pipeline was finished. To the north, almost 2,000 tons of gasoline were concealed in 100 trenches. Food supplies were draped with camouflage nets.

Montgomery enjoyed a 2-to-1 superiority over Rommel in almost every respect: troops, medium tanks, antitank guns and artillery. He was also better supplied. Moreover, Rommel himself was out of action; he had fallen ill and was

In Britain's Crusader offensive of November 1941, the Eighth Army (black arrows) relieved the siege of Tobruk and dogged Rommel across Cyrenaica to El Agheila. When the Axis forces (red arrows) rebounded in January 1942, the Eighth Army retreated to a chain of fortifications known as the Gazala Line. In June, Rommel crushed these fortifications, captured Tobruk and drove the British across Egypt to El Alamein.

Sporting the black beret that became his trademark, Lieut. General Bernard L. Montgomery nonchalantly leans against an American-made Grant tank as a shell explodes behind him in 1942. Monty—as his men liked to call him—commanded not only the respect of his men in the field but the adoration of millions at home.

forced to quit the front to undergo treatment in Austria. In his place was General Georg Stumme, a veteran of the Russian campaigns who was afflicted by acute high blood pressure.

By October 23, the Eighth Army was ready. A skilled stage manager, Montgomery had overlooked few details. To the rear, 2,000 military policemen, in white gloves and red caps, stood by to shepherd the tanks to their objectives and to direct the forward movement of water carts that would sprinkle the sand and hold down the dust. Sappers assembled 500 long-handled mine detectors, 88,000 lamps to mark the minefield gaps for the advancing armor and 120 miles of marker tape to delineate cleared paths.

Five miles away across the minefields, Stumme had no idea of the battle at hand. Montgomery's ruse had worked.

At 9:40 p.m., all along the British line the order was given: "Troop, fire!" Nine hundred guns spoke with an ear-splitting, earth-shaking roar. The barrage, unequalled since World War I, poured a storm of fire onto the Axis positions. Acres of mines went skyward, spewing geysers of rocky sand and jagged lengths of barbed wire; blockhouses crumbled and dugouts caved in; soldiers died.

Few men were more confused than Stumme. Within seconds of the start of the barrage, Stumme's communications were torn to ribbons and he was totally cut off. Early next morning he set off for the battlefront in a staff car. Jouncing through shell bursts, he was suddenly stricken by a coronary, collapsed, and died. The Axis forces were temporarily leaderless—and the battle was only a few hours old.

Montgomery's infantry had started soon after the barrage began, moving up as they had been taught, three yards apart, a steady 50 yards a minute. One man who watched them would never forget it —"line upon line of steel-helmeted figures, with rifles at the high port, bayonets catching in the moonlight, gave us the thumbs-up sign."

The sappers faced a nightmare task. Although thousands of mines had been exploded by the barrage, it was impossible to clear all of the 500,000 sown by the enemy. Instead, the sappers tried to clear lanes up to 24 feet wide to allow the tanks to advance two abreast. Despite these heroic efforts, booby traps and mines took a gruesome toll. Then a shortage of mine detectors slowed the advance. Could the mines be lifted fast enough for the armor to achieve its goal—a salient 10 miles wide, five miles deep—by dawn?

The answer was all too obvious. Struggling through the minefields, the British were pinned down by enemy fire, for most of the Axis positions remained intact. At dawn, in the north, British tanks unable to move forward were jammed behind the infantry, motors running, radiators boiling. One man likened it to "a badly organized car park at an immense race meeting held in a dust bowl."

For all the fighting spirit of his troops, Montgomery had demanded too much of them. But he still refused to call off the attack. He reasoned with clinical logic that tanks, 900 of which were still operational, were expendable. And so they were. A regiment of Staffordshire Yeomanry came under the blowtorch fire of 88mm guns. A witness, Major John Larkin, watched 27 tanks go up in sheets of flame, one by one, "just as if someone had lit the candles on a birthday cake." The Staffordshires' commanding officer broke down and wept.

On October 25, a still-recuperating Rommel flew back to North Africa, only to be told that ammunition was dangerously low and that barely enough gasoline remained for three days' all-out fighting. It had boiled down to a struggle of attrition that the Germans could not hope to win. "Rivers of blood were poured out over miserable strips of land which in normal times, not even the poorest Arab would have bothered his head over," Rommel later said.

By the third day at El Alamein, most of Montgomery's forces were still short of the objectives he had expected them to reach in eight hours. However, dramatic gains had been made in the north by the 9th Australian Division. Determined to exploit the advantage, Monty began assembling a huge assault force to seize the Coast Road and cut off Rommel's supplies.

Tough Australian infantry troops, with their bayonets fixed for hand-to-hand combat, sneak over the smoke-filled battlefield to storm an Axis strong point.

Rommel reacted to the Australian gains by moving the 21st Panzer Division to the northernmost sector of his line. It was an irrevocable decision: the gasoline shortage would not allow him to move the panzers south again if necessary.

When Montgomery learned that Rommel was shifting his elite troops, he switched his own main effort about five miles farther south. He would make the big push where the German and Italian defenses abutted. In the early hours of November 2 the fire from 360 guns hit the Axis minefields; the cold, blue desert night seemed to split apart. The barrage was so dense and so accurate, that one officer later remarked that his men "could have leaned on it."

The infantry reached its objectives by 5:30 a.m. When the tanks passed through the infantry, however, they met a screen of antitank gunfire. Tank after tank was hit and burst into flame. Still, some broke through to the gun pits, crushing German gunners under their treads. Some defenders turned and ran; others stood and fought and died.

The battle raged through most of the day. By evening Rommel was down to 31 tanks. His panzer army had been decisively defeated and he began to withdraw. He did halt his army briefly, when word came from Hitler to stand fast; but Rommel quickly resumed the withdrawal, as he put it, "to save what still can be saved." He had already lost an estimated 32,000 men, more than 1,000 guns and at least 450 tanks. A day later, Hitler authorized the withdrawal.

Although many British commanders were bitter over the cost of battle—in 12 days, 13,500 men killed, missing or wounded—Montgomery was elated. He told war correspondents, "It was a fine battle. Complete and absolute victory."

As Rommel retreated westward past Mersa Matruh and Sidi Barrani, Halfaya Pass and Tobruk, through Benghazi and on to Tripoli, a new hammer blow was in the making: Operation *Torch*. It would begin with an amphibious operation on a scale never before attempted. More than 107,000 troops—three fourths of them American, the rest British—were to land from the sea and capture Casablanca in Morocco, Oran and Algiers in Algeria, then speed eastward into Tunisia to seize Tunis and Bizerte, the major ports closest to Axis bases in southern Europe.

The sheer magnitude of the operation, commanded by General Dwight D. Eisenhower, was daunting. But it got off to a good start. Astonishingly, more than 500 American and British ships had traveled over the Atlantic unmolested by submarines. Not until noon on November 7, less than 13 hours before the first landing, did the Germans conclude that a massive movement was under way.

At Algiers, there was some French resistance, but it lasted less than 20 hours. At Oran, however, memories of Britain's 1940 devastation of French warships at nearby Mers el Kebir were still fresh. It took a concerted attack by American armor and infantry to force the city to capitulate, shortly after noon on November 10.

The following day, only minutes before an air and naval bombardment of Casablanca was to begin, the Americans received word that Admiral Jean-Louis-Xavier François Darlan, commander in chief of all Vichy forces, had ordered a cease fire. In retaliation, German and Italian divisions swarmed into unoccupied France, taking full control.

Buoyed by the success of the landings, the *Torch* forces confidently expected to make the 450-mile dash from Algiers to Tunis and Bizerte in two weeks. And for a time it looked as though they might make it. But on November 26, American armor met German armor for the first time in World War II—at a place called Chouigui. There the Americans learned an important lesson: their M3 light tanks, so efficient and responsive in field maneuvers, were no match for the brutal panzers; American 37mm cannon shells simply bounced off the 50mm armor of a Panzer IV.

Inadequate armor was not the only obstacle. By mid-December, with Allied troops stretched thin, their supply situation tenuous and air cover faltering against relentless swarms of Luftwaffe planes, two other obstacles were becoming readily apparent: the weather and the terrain. Together they made it all but impossible for Allied armor to push on. And so, with great reluctance, Eisenhower postponed the campaign until the spring. The Allies had lost the race for Tunis.

During the winter lull, the front solidified along a 200-mile mountain backbone called the Eastern Dorsal, parallel to Tunisia's eastern seacoast and 60 miles inland. In the north were the British, in the center the French XIX Corps. Below them, defending the passes at the southern end of the mountain range, was the U.S. II Corps.

On the plain between the mountains and the sea, there were now two Axis armies, the Fifth Panzer Army under Colonel General Jürgen von Arnim and Panzer Army Africa

A line of British Crusader tanks rush into the desert to hound Rommel's defeated Axis army from El Alamein westward across Egypt and Libya. On October 23, 1942, Rommel's Panzer Army Africa was taken by surprise. By November 4, the Desert Fox faced complete annihilation, and ordered a complete withdrawal.

under Rommel. The Desert Fox had arrived in Tunisia in January after a 1,400-mile retreat across North Africa with the Eighth Army on his heels. His professed aim was to instill in the Americans "an inferiority complex of no mean order."

Rommel's confidence was by no means unfounded. In fact General Eisenhower himself, after inspecting the American sector near Sidi Bou Zid, feared that the U.S. II Corps was ill-prepared to deal with an Axis onslaught. Most of the troops had never tasted combat. Among the inexperienced officers he found an alarming complacency, and their commander, instead of maintaining a strong, mobile reserve, had scattered his units piecemeal along the front. As Eisenhower finished his inspection and left the area, he resolved to issue new dispositions of II Corps defenses.

It was too late. Two hours later, Arnim attacked Sidi Bou Zid. Outgeneraled and outfought, the Americans lost two battalions each of armor, artillery and infantry, and hastily retreated across the waist of Tunisia until they reached a range of mountains known as the Western Dorsal. Here the weary men of the II Corps turned to confront their pursuers. This time an unyielding defense was crucial: one of the corridors through the mountains, Kasserine Pass, was a gateway to Algeria and the town of Tebessa—a vital Allied communications and supply base.

Afrika Korps panzers tried to storm through the pass on February 19, but were halted by artillery, antitank and small-arms fire. Then at dusk, patrols worked up into the heights, overran outposts, and descended to take the American defenders by surprise. By midnight the Kasserine defenses were close to disintegration and the next day the Axis forces broke through.

The way seemed clear for a devastating drive deep into Allied territory, but Rommel suddenly halted the advance as caution overcame confidence. He had been astounded by the abundance of captured U.S. supplies and equipment, the profusion of spare parts. His own forces were down to one day's ammunition and six days' food; his vehicles had gasoline for only 120 miles.

Rommel's radical change of heart surprised his superior, Field Marshal Albert Kesselring. "Nothing of his usual passionate will to command could be felt," Kesselring sadly observed later. In fact, Rommel was sunk in a pit of depression and suffering from jaundice and desert sores. On February 23 he pulled his troops back through the Kasserine Pass so discreetly that it was 24 hours before the Allies fully realized that he was gone.

Now the front shifted east again, back to the Eastern Dorsal, as Rommel and his men marched to meet his old enemy, the Eighth Army. On March 6, near Mareth, Rommel launched an attack to delay Montgomery's advance. Warned

American infantrymen come ashore near the Algerian port of Oran on November 8, 1942, in Operation Torch, a massive bid by the Allies to end the desert war.

by air reconnaissance, the British camouflaged a line of anti-tank guns across his path. British gunners held their fire until the panzers were close, then loosed a holocaust of armor-piercing shells, costing Rommel 52 panzers.

On that ignominious note, Rommel ended his career in Africa. He flew home to try to persuade Hitler to abandon North Africa and thereby save his soldiers from annihilation. Hitler refused, and forbade Rommel to return to Tunisia. "Africa will be held," the Führer snapped, "and you must go on sick leave." Colonel General von Arnim took charge of Army Group Africa, a new command that included both his and Rommel's armies.

The departure of Rommel coincided with the arrival of flamboyant U.S. Major General George S. Patton Jr. as commander of II Corps. With showmanship, bravado and iron-fisted discipline, Patton quickly galvanized his men into an effective fighting force. Increasing the odds in his favor, he received some tanks that were a match for some Panzer IVs, new Shermans with high-velocity 75mm guns. And in mid-March, for the first time, Patton's troops took on a panzer division and decisively defeated it.

Even so, General Alexander remained dubious of American capabilities and cast Patton's II Corps in a supporting role for the final battle of the campaign. The Germans had now retreated into a ragged, 130-mile arc stretching from west of Bizerte, on the north coast, to Enfidaville, below the Cape Bon peninsula. Allied strategy was to crush the enemy between the jaws of a great vise, Montgomery's Eighth Army inexorably driving from the south, while the Americans and British pressed the attack from the west. Patton's II Corps would participate in the initial thrust, but then would gradually be squeezed out while the British on both jaws of the vise closed in for the kill.

Patton and his deputy, Major General Omar Bradley, were outraged. Bradley flew to Algiers to protest to Eisenhower, suggesting that the U.S. II Corps be moved into position where it could go after Bizerte. Eisenhower quietly ordered Alexander to revise his plans.

On May 6, after the heaviest Allied air attack of the North African war, II Corps' infantry overcame the last Axis stronghold before Bizerte, and launched an attack aimed at the Bizerte-Tunis road. The urgency was shared by the British who began a dash for Tunis. "The rapier was to be thrust into the heart," Alexander said later.

It was less a rapier than an inundation. The dam had collapsed, and Allied forces flooded toward Bizerte and Tunis. Hundreds of tanks sped for the two ports, grinding cactus hedges to pulp and scattering goats that wandered across their route. Down the Tunis road, swerving among the vehicles, came Alexander driving his own jeep, his hands tight on the wheel, his face white with dust.

The Americans reached Bizerte on the afternoon of May 7; the British arrived in Tunis less than an hour later. On May 11, the last seven tanks of the 10th Panzer Division ran out

Lieut. General George S. Patton watches American tanks advance at El Guettar in this picture taken by LIFE's Eliot Elisofon, whom Patton called "Hellzapoppin."

as "the most capable officer on this front and the driving power behind Kesselring," Vietinghoff had only the 16th Panzer immediately available at Salerno, yet other divisions could be brought in when needed. The 16th, the sole fully equipped armored division in southern Italy, had 17,000 men, more than 100 tanks and ample artillery.

The initial Allied assault on Salerno began in the early hours of September 9, with the British X Corps responsible for the northern sector of the beachhead, while the American VI Corps went ashore to the south. The U.S. landing was spearheaded by the 36th Division, under the command of Major General Fred L. Walker. Because he expected minor opposition and saw no point in killing civilians, Walker had not requested a softening-up bombardment. That was a mistake. As the Germans opened up, the first wave of Americans scrambled for cover behind dunes and patches of scrub. Crawling through barbed wire, they worked their way past enemy tanks and machine guns, while behind them their wrecked boats and equipment floated among geysers from exploding shells.

Assault teams trying to get inland were pinned down by enemy fire. Boat schedules were disrupted, and some troops waited in vain for supporting weapons. Then at 7 a.m., while the troops were still scattered and disorganized along the beaches, the 36th Division was hit by its first large-scale tank attack—15 or more Panzer IVs moving back and forth, pouring fire into the regimental line strung across flat terrain. The battle raged past noon before the main tank assault was brought to a standstill. The 36th sorted itself out, got as far as four miles inland and seized its initial objectives.

A foothold had been gained, but there was virtually no communication with the British X Corps in the northern sector. There, following a 15-minute barrage by the Royal Navy, British troops had landed against only light opposition. But then the Germans reacted. In some parts of the beachhead, British assault forces beat off numerous tank and infantry counterattacks. Around the vital Montecorvino airfield, fighting went on inconclusively all day; at nightfall the field became a no-man's-land. Still, in the end, the British were able to establish a shaky hold on the town of Salerno and seize a beachhead. But they had been so heavily engaged that they had not been able to reach out toward the Americans on their right, and they, too, were concerned about the gap.

On the other side of the lines, General Vietinghoff saw no reason to be discouraged, in spite of the Allies' initial success. With only one division, he had managed to contain the landing within a small area and now, with reinforcements, he might be able to throw them back into the sea. He almost succeeded. Overnight the reinforcements made their presence felt on the British sector of the beachhead, while the Luftwaffe struck at Allied shipping in the Gulf of Salerno.

A crisis soon developed on the beachhead as the tempo of the fighting increased. On September 13, a German counterattack overran the 2nd Battalion of the U.S. 143rd Infantry Regiment and destroyed it as a fighting unit. With scarcely a pause the attack swept on. Between the German spearhead and the water stood but a handful of American infantrymen and two United States field artillery battalions, their 105mm guns protected by a line of improvised infantry—clerks, cooks, drivers and mechanics. On the roads nearby, Clark later said, officers were "stopping trucks, jeeps and everything else that came along. Every soldier was given a gun and put in the line." The artillery men, stripped to the waist and sweating in the September heat, slammed shell after shell into their pieces. Soon the guns were firing eight rounds per minute per gun, a rate perhaps unsurpassed by any artillery in World War II.

The enemy wavered, fell back and at sunset retreated. The American gunners had fired 4,000 rounds of ammunition on the narrow front, stopping the most serious threat against the beachhead.

Despite the repulse of the enemy, Clark was concerned that the awaited linkup with the Eighth Army would be too late. As for General Montgomery, "He was coming up, well, I won't say 'leisurely' but it sure wasn't as fast as I had hoped," said Clark. "I kept getting these messages from Monty: 'Hold on—we're coming up' and then, later, 'Hold on—we've joined hands.' I remember sending one message back where I said, 'If we've joined hands, I haven't felt a thing yet.'" Although the mere presence of Montgomery's Eighth Army moving up from the south had an effect on the

The Allied forces that invaded Sicily on July 10, 1943, sailed from Great Britain and ports along the Mediterranean from Oran to Beirut. The British Eighth Army landed with four divisions on the southeastern corner of the island, while the American Seventh Army hit the southern coast with three divisions. After the Allies landed, the Germans counterattacked the Americans at Gela, then began a gradual withdrawal to the island's northeastern corner, taking full advantage of natural avenues of retreat through the mountains. Along the eastern coast, the Germans concentrated their forces to block the narrow corridor running from Catania to Messina. To the west, they wheeled back in the direction of Messina and made their last big stand at the Etna Line while ferrying their forces across the strait to the mainland of Italy.

Americans advance toward the stronghold of Troina as the campaign in Sicily approaches its climax.

Germans, he did not make an effective connection with the beachhead troops until most of the fighting was over.

On September 18, after nine days of fighting, the Germans pulled away from the beachhead. Their withdrawal was part of a plan to fall back to the northern Apennines, making the Allies pay in sweat and blood for every mile gained. However, the successful conclusion of the first large-scale opposed landing on the European continent now meant that the Allies were in Italy—and Europe—to stay.

Once the beachhead at Salerno was secured, the drive for Naples began. The objectives of the Italian campaign were still limited: the U.S. Fifth Army would secure the port of Naples and advance as far north as the natural barrier of the Volturno River. Meanwhile, the British Eighth Army would capture the airfields around Foggia, near the east coast.

On October 1, advance units of the Fifth Army entered Naples—where German demolition teams had worked with Teutonic thoroughness. By far the worst damage was to the port. The harbor was now clogged with the wrecks of more than 130 ships. Oceangoing liners, tankers, destroyers, floating cranes, tugs, trawlers and lighters had been scuttled helter-skelter, and on top of them the Germans had piled locomotives, trucks, oxygen bottles, ammunition and mines—smothering all under a thick scum of oil.

The U.S. engineers immediately set to work rehabilitating the city—clearing the streets, repairing the sewers and the aqueduct, and putting together an ingenious electric-power system that linked a trolley substation and the generators of three Italian submarines. In the port, a salvage team used British heavy-lift crane ships, American tugs, divers, welders, mechanics and bomb-disposal experts. In just four days the first Liberty ship was able to enter the harbor to unload.

Meanwhile, Montgomery's Eighth Army on the east coast captured the airfield complex at Foggia and pressed on another 40 miles to the Biferno River. Now, from Foggia, heavy bombers could attack southern Germany, Austria and the Balkans—particularly the vital oil fields and refineries situated in Rumania.

Encouraged, Eisenhower decided at the end of September to raise the stakes of the Italian campaign by capturing Rome. Hitler, for his part, instructed Kesselring to make a stand south of the Eternal City.

In early October the Fifth Army, en route to Rome, set out to cross the Volturno in the first of many bitterly contested Italian river crossings. The Americans of the VI Corps faced the drearily familiar problems of steep hills and narrow winding roads, punctuated by easily demolished bridges and culverts. In the British X Corps sector the terrain was flat but open, offering little cover. Both corps had to cope with the Volturno itself—in flood after weeks of rain.

Bridgeheads were won at heavy cost, but by October 19 the Allies had control of the Volturno Line. "I hope I never see a mountain again as long as I live," Major General John P. Lucas, commander of the U.S. VI Corps, confided to his diary as the Allies slugged and slogged their way through the mountains north of the Volturno.

The German defenses beyond the Volturno, generally referred to as the Winter Line, were actually three different lines: the Barbara Line, the Bernhard Line and the one that Kesselring was determined not to yield, the Gustav Line. This line was anchored on a superb natural fortress, Monte Cassino, then ran across Italy to the Adriatic northwest of the Sangro River.

If the Allies could break into the wide valley of the Liri River—the gateway to Rome—they could dash 80 miles northwest to the city. But to reach the Liri Valley they first would have to overcome the Barbara Line, run the gauntlet of the Mignano Gap and then break through the main fortifications at Cassino.

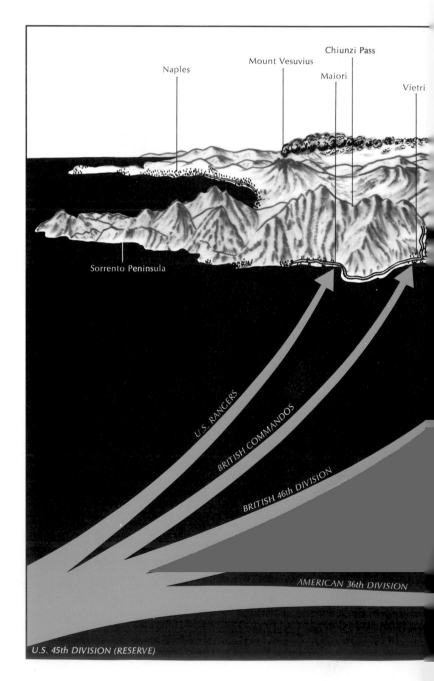

The crescent-shaped Salerno beachhead stretched from the rugged Sorrento Peninsula in the north to the town of Salerno, then south nearly 30 miles through Paestum to Agropoli. When the Allies came ashore at five different points, they found themselves hemmed in by mountains that rose more than 4,000 feet in the north and from 1,500 to 4,000 feet in the center and south. The British 56th Division was separated from the U.S. 36th Division by the Sele River and a treacherous sandbar at its mouth. With the roads leading northward from the beachhead easily defended by the Germans, the Allies faced a tough drive toward their primary objective—the city of Naples, which appears to be closer in this foreshortened drawing than the actual distance of 30 to 40 miles.

The Fifth Army took more than two weeks to push past the Barbara Line and advance 15 to 20 miles from the Volturno along a 40-mile front. Then, in early November, came their first futile effort to get through the Mignano Gap, a winding six-mile passage between steep mountains. On November 15, his troops on the verge of exhaustion, General Clark called a halt for rest and refit.

For some time now, Allied planners had been considering the problem of getting to Rome by some means easier than mountain climbing. It was General Eisenhower's belief that an amphibious end run around the enemy's lines would force the Germans to abandon their defensive positions south of Rome. If nothing else, the Germans had to be prevented from moving divisions from the Italian front to Russia or Normandy. This they would be able to do if they were allowed to build more formidable fortifications. And so a plan was born for a two-division landing on January 22 at Anzio, 35 miles south of Rome.

Before the landing, however, the Fifth Army was to launch a strong attack in the south with a threefold goal: to tie down the enemy; to draw German reinforcements from the Rome area, so that they would be unavailable to counterattack at Anzio; and to break into the Liri Valley and dash north to link up with the landing force.

By an extraordinary effort that cost many casualties, the Allies made it to the entrance of the Liri Valley by the middle of January 1944. There Clark's battle plan called for the French Expeditionary Corps—hard-fighting Algerian and Moroccan troops—to capture the heights north of Cassino while the British took the high ground at Sant'Ambrogio. That done, the American 36th Infantry Division under General Walker was to deliver the main stroke, an attack across the Rapido River in the center of the valley's mouth.

The Rapido did not look like much. It was only 25 to 30 feet wide; but the water was deep, cold and swift, and ran between banks four feet high. The marshy, mile-wide floodplain on the American side was without roads, and had been denuded of all cover and sown with mines. Every inch of the

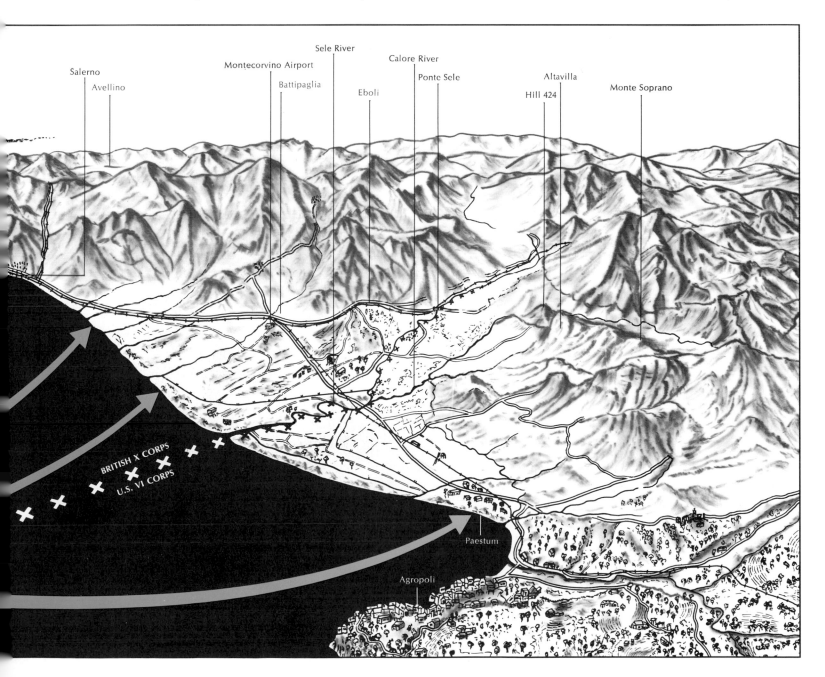

area was indeed sited for German artillery and mortar fire.

The 36th's Walker had grave doubts about the operation. "I do not know a single case in military history where an attempt to cross a river that is incorporated into the main line of resistance has succeeded," wrote Walker in his diary, and he added: "So I am prepared for defeat." Walker's gloom only increased when the French and the British were unable to secure their positions above Cassino and at Sant'Ambrogio. The 36th would be launching an attack across the Rapido without flank protection on either side.

Moreover, the division was scarcely in prime fighting condition. The outfit had been severely mauled at Salerno and battered still further on the drive north. It had been hastily patched together with green replacements and new officers not yet familiar with their men. A sense of fear and futility prevailed. "We thought it was a losing proposition," said Technical Sergeant Charles R. Rummel, "but there ain't no way that you could back out."

The attack across the Rapido began at 8 p.m. on January 20, in darkness and heavy fog. As the Germans commenced their deadly fire, what had been low morale among the troops was transformed into panic. Some men fell into the water deliberately and others refused to enter the boats at all. Of many who did make it across the river before dawn, only the sound of their weapons could be heard, diminishing as the Germans closed in on them.

Late that afternoon, under cover of a smoke screen laid down by artillery, the Americans tried again. Neither the withering response from the defenders nor the horror of the experience for the attacking troops abated. Staff Sergeant Bill Kirby, then a 22-year-old machine gun section leader, described the scene: "We were under constant fire. I never knew whether they made it or not. When we got to the other side, I had never seen so many bodies—our own guys. I remember this one kid being hit by a machine gun; the bullets hitting him pushed his body along like a tin can."

The battle raged on through the night and the next day, and most of the bridges the Americans had managed to establish were demolished one by one. Small groups of dazed and wounded soldiers made their way back across the river. Many were drowned. As night fell again, the sound of American weapons on the far bank faltered and faded.

Meanwhile, as the last attempt to cross the Rapido was failing, the Allies were making their landing at Anzio. If any of the seaborne soldiers cocked their ears to the southwest, hoping to hear the distant rumble of the guns of their com-

Under a smoke screen, a Ranger patrol clambers up a hillside near Chiunzi Pass, overlooking the plain of Naples. While the main Allied offensive unfolded at Salerno, U.S. Rangers landed at Maiori, 12 miles west of Salerno, dashed six miles inland and seized the 4,000-foot-high Chiunzi Pass. By occupying these commanding heights, the Rangers prevented the Germans from mounting a flank attack on the Salerno beachhead through the pass.

When Allied troops reached the Cassino front north of Naples in January 1944, they attempted initially to skirt the hub of the powerful German defenses at Monte Cassino and break into the Liri Valley for a quick linkup with British and American forces landing at Anzio. Troops of the British X Corps succeeded in establishing a small bridgehead across the lower Garigliano River. But the British 46th Division was thrown back when it attempted to cross the river farther upstream. On the U.S. II Corps front, two regiments of the 36th Division were repulsed in their bloody struggle to get across the Rapido River at Sant'Angelo. The fighting at Cassino and Anzio then developed into a long and costly stalemate.

rades coming up the Liri Valley to help them, there was only silence. Every GI on the German side of the Rapido was captured, wounded or dead.

The VI Corps of the Fifth Army, under Major General Lucas, had been given the task of establishing a strong beachhead at Anzio. Then Lucas was to push inland about 25 miles, seize the Alban Hills and cut Highways 6 and 7—the Germans' main supply and escape routes.

While Churchill and Alexander regarded the landing as an envelopment substantial enough to crumple the Winter Line, it was not in Lucas' nature to make Patton-style thrusts across the landscape. Just prior to the landing, he accurately predicted his own fate. "They will end up by putting me ashore with inadequate forces and get me in a serious jam," he wrote in his diary. "Then, who will take the blame?"

At first the operation went well. On January 22, the U.S. 3rd Division landed at Anzio, accompanied by detachments of Rangers and paratroopers, along with the British 1st Division and a brigade of commandos. The port was captured virtually intact, as was the nearby town of Nettuno. By the end of the day, 36,000 troops and 3,200 vehicles were ashore—but conspicuous by their absence were the

mechanized troops necessary for the kind of rapid advance that Churchill expected; they had been held back for fear of a German counterthrust on the Cassino front.

For the next nine days Lucas concentrated on getting ashore more men and supplies—while the Germans set up a formidable defense and prepared to counterattack. Finally on January 30, Lucas felt ready to launch a two-prong drive toward the Alban Hills. The British 1st Division reached Campoleone, more than halfway to the hills, before it was stopped. But the U.S. attack spearheaded by two battalions of Rangers heading for Cisterna met disaster. After three days of fighting and 5,500 casualties on each side, Lucas' VI Corps dug in behind a beachhead perimeter of barbed wire and mines.

The fortunes of the Anzio landing force and of the main body of the Fifth Army at Cassino were inextricably intermeshed. Strategically, the two forces were engaged in the same battle. Success on one front meant success on the other, and failure at either imperiled both.

As soon as the surprise landing at Anzio had diverted the attention of the Germans in the south, Clark had ordered the main body of the Fifth Army to try again to breach the Winter Line by pushing up and over the spur of jumbled

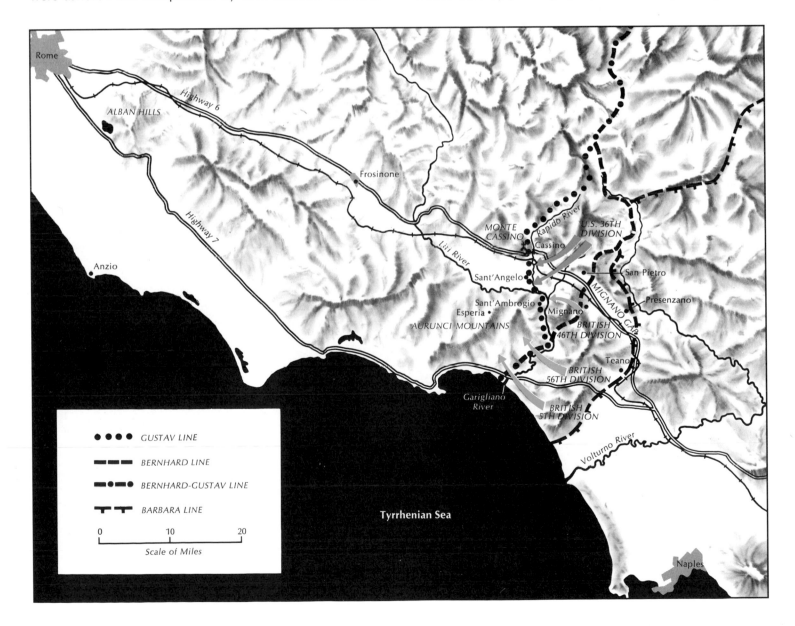

mountain peaks that culminated in the prominence of Monte Cassino. But despite enormous effort, they were unable to bypass Monte Cassino.

As a consequence the Anzio beachhead was now in dire trouble, unable to push forward and under increasing pressure from fresh German troops. Churchill fumed in frustration over Lucas' inability to wreak havoc upon the Germans. "I had hoped that we were hurling a wildcat onto the shore," he complained, "but all we got was a stranded whale." And very nearly a dead whale.

By February 16, the German forces at Anzio outnumbered the Allies by about 125,000 to 100,000. In a major counterattack, the U.S. 45th Division was pushed back toward the sea. But the beleaguered GIs dug in and refused to budge. Fighting at close range without sleep and in numbing cold, the shattered companies of the 45th Division—some completely surrounded—seemed to deny a German breakthrough by sheer force of will. Their courage and determination prevented an Allied disaster.

Finally acknowledging that they could not wipe out the beachhead, the Germans suspended the offensive on February 20. Their losses since the day of the landing totaled nearly 19,000 men. Allied casualties were equally heavy.

Two days later, Lucas was replaced by General Lucian K. Truscott as commander of the U.S. Corps. Although Lucas was blamed for the failure to achieve a spectacular result at Anzio, the real mistake was most accurately pinpointed by Field Marshal Kesselring: "The landing force was initially weak and without infantry armor. It was a half-way measure as an offensive."

When efforts to bypass Monte Cassino failed, the Allies determined to take it by storm. The job fell to General Sir Bernard Freyberg and his newly arrived New Zealand Corps, composed mainly of the 2nd New Zealand and 4th Indian divisions. Freyberg, who had won the Victoria Cross in World War I, assigned the New Zealanders to take the town, while the Indians assaulted the great fortresslike monastery above. But before any attack, the place would be bombed to destruction; Allied intelligence was convinced—wrongly as it happened—that Germans were entrenched in the historic abbey.

Leaflets were dropped on February 14 warning the abbot, some 10 monks and lay brothers, and more than 800 refugees to get out of the building at once. But before they could leave, the harried monks had to parlay with equally harried Germans to plan their departure. In the end they were still there when the raid began at 9:45 a.m. on February 15.

Over several hours, waves of bombers dropped nearly 600 tons of high explosive on the monastery. Between

waves, artillery pounded the building with volley after volley. At intervals the smoke and dust cleared, revealing the great walls in various stages of demolition. American foot soldiers watched, and wept with joy. If the men of the 34th Division had any regret, it was only that the monastery had not been bombed earlier. Inside, monks and refugees prayed and died. Perhaps 300 were crushed and buried in the rubble, or killed by artillery fire as they attempted to escape. The 80-year-old abbot and 40 others survived in the depths of the abbey's crypt.

When the raid was over it could be seen that while the monastery was in ruins, the base of the 10-foot-thick walls had not been breached; there was no easy way in for attacking troops and the wreckage would provide ideal lodgments for German mortar and machine gun crews. Yet the Indians

Weighed down with gear, Allied troops disembark from LSTs (Landing Ship Tanks) docked at Anzio, 35 miles south of Rome. The first week after the January 22 landing, the Allies brought ashore 69,000 men, 508 guns, 237 tanks and 27,250 tons of supplies. So great was the surprise achieved by the predawn landing that, of the 200 or more Germans captured, many were still in bed.

went in nonetheless. Three times they bravely attacked, but were thrown back with terrible casualties by Germans dug into the slopes. Meanwhile the New Zealanders fought their way to the southern edge of the town of Cassino before they, too, were hurled back with frightful losses.

For two days, the carnage continued, and then the firing died as the aged abbot came out of the rubble holding aloft a large wooden crucifix. Behind him stumbled a forlorn procession of monks and refugees. After they had made their way to safety, German paratroops moved into the ruins.

The Allies might well have decided to halt the attack at Cassino for the remainder of the winter. After all, having failed with their counterattack at Anzio, the Germans were no longer threatening to wipe out the beachhead; they were content to contain it. However, General Freyberg and his New Zealand Corps had no intention of giving up now.

On March 15, a tremendous bombardment by 435 aircraft, including heavy bombers based as far away as England, dropped 1,000 tons of explosive in the Cassino area; 750 Allied guns and howitzers added another 4,000 tons of shells into the target area. A British war correspondent, Christopher Buckley, described the scene: "Sprout after sprout of black smoke leapt from the earth and curled slowly upward like some dark forest. One wave had no sooner started on its return journey than its successor appeared over the eastern skyline. I remember no spectacle so gigantically one-sided. Above, the beautiful, arrogant, silver-grey monsters performing their mission with what looked like a spirit of utter detachment; below, a silent town, suffering all this in complete passivity."

After the bombardment the New Zealand infantry moved into what was left of the town of Cassino—and found Germans of the 1st Parachute Division had survived in deep tunnels and bunkers. Even after a week of close quarter combat, the Germans still held much of the town. On the mountain above, Indian soldiers fought to within 250 yards of the monastery, but German paratroopers held on. Yet another attack had failed.

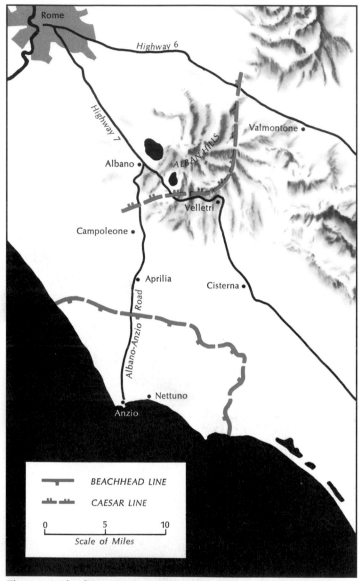

The surprise landing at Anzio was intended to relieve Allied forces stalled on the Cassino front. But the Allied commander, Major General John P. Lucas, failed to exploit the initial surprise. Instead of driving inland toward Kesselring's Caesar Line defensive to cut Highways 6 and 7, the major supply and escape routes for the German forces to the south, he halted his forces in the beachhead and built them up against an anticipated enemy counterattack. When the counterattack was launched along the Albano-Anzio Road on February 16, 1944, the Allies were driven back one and a half miles, but they had accumulated enough strength to beat off the attackers. The beachhead was saved, but the value of the Anzio operation would long be debated.

Then, on May 11, Alexander launched a coordinated assault along the main battle line from Cassino to the sea. It started with the most devastating cannonade the Italian war had seen—more than 1,600 guns along the 25-mile front firing at every known German position. The Germans were stunned, but skillfully fought back. Only in one sector, where the French attacked through the Aurunci Mountains, was there much progress. Sparked by the French advance, the Americans began to push forward along the coast while the Eighth Army steadily enlarged a bridgehead it had managed to gain across the Rapido.

On the scarred slopes around the abbey were the men of the Polish II Corps, two divisions and a brigade under Lieut. General Wladyslaw Anders. They probed the German defenses, taking severe casualties. Having lost their country to the Germans, as well as many of their families, few had much hope for the future. They fought, as they said, for revenge and honor, and they were a grim sight to the Germans who saw them coming.

After six days of fighting, the British had advanced far enough into the Liri Valley to outflank the ruins of the town of Cassino and the monastery above. That night the Germans withdrew from both places. The next day, the Poles occupied the monastery and raised their flag. In the Cassino operation they had lost nearly 4,000 men, many of whom were buried in a cemetery on a nearby ridge, beneath this inscription:

> We Polish soldiers
> For our freedom and yours
> Have given our souls to God
> Our bodies to the soil of Italy
> And our hearts to Poland.

On May 23, with the Germans in retreat the length of the main battlefront, it was time to break out of the Anzio beachhead. At 5:30 a.m., 500 Allied guns opened fire from the beachhead. At the same time, 60 light bombers struck at Cisterna. Then four divisions launched an all-out attack toward the town.

As the U.S. VI Corps lunged forward, intending to trap large numbers of retreating Germans, Clark interceded. He feared that while the Americans were occupied with the enemy, the British might slip past and enter Rome; he wanted Rome for the American Army and himself. He directed accordingly: fewer than one third of the American forces would go on striking east toward the town of Valmontone; the others were to wheel northwest toward Rome.

To Churchill, watching from a distance, this seemed outrageous. His outrage was shared by other commanders, both

Looming over the Rapido River valley, the 1,700-foot Monte Cassino was a natural observation post from which to spot almost anything that moved. Before its destruction, the Cassino abbey (inset) included a cathedral, a seminary, an observatory, a boys' college and a library some 200 yards long. Gutted by the Allied bombing, as shown in large photo, a few sections were left intact including the tomb and cell of the monastery's founder, Saint Benedict.

American and British. They felt that Clark had thrown away the chance of trapping the bulk of the German forces retreating from the Cassino area for the prestige of entering Rome first. While no one can say whether this is true, Anglo-American military relations were strained—and the Germans did in fact sidestep the Allies to get away.

At 9 p.m. on June 4, 1944, a young woman in Rome named Vera Signorelli Cacciatore saw the last of the Germans leave town. "There was a brilliant full moon," she later recalled. For half an hour after the Germans' departure, she said, "there was quiet and then someone yelled that the Americans were coming. Soon a few tanks went through the Piazza and then the soldiers were marching in the moonlight. They were silent, very tired, marching almost like robots. The people came out of the houses to cheer them but they only smiled, waved and kept on going. One company of them disappeared, then another, but finally an order was given and hundreds of soldiers came to a halt. The civilians crowded around them, patting them on the back, kissing them. The soldiers asked for something to drink, water or wine, and when they had drunk they slumped down on the stones and fell asleep.

"They slept on the street, on the sidewalks, on the Spanish steps. The stones were still warm from the sun and the Piazza seemed like an enormous bed. Next morning the air, the smell of Rome had changed. Before, Rome had always smelled of cooking, wine, dried fish, garlic. Now suddenly it was Chesterfields."

With the Americans' arrival in Rome, General Alexander's massive offensive had succeeded, but at a fearful price. Allied casualties in the drive on Rome totaled 40,000 dead, wounded and missing; the Germans lost 38,000 men. And only for a fleeting moment could the soldiers—and their leaders—revel in the glory of taking the Eternal City. On June 6, the attention of the world was diverted by the Allied landing in Normandy.

Footsore and exhausted, the Allied soldiers left Rome behind and marched north, past one hastily erected German defense line after another. The Germans were backing into the Gothic Line, a winding defense through the northern Apennines. Kesselring was skillfully consuming time, eating up the good summer weather that was so valuable to the highly mechanized Allies.

September rain and November snow came to his aid, and the Allies were soon hung up in the mountains for the winter, just as they had been hung up at Cassino a year earlier. During the cold, wet months, the Germans did what they could to strengthen their positions. But with the war going badly for them on all fronts, defeat was merely a matter of time. In fact, secret negotiations for the surrender of Kesselring's armies had begun already. But these negotia-

HEROES ABROAD, INTERNED AT HOME

Following Pearl Harbor, a wave of prejudice and hatred engulfed the 127,000 Japanese-Americans living in the U.S. Banks refused to cash their checks; insurance companies canceled their policies; milkmen and grocers refused to sell to them. "A Jap's a Jap!" declared Lieut. General John L. DeWitt, charged with the West Coast's defense. "It makes no difference whether he's an American or not."

Late in March 1942, DeWitt's men began rounding up the Japanese-Americans for evacuation; many were given as little as 48 hours to dispose of their homes, businesses and farms. Eventually they were shipped inland to internment camps—isolated barracks cities, where they lived for at least a year as prisoners.

Albeit imprisoned by their own government, many began their days by pledging allegiance to the U.S. flag. Some 8,000 Japanese-Americans also served with great distinction in the Armed Forces, in France and particularly in Italy. The 442nd Regimental Combat Team was among the most widely decorated units in the U.S. Army—with 3,600 Purple Hearts for wounds received in action, and in recognition of their gallantry, 354 Silver Stars, 47 Distinguished Service Crosses, one Distinguished Service Medal and one Medal of Honor.

Navy Secretary James Forrestal, accompanied by General Mark Clark, reviews an honor guard of Japanese-American troops in Leghorn, Italy. The soldiers were from the 100th Battalion of the highly decorated 442nd Regimental Combat Team, which saw fierce action in Italy and France.

Exiles from the West Coast arrive by the truckload at their new home in the barren, desolate Wyoming desert, the Heart Mountain Relocation Center. Each family was assigned to one room measuring 20 feet by 25 feet, in a wooden barracks covered with tar paper.

tions were hamstrung by protests from the Russians, who feared that the Americans and British would make a separate peace with the mutual foe.

The Allies' last crushing attack began on April 9, when the Eighth Army struck in the area of Lake Comacchio; and the Fifth Army, several days later near Bologna. On April 14 the Americans sliced through the last of the Gothic Line defenses in front of Bologna. By April 20, they broke onto the Po Valley plain, and their armored columns began to dash across it. A day later, the Fifth and Eighth armies linked up. As the Germans fled in disorder, armored spearheads moved in great arcs to encircle them. The German armies were disintegrating, their exhausted troops surrendering by the tens of thousands.

Allied armored units, exhilarated by victory, raced to the Austrian and French borders to seal off the Alpine passes.

Meanwhile, Italian partisans operated with increasing boldness behind the German lines. Some 50,000 strong, they made a significant contribution to the German defeat by cutting telephone wires, dynamiting bridges, roads and railroad tracks, and ambushing trucks.

On April 28 one such group of partisans ambushed a convoy of trucks passing through the town of Dongo near Lake Como. Inside one of the trucks, disguised in a German soldier's greatcoat and steel helmet, was Il Duce.

For two weeks after his arrest in July 1942, Mussolini had been held prisoner in the Hotel del Gran Sasso, deep in the Apennine mountains. Then, at Hitler's direction and under the leadership of SS Captain Otto Skorzeny, a rescue mission had been mounted. Landing in gliders on the Alpine meadow near the hotel, Skorzeny and his commandos freed the Duce and bundled him into a small Storch observation plane. The Storch bumped along the meadow, bounced off a boulder and wobbled over the edge of the plateau—to drop dizzyingly through the air before nosing up and heading away to safety.

Transported to Germany, Mussolini was escorted before Hitler, who ordered him home to organize a new Fascist state under German control in northern Italy. It was farcical, and Mussolini was now going out of his mind. He compared himself to Jesus Christ and Napoleon, and blamed his failure on the Italian people. He said his countrymen were a "mediocre race of good-for-nothings—only capable of singing and eating ice cream." When Naples was bombed, he even expressed a ghoulish delight.

The campaign for Italy, a grinding, bloody, inch-by-inch slog through mountains that seemed to go on forever, was finally coming to an end. And with it would die the Duce, hated and reviled in a country where oceans of worshipful admirers had once roared their adulation.

The Duce—flanked by Claretta Petacci and a cohort—hangs in Milan. A crowd gathered, shouting obscenities. One woman fired a pistol at Mussolini's body five times to "avenge her five dead sons."

It was as Mussolini was fleeing the Allied advance into northern Italy that he was captured by partisans on April 28, 1945. Next day, accompanied by his faithful mistress Claretta Petacci, Benito Mussolini was taken to a nearby villa. A Communist partisan ordered them out of the car, and Mussolini witnessed Claretta's death. Then, holding the lapels of his jacket, he said, "Shoot me in the chest." The partisan fired twice, and the Duce was dead. Just two years earlier, upon his arrest, he had prophetically spoken his own epitaph as well as that of the bloody era he represented. "That's my fate," he had said, "from dust to power and from power back to dust."

A SEA WAR COMMEMORATED

The Royal Navy light cruiser Manchester (left) and the battleship Rodney beat back Axis air attacks on a major convoy, steaming for Malta.

PROFILE OF A CAMPAIGN WITHOUT MONUMENTS

The French battleship Provence (left) is flanked by British warships in Alexandria in 1940. The British later shelled the Provence at Mers-el-Kebir.

On the warm spring night of May 3, 1943, the sea off the Tunisian coast was rent by a cataclysmic explosion. An Italian transport carrying an enormous cargo of artillery shells, bombs and land mines had been blown up by gunfire from three patrolling British destroyers. The thunderclap signaled the end of the battle for control of Mediterranean shipping lanes, the central drama of a three-year campaign. Italy's merchant fleet was now virtually extinct and no more of its transports would brave the "death route" southward past the British stronghold of Malta to North Africa. By contrast, Allied convoys were steaming to Malta and Alexandria almost unopposed.

For both sides, the toll had been terrible. Wrote a British veteran: "Rusting off every cape and headland, and disintegrating beneath the blue acres of the sea, lay millions of tons of merchant and naval shipping, together with the whitening bones of men from almost every race under the sun."

Though the Mediterranean war had seen some spectacular naval actions near Cape Matapan and Italy's Calabrian shores, the critical contests had been fought by submarines and aircraft operating off Sicily, Malta and the Axis-held African coast. Lieut. Commander Malcom D. Wanklyn's submarine *Upholder* alone had sunk 128,353 tons of Axis shipping and claimed the lives of thousands of German and Italian soldiers before being sunk herself. Indeed, submarines had turned out to be Britain's strongest weapon in the Mediterranean. "More than any other single arm," wrote Admiral Sir Andrew Cunningham, "they played a decisive part in cutting the Axis supply lines to Libya, helping to make possible the eventual advance of the Eighth Army to Tripoli and beyond."

No monuments mark the sites of the battle of Matapan, the surprise British air attack on the Italian naval base at Taranto or the last resting place of the *Upholder* and her crew. But the events and the fighting men are commemorated in a series of paintings commissioned by the Royal Navy and published on these pages. They were created by artist David Cobb, a reserve officer stationed at Gibraltar

British warships based at Gibraltar steam past the Rock. Ships operating from Gibraltar could strike into the Atlantic or into the western Mediterranean.

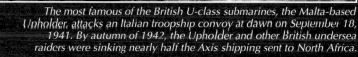

The most famous of the British U-class submarines, the Malta-based Upholder, attacks an Italian troopship convoy at dawn on September 18, 1941. By autumn of 1942, the Upholder and other British undersea raiders were sinking nearly half the Axis shipping sent to North Africa.

Braving heavy antiaircraft fire, one of the 21 Swordfish from the aircraft carrier Illustrious launches its torpedo against the Italian fleet at Taranto. The British sank or disabled three battleships and lost only two planes.

Led by the battleship Littorio, an Italian fleet turns away from a Malta-
bound convoy off the coast of North Africa on the 22nd of March, 1942.
Smoke screens laid by British destroyers prevented the Italians from
sighting on the convoy or its outgunned escort, and the British destroyers'
daring torpedo attacks finally forced the Italians to break off the action.

During the battle of Matapan, the British battleships Warspite, Valiant and
Barham demolish the Italian cruisers Fiume and Zara on the night of March
28, 1941. "Our searchlights shone out with the first salvo," Admiral
Cunningham recalled. "The Italians were quite unprepared. They were
helplessly shattered before they could put up any resistance."

A flight of Stukas attacks Malta in one of the daily raids that punished the island in the spring of 1942. The Luftwaffe almost succeeded in isolating and crushing Malta, but urgent calls for air support from German armies fighting in Libya and on the Russian front drained off the bombers, permitting the British to regain control of the air over the Mediterranean.

The carrier Illustrious bears the brunt of a concentrated dive-bombing attack by three squadrons of Stukas while on convoy duty in January 1941. The Illustrious sustained six direct hits by 1,000-pound bombs; she survived them thanks to her armored flight deck and her crew's superb damage-control work.

The aircraft carrier Eagle, torpedoed by the German submarine U-73 as she set out to accompany a convoy, lists to port before sinking with a loss of 260 lives. In addition to escorting nine British convoys, the veteran ship earlier had ferried 183 fighter planes to Malta.

The tanker Ohio, lashed between two other ships, is towed into Malta harbor at the completion of a perilous voyage. Torpedoed, struck by bombs, set on fire, twice abandoned and reboarded, dead in the water and sinking, the Ohio survived her ordeal to deliver 10,000 tons of fuel for the island's cooking stoves, dock machinery, planes and submarines.

10

In the six months since Pearl Harbor, Japan had routed the Americans in the Philippines; the Dutch in the East Indies; and the British in Burma, Malaya, Singapore and Hong Kong. Japan had also made a number of moves to threaten Australia: in January 1942, Japanese soldiers landed on New Britain and seized the port of Rabaul; in March they took Lae and Salamaua on New Guinea's northeast shore. Then, in May, they seized Tulagi in the Solomons, bringing them much closer to the vital supply lines between the U.S. and Australia. The Japanese appeared unstoppable—yet the cracks were beginning to show. In early May the Imperial Navy was checked in the Battle of the Coral Sea, and now in June, off Midway Island, it was about to suffer a blow from which it would never recover.

Under hazy spring skies, an immense flotilla of Japanese warships steamed eastward across the Pacific Ocean. They moved forward in a gigantic arc many hundreds of miles across—more than 150 vessels divided into 10 fighting groups. There were eight carriers bearing a total of 650 planes, along with 11 giant battleships, 20 cruisers, 60 destroyers, plus troop transports, supply ships and auxiliary craft. It was the final week of May 1942, and this immense force represented the greatest assemblage of naval might anywhere on earth.

Aboard the armada's flagship—the 69,100-ton *Yamato*, the world's largest battleship—rode Admiral Isoroku Yamamoto, the man who had designed the surprise attack on Pearl Harbor. His present objective: the tiny mid-ocean atoll of Midway Island, the westernmost point in the Pacific where the United States flag still flew.

Yamamoto intended to invade Midway, and replace the Stars and Stripes with Japan's Rising Sun. But this was not his only purpose. The Midway attack was also bait, intended to lure the remnants of the U.S. Pacific Fleet from Pearl Harbor, 1,150 miles to the east, so that Yamamoto could annihilate it. Such a victory, he reasoned, would give Japan supreme control over the entire western Pacific. And it would make up for the embarrassing losses a month earlier, at the Battle of the Coral Sea.

The battle plan bore all the earmarks of Yamamoto's subtlety and daring. A vanguard of 15 submarines would speed ahead to form a picket line between Midway and Hawaii. Next, a diversionary northern force would raid U.S. positions in the Aleutians, 1,800 miles to the north. While the Americans focused on this attack, the First Carrier Striking Force, under Vice Admiral Chuichi Nagumo, would launch its planes to smash Midway's defenses, so that transports could land their 5,000 troops. Then, when the Pacific Fleet steamed out of Pearl Harbor to the rescue, Yamamoto's main force, which lurked several hundred miles away, would sweep in to blast the Americans out of the water.

The odds for success seemed overwhelming. The Japanese ships outnumbered the American forces by nearly four to one. The U.S. Pacific Fleet, severely depleted in the war's opening salvos, was reduced to only eight cruisers, a mere 14 destroyers, and 19 submarines. It had no usable battleships. Of its original four carriers, the *Lexington* had been sunk in the Coral Sea engagement, and the *Yorktown* was so badly crippled that the Japanese thought she, too, had gone down. The two others, the *Hornet* and the *Enterprise*, were still operational. But Japanese intelligence told Yamamoto that both were patrolling in the Solomon Islands, thousands of miles to the southwest. The threat of a carrier-based counterattack seemed nonexistent.

PEARL HARBOR AVENGED

But Japanese intelligence was wrong on several counts. The *Yorktown* had not sunk, but was now back at Pearl Harbor undergoing hasty repairs. The *Hornet* and the *Enterprise* were also in Hawaii, having been ordered back home at flank speed. In addition, the key element in the Japanese attack—surprise—had been fatally compromised. Navy cryptologists had broken the Imperial Fleet's operational code, and every thrust and feint in Yamamoto's elaborate battle scheme lay exposed to American view. The admiral's own trap was now turned against him.

The American plan, as devised by the Pacific Fleet's new commander, Admiral Chester Nimitz, was simplicity itself. The Japanese fleet would approach Midway unmolested. Nagumo's First Carrier Striking Force would be allowed to launch its attack. But the three American carriers and their escorts would be waiting in ambush, hidden well beyond the horizon. So while Nagumo's planes were off pounding Midway's defenses, U.S. dive bombers and torpedo planes would swoop in to rain havoc upon Nagumo's ships.

On May 28, two days after Nagumo's strike force had left Tokyo Bay and steered eastward, all went according to plan. The *Hornet*, the *Enterprise*, the six cruisers and nine destroyers of Task Force 16 weighed anchor at Pearl Harbor and headed west. The force commander, Rear Admiral Raymond Spruance, was new to carrier duty; but he had a sure, slide-rule intellect and, as events would prove, a capacity for swift decision. Task Force 17—two cruisers, five destroyers, and the patched-up *Yorktown*—filed out two days later. On the *Yorktown*'s bridge stood Rear Admiral Frank Jack Fletcher, in tactical charge of both units.

The first alert came just after dawn on June 3—a report of the diversionary attack in the Aleutians. Then a Catalina

Pilots of the U.S. aircraft carrier Hornet's new and untried Torpedo Squadron 8 gather for a picture on the flight deck before taking off to attack Japanese carriers in the Battle of Midway. Only one squadron member—Ensign George Gay (front row, fourth from left)—survived the action that followed. Shot down as he attacked the carrier Akagi, he clung to a raft and watched the rest of the battle from the water.

At the epic Battle of Midway on June 4, 1942, dauntless dive bombers from the U.S.S. Enterprise deliver a death blow to the Japanese carrier Akagi. A second

enemy carrier lies ablaze in the background of this painting by eminent aviation artist R.G. Smith.

patrol bomber spotted some enemy ships closing toward Midway from the southwest. A squadron of B-17 Flying Fortresses lifted off from Midway to bomb them, followed by more Catalinas armed with torpedoes. One tanker took a hit. But the main strike force had yet to be located.

It showed up the next morning at 5:34 a.m. A Catalina pilot found Nagumo's four carriers and their escort ships heading in from the northwest. He also spotted squadrons of Japanese planes coming his way. Midway radar picked up the planes soon afterward. By 6:30 a.m. more than 100 Japanese dive bombers, torpedo bombers and Zero fighter planes were roaring over the island, bombing and strafing its runways, hangars, fuel tanks and other facilities. Midway's own fighter force—26 Buffaloes and Wildcats—had scrambled to meet them, and knocked down three bombers. But the American planes were no match for the swifter Zeros. In a 25-minute dogfight, 17 of Midway's fighters were destroyed; seven others were forced out of action. And all the while the bombs rained down.

But Nagumo's carriers were also coming under attack. Bombers from Midway struck five separate times. And while they scored no hits—indeed, they took some punishing losses—Nagumo was clearly rattled. Then a Japanese patrol plane spotted the one ingredient that the admiral had not counted on—the carriers of Task Forces 16 and 17.

The news hit Nagumo like a sledgehammer. His reserve torpedo planes were being rearmed with bombs for a second strike on Midway; now the bombs had to be removed and the torpedoes reloaded. While this was going on, the first wave of Midway raiders, shot up and low on fuel, appeared overhead, urgently requesting permission to land. When the first torpedo planes from Task Force 16 swept in, less than an hour later, Nagumo was barely ready to receive them.

Admiral Spruance, hoping to catch the Japanese by surprise, had taken a bold gamble. He had launched all his planes at once: 67 dive bombers, 29 torpedo planes and 20 fighters from the *Hornet* and the *Enterprise*. The initial strikes did not go well. Torpedo 8, dipping through a cover of scattered clouds, ran into a swarm of Zeroes, which shot down the entire squadron. Then Zeroes drove off the next squadron, Torpedo 6, gunning down ten of its bombers. A flight from the *Yorktown*, Torpedo 3, zoomed in next, and it hardly fared better. Its fighter escort took out a number of Zeroes, but more kept coming. "It was like the inside of a beehive," one pilot said later. One after another, seven bombers went down. Five others managed to release their torpedoes; all missed.

Nagumo's spirits were beginning to improve. His carriers had withstood no fewer than eight air assaults, and had sustained only minor damage. He revved up his planes for a

By August 6, 1942—the eve of the Guadalcanal campaign and two months after the Battle of Midway—the Japanese had swept across the central and southwest Pacific and were in control of all of the areas marked in color on the map. In preparation for their counterthrust, the Allies divided this vast arena into two major commands, as indicated by the white line on the map, with General Douglas MacArthur in charge of the area enclosed by the line and Admiral Chester W. Nimitz responsible for operations east and north of it.

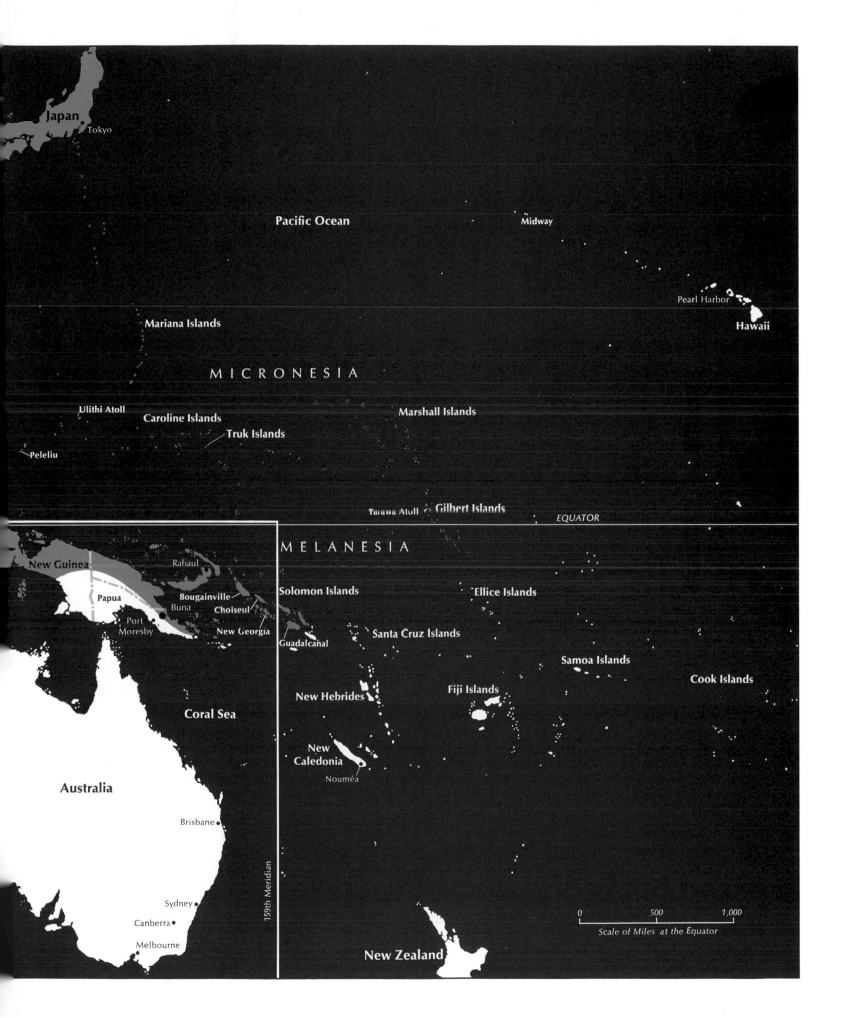

Japan

Tokyo

Pacific Ocean

Midway

Pearl Harbor

Hawaii

Mariana Islands

MICRONESIA

Ulithi Atoll

Caroline Islands

Marshall Islands

Truk Islands

Peleliu

Tarawa Atoll   Gilbert Islands

EQUATOR

MELANESIA

New Guinea   Rabaul

Papua   Bougainville   Solomon Islands   Ellice Islands

Buna   Choiseul

Port   New Georgia   Santa Cruz Islands

Moresby   Guadalcanal   Samoa Islands

Cook Islands

New Hebrides   Fiji Islands

Coral Sea

New
Caledonia

Nouméa

Australia

Brisbane

Sydney

Canberra

Melbourne

New Zealand

159th Meridian

0   500   1,000

Scale of Miles at the Equator

257

counterattack. Then came a cry from his lookouts: "Enemy dive bombers!" And one by one, little gray planes from the *Enterprise* and the *Yorktown* peeled out of the sky and came screaming down in his direction. This time, none of his Zeroes were positioned to meet them.

On the flight deck of the Japanese flagship, the *Akagi*, stood Commander Mitsuo Fuchida, who had led the Pearl Harbor air strike. Now he learned what it was like to be on the wrong end. "Black objects suddenly floated eerily from their wings," he later recalled. "Bombs! Down they came, straight toward me!" Fuchida scrambled for safety, and broke both his ankles leaping from one deck to another.

As quickly as the strike had come, it was over. A huge crater gaped amidships. The plane elevator lay exposed,

drooping and twisting, Fuchida said, "like molten glass." Then the fire started. The flames swirled aft, ignited the wooden flight deck and engulfed its bunched-up planes, setting off their fuel tanks and the torpedoes slung beneath them. Bombs that had been stacked on deck began exploding. Nagumo, and as many officers and crew as were able, transferred to nearby escort vessels.

The devastation was much the same aboard the carriers *Soryu* and *Kaga*. Four direct hits sent flames raging through the *Soryu*'s torpedo magazines, and the resulting explosions blasted a hole through the vessel's hull—leaving it, one sailor recalled, "like a skull smashed open." The *Kaga*, also hit four times, was transformed into a floating bonfire.

Of Nagumo's four carriers, only the *Hiryu* survived the

Mount Austen

Henderson Field

Ilu River

Iron Bottom Sound

onslaught. It now prepared to take revenge. A flight of dive bombers and Zeroes rumbled off its flight deck and tailed some returning American planes straight to the *Yorktown*. Twelve Wildcats from the *Yorktown*'s Combat Air Patrol rose to meet the Japanese. Ten enemy bombers went down in flames. But six others came hurtling on, boring in through the wall of antiaircraft fire. Three bombs struck home, and Nagumo's radio sputtered out a gratifying message: "Enemy carrier burning."

The fire was contained, and the *Yorktown* limped on under her own power. Then came a second attack. And this one proved fatal. Ten torpedo bombers and six Zeroes—all the *Hiryu*'s remaining planes—streaked in. A pair of torpedoes punched into the carrier's port side. Oil gushed out from ruptured fuel tanks. Sea water poured in and, at 3 p.m., the order was given to abandon ship.

Soon afterward the *Hiryu* received her own deathblow. A catch-all squadron from the *Enterprise*, along with 10 refugee dive bombers from the *Yorktown*, caught up with her in the fading glow of afternoon. Four big bombs slammed home, setting the flight deck alight. For more than seven hours her crew labored valiantly to stifle the flames, but to no avail. Shortly after midnight Captain Tomeo Kaku ordered his crew to abandon ship. He himself would stay on board, and so would Admiral Tamon Yamaguchi, who had earlier transferred from the stricken *Soryu*. Bugles sounded, and the flag of the Rising Sun came fluttering down. A portrait of the Emperor was reverently unloaded. As the last crewmen took to the boats, Yamaguchi issued his final order to nearby destroyers: "Torpedo and sink the *Hiryu*." Then he turned to Captain Kaku and said calmly, "Let us enjoy the beauty of the moon."

When news of the Midway casualties reached Yamamoto, still hundreds of miles to the west aboard his superbattleship *Yamoto*, he at first tried to rally his forces for a second attempt. But he soon faced up to the futility of this idea. "The price," he was heard to whisper, "is too high." Then he sent out a message to all the ships of his great armada, ordering them back to home waters.

The price was indeed too high. Yamamoto's ill-fated venture had cost Japan a total of four carriers, one cruiser, 322 planes, and the lives of 3,500 men. The United States had lost a carrier, a destroyer, 150 planes and 307 lives. Never again would the Imperial Navy put out to sea with such confidence of victory; never again would it launch a major offensive. As one high-ranking Japanese official later put it, at Midway "the Americans had avenged Pearl Harbor."

The Americans had achieved much more. Though few realized it at the time, Midway had changed the direction of World War II in the Pacific. The Allied retreat was over.

From now on U.S. ships, bearing crack divisions of combat marines, would roll back the tide of Japan's early advances, freeing—one after another—the island territories that had been seized in the war's opening months.

The first American targets in the South Pacific were a seaport and an airfield in the jungle-clad Solomon Islands in the South Pacific. Tulagi, part of a small island cluster near the eastern end of the Solomon chain, had once served as the region's British colonial headquarters; it boasted a superb natural harbor. Some 25 miles to the south, across a semi-enclosed span of water, lay Guadalcanal, which the Japanese occupied in June. And at grassy Lunga Point, opposite Tulagi, they were building an airfield.

The danger posed by these two positions was chillingly apparent. Together they shaped a spearhead for further enemy thrusts to the east; bombers from Guadalcanal would be able to strike at Allied possessions as far east as Samoa. Battleships moving out of Tulagi, backed by air support, could wreak mayhem on the main supply routes from the United States to Australia. The Allies would have to recapture both islands—at all costs, and as quickly as possible.

D-day was set for August 7, 1942. The 82 ships of Task Force 61 glided through predawn tropical darkness toward the ragged coastline of Guadalcanal. A carrier group split off south of the island, its planes revving up to deliver a series of devastating air strikes. The remaining vessels moved north, then west, into the stretch of water between Guadalcanal and Tulagi. Aboard the transports rode 19,000 troops of the 1st Marine Division under the command of General Alexander A. Vandegrift. As the first blush of sunrise warmed the eastern horizon, a barrage of fire from the Task Force's cruisers exploded over the targets. Marines scrambled into landing craft, and headed toward shore. The first American offensive of World War II was under way.

The assault caught the Japanese totally by surprise. On Tulagi, a radio operator tapped out a bewildered alert, then added: "Enemy forces overwhelming. We will defend our posts to the death, praying for eternal victory."

That vow was kept. The garrison there held out for 31 hours of brave, bitter fighting. Some died in suicide charges; others holed up in deep caves in the Tulagi hills and on adjacent islets, pouring machine gun fire into the approaching Marines until they were silenced by high-explosive charges tipped into the caves. Of an estimated 800 defenders, only 23 were taken alive. The assault cost the Marines 144 dead or missing, and 194 wounded. It was America's first bracing lesson in the Japanese code that held that death was preferable to the eternal dishonor of surrender.

By contrast, the landing on Guadalcanal itself went easily.

The north coast of Guadalcanal, where the heaviest fighting of the first U.S. offensive in the southwest Pacific took place, is seen in a labeled photograph taken from a Navy reconnaissance plane in late August 1942. In two days of combat along the Ilu River (foreground), 800 Japanese soldiers were killed. In the background is Henderson Field, site of the American headquarters and base for U.S. planes. Overlooking the airstrip is Mount Austen, a strategic 1,500-foot ridge that was held by the Japanese until January 1943.

The Marines swarmed ashore, unopposed, on the level sands east of the Lunga Point airstrip. The first American casualty was a man who cut his hand with a machete while opening a coconut. Next morning the Marines pushed through jungle and coconut groves toward the airfield; they met only scattered resistance. Most of the Japanese guards and construction workers had retreated into the bush.

The airfield proved to be a wonderfully rich prize. Its 2,600-foot runway was nearly completed; wharves, revetments, machine shops were already in place. More than 100 trucks and other construction equipment stood where the Japanese had left them, along with quantities of gas, oil, cement, medical supplies and food stocks. There was even a facility for making ice, which, in short order, wore a gaudily painted sign that read "TOJO ICE FACTORY. Under New Management." The Marines settled in and set to work. In just 13 days the airstrip, renamed Henderson Field, would be ready to receive the first flights of American planes.

But seizing the airstrip was not the same as holding it—as the Marines would soon learn. Already the Japanese had begun to strike back. On the morning of D-day, the first waves of Japanese Navy bombers lifted off from an island base at Rabaul, 650 miles to the west, and began hitting the ships of the invasion force. A destroyer and a transport went down; the unloading of supplies, already behind schedule, was delayed even further.

Late the following night, a more ominous danger loomed out of the darkness in the sea passage near the landing zone—soon to be dubbed Ironbottom Sound because of the quantities of shipping that would litter it. A Japanese attack force—seven cruisers and a destroyer—slid past the Allied pickets and fell upon a cluster of American and Australian escort vessels stationed off Savo Island. The Japanese released their first torpedoes at 1:43 a.m. on August 9. In the next 40 minutes two Allied cruisers plunged to the bottom, and two more were so badly damaged they had to be abandoned. The Japanese sped homeward unscathed, leaving behind them 1,023 American and Australian sailors dead, and 709 more wounded—more casualties than the Marines would suffer during the entire Guadalcanal campaign.

It was a bitter defeat, and one with repercussions for the men on Guadalcanal. Concerned over the vulnerability of his carriers to shore-based Japanese airpower, the U.S. Navy commander, Vice Admiral Frank Jack Fletcher, had already ordered the big flattops out of the area. And now, without any sort of cover, the transports waited only to pick up survivors of the Savo battle before making their own hasty departure. Some of the ships still had vital supplies of food and matériel in their holds. The Marines—10,000 men on Guadalcanal and 6,000 more on Tulagi—stood alone, undefended against air and sea bombardment.

The next Japanese attack came from land. The Imperial General Headquarters, underestimating Vandergrift's force, sent a single regiment to clear it out—2,000 troops under

Colonel Kiyono Ichiki. Destroyers bearing Ichiki's first battalions, about 1,000 men, slipped past Lunga Point under cover of darkness—the Marines at the airstrip heard their wash as they went by—and landed 20 miles down the coast.

Two nights later Ichiki ordered his men to move out. Victory seemed so certain that he had not bothered to wait for the rest of his regiment to arrive. The men crept through the jungle, forded the Tenaru River, then paused at the next one, the Ilu. There the Marines were dug in on the far bank. At 3 a.m. on August 21, Ichiki gave the order to attack. The result was a bloodbath.

As Ichiki's soldiers waded across the Ilu, bayonets fixed, the Marines cut them down with rifle and machine gun fire, and canisters shot from antitank guns. The attackers twisted and crumpled as though blasted by a wind machine. And all night they came, wave upon suicidal wave.

As the sun rose, Japanese bodies lay in heaps upon the sands of the river bank. Vandegrift sent in tanks to flush out survivors hiding in the jungle. On crossing the river their steel treads crushed and mangled the fallen Japanese—living, dead and dying—until, as Vandegrift put it, "the rear of the tanks looked like meat grinders." Of the 1,000 attacking soldiers, 800 had perished. Ichiki escaped with a handful of men and at a quiet spot on the beach he burned his regimental colors. He then committed hara-kiri.

The hitherto all-powerful Japanese Army had met its first defeat, and more would soon follow. In September the Japanese struck again at the Lunga Point airfield, this time with 6,000 men. The plan called for three simultaneous attacks—one along the coast from the west, one across the Ilu River to the east, and the third from inland, along a jungle-shrouded rise of ground that came to be known as Bloody Ridge. But the two coastal assaults were repelled, and the jungle force bogged down in rain and mud. Its thrust along the ridge also met defeat.

In October the Japanese flung in an entire division, which attacked through the jungle from the west and south. Once again the defenders, their numbers freshened with new Marine units and Army troops, turned them back. Then a Japanese Navy task force arrived in November with its own body of reinforcements. In three days of sulfurous battle against U.S. ships in Ironbottom Sound—collectively known in American Navy annals as the Battle of Guadalcanal—the task force lost a total of 13 vessels, including two battleships and a heavy cruiser.

Finally, the Japanese called it quits. On three dark nights in early February, the Imperial Navy evacuated 13,000 sick, wounded and starving survivors of the Guadalcanal invasion forces—all that were left of the 36,000 men who had fought on what Japan now called the Island of Death.

As the Marines were consolidating their position on Guadalcanal, another battle was raging in the steamy, precipitous rain forests of New Guinea, nearly 1,000 miles to the west. The Japanese had already taken most of the huge island. But the jungle-clad region of Papua, in New Guinea's southeast, was still in Allied hands, including the strategically vital naval base of Port Moresby.

An attempt to seize Port Moresby, in May of 1942, had been turned back by American carriers at the Coral Sea battle. But the Japanese were trying again, fighting overland along a steep, slithery path called the Kokoda Track. This narrow trail led from Buna on New Guinea's northeast coast to Port Moresby on its southwest coast, over the 13,000-foot-high Owen Stanley Mountains dividing the region.

Defending the Kokoda Track was a single unit of Australian riflemen, the 39th Infantry Battalion, and a small reconnaissance team of native Papuans. All through the rain squalls of July and August, the Aussies and their native guides fought a bitter, up-and-downhill holding action against the Japanese advance. Papua's rough terrain and climate were often a more brutal adversary than the Japanese. In places the track was so narrow that the front consisted of two riflemen, belly down in the mud, sniping at each other through a tangle of vines and ferns. The rains poured down in sudden, drenching cataracts, as much as one inch in five

Japanese soldiers, killed by U.S. Marines on Guadalcanal, lie half-buried in a sandbar near the mouth of the Ilu River in August of 1942. Members of Colonel Kiyono Ichiki's crack 28th Infantry Regiment, they made a futile attempt to overrun positions held by the 2nd Battalion, 1st Marine Regiment, and were mowed down by rifles, machine guns and 37mm guns.

Teetering on a makeshift footbridge on the Kokoda Track, Australian soldiers cross the Kumusi River. In spite of painful, swollen feet; damp, rotting clothes and short supply of food, the Aussies kept on with their dogged advance, even when it meant crossing flimsy wood and wire bridges under enemy fire.

261

minutes. The Aussies lived for weeks in clothing so damp it rotted from their bodies. Soles of feet, swollen to a pulp from ceaseless walking, peeled off in layers when socks were removed. Food ran short, and men began to starve, while aerial drops of supplies and provisions often missed the trail, skidding instead into jungle ravines from which they could not be recovered. Jungle fevers—malaria, dysentery, typhus, dengue—took an even heavier toll than enemy bullets.

The Japanese bore down the trail in seemingly inexhaustible numbers. By early September they had slipped through the pass across the mountains, and were advancing downslope to within striking distance of Port Moresby. The Australians knew that the city could not be allowed to fall; if the Japanese seized it they would have a clear shot at Australia, just 300 miles to the southwest.

The Supreme Allied Commander in this region was General Douglas MacArthur. He knew that to save Port Moresby he would not only have to push the Japanese back over the mountains, but also dislodge them from their bases on Papua's northeast coast. Already he had landed a combined force of 9,000 Australian and American troops at Milne Bay, on the island's easternmost tip, to secure an airbase there. Now he dispatched the 7th Australian Infantry Division to fight its way back up the Kokoda Track. And he lined up the U.S. 32nd Infantry Division for a direct assault on Buna, northern Papua's main Japanese bastion.

All through September and October, the American forces shipped out from Australia in stages. By mid-November they had occupied the marshlands surrounding Buna, and the Australians had worked their way back across the mountains, past the village of Kokoda and across the gorge of the Kumusi River. Every yard of gain was a nightmare, meeting fierce resistance by Japanese suicide squads, or finding human skeletons picked clean by jungle ants. Most ghastly of all was the evidence that the retreating enemy, his own supplies exhausted, had begun to cannibalize the corpses. Nearing the coast, the Australians made ready to assault Gona, a heavily fortified village ten miles east of Buna.

Here the offensive stalled, bogged down in jungle and swamp. The Japanese, entrenched within earth-covered bunkers connected by a maze of tunnels, turned back every assault. No weight of fire, short of a direct bomb blast, seemed to penetrate the bunkers' coconut-log construction. Allied morale began to falter, and communications between units broke down. An air strike called on a Japanese position at Cape Endaiadere hit American lines instead, killing 10 GIs and wounding 14.

MacArthur was not a man to listen to excuses, and he called in his best soldier, Lieut. General Robert L. Eichelberger, to shake things up. "Bob, I'm putting you in command at Buna," he announced, pacing the veranda of the Brisbane Government House. "I want you to relieve all officers who won't fight. If necessary, put sergeants in charge." Then he aimed his finger at Eichelberger. "I want you to take Buna, or not come back alive."

Eichelberger launched his do-or-die assault on December 5, with a two-pronged thrust by the 32nd Division. One force, moving along the coast, was stopped cold by searing enemy fire from bunkers and pillboxes. "We have hit them and bounced off," its commander reported. The other force swarmed out of the jungle to within 50 yards of the Japanese line, where it was also forced to take cover. A single platoon got through, set up a machine gun nest on the beach, and held. Throughout the next week the two American units crept forward, yard by yard, at punishing cost.

The Australians, moving in on nearby Gona, also seemed unable to pry the Japanese from their positions. Then on December 8, supported by a massive artillery barrage, they punched through. And what they found appalled them. The Japanese, their food stocks depleted, had been surviving on roots, grass and tree bark. Many had starved to death. "Rotting bodies, sometimes weeks old, formed part of the fortifications," a British war correspondent reported. The defenders had stacked the corpses against the bunkers like sandbags, and had stood on the bodies of dead comrades to aim their rifles. So vile was the stench that the last survivors had fought in gas masks.

Five days later the Americans took possession of Buna. Another full month was required to clean out the last pockets of resistance in the Buna-Gona sector. Finally, by

A dead Japanese soldier lies outside his smashed pillbox as an Australian checks for survivors. Because some Japanese would lie motionless among dead comrades, then shoot passing enemy soldiers in the back, the Aussies finally took to bayoneting every enemy corpse as a precaution.

A PUNCTUAL MEETING WITH DEATH

Only a week before his death, Yamamoto addresses Japanese pilots at Rabaul. Following the crash of his plane, Japanese searchers found Yamamoto's charred body in the jungle.

On April 14, 1943, U.S. intelligence intercepted a message revealing that Admiral Isoroku Yamamoto, Japan's naval Commander-in-Chief, would be flying to Bougainville four days later. Bougainville lay within range of U.S. P-38 fighters at Henderson Field on Guadalcanal, and Allied planners seized the chance to get rid of one of their most formidable foes.

Admiral Chester W. Nimitz, commander-in-chief of the Pacific Fleet, authorized a plan to shoot down Yamamoto's plane. The plan was approved by Secretary of the Navy Frank Knox and President Roosevelt.

Yamamoto was invariably punctual, and American planners were confident that his plane would appear over Bougainville on schedule—9:35 a.m., April 18. At that moment, 16 P-38s from Henderson spotted two Japanese "Betty" bombers, one carrying the admiral, and six Zero escorts.

As the bombers broke formation to escape, two P-38s dived to the chase. Lieutenant Thomas Lanphier, in one of the fighters, bore down on Yamamoto's plane, shot the right wing off and sent the Betty plummeting to the ground. The other plane plunged into the sea.

A shirtless and sun-tanned Lieutenant Thomas Lanphier relishes his success after downing Admiral Yamamoto's plane.

February of 1943, Japanese holdings in the region were reduced to a pair of bases, Salamaua and Lae, on New Guinea's northeast coast. But the cost of freeing Papua had been shockingly high—3,095 Allied troops killed and 5,451 wounded. Not even Guadalcanal had taken such a toll. When the fighting was over, MacArthur made a pledge: "No more Bunas."

So far in the Pacific, every Allied move had come in response to a Japanese initiative. The assault on Buna and the invasion of Guadalcanal were both envisioned as defensive actions designed to halt the enemy advance. But the recent victories wrote an end to Japanese expansion. A major Allied offensive would now begin.

On March 1, 1943, eight Japanese troop ships with destroyer escort headed out from Rabaul, a large Japanese air and naval base on the island of New Britain; their mandate was to reinforce the Imperial garrison in northeast New Guinea. The convoy was soon treated to a deadly surprise. Unrelenting waves of B-17, B-24 and B-25 bombers from the Fifth Air Force, commanded by General George C. Kenney, introduced the ships to skip bombing. The bombers, flying in low, dropped 500-pound missiles that bounced across the water like flat stones. Fitted with delayed reaction

fuses, the bombs embedded themselves in their targets' hulls before exploding.

The result was devastating. All eight transports went down, along with four destroyers. Of the 6,900 soldiers aboard the transports, half drowned or succumbed to Allied bullets. Skip bombing would destroy vast tonnages of Japanese shipping in the months ahead.

During the following year, the South Pacific's Solomon Islands raged with battle. Strategic moves by MacArthur and tough Admiral William "Bull" Halsey pushed slowly through the jungle islands with determination and vengeance. Some victories were harder won than others.

The island of Rendova, defended by only 120 Japanese, fell easily enough. There the Navy's Seabees set to work building roads and gun emplacements. For four days they labored in mud up to their knees, exposed to incessant strafing attacks by Japanese planes. On July 3, batteries of 155mm "Long Tom" guns started blasting the Japanese at Munda, on the nearby island of New Georgia.

But a landing force headed for New Georgia ran into trouble. The Army's 43rd National Guard Division, new to combat, found itself crawling through a seemingly endless tangle of jungle vegetation—dank, fetid, and heavily defended by the Japanese. Banyan trees blocked mortar trajectories, and aerial pathways had to be hewed by machete. Grenades hurled at enemy pillboxes hit tree trunks, and bounced back to explode among the Americans. Japanese patrols slipped through the perimeter at night, to slit the throats of drowsing soldiers. Morale plunged, and every day soldiers cracked up—victims of war neuroses. Two weeks

Hip-deep in water, men of the U.S. 27th Infantry Division wade ashore at Butaritari island on Makin Atoll as black smoke from enemy oil dumps hit by naval gunfire clouds the sky. Although they outnumbered the Japanese troops by more than 20 to one and were supported by tanks, the poorly trained Americans, in combat for the first time, took four days to capture lightly defended Makin and suffered 218 casualties.

THE "CAN DO" SEABEES

The island-hopping war that the Allies fought in the South Pacific depended in large measure on a rough-and-ready breed of engineers who proudly called themselves "the goddamnedest, toughest road gang in history."

Members of the U.S. Navy's Construction Battalions, known as Seabees for the initials C.B., these versatile performers could magically transform the thickest jungle or most barren atoll into a full-blown air and naval base, build roads and railroads, lay pipelines, and clear all sorts of underwater obstacles.

The speed and ingenuity of the Seabees became legendary throughout the Pacific. Recruited from the ranks of American workers, many from the construction industry, the 260,000 Seabees were for the most part already masters at their trades when they signed up. The Seabees lived by a simple code: "Can do!" No job was too big or too difficult for them to accomplish. They converted the mangrove swamps of Merauke, Dutch New Guinea, into an airstrip in eight days. On Tinian in the Marianas, they moved more than 11 million cubic yards of mud, rock and coral to build the world's largest bomber base—six strips, each a mile and a half long.

They worked with so little regard for creature comforts that one of their officers said they "smelled like goats, lived like dogs and worked like horses." But so essential were they to Allied operations that U.S. Secretary of the Navy James Forrestal said in 1945, "The Seabees have carried the war in the Pacific on their backs."

Testing a new railroad, Seabees go for a trial run on a mile-and-a-quarter-long narrow-gauge line they built in three days to haul supplies on Guadalcanal.

Building a mess hall, shirtless men lay a concrete floor before erecting a prefabricated structure. Construction crews competed to set new speed records.

Betio Island of the Tarawa Atoll lies ravaged after one of World War II's most violent battles.

had seemed time enough to cover the five miles between the beach and the airstrip. The passage took a month.

On August 5th Halsey's forces finally took Munda. Four divisions had been called in—40,000 men—to dislodge 10,000 Japanese defenders. By early September Halsey's planes were flying from the captured island of Vella Lavella.

On November 1, Halsey caught the Japanese completely by surprise at Bougainville, whose airfields would put U.S. air power within easy reach of the huge Japanese base at Rabaul on nearby New Britain. After a masterful feint at the island of Choiseul, Halsey landed two divisions of Marines and Army troops at a spot on Bougainville where the Japanese least expected an assault. And now it was the enemy who had to slog through the jungle, in a vain attempt to dislodge the Americans. The fighting raged through the winter into the spring, and by the end of April 1944, Bougainville was securely in American hands. The price of victory was 7,000 Japanese and 1,000 American dead.

Yet over the months, the island had become strategically less important; the planners had decided to bypass Rabaul and its 135,000 well-dug-in defenders. Allied aircraft had reduced Japanese air defenses to impotence and ranged over the base at will. It could safely be left to wither on the vine, while the Navy turned its attention elsewhere and Douglas MacArthur planned a steady march up the New Guinea coast to his ultimate goal—a return to the Philippines.

As the Allied forces swept up toward Japan from the south, the U.S. Pacific Fleet under Admiral Chester W. Nimitz began closing in from the east, through the flat, sandy coral atolls of the central Pacific. And if jungle fighting in New Guinea and New Georgia had been unexpectedly difficult, these barren stepping-stones offered equally stern and painful lessons.

The first targets were Makin and Tarawa atolls, in the Gilbert Island chain. Both consisted of tiny coral islets, lined up like nails in a horseshoe around a central lagoon. Jagged coral reefs shelved off in all directions, blocking access to the beaches. There were no hills to hide behind, and the few coconut palms gave virtually no cover. Assault troops, once ashore, would find little room to maneuver. At their backs they would have the sea; in front, the enemy, dug firmly into the coral. On both atolls the defenses were formidable.

No one foresaw the difficulties in November of 1943, as an armada of 200 ships from various U.S. Pacific bases zeroed in on the Gilberts. There were three dozen transports carrying the entire 2nd Marine Division, plus elements of the 27th Infantry Division—35,000 men in all—along with tanks, guns and landing craft. Protecting the transports were 12 battleships, eight heavy and four light cruisers, 66 destroyers, and 17 carriers bearing more than 900 fighters and dive bombers. Here was more than enough firepower, the planners assumed, to silence the atolls' defenses before the assault troops went in.

The landing on Makin was expected to be so easy that Admiral Richmond Turner, the amphibious force commander, and Marine Major General Holland M. "Howlin' Mad" Smith, in charge of the landing forces, decided to go there first. They would survey the victory, then quickly speed on to Tarawa, where a somewhat tougher fight was expected.

Clearing Makin took four entire days. Despite an intense pounding by Navy guns and aircraft, the defenses held up. The 27th Division's entire 165th Regimental Combat team—6,500 American riflemen—found themselves pinned down on the beach by a mere 300 Japanese troops.

At Tarawa, the situation was much worse. The main target was an airstrip on Betio, an islet in the atoll's southwest corner. Just two miles long and 900 yards across at its widest point, Betio was less than half the size of New York's Central Park. Yet this tiny chunk of real estate had been turned into the most heavily fortified bastion for its size in the world. Japanese construction crews had dug scores of bombproof bunkers deep into the coral, lined them with steel and concrete, and mounded them over with coconut logs and coral; bombs and artillery shells glanced off harmlessly. Fourteen coastal defense guns guarded the oceanfront, and 40 more artillery pieces were emplaced to barrage every beach and access route in explosive fury. The defenses were lightest on the island's lagoon side, and it was here that the assault teams would land. Even so, the obstacles were formidable. A coconut-log seawall four feet high lined the shorefront, with more than 100 machine guns aimed to fire over its lip. Artillery emplacements guarded key points.

Nevertheless, the sheer weight of the pre-invasion bombardment would surely render these defenses useless—or so the Americans believed. Since well before D-day, on

Under heavy enemy fire, U.S. Marines advance inland on Betio Island of the Tarawa Atoll in November 1943. Converted into a bristling fortress by the Japanese, the tiny island was the scene of one of World War II's most violent battles.

November 20, B-24 Liberator bombers from bases in the nearby Ellice Islands had been plastering the atoll. Then at dawn, just before the first assault waves were slated to go in, the Navy guns opened up.

The battleships *Tennessee, Maryland* and *Colorado*, along with five cruisers and nine destroyers, lobbed in 3,000 artillery rounds, or about 10 tons of high explosives per acre. "We will not neutralize Betio," promised the force commander, Rear Admiral Howard F. Kingman. "We will obliterate it." And as flame and coral dust spurted up from the battered shoreline, his prediction seemed accurate. "It's a wonder the whole goddam island doesn't fall apart and sink," one Marine muttered.

The landing barges were known to be the weakest link in the assault plan. An apron of coral shelved out 600 yards or more from shore, at an estimated depth of about five feet. The first waves headed in aboard amphibious vehicles called LVTs (landing vehicle, tracked), or "amtracs," with tanklike treads that would have no difficulty negotiating the coral. But the amtracs were in short supply; the Marines had only 125 of them. Later companies would have to make do with LCVPs (landing craft, vehicle and personnel), more popularly known as Higgins boats, which fully loaded drew about three and a half feet. Should the depth estimate be wrong, the Higgins boats were in trouble.

Trouble began well before the Marines hit the beach. Japanese shore batteries, fully operational despite the bombardment, had found the range of the transport ships just as the Marines were scrambling into the landing craft. With shells splashing down on all sides, the carefully planned assault schedule began to unravel. Then, as the amtracs and Higgins boats moved into the lagoon entrance, choppy seas and unexpected currents further upset the battle order. Many men got seasick; all were drenched. A final bombardment by Navy guns and aircraft failed to silence the shore batteries. As the first wave of amtracs chugged in toward the beach, the Japanese gunners were ready for them.

The enemy artillery began firing when the amtracs were 3,000 yards out. At 2,000 yards the machine guns opened up. At 800 yards the amtracs started waddling up onto the reef, and ran into a curtain of fire from every gun in range.

Marine Private Newman Baird was a machine gunner in one of the first amtracs. "They were knocking out boats right and left," he recalled. "A tractor'd get hit, stop, and burst into flames, with men jumping out like torches." Some amtracs blew up when Japanese guns hit their fuel tanks. Others foundered in shell holes. Others, their drivers dead at the controls, ran wildly off course, spilling shaken, wounded and dead Marines. Some reached shore, but at the wrong beaches, with ruinous consequences to the carefully orchestrated battle plan.

The Marines aboard the Higgins boats were hardly in better shape. Most of the boats ran aground at the edge of the coral, where they became easy targets for Japanese gunners. Some transferred their passengers to returning amtracs, which began shuttling stranded Marines to shore. But the number of workable amtracs was shrinking alarmingly, and most men in the later waves had to wade in, under fire, through neck-deep water.

The beachfront had been divided into three sectors, with a reinforced Marine battalion assigned to capture each sector. But with entire companies decimated in the passage

Piled on stretchers on a rubber boat, wounded Marines are towed through the water by their buddies to Higgins boats--a distance of more than 500 yards--for

over the coral, the battle plan was a shambles. A monstrous jumble of blasted amtracs and lifeless bodies littered the water's edge, while small groups of leaderless men hugged slivers of shoreline, enemy bullets peppering the sand around them. As one man later recalled, "It was like being in the middle of a pool table without any pockets."

Some platoons found shelter under a long pier that projected out across the coral. The coconut-log sea wall gave temporary shelter to the Marines who reached it, while fire from Japanese machine gun nests sprayed over their heads to strike their oncoming companions. Communications broke down, with radios too waterlogged to function. Damp flamethrowers proved useless against the Japanese bunkers.

Worst hit were the assault companies of the 3rd Battalion, 2nd Marines, who were pinned down on a beach where the shoreline curved inward. They were raked by crossfire from enemy batteries at either end. The battalion commander, Major John F. Schoettel, was hung up on the reef in a Higgins boat, unable to make radio contact with the men on shore. He believed they had been totally wiped out. Deciding to hold the rest of his companies on the reef, he radioed his superior, back in the transports: "Unable to land; issue in doubt." When a curt reply ordered him to land and work west, his response stunned all who heard it: "We have nothing left to land."

One of Schoettel's assault companies had in fact landed, however, and secured a patch of sand on Betio's northwest tip. Though one third of its men were dead or wounded, its commander, Major Michael Ryan, rallied the rest. Backed by two tanks, and some troops gathered from other companies, he led them on a sweep of the island's west coast, overrun-

ning its pillboxes and gun emplacements. But without a working radio, he could report neither his position nor his victory.

Another hero was First Lieutenant William Dean Hawkins, who led his regiment's 2nd Scout-Sniper Platoon. "Hawk," as everyone called him, had landed a few minutes ahead of the first wave in a daredevil commando strike against some machine gun posts on the pier between Red 2 and Red 3. With a flamethrower and a few grenades he and his men cleared the pier. Then he charged over the seawall to fight his way inland.

All through that day and on into the night, Hawkins never quit fighting. The next morning he was given another tough assignment: to knock out a cluster of machine guns that guarded a strong point. As his men laid down covering fire, he dashed from pillbox to pillbox, in the open, to shoot point-blank through the firing slits. Then he tossed in grenades to finish off the occupants. Taking a shrapnel wound from a mortar shell, he still kept going. "I came here to kill Japs, not to be evacuated," he told a medical corpsman. Then an explosive shell from a heavy machine gun hit him in the shoulder. "The blood just gushed out of him," a sergeant remembered. Hawkins died. He would receive a posthumous Medal of Honor.

The battle for Betio raged for three more days. A rising tide finally permitted the Higgins boats to bring in fresh battalions, and reinforcements were landed at the perimeter secured by Major Ryan in the west. Yard by yard the Marines took control. The shore batteries were silenced, the pillboxes were blasted with grenades. An explosive charge dropped down an air vent of the island's two-story, bombproof com-

evacuation to a waiting transport. The most casualties occurred the first day: 1,500 dead or wounded out of a landing force of 5,000 men.

mand post roasted the 200 men inside. The body of the Japanese commander, Rear Admiral Keiji Shibasaki, was thought to be among the charred remains.

On November 24, the island was declared secured, and with it the rest of Tarawa Atoll. Only 17 Japanese surrendered. The rest—some 4,700 troops and construction workers—had died defending it. Taking it had spent the lives of 1,027 Marines and 29 Navy officers and men. It was the bloodiest four days of the entire Pacific campaign.

Other atolls fell in the months ahead: Kwajalein in the Marshall Islands, with its large Japanese airbase; Eniwetok, where a decade hence the first H-bomb would be tested; plus about 30 others. But the slaughter at Tarawa was not repeated. American commanders developed new tactics—better landing techniques with more heavily armored amtracs, precision bombardment for smashing coral bunkers—which reduced the cost to less painful levels.

One Allied commander whose first thought had always been to minimize casualties was General MacArthur. Frontal assaults on heavily defended islands, he maintained, were an utter waste of men and time. His own master strategy, which had already driven the Japanese from Papua and much of Western New Guinea, was to throw "loops of envelopment" around the enemy, bypassing the strong points to strike at more lightly held areas beyond. "Hit 'em where they ain't, let 'em die on the vine," he declared. And true to his word, during the first eight months of 1944, MacArthur sent his forces streaking 1,100 miles along New Guinea's north coast, leapfrogging past the main Japanese redoubts, and across to the islands off its western tip.

Before setting out on this ambitious drive, however, the general had unfinished business to attend to. Thousands of enemy soldiers, refugees from the fighting in New Guinea's Huon Peninsula, were fleeing overland toward the Japanese Eighteenth Army headquarters at Madung—140 miles to the west. MacArthur sent in the 7th and 9th Australian divisions to block their route. Then he took the nearby Japanese-held ports of Sio and Saidor.

Madung lay a mere 70 miles west of Saidor, and the Japanese commander, Lieutenant General Hatazo Adachi, erroneously assumed that MacArthur would strike there next. On February 29, 1944, a task force carrying 2,500 troops of the U.S. 1st Cavalry Division headed toward the Admiralty Islands, 200 miles offshore to the north of New Guinea. Landing on a small, lightly defended bay, the troopers quickly established a perimeter. MacArthur stepped off his flagship, the cruiser *Phoenix*, to inspect the beachheads. He paused for a look at the bodies of two dead Japanese. "That's the way I like to see them," he commented.

The general had much reason for satisfaction, in fact. American bombers flying sorties from air bases in the Admiralties would sever the supply routes to Madung. General Adachi, knowing he could no longer defend Madung, moved his headquarters up the New Guinea coast to Hansa Bay.

MacArthur leapfrogged Hansa Bay as well, and another Japanese stronghold beyond it. His next move, on April 22, was a surprise assault on the old colonial seaport of Hollandia, 500 miles to the west. Hollandia fell easily, with a loss of only 152 American lives. And so MacArthur was off and running. In May, June and July he seized vital New Guinea and neighboring island airstrips. By the end of August all of New Guinea was effectively in his hands. Then on September 15 he landed, virtually unopposed, on Morotai Island in the Moluccas. His road to the Philippines, only 300 miles to the north, was now wide open.

The U.S. Fifth Fleet was also sweeping westward, at an ever faster pace. Its commander was Admiral Spruance, whose decisive action had helped win the day at Midway; now he led the most powerful armada in the world. The fleet contained no fewer than 535 vessels, including a task force of 15 fast attack carriers with 891 planes, screened by seven battleships, 21 cruisers and scores of destroyers. Packed into troop transports were 127,571 soldiers and Marines.

The armada's destination was a trio of island bases in the Mariana group—Saipan, Tinian and Guam. All three were prime strategic targets. Located 1,300 air miles southeast of Tokyo, their airfields would put the new B-29 bombers within striking range of the Japanese homeland. And Guam held a further significance: an American possession in prewar years, it would now become the first patch of U.S. territory to be recaptured from the Japanese.

As the armada approached the Marianas on June 15, 1944, almost every remaining vessel in the dwindling Japanese Navy moved up to confront it. The effort was valiant, its results predictable. Japan's First Mobile Fleet included a mere nine carriers, and an abbreviated support force of carriers, battleships and destroyers. American dive bombers and torpedo bombers thundered overhead, sinking three carriers and severely damaging the rest. Of the Mobile Fleet's 430 aircraft, only 35 remained operational. With American losses of just 130 planes—most of them ditched when they ran out of fuel—the battle went down in U.S. Navy annals as "The Great Marianas Turkey Shoot."

The landings on the three target islands however were another matter.

Some 20,000 Marines from the 2nd and 4th divisions hit the Saipan beaches on June 15, followed shortly afterward

WARFARE AT WORLD'S END

The war that had begun in Europe became the first truly worldwide conflict. Every major nation and dozens of small ones had been drawn into the struggle on either side. From the pack ice of the Arctic to the inaccessible jungles of Asia to the uninhabited Pacific atolls, every stretch of land and sea was a potential combat zone.

On the periphery of the major theaters of the war, some remote regions took on particular strategic importance. As the war in the Pacific raged, the Aleutian Islands, for example, became increasingly significant. The 1,200-mile-long chain of 70 islands just off the coast of the Alaska Peninsula could be used as a stepping-stone for an invasion of North America—or for an invasion of Japan.

The Aleutians were fiercely defended, from end to end and in all seasons, by the worst weather in the world. But the Japanese, who had fished the Aleutian waters for generations, knew the worst about the weather and were not discouraged by it. They invaded the American-occupied island chain on June 3, 1942, primarily to prevent the U.S. from using the islands to invade Japan.

The Aleutian fighting was by turns ludicrous and infuriating. The airmen lost far more planes to the weather than to enemy gunfire. The sailors fought only one sea battle—an old-fashioned ship-to-ship slugging match with damage to both sides, but no ships sunk. The soldiers fought only one important land battle—the final battle on the island of Attu in May of 1943.

That battle was the first operation of the War in which U.S. forces bypassed a strong enemy base to attack a weaker one closer to Japan—a technique they would later use over and over again in island-hopping campaigns across the Pacific. It was also the scene of the first Japanese banzai charge of the War. Of 2,300 Japanese defending the island, 29 were taken prisoner; the rest had been killed or had committed suicide. The cost to Americans was 549 killed and 1,148 wounded.

In the end, the men who campaigned in the cold north agreed with the jaundiced view of Lieut. Commander Samuel Eliot Morison, who was commissioned by President Roosevelt to write a Naval history of the War. "The Aleutians theater," he wrote, "might well be called the Theater of Military Frustration. Both sides would have done well to leave the Aleutians to the Aleuts."

Medics carry a disabled GI—one of hundreds of frostbite or trench foot victims—to a jeep for evacuation to an Attu aid station. During the Battle of Attu, 2,100 American men were listed as casualties because of trench foot, exposure and shock.

From the island of Attu, 650 miles northeast of Japan's big naval base in the Kurile Islands to Umnak, just off the coast of the Alaska Peninsula, the shortest route from Japan to the United States closely followed the Aleutians.

LIFELINE TO CHINA

In the War's Asian theater, the Japanese spring 1942 conquest of Burma was a crushing blow for the Allies, and left two major parts of the theater cut off from each other except by air. For nearly three years thereafter, the sole means of getting supplies to U.S. and Chinese forces in China was to fly the matériel over the Himalayas from India. The hair-raising 500-mile route, nicknamed "the Hump" by pilots, was the most treacherous air route in WW II.

In 1942, U.S. Army engineers began a $150 million project that would offer an alternative supply route—to be completed just 7 months before the War's end. First, the old, war-torn Burma Road leading east 600 miles from northern Burma into China was upgraded for all-weather travel. Then a new 500-mile road was carved out of the wilderness from Ledo to join the Burma Road. In total, 28,000 engineers and 35,000 native workers labored for more than two years to complete the combined Ledo-Burma Road—officially known as the Stilwell Road—for Lieut. General Joseph W. Stilwell, the senior American military commander in the China-Burma-India theater.

By the War's end both routes had taken their toll. The Hump had claimed more than 1,000 lives and nearly 600 planes. As for the Ledo-Burma Road, it was said without exaggeration that the overland route was built at the cost of "a man a mile." But the objective had been achieved: all told, Allied troops had received 650,000 tons of airlifted cargo, and 34,000 tons by overland convoy.

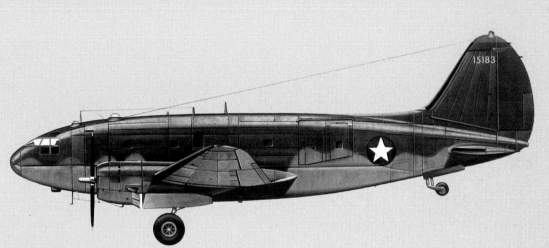

The workhorse of the Hump airlift was the C-46 Commando, the largest, heaviest twin-engine transport used by the Army Air Forces in the War. Although ungainly and problem-ridden, the plane could nonetheless operate at altitudes of more than 24,000 feet--and often had to fly that high to get over the highest peaks in bad weather. Pilots nicknamed it Ol' Dumbo, after Walt Disney's flying elephant.

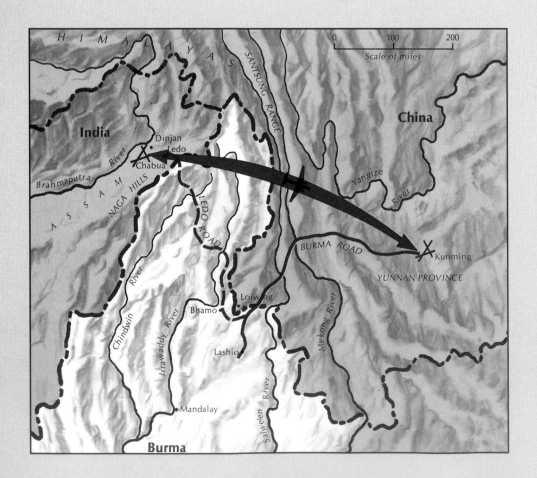

Taking off from bases near Chabua in Assam, India, U.S. Air Transport Command planes flew military cargo via the so-called Hump route (red arrow) over the Himalayas to Kunming and other points in China's Yunnan Province. Until the 500-mile Ledo Road was carved out of the wilderness, and joined with the repaired and improved Burma Road, the treacherous 500-mile sky route was the sole means of supplying Allied forces in China.

Built along 8,500-foot defiles, down steep gorges and across raging rapids, the Ledo-Burma Road stands as one of the great engineering feats of World War II.

by reserve Marine battalions and the Army's 27th Division. Battling yard by yard through mountainous terrain, against seemingly endless waves of banzai attacks, it took them more than three weeks to secure the island. The cost: 16,525 Americans killed or wounded. The 29,000 Japanese defenders died almost to a man. At the end, thousands of Japanese, fueled with *sake* wine, hurled themselves screaming at the American lines. Some had guns, but many carried no more than a grenade, or a stick tipped with a bayonet. One American soldier who faced the onslaught recalled later: "It reminded me of one of those cattle stampedes in the movies. You see the head coming and then they leap up and over you and are gone. Only the Japs just kept coming and coming. I didn't think they'd ever stop." In some places, the attackers were forced to climb over piles of their own dead to get at the Americans. Marine machine gunners had to move their weapons to keep shooting because the mounds of corpses blocked their line of fire. Not until the waves reached a command post were they finally halted by a pick-up defense of cooks, typists and staff officers. Two days later,

when the mop-up was finished, 4,311 Japanese bodies were counted in the area.

And there was a further horror after the main fighting had ended. As a well-developed longtime Japanese possession, Saipan was home to large numbers of civilians, who now joined the remaining troops in an orgy of self-destruction. Crowds of people gathered at the northern tip of the island, on a headland high above a shore of jagged coral rocks. Despite loudspeaker assurances from the Marines that captives would be well treated, parents threw their children from the cliff and jumped after them. Elsewhere, whole families swam out to sea to die. One group of 100 Japanese bowed to watching Marines, then bathed, donned fresh clothing and spread a Japanese flag on the rocks. A man distributed hand grenades, and one by one they pulled the pins and held the grenades against their bellies.

The nearby island of Tinian was taken with relative ease after a cataclysmic bombardment. But Guam, 100 miles to the south, was the scene of yet another hideous bloodbath. It took five days of desperate fighting before the Marines and

U.S. soldiers wading ashore in columns churn up the waters off Morotai Island, midway between western New Guinea and the Philippines.

Army troops could term the situation under control. Yet once again, the Japanese refused to acknowledge the inevitable. Crouched in their foxholes, the Americans in one sector could hear hysterical shrieking and laughter and the breaking of bottles. Then the Japanese came, the officers waving flags, the men brandishing pitchforks, empty bottles, and baseball bats. Artillery fire descended on the charging Japanese, and an American lieutenant later described the carnage: "Arms and legs flew like snowflakes. Japs ran amok. They screamed in terror until they died." The survivors fled back into the swamp whence they had come—to be wiped out by readjusted artillery fire. Even then, the fighting went on for two weeks. And after Guam had been declared secure, small bands of Japanese held out in the hills, guerrilla style, for months—in some cases for years.

One further stepping-stone remained. Tiny, coral-fringed Peleliu Island in the Palau chain held a major Japan airfield that had long been regarded as a threat to any advance on the Philippines. But now there was a controversy of strategy. The island was known to be heavily defended by troops dug into a network of pillboxes and 500 coral caverns—and increasingly, with the collapse of Japanese airpower in the

central Pacific, some planners argued in favor of bypassing the place. Yet in the end, Peleliu was deemed too great a threat, and on September 15, the 1st Marine Division backed by Army troops, stormed ashore after three full days of intense bombardment.

The Marine commander had briefed his men: "We're going to have some casualties, but let me assure you, this is going to be a short one. Rough but fast. We'll be through in three days." Peleliu proved to be very rough, and not at all fast; the Marines compared it to Tarawa. The deeply entrenched Japanese big guns had scarcely been touched by the massive pre-invasion bombardment, and wreaked havoc on the beaches. The Japanese defenders in their caverns had learned the lessons of Saipan and Guam; instead of fruitless banzai charges, they coolly remained hidden when overrun, then popped up to pour deadly fire into American backs. The brutal struggle went on for the better part of a month. When the island was finally taken, 10,000 Japanese had perished along with 1,529 Americans.

By then, Douglas MacArthur, with appropriate fanfare and against little immediate opposition, had finally returned to the Philippines.

With a salvo of rockets filling the sky, an LCI (R), for Landing Craft Infantry (Rocket), launches an attack on Peleliu in the Palau Islands.

THE AGONY OF PELELIU

When the 1st Marine Division landed on Pele▮▮ Island in September 1944, among those in the first assault was a noncombatant named Tom Lea, an artist and writer for LIFE Magazine. Lea was a veteran correspondent, who had chronicled life on board a destroyer in the North Atlantic and on an aircraft carrier in the Pacific; assignments had taken him to England, North Africa, India, Italy and China—but mostly he had painted, as he put it, "the backroads of war, where there was not much firing in anger." He had seen no ground combat, and nothing in his experience could ▮▮pare him for the grisly drama that was about to unfold on Peleliu.

Almost from the moment he stepped ashore, Lea was confronted by death. "I saw a wounded man near me," he wrote. "His face was half bloody pulp, and the mangled shreds of what was left of an arm hung down like a stick, as he bent over in his stumbling shock-crazy walk. The half of his face that was still human had the most terrifying look of abject patience I have ever seen. He fell behind me, in a red puddle on the white sand."

Under fire, Lea found it impossible to use the pencils and sketch pads in his knapsack. "My work consisted of trying to keep from getting killed and trying to memorize what I saw and felt." Lea survived a Japanese mortar barrage and dodged sniper fire, and experienced, as he later wrote, "the sheer joy of being alive."

On the evening of his second day, he returned to shipboard and feverishly put down, in words and sketches, the scenes that were seared into his consciousness. Later, at home in Texas, Lea turned his rough sketches into finished paintings—two of which appear on these pages.

"We saw a Jap running along an inner ring of the reef," Lea remembered, "from the stony eastern point of the peninsula below us. Our patrol cut down on him and shot very badly, for he did not fall until he had run 100 yards along the coral. Another Jap popped out running—and the Marines had sharpened their sights. The Jap ran less than 20 steps when a volley cut him in two and his disjointed body splattered into the surf."

Almost from the moment he stepped ashore on Peleliu, Lea was confronted by death. "There were dead Japs on the ground where they had been hit," he wrote. "We walked carefully up to the side of this trail littered with Jap pushcarts, smashed ammunition boxes, rusty wire, old clothes and tattered gear. Booby traps kept us from handling any of it. Looking up at the head of the trail I could see the big Jap blockhouse that commanded the height. The thing was now a great, jagged lump of concrete, smoking."

THE HOME FRONT: U.S.A.

Assembly line workers turn out 37mm antitank shells. They were among 31,000 women employed in munitions plants in 1942.

EVERYONE'S WAR

To save gas and rubber, a 35-mph speed limit was imposed; commuters formed car pools, and driving alone produced a touch of guilt.

Few wartime measures had so great an impact on home front daily life as food rationing. At the canned-fruit shelves, a woman assesses the loss to her coupon book of 12 points for a 16-cent item.

Even as Japanese bombs were still falling on Pearl Harbor, the stunning news of the attack reached most Americans via radio. For many, life would never be quite the same again—at least not for four years.

Movie stars and farm kids, professors and students, center fielders and congressmen—everyone seemed ready to join up. Army and Navy recruiting stations and civilian-defense headquarters were deluged with volunteers. All told, nearly 16 million Americans wore a uniform during the War, about four times the number who had served during World War I.

At a time when almost every ablebodied man was away in uniform, women came out of the home to work in factories and foundries, and to assume military roles hitherto performed by men. By 1943 women constituted nearly a third of the total work force, and by the time the War ended, most Americans were willing to concede that victory could not have been achieved without the contribution of women.

America's children were also indelibly touched by the War. Many grew up knowing their fathers only as pictures on bureaus; their mothers were away for long stretches, working at jobs. The youngsters pitched in with gusto to help with the war effort, making clothes for children in war-devastated lands and knitting socks for GIs overseas. In classrooms, students plunked down oceans of nickels and dimes for War Stamps and Bonds.

Across the country, shopping became a complicated and often frustrating experience. Even with coupons for rationed goods and the patience to wait in long lines, there was never quite enough to go around. Everyday items were now hard to come by—laundry soap, facial tissue, cotton diapers, thumbtacks and even hair curlers. Nylon had "gone to war," and women went back to stockings of rayon and cotton. The annoyance of such shortages was compounded by the great amount of money in the pockets of U.S. consumers—$90 billion more in 1944 than at the time of Pearl Harbor.

Most Americans at home, however, fortified their patience, drew on old Yankee ingenuity and made do. Month after month they waited, praying for good news of family members overseas. In the meantime, they patched up aging cars, drove slower and shared rides. Housewives used saccharin and corn syrup instead of sugar and stretched meats with all sorts of casseroles. Smokers revived the "roll-your-own" cigarette, and coffee drinkers rebrewed grounds. In general, spirits remained high. Homefront sacrifices stirred a sense of duty. And besides, victory was coming.

During the War, items of convenience and self-indulgence could no longer be taken for granted. At right, a New Jersey man implements his solution to the tire shortage in 1942— a retread made from soles of old shoes. The woman at left, pleased with her find, slips right into a pair of nylon hose.

Using every bit of available space in front of their home, an Oregon couple tends a Victory garden. By May 1943, 18 million Americans had planted cabbages, radishes and other vegetables at sites as various as Boston's Copley Square and Chicago's Cook County Jail.

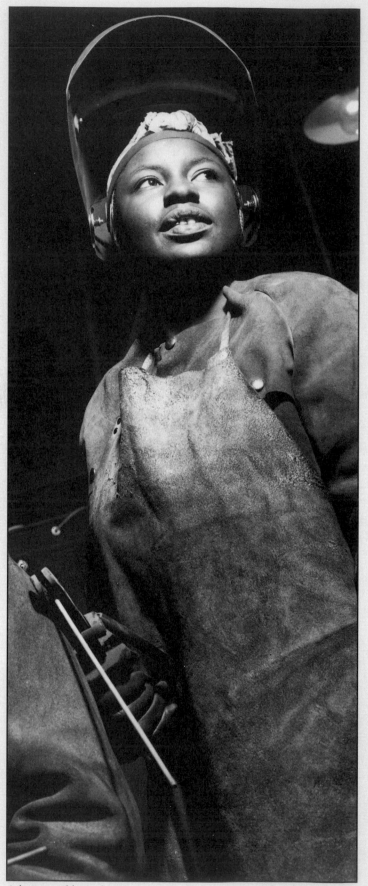

A factory welder in Connecticut wears her protective mask at the ready. The number of black women in industry rose by 11.3 percent during the War.

For soldiers stationed close to small cities or towns, even entertainment was scarce. This fortunate sergeant, in Washington, D.C., enjoys dancing with his girl friend at the USO—the United Service Organization.

Coveralled students of a motor-transport class line up in front of their vehicles in the Fort Des Moines motor pool. Women learned how to drive in convoy as well as how to free mired trucks and assemble engines.

Sixteen-year-old Roy Popp works on a transport plane's fuselage on the assembly line of a West Coast aircraft plant.

A WAVE (Women Accepted for Voluntary Emergency Service) takes aim with a pistol during target practice. Although the Navy took 77,000 women into the Women's Naval Reserve, they were never assigned to combat, and few of them ever got to leave the U.S.

IV
ON THE CREST OF VICTORY

On D-Day—June 6, 1944—Allied soldiers swarm ashore at Bernières-sur-Mer, France. The Normandy invasion was the greatest amphibious operation in history.

All through the month of May 1944, Southern England basked in sunshine, with barely a breeze ruffling the Channel. But now as June began, storm fronts were rolling in. Rain, fog and high winds swept over the Channel, driving white breakers onto the beaches of Normandy. The Allies anxiously watched the skies. Operation *Overlord*, the long-awaited invasion of Europe, was scheduled for dawn on June 5. But everything depended on the weather.

At 9:30 p.m. on June 3, Allied Supreme Commander General Dwight D. Eisenhower met with his subordinate chiefs at Supreme Headquarters Allied Expeditionary Force (SHAEF). The tension was palpable. An invasion fleet of 5,000 ships carrying 170,000 men was ready and poised; some units were already at sea. An aerial armada of 10,521 planes stood waiting on the runways. And now, Operation *Neptune*, the initial assault phase of the greatest and most complex single military thrust in history, awaited the word of a dour Scottish meteorologist named J.M. Stagg.

11

Throughout 1943, the Allies had been preparing to open a second front in France. By the spring of 1944, an extraordinary plan to land on the beaches of Normandy had been developed and an enormous build-up of men and supplies was nearing completion—the points of attack all successfully masked from the Germans by an elaborate series of deceptions. Moreover, on the eve of D-Day, General Dwight D. Eisenhower, Supreme Commander of the European invasion force, possessed superior intelligence about the enemy; he knew much about the Germans' strength, defenses, supply, communications, morale, plans. Everything was in order; nothing had been left to chance. But there could not be any control over one sovereign factor—the weather.

LIBERATION OF FRANCE

As head of the SHAEF Meteorologic Committee, RAF Group-Captain Stagg reported that the forecast for the British Isles and northern Atlantic was "very disturbed and complex." The commanders met again at 4:15 a.m. on Sunday, June 4. Stagg confirmed his dismal forecast. Air Chief Marshal Sir Trafford Leigh-Mallory said his bombers could not operate in the heavy cloud cover that was predicted. Without Allied air supremacy, the planned invasion became too risky; Eisenhower postponed D-Day by 24 hours.

All that Sunday, the storm grew in fury. When the commanders met again at 9:30 p.m., the wind was still blowing hard and torrents of rain poured from the scudding clouds. The commanders stared solemnly at Stagg. If D-Day had to be postponed again, it would have to wait two weeks until the right conditions of both light and tide would prevail again—when low tide and first light more or less coincided. The result would be devastating: in Russia, Stalin had timed a huge Soviet offensive for the first weeks of June; in

England, the assault troops were already jammed into their ships, and follow-on units were pouring into the staging areas just vacated. If the invasion were called off, a logistical nightmare would ensue, and morale would plummet.

"Gentlemen," Stagg began, "some rapid and unexpected developments have occurred over the North Atlantic." He went on to explain that there might be a brief period of improvement starting on the afternoon of Monday, June 5, and lasting till late on the evening of Tuesday, June 6. At that time the weather would again become unsettled.

Stagg was offering a gift—a hole in the weather just big enough for the initial assault force to pass through. But the final irrevocable decision—one that only the Supreme Commander could make—would still have to be delayed for a last weather report. At 4:15 a.m. on Monday, June 5, another meeting was convened. General Eisenhower waited. Then Stagg said that the fair weather interval would probably last into Tuesday afternoon. Eisenhower grinned.

"OK," he said, "we'll go."

With those words the die was cast, and a signal was flashed to the fleet: "PROCEED WITH OPERATION NEPTUNE."

In the gray predawn light of June 5 an English Coastguardsman on the Dorset cliffs watched in disbelief as thousands of ships streamed by. Below him were soldiers and tanks in landing craft; in the sky above floated barrage balloons; to the south, a whole fleet was silhouetted against the white cliffs of the Isle of Wight. When the last of the ships had disappeared over the horizon, the Coastguardsman turned for home. "A lot of men are going to die tonight," he told his wife. "We should pray for them."

The mind-boggling task of planning the invasion had fallen to British Lieut. General Sir Frederick E. Morgan back in March 1943. Appointed Chief-of-Staff to the Supreme Allied Commander—COSSAC for short, the name also used to describe his whole operation—Morgan had gathered a brilliant team of British and American officers to help him draw up the master plan.

D-Day was at first set by the Combined Chiefs for May 1, 1944. From the beginning, Morgan and COSSAC discarded old preconceptions in their search for the best area for the invasion. In the end, they deemed only two places suitable: the Pas-de-Calais coast and the Caen sector of the Normandy coast. Both were within the range of fighter air-

Presiding as Allied Supreme Commander, General Eisenhower (center) plans the invasion in a meeting with his subordinate commanders in chief: (from left) Admiral Sir Bertram Ramsay, Air Chief Marshal Sir Arthur Tedder, General Sir Bernard L. Montgomery and Air Chief Marshal Sir Trafford Leigh-Mallory. Also at the meeting, but not seen in this photograph, were Lieut. General Omar N. Bradley and Lieut. General Walter Bedell Smith.

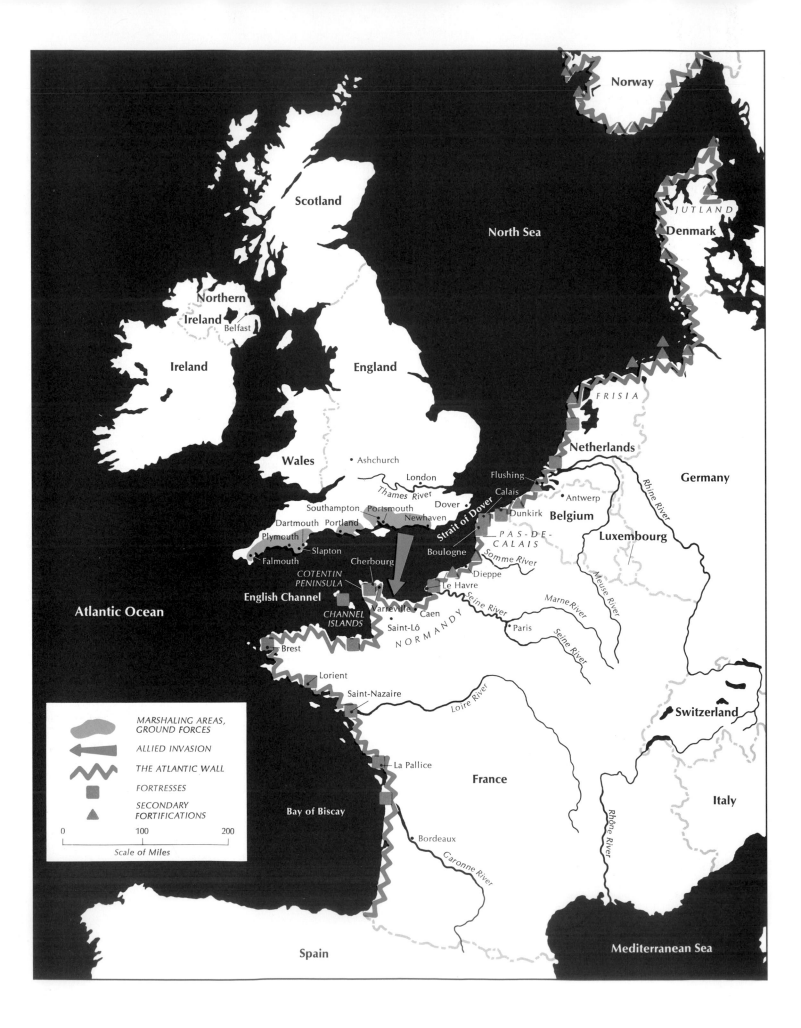

Norway

North Sea

JUTLAND

Denmark

Scotland

Northern
Ireland
· Belfast

Ireland

England

Wales

· Ashchurch

London

FRISIA

Netherlands

Germany

Flushing
Calais

· Antwerp

Rhine River

Thames River

Dover
Southampton · · Portsmouth
Newhaven

Strait of Dover

Dunkirk

Belgium

Luxembourg

Dartmouth · Portland

Plymouth ·
· Slapton
Falmouth

Cherbourg

Boulogne

*PAS-DE-
CALAIS*

Somme River

Dieppe

Le Havre

*COTENTIN
PENINSULA*

English Channel

Atlantic Ocean

*CHANNEL
ISLANDS*

Varreville
Caen
Saint-Lô

NORMANDY

Seine River

Marne River

Meuse River

Paris

Seine River

· Brest

· Lorient

· Saint-Nazaire

Loire River

Switzerland

MARSHALING AREAS,
GROUND FORCES

ALLIED INVASION

THE ATLANTIC WALL

FORTRESSES

SECONDARY
FORTIFICATIONS

· La Pallice

France

Italy

0   100   200

Scale of Miles

Bay of Biscay

· Bordeaux

Caronne River

Rhône River

Spain

Mediterranean Sea

craft based in England and both had wide beaches with large ports nearby. The Pas-de-Calais was nearer England; it was also the most heavily defended section of the French coast. On the other hand, Caen was "weakly held," according to a COSSAC report, and the nearby port of Cherbourg was big enough to handle large amounts of matériel quickly. Normandy became the strike point.

During the intricate planning of D-Day, the element of surprise was paramount. Only if Hitler could be kept guessing would the assault succeed. To that end, thousands of pieces of false information would be leaked to the enemy. Guerrilla operations, rumors, raids and acts of sabotage would bewilder the Germans and keep them off balance.

The deception that most directly affected the invasion was code-named *Fortitude*. Its purpose was first to make the Germans believe that the landing would be at the Pas-de-Calais and then, on D-Day, to convince them that Normandy was merely a feint. While the 21st Army group under General Sir Bernard L. Montgomery, ground commander of the invasion force, was secretly gathering in southwestern England, a fake army group under Lieut. General George S. Patton Jr. appeared to be assembling in southeastern England. Fake ammunition dumps, hospitals, field kitchens, troop camps, guns and planes made of canvas and scaffolding crowded the fields.

Fortitude was perhaps the most extraordinary deception of the war and behind its mask the planning went on. Morgan and COSSAC had a wealth of data with which to work. Once Normandy was chosen, frogmen, commandos and low level photo reconnaissance planes constantly monitored the state of the beaches and the German coastal defenses known as the Atlantic Wall. In May 1944 alone, French agents sent to London 700 radio reports and 3,000 dispatches on German military positions. A precise understanding of what the Allies were up against was essential—especially if they were going to avoid a repeat of the Dieppe raid of August 1942.

Designed as a morale-booster and probing action for an eventual Second Front, Dieppe had been a tactical catastrophe. Seeking to achieve surprise, the raiders, drawn mainly from the 2nd Canadian Division, were sent in without benefit of a softening-up bombardment; and they were landed directly at the fortified port of Dieppe instead of on the open beaches nearby. Intelligence reports were either ignored or faulty. Unreported machine gun nests cut down the troops as they came ashore; one regiment lost 80 per cent of its men. As the attack developed, it was directed mainly against the heaviest defenses instead of flowing around the flanks. Something might have been salvaged, but the plan was inflexible, and offered no opportunity for individual initiative.

When the survivors withdrew, they left behind more than 70 per cent of their number, 3,648 men killed or captured. The German High Command offered a scathing assessment. It was, they announced, "an amateur undertaking carried out in opposition to all good military sense."

True, perhaps, but it would not happen again. The disaster of Dieppe, said Winston Churchill, was a "mine of experience"—knowledge gained in blood that the planners of Operation *Neptune* would put to excellent use. As Lord Louis Mountbatten later wrote: "For every soldier who died at Dieppe, 10 were saved on D-Day."

One of the many lessons of Dieppe was the need for strong fire support. In planning for D-Day, COSSAC proposed that assault infantry be accompanied by guns, mortars and rockets mounted in landing craft and gunboats. Furthermore, since it was clear in retrospect that the Dieppe invaders had needed effective armor support upon landing, the 79th British Armored Division, under Major General Sir Percy C.S. Hobart, was turned loose to develop special armor for the invasion. Hobart and his staff produced an amazing variety of vehicles, the most important of which were the sea-going DD tanks, 33-ton Shermans adapted with flotation devices that allowed them to "swim" under their own power.

By May 1944, an army of 3.5 million men from Europe, Africa, Asia, North America and Australia had gathered in Britain. So had all the planes, ships, guns, tanks, trucks, ammunition, fuel, rations, clothing, medicines and other supplies required by such a huge force. "It was claimed facetiously at the time," Eisenhower wrote later, "that only the great number of barrage balloons floating constantly in British skies kept the islands from sinking under the seas."

Throughout the spring, the build-up and the strategic planning went on. The earlier date of May 1 for D-Day came and went. Finally, on May 8, Eisenhower settled on the first week in June and the countdown began. In its final version, the invasion plan called for a naval armada under the command of Admiral Sir Bertram Ramsay to begin transporting the armies across the Channel to France on D-minus-1.

Ramsay's immense naval armada was to consist of an Eastern Task Force for the British and Canadian Beaches, code-named Gold, Sword and Juno, and a Western Task Force for the American beaches, code-named Omaha and Utah. Shortly after midnight on D-Day, two aerial fleets, one British and one American, would begin dropping parachute and glider troops behind the German defenses; by daybreak, they would have secured the eastern and western flanks. Just after dawn, following a massive bombardment, five seaborne divisions would start landing between the flanks held by the airborne divisions. They were to secure their separate

On June 1, 1944, five days before D-Day, most of the million-odd German troops stationed in France and the Netherlands were dispersed along the Atlantic Wall, a 2,400-mile coastal barrier (saw-toothed line) of powerful fortresses (gray squares), lesser fortifications (gray triangles), innumerable machine gun nests and long stretches of formidable terrain. Most of the 3.5 million Allied troops in Britain were concentrated in southern England, in marshaling areas (shading) around the major embarkation ports. Across the English Channel, in the strongest sector of the Atlantic Wall, some 20 German divisions, under Field Marshal Erwin Rommel, manned the French coast between two fortresses—the ports of Cherbourg, on the Cotentin Peninsula in Normandy, and Calais, well to the northeast. The Pas-de-Calais area, the closest to England and the likeliest invasion target, bristled with the mightiest defenses of all. But the Allies had their invasion site picked: a wide stretch of the Normandy coastline west of Caen.

beachheads on D-Day, link up on D-plus-1, then expand to form a staging area and build for a breakout to Paris and the Rhine River.

On June 5, after Eisenhower had made his momentous decision, the British and American commanders left SHAEF headquarters. Dawn was breaking, and the woods were loud with the song of birds. The planners, having done all they could, went to bed. The Second Front now belonged to the men who would do the fighting.

As the invasion fleet put forth from Britain that blustery morning, minesweepers cleared 10 lanes through the Germans' mid-Channel minefields, and along these safe passages sailed the battleships and cruisers, frigates, sloops and gunboats, the tank-landing ships, troop transports and assault boats, the repair ships, ammunition ships and the hospital ships. They were approaching their final positions as the sun began to set.

Later that evening, 20,000 men of the British 6th and U.S. 82nd and 101st Airborne divisions were driven to 22 air-fields, where 1,200 transport aircraft and 700 gliders were assembled for the greatest airborne assault in history.

By midnight, the sky was filled with transport planes and gliders, their red and green navigation lights blinking fitfully in the dark. Six of the gliders bore the men of the 2nd Battalion Oxfordshire and Buckinghamshire Light Infantry and a party of Royal Engineers, all led by Major John Howard. Their assignment was to capture the bridges of the Caen Canal and Orne River, which guarded the eastern flank of the invasion beachhead.

Peering out into the darkness, Howard glimpsed for a second the ribbon of the Caen Canal. The pilot dived steeply and the land rose up. "Hold tight!" the pilot shouted. The men linked arms and sat locked together, waiting for impact on the soil of German-occupied France.

Thanks to the glider pilots' precise landings—later described by Air Chief Marshal Leigh-Mallory as the War's finest piece of airmanship—the three platoons led by Major Howard secured the Caen Canal bridge less than 10 minutes

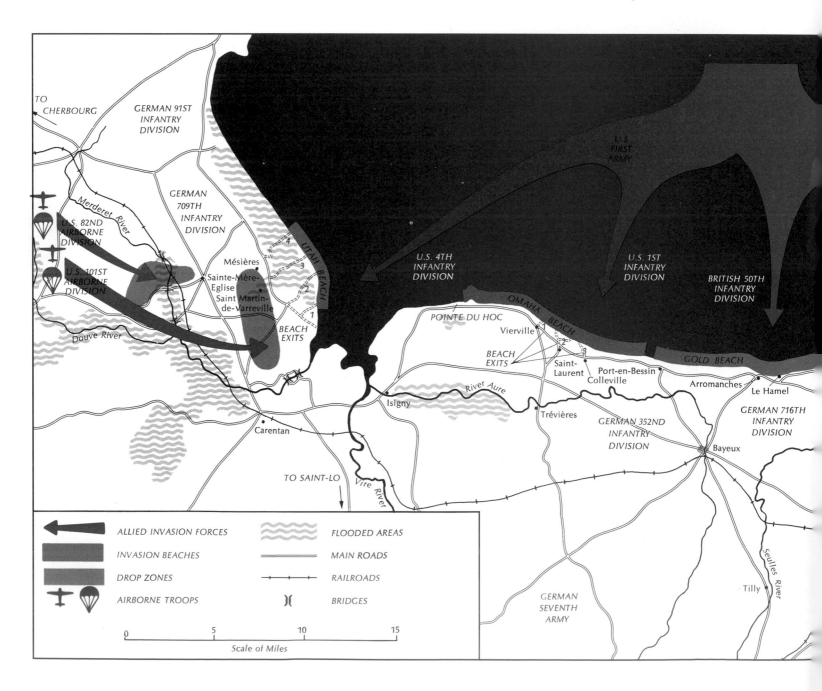

after the first glider landed. Howard's three other gliders, attacking the Orne River bridge, did not land as accurately, but were just as successful. Thus, within minutes the glider-borne strike force of the 6th Airborne had secured the first objectives of the invasion.

Perhaps the toughest mission of the British airborne division had been assigned to the 9th Parachute Battalion led by Lieut. Colonel Terence Otway. They were to storm the heavily fortified German battery at Merville. It was absolutely essential for them to succeed, since the battery commanded the left flank of the British landing beaches.

Otway's mission seemed doomed from the start. The five gliders carrying his antitank guns and jeeps broke their tow ropes and crashed into the sea. Then, to escape the flak, the pilots of the transport planes began swerving violently, scattering the battalion over 50 square miles of Normandy. Otway landed in the garden of a house that he recognized as a German headquarters. Germans began pouring out the door, and Otway and two companions ran for their lives.

As Otway prowled around in the dark, he realized that he had an impending disaster on his hands—400 of his men were missing, as were his mortars, antitank guns, jeeps and assault equipment. He had scarcely enough explosives to blow up the German guns. Still he assembled the remaining 155 men and headed for the Merville battery.

One group of paratroopers engaged the battery's machine gunners in savage hand-to-hand combat. Another party headed for the guns, battling toward the heavy steel doors in the concrete blockhouse. Incredibly, they found two of the doors still open. The attackers rushed inside, hurling grenades and emptying their guns. The German defenders were overwhelmed, and Otway's men proceeded to destroy the huge cannon—after which, the battalion signals officer took a carrier pigeon from his blouse and sent it winging back across the Channel with news that a critical objective of the 6th Airborne had been achieved.

From the outset, the American airborne operations were bedeviled by confusion and bad luck. Three quarters of the 6,500 men in the 82nd and the 101st Airborne divisions were widely scattered by their flak-dodging planes and took no meaningful part in the action. One group of 30 paratroopers, from the 82nd Airborne Division, was dropped right in Sainte-Mère-Eglise—the town they were supposed to surprise. A trooper landed in the main square and was immediately captured. Another fell on the church steeple and hung there from his parachute pretending to be dead for two and a half hours before he was cut down and taken prisoner. Two men plummeted through the roof of a house and died instantly when the mortar shells they carried exploded. A German soldier confronted some French civilians and, pointing to the body of a paratrooper hanging from a tree, shouted triumphantly, "All *kaput!*"

But the paratroopers were far from *kaput*. Enough men had landed outside town to rally and take their objective. Even though the Germans counterattacked in strength, the Americans held the town and with it, command of the vital main road between Cherbourg and Carentan.

All through the dark morning hours of June 6, while thousands of Allied paratroopers were scrambling toward their objectives and thousands of Allied ships were closing in on the Normandy coast, the Germans remained oblivious of the invasion. A few paratroopers might be making a nuisance of themselves, but nothing serious could be happening in such atrocious weather. Field Marshal Erwin Rommel, whose Army Group B defended the coasts of France and the Netherlands, was sleeping in his home in Herrlingen, where he had returned to celebrate his wife Lucie's birthday. At OKW (German Armed Forces Supreme Headquarters) in

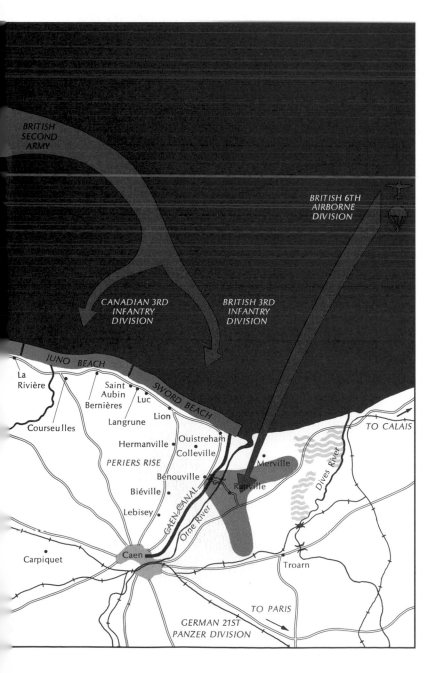

The assault phase of Operation Overlord began shortly after midnight on June 6, 1944, when three Allied airborne divisions—the British 6th, U.S. 82nd and U.S. 101st—landed near predetermined drop zones (shaded areas) in Normandy. Their objective was to secure vital inland targets in preparation for the amphibious assault. Between 6:30 and 7:35 a.m., leading elements of five U.S., British and Canadian divisions hit invasion beaches whose code names would go down in history: Utah, Omaha, Gold, Juno and Sword. Though the Allies established beachheads and seized many of their targets in each sector, they met with stiff resistance from the German forces—deployed as shown—and were prevented from taking their most important D-Day objective, the city of Caen.

Berchtesgaden, East Prussia, Adolf Hitler and his chief of staff, Colonel General Alfred Jodl, were both sound asleep.

One man who was awake was Field Marshal Gerd von Rundstedt, Commander-in-Chief-West, Paris. For hours, Rundstedt had refused to believe that an invasion was under way. But finally, the evidence was too strong to dismiss and Rundstedt ordered the Strategic Reserve—two crack armored divisions—to the Normandy coast. Had the order been implemented, it might have driven the Allies back into the sea. But at 6:30 a.m., Jodl awoke—and countermanded the order as premature.

Hitler himself rose at 10 a.m., and at first he endorsed Jodl's action. It was not until after lunch that he finally authorized Rundstedt to bring up the Strategic Reserves.

The failure of German commanders to take swift and effective action was due largely to Operation *Fortitude*, the Allies' brilliant deception. In a massive electronic conjuring trick, two groups of British motor launches appeared in the early hours off the Pas-de-Calais, each launch towing a pair of 29-foot balloons fitted with radar reflectors; altogether they produced radar images equivalent to a fleet of 10,000-ton troop transports. Meanwhile, RAF bombers dropped tons of aluminum chaff to simulate a vast air fleet overhead. German radar stations were soon reporting an enormous air and sea armada bound for the Pas-de-Calais.

The real show began at dawn, far to the southwest, along a 59-mile stretch of the Normandy coast. Suddenly the sea was full of ships and the air reverberated with a rumbling, concussive roar as salvo after salvo of naval gunfire erupted on German fortifications. Down from the skies swept waves of aircraft to bomb and strafe the beaches. Huddled in their bunkers, the German defenders lay with their hands pressed tightly against their ears. Unlike their superiors at OKW, they had no doubt about what was happening. The day of retribution, the day of invasion, had arrived.

At 6:31 a.m., almost exactly on H-Hour, 10 landing craft lowered their ramps at Utah Beach and 300 men of the 2nd Battalion, 8th Infantry Regiment, 4th United States Division, waded through 100 yards of surf to the dry sand beyond. A few minutes later, another 10 landing craft deposited the 1st Battalion just on their right. Ahead lay 500 yards of gently shelving beach surmounted by a belt of low dunes. It was oddly quiet.

Many of the Utah defenders had been killed by the bombardment, and the survivors were too dazed to react quickly. The Germans also were astonished to see tanks, the Sherman DDs, come swimming out of the sea. But the main reason was luck. The landing was in the wrong place; smoke and dust had obscured the landmarks and a strong tide had pushed the assault craft 2,000 yards south of the planned location, to a place where the beach was lightly held.

The men were elated, and none more so than Brig. General Theodore Roosevelt, the 4th's assistant divisional commander. At 57, Roosevelt was the oldest man and only general to go ashore on D-Day. He had persuaded General Omar Bradley, First Army Commander, to let him join the first wave, "to steady the boys," as he put it. And now Roosevelt made a shrewd decision. "We'll start the war from here," he said, and ordered the rest of the division to pile ashore on this relatively calm stretch of beach.

His gamble paid off. A rapid move inland deepened the beachhead, clearing the area for fresh assault waves. By 9:00 a.m., infantry and tanks had broken through the Atlantic Wall on a two-mile front between the sea and the lagoons at the back of the dunes. One by one, the strong points guarding roads inland fell, and by noon three beach exits were in American hands. Totaling the casualties at the end of the day, Roosevelt would report only 197 dead; another 60 were missing and presumed drowned. By every measure, Utah was a resounding success.

But to the southeast, on the four-mile-long crescent of beach between the towns of Vierville-sur-Mer and Coleville-sur-Mer, the bloodiest battle of D-Day was being fought. What happened on that beach would enshrine the name Omaha in American military annals, as valorous an event as Antietam or Gettysburg. And it was there that the Germans came closest to hurling the invaders back into the sea.

Omaha was not a good beach for a landing; it had been chosen because it was the only possible place on the rugged coast between Utah and the British beaches to the east. The area was dominated by 100-foot cliffs at either end, and the beach was backed by a seawall and a steep bank of coarse pebbles impassable to vehicles in most places. The four exits ran through heavily wooded ravines to stout, fortified villages. The shore between the tidelines was thickly planted with mined obstacles, and every inch of the entire area was pre-sighted for well-dug-in German machine guns, mortars, rocket launchers and cannon, some of them emplaced behind concrete walls three feet thick. Moreover, the German 716th Infantry Division, a third-rate outfit with 50 per cent foreign conscripts, had just been stiffened by the mobile, battle-hardened 352nd Infantry Division.

The American plan called for an initial assault by two regimental combat teams, the 116th and the 16th. As soon as they had gained a foothold, the remainder of the 1st and 29th Divisions of V Corps would storm ashore. The planners hoped to have a beachhead 16 miles wide and six miles deep by dusk. That was the idea.

But the troops at Omaha were in trouble from the moment they climbed into their landing craft nearly 12 miles

offshore. Immediately, ten of the slab-sided landing craft were swamped in the choppy seas; many of the 300 men on board were lost. Amphibious DUK-W transporters foundered as well in the rough water, carrying most of the first wave's artillery to the bottom. The DD Sherman tanks with their flotation devices were unable to survive either; only two of the first 29 made it to the beach. The rest sank like stones. The men hitting the beach had no armor and no heavy guns to support them in the face of murderous German fire.

Unlike the situation at Utah, only a few German positions had been knocked out by the preliminary bombardment, much of which either fell short or went long in the poor visibility. German strong points came to life as soon as the naval gunfire was lifted. Inside a bunker overlooking Omaha, near Colleville, a German commander was telephoning instructions to gunners several miles inland, where his regiment's 105mm howitzers were hidden. "Wait for the order to fire," he finished. The Germans watched silently as the American landing craft drew near.

The tide had ebbed a long way out and had yet to turn. The first line of landing craft from the awesome invasion force sped toward the shore, then lurched to a halt on the sandbars beyond the beach. The range was 400 yards.

"Target Dora," the German commander shouted into his telephone, "Fire!"

As the ramps of the landing craft dropped open and the troops rushed out, a machine gunner in the bunker got off a long, terrible burst that stitched the American line from one end to the other. An instant later, the howitzer shells came screaming over to explode among the men on the beach.

Trying to land near Vierville, the six boats of Company A of the 116th Infantry also ran into a cauldron of fire. "As the first men jumped," read the official report, "they crumpled and flopped into the water. Then order was lost. It seemed to the men that the only way to get ashore was to dive in head first and swim clear of the fire that was striking the boats. But, as they hit the water, their heavy equipment dragged them down and soon they were struggling to keep afloat. Some were hit in the water and wounded. Some drowned then and there. Those who survived kept moving forward with the tide, sheltering at times behind under-water obstacles and in this way they made their landings.

The assault on Omaha became a shambles. The engineers clearing and marking boat lanes through the obstacles made easy targets as they struggled ashore burdened with equipment and explosives. The attacking troops were mowed down at the water's edge or pinned below the sea wall or the pebble bank at the top of the beach. When subsequent waves came in, the new arrivals simply contributed to the chaos, augmenting the heaps of dead and huddles of living soldiers. The losses in the first hour were awesome.

Novelist Ernest Hemingway, serving as a war correspon-

dent, reached Omaha at the height of the battle. "One of the tanks flared up and started to burn with thick black smoke and yellow flames," he wrote. "Farther down the beach, another tank started burning. Along the line of the beach, they were crouched like big yellow toads along the high water line. As I stood up, watching, two more started to burn. The first ones were pouring out grey smoke now, and the wind was blowing it flat along the beach. On the beach, the first, second, third, fourth and fifth waves lay where they had fallen, looking like so many heavily laden bundles on the flat pebbly stretch between the sea and the first cover."

As the tide crept in, the living and the dead along the pebble bank eventually formed a motionless belt seven yards wide. Exhausted, shocked, uncertain of their bearings and unsure of where to go or what to do in the face of unrelenting German fire, the bewildered troops were slow to rally, even slower to move off the beach. But gradually, a few small groups did begin to move and pick their way over the marshy flat behind the beach and up the bluff to the plateau. By midmorning, there were 200 Americans in Vierville—enough to drive off a counterattack.

At 9:50 a.m., with the bulk of American troops still pinned down on the beach, Major General Clarence R. Huebner, commander of the 1st Division, interrupted the flow of matériel to the beach and sent in reinforcements. At the same time he called on the Navy to punch out the German guns even at the risk of hitting his own troops. "Get on them, men! Get on them!" Rear Admiral C. F. Bryant radioed his destroyers. "They're raising hell with the men on the beach! We must stop them!" The destroyers swept in so close that their keels occasionally scraped bottom as they whipped around to deliver thunderous salvos. All morning they fired, and into the afternoon. The fire was almost the only direct artillery support the infantry got that day.

By 11:00 a.m., the battle was finally beginning to go in the Americans' favor. Colonel George A. Taylor, commander of the 16th Infantry, yelled across the beach: "Two kinds of people are staying on this beach, the dead and those who are going to die. Now let's get the hell out of here!" He then led his troops forward to attack the German positions.

At the exits to the beach, fresh troops and newly-landed tanks began to capture German strong points weakened by the destroyers' ferocious bombardment. The German 352nd Division mounted a series of counterattacks, all of which were beaten off; the division spent most of its available reserves in a fruitless attempt to dislodge a battalion of tough U.S. Rangers, who had scaled the 100-foot cliffs at Pointe du Hoc and secured the western flank of Omaha Beach. Finally, at 1:30 p.m., V Corps was able to radio First Army commander Bradley on board the cruiser *Augusta*: "Troops formerly pinned down on beaches Easy Red, Easy Green, Fox Red now advancing up heights."

When darkness mercifully fell, V Corps was clinging to a precarious beachhead six miles long and not even two miles deep. Already, the Americans had sustained 3,000 casualties. Whether U.S. forces were at Omaha to stay depended on what the German defenders could throw against them in the days to follow. And that, in turn, depended on the fortunes of the British and Canadians on Gold, Juno and Sword.

Strategy on those three beaches was dictated by a threat that the Americans did not have to face: tanks. The British Second Army—75,000 strong—under General Sir Miles Dempsey, would have to take on at least one panzer division if it was to achieve its primary D-Day objectives of capturing the city of Caen and securing the eastern flank of the Allied front. This meant moving inland far and fast in order to contain an expected assault by masses of German panzers. The beachhead would be none too safe even if it extended 20 miles inland by nightfall.

Shortly before 7:30 a.m., after a two-hour naval bombardment, the gates of the landing craft clanged open. Soldiers in their hobnailed boots clattered down the ramps into the surf—and a scene far different from that facing the Americans to the west. Nowhere along the 24 miles of beaches were there natural terrain features as formidable as those at Omaha; instead of the high bluffs and steep banks

In this photo taken by Life photographer, Robert Capa, the first wave of American invaders on Omaha Beach take shelter from deadly fire behind German barriers and a disabled American tank. The beach itself was dominated by sheer cliffs 100 feet high. Three hundred yards deep at low tide, it shelved gently up to a steep bank of coarse pebbles and was impassable to vehicles in most places. The only four exits wound through deep, wooded ravines to stout little villages fortified by the Germans.

of coarse pebbles, the men of two British and one Canadian division found a gently shelving beach with a series of small summer resorts lying along a coast road, and beyond that only flat open country—good for tanks. Awaiting them were 24 companies of German infantry, with machine guns, mortars and close to 200 artillery pieces. But death on the British beaches was a random harvest rather than the grim reaping at Omaha.

The beachside German defenders were mainly from the heavily conscript 716th Division, and how an Allied soldier fared depended on where he landed and whom he faced. Some units came ashore to no opposition whatsoever; the enemy surrendered instantly. But those units that were set down before resolute defenders suffered greatly. Troops arriving in the second wave found scattered concentrations of bodies and spreading stains of blood clotting the sand. Soldiers hurt at the water's edge were dragged up the beach by comrades who feared that they would drown in the incoming tide. But British tanks lumbering up the beach ran over and crushed some of the screaming wounded men.

Still, after a few hours, most of the units with inland objectives fought their way off the beaches. Troops of the British 50th Division, who landed on Gold Beach, cut the Bayeux-Caen road, putting themselves in position to prevent tanks from reaching the vulnerable Americans on Omaha.

To the left of Gold, on Juno Beach, men of the 3rd Canadian Division were established on the fringes of both Bayeux and the Carpiquet airfield—within sight of Caen—when darkness halted operations. Canadian units linked up on their right with British troops on Gold Beach, forming a solid beachhead 12 miles long and at least six miles deep. But the Canadian left flank was still separated from Sword Beach by two and a half miles of enemy-held territory. And Sword Beach was where the real danger loomed. Somewhere behind the beach were the tanks of the 21st Panzer Division.

The 3rd British Infantry Division, held up by reefs and a tricky tide, landed late on Sword and was late starting inland. By 4 p.m., however, a battalion of the King's Shropshire Light Infantry (KSLI), with tanks and some anti-tank guns, was only three miles from the northern outskirts of Caen. But hopes of capturing the city by nightfall were dashed when they encountered a formation of 40 powerful Mark IV panzers just outside Biéville, and the first big tank battle of the invasion erupted.

General Erich Marcks, whose 84th Corps controlled the 21st Panzer, had spotted a serious flaw in the British lines. From Lebisey, a gap several miles wide reached all the way to the coast between Langrune and Lion-sur-Mer; various British units there had failed to clear out the German defend-

ers. If those defenders could be reinforced, Marcks had reasoned, the Germans might be able to maintain a wedge between the British and the Canadians and, eventually, begin to roll up the Sword and Juno beachheads. Thus, he had sent the Mark IVs plunging into the gap.

In the opening phase of the battle, Shermans of the Staffordshire Yeomanry knocked out two Mark IVs, and anti-tank guns stopped two more. Soon the British knocked out another six tanks. At this point, the two forces disengaged—the battered panzers to drive on toward the sea, the British to press toward Caen. The lead units were only two miles from Caen when they ran into intense fire from a German position too strong to attack without reinforcements. The bold push on Caen was halted and the British dug in for the night. It would be weeks before any Allied units surpassed the KSLI's high-water mark on the road to Caen.

Meanwhile half a dozen tanks of Marcks' battle group, supported by a company of infantry, slipped through British lines and reached the coast at Luc-sur-Mer, between Langrune and Lion. There they waited for reinforcements. However, as the reinforcing tanks—another 50 Mark IVs dispatched by General Edgar Feuchtinger, commander of the 21st Panzers—were on their way, a tremendous coincidence disrupted the promising plan for a counterattack.

The sky suddenly filled with planes, and before the Germans' eyes, fresh airborne forces swooped past on the way to reinforce the British 6th Airborne Division along the Orne River a few miles to the east. The vast armada numbered 250 gliders, filled with troops and supplies, towed by 250 transport planes and guarded by a great flight of fighter planes. The massive reinforcement would double the strength of the besieged and exhausted 6th Airborne, which had already been in action for 20 hours.

To the German tank crews, the enemy planes and gliders seemed to be a huge bridge reaching across the whole horizon. "We looked up," said a panzer lieutenant, "and there they were just above us. Noiselessly, those giant wooden boxes sailed in over our heads. We lay on our backs and fired and fired into those gliders, until we could not work the bolts of our rifles anymore. But with such masses, it seemed to make little difference."

The Germans lost heart. General Feuchtinger called off his counterattack toward the coast. His division had saved Caen for a while, but at terrible cost; he would end the day with the loss of 76 of his 146 tanks. He reported to his superiors: "Attack by the 21st Panzer Division rendered useless by heavily concentrated airborne troops."

For the Germans, D-Day ended as it had begun—in confusion or delusion or both. General Marcks of the 84th

BUILD-UP TIME IN NORMANDY

On June 7, the day after D-Day, the invasion entered its second critical phase. Even as the Allied dead were being gathered for shipment to England, great flotillas of ships appeared off Normandy and began pouring ashore more men and matériel.

Among the arrivals was a motley collection of vessels destined to be sunk off Omaha Beach and Gold Beach as the foundations for two huge artificial harbors that would serve until proper ports like Cherbourg and Brest could be captured and put into operation. Code-named Mulberries, these harbors would have to handle 25 divisions with all their equipment and mountains of supplies in the next 20 days. The target was 6,000 tons of supplies daily by D-plus-5, with dramatic rises thereafter.

Protected from German aerial attack by barrage balloons and resistant to storms, the rugged Mulberries accomplished everything planned for them and more. By the evening of D-plus-10, the massive movement of men and supplies had already shifted into high gear. Although the ports were still not complete, 557,000 troops with 81,000 vehicles and 183,000 tons of supplies had been brought ashore. Hordes of landing craft, freighters and outboard Rhino ferries had transformed Omaha and Gold beaches into major facilities. The supply side of the Second Front was secure.

Protected by barrage balloons, Omaha Beach swarms with ships and trucks funneling supplies inland to support the American troops.

Corps believed that the American landings at Omaha Beach had been smashed. His superiors at Seventh Army headquarters thought that the American landings were merely a sideshow compared to the British assault, and that the Americans could be dealt with at leisure. OKW in Germany was still waiting for what it was certain would be the main invasion at the Pas-de-Calais. Erwin Rommel, who felt that the war would be won or lost on the beaches, suspected that it was already lost. And poor Feuchtinger, despite his losses, kept getting orders to wipe out the beachhead at once.

For the Allies, D-Day had brought a tremendous victory. The whole vast, complex assault phase of Operation *Overlord* had worked. So effective was Operation *Fortitude* that while the German High Command had looked toward the Pas-de-Calais area, the Allies landed 152,000 troops and hundreds of tanks in Normandy without a single massed counterattack. SHAEF had secretly predicted 10,000 dead in the initial assault. In fact, no more than 2,500 men had lost their lives—while total casualties were fewer than 12,000, of whom 6,600 were American, 3,500 British and 1,000 Canadian.

The Allied commanders were elated, but they were far from complacent. The beachhead was small, the front thinly held, the supplies slow to come in. The American seaborne forces had not yet linked up with the 82nd Airborne; the Utah beachhead was isolated, and the penetration beyond Omaha tenuous. A seven-mile gap separated the British and the Americans, and the 3rd British Division was still three miles away from the 3rd Canadian. Caen remained in German hands, and without Caen as an anchor, the whole invasion front was afloat.

The Allies spent the night clinging to their patches of Normandy coastline. On the beaches, work parties prepared for the flood of men and matériel scheduled to resume at first light. Inland, infantry patrols padded carefully through the orchards and farms. The few GIs and Tommies lucky enough to catch a few winks, awoke to find the sun rising in a brilliant sky aswarm with protective fighter planes.

At Saint-Aubin-sur-Mer, just behind Sword Beach, Lieut. Colonel James L. Moulton and the men of No. 48 Commando began to clean up the mess around them. "It was a shocking sight," Moulton wrote later, "Many corpses, some of them badly dismembered, were lying among the rest of the debris of the assault: wrecked and burnt-out tanks, equipment and stores of every sort, scattered on the beach or drifted up along the water's edge; wrecked landing craft broached-to on the beach or in the sea among the beach obstacles. Among all this, several French women were walking about, picking up what tinned food they could

find—incredibly, they had small children with them, who gazed with indifferent curiosity on the shattered corpses, the broken equipment and the scattered tins of food."

But the Allies had little time to pause and contemplate. Their task was to drive ahead. By noon, a reinforced 82nd Airborne Division linked up with the forces, designated VII Corps, from Utah Beach. By nightfall, they held a bridgehead nine miles long and eight miles deep. Even the situation at Omaha was beginning to improve. The troops of V Corps were able to establish a bridgehead across the River Aure, about four miles south of the Beach.

To the east, the Germans were so heavily involved in holding Caen against the 3rd British and 3rd Canadian divisions that they could do little to slow the 50th British to the northwest. Most of the Caen-Bayeux road fell and on June 8 Bayeux was captured—the first important town in France to be liberated.

The invasion had fired Frenchmen everywhere. With D-Day, the Resistance emerged in all its fury, blowing bridges and ammunition dumps, cutting telephone lines and sabotaging the railway system. At the same time, Allied planes controlled not only the battlefield but also the approach routes to a depth of 100 miles. An SS staff officer later recalled the awful effect of those air strikes: "Our motorized columns were coiling along the road toward the invasion beaches. Then something happened. Spurts of fire flecked along the column and splashes of dust stuccoed the road. Everyone was piling out of the vehicles and scuttling for the neighboring fields. Several vehicles were already in flames. This attack ceased as suddenly as it had crashed upon us 15 minutes before. The men started drifting back to the column again, pale and shaky and wondering how they had survived this fiery rain of bullets.

"An hour later the whole thing started all over again, only much worse. The march was called off and vehicles that

Troops of the U.S. 2nd Division land on Omaha Beach on D-plus-1 and begin their trek inland to fight for the crucial high ground of Cerisy Forest, 12 miles to the south.

were left were hidden. No one dared show himself any more. Now the men started looking at each other. This was different from what we thought it would be like."

Meanwhile, from the crowded beaches endless columns of men and vehicles moved inland. One RAF liaison officer remembered "the sight of the British infantry, plodding steadily up those dusty French roads towards the front, single file, heads bent down against the heavy weight of all the kit piled on their backs, armed to the teeth; they were plodding on, slowly and doggedly towards the front with the sweat running down their faces, never looking back and hardly ever looking to the side—just straight in front and down a little on to the roughness of the road; while the jeeps and the lorries and the tanks and all the other traffic went crowding by, smothering them in great billows and clouds of dust which they never even deigned to notice. That was a sight that somehow caught at your heart."

Although the Allies were clearly winning the battle of the build-up, they had failed to expand their beachhead as swiftly as the *Overlord* planners had expected. By June 10, the American VII Corps was locked in an inch-by-inch struggle to cut the neck of the Cotentin Peninsula, and the British were still frustrated in their attempts to capture Caen. Amazingly, the German OKW still believed that the main invasion was to come in the Pas-de-Calais area, and that the intention of the Allies was to swing northeast to link up with this main landing for a concerted drive into Germany. Caen thus appeared essential to anchor their eastern flank.

The British were just as determined to capture the city, and on June 10, Montgomery launched a massive pincer attack. One arm of the pincer was the 7th Armored Division, the Desert Rats of North Africa fame. But they swiftly came to grief before the muzzles of four SS heavy tanks—50-ton Tigers mounting 88mm guns. As the Tigers opened fire from hidden positions, the lead British tank exploded in flames and shuddered to a halt, blocking the entire column. Then, as the British deployed to attack, the commander of the German unit rolled his Tiger out from cover and moved down the stalled line of British vehicles, firing as he went. The thin-skinned British personnel carriers and half-tracks exploded in geysers of flame. Armor-piercing rounds from the few British tanks that tried to shoot back bounced like peas off the Tiger's thick steel plate.

A second company of Tigers, with eight tanks, now joined the foray, and in less than 10 minutes the leading brigade of the 7th Armored Division was nothing but scrap metal. The Tigers plowed on into a nearby village where the British soldiers, supported by a handful of tanks, were holed up in houses. There, the Tommies began knocking out the Tigers with hand-held rocket launchers; finally, the Germans were

forced to retreat. But they had smashed the spearhead of an armor division and stalled the whole attack on Caen. For the next month the fighting at Caen was a standoff.

In the meantime, the Americans to the west were making slow gains. On June 12, they captured the important crossroads town of Carentan, linking V Corps at Omaha with VII Corps at Utah and giving the Allies an unbroken lodgment about 10 miles deep and 60 miles wide. Yet U.S. forces were still nowhere near Cherbourg, whose capture had been forecast for D-plus-8. The Americans had pushed isolated salients down to Villers Bocage and Caumont, but were stymied on the way to Saint-Lô. And along most of the rest of the front the offensive had slowed to a crawl.

The terrain was made to order for defense. This was hedgerow country, a patchwork of thousands of small fields enclosed by almost impenetrable hedges, thickets of brambles, vines and trees growing out of coarse earthen mounds. Each field was like a small fort: defenders dug in at a hedgerow base and hidden by vegetation were all but impervious to rifle and artillery fire. Most of the roads were wagon trails, worn into sunken lanes by centuries of use and turned into cavernlike mazes by arching hedges, gloomy passages tailor-made for ambushes, and deathtraps for tanks.

The mental and physical strain were so exhausting that many men were in a stupor. "Over a stretch of time," said a platoon leader, "you became so dulled by fatigue that the names of the killed and wounded, names of men who had been your best friends, might have come out of a telephone book for all you knew. All the old values were gone, and if there was a world beyond this tangle of hedgerows you never expected to live to see it."

While the Germans fought with great stubbornness and skill in the hedgerow country, Hitler clung to the belief that the Germans would eventually regain the initiative. In con-

In their first postinvasion meeting on D-plus-4, British General Bernard Montgomery (left), commander of all Allied ground forces in France, and Lieut. General Omar Bradley, U.S. First Army commander, discuss troop movements in a quiet field near Port-en-Bessin.

trast, both Rundstedt and Rommel were convinced that the situation on the Normandy front was hopeless. Rommel even went so far in a meeting with Hitler on June 17 as to suggest an end to the War. But for the Führer, withdrawal was inconceivable, capitulation unmentionable.

Three days before Rommel's fruitless meeting with Hitler, American troops had set out to capture Cherbourg and its port. The First Army's General Bradley used the VII Corps under Major General J. Lawton Collins as his spearhead. Collins would drive west from Carentan to the west coast of the Cotentin Peninsula, then north to Cherbourg.

It took the better part of a week for three infantry divisions to negotiate the difficult, flooded terrain and hammer their way through German defenses. Finally, on June 20, they stood wearily before Cherbourg, confronting a massive complex of concrete blockhouses bristling with automatic weapons and covered by artillery. It was quickly apparent that there would be no easy entry into the port city. The brutal, slogging fight for Normandy would continue.

When one battalion attempted to move past a crossroad on the edge of the city, machine guns opened up from houses all around. A deluge of artillery shells from nearby hills struck the command group, mortally wounding the battalion commander, injuring his staff and driving back the whole unit. Another battalion, attacking a suburb of Cherbourg, was hit by small-arms fire and an artillery barrage; within just a few minutes, 31 men were dead and 92 wounded.

For another two days the Americans slugged it out with the defenders. And then Collins broadcast an ultimatum, threatening an "air pulverization" if the defenders did not surrender. When the ultimatum was ignored, hundreds upon hundreds of Allied fighter bombers roared in to bomb and strafe for one solid hour. And still the Germans grimly hung on. For four more days, the Americans fought from street to street and house to house, flushing out the defenders with explosives attached to long poles and "beehive" charges of adhesive-covered explosives.

As the end drew near, the German commander, Lieut. General Karl Wilhelm von Schlieben, tried to rally his sag-

ging troops by handing out Iron Crosses dropped in by parachute. But he knew that the garrison was doomed. "I must state in the line of duty," he radioed Rommel, "that further sacrifices cannot alter anything."

On June 26, American troops found the underground command post where Schlieben was holed up and sent in a prisoner to demand surrender. When Schlieben refused, tank destroyers were summoned. A few rounds brought out 800 defenders, including General Schlieben.

The surrender of Cherbourg threw Hitler into a rage. He had ordered Schlieben to fight to the death "and leave the enemy not a harbor, but a field of ruins." In the end, the general had decided not to die for his Führer, but he had carried out his other orders to the very letter.

Cherbourg was in truth a field of ruins. Mines were everywhere; sunken ships blocked all the basins. The electrical system and dock machinery were destroyed, quay walls damaged, cranes toppled and twisted, and the breakwater heavily cratered. The Germans had effectively denied the Allies the harbor. Three weeks of intensive clearing would be needed before the port could begin to operate. The bulk of supplies would continue to come in over the beaches.

Nevertheless, as the end of June approached, the situation was deteriorating rapidly for the Germans. Desperately seeking to regain the initiative, Hitler ordered a counterattack with all possible forces. On June 29, elements of four panzer divisions hurled themselves at the British in a thrust aimed at Bayeux. The panzers were immediately blasted by British antitank guns and by a tremendous air and sea bombardment; even the near misses from 16-inch naval shells knocked out Panther and Tiger tanks, bowling them over like toys. The German attack spent itself in a single day.

German casualties were now rising to the point where they outnumbered replacements; German vehicles needed 200,000 more gallons of fuel than was available; and only 400 tons of the 2,250 tons of other supplies required daily were reaching the front through the crippled transportation system. To Field Marshal Gerd von Rundstedt at his headquarters near Paris, it all was evidence of the growing futility of the War. He called Field Marshal Wilhelm Keitel, chief of the German High Command, and explained the situation.

"What shall we do?" cried the distraught Keitel.

"Make peace, you fools," Rundstedt answered. "What else can you do?"

The next day the Führer's adjutant appeared at Rundstedt's headquarters with orders removing Rundstedt from command. His successor, Field Marshal Günther von Kluge, soon announced his commitment to an "unconditional holding of the present defense line."

On July 4, the British resumed their attempts to take Caen with a drive on Carpiquet. Three days later, they followed up with an attack on Caen itself. A few minutes before 10 p.m. on July 7, an armada of 500 four-engine bombers dropped 2,500 tons of bombs on the edge of the city. Early on the morning of July 9, German units began evacuating across the Orne River.

British and Canadian troops entered Caen early that afternoon, and found the streets choked with huge blocks of stone. Rescuers digging into the rubble found that the weight of the bombing had fallen on the civilian population; relatively few Germans had been in the target area. About 6,000 men, women and children had perished in the cataclysm; thousands more were injured. "The dead lay everywhere," recalled one witness, "not corpses, just the remains, fingers, a hand, a head, and pathetic personal belongings, a bottle of aspirin, rosary beads, torn and mud-soaked letters."

After Caen, came Saint-Lô, which had been a favorite leave spot for the German occupiers before June 6. Since then, Allied bombing had reduced it to rubble, and 800 civilians lay dead in the ruins.

The job of taking Saint-Lô fell to the 29th Division. But

American infantrymen advance through the streets of battle-scarred Carentan, won from the Germans on June 12. The capture of the crossroads town consolidated the Allied beachheads, which freed the U.S. V Corps and VII Corps to attack toward the port city of Cherbourg.

Normandy's hedgerows, compact earthen mounds covered with thornbush and trees, stretched before the Allied invaders like a never-ending obstacle course. So dense was the vegetation that tanks had to be armed with steel blades (top right) to slice through. Sometimes infantrymen going around the hedgerows found themselves staring eye to eye at a startled German. For nerve-racked soldiers, searching for the snipers (bottom right) was a deadly game of hide-and-seek.

301

first one attacking American battalion, then another, was pinned down and decimated by sheets of German machine gun and artillery fire. Finally, on the night of July 17, riflemen of the 116th Infantry Regiment broke through to relieve the two isolated battalions. The following morning, a task force picked its way through antitank, artillery and mortar fire to a square close to the town cemetery. Spreading out from there, teams of infantry, tanks and tank destroyers methodically obliterated the enemy's strong points. By 5 p.m., Saint-Lô was in American hands.

While his troops were still struggling toward Saint-Lô, Bradley had ordered that a large mess tent be set up next to his command-post truck and provided with the biggest available map of the Normandy beachhead, a map that would depict in detail every road and terrain feature in the area. The general also required that the tent be equipped with a wooden floor: recent rains had turned the countryside into a sea of mud, and Bradley expected to do a lot of pacing.

For two nights, Bradley moved back and forth in front of the map, sketching in division and corps boundaries with colored pencils. By the time he was done he had devised a plan that would accomplish nothing less than a breakout from the Normandy beachhead in which the Allies had been penned for more than a month. Code-named *Cobra*, the operation would result in what Omar Bradley, with a certain pride of authorship, later described as, "the most decisive battle of our war in western Europe."

Bradley's plan called first for such heavy bombing of the battle area that the Germans would be unable to fight back immediately. Then, attacking on a narrow front, two infantry divisions would tear a gap through the enemy positions and hold back the sides for a motorized infantry division to come through on a 15-mile dash to Coutances. Two armored divisions would then follow: while one protected the eastern flank, the other would barrel 30 miles

south to Avranches and turn the corner into Brittany.

Unless *Cobra* was quick and decisive, Bradley warned his staff, "we go right back to this hedge fighting and you can't make any speed. This thing must be bold."

On July 10, Bradley briefed his immediate superior, General Montgomery. Meaning to help, Montgomery ordered General Dempsey's First British Army to make a "massive stroke" in the Caen-Falaise area. In notifying Eisenhower of the operation, which would be called *Goodwood*, Montgomery said that it might produce "far-reaching results," but only if it was backed by "the whole weight" of Allied air power.

In fact, as one of Montgomery's aides soon informed the War Office in London, *Goodwood's* main purpose was "to muck up and write off the enemy troops," thereby diverting German attention from *Cobra*. But because of Montgomery's glowing prediction and the demand for massive air support, Eisenhower supposed that *Goodwood* was aimed at a second long-awaited breakout—this one from the Caen area.

Thanks to Field Marshal Rommel, the Wehrmacht's Army Group B was prepared for *Goodwood*. Having deployed his 13 divisions in five defensive zones along a 70-mile front, Rommel made a final inspection on July 17 and then headed back to headquarters. En route, his car was spotted by British fighter-bombers. Rommel called to his driver to take cover, but the planes swooped down to strafe so swiftly that the driver was killed at the wheel. The car hurtled into a tree and the Field Marshal was thrown to the road. Suffering from a concussion, Erwin Rommel, one of the greatest of the great German military minds, was sent home to a long-term recuperation, his luminous career at an end.

Operation *Goodwood* began at 5:30 a.m. on July 18 with a 45-minute air bombardment by 1,000 RAF Lancasters and Halifaxes, followed by a pounding from 571 American Eighth Air Force heavy bombers. Wrote an infantryman who watched from the ground: "The bombers flew in majestically

A U.S. Navy Salvage ship in Cherbourg harbor moors alongside an overturned 550-foot-long whaler that was later used to extend a rebuilt pier. When the Allies finally captured the badly needed port at the end of June 1944, they already had in hand reconstruction plans for the rebuilding of the harbor. But when the damage was surveyed, it proved to be more extensive than anyone had foreseen. Still, the salvage operation proceeded at a fever pitch and three weeks after the capture of Cherbourg four Liberty ships were able to unload the first supplies in the harbor.

The gaunt remains of the cathedral of Notre-Dame rise from the ruins of Saint-Lô, a strategic Normandy crossroads town that was almost 95 per cent destroyed before troops of the U.S. 29th Division captured it on July 18, 1944. The devastation brought about by more than a month of Allied bombing and shelling was intensified by a two-day German artillery and mortar barrage. So great was the destruction that many U.S. troops fell into an awed silence upon entering the rubble-choked streets. Said one soldier: "We sure liberated the hell out of this place."

and with a dreadful, unalterable dignity, unloaded and made for home." Yet despite the intensity of the air assault, the backbone of the German defense system, the 88mm guns on the Bourguébus Ridge, escaped serious damage.

When the British VIII Corps moved forward, it advanced more than three miles in little over an hour, and by noon it appeared on the verge of a complete penetration. Then, however, from the Bourguébus Ridge came fire so effective that the Germans referred to exploding British tanks as "Tommy cookers" and "Ronson lighters" because "they light up the first time." The British faltered and fell back.

For two more days, the VIII Corps and Canadian II Corps persevered, and only when a thunderstorm turned the ground beyond Caen into a swamp did Operation Goodwood come to a halt. Montgomery declared himself satisfied. He had taken 2,000 prisoners, secured all of the Caen area and seized 34 square miles of territory. But Goodwood's cost was immense. The British had lost more than 3,500 men and the Canadians suffered 1,956 casualties. Tank losses amounted to 36 per cent of all British tanks on the Continent.

At one point during the fighting, Montgomery had issued

a communiqué saying that the British and Canadians "broke through" into the area east of the Orne and southeast of Caen. The choice of words was unfortunate: it gave the impression that Goodwood had produced a real breakout. When Eisenhower learned differently, he was furious, and there were rumors that Montgomery was going to be fired. Responding quickly, Montgomery explained that some "misunderstandings" had arisen, and Eisenhower finally decided to swallow his wrath.

Despite the controversy, Goodwood had actually chewed up four enemy divisions, and it was growing clear to the Germans that the Allies could not be held back much longer. On July 21, the day after Goodwood petered out, Field Marshal von Kluge wrote to Hitler that "the moment is fast approaching when our hard-pressed defenses will crack." General Alfred Jodl, Chief of the German Armed Forces Operations Staff, read Kluge's letter and suggested that the Führer think about withdrawing from France.

Surprisingly, Hitler agreed. Yet before the idea could be implemented, fighting erupted again. After a four-day delay because of rain, Operation Cobra had begun.

During his intense study of the huge map, Omar Bradley's

attention had fastened on an old road running east-west from Saint-Lô to Périers. Built by the Romans, the road was ruler-straight; it could serve as a dividing line, readily recognizable from the air, that would set off the Americans on the north side of the road from the Germans on the south. At a July 19 conference in London with Air Chief Marshal Leigh-Mallory, Bradley thought he had "a clear understanding" that Allied planes would make lateral bomb runs, parallel to the Saint-Lô-Périers road, instead of coming in over the heads of American troops and risking a deadly shortfall.

Now, on July 24, one hour before *Cobra's* scheduled 1 p.m. air bombardment was to begin, American troops in the battle zone pulled back 1,200 yards so as to create a safety zone. The sky was overcast, and Leigh-Mallory, who had flown to Normandy to witness the operation, decided to postpone the bombing because of the unsettled weather. His message reached England only a few minutes before the first of 1,600 bombers started arriving over the target area.

Unaware that they were supposed to turn back, three groups of fighter-bombers flew over the heads of American troops and then out over the German positions. Large numbers of heavy bombers also failed to get word of the cancellation, but visibility was so limited that the first 500 of these planes did not release their bombs and only 35 aircraft in the second formation dropped theirs. But more than 300 bombers in the third formation unloaded 550 tons of high explosive and 135 tons of fragmentation bombs.

Tragically, some of the bombs fell on American positions, killing 25 men and wounding 131. Bradley was incensed—not least because the bombers had flown over the heads of American troops rather than parallel to the Saint-Lô-Périers road, as he had expected.

When Bradley protested to Leigh-Mallory, the air chief said he would check into the matter. Later, he called Bradley back and reported that the overhead approach to the target had been deliberate. Air planners had opposed a lateral run because it would have meant entering the rectangular target area from its narrow side, crowding the planes dangerously close together. Leigh-Mallory made it clear that if Bradley wanted the air bombardment resumed, he would have to agree to let the planes come in over the heads of the troops. Bradley had no choice but to acquiesce, and the stupendous assault was rescheduled for 11 a.m. on July 25.

The U.S. troops on the ground were elated as bombs began to tumble from the planes. "We spread our feet and leaned far back trying to look straight up, until our steel helmets fell off," wrote Correspondent Ernie Pyle. "And then the bombs came. They began like the crackle of popcorn and almost instantly swelled into a monstrous fury of noise that seemed surely to destroy all the world ahead of us."

But then, Pyle recalled, there slowly "crept into our consciousness a realization that the windrows of exploding bombs were easing back toward us, flight by flight, instead of gradually forward, as the plan called for. Then we were horrified by the suspicion that those machines, high in the sky and completely detached from us, were aiming their bombs at the smoke line on the ground—and a gentle breeze was drifting the smoke line back over us! An inde-

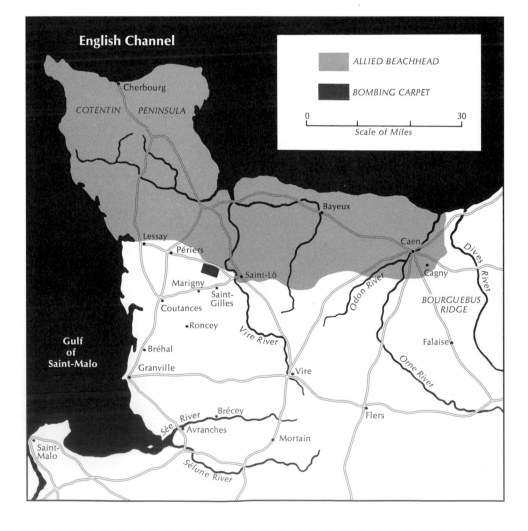

English Channel

ALLIED BEACHHEAD

BOMBING CARPET

0   30
Scale of Miles

By the third week in July 1944, the Allies controlled a large part of Normandy, including all of the Cotentin Peninsula, and were ready to break out of their beachhead. For the offensive, Lieut. General Omar N. Bradley devised a plan whereby Allied planes would "carpet bomb" a rectangle measuring three and a half by one and a half miles (shown in red) south of the Périers-Saint-Lô road. The bombing was designed to tear a hole in the German lines through which the U.S. First Army could plunge south toward Coutances and Avranches, and achieve the crucial breakout.

scribable kind of panic came over us. And then all of an instant the universe became filled with a gigantic rattling as of huge ripe seeds in a mammoth dry gourd. It was bombs by the hundreds, hurtling down through the air above us."

For the second time in two days, Allied bombs had fallen on Americans: this time 111 men were killed, including Lieut. General Lesley J. McNair, a senior staff officer from Washington who was present as an observer, and another 490 were wounded. But the Germans had suffered even more: 1,000 men of Panzer Division Lehr had perished, and the division commander later reported "my lines looked like the face of the moon, and at least 70 per cent of my troops were out of action—dead, wounded, crazed or numbed." Only a dozen of his tanks remained operational.

As Bradley's ground attack got under way, the town Saint-Gilles fell on July 27, then Marigny. Bradley determined to go all out. To prevent the Germans from regrouping behind the Sée River, he ordered George Patton, who had been waiting impatiently in an apple orchard for his Third Army to become operational on August 1, to get himself personally involved in the fight right now. Bradley gave Patton command of his own VIII Corps and told him to get to Avranches in a hurry.

Patton put two armored divisions at the point of the VIII Corps and started barreling south. Coutances fell on July 28, but the units had no time to savor victory as the race to Avranches continued. The speed of the Americans' advance actually spread confusion through their own ranks. While racing across the countryside, units were getting out of touch and running into one another. In order to keep the momentum going, generals directed traffic at intersections.

For the Germans, the situation had become what Kluge called a "Riesensauerei"—roughly, one hell of a mess. As their vehicular columns fled pell-mell to the south, burning trucks and tanks lined every road, unused mines lay scattered along the highways and, in the haste of withdrawal, German troops neglected to set off bridge demolitions.

Realizing that his left flank along the Cotentin east coast had collapsed, Kluge ordered troops to race to Pontaubault, four miles below Avranches, to make sure that the Americans did not seize a bridge there across the Selune River. But when the first German elements arrived on July 31, they found Americans already holding the bridge.

Cobra had torn a funnel-shaped hole in the German defenses that was 10 miles wide at Avranches and narrowed to a single road and the bridge at Pontaubaut. Casualties were light and morale soared at the sight of German prisoners who, as an officer put it, were "so happy to be captured that all they could do was giggle." Of the 28,000 enemy soldiers captured by the First Army in July, 20,000 were bagged during the last six days of the month.

Now there was nothing to stop the Americans from entering Brittany or from turning toward Paris. The grim push through the hedgerows gave way to electrifying thrusts.

The breakout was accompanied by a shift in high command. Bradley took over the new U.S. Twelfth Army Group, made up of the old First Army now under Lieut. General Courtney H. Hodges and the Third Army under Patton.

When the Third Army rolled off its mark on August 1, it included the VIII Corps already in action under Patton's direction and the XV Corps. In 48 hours, Patton squeezed two armored divisions through the opening at Pontaubault. On their heels came other units, wriggling along the highways clogged with debris and dead animals, past wrecked vehicles and through shattered villages and towns. As the American tanks and motorized units debouched into the verdant, wide-open countryside of Brittany, the whole character of the fighting abruptly changed. "Suddenly the war became fun," a correspondent later wrote. "It became exciting, carnivalesque, tremendous. It became victorious and even safe."

Patton and his divisional commanders were old cavalry-

The dazed expression on the stubbled face of this German paratrooper mirrors the ferocity of the Allied attack in the Argentan-Falaise pocket. At right, two French women waste no time knocking down the signs of German occupation in a newly liberated town.

men, brought up in the hell-for-leather tradition by which horsemen rode off in a cloud of dust and chased the enemy over the landscape. The armored divisions traveled so fast that they frequently got out of radio range. Supply outfits had to struggle to catch up with tanks and motorized infantry, and service them on the run. "Within a couple of days we were passing out rations like Santa Claus on his sleigh, with both giver and receiver on the move," said one armored-division officer. "The trucks were like a band of stagecoaches making a run through Indian country. We got used to keeping the wheels going, disregarding the snipers and hoping we wouldn't get lost or hit."

Patton's orders were to overrun Brittany and capture some ports to ease the critical supply situation. The 6th Armored Division was to grab Brest, Brittany's biggest port; the 4th Armored would seize Lorient and Vannes.

It turned out to be a bitterly frustrating operation. A mix-up in orders cost the 4th Armored Division a whole day and enabled the German garrison at Lorient to prepare for the American assault. The 6th Armored Division lost a crucial day through a similar foul-up. It reached the outskirts of Brest on August 6, only to find that the Germans, under orders from Hitler to deny the city to the Allies at all cost, were ready to resist fiercely. It would be six weeks before Brest fell.

Meanwhile, at the base of the Brittany peninsula, infantrymen of the 83rd Division launched an attack on Saint-Malo. The commander of the heavily fortified town, Colonel Andreas von Aulock, had sworn to make it "another Stalingrad." When the inhabitants pleaded with him to spare the old town—home of the 16th-century explorer Jacques Cartier—Aulock referred the request to Hitler, who replied that in warfare there was no such thing as a historic city. "You will fight to the last man," he said, and Aulock, in turn, told his troops: "Anyone deserting or surrendering is a common dog."

The German defenses at Saint-Malo were dominated by an 18th-century fort known as the Citadel, dug into a rocky promontory close to the harbor. For more than a week, bombardments hammered the stronghold. Finally, even Aulock had had enough, and on August 17—just before planes were to drop napalm—a white flag was raised over the Citadel.

The Brittany campaign had liberated thousands of square miles, but the failure to capture even a single port intact was a major frustration. For the time being, however, this disappointment was obscured by momentous developments to the east. There, the Third Army's XV Corps, under Major General Wade H. Haislip, had emerged on August 5 from the bottleneck at Pontaubault and headed southeast for Mayenne and Laval. In less than half a day, the corps covered 30 miles. Haislip's tanks then pushed 45 miles farther to Le Mans. American troops were now 85 miles southeast of Avranches and threatening to encircle the two German armies west of the Seine.

Hitler still clung to the notion that the situation could be retrieved. He ordered Kluge to attack to the west through Mortain to reach the coast at Avranches, thereby separating the U.S. First and Third armies. Then Kluge was to turn north and throw the Allies into the sea.

By August 6, four panzer divisions were ready to strike. Directly in their path, in the vicinity of Mortain, was the American 30th Division, a veteran outfit that had spent a grueling 49 days in the hedgerows and was just now returning from a rest area. When the Germans attacked in force, panzers quickly penetrated four miles along the road to Avranches. The enemy was perilously close to breaking through the 30th Division—so close that the division commander could later say, "with a heavy onion breath the Germans would have achieved their objective."

But then air power came to the rescue. The Germans expected a thick fog on the morning of August 7, and were counting on it to conceal their movements. But the day dawned bright, and they were forced by overwhelming Allied air power to hide in the forests under camouflage nets. Roaring overhead by the hundreds, Allied aircraft bombed and strafed concentrations of vehicles wherever they appeared. "We could do nothing against them, we could make no further progress," said Major General Heinrich von Luttwitz, commander of the 2nd Panzer Division. Hitler's desperate counterattack had clearly failed.

The next day, the Canadian First Army launched an attack down the Caen-Falaise road spearheaded by 600 tanks. The assault drove three miles into German defenses and raised the specter among German commanders of a linkup with Haislip's forces that would completely cut off Army Group B. Field Marshal Kluge thought it madness to go on sticking

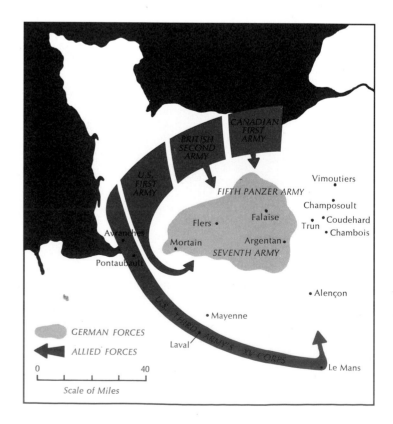

Following the breakout from the Normandy hedgerow country at the beginning of August 1944, troops of the U.S. Third Army dashed 85 miles to the southeast from Avranches. Meanwhile, the Canadian First Army, the British Second Army and the American First Army pressed in on the Germans from the north and west. The combined actions of these three armies threatened the German Fifth Panzer and Seventh Armies with encirclement, but Hitler, who was determined to drive a wedge between the American forces, ordered his Seventh Army to counterattack to the west through Mortain toward Avranches. The attack succeeded only in making the Germans more vulnerable to the threatened encirclement.

CANADIAN FIRST ARMY

BRITISH SECOND ARMY

U.S. FIRST ARMY

FIFTH PANZER ARMY

Vimoutiers

Champosoult

Flers •   Falaise   Trun • Coudehard

Avranches   • Chambois

Mortain   Argentan
SEVENTH ARMY

Pontaubault

U.S. THIRD ARMY'S XV CORPS

GERMAN FORCES

ALLIED FORCES

• Alençon

• Mayenne

Laval

Le Mans

0   40

Scale of Miles

his head deeper into the noose at Mortain. He must pull out now or face the possibility that all of Army Group B would be destroyed.

However, on August 9, Hitler ordered a renewed and even stronger attack toward Avranches. His officers in the field were astonished and appalled. The Seventh Army chief of staff later called the order "the apex of conduct of a command ignorant of front-line conditions, taking upon itself the right to judge conditions from East Prussia."

The new attack failed dismally—in no small measure due to a drama of great courage and tenacity that was being played out near Mortain, on a hill called 317. Throughout the German counteroffensive, the hill had been a key objective because of the excellent observation it afforded. But on that hill was the 2nd Battalion, 120th Infantry, 30th Division —and the Germans had never been able to push them off.

From the start, the 2nd Battalion had been cut off and surrounded. Twice the Germans demanded surrender, and twice the Americans refused. C-47 cargo planes dropped food and ammunition: howitzer gunners, with shells normally used to scatter propaganda leaflets, lobbed bandages and morphine to the beleaguered battalion.

For five days it went on—until August 11, when the Germans finally broke off their counteroffensive. The 2nd Battalion, by then known as the "Lost Battalion," had suffered almost 50 percent casualties, 300 of the 670 men on Hill 317. But not only had they stymied the Germans, their observations of enemy movements made it possible for Allied planes and artillery to exact a heavy toll, including at least 100 tanks.

During the Lost Battalion's ordeal, Bradley had ordered Haislip to turn north after capturing Le Mans. On August 12 his tanks went roaring past Alençon, and the next day they came within sight of Argentan. Haislip was sure he could reach Falaise and link up with the Canadians pushing down from the north; together they could prevent the escape of the two German armies in Normandy.

But then, in one of the most controversial orders of the War, General Bradley told Haislip to halt where he was. Bradley later explained that he wanted to avoid a head-on collision between Americans and Canadians and a "calamitous battle between friends." He also feared that Haislip's corps might cross the boundary separating Montgomery's Twenty-first Army Group from Bradley's Twelfth Army Group. It was necessary, Bradley felt, to await Montgomery's invitation to penetrate farther into the zone reserved for British-Canadian operations. No such invitation was forthcoming. Also, the Germans inside the unclosed pocket were about to stampede through the Argentan-Falaise gap and might trample any thin line of American troops that

Flanked by some of his top subordinates and his English bullterrier Willie, Third Army commander George S. Patton Jr. waits for General Dwight D. Eisenhower to show up for a meeting. Throughout August, Patton pushed his armored spearheads up to 70 miles a day. By August 31, his army had reached Brest in the west and Verdun in the east, liberating almost 50,000 square miles of territory in the process. But then something happened over which he had no control: he ran out of gas.

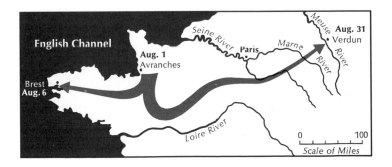

could be established there. Bradley preferred "a solid shoulder at Argentan to a broken neck at Falaise."

Montgomery's failure to invite Bradley into his zone may have stemmed from the fact that the Canadians were preparing to resume their attack toward Falaise. That assault came on August 14 and took them to within three miles of the city. The Germans were now confined to a pocket 40 miles long and shaped like a horseshoe with a 25-mile opening in the east. The Canadians near Falaise held the northern prong, Haislip's XV Corps south of Argentan the southern prong. The gap was narrowing. Most of the pocket lay within the range of Allied artillery, and all of it was vulnerable to air attack. Eisenhower later described it as "one of the greatest killing grounds" of the War.

Hitler wanted Kluge to attack. On August 16, however, Kluge recommended that the troops be immediately withdrawn from the pocket. "No matter how many orders are issued," Kluge said, "the troops cannot, are not able to, are not strong enough to defeat the enemy. It would be a fateful error to succumb to a hope that cannot be fulfilled." Without Hitler's permission, Kluge ordered the first of his troops to start withdrawing that night. Several nights would be needed to get them all out—if the sides of the pocket could be kept from closing in and the exit held open.

The Canadians entered Falaise on August 16, and the gap was now only 20 miles wide. The next day, they churned to within two miles of Trun, northeast of Argentan. At this point, Hitler decided to relieve Kluge, whom he blamed for the disaster. In little more than two weeks, the Western Front had disintegrated into chaos. Two German armies were on the brink of destruction. On August 18, the Canadians took Trun and the Americans almost reached Chambois. The gap was less than 10 miles.

Field Marshal Walther Model assumed command of Army Group B at midnight, August 18. Before leaving for Germany by car, Kluge wrote Hitler an eloquent plea to end the War. Then, on the road to Metz, he took his life by swallowing potassium cyanide. In a farewell letter to Hitler, the fallen field marshal had pleaded with the Führer to "show now that greatness that will be necessary if it comes to the point of ending a struggle which has become hopeless."

That night the pocket was only six miles deep and seven miles wide. Under savage artillery fire, remnants of German divisions improvised task forces. Stragglers and service units moved wearily along roads, and fields were clogged with wreckage and the dead. When the morning mist rose on August 19, the gap was barely open. The Germans still coming through it were pounded mercilessly by Allied aircraft.

Trucks, tanks and guns went flying through the air. Flames leaped skyward from burning gasoline tanks. Ammunition exploded. Crazed horses ran wild. A Canadian soldier named Duncan Kyle later recalled: "I remember wishing that the Germans didn't have to use so many horses. Seeing all those dead animals on their backs, their legs pointing at God's sky like accusing fingers, their bellies bloated, some ripped open. That really bothered me."

The defeat was the worst suffered by the Germans since 275,000 Axis soldiers surrendered in Tunisia in May 1943.

In the Argentan-Falaise pocket, approximately 10,000 men were killed and 50,000 captured, and 220 tanks were destroyed. However, among the estimated 40,000 Germans who escaped were an army commander, four corps commanders and 12 division commanders, critically needed combat leaders who would fight again.

Even for those who got out of the pocket the ordeal was not over. They were threatened by another encircling arm, formed by the two divisions that Bradley had sent from Argentan to drive to the Seine. On the night of August 19, in torrential rain, American soldiers walked single file across a narrow dam in the Seine. At daybreak others paddled over. By nightfall on August 20, a substantial force was across the river and ready to move toward Germany.

As British, Canadian and American units surged eastward, they left a large part of northwestern France liberated. And now it was time to mount yet another invasion by landing on the famed Riviera beaches of the Mediterranean coast in southern France. Originally code-named *Anvil*, the operation had been long in the making—and was a subject of some dispute. The idea of assailing southern France had been officially suggested as early as August 1943, as a small-scale diversion to help the Normandy assault. Later, Stalin urged that it be upgraded to a major project, and President Roosevelt concurred.

Winston Churchill, however, stood in strong opposition: in furtherance of Britain's interests in the eastern Mediterranean, he wanted to use the troops earmarked for *Anvil* to drive north from Italy into Yugoslavia through an Alpine pass known as the Ljubljana Gap ("that gap," said Eisenhower, "whose name I can't even pronounce"). Outvoted by his peers, Churchill finally went along, and even permitted himself a rueful joke about his resistance: after *Anvil* was renamed *Dragoon* for security reasons, Churchill declared that the new designation was entirely fitting, since he had been dragooned into accepting the operation. Assigned to assault a 45-mile stretch of the Riviera were the 94,000 men of Major General Alexander M. Patch's Seventh Army, which consisted of the U.S. VI Corps, commanded by Major General Lucian K. Truscott, and the Free French forces led by General Jean de Lattre de Tassigny.

In the predawn hours of August 15, 1945, paratroopers of the American-British 1st Airborne Task Force dropped out of the sky in a successful effort to seize the roads by which German reinforcements could reach the beachhead. Not long after, 1,300 Allied bombers began pounding the Riviera, and at about 7:30 a.m., Allied warships unleashed a furious bombardment of 16,000 shells in 19 minutes. After that, the landings themselves went like clockwork.

On D-plus-1, the French returned in force to their home-land. "I kept my eyes closed so as not to be aware of too much too soon," one French soldier recalled. "And then I bent down and scooped up a handful of sand, with the feeling that what I was doing was a private act, separate from anybody else's."

The hard-bitten de Lattre had no time for patriotic reflections. He had undertaken to race eastward and launch simultaneous attacks against the two great ports of Toulon and Marseilles. For Army B, as de Lattre's force was now designated, the job required some hard and often untidy fighting. On the streets of Marseilles, de Lattre later recalled that, "In a few yards one passed from the enthusiasm of a liberation boulevard into the solitude of a machine-gunned avenue. In a few turns of the track, a tank covered with flowers was either taken by the assault of pretty, smiling girls or fired at by an 88mm shell."

At any event, both Marseilles and Toulon surrendered on August 28, and de Lattre sent a proud message to Charles de Gaulle: "Today, D-plus-13, in Army B's sector there is no German not dead or captive."

For General Truscott and his VI Corps, speed was all-important in a race to Montélimar, far to the northwest of the Riviera beachhead. Just north of the town, National Highway 7 ran through a narrow defile between the Rhone River and a 1,000-foot-high ridge. If Truscott could beat the Germans to the bottleneck, he could plug their main route of retreat from southern France.

Nothing if not aggressive, the VI Corps commander kept his tanks roaring through the countryside at top speed, while infantrymen rushed ahead at what they called the "Truscott trot," a pace just short of double time. But the fleeing Germans were even faster: their main body managed to escape, leaving behind only a rear guard who had little choice but to surrender or die. Most chose to surrender—including 20,000 who gave themselves up in a single group.

Symbolically, *Anvil-Dragoon* ended on September 11, 1944, when some of de Lattre's men linked up with soldiers of Patton's Third Army in the town of Saulieu, 40 miles west of Dijon. The invasion had accomplished much: southwestern France, almost one third of the nation, was liberated; the captured ports would inject into the war a total of 905,000 American soldiers and 4,100,000 tons of matériel. U.S. Chief of Staff George C. Marshall called the operation "one of the most successful things we did."

As the Allies' massive seaborne invasion force was nearing the Riviera on August 14, 1944, events in northern France were about to take a dramatic turn. Hanging in precarious balance was the future of the renowned City of Light—Paris.

Along the bomb-ravaged road between Caen and Falaise, a Canadian casualty is tended by a medic while a German tank burns only a few yards away. In August 1944, fighting raged along the 21-mile-long road from Caen to Falaise for nine days as the Canadian First Army battered its way through the tough German defenses. The Canadian advance—which produced more than 2,000 casualties—was, in General Eisenhower's eyes, a remarkable achievement. "Ten feet gained on the Caen sector," the Supreme Commander said, "was equivalent to a mile elsewhere."

Although General Eisenhower was well aware of the spiritual uplift that the liberation of Paris would give to the French, and indeed to the whole Allied world, his primary objective clearly lay elsewhere. If his armies could thrust to the Rhine, now only 250 miles away, before the Germans had time to regroup, the War might be ended in short order. In addition, Ike wished to avoid street fighting in Paris, and he knew that maintaining the city, once it was freed, would be an enormous drain on Allied resources.

Thus, reflecting Eisenhower's thinking, General Patton informed the commander of the U.S. XV Corps, General Haislip, that there would be no immediate Allied attempt to liberate the French capital. Instead of forging on to Paris, Haislip would keep part of his corps at Argentan and send two divisions only as far as Dreux, 45 miles short of Paris.

Deeply disappointed, Haislip begged Patton at least to let Major General Jacques Leclerc's French 2nd Armored Division march on Paris. "George," he said, "you are wrong, you know. It will mean more to the French than anything else to think that the only division they have in Europe is the first one to get into Paris."

"Oh, to hell with that," replied Patton. "We are fighting a war now."

But Eisenhower and Patton had reckoned without the steel will of Charles de Gaulle. Although de Gaulle headed the French Committee of National Liberation from his headquarters in Algeria, he realized that in order to establish himself as the unquestioned leader of France itself, he would first have to be recognized as the liberator of Paris. He knew also that if the strident Communist factions in the Resistance were able to spur the city's civilian population to a successful uprising against the Germans before he got to Paris, then "on my arrival they would bind my brows with laurel, invite me to assume the place they would assign me, and thenceforth pull all the strings themselves."

Against that unacceptable prospect, de Gaulle had been preparing with consummate skill. As Allied troops swept eastward across France in August 1944, teams of Gaullist administrators, police and even a traveling court-martial board followed close behind, taking control of local governments. Moreover, Leclerc's French 2nd Armored began squirreling away enough gasoline and ammunition to get the division to Paris without American help.

Still, the hopes of the Free French for regaining Paris intact might very well have been dashed had it not been for, of all people, the city's German commander. He was Major

General Dietrich von Choltitz, a pudgy little man with a fearsome reputation as the wrecker of Sebastopol and other cities. It was a role that Choltitz did not fancy for himself. "It has always been my lot," he explained, "to defend the rear of the German army. And each time it happens I am ordered to destroy each city as I leave it."

Now, summoned to Hitler's headquarters, Choltitz was aghast at the Führer. "Saliva was literally running from his mouth," Choltitz recalled. "He was trembling all over and the desk on which he was leaning shook with him." Choltitz was even more dismayed by Hitler's orders: if the Wehrmacht were to pull out of Paris, the city "must be utterly destroyed. Nothing must be left standing, no church, no artistic monument." Even the water supply would be cut off, so that—in the Führer's words—"the ruined city may be a prey to epidemics."

Back in Paris, Choltitz was haunted by his conviction that the man to whom he had sworn blind obedience was mad. As a dutiful German soldier, he was prepared to defend Paris against the advancing Allies. Yet he knew that if he carried out Hitler's directives, history would damn him as the man who destroyed one of the world's most glorious cities.

On August 19, Communist Resistance forces called for an uprising in Paris. The next day, rival Gaullists seized police headquarters. Soon, sharp gunfights could be heard across the city as well-organized Resistance bands—Communists and Gaullists alike—attacked police substations, post offices and government buildings. By nightfall, the Germans suffered more than 150 casualties. And as the violence mounted over the next several days, with the Resistance making steady gains, Choltitz struggled with his dilemma.

At the same time, General Eisenhower was in the process of changing his mind about Paris. Just as Choltitz dreaded an enduring infamy as the destroyer of Paris, Eisenhower had no desire to be responsible for the city's ruin by doing nothing to save it. Finally, as Eisenhower himself later put it, "My hand was forced by the actions of the Free French forces inside the city." At a conference with Omar Bradley on August 22, Ike made known his decision. "Well, what the hell, Brad," he said. "I guess we'll have to go in."

Returning to his own headquarters at Laval, Bradley gave the good news to a waiting General Leclerc, whose French 2nd Armored Division had been selected to lead the way. Around dusk Leclerc leaped from his plane on the field at Argentan and cried: *"Mouvement immédiat sur Paris!"*

By then, General Choltitz had made his own compromise between conscience and duty: having preserved Paris, he would nonetheless defend it. Leclerc would have to fight his way in. And so he did. At precisely 9:22 p.m. on August 24, 1944, the first Free French tank arrived in the heart of Paris.

The bells of the French capital—silent for four years—began to ring, first from the south tower of Notre-Dame, then from Sacré-Coeur in Montmartre, then throughout the length and breadth of the city.

Sitting at a candlelit dinner table at the elegant Hôtel Meurice, a young German woman heard the pealing of the bells and turned to her companion. "Why are they ringing?" she asked. Replied General von Choltitz: "Why are they ringing? They are ringing for us, my little girl. They are ringing because the Allies are coming to Paris."

The next day, Choltitz formally surrendered his German forces in Paris to Leclerc.

Elsewhere along the 200-mile front in northern France, Allied spearheads were already crossing the Seine. Eisenhower's plan was for Montgomery's army group to surge northeastward through Belgium and into the Ruhr, Bradley's to drive eastward through France and lunge into the Saar. But Montgomery vehemently disagreed with this idea. He argued for a single, massive thrust through Belgium, the two army groups side by side, 40 divisions strong, to overwhelm the Germans and end the war. Attacking in two columns, he contended, would spread supplies too thin; the front would be weak everywhere, the advance would peter out, winter would set in and the war would drag on.

Eisenhower rejected Montgomery's argument. To confine both army groups to one sector, he felt, would invite a German counterattack in another. But as a compromise, he would split the Twelfth Army Group; General Hodges' First Army would be sent into Belgium alongside Montgomery, and Patton's Third Army would drive into the Saar by itself. Eisenhower gave first priority on supplies to the major thrust into Belgium. Patton, for now, would get less.

As the Allied armies plunged across the Seine toward Belgium and Germany, the pursuit of the disintegrating enemy forces turned into a headlong rush. Soldiers rode on tanks and in trucks, jeeps and captured German vehicles. Progress was seldom interrupted for long. The countryside became a blur.

On the morning of August 31, six armored columns passed Reims and rolled through the Argonne Forest. By noon, they were across the Meuse. Patton was less than 60 miles from Germany, but his supply lines were stretched too thin. With no opposition in sight, Patton was forced to park his armor because the gas tanks were dry. His appeals for more gasoline came to no avail. "My men can eat their belts," he bellowed, "but my tanks have gotta have gas."

In the meantime, in the center of the advance, Hodges' First Army also made impressive gains, crossing into Belgium, cutting off and encircling part of the Fifth Panzer

Hundreds of parachutes, streaming from U.S. transports on August 15, 1944—D-Day in southern France—drop men and supplies to the 1st Airborne Task Force, whose American and British paratroopers had landed in the dark near Le Muy, 12 miles behind the invasion beaches. By the time of this drop, the soldiers had achieved their main objective: setting up roadblocks to keep German reinforcements from reaching the beachhead.

Army, some 25,000 men. But a shortage of gasoline forced Hodges to stop one entire corps for three days. His other two corps kept moving, but as they thrust through Luxembourg and Belgium and approached the German border, trucks ran out of gas and the advance sputtered. The First Army, like the Third, was coming to the end of its tether.

To the left of the Americans, the British and Canadians made great strides along the French coast. On August 30, elements of the Canadian First Army liberated Rouen. During the first week of September, the Canadians invested Le Havre, Boulogne, Calais and Dunkirk, and seized the V-1 launching sites in the Pas-de-Calais. On the Canadians' right, the British Second Army liberated Amiens on August 31, entered Belgium and took Brussels on September 3. The next day the British captured a major prize, the port of Antwerp, before the Germans could demolish it.

On September 10, Montgomery appealed again for one big thrust into Germany, and offered a bold and daring scheme as a preliminary. He proposed dropping three divisions of the First Airborne Army, the Allies' strategic reserve, along a highway connecting the Dutch cities of Eindhoven, Nijmegen and Arnhem. They would seize bridges that spanned canals and large rivers, clear the highway and hold it open. This was Operation *Market*. Then, in a venture called *Garden*, British armored units would dash up the highway, across the bridges and through the cities to link up with the airborne troops, establishing a foothold east of the Rhine. Soon after, Montgomery would drive all the way to the Zuider Zee, then wheel east, outflanking the German West Wall, and go on to seize the Ruhr.

The boldness of the concept startled Montgomery's fellow commanders. "Had the pious, teetotaling Montgomery wobbled into SHAEF with a hangover, I could not have been more astonished," General Bradley later recalled. Eisenhower, in his turn, was intrigued. He had been itching to use his airborne reserve, most of which had dropped into Normandy during the invasion and later returned to England. Three and a half divisions of paratroopers and glider infantry—the U.S. 82nd and 101st Airborne, the British 1st Airborne and a Polish brigade—were rested, retrained and ready for more action. Ike again rejected Montgomery's demand for one massive thrust, but he gave his approval to *Market-Garden*.

Allied commanders believed that German troops in the target area were few, ill-trained, and capable of mustering only a feeble defense. They persisted in that belief despite disturbing evidence to the contrary. In one instance, after Allied intelligence had confirmed Dutch Resistance reports that two German panzer divisions had stopped in the vicinity of Arnhem to rest and refit, Eisenhower's chief-of-staff,

General Walter Bedell Smith, carried the disquieting information to Montgomery. But, Smith wrote later, "Montgomery simply waved my objections airily aside." Similarly, a British intelligence officer upset by aerial photographs showing enemy tank congregations became "such a pain around headquarters that on the very eve of the attack I was removed from the scene. I was told to go home."

On Sunday, September 17, from 24 airfields in Britain, 1,545 C-47s and 478 gliders, protected by 1,131 fighter planes, took to the air—the British 1st Airborne Division bound for Arnhem, the U.S. 82nd Airborne for Nijmegen, the U.S. 101st Airborne for the vicinity of Eindhoven. Soon, 16,500 parachutists and 3,500 glider troops were landing.

The "Red Devils" of the 1st Airborne, under Major General Robert E. Urquhart, came down on the north bank of the Lower Rhine, eight miles west of Arnhem, and started for the huge highway bridge there. They had dropped close to the headquarters of German Army Group B. Field Marshal Model, thinking the British were raiders sent to kidnap him, raced 18 miles by car to the headquarters of Lieut. General Wilhelm Bittrich, commander of the 2nd SS Panzer Corps. Model found that Bittrich had already reacted to the invasion—with great foresight, as it turned out.

Bittrich had a hunch that the Allies were bent on forging a bridgehead across the Rhine and would need the bridges at Arnhem and Nijmegen. He quickly committed his 9th and 10th SS—the panzer divisions whose presence in the *Market-Garden* area Montgomery had ignored. Bittrich sent the 9th to Arnhem, the 10th to Nijmegen. A couple of hours later, the Germans found a copy of the entire *Market-Garden*

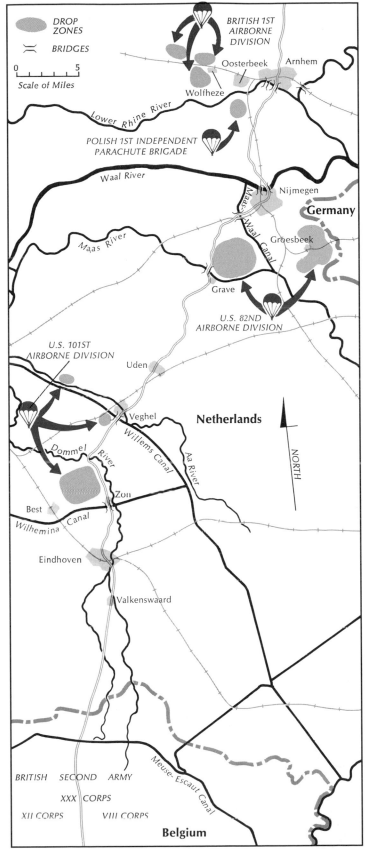

DROP
ZONES

⊃⊂ BRIDGES

0   5
Scale of Miles

BRITISH 1ST
AIRBORNE
DIVISION

Oosterbeek   Arnhem

Wolfheze

Lower Rhine River

POLISH 1ST INDEPENDENT
PARACHUTE BRIGADE

Waal River

Nijmegen

Germany

Maas River

Groesbeek

Grave

U.S. 82ND
AIRBORNE DIVISION

U.S. 101ST
AIRBORNE DIVISION

Uden

Veghel   Netherlands

Dommel River

Willems Canal

Aa River

NORTH

Best

Zon

Wilhemina Canal

Eindhoven

Valkenswaard

Meuse-Escaut Canal

BRITISH   SECOND   ARMY

XXX   CORPS

XII CORPS   VIII CORPS

Belgium

Operation Market-Garden, the Allied invasion of the Netherlands, began on
September 17, 1944, when Anglo-American airborne troops landed near
Arnhem, Nijmegen and Eindhoven. They were to seize seven vital bridges
and hold open a corridor for tanks of the British Second Army to drive into
Germany and bring about an early end to the War.

plan in a wrecked American glider. It included the schedule
and location of reinforcement and supply drops.

The Germans cut the main roads to Arnhem, and only the
500 men of Lieut. Colonel John D. Frost's 2nd Battalion, 1st
Parachute Brigade, made it to the north end of the bridge.
They attacked across the bridge during the night but were
thrown back, and the Germans laid siege to the houses the
paratroopers held. The other two battalions of the 1st
Brigade were forced to make a stand in Oosterbeek, a western suburb of Arnhem.

Near Nijmegen, the U.S. 82nd Airborne rushed to capture its bridge objectives. By the end of the day, only a railroad bridge and a 1,960-foot highway bridge over the Waal
River remained in German hands. First contingents of the
10th SS Panzer Division rolled across the span and dug in
around a traffic circle at the south end. Men of the 82nd got
to within one block of the bridge and were stopped. The
Germans clung tenaciously to the bridge. American troops
could only await reinforcement from the ground force
advancing up the corridor.

In the southernmost sector near Eindhoven, the U.S. 101st
Airborne landed to the north of the city and seized four rail
and highway crossings over the Aa River and Willems Canal.
Then they turned to the highway bridge over the Wilhelmina
Canal at the village of Zon. When they were within a stone's
throw of the canal, a tremendous roar went up and debris
rained down on them. The Germans had blown the bridge.
Working feverishly, engineers built a wooden footbridge
across the wrecked span. Repairing it for vehicular traffic,
however, would require heavy equipment that the paratroopers lacked. That, too, would have to wait until the
armored column arrived.

The armored move to link up with the paratroopers was a
maddening, stop-and-go affair that threw the operation's
timetable out of kilter. In the vanguard of the British Second
Army's XXX Corps, commanded by Lieut. General Brian C.
Horrocks, the Guards Armored Division had scarcely
crossed the Belgian-Dutch border on September 17 when
concealed antitank guns knocked out nine tanks, and the
advance jarred to a halt. Not until late afternoon September
18 did the column enter Eindhoven—24 hours behind
schedule. The Zon bridge was destroyed, so engineers laid a
pontoon bridge over the canal. The next morning the tanks
raced across toward Nijmegen. The advance began to look
like a thrust again—until a few hours later, when it met stiff
resistance at the bridge over the Waal at Nijmegen. Arnhem
was only 11 miles away.

German reinforcements were pouring into the area.
Elements of the 1st Parachute and Fifteenth armies stabbed
viciously at the British column all along the 65-mile corri-

dor. Allied supply drops on September 18 and 19 failed. Forewarned by the captured plans, the Germans overran some drop zones, and bundles of ammunition and food fell into their hands.

Planners had estimated that the troops at Arnhem could hold out for only four days without relief. On September 20, the fourth day, their fate rested on the outcome of a desperate measure conceived by the 82nd Airborne commander, Brigadier General James M. Gavin—an amphibious assault across the Waal, in broad daylight, to take first the railroad bridge and then, simultaneously from both ends, the all-important highway bridge. In late afternoon, as artillery and tanks pounded the German defenders, the first wave of paratroopers, 260 men, launched their craft. Some of the 33 flimsy plywood-and-canvas boats flipped over as the soldiers climbed in. Others were overloaded and sank. Seized by the current, still others were swept in circles. The Germans opened up with machine guns and mortars. Recalled a British officer who watched from the south side of the river: "It was a horrible, horrible sight. Boats were literally blown out of the water. Huge geysers shot up as shells hit and small-arms fire from the northern bank made the river look like a seething cauldron."

Only about half of the boats reached the north bank. After depositing the survivors, they returned for more men. The remnants of the first wave went on to take the northern end of the railroad bridge, trapping German soldiers on the span itself. As the Germans on the bridge tried to escape at the north end, they met concentrated machine gun fire. More than 260 were later found dead on the structure.

Their numbers swelled by succeeding waves, the paratroopers then advanced on the highway bridge. At the same time, a British armored attack on the other side of the river cracked the German perimeter around the traffic circle at the foot of the span. Through an inferno of burning buildings and shellfire, four British tanks made a wild dash up the bridge approaches and rumbled onto the bridge. Three made it across, to be met by the jubilant U.S. paratroopers who had survived the waterborne assault. The triumph soon turned sour: exhausted and running low on ammunition, the British tankers hunkered down for the night instead of rushing to rescue their comrades at Arnhem.

All this time, Col. Frost and his dwindling force, surrounded and under constant shellfire, had been holding out in houses near the Arnhem bridge. They were short of medical supplies and ammunition and their rations were gone. By the night of September 19, only half of Frost's original 500 men were capable of fighting. The following day, the number dwindled to about 150. In the cellars of the shell-pitted houses, the wounded, swathed in filthy bandages, were jammed so tightly that medics found it difficult to treat them.

On the 20th, Frost concluded that continued resistance was senseless. Shortly before dawn the next day, he ordered the survivors of his gallant band to try to escape, two or three at a time. Only a few who melted into the darkness got away. Most were captured, including Frost.

A little over two miles away, the rest of Urquhart's Red Devils had been forced into a U-shaped defensive position, the open end facing the bend of the Lower Rhine. By September 21 the perimeter had been reduced to a pocket only a mile deep and a mile and a half wide. Pounded mercilessly by artillery, harassed by snipers, the paratroopers

German soldiers dash across a rubble-cluttered street in Arnhem (left), while British paratroopers cautiously advance through the ruins of a house (right).

held out, still waiting for the armored column from Nijmegen. Six miles short of Arnhem, as the column rolled along the elevated, exposed highway, a single German artillery piece knocked out the lead tanks. Once again the armor ground to a halt.

Three days later, with medical supplies exhausted and the wounded in pitiful condition, General Urquhart arranged a truce and turned his wounded over to the Germans. On the following day, Montgomery ordered a withdrawal to save the remnants of the 1st Airborne. That night, in a driving rain that helped muffle the noise of movement, the exhausted survivors left their foxholes and made their way to the north bank of the Lower Rhine. They were met by boats sent up from the XXX Corps and paddled by Canadian and British soldiers. During the night, under sporadic machine-gun fire, scores of men were ferried to the south bank. Still, at dawn, hundreds remained at the river's edge. Many plunged into the swift water. Some were swept away by the current or dragged down by the weight of their clothing. Others stripped and swam across. The remainder, too weary or too sick to swim, were captured.

The ordeal at Arnhem was over at last. Of 10,000 British troops who landed and fought, fewer than 2,200 made it back across the river. For the time being, the 1st Airborne Division ceased to exist. Operation *Market-Garden*, one of the most gallant but disastrous ventures of the War, came to a close with the Germans still holding the Arnhem bridge.

In one sense *Market-Garden* achieved its objectives. The Allies had won a corridor 60 miles long in the Netherlands, but they had failed to gain a bridgehead over the Rhine or to outflank the West Wall for a drive into the Ruhr. They had paid a stiff price—17,000 men dead, wounded or captured. The bright vision of a quick end to the War evaporated. A long, hard winter loomed ahead.

The northern end of the 2,000-foot-long highway bridge (near top of picture) at Arnhem was the scene of vicious fighting between the British and the Germans.

12

By August of 1944, after five years of war, the German Wehrmacht had lost 3,360,000 men killed, wounded or missing, and some of its finest units were mere shadows: the proud Panzer Lehr Division, for example, was down from 17,000 men and 190 tanks to a pair of understrength companies with five tanks. The Luftwaffe had been overwhelmed; German cities were in ruin, and industries, communications and transport were under constant attack by Allied bombers. It seemed impossible for Germany to manage anything but a fighting retreat. Yet Adolf Hitler was preparing one last desperate throw of the dice, a massive counterattack in the West—a vicious thrust that would enter history as the Battle of the Bulge.

Day after day, all through August of 1944, grim reports from the far-flung battlefronts had greeted the Führer at Wolf's Lair, his secret headquarters in East Prussia. On the Eastern front, the Russians had destroyed 25 German divisions and were overrunning Poland and Rumania. In Italy, the Allies were 155 miles north of Rome and attacking the last German defensive line before the Alps. French, American and British forces had virtually annihilated two German armies after breaking out of the Normandy beachhead.

Even so, Hitler still believed that the tide of battle could be reversed. The Allied armies had come so far so fast, he reasoned, that they would have to halt until their supplies caught up and their exhausted troops were rested, refitted and reinforced. The delay would allow him to regroup his forces behind the West Wall, Germany's belt of fortifications stretching north from Switzerland to Holland. A resolute stand there would give him time to mount a major counteroffensive, a surprise blitzkrieg that would send the Allied armies reeling back in defeat.

Hitler planned the counteroffensive himself. Secretive by nature, he had become paranoid about security ever since July 20, when a time bomb, planted by anti-Nazi Lieut. Colonel Claus von Stauffenberg, had exploded in a conference room at Wolf's Lair. Hitler had escaped with superficial injuries, but he concluded that the whole army was plotting against him. He therefore confided his intention to counterattack to only a few trusted advisers.

As far as he could, the Führer developed the plan alone. On September 16, he called Field Marshal Keitel and several top-ranking generals to a special meeting.

"I have just made a momentous decision," he said in a theatrical display. "I shall go over to the counterattack!" He jabbed his finger at a map. "Here, out of the Ardennes, with the objective—Antwerp!"

While the generals sat stunned, Hitler explained. A powerful attack group would break through the thin shell of American defenders in the Ardennes and race across the Meuse River to capture the Belgian port, which the British had occupied on September 4. This bold thrust would split the American and British armies, isolating the British in the north and driving them to the sea in "another Dunkirk." The Ardennes was admittedly a region of difficult terrain, but German commanders knew the territory and the vital roads that would speed the panzer divisions on their way.

Hitler brushed aside objections. There was no need, he said, to fear the Allies' alleged advantage in strength. Before the commanders departed to breathe life into his grand design, Hitler swore them to secrecy.

By the end of September, German units had regrouped and were standing to fight all along the front. When they

Advancing through the dangerous Hürtgen Forest, mud-splattered infantrymen of the U.S. 4th Division clamber out of a gulch clotted with barbed wire, felled trees and other debris. American GIs frequently lobbed grenades or small charges of TNT ahead of them in order to set off any mines or booby traps that German soldiers might have placed in their path. More than 25 per cent of the Americans who fought in Hürtgen Forest were casualties.

THE LAST GREAT GAMBLE

were forced to retreat, they did so in good order, after exacting a heavy toll. This the men of the American VII Corps discovered as they pushed east through the killing ground of the Hürtgen Forest. Laced with mines and booby traps, the 10-mile-deep forest was a chamber of horrors for the GIs.

By December 13, when units broke into the open on the far side of the forest, more than 24,000 American soldiers had become casualties. The Germans had suffered losses of about the same magnitude. But they had covered themselves with glory: they had bought precious time for Hitler to ready his massive Ardennes counterattack.

The main force, the Sixth Panzer Army under SS General Josef Dietrich, would break through the northern part of the Ardennes front, cross the Meuse River, then wheel northwest for Antwerp. On that army's left flank, the Fifth Panzer Army under Lieut. General Hasso von Manteuffel would also cross the Meuse to Brussels and Antwerp. Protecting the southern shoulder of the breakthrough area would be General Erich Brandenberger's Seventh Army, while the Fifteenth Army under General Günther Blumentritt would cover the salient's northern shoulder.

To sow confusion and terror among enemy troops, Hitler organized a panzer brigade led by Lieut. Colonel Otto Skorzeny, the daredevil commando who had rescued Mussolini in September 1943. Skorzeny's men, some of them dressed in American uniforms and equipped with captured American tanks, arms and identification, were to race for the Meuse, seize several bridges, commit sabotage and create consternation in the American rear areas. A 1,000-man parachute force under Colonel Friedrich von der Heydte would land behind American lines, open roads for German armor and block enemy units from interfering with the panzers' progress.

To prevent detection by the Allies, all the units in the German offensive were to be held at least 12 miles from the front until Hitler gave the order for the final assembly. Then troops and tanks would move up on a rigid timetable.

On the nights of December 11 and 12, Hitler had explained his offensive in detail: "This battle is to decide whether we shall live or die. I want all my soldiers to fight hard and without pity. The battle must be fought with brutality, and all resistance must be broken in a wave of terror."

On December 12, all units had been alerted for movement. The following night they took up positions on a base line opposite the Ardennes, with the force assembled opposite Aachen slipping down from the north. To muffle the sound of traffic, wagon wheels and horses' hooves were padded with straw, and low-flying aircraft zoomed over the assembly areas to drown out engine noises.

By the night of December 15, twenty reequipped and reinforced German divisions were poised for the jump-off, with five more in reserve. The whole powerful force of approximately 300,000 men, 1,900 pieces of artillery, and 970 tanks and armored assault guns had been brought up to the assembly lines in utmost secrecy. Radio silence was strictly enforced; tanks and vehicles heavily camouflaged;

nearly 10,000 carloads of ammunition and supplies moved up during the nights by trains that had been hidden by day in tunnels and forests.

The Americans and British ignored reports of the German preparations. On December 12, an intelligence summary issued by General Omar Bradley's Twelfth Army Group headquarters declared: "It is now certain that attrition is steadily sapping the strength of German forces on the western front." On visiting General Troy Middleton's VIII Corps headquarters at Bastogne, Bradley was surprised to hear Middleton say that the long 85-mile front assigned to him in the Ardennes was too thinly held. "Don't worry, Troy," Bradley assured him, "they won't come through here."

On the morning of December 16, four German armies struck at the Ardennes in the early darkness.

All along the front, from the medieval town of Echternach in the south to the honeymoon resort of Elsenborn in the north, American units were shaken from their sleep by the thunder of artillery. Shells screamed, the ground trembled, trees were splintered and ugly black patches appeared in the six-inch blanket of snow. The shells came in all sizes—from mortars, multiple rocket launchers, howitzers, 88mm and 14-inch railway guns.

GIs leaped out of sleeping bags, grabbed their weapons and dived for foxholes. Forward observers reached for field telephones only to find the wires cut by the shelling. Switching to radios, they found their wavelengths jammed by the martial music of German bands. One officer who did reach his commander by phone was interrupted in mid-sentence by a German voice announcing triumphantly, "We are here!" The Volksgrenadier who had tapped the phone was from an advance party that had crossed the Sûre River.

After an hour, the shelling let up and the morning mists were bathed in an eerie glow as the Germans bounced powerful searchlight beams off low-hanging clouds to light up the American positions. Through this "artificial moonlight," German infantrymen advanced—spectral figures in snow-white camouflage suits or mottled battle dress. In foxholes and bunkers, GIs braced themselves for the attack.

The Sixth Panzer Army of SS General Josef Dietrich, a burly Nazi veteran, was made up of nine divisions, but his hopes lay in two elite units that shared a reputation for ferocity in battle: the 12th SS Panzer Hitler Youth Division and the 1st SS Panzer Division. These two were to drive ahead quickly to take control of the Elsenborn Ridge and the Malmédy Road and stop American reinforcements from pouring down from the north to choke off the advance.

The spearhead of the 1st SS Panzer Division was built around the 1st SS Panzer Regiment commanded by 29-year-old Lieut. Colonel Joachim Peiper, a hard-boiled bravo with the kind of fanaticism Hitler admired. His regiment was reinforced to a strength of 4,000 men and 127 tanks, including 42 mammoth Royal Tiger tanks.

Pushing forward, preparing to attack, Peiper's regiment was ordered to move west to the village of Lanzerath. Here, from a hill overlooking the village, a gallant platoon of U.S. infantry under Lieutenant Lyle J. Bouck Jr. had held up the advance of an entire German parachute battalion all day before being overrun. In doing so, they had blocked one of the roads earmarked for the main German drive.

Peiper pulled into Lanzerath after midnight and called for the paratroop commander, who admitted that his troops had been unable to break through because "the woods up the way were full of Americans." Furious, Peiper stormed out and commandeered a battalion of paratroop infantry. At 4 a.m he set out to attack the next villages up the road. In the village of Honsfeld, his men caught the Americans by surprise. A GI in one house opened the door, saw a giant Tiger tank rumbling past and slammed the door in a hurry. "My God!" he exclaimed. "They're German!"

In the onslaught that followed, Hitler's directive that the offensive must be "preceded by a wave of terror and fright" was given its first expression. In one house, 22 Americans were surrounded by the SS troops. A German 88mm gun was methodically pulverizing the building when a white flag appeared in a window. A dozen Americans walked outside to surrender, and were shot down. Elsewhere, Peiper's men rounded up about 200 prisoners and as they were herded to the rear, a German tank opened fire on them.

Peiper's troops moved up to Büllingen, hoping to refuel from an American supply dump there. On their way, they shot a half dozen more American prisoners. They then forced 50 American prisoners to fuel their tanks. In the town itself, the slaughter continued; about 30 Americans were shot. Another group, marching with hands on their heads, was also fired on. But the worst was yet to come.

As Peiper's advance guard arrived at Baugnez, south of Malmédy, it ran into an American artillery battery and opened fire. Panicky GIs scrambled for cover in a ditch, while the rest dashed for a nearby patch of woods. In all, about 120 men in the ditch were surrounded, and crawled out with hands in the air. While the GIs were being searched, a tank crewman said in formal English, "First SS Panzer Division welcomes you to Belgium, gentlemen." The prisoners were then lined up and prodded into a pasture. Some panzers and half-tracks rolled up, and opened fire. The Americans crumpled to the ground, most of them dead or wounded, a few feigning death. The SS troops then walked among the bodies, pumping bullets into GIs who

showed signs of life, or crushing their skulls with rifle butts.

News of the killings, which came to be called the Malmédy Massacre, spread rapidly through the frontline units; it had an electrifying effect. American resolve stiffened, and some units vowed that they would take no prisoners in SS uniform.

Meanwhile, some of Skorzeny's commando teams were succeeding beyond their leader's wildest dreams. Trained in the techniques of infiltration and sabotage, 150 English-speaking Germans wearing American uniforms and carrying false identity papers had set out in 30 captured American jeeps. The nine commando teams that managed to penetrate American lines had a devastating psychological impact. One unit blocked off key roads with white tape—the GIs' signal for minefields ahead. Another told an American officer such a lurid tale of German successes that the American withdrew his unit. A group seized by GIs near Liège told an outrageous story of a plot to assassinate General Eisenhower at his Versailles headquarters. The Americans accepted the whole yarn. Surrounded by a triple guard, Eisenhower became a virtual prisoner in his headquarters.

The paratroop operation under Colonel von der Heydte proved a failure, however. His planes ran into strong head winds and antiaircraft fire en route to the drop zones; the formation was widely scattered. Ironically, the most successful airdrop was a fake: about 300 dummies dressed as paratroopers came to earth near Belgium's Elsenborn Ridge, causing considerable confusion until they were identified for what they were.

In the meantime, the most important battle on the northern Ardennes front was developing rapidly around Elsenborn Ridge, which dominated two roads feeding the route to the Meuse River via Malmédy. Dietrich's Sixth Panzer Army had to gain control of these feeder roads to launch the 12th SS Panzer Division westward. The principal feeder route ran

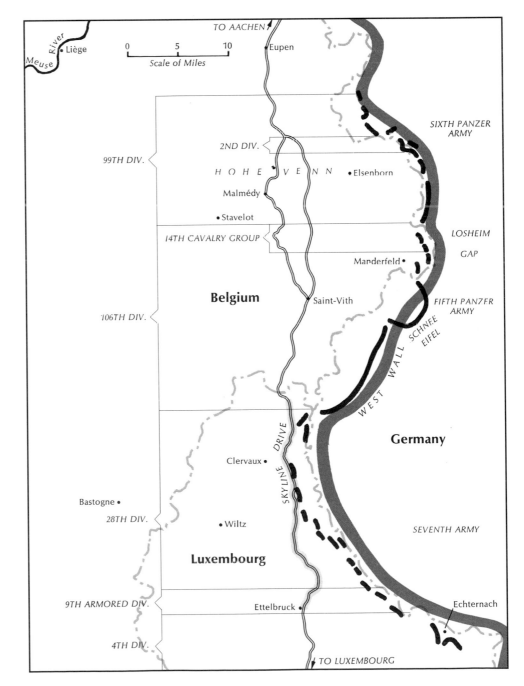

On December 16, 1944, more than 250,000 Germans attacked 83,000 American troops deployed thinly along the 85-mile Ardennes front (broken line). In the north, the Sixth Panzer Army struck the U.S. 99th Division and threatened to cut off the U.S. 2nd Division, attacking into Germany through the West Wall. In the center, the Fifth Panzer Army hit the 106th Division, the 14th Cavalry Group and part of the 28th Division. In the south, the Seventh Army clashed with elements of the U.S. 4th, 9th Armored and 28th divisions.

through Losheimergraben, and Dietrich assigned his 12th Volksgrenadier Division to capture the village. The second road went through the twin villages of Krinkelt and Rocherath, and the 277th Volksgrenadier Division was ordered to seize them and overrun the ridge.

Dietrich anticipated no trouble from the American division in this area—the 99th, commanded by General Walter E. Lauer. Its troops were known to be inexperienced, and were holding a line long enough to require four to five divisions. But his low estimate of their fighting was ill-founded. And his intelligence section had made a critical error: it had informed him that the veteran U.S. 2nd Division was resting far to the rear. In fact, on the day Hitler launched his blitzkrieg, two of its regiments were attacking into Germany just north of the Sixth Panzer Army's planned thrusts.

Dietrich launched his two Volksgrenadier divisions on the morning of December 16, and at once ran into trouble. In a series of close-quarter skirmishes, the raw GIs of the 99th fought with unexpected determination. By early afternoon the grenadiers had made so little headway that Dietrich ordered tanks into action. One American antitank gunner stood his ground against a huge Tiger tank as it roared down the road. His first shot knocked off a tread. He reloaded and fired again. The Tiger burst into flames, and as its crewmen scrambled out, they were picked off by rifle fire.

Six miles to the north, in the Krinkelt-Rocherath area, the 99th Division fought off two major grenadier assaults, in one case driving the Germans back to within 400 yards of their starting point. But by nightfall, all the tanks of the 12th SS Panzer Division had been committed to the battle, and the Americans were in a precarious position. Nevertheless, at midnight, Lauer reported to V Corps commander, General Leonard T. Gerow, that the situation was in hand.

Gerow was not reassured. His superior, Lieut. General Courtney H. Hodges, had not yet called off the 2nd Division's attack into Germany. Gerow knew that if the division had to retreat, its route would be the Krinkelt-Rocherath road, which the Germans might cut at any moment. Early on December 17, Hodges realized that Gerow's front was in serious trouble, and made two important decisions. He gave Gerow permission to defend his position as he saw fit, and ordered the 2nd Division to withdraw.

Anticipating the order, 2nd Division commander Major General Walter M. Robertson had spent the previous day mapping out a plan for a daylight withdrawal under enemy fire, a tactic known as "skinning the cat." His attacking units would pull back through their rear battalions, which would cover their withdrawal. The rear battalions—now in front—would then fall back through the former front units, until the entire force was safely back in the Krinkelt-Rocherath area, seven miles to the south. Then, with the 2nd Division holding off the Germans, the men of the 99th could pull back to form a defensive position on Elsenborn Ridge, where they would be joined later by the 2nd.

The maneuver was fraught with peril. In the winter fog and snow, frontline troops could easily be mistaken for the enemy, and mowed down by their own rear units as they withdrew. If closely pursued by Germans, the withdrawing troops could not be covered safely with fire from the rear units. Aware of the pitfalls, Robertson personally supervised the 2nd Division withdrawal, frequently directing traffic.

As these moves were taking place, German tanks and infantry renewed their assaults on the 99th. One battalion was nearly destroyed; another had to retreat so hastily that it left many wounded men behind. East of Krinkelt-Rocherath, the exhausted Americans were pushed back through the thin second line of defense, manned by a battalion of the 2nd Division's reserve regiment, the 23rd.

Storming an enemy position, infantrymen of the 2nd Panzer Division sprint over a muddy road blocked by abandoned U.S. vehicles.

Eventually the Germans brought up Tiger tanks and drove one company back under point-blank cannon fire. Private First Class Richard E. Cowan covered the company's withdrawal with its only remaining machine gun. Cowan cut down wave after wave of enemy troops. An 88mm shell from a Tiger tank exploded so close that he was knocked from his weapon, but he jumped back and fired until his ammunition ran out. Then he trudged toward Krinkelt.

Such gallantry slowed the German onslaught long enough to permit the 2nd Division's 9th and 38th regiments to withdraw safely to the twin villages. Throughout the night the battle for Krinkelt raged on, while the retreating 99th continued toward Elsenborn Ridge.

Just before daybreak, tanks of the 12th SS Panzer burst into Rocherath, and were hurled back by artillery from Elsenborn Ridge and by bazookas, antitank mines and cans of gasoline poured on the tanks and set afire.

By nightfall on December 18th, the complex withdrawal was completed—and not a single one of the 12th SS panzers had broken through to the Malmédy road. Two days later, the 2nd Division, with reinforcements, was solidly dug in on Elsenborn Ridge. Three times the Germans tried to break through the defenses, and three times were driven back. The failure of these assaults made it obvious to the German High Command that the battering-ram tactics of the Sixth Panzer Army would not dislodge the Americans from Elsenborn Ridge. At a cost of 6,000 casualties, the green troops of the 99th Division and the veterans of the 2nd had dealt the Germans a critical blow. Henceforth, Manteuffel's Fifth Panzer Army to the south would have to carry the main weight of Hitler's offensive.

General Manteuffel had persuaded the Führer that, on December 16, the infantry should attack first, rather than the panzers, as Hitler had planned; the foot soldiers would open paths for the armor, clearing out enemy tank destroyers. Small units would infiltrate the enemy frontline positions before the artillery opened fire. In some areas, special storm battalions would move forward stealthily, bypass enemy positions and penetrate deep into rear areas before the Americans could effectively react. Over most of his 28-mile front, tanks would not go into action until dark at the end of the first day. Navigating by artificial moonlight, they would speed forward to exploit infantry breakthroughs.

Manteuffel's clever planning got his army off on the right foot. In the predawn darkness of December 16, his storm battalions penetrated American lines and advanced rapidly. But while Manteuffel's vanguards pressed forward, many small bypassed American units formed pockets of resistance in what had become the German rear.

All of a sudden, two U.S. 28th Division regiments had found themselves fighting two entire German corps. The 112th Regiment, defending a six-mile front, held off the German infantry through the first day. But, by the night of December 17, the Americans were forced back to the west bank of the Our River; most of the men slipped across a bridge at Ouren. One patrol reached another bridge and found it guarded by Germans. The patrol lined up in formation and, with their sergeant shouting commands in German, marched safely across in the dark under the noses of the guards.

Manteuffel's main thrust hit to the south of the 112th in the zone of the 110th Regiment. Spread over a 15-mile front along a road known to Americans as Skyline Drive, the 110th was attacked by three German panzer divisions. Its commander, Colonel Hurley E. Fuller, was at headquarters in a hotel in Clervaux, a resort town five miles west of the front. At the start of the attack, his telephones were knocked out and radio wavelengths jammed. Gradually, from isolated reports, he learned that German infantry and tanks had crossed the Our and were heading west en masse. Scraping together a dozen or so tanks and about 200 men, mostly headquarters clerks and cooks, Fuller prepared for defense.

By dawn of December 17, Volksgrenadiers were attacking a château on the outskirts where Fuller's headquarters company was billeted. All morning Fuller's men fought and lost skirmishes, and by late afternoon panzers were heading into town. At dusk, explosions shook the floor under Fuller's feet and machine gun fire slammed into the plaster above his head. Quickly, he gathered up his staff, and with a blinded soldier hanging onto his belt, led the way out of a rear window, up a steel ladder and onto a cliff behind the hotel.

Below, Clervaux was an inferno. Tanks rumbled through the streets firing point-blank at houses where GIs were still holed up. In the burning château, a hundred men of the headquarters company held out. When German troops stormed through the building, they found nearly everyone

A heavily armed SS panzer trooper radiates the confidence and excitement that pervaded the German armies after their early victories in the Ardennes.

dead or wounded. They encountered one strange sight: in a baronial hall deep in the château a lone American soldier sat playing the piano while rubble sifted down over him.

The Germans now rolled west past Clervaux, and by December 19 had forced the defenders back to a perimeter being set up around Bastogne. Colonel Fuller was taken prisoner near Wiltz, an important road junction along the southern route to Bastogne. There, his executive officer, Colonel Daniel B. Strickler, took over the defense of Wiltz. But by the evening of December 19, the Germans were poised to overwhelm the town.

By now, the GIs were numb with weariness; many units were out of ammunition. Strickler called the unit commanders together and told them to find their way out and head toward Bastogne. He himself stayed at his command post until 11 p.m., destroying maps and equipment. Then with a staff officer and driver, he climbed into a jeep and roared to the outskirts of Wiltz with bullets flying around them. Forced by heavy fire to abandon the jeep, Strickler and his companions made good their escape on their feet and bellies, crawling into the woods outside the town.

For three days without food, Strickler and a small band of men stumbled westward through the snow, hiding from the Germans by day and moving by night through underbrush and pine forest. Finally they were halted by American sentries near the village of Vaux-les-Rosières. It turned out to be the new headquarters of their own division. Strickler, who had been reported killed at Wiltz, was greeted, he said later, "like a ghost come to life."

While the remnants of the 28th Division were pulling back, disaster was befalling the 106th Division on the rugged Schnee Eifel, the ridge protruding dangerously through Germany's West Wall defenses. The 106th commander, Major General Alan W. Jones, had disliked and distrusted his positions from the start. Attacking forces could flow along roads at both ends of the ridge and link up at Schönberg to his rear, trapping his 422nd and 423rd regiments defending the ridge. His 424th Regiment had the Our River at its back, leaving little room to maneuver. Still, Jones understood that the Schnee Eifel was a strategic position, and had to be held.

Jones's worst fears were realized on the first day of the German offensive. Manteuffel sent three Volksgrenadier regiments in a two-prong pincer attack around the edges of the ridge. By nightfall the 106th was in grave peril. The 424th Regiment was driven back to the Our River and the two regiments on the Schnee Eifel were threatened with entrapment. By 8:30 the next morning, converging German forces had linked up at Schönberg. The trap snapped shut.

That afternoon Jones ordered his two trapped regiments to fall back to the west bank of the Our. But so busy was the radio traffic that they did not receive his message until after midnight—and then it was followed by another order to attack panzer concentrations along the road from Schönberg to Saint-Vith, then move to protect Saint-Vith.

When Colonel George L. Descheneaux Jr. of the 422nd read this message, he bowed his head and said in despair, "My poor men, they'll be cut to pieces." The men were running out of ammunition, and were being called upon to make their way over rugged, unfamiliar terrain and attack panzers. But orders were orders; his outfit and Colonel Charles C. Cavender's 423rd Regiment got ready to attack.

They moved out at about 9 a.m., leaving their wounded behind in the care of aid men. Through rain and fog, they stumbled over gullies and ravines, slipping and sliding through the mud and slush; many units were soon lost or stranded in the woods. The following morning both regiments came under heavy fire. Finally surrounded by German tanks and infantry, and with casualties mounting, the two regiments were forced to surrender. Some 7,000 men were marched off into Germany. The survivors of the division's remaining regiment, the 424th, supported by tanks of the 9th Armored, withdrew safely across the Our and set up a new front line east of Saint-Vith.

Manteuffel's Fifth Panzer Army had won tremendous victories, destroying the 106th Division and shattering the 28th. Yet they had been won at the high cost of time. Manteuffel had planned to capture both Saint-Vith and Bastogne by the night of December 17. But on that night, Colonel Fuller's men were still holding out in the Clervaux area, and Colonel Strickler did not abandon Wiltz until two nights later. Even the ill-fated 106th Division managed to hold on until December 19, tying up German units that had urgent assignments farther to the west.

Fierce fighting by outnumbered and outmaneuvered GIs had granted the American command enough time to defend two key road junctions in the path of Manteuffel's army: Saint-Vith and Bastogne.

On December 19, Eisenhower met with his top field commanders at Verdun to formulate a strategy to halt the Germans. The situation appeared to be getting worse by the hour: Peiper's panzers were racing unchecked to the west; Manteuffel's legions were pouring through a 30-mile gap between Saint-Vith and Bastogne, and had already driven a deep salient, or bulge, into the American front. Rumors were rife of enemy commandos in American uniforms popping up behind every bush. But Eisenhower injected a note of optimism. "The present situation," he told his generals, "is to be regarded as one of opportunity for us and not of disaster."

Advancing from tree to tree, infantrymen were exposed to "tree bursts," artillery shells that exploded on trunks and branches, spraying a rain of splintery death over a wide area below. If a man threw himself flat on the ground, he only made himself a bigger target for a tree burst.

General Patton grinned and said, "Hell, let's have the guts to let the sons of bitches go all the way to Paris. Then we'll really cut 'em off and chew 'em up!"

"No," Eisenhower responded quietly. "The enemy will never be allowed to cross the Meuse."

Advantageous conditions were already developing. At the southern end of the Ardennes, where General Brandenberger had launched four divisions of his Seventh Army, the exhausted veterans of the vastly depleted U.S. 4th Infantry Division were fighting with courage and skill against Brandenberger's best division, the 212th Volksgrenadiers. Although forced to yield ground, the Americans were to blunt the attack of the entire Seventh Army for five days.

To the north, a lone combat command of the 9th Armored Division pulled back, holding the German penetrations to less than five miles. Further along the line, one regiment of the 28th Infantry Division had restrained infiltrating Volksgrenadiers for nearly two days while falling back across a branch of the Sûre River; the Americans blew the bridges behind them and eventually joined forces with 9th Armored and 4th Infantry Division units to the southeast. Together with most of the 10th Armored Division, these units and the newly arrived 5th Infantry Division established a new line of defense stretching from the Echternach area in the east to the village of Grosbous, almost 20 miles to the west.

The net result was a signal American success. At the cost of about 2,000 casualties, the GIs had established a solid line of defense blocking any enemy expansion to the south. This southern shoulder, together with the matching shoulder formed by the Americans on Elsenborn Ridge, restricted the enemy onslaught to the central portion of the Ardennes. From these anchors, Eisenhower decided, U.S. forces would build strong positions outward along both flanks of the enemy salient. They would then sever the narrow attack corridor and cut off the enemy heading for the Meuse. The counterattack would be launched initially by troops of Patton's Third Army, which would slice north through the German flank and relieve the vital road center of Bastogne.

Eisenhower asked Patton when he could attack. "On December 22, with three divisions," Patton replied. The other generals stirred in disbelief. Patton was proposing a movement of enormous complexity: to pull three divisions out of line, wheel them northward and launch an assault—all in three days. But Patton and his staff had foreseen the German attack and had drafted plans to deal with such an emergency. Now Patton was enjoying the situation. He lit up a cigar and pointed to the German penetrations on the map. "This time the Kraut has stuck his head in a meat grinder," he said. "And this time I've got the handle."

In the north-central sector of the Ardennes, the key to the struggle was the town of Saint-Vith with its six paved high-

ways radiating from its center. Initially Manteuffel's panzers, using the blitzkrieg method of bypassing centers of resistance, had swept past the town. But the farther their spearheads traveled, the more the Germans needed to oust the Americans from Saint-Vith in order to ferry supplies forward. The chief responsibility for defending the town was given to Brigadier General Robert W. Hasbrouck's 7th Armored Division, which reached the horseshoe-shaped defense line east of Saint-Vith on the night of December 17.

For two days the Germans jabbed at the hastily formed, 15-mile-long perimeter, striking first in one place then another. Hasbrouck juggled his troops to meet each new threat, forcing the Germans back, and leaving behind smoking tanks and piles of dead infantry. The German High Command lost patience; American control of the road hub was stalling the entire Fifth Army offensive.

On the morning of December 21, following a heavy artillery bombardment, wave upon wave of tanks and infantry were hurled against the perimeter. "The Krauts kept boring in, no matter how fast we decimated their assault squads," later wrote Major Donald P. Boyer Jr. of the 38th Armored Infantry Battalion. "Always there were more Germans, and more Germans, and then more Germans."

By 8 p.m. the American lines had been pierced in at least three places, and tanks were rolling through the streets of Saint-Vith. Of the original 1,142 men in Boyer's battalion only 100 were still in condition to fight. Brigadier General Bruce C. Clarke of Combat Command B ordered his men to move back to a new line being formed west of the town.

Meanwhile, Major General Matthew B. Ridgway of the XVIII Airborne Corps was planning to set up an oval-shaped perimeter between Saint-Vith and Vielsalm. Soon dubbed the "fortified goose egg," it was to be held by Hasbrouck's troops and supplied by airdrops. Neither Hasbrouck nor Clarke liked the idea. Their troops were spread out and exhausted. Moreover, the goose egg contained a dense forest and only one decent road—hardly terrain for a mobile armored defense. Sarcastically Clarke called the operation "Custer's Last Stand." That label almost proved prophetic.

Even as the oval perimeter took form, the Germans began piercing it. By December 22, some 6,000 of the original 22,000 troops at Saint-Vith had been killed or wounded. Field Marshal Bernard Montgomery, who was now temporary commander of American Forces in the north, ordered a withdrawal.

Early on December 23, throughout the goose egg, motors roared to life and vehicles started moving over roads and fields that had miraculously frozen overnight. With a 7th Armored task force covering their withdrawal, the defenders of Saint-Vith slowly streamed over the Salm River to safety behind the lines of the 82nd Airborne, which had set up a defense to the west. Bruce Clarke stood in a field directing traffic. He looked at his men as they went by; they were dirty, unshaven, red-eyed and gaunt, and he was proud of every one. When the last truck had passed, Clarke climbed heavily into his own jeep and told his driver to bring up the rear of the column. He had not slept lying down for seven days; now, he fell fast asleep.

Although Saint-Vith was lost in the end, the 7th Armored and its supporting units had tied up an entire enemy corps for nearly a week, blocking crucial supply routes. And the Allies were now flooding the Ardennes with reinforcements. Among them was the U.S. 30th Infantry Division whose deployment along the Amblève River set the stage for a showdown with Lieut. Colonel Peiper and his SS troopers, who had run amok near Malmédy.

After passing Malmédy on December 17, Peiper's SS troops had pushed westward toward Ligneuville, where his men shot eight more American prisoners. By dusk his panzer column had advanced along the south bank of the Amblève River to the heights across from the village of Stavelot. As the lead tank approached the Stavelot bridge, it was knocked out by mines. Peiper sent 60 men ahead on foot to

A Medical Service ambulance, hit by a German plane despite Red Cross markings, burns during the Battle of the Bulge. The driver and patients perished.

324

storm the bridge; they were driven back. His tanks were now low on fuel and his men had not rested for almost three days. Bone-tired himself, he decided to close down for the night. The delay gave the Americans a few precious hours to bolster their defenses.

At dawn, two Panther tanks charged the bridge. The first Panther was set afire, but still crossed over and crashed through a roadblock. Another tank shot the gap, followed by other vehicles and infantrymen who drove the Americans back to the village square. Peiper now ordered the bulk of his column to head for his next objective, Trois-Ponts, leaving a sizable detachment to deal with Stavelot. The SS troops continued their onslaught, shooting eight American prisoners and firing on civilians. Discovering 26 Belgians huddled in a cellar, they hurled in grenades. Before the killing subsided in Stavelot, 101 people were murdered.

In the end, Stavelot was held. Peiper's position was discovered in time for American engineers to blow up a bridge, thwarting his arrival at Trois-Ponts. His column was scattered, but he regrouped, and headed for the crossroads of Habiémont. There, a squad of American engineers under Lieutenant Alvin Edelstein had just wired the bridge. Around 5 p.m., the engineers spotted the panzers approaching. A Tiger fired its 88mm cannon at them, but the shot was off target. Corporal Fred Chapin waited with the detonator in his hand. Edelstein yelled, "Blow! Blow!" Chapin turned the key and, to his relief, saw the familiar string off blue flashes, followed by a thunderous blast. The engineers escaped.

Since Peiper carried no heavy bridging equipment, he had no choice but to head back and find another route. Retreating northward, he seized the towns of La Gleize, Cheneux and Stoumont, and attempted to turn them into a fortified triangle. By then, however, he was boxed in by the 30th Infantry and 82nd Airborne divisions. Ten miles to his rear, the bulk of the 1st SS Panzer Division was unable to cross the Amblève River at Stavelot, which had been recaptured, or to cross the Salm River near Trois-Ponts. Cut off from fuel, ammunition and food, Peiper's spearhead fought fiercely for several days, but was driven back into a pocket around La Gleize. By the afternoon of December 23, Peiper realized his only hope was to get back to his own lines.

Early the next day, the remnants of his troops—some 800 men out of the original 4,000—left La Gleize silently and on foot, and headed into the woods. That night, Christmas Eve, the tired Germans ran into American outposts south of Trois-Ponts. A firefight followed. Then Peiper and his men slipped away in the dark, swam across the icy Salm River, and made contact with German units four miles to the east. Behind them they had left a trail of 353 prisoners of war and 111 civilians, killed in cold blood.

While battered American troops were desperately delaying Manteuffel's panzers around Saint-Vith, the biggest and longest fight of what would forevermore be known as the Battle of the Bulge was shaping up at Bastogne, 30 miles to the southwest. A drab market town of 3,500 inhabitants, Bastogne was fated to be a battlefield because of the seven paved roads that radiated from its central square. These roads included the main east-west highways vital to Hitler's thrust toward Antwerp. In the American camp, Eisenhower had also realized Bastogne's importance. In fact, as early as December 17, he had alerted three divisions—the 10th Armored and the 82nd and 101st Airborne—for movement to the general area.

On the night of December 17, the acting commander of the 101st Airborne, Brigadier General Anthony C. McAuliffe, called an emergency meeting of his officers. In his quiet, undramatic manner, he explained that the 101st had been ordered to move out early the next morning to the Belgian town of Werbomont. "All I know," he said, "is that there has been a breakthrough, and we have got to get up there."

As the division's 11,000 men began moving out next morning, McAuliffe sped on ahead and called on General Middleton's VIII Corps headquarters in Bastogne to gain more information. To his concern, he found the roads outside the town clogged with troops heading away from the front. "There has been a major penetration," Middleton told him. The headquarters was now being withdrawn to Neufchâteau and McAuliffe's orders had been changed; the 101st was to defend Bastogne—and hold it at all costs.

Soon after, Middleton received a welcome arrival, his old friend Colonel William L. Roberts, whose Combat Command B of the 10th Armored Division was rushing toward Bastogne from France. Indicating on his map the three German columns converging on Bastogne, Middleton said he needed three combat teams. "Move with utmost speed," he ordered. "And Robbie, hold those positions at all costs."

The first of the 101st Airborne to arrive around Bastogne were the men of the 501st Parachute Infantry Regiment, commanded by Lieut. Colonel Julian J. Ewell. McAuliffe decided to dispatch Ewell and his regiment to the east of Bastogne to reinforce Team Cherry, one of the three armored groups of Combat Command B. At 6 a.m. on December 19, Ewell sent his 1st Battalion to reconnoiter the road going east to Longvilly. "Take it slow and easy," he told its commander. "I don't want you to beat the enemy to death."

Ewell's caution paid off. When the 1st Battalion reached the outskirts of the village of Neffe, it ran into what seemed to be a German roadblock. Though no one yet knew it, they had encountered the vanguard of the formidable Panzer Lehr Division under Major General Fritz Bayerlein.

A head-on attack was out of the question. Ewell told the 1st Battalion to hold its ground, and brought forward his 2nd and 3rd battalions to form a solid front. He then called up the divisional artillery. Zeroing in on the German forward positions with 105mm howitzers, the gunners began a steady, killing fire.

The winter fog was so thick that Bayerlein could not see what was going on, and the heavy shelling convinced him that he faced a larger force. Badly shaken, he went off to a cave near the Neffe railroad station to set up a command post and analyze the situation. As a result, the Panzer Lehr spent the whole day probing at one American outpost after another, but failed to make a concerted drive on Bastogne. The defenders of the town had survived their first crisis.

While Ewell's men were fighting, another serious threat developed at Noville, a village six miles northeast of Bastogne. Twenty-six-year-old Major William R. Desobry of Combat Command B, leading a team of 15 Sherman tanks, a platoon of tank destroyers, and armored infantry, arrived at the village at about 11 p.m. on December 18. There, retreating GIs told him that the crack 2nd Panzer Division was hot on their heels. Desobry posted roadblocks on the roads north and east and got set for battle.

Before dawn, German tanks hit two of his roadblocks. Desobry's men beat back the attacks. Then at 7:30 they followed his order to fall back to Noville. A heavy fog settled in, but the nervous defenders could hear out front the rumbling and clanking of enemy tanks. When the fog lifted at 10 a.m., they saw to their horror that the countryside was crawling with German Tigers and Panthers; 30 tanks could be seen nearby, and a dozen more ranged on distant ridges.

The Americans threw everything they had at the Germans—bazooka rockets, antitank rounds, .50-caliber machine gun fire. Frustrated, the Germans rained a heavy barrage of shells on the village, killing men, setting fires and leveling houses. The Americans launched a counterattack, advancing only 500 yards before being pinned down. The Germans replied with an attack of their own, and continued their bombardment. An 88mm shell burst outside the American command post, seriously wounding Desobry.

All night long the GIs kept fighting and dying as the panzers kept up the pressure. Finally at noon, the survivors were ordered to fall back on the village of Foy. The fight at Noville had been grisly. A GI who passed through the village later said: "We found all manner of horrors. Stuff like a galosh with a foot still in it, a headless paratrooper, a blackened tree stump which turned out to be a cremated Kraut sitting in a foxhole—all that sort of mincing-machine warfare."

Yet that grim defense had delayed the powerful 2nd Panzer for almost 48 hours. When the commander of 2nd Panzer radioed for permission to attack Bastogne, an angry staff officer spat back, "Forget Bastogne and head for the Meuse." The High Command had decided to leave the capture of Bastogne to Bayerlein's Panzer Lehr and Brigadier General Heinz Kokott's 26th Volksgrenadier Division.

By December 20, General McAuliffe was playing with a full hand. The entire 101st Airborne was on the scene along with all of Colonel Roberts' Combat Command B of the 10th Armored and the 705th Tank Destroyer Battalion. These forces were deployed in a defensive arc around Bastogne. In the center were seven battalions of artillery, including three with long-range howitzers.

That day the defense line was tested at two spots, and in both cases the Germans were finally repulsed. Nevertheless on the night of December 20 other German troops encircled Bastogne to the north and south. The Americans were now trapped inside a lumpy ring five miles in diameter.

The encirclement of Bastogne was followed by a lull in the fighting that lasted two and a half days, while the Germans massed for new attacks. As an airborne division, the 101st was used to being on its own. But they did worry about the lack of supplies. Artillery shells were so short that McAuliffe ordered severe rationing. To a protesting officer, he said tongue-in-cheek, "If you see four hundred Germans in a hundred yard area and they have their heads up, you can fire artillery at them. But not more than two rounds."

This vast American fuel dump—more than 400,000 five-gallon jerry cans of gasoline lining five miles of roadway between the Belgian towns of Stavelot and Francorchamps—lay just one mile from Joachim Peiper's gas-starved panzers after they crossed the Stavelot bridge on December 18. But American units retreating along the Francorchamps road turned back reconnoitering German tanks by setting up an immense flaming roadblock in which 124,000 gallons of fuel were consumed.

American antiaircraft gunners watch a high-speed dogfight between German interceptors and U.S. fighter-bombers flying escort for cargo planes bound for Bastogne.

Rifle ammunition was also low, food dwindling fast and medical supplies dangerously skimpy. The 101st's medical unit, including most of its surgeons and equipment, had been captured on December 19. Virtually the only painkiller on hand was brandy.

At 11:30 a.m. on December 22, Sergeant Oswald Butler of the 327th Glider Infantry Regiment saw four Germans walking toward the farmhouse he was occupying on the perimeter's southern rim. On the field telephone he reported, "There're four Krauts coming up the road. They're carrying a white flag. It looks like they want to surrender."

The Germans carried a message, and asked to see the American commanding general. Major Alvin Jones held the emissaries at his company command post and took the message to divisional headquarters. "It's an ultimatum, sir," Jones said to Lieut. Colonel Ned D. Moore, the 101st's chief of staff. Moore handed the document to McAuliffe. "They want you to surrender," he said.

The general looked briefly at the message. "Aw, nuts!" he said and left the room. When reminded that the German emissaries still awaited a reply, he was stumped. "Well," he said, "I don't know what to tell them."

Replied operations officer Lieut. Colonel Harry Kinnard, "That first crack you made would be hard to beat, General."

"What was that?" McAuliffe asked.

"You said, 'Nuts!'"

McAuliffe snapped his fingers. "That's it!"

Everyone laughed and a sergeant typed up the answer. The note read: "To the German Commander: Nuts! The American Commander."

McAuliffe gleefully handed the reply to Colonel Joseph H. "Bud" Harper, commander of the 327th Glider Infantry Regiment, who had just arrived, and asked, "Will you see that it's delivered?"

Harper beamed. "I'll deliver it myself!" At the command post he handed the note to the awaiting German major, and said, "If you don't understand what 'Nuts' means, in plain English it's the same as 'Go to hell.' And I will tell you something else—if you continue to attack, we will kill every goddamn German that tries to break into this city!"

The Germans saluted formally. "We will kill many Americans," the captain declared.

"On your way, bud!" growled Harper. Then he added impulsively, "And good luck to you." As the Germans receded, he wondered what had come over him to make him wish his enemies good luck.

On December 23, the damp, foggy weather broke; the day dawned bright and very cold, turning sodden boots to icy slabs. Most importantly, it also provided fine flying weather for the first time in days, and Bastogne received word that an airdrop was in the works. Just before noon, the first of 241 C-47 cargo carriers droned over the drop zone. Red, blue and yellow parachutes billowed like fantastic Christmas ornaments, floating downward with priceless gifts

of ammunition, medical supplies and food. Almost 140 tons of matériel were successfully dropped.

Though the cold snap had made it possible to supply Bastogne, it also helped the Germans. Now that the ground was frozen, their tanks and half-tracks were able to maneuver across previously muddy terrain. Colonel Heinz Kokott and his 26th Volksgrenadiers, reinforced by the tanks and infantry of the Panzer Lehr, pressed his attack, aiming to smash into Bastogne from the southeast. At dusk they began blasting the already ruined town of Marvie and soon took Hill 500, a low knob south of the village defended by a single U.S. infantry platoon. In overrunning Hill 500, the Germans opened a crack in Bastogne's outer defenses. Now they sought to widen it, charging toward Marvie, screaming and setting off flares that illuminated the snowy landscape.

Repulsed with heavy losses in the southeast, Kokott now decided to deliver his knockout punch on Christmas Day in the northwest sector defended by Lieut. Colonel Steve A. Chappuis and his 502nd Parachute Infantry Regiment. December 24 was relatively quiet as Kokott shifted his troops around and Manteuffel, warned that units of Patton's Third Army were on their way, sent the 15th Panzer Grenadier Division as reinforcements.

Christmas Eve turned into a nightmare in Bastogne, where Luftwaffe bombers made heavy raids. But even while the bombs were falling, an impromptu soldiers' choir gathered in the vaulted chapel of the town's seminary, and wounded men lined the cold stone floor all the way up to the altar, wrapped in colored parachutes from the supply drops to keep warm. As the choir sang "Silent Night, Holy Night," they joined in.

At 1:30 a.m. on Christmas morning, heavy German artillery fire heralded Kokott's all-out attack. In the wake of the shells, white-clad Volksgrenadiers burst into the village of Champs and grappled hand-to-hand with a company of Chappuis's paratroopers. The colonel coolly withheld rein-

forcements, expecting a heavier blow to land elsewhere.

He was right. At daybreak, Harper's glider troops south of Champs saw 18 white-camouflaged tanks, with squads of panzer grenadiers clinging to them, roar down a snow-covered hillside, firing at the GIs in their foxholes. The Americans returned the fire, dropped deep into their holes as the tanks roared over their positions, then raised up and fought the German infantry who followed.

Kokott seemed to have his breakthrough. At 5:45 a.m. Christmas morning a German tank section leader sent a message saying he was on the edge of Bastogne itself, roughly a mile from McAuliffe's command post. But as the panzers headed into the town, they ran into a maelstrom of fire. One tank was captured intact; the rest were destroyed. Of the 18 German tanks that had gone into action, not one survived.

Meanwhile the other section of this tank group had turned north hoping to take Champs from the rear. This was what Chappuis had been waiting for. He swiftly deployed two companies facing south toward the oncoming Germans and placed some tank destroyers in a wood alongside the enemy line of attack. As the panzers came on, the paratroopers fell back into the trees. The onrushing tanks then turned, bypassing the wood, and headed for Champs—exposing their vulnerable flanks to the hidden tank destroyers. A slaughter followed. The high-velocity 76mm American guns swiftly knocked out three panzers, and armor-piercing bazookas got two more. Only one tank made it to Champs—to be destroyed.

On the afternoon of December 26, the lead units of Patton's relieving 4th Armored Division were just four miles south of the town. The 37th Tank Battalion was led by Lieut. Colonel Creighton W. Abrams, who one day would be Chief of Staff of the U.S. Army. He and Lieut. Colonel George L. Jaques of the 53rd Armored Infantry Battalion discussed how they would attack. The target would be the village of Sibret, known to be heavily defended by Germans. Suddenly a fleet

A rifleman, a machine gunner and tanks of the 4th Armored fight to hold open the corridor to Bastogne against counterattacking Germans. A tanker said that the corridor was "so narrow you can spit across it."

of cargo planes materialized over Bastogne, dropping their parachute supplies as they dodged puffs of enemy flak. Galvanized by this evidence of the 101st's urgent shortages, Abrams and Jaques decided to strike directly north into Bastogne through the village of Assenois, even though it risked a German flank assault from Sibret.

By radio, Abrams asked headquarters to authorize the new attack. Patton replied, "I sure as hell will!" Standing up in the turret of his tank, Abrams stuck a big cigar in his mouth and announced: "We're going in now. Let 'er roll!" Dusk was settling as Abrams' support artillery sent volley after volley crashing into Assenois. Then the armored attack started down the slope. Leading the way were five new 40-ton Shermans, headed up by Lieutenant Charles Boggess.

The tanks raced into the village, spitting fire. Troops leaped from the Shermans' decks. Shooting, bayoneting and clubbing, they worked their way from house to house. A 19-year-old private, James R. Hendrix, armed only with a rifle, took on the crews of two German 88mm artillery pieces that were pounding the Shermans. "Come on out!" shouted Hendrix. A German poked his head up from a foxhole. Hendrix shot him in the neck. Running to the next foxhole, he smashed another German in the head with the butt of his rifle, and charged straight at the muzzles of the two big guns. The crews came out with their hands up. (Hendrix's brief one-man war would win him the Medal of Honor.)

Leaving Assenois, Lieutenant Boggess now moved toward Bastogne at top speed, his forward machine gunner spraying the tree line along both sides of the road. Then, in the gathering darkness, he saw some men duck into foxholes—but they did not look like Germans. Boggess took a chance. Standing up in his turret, he shouted, "Come here! This is the 4th Armored!"

Suspiciously, a few helmeted heads poked out of the foxholes. Then a figure emerged, and started walking forward, keeping Boggess covered with his carbine. Suddenly he broke into a smile, stuck his hand up toward the turret and said: "Second Lieutenant Duane J. Webster, 326th Engineers, 101st Airborne Division."

By this time commanding officer Captain William Dwight had made his way up a hill to a 101st observation post. General McAuliffe was waiting to greet the new arrivals. "Gee," the general said, "I am mighty glad to see you." The siege of the 101st Airborne, Bastogne, was lifted.

On December 23, Major General Ernest N. Harmon, commander of the U.S. 2nd Armored Division, had been eating lunch with his staff at their new command post at Havelange, 19 miles east of the Meuse River. His "Hell On Wheels" division had arrived just the day before after an exhausting forced march of 70 miles from the area of Aachen. He had been told not to expect any action for at least a week, and he was relaxing over coffee when a very excited young officer wearing a bloody bandage pushed his way into the room. Lieutenant Everett C. Jones bore startling news. His patrol had been fired on by German tanks just 10 miles to the south. His armored car had been hit, but he and his crew had escaped.

Jones' news electrified Harmon. He jumped up from the table, ran across a snowy field to the bivouac of a tank battalion, and asked the tank commander how long it would take to get his outfit on the road. Five minutes, was the reply, provided radio silence was lifted.

"Radio silence is lifted here and now," said Harmon in the throaty growl that had earned him the nickname Old Gravel Voice. "You get down that road and start fighting. The whole damned division is coming right behind you."

In five minutes, the lead company of Shermans was rolling south, and another tank contingent rumbled southeast a little later. Seventeen miles below them, stretched out in a long column, lay the 2nd Panzer Division—the vanguard of the German offensive. By the evening of December

The bodies of German soldiers caught in a cross fire from American machine guns litter a shell-pocked open field to the northwest of Bastogne on Christmas morning, 1944. Most of the attacking infantrymen were mowed down in tight clusters as they advanced behind Mark IV tanks; others, riding on the tanks into battle, were shot off the decks. The Americans knocked out the Mark IVs soon afterward.

23, its leading elements were within 15 miles of the Meuse. But it was traveling alone, having outdistanced both the 116th Panzer Division and the Panzer Lehr. By December 23, it was not only badly strung out, but its men were exhausted and their tanks running out of fuel.

No one realized the division's precarious position more than Manteuffel who, obsessed with the idea of reaching the Meuse, had ordered the Panzer Lehr to break off its attack in the Bastogne area, and had personally led the division from Saint-Hubert to the Rochefort area about 15 miles from the river. But his 116th Panzer Division was having trouble. Before daylight on December 24, the punch Harmon had aimed at the head of the 2nd Panzer struck home as a task force sent south collided with an outriding panzer column probing north. The results were spectacular.

A jeep patrol ahead of the American tanks heard the rumble of approaching armor and raced back to warn the column. Lieut. Colonel Hugh R. O'Farrell, the task force commander, had barely time to warn his Shermans off the road and into a grove of trees. When the German column appeared, the Americans opened fire, catching the panzers by surprise and annihilating the entire column.

This stunning success was merely the opening round in a great tank battle. On the afternoon of Christmas Eve, Harmon called VII Corps headquarters. "One of my patrols just spotted Kraut tanks coiled up near Celles," Old Gravel Voice rasped excitedly. The village of Celles was just four miles from the Meuse, and the 2nd Panzer tanks were holed up in a nearby forest. "Belgians say the Krauts are out of gas," Harmon went on. "Let me take the bastards!"

When headquarters authorized the attack, he hollered, "The bastards are in the bag!" He then deployed two combat groups—one plunging southwest to Celles to encircle the panzers, the other driving southeast to stop any further German advances toward the Meuse.

The fight to annihilate the 2nd Panzer in the Celles pocket raged for three days. At one point, American tanks were attacked by 45-ton Panther and 57-ton Tiger tanks of the Panzer Lehr, which was trying to break through to rescue the trapped German troops. Shermans could not stop these monsters, but fighter-bombers could—and, as it happened, some rocket-firing British Typhoons were on call. To guide them to the targets, the Americans arranged to send up a small Piper Cub plane with an artillery observer who knew where the tanks were located.

Shortly afterward, the 2nd Armored was treated to an aerial show. A squadron of Typhoons flew over, homing in on the Piper Cub. As the Cub dived low to point out the tanks, the Typhoons came swooping down with rockets blazing, leaving a trail of burning hulks in their wake.

Two more rescue attempts were made by the Panzer Lehr, and again both were stopped by fighter-bombers called in by radio. Worn down in a hard struggle, the 116th was forced to dig in and was soon finished as an offensive threat in the Battle of the Bulge. Elements of yet another German division—the 9th Panzer—were thrust into the whorl of combat at the tip of the Bulge. Seizing control of a road junction at Humain, a village northeast of Rochefort, they took a terrible pounding from the 2nd Armored Division, and finally, on December 27, Humain fell to the Americans.

Later that night, in a brief report of the battle, Harmon wrote, "Attached is a list of spoils we took—including some 1,200 prisoners. Killed and wounded some 2,500. A great slaughter." In addition, they had destroyed or captured 82 tanks, 83 field guns and 441 vehicles. More important, one arm of Hitler's offensive had been smashed.

While Harmon's tank battle had been unfolding, the 2nd SS Panzer Division was mounting another threat 40 miles east at Baraque de Fraiture, a crossroads hamlet with a broad paved highway leading north to the town of Manhay. The isolated hamlet was situated atop a 2,139-foot plateau, and lay along the boundary between the American 82nd Airborne and 3rd Armored divisions. Both were stretched thin and neither had assumed responsibility for the crossroads until Major Arthur C. Parker III happened along.

Parker's outfit, the 589th artillery battalion, had been far out on the Schnee Eifel ridge, protruding into German territory when the German offensive struck. Except for a handful, all the men of the 589th had been killed or captured, but Parker had led the survivors off the ridge and struggled westward until reaching Baraque de Fraiture. A glance at his map showed him clearly that this was a crucial junction. So Parker stopped retreating then and there. He immediately set up three howitzers to cover the crossroads and began collar-

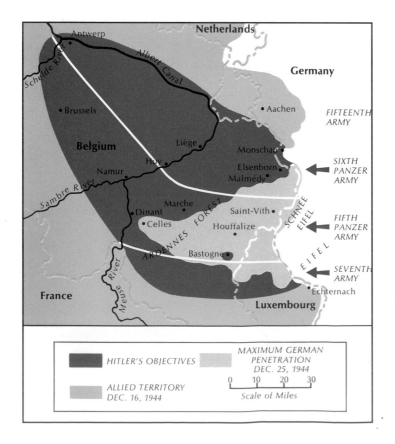

HITLER'S OBJECTIVES

ALLIED TERRITORY
DEC. 16, 1944

MAXIMUM GERMAN
PENETRATION
DEC. 25, 1944

0   10   20   30
Scale of Miles

Hitler's master plan for the Ardennes counteroffensive called for the Fifth and Sixth Panzer armies to break through to Antwerp while the Seventh and Fifteenth armies protected their flanks. Had the Führer's plan succeeded, the Germans would have seized a vast chunk (red area) of Belgium and Luxembourg. But at their maximum penetration, the attackers managed only to bend the Allies' line back in a wedge-shaped bulge (gray area), from which the famous battle got its name.

ing a ragtag assortment of retreating troops to help out.

Parker's scratch outfit withstood a number of probes by enemy patrols. Word of these hit-and-run attacks reached Major General James M. Gavin of the 82nd Airborne, who recognized that if the Germans broke through and thrust north toward Manhay, the enemy would be in his rear. Gavin therefore sent a company of glider troops to bolster Parker's motley group, and a battalion to the town of Fraiture, a mile north of the crossroads.

On the afternoon of December 23, German artillery pounded the junction for 20 minutes. The Americans, heavily outnumbered, stood their ground for more than an hour before they were overwhelmed. Major Parker was seriously wounded, but his valiant stand had provided the time the Americans desperately needed to bring in troops to stop the drive. GIs in the Bulge renamed Baraque de Fraiture "Parker's Crossroads."

As reinforcements poured into the path of the Germans on Christmas Eve, Field Marshal Montgomery arrived at XVIII Airborne Corps headquarters. The Field Marshal had come to "tidy" the front line, as he put it, by giving up some ground to form a strong, consolidated position. Gavin protested that the 82nd Airborne was used to fighting in surrounded positions; he was concerned that a retreat might have a disastrous effect on the division's morale. But his arguments failed to sway his superiors. That night the 82nd withdrew to new defensive positions on high ground to the north, and by Christmas morning had dug in, planted mines and strung wire.

Then, on December 27, two German divisions attacked, and finally took Manhay. But to the Americans' relief, instead of continuing to attack north, the enemy pivoted west, intent on relieving the pressure on the 2nd Panzer trapped at Celles. Driving west, they took the town of Grandménil, only to lose it in a counterattack by the 3rd Armored. A battalion of the 517th Parachute Infantry Regiment then recaptured Manhay.

At Manhay in the north and Celles in the west, the Germans reached the high water marks of the Battle of the Bulge. Hitler's great gamble had failed. Not a single German tank crossed the Meuse.

But the Battle of the Bulge was not yet over. Battered and weary, the Allied forces still had to push the German armies back—fighting not only against stubborn soldiers experienced in winter warfare, but also against winter itself.

Two days before the New Year, the Allies launched their counteroffensive. A pincer movement designed to cut off the Bulge at the waist, it called for the U.S. Third Army to strike north and the U.S. First Army to push south, the two armies meeting at the village of Houffalize to trap all German forces in the tip of the Bulge.

The Germans, however, fought back with ferocity, and the Americans found the going rough. Day after day soldiers wallowed helplessly through the snowdrifts, and tanks skewed crazily on the icy roads. GIs stuffed sheets of newspaper into their boots and jackets for added insulation; they heated pebbles in cans over fires, then dumped the hot pebbles into their wet socks and their socks into their wet boots to dry them out. They also learned that a wounded man had to be kept moving or he would quickly freeze to death.

On New Year's Day, Hitler launched what was called "The Great Blow," aimed at eliminating Allied air power that was proving so lethal. At 8 a.m. hundreds of fighter aircraft were unleashed over Belgium, Holland and northern France. Streaking in just above the treetops, they savagely pounded Allied airfields for two hours. The Great Blow, in one sense, was a huge success: by 10 a.m. a number of bases and 206 Allied aircraft had been destroyed or damaged. But it was also virtual suicide; the Luftwaffe lost 300 planes and 253 trained pilots. The damage was so great that the Luftwaffe never again took to the skies in appreciable numbers.

On January 8, Hitler authorized a withdrawal from the tip of the Bulge—a clear sign he had given up his offensive as a lost cause. By January 16, the two American armies had linked up at Houffalize to clamp the pincers shut. On January 23, Saint-Vith was retaken. By then, the remnants of the Sixth Panzer Army had been ordered to the Eastern Front to attempt to cut short a big Russian offensive. Other retreating German units trudged back toward Germany in the bitter cold and snow, sick with dysentery, wounds, fatigue and defeat, their long, winding columns harried ceaselessly by pursuing tanks, artillery and fighter-bombers.

Many Germans never made it home. When the German losses were finally added up, the cost of Hitler's desperate gamble was about 100,000 casualties. The Americans also paid a stiff price; 80,987 casualties, including 19,000 killed, and 15,000 captured.

On January 28, 1945, the Battle of the Bulge was officially declared over. Although the German armies would rally to defend their homeland, the last great assemblage of the Third Reich's precious reserves of men and matériel had been expended in the Ardennes.

The body of an American soldier killed during the Battle of the Bulge is carried in from a snowy Ardennes field by German prisoners. The six-week battle—the biggest in Western Europe during the Second World War—claimed more than 180,000 American and German casualties.

13

The legions that Hitler sent forth to conquer the world were now reduced to fighting for their own homeland. Their drive into Russia had long since been reversed, and now a resurgent Soviet army stood poised on the banks of the Oder River, deep within German soil. In the west, their ranks whittled down to no more than a million battle-weary men, the defenders faced the full might of the Allied war machine: 3,725,000 American, British, Canadian and French troops under General Eisenhower, with a numerical superiority of 10 to 1 in tanks, 3 to 1 in planes, and at least 2.5 to 1 in artillery. The crushing of Hitler's Reich—which the Führer had once boasted would flourish for 1,000 years—appeared to be a matter of only a few months, perhaps even weeks away.

In the chill predawn hours of February 8, 1945, the mightiest artillery barrage of the war in Western Europe exploded across the border between Holland and Germany. More than a thousand Allied field guns, their muzzles steaming in an early morning drizzle, lobbed half a million shells at the Wehrmacht's defenses. Then, as the drizzle hardened into a driving rain, a massive attack force of British XXX Corps infantry and armor, seven divisions strong, swept forward into German territory.

At last the end of the war with Germany was in sight. But two major obstacles blocked Allied progress into the enemy's heartland. The first was the steel and concrete West Wall fortifications that stretched from the mountains of Switzerland to the watery lowlands of the Dutch frontier. Four years in the building, 20 miles deep in places, the Wall comprised more than 3,000 pillboxes and blockhouses with interlocking fields of fire, supplemented by row upon row of so-called dragon's teeth—concrete pyramids, from two to five feet high, designed to stop tanks.

Beyond the West Wall, 20 to 90 miles deeper into Germany, lay the second great obstacle—the swift, majestic torrent of the Rhine River. Nearly half a mile wide in places, swirled by treacherous currents, and with steep hills and rocky crags lining either bank, the Rhine formed a natural moat against attack.

The river also served Germany in other ways. The main artery of travel between southern Germany and the North Sea, it was vital to the transport of troops and supplies. Moreover, the waterway was intimately bound with Germany's national mystique, its history, culture and legends. Hitler's forces had been ordered to defend it to the end.

For the Allies, crossing the West Wall and the Rhine would be no small undertaking. The very size of the Allied force—seven armies, totaling 85 combat divisions and nearly four million men—meant that the logistics would rival those of the Normandy invasion. Furthermore, a dispute on strategy had erupted between the Allied generals.

The British view, strongly argued by Field Marshal Bernard L. Montgomery, called for a single powerful thrust through the northern edge of the West Wall, and a quick dash to the Rhine, followed by a concentrated push toward Berlin across the broad, open landscape of the north German plain. By heading across the north, Montgomery's forces would be able to reach such key German ports as Bremen and Hamburg before the Russians did—a primary concern to the British, who did not want Stalin to gain a foothold on the North Sea. Since Montgomery's own two armies—the Canadian First and the British Second—were already focused on the northern sector, they could lead the assault. The American forces would then fall in behind.

ACROSS THE RHINE

Not surprisingly, the American generals took exception to this plan. Lieut. General Omar N. Bradley, for one, had already handed over his Ninth Army, one third of his force, to Montgomery's command, and he now faced the possibility of losing other units as well. (A week or so earlier, when asked by Allied Headquarters to detach several divisions to clean out some pockets of enemy resistance in France, the usually soft-spoken Bradley had exploded over the telephone. "I trust you do not think I am angry," he shouted, "but I want to impress upon you that I am goddam well incensed.") What American commanders envisioned was a simultaneous advance along the entire stretch of the western border, with several Rhine crossings at widely separated points. Such a broad-front strategy would give the Americans an equal share in the assault. It also had the merit of flexibility, with each commander free to exploit the opportunities in his own sector.

The attack plan that emerged was a finely wrought compromise between the two. Montgomery won top priority for his thrust in the north, but failed in his attempt to take overall command and to impose a static defense on U.S. forces. Instead, the American forces were to go on the "aggressive defensive." Wrote Eisenhower in a letter to Montgomery: "The more Germans we kill west of the Rhine, the fewer there will be to meet us east of the river."

The Allied offensive was to be made up of a precise interweaving of no less than four operations. The initial thrust—code-named *Veritable*—was to begin on February 8 and consist of a massive, lightning-fast assault by Montgomery's forces across the Dutch border into Germany's Rhine lowlands. Two days later, in Operation *Grenade*, the U.S. Ninth Army, under Lieut. General William H. Simpson, would move up from the south and connect with Montgomery's Canadians to clear the west bank of the Rhine.

Once those units reached the Rhine, Bradley's two remaining armies would swing into Operation *Lumberjack*: the U.S. First Army, under Lieut. General Courtney H. Hodges, would push through the wooded highlands of the Eifel region, while Lieut. General George S. Patton's Third Army moved forward on Hodges' southern flank. *Lumberjack* was expected to begin on February 23. Finally, after a three-week pause, Operation *Undertone* would launch Lieut. General Jacob L. Devers' Seventh Army toward the Rhine's southern reaches through the heavily industrialized Saar Basin.

One preliminary maneuver would have to take place before Simpson's Ninth Army could roll into action. The Germans had to be prevented from blowing up the complex of dams that controlled the flow of the Roer River. Therefore, if the dams were opened, Operation *Grenade* would begin with a washout.

The task of securing the dams fell to the First Army's 78th Division. The first battalions jumped off on the night of February 5, and threaded their way through steep, densely wooded uplands toward the mighty Schwammenauel, the largest dam. Opposing them were 6,000 troops of the 272nd Volksgrenadiers, a collection of teenage boys, elderly men, sailors, airmen and rear echelon personnel with only six weeks' infantry training. But the Volksgrenadiers fought with fanatic ferocity, and delayed the Americans in a three-day firefight. When the first U.S. unit finally reached the Schwammenauel on February 9, the dam had already been breached. Nearly 111 million cubic yards of water cascaded down the Roer, raising its level by five feet and submerging the landscape on either side. Operation *Grenade* would have to wait.

In Aachen, near Germany's border with Luxembourg, a sign written in German and English and posted by American GIs holds up the Führer's promise to ironic commentary. On October 21, 1944, after approximately 75 Allied air raids and weeks of American artillery bombardment, the battered city capitulated—signaling the first Allied breach of Germany's border defenses.

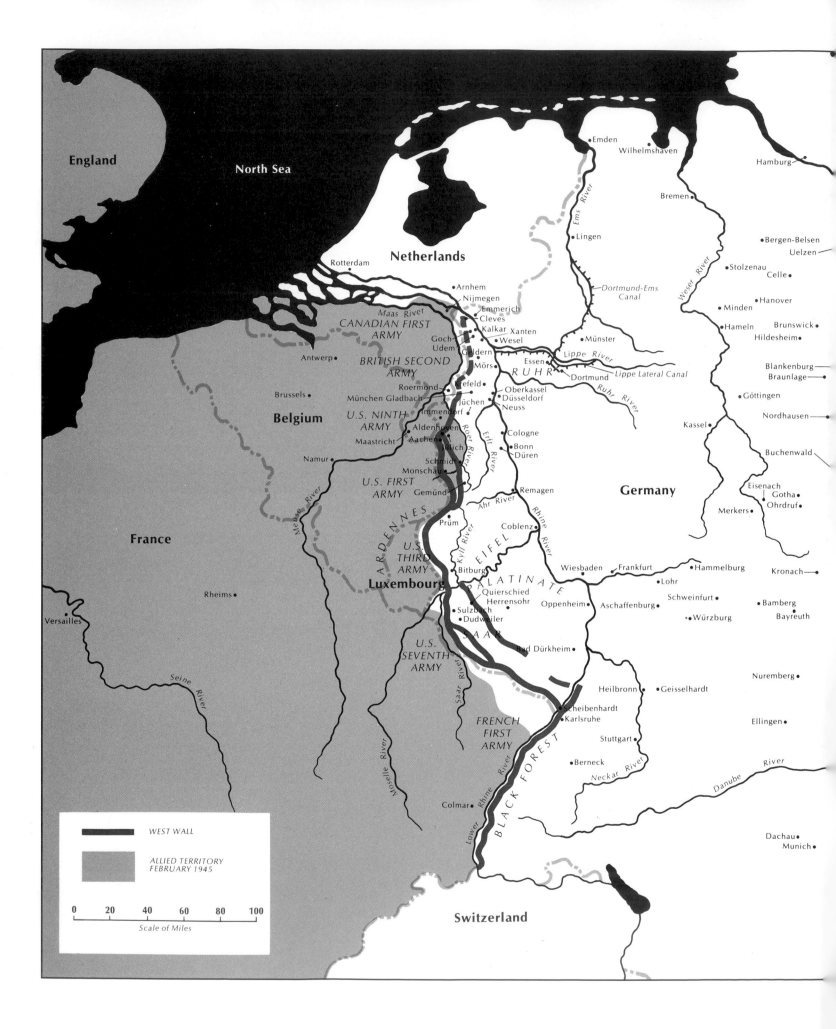

England

North Sea

Netherlands

Emden
Wilhelmshaven
Hamburg

Bremen
Bergen-Belsen
Uelzen

Rotterdam
Stolzenau
Celle

Arnhem
Nijmegen
Emmerich
Cleves
Kalkar
Xanten
Wesel

Maas River

CANADIAN FIRST
ARMY

Goch
Udem
Geldern
Mörs
Münster
Hanover
Minden
Hameln
Brunswick
Hildesheim

BRITISH SECOND
ARMY

Antwerp

Roermond
Crefeld
München Gladbach
Jülich
Immendorf

Lippe River
Lippe Lateral Canal
Dortmund-Ems
Canal

Weser River

RUHR
Dortmund
Essen
Oberkassel
Düsseldorf
Neuss

Blankenburg
Braunlage

Brussels

Belgium

U.S. NINTH
ARMY

Aldenhoven
Aachen
Maastricht
Jülich
Schmidt
Monschau
Gemünd

Cologne
Bonn
Düren

Göttingen

Kassel

Nordhausen

Namur

Ruhr River

Erft River

Roer River

Buchenwald

U.S. FIRST
ARMY

Prüm

Ahr River
Remagen
Coblenz

Rhine River

Eisenach
Gotha
Ohrdruf

France

ARDENNES

Meuse River

Merkers

EIFEL

Kyll River

U.S.
THIRD
ARMY

Luxembourg

Bitburg

PALATINATE

Wiesbaden
Frankfurt

Hammelburg
Kronach

Rheims

Lohr

Schweinfurt

Quierschied
Herrensohr
Sulzbach
Dudweiler

Oppenheim
Aschaffenburg

Bamberg
Bayreuth

Versailles

SAAR

Würzburg

U.S.
SEVENTH
ARMY

Saar River

Bad Dürkheim

Nuremberg

Seine River

Heilbronn
Geisselhardt

FRENCH
FIRST
ARMY

Scheibenhardt
Karlsruhe

Ellingen

Stuttgart

Moselle River

Berneck

BLACK FOREST

Neckar River

River

Danube

Colmar

Lower Rhine River

Dachau
Munich

WEST WALL

ALLIED TERRITORY
FEBRUARY 1945

0   20   40   60   80   100

Scale of Miles

Switzerland

Germany

334

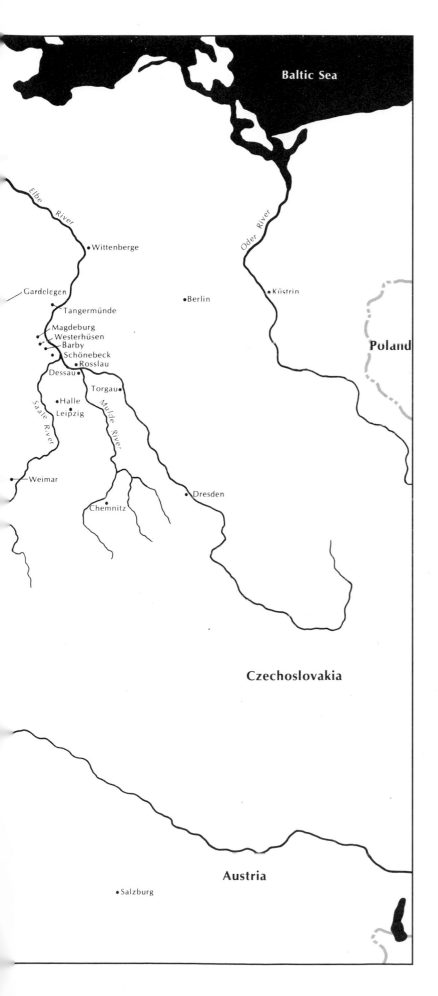

Baltic Sea

Elbe River

• Wittenberge

Oder River

— Gardelegen

• Berlin   • Küstrin

• Tangermünde

Magdeburg
Westerhüsen
Barby
• Schönebeck
• Rosslau

Dessau

Poland

Saale River

• Halle   Torgau
Leipzig

Mulde River

— Weimar

• Dresden

Chemnitz

Czechoslovakia

Austria

• Salzburg

Meanwhile, Montgomery's forces had jumped off on schedule the day before. His most brilliant deputy, Lieut. General Sir Brian G. Horrocks, led the attack, moving out with the British XXX Corps along a six-mile front. Directly ahead rose the dense evergreen forest of the Reichswald, its environs studded with West Wall pillboxes and fieldworks. Beyond lay the ancient towns of Cleves and Goch, both ringed with minefields, barbed wire and antitank ditches. On either flank spread the waterlogged lowlands, the flood that covered them swelled by a pelting rain. And confronting Horrocks, determined to hold at any cost, were 10,000 soldiers of the German 84th Division, augmented by 2,000 to 3,000 troops of the First Parachute Army under Lieut. General Alfred Schlemm, a tough shrewd veteran of the Eastern Front.

With seven divisions under his command, and 500 tanks to the Germans' 50, Horrocks believed that he had more than enough force to overrun the enemy. But weather and terrain conspired against him and it took the better part of two weeks for the XXX Corps to bull its way through the German defenses.

The advance through the Reichswald was a grueling yard-by-yard battle. Horrocks' men were raked by enemy fire amid the tangled conifers and wallows of icy, waist-deep water. To make matters worse, heavy rain grounded Allied air support and rendered the already swampy forest floor almost impassable. From his command post—a wooden platform his engineers had built for him partway up a large tree—Horrocks watched his unhappy troops slog forward. Among them were some of the British Empire's oldest and finest regiments.

Elements of Horrocks' 15th Scottish Division, moving along a road on the Reichswald's northern fringes, made their way to the ancient town of Cleves—a key objective of Operation *Veritable*. The division, however, was unable to enter Cleves with its tanks. The town's streets were pocked with craters and piled high with rubble—the result of a previous visit by Royal Air Force raiders in which the crews had unaccountably used high-explosive bombs instead of the incendiaries Horrocks had specified. In the three days required to clear a way into the town, the Germans brought up heavy reinforcements; it took the 15th Scottish another two days of hand-to-hand fighting to capture Cleves, and by then, further reinforcements awaited the British on the road to the Rhine.

Seven miles to the south, three divisions converged on the town of Goch—a particular prize whose capture would enlarge the constricted front. There, at the anchor of the German defense line, die-hard units fought on for 48 hours even after the German commander surrendered.

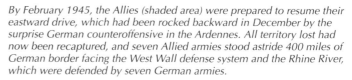

By February 1945, the Allies (shaded area) were prepared to resume their eastward drive, which had been rocked backward in December by the surprise German counteroffensive in the Ardennes. All territory lost had now been recaptured, and seven Allied armies stood astride 400 miles of German border facing the West Wall defense system and the Rhine River, which were defended by seven German armies.

Finally, on February 23, Horrocks was able to send a message of victory and congratulation to his troops. "If we continue our efforts for a few more days," he told them, "the German front is bound to crack." Already he had taken 12,000 German prisoners. German dead were estimated at 8,000. But the cost to his own men was painfully high: 6,000 dead and wounded.

That same day, some unqualified good news arrived from the south: Simpson's Ninth Army was crossing the Roer.

Two weeks after the Germans had flooded the river, the waters were still dangerously high. Nonetheless, Simpson's men had pushed off. Along a 17-mile stretch of river, at precisely 3:30 a.m., infantry strike teams and combat engineers from six divisions moved out in eight-man assault boats. Hoping to catch the Germans by surprise, Simpson had ordered radio silence; and he had eliminated the usual pre-strike pounding by Allied aircraft, contenting himself with a brief, but devastating, artillery barrage.

Once in the river, the assault teams battled strong currents that threatened to swamp their boats and swept them beyond their designated landing points. Boats slammed together and crashed against bridges and floating debris. Reaching the far bank, each unit fanned out quickly as a deadly rain of German mortar and machine gun fire smashed into the footholds. Worst hit were the engineers, whose job it was to span the river with pontoon bridges to carry the rest of the troops across. Even so, losses were slight—31 men killed in the first day of fighting.

By nightfall, nearly 25,000 infantrymen were across the Roer, and over the next few days their numbers swelled tenfold. By February 27, Simpson had 378,000 troops pushing forward on the far bank, along with tanks, guns and equipment. Splitting his forces, he dispatched his XVI Corps north to link up with the British. The rest he sent speeding directly across the lowlands toward the Rhine.

Germany's forces were hardly sufficient to defend the Rhine's approaches. Field Marshal Gerd von Rundstedt, the Wehrmacht commander in the West, had told Hitler as much, repeatedly begging leave to move his divisions to more strategic positions on the east bank. Hitler repeatedly turned him down. "Withdrawal behind the Rhine is unthinkable," the Führer declared.

But eventually even Hitler had to admit the truth. Though he never gave permission to retreat—such action "would only mean moving the catastrophe from one place to another," he muttered—he did issue orders for blowing the Rhine bridges, should retreat become necessary. No bridge could be allowed to fall into Allied hands, and any commander who failed to destroy his bridges in time would be summari-

ly executed. The same fate, Hitler added, awaited anyone who blew up a bridge too soon.

The ticklish task of deciding precisely the right or wrong moment to destroy a given bridge was left to the commander of each area. The First Parachute Army's General Schlemm later told an American interrogator: "Since I had nine bridges in my sector, I could see my hopes for a long life rapidly dwindling."

Meanwhile, the Allied commanders fully expected the bridges to be down by the time they reached the Rhine. Their forces would have to cross in the same manner that Simpson's men had leaped the Roer—in assault boats, amphibious troop carriers, and on scores of pontoon bridges strung across the river by combat engineers. But every bridge that could be captured intact meant a giant step forward. And so began a race for the bridges.

The forces closest to the Rhine were Montgomery's British and Canadians in their new positions at Cleves and Goch. A mere 20 miles of farmland and forest divided them from their crossing sites opposite the small east-bank city of Wesel. A major German communications center, Wesel was also the conduit point for the shipping of badly needed coal and steel to the rest of Germany. Montgomery's forces, half a million strong, faced fewer than 100,000 defenders.

The Allied plan was to move across a crescent of high ground, dubbed the "Hochwald layback," while securing the fortified towns of Kalkar and Udem at either end. Then the attackers would speed east through a natural gap between the forests of Hochwald and Balbergerwald. The plan seemed easy enough—except that each of these points was held by Schlemm's First Parachute Army, perhaps the toughest soldiers in the Wehrmacht. Dug in behind a daunting network of barbed wire and minefields, and with high-velocity 88mm antiaircraft guns aimed horizontally along the tank routes, the German paratroopers would prove all but unbudgeable.

The assault on the Hochwald layback, spearheaded by the 2nd and 3rd divisions of the Canadian II Corps, began two hours before dawn on February 26. At dawn the next day the ridge was still in German hands, its slopes a charnel house of bullet-riddled, bayoneted bodies. The fighting continued for four more days, with a savage hand-to-hand intensity, before the Canadians could push across the northern end of the ridge. The Canadians had matched the foe in their ferocity. As one Allied chronicler of the battle put it, "The idea that the only way to end the War was to kill the Germans in front of them had struck home."

To the south, a breakthrough was just as difficult to achieve. On February 27, the Canadian 4th Armored Division rolled down the far slope toward the gap along the

As the rising sun shines through a shell-gutted house, infantrymen of the U.S. 29th Division hurry across a footbridge over the Roer River in western Germany. Nearly two dozen Roer bridges were built by the engineers of the U.S. Ninth Army in only four days.

railway between the Hochwald and the Balbergerwald. Followed by infantry, the armor was to sweep east toward the town of Xanten, close to the Rhine's west bank. But the Germans stopped them cold at the gap. A single battalion of Schlemm's paratroopers, supported by heavy mortars and the fearsome 88s, held the Canadian tanks in the narrow forest corridor for six days and nights. Wedged together, the antagonists battled at a distance of only a few yards; attack and counterattack merged into one.

It was sheer strength of manpower that overwhelmed the Germans in the end. On March 2, the first Ninth Army unit, a motorized task force of the XVI Corps' 35th Division, linked up with the Canadians. Schlemm pulled back to his final defense position at the barricades at Xanten. There, his troopers fought with the desperate fury of men with their backs to the wall. Then, with a grudging consent from Hitler, the general finally began moving his forces across the Rhine to Wesel.

During their fighting retreat, Schlemm's paratroopers had blown seven of the nine bridges in their sector, and now it was time to complete the job. At 7:00 a.m. on March 10, with all but a rear guard evacuated from Xanten, two tremendous explosions shattered the morning air. The Wesel bridges collapsed into the Rhine. The battle for this stretch of the west bank was over. It had been savage and costly, but with moments of heroism on both sides. As the German paratroopers taken at Xanten were marched off to holding pens in the rear, the staff of a British brigade that had helped capture them stood respectfully at attention. "The German garrison at Xanten," said the colonel in charge, "were very gallant men."

As the battle raged in the northern sector, the main force of Simpson's Ninth Army in the southern sector had raced toward the Rhine against little resistance. On the night of March 2, they reached Neuss, opposite the great industrial city of Düsseldorf. Several American tanks were already rumbling across the bridge at Ürdingen when the Germans blew it up.

Nearby, at Oberkassel, Simpson tried a less direct tactic. The commander of his 330th Infantry Regiment had the bright idea of painting out the white star insignia on his tanks and applying German crosses. Hoping to pass unnoticed through the Germans and snatch the bridge from under their noses, he had German-speaking GIs standing in the turrets. The ruse seemed successful, until the moment the lead tanks reached the bridge itself. Then sirens sounded, and a massive explosion sent the structure tumbling into the Rhine.

No such frustrations slowed the advance of Bradley's two armies along the front's middle sector. As part of the overall

Allied strategy, his *Lumberjack* offensive could go ahead only after Montgomery's northern forces had reached the Rhine. When they did, in the final days of February, the U.S. First and Third armies surged forward with the pent-up energy of a three-week wait.

Hodges' First Army had already carved out a salient across the Roer. Now it sped east against light opposition, leaped the Erft River, and descended on the great cathedral city of Cologne. A swift tank attack on March 5 secured Cologne airport, and the next morning, men of the VII Corps marched into the city itself. Once the proudest German metropolis west of the Rhine, Cologne now stood a blackened, shell-blasted ruin—the result of incessant Allied bombings. Cologne, as one GI put it, was little more than a mass of "wrecked masonry surrounded by city limits." But its capture marked a significant Allied triumph.

The bridge at Cologne had been transformed into rubble by the fleeing Wehrmacht. But 30 miles to the south, at the little resort town of Remagen, was a span that the Germans had not yet destroyed. One day after the victory at Cologne, a tank-infantry unit of the First Army's III Corps came upon the prize and could not believe their eyes.

The German defenders retreated to a railroad tunnel in a steep bluff at the far end. There, a steady pounding by high-explosive and phosphorous shells from advancing American tanks kept them pinned inside. The Germans had attached a string of demolition charges to the span, and the bridge commander flipped the electric switch that should have set them off. Nothing happened; the wires had been severed. A volunteer ran forward to trigger an emergency igniter by hand. There was an ear-cracking roar as 650 pounds of high explosives went off. The bridge shuddered and seemed to rise, then settle back on its foundations. But still it stood—the charge was only half as powerful as that needed to do the job. Moments later, the first American platoons dashed across the bridge. The Allies had crossed the Rhine.

News of the Remagen triumph traveled quickly up the line to Bradley's headquarters. "Hot dog, Courtney," Bradley shouted over the phone to Hodges. "This will bust 'em wide open. Shove everything you can across!" Eisenhower, too, could hardly control his jubilation. Looking back, he described the event as "one of my happy moments of the

Seized by American troops on March 7, 1945, the Ludendorff Bridge at Remagen enabled the U.S. First Army to establish a strong foothold on the east bank of the Rhine. But the bridge had been seriously damaged by demolition charges set by the retreating Germans. Although American engineers (right) worked around the clock to make repairs, the weakened span collapsed (center and far right) into a mass of twisted rubble 10 days after its capture.

war." Even Montgomery—who had intended to be first across—expressed his measured approval. "It will undoubtedly be an unpleasant threat to the enemy," he allowed.

The reaction in Berlin was understandably grim. Hitler, casting about for scapegoats, fixed upon the 69-year-old Rundstedt. The hero of the blitzkrieg in France and Holland was given a medal and packed off into retirement. His replacement was Field Marshal Albert Kesselring, called home from his command in northern Italy.

There was little Kesselring could do in any case. Besides its losses in the north and center, the Wehrmacht was sorely pressed in the south, where Patton's Third Army was galloping forward in a headlong cavalry charge.

Even before the launching of *Lumberjack*, the aggressive Patton had jumped into action. He had pushed through the West Wall fortifications along the Luxembourg border, taken the key communication centers of Prüm and Bitburg, and fanned out across the Eifel uplands—all the while netting 1,000 German prisoners a day. Then on March 5, his forces crossed the Kyll River and struck east for the Rhine. By March 7, the day of Remagen, tank crews of Patton's 4th Armored Division were overlooking the river north of Coblenz. They had made the 55-mile dash from Bitburg in 48 hours—boldly carving a salient through enemy lines that was no wider than the road on which they traveled.

The next day, Patton's forces linked up with elements of Hodges' First Army. An Allied noose had begun to tighten around the German troops that remained in the Eifel.

Other Third Army units were cutting south in an even more ambitious operation—in conjunction with General Devers' Sixth Army Group. Operation *Undertone* was to envelop the heavily industrialized Saar-Palatinate region. More than 3,000 square miles in extent, the region was triangle-shaped, with the Rhine as its base. With coalfields, steelworks, chemical plants and munitions factories, it was an economic cornerstone of the German war effort. As originally conceived, the operation called for Devers' Seventh Army to break through the West Wall defenses from the south, while the French First Army, also under his command, guarded the eastern flank. Now Patton would throw in troops from the west and north.

D-day for *Undertone* was March 15, but Patton, impatient as always, jumped the gun. From a salient at Trier, just across the Moselle River, his XX Corps moved out two days early, to assault the Palatinate's forested Hunsrück Mountains. So rugged was this area that its defenders, the German Seventh Army, had thought it unsuitable for tanks. But by March 15 the tank battalions of the XX Corps were clanking downslope toward the valuable industries of the central Saar.

Devers' Seventh Army, led by Lieut. General Alexander M. Patch, moved out on schedule, assailing the West Wall barricades with 15 full divisions. A ferocious five-day battle ensued, with engineers blasting pillboxes and antitank dragon's teeth with hand-placed explosives. Then resistance collapsed. The Wall's defenders fled east across the Rhine.

The most brilliant coup was Patton's, however. His XII Corps had charged south from Coblenz, moving fast along the Rhine's west bank. By March 22, the vanguard 5th Infantry had discovered a riverside cove, hidden among the terraced vineyards of Oppenheim. That night six battalions of the 5th Infantry piled into rafts and assault boats, and paddled across the river. They found a single platoon of Germans guarding the far bank.

The next morning, as his engineers were stringing their pontoon bridges, Patton reported his success to Bradley. "Don't tell anyone," he whispered, "but I'm across."

"Well, I'll be damned," Bradley responded. "You mean across the Rhine?"

"Sure am. I sneaked a division over last night. But there are so few Krauts around they don't know it yet."

But even the merit of tactical secrecy could not suppress Patton's urge to proclaim his triumph. Later that day he phoned Bradley again. "Brad, for God's sake, tell the world," he shouted. "I want the world to know that the Third Army made it before Monty starts across."

Montgomery's assault on the Rhine—code-named Operation *Plunder*—was scheduled for March 24. A man of exquisite deliberation, the field marshal believed that no battle should be joined without the most meticulous planning; the impetuosity of the Americans was not his cup of tea.

The preliminary groundwork for the crossing in the Wesel sector had been taking shape for more than a month. Even as the conflict raged at Cleves and Xanten, first-strike teams

THE ALLIED TACTICAL AIR FORCE

Tactical air power—the use of planes to support troops in the field rather than for the strategic purpose of undermining the enemy's overall war-making ability—was pioneered with awesome effect by the Luftwaffe. But by mid-1943, the British and Americans had seized the lead in developing tactical air techniques, and their hard-hitting sorties ultimately helped tip the balance in their favor on the battlefields of Western Europe.

The Allies employed tactical air power in a three-stage pattern, using planes of all types—even heavy bombers normally used on strategic missions. First, the planes flew well ahead of the ground assault forces, attacking Luftwaffe planes and bases in the chosen zone to achieve local air superiority. Then, to isolate enemy ground forces in the battle area, bombers and fighters plastered rail lines, highway junctions, truck convoys and trains. Bridges were bombed and shipping disrupted, preventing supplies and reinforcements from reaching the front. The bombing also obstructed German troops who were trying to leave the combat zone and establish defense lines elsewhere.

Finally, as Allied ground forces moved forward, fighter-bombers hit the enemy troops and strong points that stood in the way of the advance. These dangerous operations were executed by the airmen of the British Second Tactical Air Force, the U.S. Ninth Air Force and the U.S. First Tactical Air Force. All had received months of special training for the job.

By mid-1944, Allied mastery of the skies was so complete that the German infantry in the combat zone made a bitter joke of their plight. They claimed to have a foolproof method of identifying aircraft overhead: if the plane was silver, it was American; if dark in color, British; if it could not be seen at all, it was German.

A pall of smoke blankets the Luftwaffe's airdrome at Chateaudun, south of Paris, while two Consolidated B-24 Liberators make their final bombing passes.

A British Beaufighter fires rockets at a ship in the North Sea. By mid-1944, Allied tactical air forces were constantly striking targets on land and sea, and in the air.

Entangled track and demolished trains litter the railway marshaling yard near Limburg, Germany. The yard was struck by bombers of the U.S. Ninth Air Force.

of the British Second Army had been training with assault boats on a quiet stretch of the Maas River, to the rear. A total of 1.25 million British and American troops would take part in *Plunder*, and 300,000 tons of matériel would be required. To pave the way for this massive force, Montgomery ordered nine bridges to be thrust across the Maas. Rail lines were extended, airfields built and roads widened.

The sheer immensity of these preparations could not be disguised. But to keep the Germans guessing as to the exact place of the crossing, Montgomery had his engineers build a string of phony staging areas, with dummy guns installed in fake emplacements, and fake depots housing plywood vehicles. Simpson, whose Ninth Army would join in the assault, entered into the deception with gusto. At a site near Krefeld, a city he had taken after his breakout from the Roer and one that was 20 miles south of the crossing, he set up an enormous bridge park. Every day a treadway bridge company would roll in and unload its assault boats, pontoons and other equipment. Then by night it would replace the genuine articles with dummies. Sure enough, in time, the

Luftwaffe showed up, and expended its dwindling resources bombing these paper-and-plywood stage props.

For all the subterfuge, the Germans were not entirely fooled. Kesselring, for one, had no illusions. Nearly 100,000 German soldiers had been sacrificed in Hitler's vain attempt to hold the Rhine's west bank. Now Kesselring's forces had been reduced to the remnants of the once-powerful First Parachute Army—a mere 13 divisions, all understrength—and some 30,000 soldiers from local militia units. The Rhine's east-bank fortifications consisted in large part of hastily dug rifle and machine gun pits that offered little protection. As he later said, "I felt like a concert pianist asked to play a Beethoven sonata before a large audience on an ancient, rickety and out-of-tune instrument."

On the afternoon of March 23, Montgomery notified his commanders to be ready to go. "Two if by sea" were the code words; puckishly, he borrowed a part of the signal that had sent Paul Revere galloping through the Yankee countryside in 1775 to warn that the British were coming. In a final message to his troops, couched in man-to-man terms, he promised, "the enemy has in fact been driven into a corner, and he cannot escape. Over the Rhine, then, let us go. And good hunting to you on the other side."

The assault worked with the precision that Montgomery so greatly prized. As darkness fell, the entire 22-mile front opposite Wesel lit up with an orchestrated barrage by 3,500 field guns plus 2,000 antitank and antiaircraft guns and rocket launchers. Then at 9:00 p.m., the British jumped off. Amphibious personnel carriers known as "buffaloes" slid into the Rhine, bearing four battalions of the Second Army's 51st Highland Division; the leading wave landed on the far bank in less than seven minutes. At 10:00 p.m. the 1st Commando Brigade slipped across, and by 10:30 it was forming up on Wesel's outskirts, ready to move in.

The Americans' turn came next. All along the west bank, thousands of troops were massed and ready to pour across. At 2:00 a.m., the Ninth Army's 30th Division headed for the east bank, three regiments abreast, followed an hour later by two regiments of the 79th Division. At their beachhead, just south of Wesel, the divisions swiftly overran the enemy's forward position. By the following day, they had pushed inland as far as six miles. And Ninth Army engineers had put up the first of *Plunder*'s Rhine bridges—a 1,150-foot pontoon treadway that they completed in a record nine hours.

Meanwhile, at Montgomery's tactical headquarters, the field marshal was coping with a problem he would have preferred to avoid: the presence of Prime Minister Winston Churchill. The P.M. had flown in from England in time for tea on March 23. The next morning, Montgomery and his illustrious guest motored to a hill overlooking the Rhine near

During the last and biggest one-day airborne operation of the War, on March 24, 1945, the paratroopers of Operation Varsity helped Allied ground troops establish a bridgehead across the Rhine around the town of Wesel. In this photograph taken by Life photographer Robert Capa, U.S. troops move swiftly through an orchard toward their objective—a farmhouse full of German soldiers and civilians. The house was quickly taken, and the GIs pushed on. Some 3,500 German soldiers were captured that day.

Xanten. The best of the show that Churchill wanted to see was about to begin.

In addition to the rivers crossing, Montgomery had laid on a massive aerial assault, code-named Operation *Varsity*. Shortly before 10:00 a.m. on March 24, an armada of British and American planes began passing overhead. First came the paratroop transports, American C-46s and C-47s, in parallel columns. And close behind them flew the tug planes—Fortresses, Liberators, Lancasters, Stirlings, Halifaxes, each with two infantry-bearing gliders in tow. For 3 hours and 32 minutes the planes flew past, the 3,044 transports and gliders carrying 21,680 troops of the U.S. 17th and British 6th Airborne divisions. High above them, 900 fighters provided a protective umbrella, and another 2,100 fighters ranged out to screen the area against possible attack by the Luftwaffe.

The objective of this great force was the Diersfordterwald, a stretch of high, wooded ground north of Wesel. German antiaircraft batteries knocked out scores of aircraft. "Our plane was a hell of a lot hit before we got out of it," reported Robert Capa, *Life* magazine's famed combat photographer who jumped with the 17th Airborne. But the vast majority got through to release their gliders, or to disgorge their paratroopers—"black dots, transforming into silken flowers," Capa recalled.

More than 500 Americans and British died in the assault, and 1,250 were wounded. But by evening their comrades had wiped out all resistance at the landing site, and had linked up with the British commandos at Wesel. On the ground, on *Plunder*'s left flank, the Second Army's 51st Highland Division had also suffered painful losses. But the next day, this area, too, was largely secured.

By March 28, the Allies had expanded their east-bank foothold into a solid bridgehead 35 miles wide and up to 20 miles deep. Twelve new bridges spanned the Rhine, and troops were pouring across them by the scores of thousands every 24 hours. In a message to his commanders, Montgomery wrote finis to *Plunder* in one terse sentence: "We have won the Battle of the Rhine."

With this great obstacle behind them, the Allies now faced a choice. They could focus their strength on the northern sector, as in the original plan, with Montgomery grinding across the well-defended north German lowlands toward Berlin. Alternatively, the thrust might be launched from the center, thus exploiting the rapid gains already made there. This second course would allow the Russians to liberate Berlin.

Up to now nearly everyone had expected the Allied armies to make a dash for Berlin, seeking to get there before the Russians. The German capital was a goal of long-range political consequence, and Churchill, for one, virtually demanded that the British and Americans share in its capture. But Eisenhower, as Supreme Commander, refused to oblige: an assault on Berlin might cost an additional 100,000 Allied casualties, he pointed out. Besides, it was believed that the Russians were already so close to the city that it would be a waste of Allied manpower to make an attempt. Instead, Eisenhower decided to concentrate the thrust from the middle sector and halt before Berlin at the Elbe River.

Already two American divisions were slashing into the new offensive's immediate target—the heavily industrialized Ruhr Valley. Stretching eastward from the Rhine between Simpson's Ninth Army at Wesel, and Hodges' First Army bridgehead at Remagen, the Ruhr's 2,000 square miles contained 75 percent of Germany's remaining industry. Concentrated there were 18 large manufacturing cities; three of them—Essen, Düsseldorf and Dortmund—were each nearly as large as Pittsburgh. An immense coal deposit, 10 miles wide and 40 miles long, paralleled the Ruhr River, and supplied the Reich with 69 percent of its coal. This, plus hydroelectric power from the Ruhr dams, gave enough power to run more than 2,500 factories, blast furnaces, drop forges and other plants. So densely populated was the

In another Robert Capa photograph, taken near the town of Wesel, a soldier crouches low in a muddy stream, sheltering himself from German fire. With one hand he clutches his carbine; with the other he grasps a slender tree trunk for balance.

THE ENGINEERS

Accompanying every division were supporting units of engineers whose multifold responsibilities made the sweep through Western Europe possible. They took on such varied tasks as building—or destroying—roads, railways, and pipelines; "delousing" minefields; restoring enemy-wrecked ports; and repairing aqueducts.

At no time were the engineers' special skills so critical as during the final drive into the heartland of the Third Reich. For in order to reach their objective of the Elbe River, the Allies would have to leapfrog across the Roer and the Erft rivers before the final big jump across the Rhine—all after the retreating Germans had destroyed most of their bridges.

Transporting the massive bridging materials and big landing craft to forward depots was one of the engineers' most rigorous challenges. Still by March 1944, American engineers alone had stockpiled 124 landing craft, 1,100 assault boats plus enough lumber, pontoons and prefabricated structural sections to build 62 bridges across the Rhine.

Each bridge was thrown across the Rhine on time, and in record speed. "It was almost like maneuvers," said one observer. The operation was like clockwork, the result of long practice in synchronized teamwork.

While one gang of engineers lowered strings of inflated pontoons into the water, other teams in boats pushed the pontoon links into place. No sooner were the pontoons in position than other engineers began bolting on the treadway. The task of assembling the bridges went so fast that the engineers sometimes astounded themselves. One treadway bridge, scheduled to be finished in 36 hours, was opened for traffic in just nine hours.

With almost 100 Allied bridges of

Ninth Army engineers tug on a rope to release the anchor of an antifrogman barrier before hauling it across the Rhine by launch.

A U.S. Third Army engineering crew joins together sections of a steel treadway bridge.

every sort spanning the Rhine by late March, British and American engineers were determined that none of their hard work would be undone: they bulldozed gun emplacements at a bridge's approaches and dug in batteries of antitank guns. Upstream of most bridges, the engineers installed three barriers: a wire-cable boom capable of halting large vessels, a log boom to detonate floating mines, and a net to entangle one-man submarines or frogmen. Would-be saboteurs were further discouraged by night patrols, which periodically detonated TNT charges in the water.

The Germans mounted numerous attacks of one sort or another against the bridges. But the engineers could proudly report that not a single bridge that they had built was knocked out by enemy action.

Engineers wait for another section of a Bailey bridge to be brought up and fitted into place.

region, particularly in its northern reaches, that its entire 50-mile length could be traversed by streetcar.

Allied bombers had begun pounding the Ruhr cities as far back as 1942, and the raids had steadily increased in frequency and fury. Essen alone had been hit 272 times. After each raid, the people of the Ruhr had put out the fires, repaired the furnaces and restarted the assembly lines again. Yet in time, the sheer weight of bombs had overwhelmed human determination, until the Ruhr was operating at only a fraction of its former capacity. Nevertheless, the only sure way for the Allies to put the Ruhr out of business for good was to occupy it.

Eisenhower, however, decided to avoid a direct, frontal assault. Instead, he would seal off the Ruhr in a classic pincer maneuver. A Ninth Army force, led by the 2nd Armored Division, would move along its northern boundary, while the First Army's 3rd Armored Division sliced up from the south. Then, having enveloped the entire region in a giant

bear hug, the two forces would squeeze to death the German armies trapped inside.

Almost 320,000 Germans had been assigned to defend the Ruhr, including Luftwaffe units and more than 200,000 soldiers of Army Group B. Their commander was Field Marshal Walther Model, a ruthless and aggressive tactician. But now Model made a mistake. Thinking that the Allies would continue to consolidate their bridgeheads along the Rhine's east bank, rather than launch a pincer maneuver to encircle the area, he grouped most of his forces along the river to block any riverside drive. He spread the rest of his men thin—much too thin—along the northern and southern flanks of the Ruhr. And, in the end, this proved fatal.

General Hodges' First Army barely paused to catch its breath. On March 25, seven divisions sliced east from Remagen, broke through the German lines, and rampaged out across the countryside. By the end of the second day, tanks of the 7th Armored Division had driven 50 miles east,

With bridges in place, trucks carrying men and matériel of the U.S. Ninth Army roll across the Rhine near Wesel, heading inland to seal off German escape routes.

and captured 12,500 Germans. Soon the tankers were bearing down on the city of Limburg.

To the north, Simpson's Ninth Army drove ahead on a broad front, advancing virtually at will. In the vanguard rode the powerful "Hell on Wheels" 2nd Armored Division in a column 72 miles long. The reconnaissance units raced ahead, bypassing German resistance, disrupting communications, cutting supply routes between the Ruhr and Berlin—and moving so rapidly that they ran off their maps. Officers used old Baedeker guidebooks to find their way.

The 3rd Armored Division was now knifing north toward its rendezvous with the 2nd Armored at the Ruhr's far end. The division set out at 6 a.m. on March 29. Its first night's destination was Paderborn, a city near the Lippe River, 60 miles ahead. Sixty miles through enemy territory was a substantial distance for any tank unit, and the commander of the lead battalion, Lieut. Colonel Walter B. Richardson, was incredulous. How could he do it? "Just go like hell," his commanding officer said.

All day long the tanks raced north in columns. Without stopping, they knocked out a passenger train and rolled through several undefended military installations. Through the eastern reaches of the Ruhr they rumbled, passing farmsteads and small villages huddled in the wooded hills. Their crews saw many dismayed villagers, but met only sporadic resistance. En route, the tankers found a warehouse full of champagne. At dusk, Richardson's men were slowed by fog. By midnight, they had made 45 miles. The only casualties were some tankers Richardson detailed to clear out a small German unit en route—and a batch of hangovers.

An SS panzer training center was situated on the road to Paderborn, and at dawn the next day, Richardson found himself under fierce attack by a battle group of about 60 Panther and Tiger tanks. The American task force punched through the panzers until it was only six miles from Paderborn—and then Richardson learned that he had been cut off by the Germans. Richardson and his men dug in to await the rest of the 3rd Armored led by Major General Maurice Rose.

Toward dusk on March 30, Rose was leading a force toward Paderborn when a flurry of small arms fire from a nearby woods separated the general from his column. Suddenly German tanks loomed out of the gloom. Although Rose's jeep driver swerved off the road in a desperate attempt to escape, a Tiger tank now barred the way. Atop the tank turret, an SS man motioned with his burp gun. Rose, an aide and the driver dismounted and carefully started unbuckling their pistol belts. Just then, something startled the German. He ripped off a burst. The aide and the driver dived into a ditch. But Maury Rose pitched forward, dead—one of the 12 American general officers to be killed in action during the War.

By daylight on March 31, the German counterattack had petered out and three divisions moved up to bolster the 3rd Armored's advance. But the German attack had been sharp enough to cause a slight adjustment in Allied plans. Paderborn was scratched as a destination. The division turned toward Lippstadt, 25 miles to the west. And there, on April 2, the day after Easter, it linked up with the vanguard units of Simpson's 2nd Armored Division.

The Ruhr was now encircled; all that remained was to deal with the Germans still inside. Some fought on with savage, futile courage. Hitler had told Model to defend "Fortress Ruhr" to the last man, and Model was a soldier who carried out orders. But inside the encircled pocket, Model saw his position deteriorating rapidly.

On the north side of the Ruhr River, however, GIs were finding the going rough. This was the region known to Allied bomber crews as "Flak Alley," for the 2,400 powerful 88mm and 128mm antiaircraft guns emplaced there. Now the defenders turned the guns on U.S. tanks, and the effect was punishing. When the tanks finally pushed through, the Americans found moonscape cities of rubble, and a permeating stench of sewer gas, decay and death. Still the

Seventh Army GIs scramble out of an assault boat and up the muddy east bank of the Rhine near Worms, south of Oppenheim.

Germans fought on, many giving their lives to hold a slag heap or a cellar.

On the Ruhr's southern flank, the Americans had an easy time in some sectors and ran into staunch resistance in others—especially along the routes that Model had originally believed the Americans would take in breaking out of their Remagen bridgehead.

Southeast of Cologne, the 78th Infantry Division stormed across the Sieg River in plywood boats, and started speeding eastward. Advance patrols began taking towns by telephone. Racing into an undefended town, the troops would quickly seek out the local telephone exchange. A German-speaking GI would call ahead to the next town and ask to speak to the Bürgermeister or local military commander. "This is the American Army," he would say. "Your town is next on our list for wipeout if you don't surrender. So get the white sheets out!" The tactic was remarkably effective.

By April 6, scarcely more than a week after the Ruhr offensive began, the German perimeter had shrunk to a tiny segment of the Lippe Lateral Canal centered on Dortmund and Essen. By April 11, the Germans were falling back rapidly in all quarters; the Ruhr pocket was reduced to an average diameter of about 16 miles, and the Germans' dwindling defenses seemed likely to collapse at any minute.

On April 15, under a flag of truce, Model received a carefully composed letter from an American general. He was Matthew B. Ridgway, commander of the XVIII Airborne

Corps, and he wrote: "Neither history nor the military profession records any nobler character, any more brilliant master of warfare, any more dutiful subordinate of the state, than the American general Robert E. Lee. Eighty years ago this month, his loyal command reduced in numbers, stripped of its means of effective fighting and completely surrounded by overwhelming forces, he chose an honorable capitulation.

"The same choice is yours now. In the light of a soldier's honor, for the reputation of the German officer corps, for the sake of your nation's future, lay down your arms at once."

Model rejected Ridgeway's plea. But he knew that it was all over, and that further slaughter would accomplish nothing. However, he had given Hitler his oath to resist to the end, and he would not dishonor it. Now that organized resistance was pointless and indeed impossible, he had in mind a way out of his dilemma—an unorthodox way, to be sure, but not a dishonorable one.

A command that did not exist, Model reasoned, could not surrender. He simply disbanded Army Group B in place. Any combat units that wished to fight on might do so. The rest could go home.

But Model himself would not give up. "A field marshal," he said, remembering Friedrich von Paulus at Stalingrad, "does not become a prisoner. Such a thing is just not possible." Then he went into the countryside. Field Marshal Walther Model ended his life with a single shot. The battle for the Ruhr was over.

Every farm boy in GI uniform knew the old saying about snakes with broken backs: their tails were supposed to twitch until sunset before they died. That was the condition of the Wehrmacht in April 1945.

Along the entire Western front, Allied armies were advancing almost at will against broken divisions, corps and armies. In the north, Montgomery's Canadian First Army spread across lower Holland, and rolled on toward the estuary of the Weser River and the German naval base at

The empty streets and crumbling buildings of Soest, in the northeastern Ruhr, are patrolled by men of the 95th Infantry Division. A key rail junction, Soest was fiercely defended by the 116th Panzer Division; the town finally fell on April 6 after a punishing attack by U.S. fighter-bombers that killed 300 Germans.

Thousands of surrendered German soldiers mill about in a compound in the Ruhr. When the Ruhr pocket had been reduced, the final tally of German prisoners came to 317,000—more troops than had surrendered to the Russians at Stalingrad. The Americans could only accommodate all the prisoners by hastily fencing them in open fields with barbed wire fences.

TELLING THE TRUTH TO THE WORLD

Dwight D. Eisenhower, Supreme Allied commander, was shaken and enraged by what he saw at Ohrdruf, the first concentration camp to be liberated by the Allies. Rushing to U.S. Third Army headquarters, Ike sent cables to Washington and London, urging that legislators and journalists be brought in to view the horrors of the camp.

From then on, dozens of news reporters and others accompanied the troops into each newly discovered camp. Radio-journalist Edward R. Murrow rode with U.S. Third Army tanks into Buchenwald. Marguerite Higgins, the well-known reporter for the New York *Herald Tribune*, reached Dachau with the first Allied troops. Pennsylvania Congressman John Kunkel visited Buchenwald; when reporters asked his opinion, he said grimly; "If you tried to tell the actual facts, you'd get into filth and obscenity that would be unprintable."

The Allied commanders ordered townspeople from adjacent communities to inspect the camps. The local citizens were spared nothing. They saw the stacks of corpses, the gallows and the ovens in which the dead had been cremated.

Nearly all of the Germans were profoundly affected. After a tour of the Ohrdruf camp, the mayor of the town and his wife hanged themselves. Some Germans admitted that they had realized terrible things were going on in the camps, but insisted that they had been powerless to effect any change. Still others, however, said that they had known nothing of the atrocities—a view derided by a correspondent for *Yank* magazine. Many of the prisoners, he wrote, had, after all, been in plain sight. "They collapsed of hunger at their benches and no one asked why. They died along the road on the long walk back to camp and no one expressed surprise. The good citizens shut their eyes and their ears and their nostrils to the sight and sound and the smell of this place."

A recently liberated prisoner at Buchenwald confronts and accuses one of his former captors. At every camp, the freed prisoners took revenge on their former captors, and the Allies were in no hurry to stop them. Most inmates, however, were content to curse and spit at their tormentors.

An SS sergeant major at Bergen-Belsen (left) carries a victim for burial in a mass grave (right). The Allied commanders were bent on teaching the German people an abject lesson. On their orders, citizens of nearby towns, and captured Germans who had run the concentration camps, were required to load the corpses into trucks and horse-drawn wagons and carry them to burial grounds deliberately chosen in prominent places to remind the Germans of the atrocities.

German townspeople stand shocked and weeping during a tour of the Buchenwald camp. They had seen a truck loaded with corpses, and an American officer had described the SS atrocities committed there.

Wilhelmshaven. Below the Canadians, the British Second Army pushed east toward the Elbe, and northeast toward the North Sea ports of Bremen and Hamburg. In the south, below the Ruhr, Patton's Third Army was knifing southeast toward Chemnitz, scarcely 20 miles from the border with Czechoslovakia. On Patton's right, the U.S. Seventh Army struck into southern Germany, toward Bavaria and Austria. And the French First Army drove south into the Black Forest, intent on settling scores with the hated "Boches"—a derogatory term for Germans—before the war ended.

In many places, the defenders were exhausted and more than ready to surrender. By mid-April, most front-line American divisions were collecting between 2,000 and 5,000 captives a day. "If you fire your pistol into the air, a dozen Germans will come rushing in to be taken prisoner," said a U.S. infantry officer. A GI of the 78th Infantry, heading for a regimental collecting point with 68 bedraggled POWs, found that he had 1,200 in tow by the time he arrived.

Yet the Wehrmacht's tail kept twitching viciously in bloody clashes along country roads between towns with soon-forgotten names. "You thrust past huge roadblocks where the Germans had hastily improvised defenses," reported Time-Life correspondent Sidney Olsen, following an armored divison on its drive eastward. "Around these lie the old familiar signs of another lost German battle, the scattered helmets, the ripped off pants legs and coat arms where wounds were dressed, the golden sprinkles of ammunition, the smashed machine guns and still-smoldering trucks in the ditches." And miles later, wrote Olsen, "you come to the debris of war again, a bend in the road where the fleeing Germans turned for a delaying action. The trucks, guns and equipment are scattered colorfully over the field, the scene much like a littered picnic ground where the picnickers will never yawn awake again."

And then there was the horror of the concentration camps. It was in April that the Allies came upon the first of many death camps when the 4th Armored Division took

Ohrdruf, near Kassel in southern Germany. The existence of these camps was as yet nearly unknown to the Allied world. The hellhole at Ohrdruf was crowded with starving slave laborers; unburied corpses lay everywhere. When General Patton came to see the appalling scene, he vomited.

The first Allied unit to reach the Elbe was the "Hell on Wheels" 2nd Armored Division. Moving on from the Ruhr, the tankers bridged the Weser near Hameln, the town of Pied Piper legend. Hameln was a pretty spot—but not for long. Strongly defended by an SS unit, it took a severe pounding from the American guns. Then the tankers sped toward the Elbe across open, rolling countryside. They met a roadblock of 88mm guns, outflanked it and accepted the surrender of a 1,700-man German unit marching along the autobahn. On the evening of April 11, the lead columns reached Schönebeck, on the Elbe's west bank.

The next day, two more Seventh Army units attained the river. The 329th Infantry Regiment, part of the 83rd Division, had sped its advance by commandeering an assortment of civilian vehicles—trucks, fire engines, even horse-drawn wagons; GIs dubbed it the "Ragtag Circus." On April 12, the Ragtag Circus invaded Barby, a few miles upstream from the industrial center of Schönebeck. And 50 miles to the north, the 5th Armored Division reached the Elbe at Tangermünde.

Defense of the area had been entrusted to 45-year-old Walter Wenck, one of Hitler's youngest, feistiest generals. Wenck's command was the hastily recruited Twelfth Army, itself a motley gathering of 50,000 panzer trainees, cadets from officer schools, convalescents from Berlin hospitals, and conscripts from a paramilitary labor unit. But Wenck wielded this force with great tactical brilliance in a series of hit-and-run guerrilla thrusts. By April 13, the U.S. 2nd Division had carved out a bridgehead on the Elbe's far bank, and sent three battalions across. Wenck swept down and caught the Americans by surprise. The next day the battalion was forced to withdraw, with a loss of 330 men. It was the 2nd Armored's only defeat in almost three years of combat.

As the Allies in central Germany fought to mop up the pockets of resistance between the Weser and the Elbe, a more vicious battle was commencing to the south. The medieval walled city of Nuremberg, at the edge of the Bavarian highlands, was a shrine of Nazism—"the most German of all German cities," as Hitler put it. An entire corps of Patch's Seventh Army was now heading that way. And Nuremberg's garrison, the crack 13th SS Corps under General Max Simon, could be expected to defend the city with religious tenacity.

The attack on Nuremberg began on April 15. The U.S. XV Corps, reinforced by the 42nd Division, surrounded the city with a cordon of armor and infantry. The following day the

A 15-year-old German soldier bursts into tears after being taken prisoner near Giessen, southeast of Paderborn. Though many youngsters, hastily recruited as Germany scraped the bottom of its manpower barrel, lost their boyish bravery after firing a few shots, others fought doggedly until disabled or killed.

cordon started to close, and as the GIs advanced, they began to understand the depth of the Nazi commitment. Hundreds of 88mm guns opened up in front of them, hurling shrapnel shells fused to burst overhead, spewing fragments of hot metal for hundreds of yards. Whole platoons of Americans lay dead, or writhing in agony. Sorties of Messerschmitts and Focke-Wolf 190s screamed in to bomb and strafe in the heaviest German air attack since the Rhine crossing.

One by one the 88mm guns were silenced, the planes shot down. Inexorably, the noose continued to tighten. On April 18, the 45th Division overran the enormous Luitpold Arena, hallowed site of the great Nazi party rallies. German prisoners who witnessed this desecration broke down and wept. The following day the GIs breached Nuremberg's medieval walls and moved into the central city. There they fought house by house, cellar by cellar, against both soldiers and civilians who blasted them with rifles and antitank

Panzerfaust weapons. German corpses were another hazard; many had been booby-trapped.

April 20 was Adolf Hitler's birthday, and on its eve Nuremburg's Nazi leader, Gauleiter Karl Holz, sent him a final message. "All antitank guns have been destroyed. There is an acute shortage of ammunition," he wrote. But morale, Holz reported, was high: "All party members greet each other with 'Heil Hitler!' Our faith, our love, our life belongs to you, my Führer." The next day the city fell. Holz put a bullet through his temple.

By now, the Allies controlled most of Germany west of the Elbe. Montgomery's forces were poised to take Bremen, and had driven to within 60 miles of fire-gutted Hamburg. Magdeburg was taken, and Leipzig had surrendered. Patton's Third Army was running on a line south to Bayreuth. And the French Seventh Army was about to capture Stuttgart.

The war in the west was virtually over.

Reclining in the turret of his armored car, a Ninth Army soldier returns the curious attention of hundreds of civilians in the just-captured town of Jüchen.

LIFE UNDER THE BOMBS

German civilians pick their way through the bombed-out city of Hamburg—one of 72 German cities that Allied bombers ravaged between 1942 and 1945.

ENDURING AN ENDLESS RAIN OF MISERY

For three years, beginning in 1942, the cities of Germany endured a campaign of strategic bombing unprecedented in human history. By night, British bombers flew so-called saturation raids that were as unselectively ruinous as the name suggests. By day, waves of American planes sought to pinpoint important military and industrial targets but their bombs sometimes struck homes or office buildings instead. As many as 1,600 bombers roared over a city in a single raid; often they returned a day later—and again and again until it seemed to beleaguered Germans that the bombing never stopped. Official estimates of the bomb tonnage that fell on Germany begin at one million tons. The bombs wiped out more than 11 million dwellings and an estimated half million civilian lives.

The average air-raid shelter—a cellar in a house or business establishment—provided uncertain protection. A direct hit on the structure above might cave in the shelter and crush everyone within it. Or the refugees might survive the bombs and the wreckage above, only to be trapped below ground and die of asphyxiation. For those who remained aboveground during a raid to muster what defenses they could against the relentless pummeling, the terrors were manifold. Among the worst were incendiary bombs, which ignited on impact and spread fire everywhere. "I saw people tearing off their clothes as they caught fire," a survivor recalled. When the Allied bombers dropped incendiaries in quantity—and in a typical raid, a half million were dropped—they generated fire storms. These moving towers of flame reached a mind-boggling 1,800 degrees F., and tore through the streets with a shrill howl that one German remembered as "terrible music."

By the end of 1944, Berlin alone had experienced 24 major raids, and Germans everywhere felt their cities had been bombed into a new Stone Age. "There was no water, no light, no fire," one survivor recalled. Thousands of city dwellers fled, but most stayed where they were, clinging stubbornly to what was left of their homes, and doggedly getting on with life in the midst of destruction.

B-24s drop their high-explosive payload on German installations. A large formation could release up to 100 tons of bombs a minute.

In the aftermath of an air raid, a gas-masked mother wheels her baby past a Berlin theater advertising a film appropriately titled "Journey into the Past."

357

In a Hamburg bomb shelter, Germans lie dead from carbon monoxide poisoning. The gas, which resulted from incomplete combustion, accounted for up to 80 per cent of incendiary bomb casualties.

A soldier helps a desolate family through rubble-strewn Mannheim.

Distressed civilians pause in a bombed-out street in Berlin. One German remembered that people "staggered like sleepwalkers" after a raid.

Hesitantly smiling women and children while away the night in an air-raid shelter. Women with small children to round up found the sudden alerts particularly distressing; to be on the safe side they began gathering at the shelters at 6 o'clock in the evening.

As a Munich couple run for shelter with a few belongings in their arms, firemen fight the blaze raging behind them. Approximately 150,000 persons were employed full time in fire fighting throughout Germany.

In a poignant gesture to tradition, a man places a wreath on a Cologne rubble heap at Christmas time 1944. His family lay dead and buried under the wreckage.

Incongruously decked with Christmas trees, a Berlin gym serves as a temporary morgue in December 1944. In the last year and a half of the war, 77,750 civilians reported missing throughout Germany were never found.

Atop Dresden's town hall, a sandstone figure gestures with eerie serenity toward the ruins of the city's old quarter, ravaged in a fire storm set off by Allied bombing in February 1945. A British pilot wrote: "For the first time in many operations I felt sorry for the population below."

14

On February 18, 1943, just over a fortnight after Field Marshal Friedrich Paulus and the pitiful remnants of his Sixth Army had trudged into captivity at Stalingrad, Minister of Propaganda Joseph Goebbels proclaimed a state of "Total War." The German masses responded to the new austerity with a spirit of national self-sacrifice. But in return, they expected results. On March 15 they got what they wanted, when German armies won—for the second time—the city of Kharkov. With this great victory, the Red Army's winter offensive was halted and the front stabilized.

In the spring of 1943, a foreboding quiet hung over the Eastern front. During that period, Colonel General Heinz Guderian, the great tank commander who had only recently been restored to Hitler's good graces after being relieved of his command in 1941, posed a crucial question: "My Führer, why do you want to attack in the East at all this year?"

"You are quite right," replied Adolf Hitler. "Whenever I think of this attack, my stomach turns over."

Yet despite Hitler's queasiness, he had little choice: his standing with both the *Herrenvolk* ("master race") and his European allies was built on the success of his armies—and neither constituency would be satisfied with a spring and summer of static defense in Russia. Thus, dreading the time when the mighty foes would grapple again, Hitler settled for a limited offensive. He lacked the means for an all-out blow, but he might forestall a major Russian campaign by mounting his own spoiling, or preemptive strike.

The arena would be a salient, reaching about 90 miles westward into German-occupied territory, which had been created by the fighting after Stalingrad. Code-named *Zitadelle* (Citadel), the new German plan called for a short, sharp surgical operation in which General Walter Model's Ninth Army would attack from the north while Colonel General Hermann Hoth's Fourth Panzer Army drove up from the south. The converging assaults would snip off the salient at its eastern base, entrapping the Soviet armies inside the pocket.

Situated almost astride the salient's baseline was a city of little renown that would give its name to one of the decisive conflicts of world history—the Battle of Kursk.

Yet even after he had made his decision to launch *Citadel*, Hitler remained hesitant. A new generation of tanks—the heavy Tiger, the medium Panther and an odd contraption known as the Ferdinand—was just beginning to come off the assembly lines, and Hitler wanted to wait until they could be thrown into the offensive in large numbers.

Eventually, after the bugs had been worked out and the crews trained, the heavily armed and armored Tiger proved superior to its Russian equivalent, the KV1, but the sleek, speedy Panther was outmatched by the Soviet T-34 because, as one German general put it, the new tank was "easily set ablaze, the oil and fuel systems were inadequately protected." As for the Ferdinand, it was a fiasco. The brainstorm of Dr. Ferdinand Porsche, whose eccentricity Hitler mistook for genius, the Ferdinand was an elephantine tank-destroyer that was helpless in anything but head-on combat.

On May 3, originally set as the earliest date for starting *Citadel*, Hitler summoned his senior commanders to Munich. There, during a daylong discussion, the Führer seemed especially impressed by a distressing report from

THE SOVIET JUGGERNAUT

Model: there was an enormous buildup of Soviet forces within and around the Kursk salient. It almost appeared as if the Russians were counting on the German attack.

Although Hitler seemed briefly swayed, he finally bowed to overriding political considerations and decided to go ahead with the offensive—at some indefinite time.

In fact, Model was dead right. Thanks to the astounding efforts of an extraordinary espionage apparatus led by a spy called Lucy, the Soviets not only knew about *Citadel* but had made such massive preparations to meet it that they would have been greatly disappointed by its cancellation.

Although the Lucy network remains shrouded by secrecy, it is known that Lucy was the code name for Rudolf Rössler, a German veteran of World War I. An anti-Nazi, he was now residing in Switzerland, where he was well established in espionage circles. Judging by the accuracy of his information, Lucy had access to the topmost levels of the German High Command, and he had kept the Soviets informed about *Citadel* since the operation's conception.

Turning the Kursk salient into a gigantic fortress, the Russians crammed it with 977,000 men, more than 3,300 tanks and assault guns, 20,000 guns and mortars and nearly 3,000 aircraft. Confronting Model in the north was the Central Front under General Konstantin K. Rokossovsky who, having somehow survived Stalin's 1930s military purges, had emerged from the torture chambers with a mouthful of metal teeth—and a steel will. Facing Hoth's panzer army to the south was the Voronezh Front, commanded by General Nikolai F. Vatutin. Although Vatutin had been a staff officer throughout his career, he had what one of his juniors described as "a strong dash of romanticism in his makeup." Accordingly, in 1942, he had asked Stalin to give him a combat command.

As if the masses of Russian men and matériel within the

Two Red Army infantrymen, one of them armed with an antitank rifle and the other carrying a submachine gun, sprint past a knocked-out German Mark III tank during a small-scale attack in the battle for Kursk.

bulge were not enough, another powerful reserve had been built up about 100 miles southeast of Kursk. Designated by the deceptively static name of the Steppe Military District, it was commanded by General Ivan S. Konev, once a political commissar but now a ferocious fighting leader.

Even while Hitler hemmed and hawed, the Germans assembled their forces for a colossal clash. Gathered around the salient's 250-mile perimeter were 570,000 men, nearly 2,500 tanks and self-propelled guns, 10,000 field guns and mortars, and almost 2,000 aircraft.

Finally, by July 1 Hitler was ready to set *Citadel* in motion. During a meeting that day with top commanders at his Rastenburg headquarters in East Prussia, the Führer announced his decision: *Citadel* would begin on July 5. Hitler added a special caution: "This time we must make absolutely sure that nothing of our intention is betrayed either through carelessness or neglect."

By that evening, the Soviets had been informed of the impending attack.

The July 5 dawn was shattered by the thunder of German guns and the howl of Stukas overhead. Hoth's tanks rumbled into the maelstrom of Kursk while Soviet 76mm guns answered instantly, their roar in satanic symphony with the wail of "Katyusha" rockets and the crackle of 90 Ferdinand tank-destroyers along with small arms fire.

The Russians had expected that Hoth would take the direct route north—through the town of Oboyan and the city of Kursk—for his linkup with Model. But one senior officer, General S. Krivoshein, commander of the First Tank Army's III Mechanized Corps, was not so sure. "Hoth is a cunning fox," he told his chief-of-staff. "Will he really do the obvious?"

Hoth would not. Although his orders from Hitler's headquarters specified unmistakably that he must strike through Oboyan, he knew that the movement straight north would expose his right flank to Russian tank reserves coming from the east. He therefore amended his plan: the 48th Panzer Corps would feint toward Oboyan, then turn east toward Prokhorovka. Meanwhile, the 2nd SS Panzer Corps would drive directly toward Prokhorovka.

Squarely in the path taken by the 2nd SS Panzer Corps was the Soviet Sixth Guards Army, commanded by General I.M. Chistyakov. A noted trencherman, Chistyakov had just sat down beneath an apple tree for his second breakfast of the morning—a repast of cold mutton, scrambled eggs and chilled vodka—when shells started crashing about and a breathless aide reported that German tanks were even then rolling toward his headquarters.

Heavy reinforcements were thrown in to repair the lines of the Sixth Guards Army, but before nightfall brought the assault to a halt, the 2nd SS Panzer Corps had fought 11 miles into the Kursk salient.

North of the salient, Model had decided to lead his attack with infantry and then, after discovering soft spots in the Soviet defenses, to exploit the weaknesses with armor. And perhaps to confound the enemy with sheer size, perhaps because he could not figure out what else to do with the tank-destroyers, Model decided to send his 90 Ferdinand tanks along with the infantry.

When the time came, Model aimed his main thrust at the left flank of Rokossovsky's line. As the outlandish Ferdinands waddled into battle, some were halted by mechanical failure; others plowed on until they lost their infantry support, allowing Russian soldiers to leap aboard the slowly moving vehicles and squirt flamethrowers through the engine ventilation slats. Few of the Ferdinands survived, and German infantrymen found the going almost equally hard. By noon, the report made by an aide to a regimental commander was

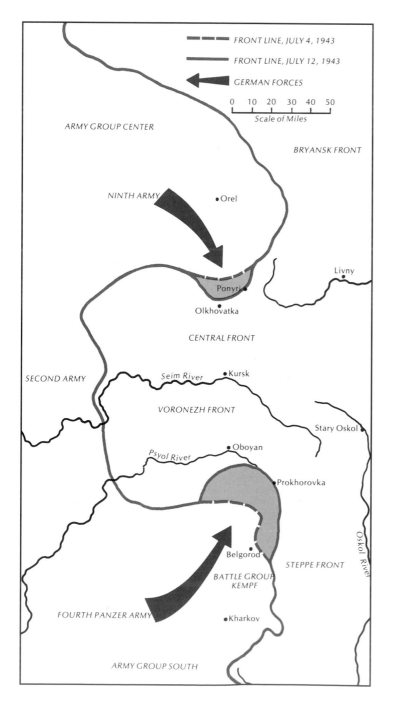

Operation Citadel, the German plan to destroy the Soviet forces in the Kursk salient, called for a gigantic pincers movement. The German Ninth Army was to attack southward from Orel while the Fourth Panzer Army and Battle Group Kempf drove northward from Belgorod. The jaws of the pincers were to snap shut at the town of Kursk. Defending the salient against the Germans were three Soviet army groups, the Central Front in the north, the Voronezh Front in the south and the Steppe Front, which was in line to the south and east.

typical: "3rd Battalion is unable to get beyond the second enemy trench on the right-hand slope. 1st Battalion is stuck in a minefield in the ravine. Some companies have lost nearly all their officers and about half their men. The Russian defensive fire is indescribable."

Although by nightfall, Model's men had fought a bare six miles within the Soviet defenses, he still intended to seize a line of hills about 13 miles within the Soviet defenses. From the 400-foot-high ridge Model would be able to see Kursk, 40 miles to the south, and his troops would have a downhill run all the way.

But General Rokossovsky was ready. He had already transformed the ridge's slopes into a warren of underground bunkers and connecting trenches, antitank strongholds, rocket-launcher emplacements, machine gun nests. Every woodland copse, every farmhouse and field, every gully and bump in the land bristled with men and weapons.

For nearly a week, Model persisted. He attacked first at the western end of the 15-mile-wide front, then at the eastern end. Day and night, the battle for the hills raged hand to hand and steel against steel with unrelenting ferocity until, at its peak, as many as 1,200 tanks and self-propelled guns and 3,000 artillery pieces were engaged. Finally, after a building-by-building brawl in the dreary little town of Ponyri at the eastern end of the line, the struggle ebbed toward its end. And still Model was on the wrong side of the ridge. Clearly, if the Germans were now to achieve a decisive break-through, it must come from Hoth's force in the south.

Since surprising Chistyakov at his breakfast, elements of the 2nd SS Panzer Corps had clawed a wide gap in the Sixth Guards Army defenses on their way to Prokhorovka. To finish off the Soviet First Tank Army at Prokhorovka, Hoth ordered an all-out attack on July 12. By fateful coincidence, the Red Army was gathering to strike at the same time in the same place.

On the evening of July 11, after a forced march of more than 225 miles, the Fifth Guards Tank Army of the Steppe Front arrived at the northeastern end of the Prokhorovka corridor. Now, in the early morning of July 12, 1943, the Soviet armored army's commander, Lieut. General Pavel A. Rotmistrov, stationed himself on a hillock. From there, he would be able to watch while his tanks delivered what he expected to be a fatal blow to Hoth's panzers.

Beneath Rotmistrov lay the Prokhorovka passageway, only a few miles wide, constricted on the Soviet right by the Psyol River and on the left by a steep railway embankment. Into that alley barreled Rotmistrov's tanks, 850 strong—almost all T-34s. At about the same instant, into the opposite end of the corridor roared 600 tanks of the 2nd SS Panzer Corps, including about 100 Tigers, at their best speed on a headlong collision course.

From his vantage point on the knoll, Rotmistrov had a panoramic view of the explosive clash: "The Russian tanks met the German advanced formation flat out. Both sides' tanks were mixed up together, and there was no opportunity, either in time or space, to disengage and reform in battle

In July 1943, at the Battle of Kursk—the greatest tank battle ever fought—a lucky German leaps clear of a Mark IV tank, set aflame by a Soviet shell. "When they hit one of our panzers," a crewman wrote, "there is an explosion, too loud, thank God, to let us hear the cries of the crew."

order. In no time at all, the sky seemed to be palled by the smoke of the various wrecks. The earth was black and scorched, with tanks burning like torches."

Although they could not match the brute strength of Hoth's Tigers, the T-34s used their greater agility with telling effect. Recalled a German tank commander: "Soon many of the T-34s had broken past our screen and were streaming like rats all over the battlefield." Amid the blinding, stifling clouds of dust flung up by churning tank tracks the struggle raged until, imperceptibly and with their guns still blazing, the Germans were forced onto the defensive.

Still, the day ended with the panzers holding their ground, while Rotmistrov retired to regroup. Each side had lost at least 300 tanks, but both remained full of fight and were ready to renew the battle. Moreover, the Germans had ample cause to believe that victory was close at hand.

When Hoth had started his thrust toward Prokhorovka, Battle Group Kempf—three panzer and three infantry divisions under Lieut. General Werner Kempf—had been assigned to cover the right flank of the 2nd SS Panzer Corps. During the drive, however, Kempf had lagged behind, and only now, on July 13, did his armor arrive on Prokhorovka's smoking battlefield. An earlier arrival of Kempf's 300 tanks might well have swayed the conflict in Hoth's favor.

By now, however, it was all academic. Incredibly, on that very day, Adolf Hitler ordered an end to Operation *Citadel*.

The reason lay on a faraway front: three days before, Allied troops had landed on Sicily and Italian resistance had collapsed forthwith. Now, fearful of a threat to his southern flank in Europe, Hitler needed troops for the defense of the Italian mainland. "And since they can't be taken from any other place," he declared, "they will have to be released from the Kursk front. Therefore I am forced to stop *Citadel*."

German casualties in the momentous battle of Kursk included nearly 30,000 dead and more than 60,000 wounded. Russian losses, although never disclosed, were certainly comparable. In terms of matériel, Soviet General Ivan Konev was encouraged to claim that Kursk was the "swan song of the German armor." Most important, Kursk had set into irresistible motion the Red Army avalanche.

On July 12, the very day that Model's drive toward Kursk had sputtered to a stop, a massive Soviet attack had started behind his back to the north. At first light on that day, Red Army forces exploded from their starting lines, plunging headlong into thickets of man-high thistles, which had grown up on lands devastated during the 1941 invasion.

The assault, code-named Operation *Kutuzov*, was part of a dual Soviet effort to drive the Germans from two salients that sandwiched the Kursk bulge. The salient in the north centered on the city of Orel; the other, in the south, con-

tained the prizes of Belgorod and Kharkov. With both the Orel and the Belgorod-Kharkov pockets cleared, the Red Army then would erupt along a 600-mile front and surge toward the Dnieper River. At stake was the strategic possession of the rich Donets Basin—which Hitler was determined to hold and Stalin equally intended to recapture.

For Operation *Kutuzov*, the Red Army amassed overwhelming superiority: 1,286,000 troops against fewer than 600,000 Germans within the Orel salient; 2,400 tanks and self-propelled guns against 1,000 for the enemy; 21,000 Soviet guns against 7,000; and more than 2,000 aircraft, about twice the Germans' strength.

At first, the Russians made steady progress. By nightfall of July 13, they had advanced 16 miles. But that day Hitler placed the Second Panzer Army under Model's direct command. Though Model had failed in his offensive against Kursk, Hitler knew the general was as tenacious a defensive fighter as the war had produced. For more than three weeks the opposing armies traded blows, and not until August 5 did the Russians finally fight their way into the heart of Orel.

They found the city in ruins—and the Germans gone. Model and his armies had skillfully withdrawn to a prepared defensive line at the western end of the Orel salient.

Meanwhile, 150 miles to the south, the offensive against Belgorod-Kharkov got under way on August 3. Jumping off at dawn, the Soviet infantry pushed deep into German positions within three hours. At noon, Vatutin's tanks ripped a wide gap between the Fourth Panzer Army and Battle Group Kempf. The Germans fell back to form a new defensive line north of Kharkov. Then, at 6 a.m. on August 5, the same day that Orel fell, Soviet troops broke into Belgorod.

That night, Moscow shook to the thunder of 12 salvos fired from 124 guns in celebration of the twin victories. Many citizens, awakened from their slumber and believing that an air raid was in progress, hastily took to their shelters. The Red Army's successful assault on Belgorod had covered 15 miles in two days. To reach Kharkov, another 45 miles to the south, would take 17 more days of vicious fighting.

Swinging around to the west, Vatutin attempted to move

The commanding officer of Army Group South, Field Marshal Erich von Manstein, greets Adolf Hitler on an airfield in the Ukraine on the 8th of September, 1943. In talks later that day, Manstein pleaded desperately for either reinforcements or permission to retreat, but he received neither.

on Kharkov but was blocked near Akhtyrka, 60 miles from his goal. Rumbling in from the east, armored elements of Konev's Steppe Front actually reached Kharkov's outskirts, where they stalled. At that point, a frustrated Vatutin called upon General Rotmistrov's redoubtable Fifth Guards Tank Army to try its luck from the northwest.

On the morning of August 19, Rotmistrov's tanks attacked head-on and throttles out across a yellow sea of giant sunflowers. From behind the flowering field, German guns blazed. The Russians reeled back, leaving behind no fewer than 184 wrecked T-34 tanks. Next day Rotmistrov struck again with 200 T-34s. Across the field they roared—and again fell back before a solid sheet of German fire. About 150 Soviet tanks were left ablaze on the battlefield.

But Rotmistrov persisted. At midnight on August 20, he returned with 160 tanks. In a wild melee, Soviet and German tanks fired at murderously close range, sometimes colliding with a screech of metal. When Rotmistrov retired, another 80 tanks were left smoking amid the carnage.

Even so, the battered victors were hardly better off than the vanquished. In overall command of Army Group South, Field Marshal Erich von Manstein realized that his defenders could not suffer another such blow and that his entire Eighth Army (a new designation for Battle Group Kempf) was in peril of being cut off. Manstein therefore decided to abandon Kharkov. "I'd rather lose a city than an army," he told his chief-of-staff. Thus, on August 22, with Hitler's resentful permission, the ruined city changed hands for the fourth—and last—time during the War.

With the entire line of his Army Group South under heavy pressure, Manstein saw that the Donets region would have to be abandoned in favor of a defensive line on the Dnieper. Hitler, of course, was adamantly opposed. To air their differences, the two met three times over a two-week period: on August 27, at the Führer's *Werewolf* headquarters in the southwest Ukraine; on September 3, at the Wolf's Lair headquarters in East Prussia; and on September 8, at Manstein's headquarters at Zaporozhye.

Each time, Manstein's pleas met with flat refusals. But finally, on September 14, Hitler's obstinacy was overwhelmed by the rush of disastrous events: the forces of Vatutin's Voronezh Front shattered Manstein's northern wing, swept southwest and soon reached Okop, 75 miles from Cherkassy on the Dnieper's great bend. Farther north, troops of Rokossovsky's Central Front probed to within 46 miles of Kiev.

Bowing to urgent necessity, Hitler at last gave permission for Manstein to withdraw to the west. Field Marshal Hans Günther von Kluge, in command of Army Group Center, was allowed to withdraw as well. A race for the Dnieper River bridges began. As a German lieutenant wrote, "Everyone is making for the great river, which we hope will give us a safe defensive line again."

By September 15, the average distance between Manstein's positions and the far side of the Dnieper was about 100 miles. Once at the river, the Eighth Army, the First Panzer and the Fourth Panzer armies—750,000 strong—would be crowded across only six bridges on a 280-mile stretch of the river.

Much of the race was run on a muddy track, with unseasonable rains miring machines and men, and the result was a photo finish. On September 21, the Fourth Panzer Army's 24th Corps, with the Soviet Third Guards Tank Army hard on its heels, began to cross the Dnieper at Kanev, 65 miles south of Kiev.

That night, the call of a bittern sounded on the Soviet side of the Dnieper at the so-called Bukrin Bend, 10 miles north of Kiev—where the Germans had not yet deployed. That call was, in fact, a signal from Guards Private I.D. Semyonov, crouched amid the reeds on the marshy ground. Three other soldiers crept up to join him and silently, with sacks wrapped around their oars, the group crossed the Dnieper in a skiff that had been hidden among the reeds. Soon after, 120 partisans and the bulk of a submachine gun company followed, and next morning most of a battalion came across.

The Russians now had their bridgehead across the Dnieper. They immediately set about doing everything possible—including a badly botched paratroop operation on

Riding a jury-rigged raft, Soviet soldiers cross the Dnieper under German fire. At the Lyutezh crossing, according to a Soviet account, the Red Army troops were ferried by a wizened peasant woman who said to them: "Even though I am old, I still have enough strength left to help you, my sons."

September 24—to enlarge the foothold. By the end of the week, the Twenty-seventh and Fortieth armies, together with all the infantry of the Third Guards Tank Army, were packed into the bridgehead, which measured 6.5 miles wide and 3.5 miles deep. And there they stayed despite their repeated attempts to burst through the crack German 24th and 48th Panzer corps.

Meanwhile other Red Army troops tried valiantly to cross the Dnieper elsewhere. Riding on skiffs or crude rafts, clinging to empty metal drums and door frames and garden benches, they managed to establish 23 small bridgeheads before the end of September. One of the incursions, all but unnoticed in the German High Command's preoccupation with Bukrin, was achieved on the night of September 26 by a tiny advance unit of the Soviet Thirty-eighth Army.

At about 4:00 a.m., 22 men of a platoon led by Sergeant P.P. Nefedov succeeded in bringing four fishing boats to the west bank at Lyutezh, 12 miles north of Kiev. By September 30, two infantry regiments and part of a heavy mortar regiment had crossed, but they were unable to enlarge their position in the face of burgeoning enemy strength. On October 3, however, the small success caught the eye of General Vatutin, who decided to give Lyutezh a try.

To develop the bridgehead, Vatutin would need a heavy infusion of armor. He summoned Lieut. General A.G. Kravchenko, commander of the Fifth Guards tank force, which was situated a few miles south of the 300-yard-wide Desna River. Kravchenko, explained General Vatutin, would have to ford his tanks across the Desna before advancing to the Dnieper.

Kravchenko found a place where the river was only seven feet deep—still considerably more than the wading depth of his T-34s. "We therefore had to turn our tanks into makeshift submarines," Kravchenko wrote later. "All slits, hatches and covers on the tank hulls and the turrets were made watertight with putty or pitch. The ford was marked out by two rows of posts. The tanks then drove off in low gear through the strange corridor, the drivers steering blind to the orders of their commanders, who sat in the turrets."

Ninety T-34s splashed across the Desna—only to face the far deeper, wider Dnieper a few miles beyond. There, Soviet troops found two barges, capable of carrying three tanks each. On the night of October 5, ten crossings were made, ferrying 60 tanks. Next day, the Lyutezh bridgehead was expanded to six miles wide and four miles deep. To go farther, Kravchenko would require more armor—much more.

Not until mid-October did Soviet authorities finally give up on the Bukrin bridgehead and agree to focus on Lyutezh. For his attack, Vatutin made no pretense at finesse: he crammed the Lyutezh bridgehead with firepower, including 2,000 cannon and mortars and 500 rocket launchers.

On the night of November 4, after Vatutin's first waves had punched a six-mile hole in the German lines, the armor of the Third Guards Tanks Army staged one of the War's wildest charges. With the soldiers of two rifle divisions riding on their hulls, the tanks struck with headlights on, sirens howling and guns blazing. Roaring into the open, they swung south—toward Kiev, which fell on November 7.

After Kiev, the German defense stiffened, and counterattacks held the Russians to a bridgehead across the Dnieper between Cherkassy and Nikopol. As the year neared its end, an unseasonal thaw turned the landscape to mud for a

month; and when winter returned, the bitter weather halted most major military movements. For a while, the fighting was overshadowed by top-level Allied diplomacy.

In October, Soviet Foreign Minister Vyacheslav M. Molotov had met in Moscow with U.S. Secretary of State Cordell Hull and British Foreign Minister Anthony Eden to lay the groundwork for a subsequent summit conference in Teheran to be attended by the Big Three—Stalin, Roosevelt and Churchill.

The Moscow sessions settled a number of issues, pending final agreement at the summit. The Americans and British agreed to launch a cross-Channel invasion of France in the spring of 1944, and Molotov declared himself satisfied on that score. For the U.S., Cordell Hull attached the highest priority to a Four Power Declaration—to be signed by the United States, Great Britain, the Soviet Union and China—on the absolute need for an effective postwar peace-keeping organization. After some grumbling about China's inclusion, Molotov agreed; the United Nations was now a healthy embryo, and Hull was well pleased.

Anthony Eden, however, did not have a successful time in Moscow. The British were deeply concerned about the postwar status of Eastern Europe, particularly the future independence of Poland, that much-abused nation on whose behalf Britain had gone to war. Fearing that Stalin meant to set up a puppet Communist government in Poland, Eden sought to persuade Hull to join Britain in an appeal for assurances of Soviet good intentions. Eden got nowhere. "I don't want to deal with those piddling little things," Hull told an associate. "We must deal with the main issues." Thus Eden was more or less forced to let the matter rest until Teheran.

At the conference itself on November 28, Josef Stalin was by turns the amiable host and bullying dictator. At one point, Roosevelt happened to speak to him while he was reading a document. Stalin snarled at the President of the United States: "For God's sake, let me finish my work."

Nevertheless, the Big Three reached their agreements—all except on the matter of Poland, for which no pledges were forthcoming. "There is no need at the present time to speak of any Soviet desires," remarked Stalin. "But when the time comes, we will speak."

And that seemingly offhanded remark, in retrospect, was as much a threat as a promise.

Whenever Stalin was not preoccupied by world politics in the autumn of 1943, he and his high command devoted their time to planning three winter offensives aimed at clearing the Germans from the Soviet Union. The attacks, later known to the Soviets as the "three blows," envisioned lifting the siege of Leningrad, driving westward from the Dnieper, and ousting the enemy from the Crimean Peninsula.

Although Leningrad, by now receiving adequate supplies, was no longer of prime strategic significance, the heroism of its citizens surpassed other considerations and demanded that the city be freed from German menace.

On January 14, 1944, the Leningrad Front's Second Shock Army pushed off to the southeast from a Gulf of Finland bridgehead at Oranienbaum, west of Leningrad; the front's Forty-second Army attacked from the Pulkovo Heights in the city's southern suburbs. The two forces quickly linked up, and on January 27, with the German Eighteenth Army on the run and Leningrad now beyond the reach of enemy guns, citizens poured into the city's streets to hear their liberation announced over loudspeakers.

It was a moment of rare emotion, and poet Olga Berggoltz marveled at the sight of "shell-pitted, bullet-riddled, scarred Leningrad, with its plywood windowpanes. Despite all the cruel slashes and blows, Leningrad retained its proud beauty. In the bluish, roseate, green and white of the lights, the city appeared to us so austere and touching we could not feast our eyes enough upon it."

Four days later, Hitler replaced the commander of Army Group North with Walter Model, known by now to the German High Command as "the lion of the defense." Between them, Hitler and Model devised a new strategy called *Schild und Schwert* (Shield and Sword). In theory, the plan held that retreats were permissible if they were preludes to attack. In practice, it authorized Model's withdrawal to the so-called Panther Position, a heavily fortified line about 150 miles southwest of Leningrad.

The arrival of Army Group North in the Panther Position coincided with a spring thaw that finally brought the Soviet advance to a standstill. A lull settled in on the northern end of the Eastern Front.

In the Ukraine to the south, the second of the Red Army's three blows had been launched on Christmas Eve, 1943. The offensive was a westward drive by three Soviet army groups intended to liberate the remainder of the region. By mid-January, Vatutin's First Ukrainian Front had thrust 60 miles, still 40 miles short of Vinnitsa, Manstein's headquarters on the upper Bug River. Meanwhile, Konev's Second Ukrainian Front had captured the industrial city of Kirovograd and was heading for Pervomaisk on the lower Bug.

At that point, however, Vatutin and Konev changed their plans after spotting a chance to surround a huge number of Germans. The result of their opportunism was the Cherkassy pocket, a hellhole that became known to the Germans within it as the Witches' Caldron.

In their westward drives, Vatutin and Konev had created between their flanks a German-held salient that pressed down on the Dnieper River like a giant thumb. Although the

During the German retreat in September 1943, an ingenious device, the "trackwolf," rips up railroad ties (far left) and German demolition troops lay mines along a village road (near left). Code named Operation Scorched Earth, the German plan to destroy everything in the wake of their retreating armies was devastatingly successful. Yet when the German forces crossed the Dnieper, the Red Army was still pressing remorselessly on their heels.

German troops there were clearly exposed to Soviet assault, Hitler imagined that he could somehow use the salient as a base for regaining possession of Kiev. Accordingly he had crammed the First Panzer and Eighth armies within the long, horseshoe-shaped line. Now, with Stalin's permission, it was agreed that Vatutin would attack from the north and Konev would come up from the south to pinch off the salient.

Konev struck early on January 24, 1944, and Vatutin's forces kicked off the next morning. Their success was perhaps best described by General Nikolaus von Vormann, whose 23rd Panzer Division was in the path of the onslaught: "Regardless of losses—and I really mean regardless of losses—masses of Soviets about midday streamed westward past the German tanks which were firing at them with everything they had. It was an amazing scene, a shattering drama. There really is no other comparison—the dam had burst and a huge flood was pouring over the flat land."

On January 28, the Soviet spearheads met. Although the First Panzer Army had escaped, two corps of the Eighth Army were trapped in a 1,200-square-mile area near the city of Cherkassy. Probably because they had overestimated the size of their bag, Vatutin and Konev concentrated on tightening their grip on the pocket rather than pushing their main front westward. That left open the possibility that a German relief force, with only 25 miles to travel, might be able to break through to the encircled soldiers.

Manstein was just the man to try. On February 4, a relief column comprised of the 3rd Panzer Corps and the 47th Corps set out to the rescue. Although gluey, knee-deep mud made the advance an ordeal, by February 14 the 3rd Panzer Corps had established a bridgehead across the deep, fast-flowing Gniloi Tikich River at the large village of Lysyanka. Only two more Soviet positions, the village of Dzurzhentsy and close beside it an eminence designated as Hill 239, blocked the way to the pocket.

In a blinding snowstorm, a strong force attempted to capture the village and the hill—while Germans inside the pocket tried to fight their way out to link up with their rescuers. Both efforts met with furious Soviet opposition. "In one place," wrote a German soldier, "we have to throw ourselves down and let the tanks roll over us, as they told us to do in the training manual. Rumbling, rattling, and whirring, the vast tonnage of a T-34 thunders over us, while the screaming, clanging chains roll past us on both sides."

The Soviets held, and next day Manstein concluded that a relief was impossible. The troops in the pocket would simply have to get on their feet and make a grand run for Hill 239 and Dzurzhentsy.

The breakout began at 11:00 p.m. on February 16. Moving in silence and using only knives and bayonets, lead

THE HARD-HITTING STALIN II: LIGHTEST OF THE HEAVY TANKS

The Stalin II, an improved version of the Josef Stalin heavy tank, was a deadly combination of extremes. It weighed 52 tons—about 15 tons less than other heavy tanks. Yet it was armed with the biggest main gun of any World War II tank and was protected by some of the heaviest armor.

The Soviet engineers pulled off these feats by giving the tank a low profile (8 feet 11 inches); this saved weight and made the Stalin II an especially hard target to hit. More weight was saved by their canny positioning of the armor, skimping in some places but piling it on—up to six inches thick—in the frontal areas most vulnerable to attack. A panzer commander who confronted the Stalin IIs was dismayed to discover that "although my Tigers began to hit them at 2,200 yards, our shells did not penetrate until half that distance."

Of course, the Stalin II tank paid a price for these advantages. With its low profile came cramped quarters for the four-man crew. Space was at such a premium that the tank went into battle with only 28 rounds for its main gun, 56 fewer than Germany's Tigers, and it carried two fuel tanks in a dangerously exposed position on the hull behind the turret.

regiments cut through enemy lines. Before the Russians realized what was happening, the regiments pushed all the way to Lysyanka. Others followed, but many were less fortunate. Passing to the east of Dzurzhentsy, they ran into heavy fire and were forced to turn south. To reach Lysyanka by that route, they had to cross the Gniloi Tikich River, a mile and a half south of the bridge seized by the 3rd Corps. And even then, the only way to get to the other side was to swim.

By the next afternoon, the scene was one of utter horror. Thousands of German troops crowded toward the 50-foot-wide river and pushed down the steep east bank to swim across. Meanwhile, Soviet T-34s fired high-explosive shells at the milling mass. Although the temperature was 23 degrees F., many of the soldiers stripped and attempted to swim, only to be battered by ice floes swirling in the strong current. Their bodies, along with corpses of horses, rolled and bobbed and drifted downstream.

In all, 30,000 of the 45,000 troops who had been in the pocket on February 16 made good their escape. But the repercussions of the battle extended far beyond the losses of men and territory. Manstein's effort to relieve the troops in the Cherkassy pocket had weakened the German line to the north and south, and the Red Army took swift advantage of the opportunity.

On March 4, 1944, the First Ukrainian Front, now under Georgy Zhukov—Vatutin had been mortally wounded in an attack by anti-Soviet Ukrainian guerrillas—resumed its westward offensive. Konev's Second Ukrainian Front joined in the following day, and General Rodion Malinovsky's Third Ukrainian Front the day after that. As the Red Army rolled relentlessly over the vast countryside, Hitler desperately tried to stave off the avalanche: on March 30, Manstein was replaced by Walter Model, now elevated to field marshal status, and in command of Army Group South, which was renamed Army Group North Ukraine.

Such cosmetic changes were of no help. By mid-April the German Fourth Army had its back to the Carpathian Mountains, its line dipping into Rumania for a 120-mile stretch. Farther south, two other German armies, the Sixth and the Eighth, were in shambles, stranded beyond the Dniester River without adequate clothing or food.

Meanwhile, through February and March, Marshal Aleksandr W. Vasilevsky, chief of the Soviet General Staff, and Lieut. General F.I. Tolbukhin, commander of the Fourth Ukrainian Front, had worked on a plan for the Crimea.

On the German side, there was widespread agreement that Colonel General Erwin Jaenecke's outnumbered Seventeenth Army should quit the Crimea. But, predictably, Hitler said no. Then on April 7, the Führer got some misguided support from Colonel General Ferdinand Schörner, the newly appointed commander of Army Group South Ukraine. Upon completing his inspection of the Crimean defenses, Schörner pronounced them in excellent shape and made one of history's shortest-lived military prognostications—that the peninsula could be held "for a long time."

Next day, Tolbukhin's troops were repulsed at the Perekop Isthmus, the principal access from the mainland, but managed to get across the Sivash, the shallow fringe of water between the peninsula and the mainland. The Seventeenth Army tumbled back. By nightfall on May 7, Soviet forces had scaled the Zapun Heights, the key to Sevastopol's southern defenses.

"The sky above Sevastopol is a glowing red," said a Soviet reporter, "filled with the droning of motors and roar of explosions. The Germans have set up antiaircraft guns and the curtain of fire they raise at night is so thick it seems as if a many-colored rainstorm has burst over the city."

On the night of May 8, Hitler belatedly gave the order to evacuate his remaining forces by sea. But the operation was mismanaged, and more than 26,000 troops were left on the beach to be taken prisoner.

"The promontory," a Soviet officer wrote later, "was packed with German tanks, vehicles, guns, and mortars. The human corpses had been cleared away, but a nauseating stench still hung in the air. As far as the eye could scan, the sea was covered with swollen carcasses of horses that were slowly rolling over on the waves and bursting in the heat."

Thus, by the spring of 1944, the Russians' three blows had pounded and twisted the German line and driven it westward as much as 300 miles. Only in the center,

Soviet troops swarm through the ruins of Sevastopol in May 1944. They recaptured the Black Sea port in just four days' fighting. In that year of victories the Red Army slashed at the Germans all along the Eastern Front, from the Baltic Sea in the north to the Black Sea in the south.

A column of 57,600 German soldiers—all of them captured during the Soviet Army's stunning victory in Belorussia—marches through Moscow on July 17, 1944. The grim procession, led by 19 German generals and liberally photographed from a special press truck, was staged primarily to correct a mistaken impression of American and British journalists, who had been speculating that the Germans had withdrawn most of their troops from Belorussia before the Soviet offensive began.

Belorussia, had the German armies been able to hold. There in a great domain of forested and lake-studded lowland between the Baltic States and the Ukraine, their trial of blood and steel was soon to come.

In Belorussia, the 450-mile front of Field Marshal Ernst Busch's Army Group Center ran along the upper ridges of the Dnieper and bulged to within 300 miles of Moscow. Although Soviet advances to the north and south had left Busch's flanks dangerously exposed, German intelligence had predicted that the big Soviet summer offensive of 1944 would bypass Belorussia in favor of a thrust in the south toward the Balkans. Hitler agreed. As he saw it, Stalin could not pass up the opportunity to grab Rumania, Bulgaria and Hungary—countries long coveted by the Russians.

With those factors in mind, Busch remained reasonably confident as Hitler stripped his forces in order to reinforce the southern sector of the Russian front. During May, Army Group Center was reduced to 400,000 men from a peak of nearly a million; Busch also lost 33 per cent of his heavy artillery, 50 per cent of his tank destroyers and 88 per cent of his tanks. As it turned out, Hitler had made a monumental strategic blunder.

To Stalin, Belorussia represented a major opportunity: if the Soviets could nip off the bulge with a powerful pincers attack from north and south, they could then strike at will toward the Baltic States, East Prussia and central Poland without worrying about the security of their flanks or rear.

Stalin named and timed his offensive in Belorussia with heavy-handed historical symbolism. He called the attack Operation *Bagration*, after a Russian warrior who had won fame fighting another Western invader—Napoleon. And he set the start for June 22, the third anniversary of Hitler's invasion of the Soviet Union.

Planning and coordination were turned over to marshals Vasilevsky and Zhukov, who assembled a force of 2.5 million men and developed a strategy that called for a classic envelopment. Lieut. General Ivan D. Chernyakhovsky's Third Belorussian Front, with help from the First Baltic Front under General Ivan K. Bagramyan, would attack toward Minsk from the northeast. Marshal Rokossovsky's First Belorussian Front would swing toward Minsk from the southeast. General Matvei V. Zakharov's Second Belorussian Front would attack directly to the west, driving the Germans into the closing jaws of the trap.

Operation *Bagration* unfolded over a three-day period, with Soviet forces attacking the German northern flank on June 22, the central sector on June 23, and the southern end on June 24.

In the north, the Russians slammed into Colonel General Georg-Hans Reinhardt's Third Panzer Army in the Vitebsk area. By June 24, the situation had become so serious that Reinhardt called General Kurt Zeitzler, Hitler's chief-of-staff, to warn that his 53rd Corps, numbering 35,000 men, would be encircled if they were not quickly withdrawn from Vitebsk. Zeitzler told Reinhardt to hold the telephone line open while he talked to Hitler. After 10 minutes, Zeitzler reported the Führer's order: "Vitebsk will be held."

Three hours later, Hitler changed his mind and gave permission for the 53rd Corps to pull out—stipulating, however, that one division "remain in Vitebsk and continue to hold out." For the sacrificial role, Reinhardt reluctantly chose the 206th Infantry Division under Lieut. General A. Hitter.

In the end, Hitter's outfit was easily overwhelmed and the general himself was among those captured. But the other three divisions of the 53rd Corps fared no better. As their corps commander, Major General Friedrich Gollwitzer, tried to lead them to safety, they found themselves mercilessly squeezed by the enemy. "No one knew what was going on," a German sergeant major later recalled. "There were Russians behind us, to the right and to the left. We fired. My God, but it was useless. It was like firing at the ocean waves with the tide coming in."

On June 27, Gollwitzer surrendered to General Chernyakhovsky's forces. In captivity, he vented his bitterness. "The responsibility for what has happened is not the Army's," he told Chernyakhovsky. "It's Hitler's."

In the central section, the attack by Zakharov's Second Belorussian Front almost immediately threw the Germans into confusion. Under the strain, battle-hardened German officers began to crack up. Soviet correspondent Ilya Ehrenburg reported that a German general was found wandering aimlessly in a patch of woods near the fortified town of Mogilev, repeating to himself: "I'm a German, not a louse."

At the southern end of the line, Marshal Rokossovsky was trying to prove a point. Before he could advance on Minsk, he would have to capture or neutralize the fortified town of Bobruisk—located at the northern edge of the immense Pripyat Marshes, which restricted armored vehicles to relatively narrow corridors of dry ground. Long before Operation *Bagration* began, Rokossovsky had decided that conditions dictated a double-pronged attack on Bobruisk, and in so doing he ran afoul of Stalin, who preferred a single, massive blow.

Rokossovsky's tactical heresy had been sharply debated at a Moscow meeting on May 22. At his first mention of a two-pronged assault, Stalin interrupted, declaring, "The defense must be breached in one place."

When Rokossovsky argued, he was contemptuously told to "Go out and think it over again."

He did, and upon his return to Stalin's study the dictator asked: "Have you thought it through, General?"

"Yes, sir, Comrade Stalin," said Rokossovsky.

"Well then, that means we'll strike a single blow?" Stalin asked rhetorically.

"Two blows are more advisable, Comrade Stalin," answered Rokossovsky while others in the room sat in stunned silence.

"Go out and think it over again," said Stalin. "Don't be stubborn, Rokossovsky."

In an adjoining room, Rokossovsky was soon joined by Foreign Minister Molotov and Secretary of the Central Committee Georgy M. Malenkov.

"Don't forget where you are and with whom you're talking," warned Malenkov. "You are disagreeing with Comrade Stalin."

"You'll have to agree, Rokossovsky," Molotov added. "Agree—that's all there is to it."

When Rokossovsky was again ushered into Stalin's presence, the dictator relentlessly asked: "So what is better—two weak blows or one strong blow?"

Said Rokossovsky: "Two strong blows are better than one strong blow."

Stalin silently smoked his pipe. Then he walked over, put a hand on Rokossovsky's shoulder and told the others: "You know, Rokossovsky is right. And generally I like a commander who sticks to his guns. I confirm your decision, Comrade Rokossovsky."

Now, beginning with a massive bombardment at 4:00 a.m. on June 24, Rokossovsky translated his obstinacy into action. To spearhead the southern arm of the attack against Bobruisk, the Sixty-fifth Army's Lieut. General P.I. Batov had chosen for his main advance a 500-yard section of swampy ground that the Germans considered impassable. He ordered his infantry to weave willow branches into wooden frames resembling snowshoes. With the lightweight frames fastened to their boots, Batov's men crossed the swamp without sinking into the ooze. Caught off guard by the unexpected direction of the assault, the German Ninth Army's 41st Panzer Corps was soon reeling under the Soviet blows.

Rokossovsky's northern arm, with Lieut. General

Aleksandr Gorbatov's Third Army in the lead, ran into heavy resistance. After four hours of bitter fighting, Gorbatov called for support from the Sixteenth Air Army. "The sky was in tumult," wrote Soviet correspondent Vasily Grossman, "with the rhythmic roaring of the dive bombers, the hard, metallic voice of the attack planes, the piercing whine of the Yakovlev fighters." By nightfall, the Sixteenth Air Army had logged 3,200 sorties against the German positions. Gorbatov's infantry resumed its attack and by noon of the following day the Germans' last trench line had fallen.

On June 27, Batov's and Gorbatov's forces linked up west of Bobruisk. With a fearlessness born of desperation, the Germans repeatedly tried to hack their way out of the Soviet encirclement. "The whole area," Rokossovsky wrote later, "soon began to look like a huge graveyard strewn with mauled bodies and mangled machines."

Rokossovsky's two-pronged strategy had succeeded. By the time Bobruisk fell on June 29, about 50,000 Germans had been killed and another 20,000 captured by the stubborn marshal's forces.

Hitler reacted characteristically to the disasters that had so far befallen his forces in Belorussia: Field Marshal Busch was sacked in favor of Field Marshal Model, the "fireman" who responded to all alarms and emergencies. Still committed to a rigid defense, the Führer fixed a new line running north and south from the town of Berezino on the Berezina River, 60 miles east of Minsk. So far, and not one step farther, would the German armies pull back.

Again, the Führer was too late: the armored spearheads of Rokossovsky and Chernyakhovsky were already closing in on Minsk. Thousands of Germans now surrendered or wandered off. A Belorussian farmer, armed only with an ancient rifle, herded 750 German soldiers toward the rear. They had stumbled out of the forests and swamps and surrendered to women farm workers, who had locked them in barns.

On July 3, Rokossovsky and Chernyakhovsky joined hands west of Minsk, trapping an additional 100,000 Germans. Even those Germans who had managed to escape from Minsk gained only temporary deliverance from the Soviet juggernaut. On July 4, Stalin ordered Chernyakhovsky to push northwest from Minsk toward Lithuania, while Rokossovsky was sent southwest toward Brest-Litovsk on the Bug River. Zakharov's forces were left behind to comb the forests and swamps for survivors of Army Group Center.

By July 11, when Zakharov had finished mopping up, the dimensions of the German debacle had become clear. During the course of Operation *Bagration*, Soviet forces had destroyed Army Group Center, ripping a hole 250 miles wide in the middle of the German line. Twenty-eight German divisions had ceased to exist, and between 300,000 and 350,000 men had been killed or captured. They could not be replaced. Just as the Battle of Kursk had crippled the German panzers, so the Battle of Belorussia had fatally weakened the Wehrmacht in the east.

Two ravishing possibilities now beckoned to Stalin. He could send Soviet forces due west into Poland. Or he could send his southern armies into the Balkans.

He did both. In the late summer of 1944, the 10 Soviet armies of the Second and Third Ukrainian fronts burst into Rumania and soon fanned out into Bulgaria, Yugoslavia and Hungary. By then, even more powerful Soviet forces had swarmed across the border into Poland, where they would be willing witness to a nation's tragedy.

Now, the shortest distance to Berlin was a straight line across Poland, and Josef Stalin had plans for that war-battered country. He could not and would not have an unfriendly wartime regime at his Army's rear as it advanced on Berlin, and after the War he wanted a submissive nation interposed between the Soviet Union and a possibly resurgent Germany. Stalin therefore intended to install in Poland a government perfectly attuned to Soviet political, social and economic arrangements. Poland, in short, would be Communist.

In Poland, Stalin would use the Red Army as a political weapon, wielding it or withholding it to serve his purposes. His political maneuvers would soon lead to the bloody and abortive Warsaw Uprising.

The campaign for Poland began in mid-July, 1944, with an enormous two-pronged assault by Rokossovsky's First Belorussian Front. While Rokossovsky's right flank was advancing beyond Minsk, his six-army left flank stood poised near the 1939 Soviet-Polish frontier. Rokossovsky's next objectives in Poland were Lublin, 60 miles beyond the border, and Warsaw, 105 miles northwest of Lublin.

On July 22, as Red Army troops neared Lublin, Radio Moscow announced the formation of a Polish Committee of National Liberation. The Lublin Committee, as it became known, was portrayed by Soviet authorities as a broadly representative group with only three Communists among its 15 members. The Committee was therefore said to be a more worthy government for a liberated Poland than the Polish government-in-exile in London under Prime Minister Stanislaw Mikolajczyk. The Lublin Committee came out wholeheartedly in favor of a Soviet-Polish border that would give the Soviet Union 40,000 square miles of pre-war Poland.

The next day, Soviet tanks entered Lublin, and by July 30 they were within five miles of Warsaw. There they stopped. Rokossovsky explained later that, "Our supply lines were

stretched out over hundreds of kilometers and could not provide all that was needed to maintain our advance."

By then, Radio Kósciuszko, a Moscow station named after an 18th-century Polish military hero, had already aired the first of many appeals to Warsaw, urging an uprising against "the Hitlerite vermin." The broadcast concluded with the cry: "Poles, the time of liberation is at hand! Poles, to arms! There is not a moment to lose!"

Such urgent calls for an insurrection were specifically addressed to the People's Army, sponsored by the underground Polish Communist Party. But as Moscow knew, the People's Army had a potential fighting force in Warsaw of only 500 men and women. Any uprising would have to come from a stronger resistance group.

The strongest by far was the Home Army—the fighting arm in Poland of the Mikolajczyk government in London. Its national commander, General Bór (the nom de guerre of Tadeusz Komorowski), claimed that its membership totaled 380,000. The Warsaw commander, Colonel Monter (Antoni Chruściel) had 40,000 fighters in the city.

The Home Army leaders were determined to free Warsaw not only for national pride but also to establish the authority of the Mikolajczyk government before the Red Army could arrive and install a Communist regime. Bór calculated they would have to strike soon, for it seemed certain that Soviet forces would enter Warsaw within a week.

Late on the afternoon of July 31, while Bór was meeting with staff officers in a downtown apartment, Colonel Monter burst in with news that Soviet tanks were approaching Praga, a Warsaw district on the Vistula's eastern bank. Although Bór was authorized to start an uprising on his own authority, he called in and briefed Jan S. Jankowski, the civilian representative of the London government. "All right. Go ahead," said Jankowski. Bór then told Monter: "Tomorrow, at 1700 hours, you will go into action."

Excitement ran high in the Home Army, and scattered shooting broke out at 3:00 p.m., two hours ahead of schedule. By five o'clock, fights were raging all over the city. The uprising was off to an enthusiastic if haphazard start.

That night, Poles controlled the heart of Warsaw—the Old Town, the Inner City and the Vistula quarter. Wherever they held sway, the insurgents began constructing a maze of cobblestone barricades and passageways, breaking through cellar walls and opening manholes that led to Warsaw's labyrinthine sewer system.

For the first few days, it seemed that the Home Army might actually triumph. Of the 13,000 German troops in the vicinity, about 8,000 were pinned down guarding bridges, factories and other installations. The German commander in Warsaw, Lieut. General Reiner Stahel, was himself besieged in his headquarters, a historic palace in the Inner City. However, as it happened, real authority for suppressing the uprising was out of the inexperienced hands of Stahel. Instead, it belonged to the SS chief, Heinrich Himmler, who had overall responsi-

Soldiers of the Home Army sprint across a Warsaw street during the first days of the uprising, when buildings were still largely undamaged by shelling.

bility for counterinsurgency and antipartisan warfare.

Himmler instantly saw a bright side to the Warsaw situation. It would, he told Hitler, give the Germans a chance to destroy Warsaw, "the head, the intelligence of this 16 to 17 million Polish people, this people that has blocked us in the east for 700 years."

To do the dirty work, Himmler selected SS General Erich von dem Bach-Zelewski, who had made a reputation fighting partisans in Belorussia. Assigned as Bach-Zelewski's instruments of destruction were two of the most disreputable units in the German armed forces: the Dirlewanger Brigade and the Kaminski Brigade.

SS Colonel Oscar Dirlewanger, commander of the brigade that bore his name, was a notorious drunkard and liar who was said to have been convicted of rape, robbery and several other crimes; he was well regarded by Hitler and Himmler. His equally infamous outfit had about 900 troops when it went into Warsaw and required 2,500 replacements during the fighting. As for the 7,000-man Kaminski Brigade, it was an unruly force of violently anti-Communist Ukrainians led by Mieczyslaw Kaminski, another drunkard and womanizer.

On Saturday, August 5, the Dirlewanger and Kaminski brigades went to work. Their first target was the working-class district of Wola, where they ordered the inhabitants into the streets for "evacuation to the rear." The rear proved to be the nearest open space—a park, a square, a cemetery. There, thousands of Polish men, women and children were crowded together and shot. The Poles later estimated that 38,000 died in Wola and the nearby district of Ochota.

In military terms, however, the day's results were meager. Dirlewanger's column progressed only a half-mile into Wola. Kaminski penetrated no more than a few hundred yards before he came on a vodka distillery, and that crucial objective halted his advance. (For this and other derelictions, the Germans shot him several weeks later.) Bach-Zelewski quickly realized that the two brigades were good for little more than murder and looting. To subdue Warsaw, new troops would be needed.

Meanwhile, Moscow had fallen silent. No more appeals for an uprising were heard, and the radio and newspapers made no mention of what was happening in Warsaw. On August 5, after Prime Minister Churchill had appealed to Stalin to aid the Poles, the dictator replied: "I think the information given you by the Poles is greatly exaggerated and unreliable. They have neither guns, aircraft nor tanks. I cannot imagine detachments like that taking Warsaw."

Perhaps most callous of all was Russia's refusal to permit U.S. B-17s, flying from London, to land at Soviet bases for necessary refueling after dropping supplies to Warsaw's resistance fighters. (With a shorter flight from southern Italy, British bombers did manage to parachute weapons to the insurgents.) In reply to a request from W. Averell Harriman, the U.S. Ambassador to the U.S.S.R., the Kremlin coldly replied: "The Soviet government does not wish to associate itself directly or indirectly with the adventure in Warsaw."

For General Bór and the Home Army command, Stalin's indifference meant the end of a dream.

By then, Bach-Zelewski had been heavily reinforced and was ready to put down the Poles once and for all. He began on August 12 with an infantry attack, backed by heavy shelling and dive bombing, against the Old Town. Day after day, the bombs and shells kept falling. Steadily the Poles gave ground. No rain had fallen in 10 days; drinking water was scarce and dust was everywhere. The sun was so hot it softened asphalt pavement. The dead, unburied or in shallow graves, decomposed quickly, filling the air with a stench and attracting billions of fat, greenish-blue flies. With the flies came an epidemic of dysentery.

On August 19, the Germans launched their heaviest assault so far against the Old Town—a whirlwind of dive bombers and artillery followed by infantry sweeps. Later, Bór would recall the devastation: "The ancient houses had collapsed across streets, forming gigantic barriers of hundreds of thousands of bricks. Nothing but ruins now remained." On August 22, Bór and his headquarters withdrew from the Old Town, taking the stinking route through the sewers to the Inner City, where they continued to hold out.

In Moscow, Josef Stalin perceived that the uprising was nearing its end, and for reasons known only to himself, he now began handing out tidbits of encouragement—enough to persuade Bór to break off surrender discussions that had started with the Germans.

"The Germans will pay dearly for the ruins and blood of Warsaw," Radio Moscow proclaimed to the Poles. "Help is coming. Victory is near. Keep fighting."

In one gesture, a few antiquated Soviet PO-2 biplanes flew low over the city, dropping supplies. In another, Stalin informed the British and Americans that they could, after all, use Ukrainian air bases for supply flights to Warsaw. On September 18, the U.S. availed itself of the offer, with 110 B-17s dropping 1,284 containers on Warsaw. Unfortunately, all but 288 fell into German hands—whereupon Stalin withdrew permission for use of his bases.

As Warsaw's hopes dwindled, Bór sent a radio message to Rokossovsky's headquarters, saying the insurgents would hold out if Soviet ground forces came to their aid soon—very soon. Rokossovsky's station acknowledged the message but did not answer. In London, Mikolajczyk asked the Soviet ambassador to send Bór's message to Stalin; he

Fifty miles from Berlin, Soviet soldiers wrestle a 76.2mm field gun across the Oder River late in January of 1945. In the race to the Oder, Marshal Ivan Konev's First Ukrainian Front managed to beat Marshal Georgy Zhukov's First Belorussian Front by nine days.

refused. Churchill then sent it himself. There was no answer.

Thus, at 9:00 p.m. on October 2, Polish delegates signed a document of surrender. Bach-Zelewski then asked them to join him in a moment of silence for the dead of both sides. The Poles had many to remember: about 180,000 civilians and 18,000 Home Army fighters. The Germans had lost 10,000 dead, 7,000 missing, and another 9,000 wounded.

And now, in accordance with the wishes of Hitler and Himmler, the systematic destruction of Warsaw began. When Soviet troops finally entered the Polish capital in mid-January, 1945, Warsaw was dead.

On January 16, the day before the Russians took Warsaw, Hitler was once again looking for scapegoats among the "weaklings and traitors" who had failed him. He fired the commander of Army Group A and ordered General Ferdinand Schörner to take over. But with the Eastern Front rapidly crumbling, there was little that could be done to stem the Soviet tide. The war was coming home to Germany at express-train speed.

On January 12, Stalin had launched the greatest Soviet offensive of the war. From five separate bridgeheads on the Vistula, three Russian armies pushed off north to Danzig, west to the Oder River and south to Cracow and Breslau. A fourth army drove hard for East Prussia in the north.

The roads leading to the Oder River and Germany were soon filled with refugees. For the first time, the pitiful columns that had long been familiar on the Eastern Front were composed of German civilians.

On January 24, armored columns of Konev's First Ukrainian Front reached Breslau. A day later, the main force

of Zhukov's First Belorussian Front reached Poznań, 140 miles east of Berlin. From there to the German capital, the road was wide open. By the first day of February, troops and tanks of the two fronts had reached the Oder and were preparing to cross it. The Germans were thoroughly demoralized. As Stalin flew south for his fateful meeting with Roosevelt and Churchill at Yalta in the Crimea, Berlin was virtually in Stalin's pocket.

On February 3, 1945, Franklin D. Roosevelt's C-54 transport, the Sacred Cow, landed at Saki airfield on the Crimean Peninsula. Spectators were shocked by the appearance of the President, who had been under treatment for an enlarged heart and high blood pressure. Lord Moran, Churchill's physician, described him as "old and thin and drawn." Even so, Roosevelt had traveled halfway around the world because Stalin had refused to leave the Soviet Union, citing his need, as supreme commander, to remain on Russian soil.

Roosevelt's ultimate destination was Yalta, 80 miles away on the Black Sea coast, known as the Russian Riviera. There, he would meet with Stalin and Churchill in a final conference. It would be his last chance to resolve the problems discussed at Teheran in 1943: Soviet entry into the war against Japan; the postwar borders and government of Poland; the political freedom of other liberated peoples of Eastern Europe; the postwar treatment of Germany; and the number of seats that the Soviet Union would receive in the United Nations.

Driven to Yalta, Roosevelt was ensconced in the Livadia Palace, formerly Czar Nicholas II's summer retreat, while Churchill was quartered five miles away in the Vorontsov Villa. Stalin reached Yalta on the morning of February 4,

with every reason to feel in high fettle. In January, his armies had finally taken Warsaw, then surged across Poland to the Oder River, on whose banks they now stood, a mere 40 miles from Berlin. That night and during the remaining seven days of the conference, the Big Three debated momentous issues of war and peace.

An early topic for discussion was Poland. It was suggested that Stalin contact the Soviet-supported Lublin Poles and arrange for them to meet with representatives of London's democratic faction led by Stanislaw Mikolajczyk. In response, Stalin protested that the "émigré" Poles—as he derisively called them—had collaborated with the Germans. The next day, he said he had tried to telephone the Lublin Poles but could not reach them. Then he abruptly changed the subject to something that would please his allies: the United Nations charter.

Previously, the Soviet Union had insisted that it receive 16 votes in the United Nations—one for each "free and independent" Soviet republic. Now, Stalin dropped that demand; instead, votes for the Soviet Union, the Ukraine and Belorussia would be sufficient. Later, Ambassador Harriman recalled: "We were greatly relieved that he reduced his demand from 16 to two extra votes."

The Americans were also relieved when Stalin agreed to go to war with Japan within two or three months of the German surrender. But Stalin's price was high: he said that unless the Soviet Union was given the Kurile Islands and the lower half of Sakhalin Island (just north of Japan), along with leases on the ports of Dairen and Port Arthur and permission to run railroads in Manchuria, he would not be able to make the Russian people understand why they were fighting Japan. In an agreement not made public for one year—nor revealed to the Chinese leader, Chiang Kai-shek—Stalin got most of what he wanted.

To Churchill, the Far East seemed "remote and secondary." He was far more concerned with preventing the Soviet Union from dominating postwar Europe. Stalin wanted to dismember Germany into helpless principalities controlled by the Big Three. Churchill insisted that France's participation would be vital in the inevitably long Allied occupation of Germany. Who knew, he asked, how long the United States would keep its forces in Europe? Britain needed a strong France in order to help bear any future attack by a resurgent Germany.

Roosevelt said that an American presence in Europe of two years or so would be sufficient. Suddenly, recalled H. Freeman Matthews of the American delegation, "I saw Stalin's eyes light up. Nothing could have pleased him more." Stalin gave in on the issue of French participation.

On the point of German reparations, however, Stalin was adamant and grim. According to Roosevelt's top adviser, Harry Hopkins, "Stalin rose and gripped the back of his chair with such force that his brown hands went white at the knuckles. He spat out his words as if they burnt his mouth."

Stalin wanted Germany to hand over $20 billion worth of goods, factories and equipment, with half of it going to the Soviet Union. Churchill objected that the figure was too high; he feared that the burden would leave Germany unable to feed itself and thus make it a ward of the Allies. A protocol was signed stating that $20 billion was only "a basis for discussion," although Stalin would later claim that Roosevelt and Churchill had agreed to that amount.

When Poland again raised its persistent head, Soviet Foreign Minister Molotov read a formal proposal that the country's border with Germany be moved westward to the

Winston Churchill, Franklin D. Roosevelt and Josef Stalin sit for formal photographs in the ornate courtyard of the Livadia Palace following the final meeting of the Yalta Conference. At Churchill's right, the British Minister for War Transport, Lord Frederick J. Leathers, gazes skyward in apparent dismay at the tedious picture-taking session. Behind the Big Three stand (from left) British Foreign Secretary Sir Anthony Eden, U.S. Secretary of State Edward R. Stettinius, British Foreign Undersecretary Sir Alexander Cadogan, Soviet Foreign Minister Vyacheslav M. Molotov and W. Averell Harriman, American Ambassador to the Soviet Union.

line of the Oder and western Neisse River—deep in German territory—to make up for land to be given the Soviet Union in eastern Poland.

"It would be a pity," Churchill said, "to stuff the Polish goose so full of German food that it died of indigestion." Such a shift in the border, he argued, would require moving 6 million Germans from Silesia and East Prussia alone. Stalin dismissed that point by insisting that most Germans had already fled the areas in question.

Eventually, Churchill and Roosevelt agreed not to oppose the Soviet boundary proposals, and to establish a "Polish Provisional Government of National Unity" to embrace all Polish factions. When Admiral William D. Leahy, Roosevelt's chief military aide, read the document, he protested: "Mr. President, this is so elastic the Russians can stretch it all the way from Yalta to Washington without even technically breaking it." Roosevelt agreed, but said it was "the best I could do for Poland at this time."

Future events would of course prove Leahy right.

Amid a barrage of last minute amendments and changes in the Yalta documents, the conference ended on February 11 when the three leaders signed the final communiqué over lunch in the Czar's billiard room at the Livadia Palace.

Let Stalin sign first, suggested Roosevelt, "He has been such a wonderful host." Churchill jokingly nominated himself to sign first because he was the oldest of the Big Three. Stalin agreed, saying that if he signed first, everyone would think he had run the conference.

In fact, he had.

15

Standing on the bridge of the cruiser *Nashville*, General Douglas MacArthur surveyed the scene before him. Earlier that morning, October 20, 1944, the men of the U.S. Sixth Army stormed virtually unopposed onto the east coast of Leyte in the central Philippines. MacArthur donned a fresh, starched uniform, pocketed a revolver and boarded a landing craft for a trip to the beachhead.

The vessel grounded in shallow water about 35 yards from the shore and a beachmaster, too busy to remedy the problem, snapped, "Let 'em walk." MacArthur and his party waded through knee-deep water. Arriving on dry land, the general made a brief speech, his voice quavering with emotion. "People of the Philippines," he began, "I have returned."

Behind that moment lay two and a half years of bitter frustration, of heated disputes about strategy, of exhausting campaigns in suffocating jungles. Immediately ahead—and necessary if MacArthur was to remain in his beloved Philippines—loomed the greatest battle in the history of naval warfare. No fewer than 282 warships would be involved in active combat, and the enormous conflict would be fought out in an expanse of water larger than France.

In part, the Battle for Leyte Gulf would be the result of misconceptions on both the American and Japanese sides. In September, after his Third Fleet had launched a series of air raids against the Philippines, Admiral William F. "Bull" Halsey had become convinced that Leyte was "wide open." Halsey proposed that it be substituted for Mindanao as the first American objective. With MacArthur's enthusiastic support, the Joint Chiefs of Staff agreed.

In fact, the Japanese in the Philippines were not quite as helpless as Halsey thought. Their lack of response to Halsey's raids had been part of a scheme called the *Sho-Go* (Victory Operation), which called for all Japanese forces to husband their resources for a single decisive battle. But the Japanese too had miscalculated: convinced that the Americans were actually aiming at Luzon, they had set General Tomoyuki Yamashita's Fourteenth Area Army to building impregnable inland defenses on the Philippines' largest island. Meanwhile, Leyte and the archipelago's other islands were left to fend largely for themselves.

Not until October 18—after an American invasion fleet had already appeared in Leyte Gulf—did Japanese Imperial Headquarters finally decide that *Sho-Go*'s climactic battle would be fought on Leyte instead of Luzon. On that day, Admiral Soemu Toyoda, commander of Japan's Combined Fleet, made a decision that he said was "as difficult as swallowing molten iron." He committed the Japanese Navy to an effort at Leyte that offered the last real chance to stem the enemy tide—or be obliterated in the process. Toyoda knew

When U.S. forces in the Philippines surrendered in May 1942, General Douglas MacArthur's pledge to return seemed at best a valiant dream. "The road back," MacArthur himself acknowledged, "looked long and difficult." But within two and a half years the Americans were ready to return. By September 1944, the great forces of MacArthur and Admiral Chester Nimitz were poised only 300 miles from the southernmost Philippine island, Mindanao.

The Philippine archipelago—more than 7,000 islands stretching 1,000 miles south from Luzon to Mindanao—became the most important land and sea battleground in the Pacific war because of its strategic location off the coast of Southeast Asia (inset). Japan needed to keep the islands to protect the shipping lanes to their sources of raw materials in the Dutch East Indies and Southeast Asia. The Allies wanted to retake the Philippines to establish air bases and staging areas for an invasion of Japan.

THE PACIFIC REGAINED

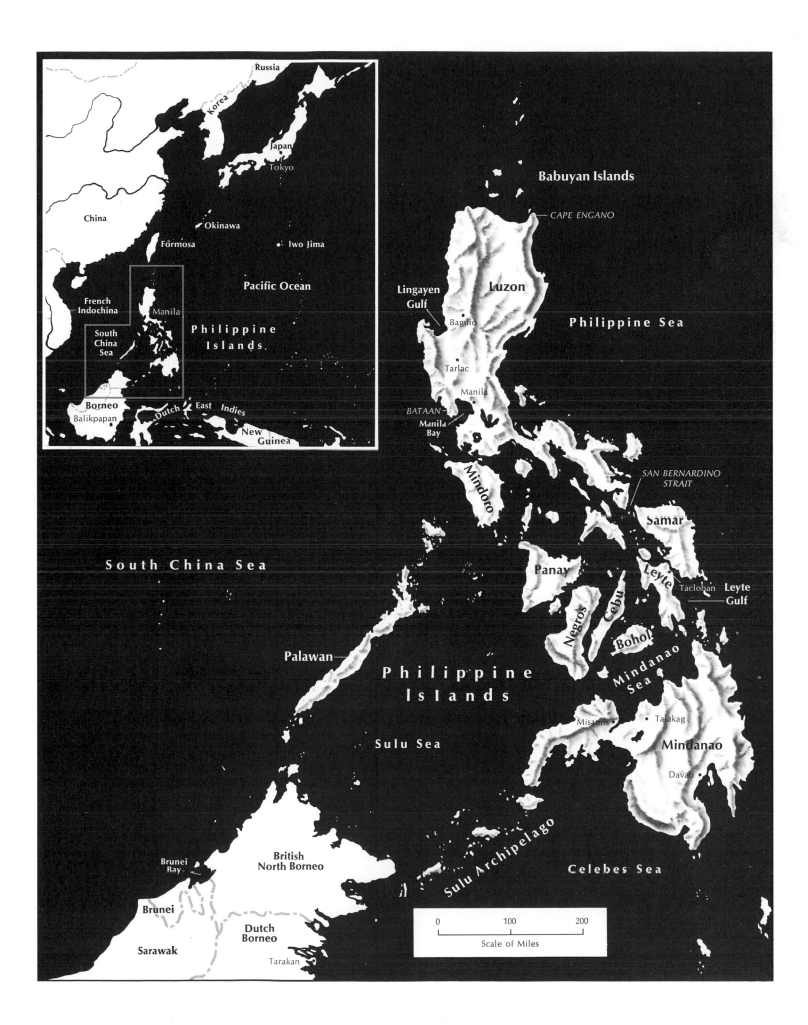

Russia

Korea

Japan
Tokyo

China

Okinawa

Formosa
Iwo Jima

Pacific Ocean

French Indochina

Manila

Philippine Islands.

South China Sea

Borneo
Balikpapan

Dutch East Indies

New **Guinea**

Babuyan Islands

CAPE ENGANO

Luzon

Lingayen Gulf

Baguio

Philippine Sea

Tarlac

Manila

BATAAN

Manila Bay

Mindoro

SAN BERNARDINO STRAIT

Samar

South China Sea

Panay

Leyte

Tacloban

Leyte Gulf

Palawan

Negros

Cebu

Bohol

Philippine Islands

Mindanao Sea

Misamis

Talakag

Sulu Sea

Mindanao

Davao

Sulu Archipelago

Celebes Sea

Brunei Bay

British North Borneo

Brunei

Dutch Borneo

Sarawak

Tarakan

0   100   200

Scale of Miles

that even if his plan was successful, it would cost him half of his warships.

According to the Japanese plan, Vice Admiral Takeo Kurita's powerful Center Force, which included the mammoth battleships *Musashi* and *Yamato*, would be the upper arm of a pincers movement that Toyoda hoped would wipe out the American invasion force. Kurita would approach the Philippines from Singapore via Borneo, steam eastward through San Bernardino Strait between Luzon and Samar and emerge in the open sea. Then Kurita would come roaring down from the north upon the Americans in Leyte Gulf at dawn on October 25.

At the same time, Vice Admiral Shoji Nishimura's Southern Force would act as the lower prong of the pincers. It would transit Surigao Strait and enter Leyte Gulf from the south with seven older, slower warships.

A third segment of the divided fleet, Vice Admiral Jisaburo Ozawa's Northern Force, was weak but indispensable to Toyoda's hopes. It consisted of two battleships, 11 light cruisers and destroyers—and four aircraft carriers with a total of only 116 planes aboard. Ozawa's was a sacrificial mission: he would act as a decoy, clearing the way for Kurita and Nishimura to strike unopposed by luring Halsey's Third Fleet carriers northward away from Leyte Gulf.

The Japanese plan began to unravel almost at once. At 1:16 a.m. on October 23, the U.S. submarine *Darter* was patrolling in the western Philippines when its radar screen was suddenly filled with a mass of blips—Kurita's Center Force, whose whereabouts had been a worrisome mystery for four days. Joined by a nearby submarine, the *Dace*, the *Darter* pumped four torpedoes into a cruiser, and saw it go down. The *Dace* sank a second cruiser and the *Darter* subsequently crippled a third. Later, the *Darter* ran aground on a reef and its men were taken aboard the *Dace*.

But the *Darter* had radioed the Third Fleet of the Japanese presence, and next morning a search plane spotted the Center Force steaming through the Sibuyan Sea.

Meanwhile, the Third Fleet itself had been spotted and a force of 200 Japanese planes based on Luzon and Formosa rose to attack. But the radar-equipped Americans were ready; Hellcat fighters shot down about 70 of the enemy and scattered the rest—all but one "Judy" bomber that slipped through to plant a 550-pound bomb deep in the hangar deck of the light carrier *Princeton*. Exploding among the packed torpedo planes, the bomb turned the carrier into an inferno; 108 men died and another 420 were wounded before the flaming hulk of the *Princeton* was finally scuttled.

But the sinking of the *Princeton* had cost the Japanese their air cover for Kurita's Center Force. And throughout the day, American carrier planes hammered the Japanese fleet at will. The first waves damaged the cruiser *Myoko*, which also was forced to retire, and damaged the huge *Yamato* (which survived the battle, only to be sunk by other American planes six months later). But for *Yamato*'s sister, the 68,000-ton *Musashi*, death was drawing near.

The *Musashi*'s torment began shortly after 10:30 a.m., when it took hits from a bomb and a torpedo. Protected by its 16-inch armor plate, the *Musashi* shuddered but steamed on. By then, it was under constant, merciless attack. During the next five hours, the *Musashi* suffered direct hits from 17 torpedoes and 19 bombs. After one furious onslaught, an American officer wrote, "The big battlewagon was momentarily lost under the towering fountains of near misses and torpedo hits, soaring puffs of white smoke from bomb hits and streaming black smoke from resultant fires. Then the long, dark bow slid out of the caldron, slowing. *Musashi* stopped, down by the head and burning."

Still, several more massed attacks were required before the *Musashi* began to go down. Finally, a Japanese sailor played the national anthem on a trumpet. To save the dying battleship's flag, sailors lowered it and wrapped it around the waist of a strong swimmer. Only then did the ship's executive officer order: "All crew abandon ship."

Swimming away from the *Musashi*, one sailor looked back and saw its stern pointing straight up, silhouetted against the setting sun. Then the great warship plunged beneath the sea with loud suckings and underwater explosions. Destroyers later picked up survivors, but 1,023 men and officers—almost half the crew—had perished.

With the *Musashi* gone and the *Yamato* and two other battleships damaged, Admiral Kurita estimated that enemy planes could make as many as three more strikes on his slow-moving fleet before sunset. He prudently reversed course in order to delay his transit of the dangerous San Bernardino Strait until after dark.

Kurita's maneuver threw the Japanese timetable hopelessly out of kilter. Yet though Admiral Nishimura, commanding the southern arm of the Japanese pincer, knew that Kurita would be unable to keep his scheduled dawn rendezvous in Leyte Gulf, he continued toward Surigao Strait, relishing the prospect of engaging the Seventh Fleet in a night battle.

Awaiting him in the darkness was Vice Admiral Jesse B. Oldendorf, commanding the warships of Vice Admiral Thomas C. Kinkaid's Seventh Fleet, assigned to support the Leyte landings. Five of Oldendorf's six battleships were relics of Pearl Harbor, where they had been raised or reconditioned and then returned to service. Nishimura's two battleships were of World War I vintage and had spent most of the present war on training assignments. Nishimura also had one cruiser and four elderly destroyers, while Oldendorf

deployed eight cruisers, plus 28 destroyers and 39 PT boats.

As Nishimura's force paraded single file into the southern approaches of Surigao Strait, it was ambushed by American PT boats that launched their torpedoes but did little damage. They did, however, provide Oldendorf with precise information about Nishimura's location, course and speed.

A few miles farther north, the Japanese entered a deadly gauntlet of American and Australian destroyers that raced back and forth on both sides of Nishimura's column, firing torpedoes as they went and then turning and speeding away before the Japanese guns could find them. The battleship *Fuso* blew up; Nishimura's flagship, the battleship *Yamashiro*, took hits, and two of his destroyers were sunk.

Still, Nishimura came on and, as he approached, Oldendorf's battleships and cruisers steamed directly across his path, thereby crossing his "T"—a classic maneuver in which one fleet in battle-line formation cuts in front of an enemy column. Crossing the "T" had the advantage of allowing every ship in Oldendorf's battle line to fire broadsides at Nishimura's ships, which could use only their forward guns to return the fire. "We were in an ideal position," said Oldendorf's flagship commander, "a position dreamed of, studied and plotted in War College maneuvers and never hoped to be attained."

Shortly before 4 a.m., as the lead Japanese ship closed the range to 15,600 yards, Oldendorf gave the order to fire. To the commander of a U.S. destroyer squadron, the opening barrage was "the most beautiful sight I have ever witnessed. The arched line of tracers in the darkness looked like a continual stream of lighted railroad cars going over a hill." Within 18 minutes, American battleships fired 270 shells from their 14- and 16-inch guns; cruisers fired more than 4,000 rounds of 6- and 8-inch shells. When the din died away, all but one of Nishimura's remaining ships, a destroyer, had been crippled or sunk. No U.S. vessels were lost.

As the battle was ending, Vice Admiral Kiyohide, Admiral Shima's rear-guard section of the Southern Force, had passed into Surigao Strait. To his dismay, Shima found only dense smoke and the burning hulks of Japanese ships. He retreated before Oldendorf's guns could get him too; his only contribution to the Japanese effort was to inform Kurita that there would be no Southern Force to meet him in Leyte Gulf.

But if the delay of Admiral Kurita's Center Force had been lethal to Nishimura, it would almost prove fatal to the Americans as well. Upon learning that Kurita had withdrawn, Admiral Halsey had assumed that the Center Force was gone for good, and he turned his attention to what he thought was bigger game.

Throughout the day of October 24, Halsey's planes had searched for the carriers he felt sure must be part of the mas-

The "invincible" Musashi (foreground)—one of the world's two largest battleships—succumbs to U.S. air attacks in the Sibuyan Sea during the critical Battle of Leyte Gulf on October 23-25, 1944.

sive Japanese operation. Finally, at 5:30 p.m., a scout spotted Admiral Ozawa's decoy carriers 300 miles north of San Bernardino Strait. Now, Halsey reckoned, he had "all the pieces of the puzzle." He had no way of knowing that Ozawa's four carriers had only a few planes left on board.

At that point, Halsey had three options: he could keep the Third Fleet where it was; he could send his carriers after Ozawa and leave his battleships to guard San Bernardino Strait; or he could rush north with his entire Third Fleet to destroy the Japanese carriers. Nothing if not aggressive, Bull Halsey chose the all-out attack. He had swallowed the bait.

After that, mistake compounded mistake. Even before discovering Ozawa's whereabouts, Halsey had sent an alert to Third Fleet commanders to be ready "when directed by me" to form a strong, fast detachment of warships, to be designated Task Force 34, which would confront Kurita if he emerged from San Bernardino Strait. But then, after deciding that Kurita was no longer a threat, Halsey had taken the ships designated for Task Force 34 along on the chase after Admiral Ozawa.

As it happened, the Seventh Fleet's Admiral Kinkaid had received a copy of Halsey's alert—but it was missing the crucial triggering stipulation. Kinkaid therefore assumed that Task Force 34 had in fact been formed and that it was guarding San Bernardino Strait. Thus, the penalty of a command divided between Admiral Chester Nimitz' Third Fleet, and the Seventh Fleet, part of "MacArthur's Navy," was that San Bernardino Strait was unguarded and no one knew it.

And Kurita was on the way. Having turned his battered but still-potent Center Force around again, he had taken advantage of the darkness to negotiate San Bernardino Strait and veer southward along the coast of Samar Island, heading for Leyte Gulf. At daybreak on October 25, lookouts sighted on the horizon what Kurita judged to be "a gigantic enemy task force, including six or seven carriers accompanied by many cruisers and destroyers."

In fact, what the Japanese had spotted was a puny Seventh Fleet force that had inadvertently got in Kurita's way. Assigned to provide air cover and antisubmarine patrol for the Leyte landings was Taffy 3, comprised of three destroyers, four destroyer escorts and six escort carriers under Rear Admiral Clifton A. F. Sprague. The so-called "jeep" carriers were actually merchant ships fitted with short flight decks. They carried about 28 planes each, could attain a top speed of only 17 knots (half the pace of Kurita's battleships), and were equipped with only 29 light guns that could not even dent the Japanese battlewagons.

Sprague's first warning came at 6:45 a.m., when an Avenger torpedo bomber pilot on routine patrol radioed that a large Japanese force was approaching at high speed. Disbelieving at first, Sprague was convinced only when the enemy warships, with their distinctive pagoda-shaped masts, hove onto the northern horizon.

Then Sprague wasted no time. He swung his carriers east into the wind and launched all his operational planes. He instructed his ships to throw up smoke screens, alerted his destroyers and radioed for help.

Within minutes, the 18-inch guns of the immense Yamato and the 14-inch guns of the other Japanese battleships opened fire. To Sprague, "it did not appear that any of our ships could survive another five minutes." Then Providence intervened: a rain squall appeared, and Taffy 3 ducked into it. For the next three hours, Sprague eased south, playing a deadly game of hide-and-seek, while his planes stayed aloft almost continually. Even after their scant supply of bombs and torpedoes was gone, pilots made dry runs to trick the Japanese into dodging off course. One airman made 20 attacks—half of them without any ammunition.

Under the shaky cover of the planes, Sprague's destroyers and escorts recklessly shielded the carriers. The destroyer Johnston, for example, was in the thick of the fight all morning. Struck by three 14-inch shells ("It was like a puppy being smacked by a truck," one officer said later), the Johnston nonetheless dashed in to draw fire from five Japanese warships that were bearing down on a crippled American carrier, the Gambier Bay. Even so, the Gambier Bay was sunk, and the Johnston suffered more hits.

Still, the Johnston returned to the fray—until, according to its action report, at "about 0930 we found ourselves with two cruisers dead ahead of us, several Jap destroyers on our starboard quarters and two cruisers on our port quarter . . . An avalanche of shells knocked out our lone remaining engine." As the Johnston went dead in the water, its skipper, Commander Ernest Evans, gave the order to abandon ship. Still under fire, the destroyer went down, taking with it 186 of its 327 men, including Evans.

Admiral William F. "Bull" Halsey, commander of the U.S. Third Fleet during the Battle of Leyte Gulf, won the admiration and affection of his men for his aggressive leadership, considerate treatment and plain good humor. One of his sailors voiced the general opinion to a fellow seaman on board the admiral's flagship: "I'd go through hell for that old son-of-a-bitch." Halsey, unseen but close enough to hear the remark, confronted the sailor and said with mock severity, "Young man, I'm not so old!"

American LSTs moored to hastily built jetties near the Leyte port of Tacloban spew ashore tons of equipment needed for the construction of the airfield at rear. So supplied, Army engineers laid a 2,500-foot runway of steel matting in just two days.

While Taffy 3 was fighting its lonely battle, Halsey was attacking Ozawa's decoy force 300 miles to the north. By midmorning, one Japanese carrier had been sunk and three more damaged. Throughout the morning, Halsey had been receiving frantic messages from Kinkaid, requesting help for Taffy 3, and at 10 a.m., he was handed a remarkable radiogram from Admiral Nimitz. Like Kinkaid, Nimitz had been deceived by Halsey's original contingency order for the formation of Task Force 34. Now, Nimitz's message read: "WHERE IS RPT WHERE IS TASK FORCE 34 RR THE WORLD WONDERS."

In fact, the phrase "the world wonders" was no more than the nonsense padding routinely added to secret dispatches to befuddle enemy cryptographers, but Halsey took it as a sarcastic comment on his decision to steam north. According to one of his officers, "the 'Old Man' was fit to be tied." The message was, however, sufficient to cause Halsey to turn his back "on the opportunity I had dreamed of since my days as a cadet." Leaving Admiral A. Pete Marc Mitscher with two carrier groups to finish off Ozawa's three remaining carriers, Halsey swung Vice Admiral Willis Lee's fast battleships—activated, at last, as Task Force 34—toward the south in a race against time.

As Task Force 34 sped south, the battle between Kurita and Taffy 3 took an incredible turn: although the Japanese clearly held the upper hand, they still did not know it. Kurita's ships suddenly began to retire the way they had come. As Kurita later explained, "I intercepted a message that help would come to the American force in two hours."

The sight of Kurita's departing force left Sprague dumbfounded. "I could not believe my eyes," he said afterward. "It took a whole series of reports from circling planes to convince me. I could not get the fact to soak into my battle-numbed brain." The reaction of his chief quartermaster epitomized the spirit of Taffy 3. "My God, Admiral," he exclaimed, "they're going to get away."

The Battle for Leyte Gulf was a tremendous victory for the U.S. Navy. The Americans had lost one light carrier, two escort carriers, two destroyers, one destroyer escort and fewer than 3,000 men. The Japanese had lost four of their remaining carriers, three battleships, six heavy cruisers, four light cruisers, nine destroyers and about 10,000 lives. The Japanese Navy was knocked out of the War for good. The U.S. now controlled the waters around the Philippines and MacArthur's Sixth Army was ashore on Leyte.

While the Navy was grappling at sea, troops of Lieut. General Walter Krueger's Sixth Army, which possessed six divisions totaling 200,000 men, were taking their first major objectives on Leyte: Tacloban, the provincial capital, and Dulag, about 14 miles to the south. With airfields captured at Tacloban and Dulag, along with five other airstrips in the Leyte Valley, Krueger meant to establish not only installations for fighter planes but bases from which heavy bombers would be able to strike anywhere in the Philippines and even range as far as Formosa and the China coast.

Krueger's ambitious timetable was, however, soon set back by an abnormally heavy monsoon that dumped 35 inches of rainfall onto the valley and transformed the planned airfield complex into a quagmire. Until the bases became operational, MacArthur's Leyte forces would lack control of the air.

That situation was made to order for General Yamashita, the Japanese commander in the Philippines. With his transports relatively safe from the skies, Yamashita began pouring in reinforcements. Eventually, he would add 45,000 to the original 12,500 soldiers of his Leyte command. The influx of enemy troops, the scarcity of U.S. planes, the soggy Leyte terrain—all would combine to make the campaign longer and more bloody than anyone had anticipated.

Nonetheless, the Americans continued to press ahead. On Krueger's left flank, elements of the XXIV Corps moved

south along the coast, then crossed the island and reached the west coast. From the beachhead, other units of the XXIV Corps pushed inland to the spine of rugged mountains that ran down Leyte's center. In the northern sector, however, Major General Franklin C. Sibert's X Corps ran into trouble.

There, the fishing port of Carigara loomed as a tactical keystone. It commanded a road that looped around the central mountains, swinging southwest to the main Japanese base at Ormoc, and southeast to the main American base at Tacloban. Whether for defensive or offensive purposes, the army that held Carigara and its surrounding hills would have the upper hand.

To coordinate with the overland attack of Sibert's 24th Division from the south, part of the 1st Cavalry Division made an amphibious landing near Carigara. But as its patrols probed toward the town, they met with increasing opposition, and Sibert cautiously ordered a halt until the full weight of the X Corps Artillery could join the 24th Division. The delay would prove costly.

At this point, local Japanese commanders evacuated Carigara and set up a new line of defense on the heights to the southwest. When troops of the 24th Division entered Carigara on November 2, they found, according to an American combat reporter, that "the streets were empty and the houses were silent hulks and there was only the distant boom of the surf."

Next day, the unsuspecting advance guard of the Japanese 1st Division, which had been rushed to reinforce Carigara, approached the town unaware that it was already occupied by the Americans. Upon suddenly coming face to face with a battalion of the American 24th Division, the Japanese coolly made a fighting withdrawal to a point near the town of Limon where the narrow, winding road to Ormoc ran through a series of steep ridges. There they dug in.

In so doing, they chose a formidable natural defense line of razor-back spurs that branched off in every direction, commanding almost every approach. Tall, knife-edged cogon grass covered the slopes, and trees filled the valleys and ravines. To the Americans who fought there, the heights would become known as "Breakneck Ridge," and the struggle for it would be the toughest clash of the Leyte campaign.

Amid the rocks and thickets of Breakneck Ridge, the Japanese fought from foxholes known as *takotsubo*—octopus traps. They were about four and a half feet deep, and each had a man-sized cavity scooped out of its side. Huddled there, a Japanese was safe from a shell bursting directly above or from a passing American spraying the hole with automatic rifle fire.

As the struggle for Breakneck Ridge swirled in and around the spurs and ravines, both sides fought savagely, frequently hand to hand. Often, it was impossible to tell where the front was or who held which height. Even when tanks found it possible to move on slopes made slick and muddy by constant rain, riflemen had to defend them against Japanese darting from foxholes to slap mines on the treads.

Not until November 12 did the 21st Infantry of the 24th Division finally take the crest of Breakneck Ridge; nearly two more weeks of battle were required to drive the enemy from the slopes beyond. By then, the Americans had suffered about 1,500 casualties, killed an estimated 5,250 Japanese—and advanced a mere two miles.

During the brawl for Breakneck Ridge, General Krueger had suggested that landing a division near Ormoc, the port of entry for all Japanese supplies and reinforcements, would wrap up the Leyte campaign in short order. Although MacArthur at first demurred because he could not spare the shipping, the Ormoc operation was finally scheduled for December 7, when Major General Andrew D. Bruce's 77th Division put ashore about four miles south of the town. The Japanese had dispersed their strength in the area: part of their 26th Division, for instance, was away on an abortive effort to seize U.S. air bases at Burauen. Thus, against weak opposition, Bruce's troops started toward Ormoc.

On the morning of December 10, after a 15-minute artillery bombardment fired by every gun in the division, amphibious tanks rumbled into Ormoc. At the same time, landing craft with rocket launchers swept into Ormoc Bay, and their high-explosive missiles smashed the town's center.

Ormoc, the wellspring of enemy resistance, was finally in American hands, and although several weeks of bloody mopping-up remained, the Leyte campaign deemed "decisive" by the Japanese was over to all intents and purposes. The Japanese toll was 60,000 lives, while American casualties came to 3,500 killed and 12,000 wounded.

MacArthur was later to say that the Leyte battle was "perhaps the greatest defeat in the military annals of the Japanese Army." But by no means did the fall of Leyte mean the end of fighting in the Philippines. Luzon lay ahead.

For Luzon, MacArthur had a plan that generally resembled the one successfully used by the Japanese three years earlier. It called for an initial landing at the best site: Lingayen Gulf, halfway up the island's west coast. From there, the Americans would drive 110 miles south to their primary objective, the capital city of Manila, over the best route available: Luzon's broad, flat central plain. It all seemed textbook perfect—but General Yamashita had other ideas.

A hardened realist, Yamashita held little hope for victory on Luzon. By mid-December, Japan had only 200 planes left on the island, and a feeble naval force of about 180 one-

man suicide motor boats. Though Yamashita's army numbered more than 275,000 soldiers, they were poorly equipped and hastily organized. Yet despite the overwhelming odds, Yamashita could—and would—fight a delaying action aimed at preventing the Allies from using Luzon as a base to attack Japan.

To that end, Yamashita ordered most of his troops to withdraw from coastal areas into Luzon's rugged interior. Yamashita's 152,000-man main force prepared defensive strongholds in the mountainous north. A second group of 80,000 was sent to hold southern Luzon and the hills east of Manila controlling the city's water supply. A third force of 30,000 was deployed in mountains west of the plain, overlooking the giant Clark Field complex.

In early January 1945, an 850-ship invasion fleet carrying troops of General Krueger's Sixth Army set forth from Leyte Gulf on the six-day journey to Lingayen Gulf. Sailing through Surigao Strait, the fleet passed Mindanao and headed north along the west coasts of Panay, Mindoro and Luzon. All along the way, it ran a murderous gauntlet of attacks from Japan's newest and most desperate weapon—Kamikaze suicide pilots who crash-dived their bomb-bearing planes onto Allied ships.

The Kamikaze assaults came to a crescendo on January 6, just as the invasion fleet entered Lingayen Gulf. One flaming Kamikaze plowed into the bridge of the battleship *New Mexico*, killing 29 men, including its captain. Thirty-nine men died and the cruiser *Louisville* was knocked out of action by a plane that exploded on its bridge. In the worst day for the U.S. Navy in more than two years, 11 vessels were badly damaged, a minesweeper was sunk, a cruiser crippled and hundreds of sailors killed.

But the fleet steamed on, and at 9:30 a.m. on January 9, 1945, nearly 70,000 Sixth Army soldiers began streaming ashore. Because of Yamashita's strategy, nearly all of the Japanese were gone, and the Americans quickly secured a 20-mile-long beachhead. The town of San Fabian was easily taken, and four frightened Japanese defenders won dubious fame by trying to escape dressed as women.

For the men of Major General Oscar Griswold's XIV Corps, the southward march resembled a holiday parade: they were cheered from town to town by Filipino civilians who regaled them with traditional Philippines feasts of chicken, bananas, coconuts and rice cakes. In a week, the XIV Corps pushed inland 25 miles, its pace hampered only by the fact that Krueger did not wit it to open a potentially vulnerable gap between itself and Major General Innis Swift's I Corps, on the eastern edge of the plain. There, Swift had met with stiff resistance from the forward line of Yamashita's mountain stronghold.

But Douglas MacArthur was impatient, and he was accepting no excuses. By January 17 he was so exasperated that he issued a formal order to Krueger to get his people moving on to Manila. MacArthur wanted the capital captured as quickly as possible, to obtain its port facilities and also to free the Allied prisoners there; they were known to be starving and were in danger of Japanese reprisals. At that, Griswold's troops stepped up their southward pace, but on January 23 they ran into forward elements of the 30,000-man force that Yamashita had left to hold Clark Field and the Zambales Mountains to the west.

The defenders threw everything they had into the fight for Clark Field. "The Japanese were using their antiaircraft guns as antipersonnel," recalled one GI, "and that's how I got wounded." Yet after a week of hard fighting, the superior American firepower prevailed. By January 30, Clark Field and the ridge line to the north were clear of Japanese.

Griswold soon put his troops back on the road to Manila, but MacArthur was still dissatisfied. He drove south in his jeep to check on the progress of a regiment that Griswold had sent ahead to take Calumpit, a vital river crossing 25 miles northwest of Manila. After the visit, he sent Sixth Army

The invasion of Luzon, the strategic prize of the Philippines, was a multiple-assault offensive aimed at liberating Manila and its superb harbor. Between January 9 and February 16, 1945, U.S. forces launched separate assaults on Luzon and nearby Corregidor at the points indicated. The Japanese resisted stubbornly at Clark Field, ZigZag Pass and other marked positions, but their main force took up defensive positions in the north.

389

Just seconds before its crash, a Kamikaze plane (top)—set afire by an antiaircraft shell—plummets toward the flight deck of the carrier Essex. The ship was only lightly damaged. The Kamikazes (bottom) performed a few simple rituals before embarking on such death flights: as a parting gesture, the commander at bottom offers his pilots a cup of sake before they fly off to attack U.S. ships in Leyte Gulf.

ASSAULT BY KAMIKAZE

On October 19, 1944, Vice Admiral Takijiro Onishi, commander of Japan's First Air Fleet, announced a shocking plan during a staff meeting on Luzon. "As you know the war situation is grave," he said. "There is only one way of assuring that our meager strength will be effective to a maximum degree. That is to organize suicide attack units composed of Zero fighters armed with 550-pound bombs, with each plane to crash-dive into an enemy carrier."

The admiral made his proposal knowing that single suicide planes often did more damage than a whole squadron flown by men intent on surviving to fight again. Earlier, several pilots had impulsively crash-dived into enemy ships with devastating effect. What shocked the admiral's officers was the idea of making such attacks an official operation.

Nevertheless, a suicide air corps was formed that night. It was named Kamikaze, or Divine Wind, after the legendary typhoon that saved Japan from a 13th-century Mongol invasion. And it quickly attracted an excess of volunteers—two or three times more men than planes available. Some men showed their eagerness to join by writing their applications in blood. As a rule, expert fliers were rejected since they were needed as teachers and escort pilots; generally, the volunteers were inexperienced youths.

But what the Kamikazes lacked in training, they made up for in fervor. Some were inspired by Japanese religious and military traditions of self-sacrifice. "How I appreciate this chance to die like a man!" one such pilot wrote. Others, resigned to being killed in combat anyway, welcomed the opportunity to die magnificently sinking an important ship.

In the Philippines, 424 of these men embarked on suicide missions; they destroyed 16 ships, damaged 80 others. For the Americans, they were not only a devastating force but a puzzle. "There was a hypnotic fascination to a sight so alien to our Western philosophy," wrote Vice Admiral Charles R. Brown. "We watched each plunging Kamikaze with the detached horror of one witnessing a terrible spectacle rather than as the intended victim. And dominating it all was a strange admixture of respect and pity."

The first ship sunk by the suicide pilots, the U.S. escort carrier St. Lo spews flame and smoke off Samar on October 25, 1944.

headquarters a sharp rebuke: "There was a noticeable lack of drive and aggressive initiative today in the movement toward Calumpit." The town was captured the next day.

With the successes at Clark Field and Calumpit, the Luzon campaign entered a new phase—one that was vintage MacArthur, with amphibious landings, paratroop jumps and daring dashes.

On January 29, some 40,000 men of Major General Charles P. Hall's XI Corps came ashore unopposed at San Antonio on Luzon's west coast, just to the north of the Bataan Peninsula. Pushing inland, the corps was stalled by strong enemy positions in the Zambales Mountain foothills above a narrow, serpentine road that the Americans called Zigzag Pass. Not until February 7—and then only with help from U.S. planes that dropped heavy doses of napalm—did the XI Corps break through Zigzag Pass and go on to establish a line reaching from Subic Bay to Manila Bay. Bataan Peninsula had been sealed.

Another operation was launched on January 31, when 8,000 men of the 11th Airborne Division, part of Lieut. General Robert Eichelberger's Eighth Army, came by boat to Nasugbu Bay and raced northeast toward Manila, 55 miles away. They were joined on the way by their own division's 511th Parachute Regiment, which had been air-dropped on Tagaytay Ridge, an important tactical position south of Manila. Although most of the paratroopers jumped too soon and landed in a forest of banana trees, they survived to link up with the main body from Nasugbu Bay. On the evening of February 4, the combined force arrived in Manila's southern outskirts, where it was brought up short by a defensive line of steel and concrete pillboxes.

The most dramatic operation of the Manila squeeze came after MacArthur, on February 1, visited Guimba, the assembly area of the XIV Corps' 1st Cavalry Division. While there, it occurred to him that a lightning attack on Manila might liberate the 4,000 Allied civilians interned since 1942 at Santo Tomás, a university now converted into a Japanese prison camp. Summoning Major General Vernon D. Mudge, the cavalry division's commander, MacArthur urged: "Go to Manila. Go around the Nips, bounce off the Nips, but go to Manila. Free the internees at Santo Tomás."

Mudge did exactly what he was told. After a wild ride down Highway 5 from Guimba at speeds of up to 30 miles

an hour, the first of his two "Flying Columns" roared into Manila at dusk on February 3, 1945—the first American troops to enter the Philippine capital since December 1942. Guided by Filipino guerrillas, Mudge's tanks sped down Rizal Avenue and crashed through the gates of Santo Tomás.

The Japanese inside were quickly put to flight, and the internees swarmed joyfully around the liberators. Recalled one accompanying newsman, "Hands grabbed me and lifted me and carried me, equipment and all, onto the stairs." Though their repatriation was still a long way off, the men, women and children of Santo Tomás joined together and thankfully sang "God Bless America."

On the day after Mudge's arrival, infantrymen of the 37th Division also entered Manila from the north to be confronted by 20,000 Japanese defenders, largely comprised of Naval troops under hard-bitten Admiral Sanji Iwabuchi. When General Yamashita had ordered his soldiers to head east from Manila, Iwabuchi had considered it his duty to remain in the capital and keep its harbor out of American hands for as long as possible. Not only did he deploy his force for a last-ditch defense of Manila, but he ordered about 5,000 other troops to fight to the death for Corregidor 25 miles southwest at the mouth of Manila Harbor.

Surprisingly, since Iwabuchi had done all he could to turn the small island called "The Rock" into an impregnable fortress, Corregidor fell before Manila.

To crack Corregidor, the emotional symbol of American heroism and defeat, MacArthur and Krueger decided on a combined air and sea attack. At 8:30 a.m. on February 16, troops of the 503rd Parachute Infantry Regiment jumped from C-47 transports, aiming at two tiny drop zones on the island's 600-foot-high cliff-sided plateau. Many of the paratroopers missed their zones, crashing into buildings and trees, while others floated out to sea. But the rest collected themselves and set up machine guns and 75mm howitzers to cover the seaborne landing.

The invasion flotilla consisted of 25 landing craft carrying men of the 34th Infantry Regiment, 24th Division—veterans of Breakneck Ridge—who hit the beach virtually unopposed and scrambled 200 yards inland toward a rocky mass called Malinta Hill. Clambering to the summit, they felt lucky to find it deserted.

But the inside of the hill was chock-full of Japanese, con-

Repeating an earlier triumphant gesture, General Douglas MacArthur strides through shin-deep water to the island of Luzon on January 9, 1945. MacArthur had fought for almost three years to fulfill his pledge to return to the Philippines. His first walk ashore had occurred on Leyte on October 20, 1944.

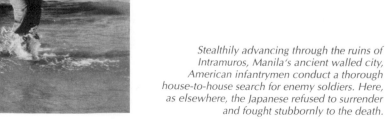

Stealthily advancing through the ruins of Intramuros, Manila's ancient walled city, American infantrymen conduct a thorough house-to-house search for enemy soldiers. Here, as elsewhere, the Japanese refused to surrender and fought stubbornly to the death.

cealed in the network of American-made tunnels along with 35,000 artillery shells, 2 million rounds of rifle and machine gun bullets, 80,000 mortar shells, more than 93,000 hand grenades and a ton of TNT.

For nearly a week there ensued what one American described as "a massacre in a lunatic asylum." Every day, demolition officers would seal off the tunnel exits. Every night, the Japanese would dig their way out and vainly assault the American positions. The charges were invariably repelled, usually with heavy casualties.

Then, on February 21, part of Malinta Hill blew up. About 2,000 Japanese inside the hill had intended to open blocked exits with a small-scale explosion, but there was too much blasting powder in the tunnels. What was meant as a controlled demolition became an inferno. Flames shot out of tunnel mouths, and as many as 1,400 Japanese died.

From Malinta Hill, the Americans pressed eastward for five days. Then, suddenly, Corregidor's remaining under-ground defenders detonated another arsenal, causing an explosion even greater than the Malinta blowup. It showered the offshore fleet with rocky debris, shook the entire island and lifted the top off a knoll at the eastern end. An American officer on the knoll was hurled 30 feet through the air. When he came to, he was shocked at what he saw: "Utter carnage, bodies laying everywhere, everywhere."

Two hundred Japanese died in the blast, bringing total Japanese casualties to about 4,500 and ending the fight for The Rock. The Americans suffered 1,200 casualties—more than one quarter of their original assault force.

By then, back in Manila, Admiral Iwabuchi was making a last stand south of the Pasig River. The core of his defense was Intramuros, the original walled city built by the Spanish in the 16th century. Intramuros was enclosed by stone walls up to 40 feet thick and averaging 16 feet high. Around it lay a city in ruins. Iwabuchi's men had blown up the entire port area and all bridges, as well as the municipal water supply

and electric power system. The blasts ignited wind-driven fires until the entire northern half of the city was ablaze.

Seeking to protect Manila's 700,000 inhabitants as far as he could, MacArthur had prohibited air attacks and at first even forbade artillery fire. But as U.S. casualties mounted in the vicious, block-by-block fighting, the big guns finally had to be called in. "Day and night the shelling goes on," wrote Time Magazine Correspondent William P. Gray. "How many hundreds or thousands of civilians already have died outside Intramuros, nobody knows. Hundreds of city blocks are burned and flattened."

On the morning of February 23, after six days of bombardment, the 37th Division assailed the 150-acre enclave of Intramuros from two sides. A battalion of the 129th Regiment crossed the Pasig in assault boats and entered the ancient citadel from the north. On the east, the 145th Regiment sent one battalion through a breach blasted in the wall and another battalion stormed through a gate.

But the Japanese fought on, making good use of an extensive tunnel system and the old Spanish dungeons. The underground hide outs became death traps as Americans tossed in hand grenades, turned on flamethrowers, or poured gasoline down air holes and ignited it. Finally, on February 24, a company of the 145th Regiment advanced through an underground tunnel and, using grenades and bazookas, eliminated the last pocket of resistance in Intramuros. The old walled city was in ruins.

Still, other Japanese held out in large government buildings near Intramuros, and not until March 3 did the battle for Manila come to an end—one month after it had begun.

The liberation of Manila was a brutal, costly affair. More

than 16,000 Japanese had been killed, while the U.S. suffered 1,000 killed and 5,500 wounded. And amid the sprawling ruins lay the bodies of more than 100,000 Filipinos who had perished during the fighting.

In freeing Manila, Douglas MacArthur achieved his most cherished hope. Yet even then, General Yamashita and his main force were still at large in the mountain strongholds of northern Luzon. Fighting and retreating, retreating and fighting, Yamashita reached his final redoubt in the high Central Cordillera late in June. There he would remain until Japan itself surrendered.

One of the reasons Yamashita and his men were able to survive for so long was that Krueger's Sixth Army had been stripped of two divisions and part of another, which were turned over to General Eichelberger's Eighth Army for MacArthur's next campaign: to seize the major islands of the central and southern Philippines that had been skipped on the way to Leyte and Luzon.

Although many of the bypassed islands were of little strategic consequence, MacArthur had pledged to liberate all of the Philippine islands—and the Filipinos had taken him at his word. "We had total faith in the American

Cases of foodstuffs and ammunition are being unloaded on the hangar deck of a U.S. carrier (above) at the Navy's immense base on Ulithi atoll in the western Caroline islands. The ship was scheduled to depart shortly with another carrier and a destroyer, seen moving in the background. Camouflaged carriers (right) riding at anchor in Ulithi's vast lagoon, form what their crewmen proudly called Murderer's Row. The camouflage was designed to mislead the Japanese as to a ship's true size, type and direction of movement.

promise to come back," recalled one guerrilla leader. "We never faltered in our hope."

In evidence of that trust, resistance groups had sprung up throughout the Philippines, and when the Americans returned in force to the islands in October, 1944, they were supported by some 250,000 guerrillas. They had proved to be valuable assets on Leyte and Luzon—and they would be priceless in the southern Philippines.

Eichelberger's first task was to capture islands that dominated the Visayan Passage south of Luzon, where the Japanese threatened American supply convoys plying between Leyte and Luzon. Kicking off on February 19, the Eighth Army found the going easier than expected. Some islands had already been taken over by Filipino guerrillas. On others, the Japanese had followed General Yamashita's strategy of retreating inland to strong positions in the hills. In such places, the Americans could spend a few days and then move on, relying on guerrilla units to keep the Japanese bottled up—or to eliminate them.

On Palawan, a long island stretching southwestward from Mindoro, the Eighth Army encountered three Americans who emerged from the jungle with a tale of horror to tell.

They had been prisoners of the Japanese until December 14, 1944, when their captors spotted a U.S. fleet bound for Mindoro. Mistakenly believing that Palawan was about to be invaded, the Japanese panicked. Prisoners were herded into air-raid shelters, doused with gasoline and set afire. About 150 died. The three now safe with the Eighth Army had escaped and—like hundreds of other Americans left behind by the disaster of 1942—owed their lives to Filipino guerrillas who had given them refuge.

The guerrillas, in fact, controlled much of the southern Philippines. The four major Visayan islands—Panay, Cebu, Negros and Bohol—were virtual walkovers for Eichelberger's Eighth Army and were declared secure by mid-April. The campaign for the huge island of Mindanao was more difficult and protracted, yet once again the powerful presence of guerrillas was a boon to the Americans.

The Japanese had 43,000 troops on Mindanao, the main body situated around the southeastern port of Davao, while the remainder were strung out along a highway running down the center of the island. However, the two Japanese concentrations were effectively cut off from each other by guerrillas who infested the intervening hinterland.

The original plan was to land General Sibert's X Corps, composed mainly of the 24th and 31st divisions, on Mindanao's west coast at the port of Malabang. From there, the 31st Division would swing north to take on the Japanese in the center of the island, while the 24th would push east to fall upon Davao from the rear.

A combat landing at Malabang was, however, rendered unnecessary by welcome news from one of the Philippines' most accomplished guerrilla leaders—a man who styled himself "General" Fertig.

He was, in fact, Lieut. Colonel Wendell W. Fertig, a U.S. Army engineer who had been sent to Mindanao before its surrender to the Japanese. Afterward, in the course of his search for a resistance group to join, he had come upon competing guerrilla bands, but no real organization. To impress rank-conscious Filipinos, Fertig put on the silver stars of a brigadier general (fashioned for him by a Moro tribesman) and set up as a guerrilla commander near the town of Misamis in northwestern Mindanao.

Fertig's proclamation that he desired all resistance units to serve under him was carried by runners to other guerrilla leaders, and soon emissaries from all over Mindanao were flocking to his headquarters. Some leaders agreed to cooperate and others did not, but all were impressed with what was happening at Misamis: professional soldiers drilled raw recruits, technicians fashioned new springs for old rifle bolts, and women's auxiliaries made badly needed uniforms, bandages and bullets. Fertig also ensured the allegiance of Mindanao's fiercely independent Muslim Moros by paying them 20 centavos and one bullet for each pair of Japanese ears they brought in.

Even Douglas MacArthur, when he heard of Fertig's activities, recognized his achievements—although not his self-promotion to general—and designated him "to command the Tenth Military District (islands of Mindanao and Sulu)."

Shortly before Sibert's scheduled Malabang landing on April 17, a unit of Fertig's guerrillas took the nearby airfield and radioed that Malabang was undefended. The American plans were immediately changed: a token force landed at Malabang while the bulk of the 24th Division swarmed ashore at lightly defended Parang, 17 miles to the east and that much closer to Davao. Fertig and his fellow guerrillas had done their job, and now it was time for the heavy firepower and manpower to take over.

While the 31st Division turned north to fight a series of brutal engagements with the Japanese before clearing the center of the island, the 24th Division headed east on what was to be the longest overland march of any American unit in the Pacific war—through more than 100 miles of stifling jungle. For the first leg of the trek, it was also one of the most bizarre. While some elements trudged wearily along a road that was only a tangled trail in places, other units cruised up the parallel Mindanao River in a makeshift fleet of shallow-draft vessels followed by four Navy subchasers that had been armed with rocket launchers and other heavy weapons. As Eichelberger said later, "There hasn't been a military adventure quite like it since Federal gunboats operated on the lower Mississippi during the Civil War."

At any rate, the men of the 24th traversed the island in just 10 days, and less than a week later, swept unopposed into Davao. Like Manila, the city was in ruins. The Japanese had destroyed everything they could, and then had retreated into the hills, where they bitterly contested every inch of ground with cleverly emplaced artillery, machine guns, rockets and mortars. Nearly two months would pass before General Eichelberger could report to MacArthur that operations had concluded everywhere on Mindanao. The campaign had cost the U.S. Army 820 men killed and nearly 3,000 wounded; the Japanese had lost nearly 13,000 dead in their fierce, but futile defense of the island.

For the Americans and Japanese, Mindanao was the last major battleground in the Philippines. As for the Filipinos, they had more than lived up to the declaration of one guerrilla leader: "If the least we can do is fertilize the ground where we fall, then we grow a richer grain for tomorrow's stronger nation."

Despite the magnitude of MacArthur's accomplishments in the sprawling Philippines, his efforts were only part of the American strategy in the Pacific. In mid-February 1945, just as MacArthur's men embarked on their sweep through the islands of the Visayan Passage, Nimitz' Navy plunged U.S. Marines into the abattoir of a place called Iwo Jima—Sulfur Island. And in the beginning of April, shortly before the Eighth Army launched its climactic campaign on Mindanao, forces under Nimitz brought the war to Japan's doorstep by landing on Okinawa in the Ryukyu Islands.

Although Chief of Naval Operations Ernest J. King strongly favored Formosa as the next step toward the conquest of Japan, in late September of 1944, Nimitz had presented compelling arguments for Iwo Jima and Okinawa.

Iwo Jima was only eight square miles of rock and ash in the aptly named Volcano group of the Bonin Chain, but it lay about 660 miles southeast of Tokyo on the direct route from the Marianas to the Japanese capital. In Japanese hands the island was a threat to the B-29s that would soon begin flying out of Saipan, Tinian and Guam. But in U.S. possession, Iwo could serve as a fighter base to support the big bombers on their way to Japan.

As for Okinawa, situated a mere 350 miles southeast of

Toiling under enemy fire, Marines pass boxes of ammunition ashore from LSTs and LSMs on D-day at Iwo Jima's Red Beach. This onerous chore fell to the men because trucks bogged down in the soft volcanic sand, and there were not enough tracked vehicles to take up the slack.

Kyushu, the southernmost of the Japanese home islands, it offered a nearly ideal bomber base. Along with a satellite island, Ie Shima, Okinawa had room for airfields sufficient to handle about 800 bombers and the necessary fighter escorts. Moreover, Okinawa might also accommodate the armies of men and the mountains of supplies that would be required for an invasion of Japan.

King reluctantly yielded, and the invasion of Iwo Jima was scheduled to begin February 19, some six weeks before Okinawa. It called for the largest Navy-Marine operation ever mounted. As commander of the amphibious force, Vice Admiral Richmond Kelly Turner was given 485 vessels, including eight old battleships. The lion's share of the killing and dying was assigned to 70,647 Marines of the 4th and 5th divisions, with the 3rd Division held in reserve.

Yet despite the massive assemblage of force, no one had any illusions about the situation at Iwo Jima. Even the bellicose Lieut. General Holland M. Howlin' Mad Smith, who would command the Marine expeditionary force en route to the island, made a gloomy prediction after studying aerial reconnaissance photographs that showed the island's defenses steadily being expanded. The invasion, Smith said, would cost 15,000 casualties. As it turned out, Smith's estimate was optimistic.

To soften up Iwo, B-24s and B-29s from the Marianas, later joined by carrier planes, began in late November a record 74 straight days of bombing attacks, dropping nearly 6,000 tons of high explosives on the small island. And as D-day approached, American warships arrived to add the awesome weight of their heavy guns. No island had ever suffered such methodical punishment as a prelude to invasion.

On Iwo Jima, however, the titanic thunder did little more than keep the Japanese defenders awake in their underground strongholds. Awaiting the Americans with about 21,000 men was Lieut. General Tadamichi Kuribayashi, who had taken cavalry training in Texas in the 1920s and had immense respect for the United States. "The U.S.," he once wrote to his wife, "is the last country in the world Japan should fight." Yet whatever his feelings about Americans, he now intended to devise a plan for Iwo Jima's defense.

Kuribayashi would neither fight for the island's beaches nor permit his men to waste their lives in suicidal banzai attacks. Instead, he planned, almost his entire garrison would go underground in an intricate network of bunkers, caves and command posts. The scheme took some doing: few places were less suited to underground construction than the volcanic Iwo, where the heat at a depth of 30 feet was so intense that it was impossible to work there for more than five minutes at a time.

But Kuribayashi was undismayed—and, with the help of engineer specialists, a construction battalion and Korean conscripts, the job was done. In its final form, the system included scores of underground citadels connected by 16 miles of tunnels. Stocked with food, water and ammunition, provided with electricity, and equipped with internal communication systems, the hidden installations terminated on

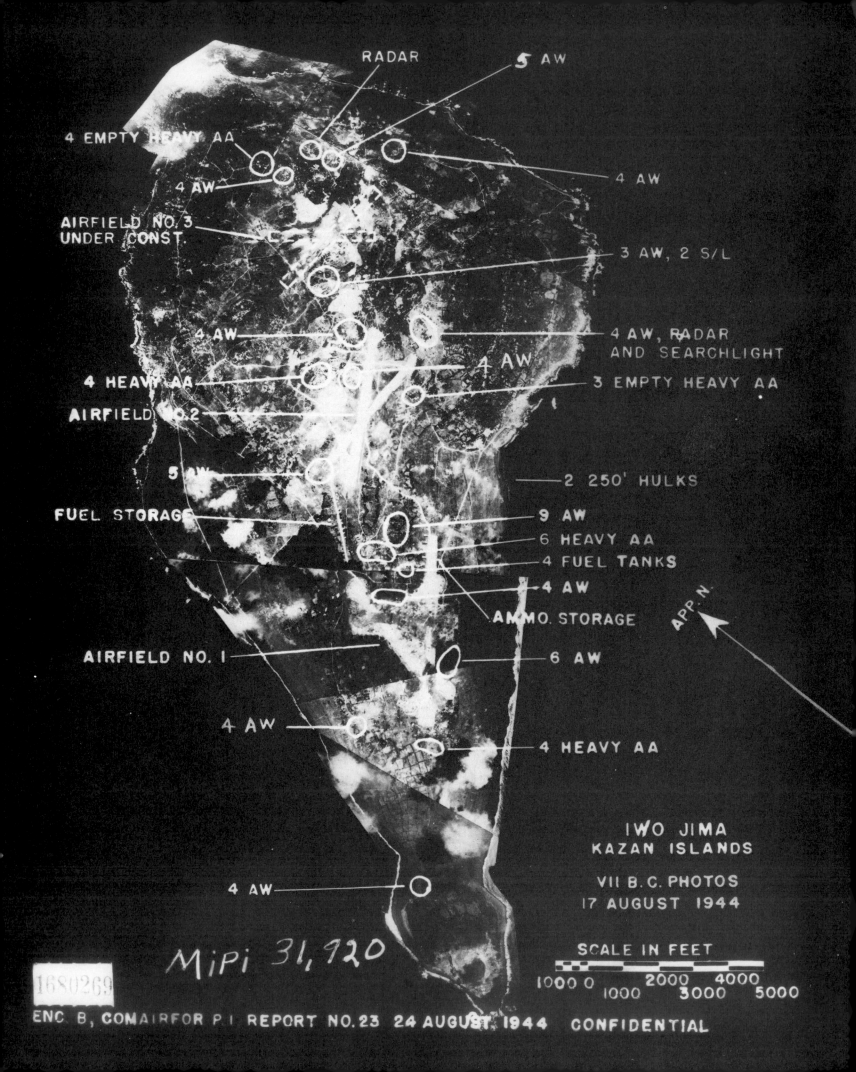

RADAR

5 AW

4 EMPTY HEAVY AA

4 AW

4 AW

AIRFIELD NO. 3
UNDER CONST.

3 AW, 2 S/L

4 AW

4 AW, RADAR
AND SEARCHLIGHT

4 AW

4 HEAVY AA

3 EMPTY HEAVY AA

AIRFIELD NO. 2

5 AW

2 250' HULKS

FUEL STORAGE

9 AW

6 HEAVY AA

4 FUEL TANKS

4 AW

AMMO. STORAGE

AIRFIELD NO. 1

6 AW

APP. N.

4 AW

4 HEAVY AA

IWO JIMA
KAZAN ISLANDS

VII B.C. PHOTOS
17 AUGUST 1944

4 AW

MiPi 31,920

SCALE IN FEET

1000 0   2000   4000
  1000   3000   5000

1680269

ENC. B, COMAIRFOR P.I. REPORT NO. 23 24 AUGUST 1944   CONFIDENTIAL

the surface in concrete blockhouses and pillboxes. In all, Iwo bristled with some 800 gun positions.

Kuribayashi built most of his warrens inside Mount Suribachi, the 556-foot eminence that commanded the south end of Iwo, and in the tortuous, boulder-strewn ridges and ravines of the island's north end. Between those areas of concentration lay two coveted airstrips, relatively undefended but so situated that an enemy driving toward them would be subjected to withering fire from both flanks.

At 8:59 on the morning of February 19, 1945, the first American LTVs lumbered ashore on Iwo Jima, precisely one minute ahead of schedule. After that, the invasion seemed to move in slow motion. The beaches were not only steep, rising in a series of terraces as high as 15 feet, but they were composed of volcanic sand so loose that neither tracked vehicles nor men afoot could get a firm grip on the stuff. The difficulties of moving soon created a mammoth pileup of men and materiel along the 3,500 yards of beachhead.

Nonetheless, at a point where Iwo Jima was only 1,500 yards wide, the 27th Marines of the Fifth Division had managed by late to push across the island and held a fingernail grip on the largest airfield.

The situation on the flanks was far more foreboding. At the extreme left, the 5th Division's 27th Marines, confronted by a wall of fire from concealed Japanese positions, failed even to reach the foot of Mount Suribachi. To the north, the 4th Division was hung up for hours while trying to seize a heavily fortified hill, surmounting a rock quarry studded with pillboxes and blockhouses. As 16 Sherman tanks waddled toward them, the Japanese troops of Captain Masao Hayauchi's 12th Independent Anti-Tank Battalion battled back until their guns were knocked out. Then, with no other way to fight, Hayauchi clutched a demolition charge against his chest and threw himself against a Sherman's steel side, blowing himself up but failing to stop the tank.

By 4:30 p.m., the quarry was taken—but the effort had cost the 25th Marines' 3rd Battalion 550 of its 700 men. The Americans were still far short of D-day's objectives.

Next morning the 27th Marines turned again to the grim work of reducing the Suribachi defenses. Although artillery plastered the prominence, it was a job for men afoot, for carbine, M-1 and bayonet, for Browning automatic rifle, grenade, satchel charge and flamethrower. Still working toward the foot of Suribachi, the men developed a technique. One Marine, lugging a flamethrower or satchel charge and covered by his companions, would crawl up to what he hoped was the blind side of a pillbox. Then, edging toward a firing slit or ventilator, he would shove in the explosive or let loose a roaring tongue of yellow flame.

By late afternoon, the 27th Marines had inched to the mountain's base. Within it, 1,200 Japanese were still free to move through interconnecting tunnels to the best-situated firing points on the surface. On D-plus-2, as they climbed the flanks of Suribachi, the Marines could hear Japanese talking from deep below. They sent for drums of gasoline, poured it into rock fissures that led downward, and set the fuel afire.

When night fell on D-plus-3, only about 300 Japanese remained alive inside the mountain. In accordance with the deathbed instructions of their commander, who had been mortally wounded, many of them crept out and headed north to report to Kuribayashi. Led by a Navy lieutenant, about 20 of them made it. After locating Captain Samaji Inouye, commander of Iwo's Naval guard, the lieutenant reported that Suribachi was lost. But Inouye was a traditionalist to the core. "You traitor, why did you come here?" he shouted. "You are a coward and a deserter. I shall condescend to behead you myself."

The lieutenant knelt and meekly bowed his head. Inouye drew his sword and raised it. But it never fell—Inouye's junior officers tore it out of his grip. Captain Inouye began to weep. "Suribachi's fallen," he moaned. "Suribachi's fallen."

Not quite. Not until 8:40 a.m. on D-plus-4, when four Marines reached Suribachi's crest and gazed into the volcano's crater. They saw a battery of machine guns and stacked ammunition—but not a living soul. Scrambling back down, they reported to Lieut. Colonel Chandler W. Johnson, commander of the 2nd Battalion, 27th Marines, who instructed his executive officer to lead a larger party to the top. "And put this up," Johnson ordered, handing his exec a small American flag.

At the summit, the men found a 20-foot section of iron pipe. The flag was lashed to the pole. Half a dozen men grabbed it and planted it. Meanwhile Private First Class James A. Robeson, aged 16, spotted a Japanese soldier with a rifle who sprang from a cave in the crater wall. Robeson dropped him with a burst from his Browning automatic rifle. Then from the cave came a Japanese officer brandishing a sword and running toward the flag. He was felled by a rifle volley from the Marines.

From the foot of the mountain, Lieut. Colonel Johnson saw the flag go up. He quickly realized that it had become a symbol of history. "Some sonofabitch is going to want that flag," he said, "but he's not going to get it. That's our flag." A corporal, sent to scrounge another flag, got one from a landing craft at the beachhead. A proper banner, almost twice the size of the one already flying, it was raised about two hours later.

On D-plus-4, Major General Harry Schmidt, V Amphibious Corps commander on Iwo, reiterated his prein-

An early intelligence map of Iwo Jima, completed on August 24, 1944, details defenses on the island. To make the map, camera-equipped B-24s took pictures of different sections of the island during the bombing runs of August 17, and a dozen photographs were later pieced together by aerial reconnaissance experts. The superimposed notation "AW" marks the location of automatic weapons; "AA" indicates antiaircraft guns.

vasion prediction—it would take 10 days to capture the island. With Suribachi taken, about a third of Iwo was in U.S. hands. But the rest of it, to the north, included the island's roughest terrain and Kuribayashi's toughest defenses. And as murderous days merged into flaming nights, the names of such places as the Meat Grinder and Death Valley were entered into Iwo's lexicon of horror.

Deeds of individual courage became almost commonplace. On D-plus-6, for example, when the man next to him was hit by sniper fire, Private First Class Douglas T. Jacobson went beserk and dropped his own rifle, picked up the fallen man's bazooka, raced up to a Japanese 20mm gun emplacement and knocked it out. Still running, he destroyed another pillbox, then a concrete blockhouse. Before he cooled off, Jacobson had killed 75 Japanese—and earned one of the 27 Medals of Honor (including five in a single day on D-plus-12) that were bestowed for heroism on Iwo Jima.

As the Americans inched forward in the Meat Grinder, a broad amphitheater whose defenses included a three-story blockhouse and numerous tanks buried up to their turrets, entire units were virtually eradicated. One of them, Company E, 2nd Battalion, 24th Regiment, lost six comman-

ders in three days. There was no need for a seventh—Company E had ceased to exist as a military unit.

But raw courage was by no means exclusive to Americans. By the night of D-plus-17, Captain Inouye, the Navy officer who had wept over the fall of Suribachi, and about 1,000 of his men were encircled by two Marine regiments. A member of Japan's hereditary warrior class, Inouye intended to defy General Kuribayashi's orders and die as his ancestors would have done—at the head of a banzai charge. Planning to break through the enemy lines and go all the way to Suribachi, where he would once more raise the Japanese flag, Inouye and his men crept to within 10 yards of a U.S. battalion command post, then charged, screaming.

Captain Inouye was last seen by his orderly brandishing his sword and shouting "*Tsukkome*!" ("Charge!"). In the morning, the Marines counted 784 Japanese bodies.

For General Kuribayashi, the end was approaching. On D-plus-23, in his cave at Iwo's northern tip, he listened to one of a series of special radio programs from Tokyo designed to bolster Japanese morale. A choir sang "The Song of Iwo Defense," composed by men under his command before the American landing. On D-plus-26, Major General

Watching out for enemy action on heavily defended Mount Suribachi, a Marine sniper hugs a steep volcanic slope above the beach, where landing craft are pouring in men and supplies.

A Marine takes down the small U.S. flag first hoisted above Suribachi, while his companions in the background raise a larger flag. The Marines knew that the flag would stand forever as a symbol of courage and sacrifice, and they wanted to make sure they kept the original.

Graves B. Erskine, whose 3rd Marine Division had been summoned from reserve, sent two Japanese prisoners to Kuribayashi's headquarters; they carried a letter from Erskine saying that Kuribayashi's position was now hopeless and suggesting that he could surrender with honor.

No reply came.

Although Kuribayashi's body was never found, his compatriots believed that he lived to take part in a final gesture of national honor—a foredoomed attack in which 262 Japanese and 53 Americans were killed. Reportedly the general was badly wounded and later committed suicide, thereby adding his name to the melancholy list of more than 19,000 Japanese and 6,821 Americans who lost their lives on Iwo Jima. For the Marine Corps the battle had the ignominious distinction of being the highest casualty rate of any engagement in their proud 168-year history.

It was D-plus-35—March 26, 1945—and only six days remained before the invasion of Okinawa.

American planners had expected the worst. Okinawa was 60 times the size of Iwo and, according to U.S. intelligence estimates, it harbored about 75,000 Japanese troops (in fact, the number was more than 100,000). Moreover, the enemy would surely put up a desperate fight for an island that was logically the last stop on the way to Japan.

Astoundingly, troops of the newly created U.S. Tenth Army, which was comprised of two Army and two Marine Corps divisions, met with virtually no opposition when they landed on a long, straight stretch of sandy beach fronting the village of Hagushi on Okinawa's lower western coast. As a Marine lieutenant recalled, the vista inland from the beach was one of "furrowed fields or patches of ripe white winter barley, and tiny bright field flowers were scattered over the light earth. We were all incredulous, as if we had stepped into a fairy tale."

Not until later would cynics point out that the date was April 1—April Fool's Day.

South of the landing site, from the ramparts of Shuri Castle, a 15th century fort that had housed Okinawa's feudal kings, Lieut. General Mitsuru Ushijima had watched the Americans swarm ashore without visible concern. Ushijima had no intention of defending the beaches. Indeed, he had written off the entire northern two thirds of Okinawa as requiring too great a dispersal of his forces.

Instead, Ushijima would make his stand in the south, where he meant to chew up the Americans piecemeal as they labored through a succession of jagged ridges, some ris-

In the invasion of Okinawa, the main assault force of four divisions went ashore on the west coast (straight arrows) while one division made a feint (curved arrow) at the south coast. Of the four outfits that landed at once, the 1st and 6th Marine divisions were assigned to move north and east, leaving the 7th and 96th Infantry divisions to attack the principal Japanese line of defense in the south.

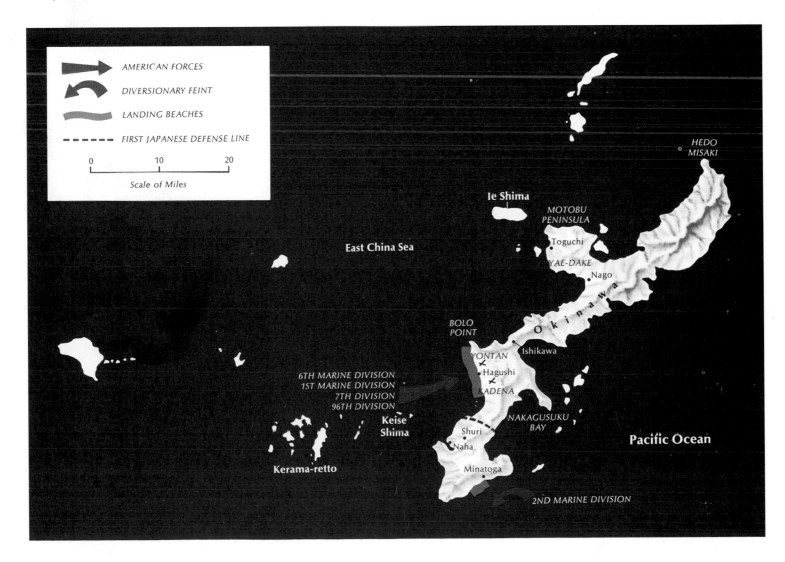

AMERICAN FORCES

DIVERSIONARY FEINT

LANDING BEACHES

FIRST JAPANESE DEFENSE LINE

0   10   20

Scale of Miles

HEDO MISAKI

Ie Shima

MOTOBU PENINSULA

Toguchi

East China Sea

YAE-DAKE

Nago

BOLO POINT

Okinawa

Ishikawa

YONTAN

Hagushi

KADENA

6TH MARINE DIVISION
1ST MARINE DIVISION
7TH DIVISION
96TH DIVISION

NAKAGUSUKU BAY

Keise Shima

Shuri

Naha

Pacific Ocean

Kerama-retto

Minatoga

2ND MARINE DIVISION

ing to 300 feet. There, in addition to the usual array of blockhouses and pillboxes, underground chambers and tunnels, Ushijima's purposes would be served by an ancient Okinawan funerary custom. Families preserved the bones of their dead above the ground, inside masonry burial vaults. These tombs, studding the hillsides by the thousands, were ready-made mortar pits and machine gun nests.

And so it came to pass that the 6th Marine Division, parading northward with the 1st Marine Division behind it, by April 13 stood at Hido Misaki at the northernmost tip of Okinawa. At that same time, the U.S. Army was still bloodily engaged in trying to seize a rocky hogback named Kakazu Ridge—which was no more than the first of several Japanese defense lines in the south.

The troops attacking southward had been in trouble from the start. The 7th Infantry Division, assigned to the eastern half, took seven days to advance just 6,000 yards—and suffered more than 1,120 casualties. On the western side, the 96th Infantry spent three days capturing one hill alone—Cactus Ridge—whose possession was vital because it lay only 1,200 yards north of the even more crucial Kakazu Ridge.

To Lieut. General Simon Bolivar Buckner Jr., the Tenth Army's commander, the lack of progress was especially galling because victory on Okinawa was necessary before he could get on with his heart's desire—the invasion of Japan itself. The son and namesake of a Confederate general in the American Civil War, Buckner was fond of expressing his hopes in a toast pronounced over a bourbon and water: "May you walk in the ashes of Tokyo."

Now, after moving his headquarters ashore on April 14, Buckner let it be known in his drillmaster's voice that he expected Ushijima's first defense line to be broken without further delay. Buckner gave weight to his demand by shuffling his own forces: brought out of reserve, the 27th Infantry Division replaced the 96th in front of Kakazu Ridge; the 96th was shifted to the center of the line, and the 7th Division was assigned to the eastern third.

Buckner's big push got under way on April 19, preceded by the most massive and concentrated artillery pounding of the Pacific war. By nightfall it had clearly failed. Not one of the divisions had been able to break through. Especially discouraging was the performance of the 27th Division, which attempted both a frontal assault on Kakazu Ridge and an end run by tanks around the heights. The head-on attack was stopped by withering fire from the ridge. Of the 30 tanks that set out to skirt Kakazu, 22 were destroyed by mines, antitank guns, artillery and mortar fire. The loss was the greatest incurred by U.S. armor for any one day on Okinawa.

Adding to Buckner's woes, Admiral Nimitz flew in from Guam on the night of April 23 to lay down the law: unless Buckner could get his operation going within five days, Nimitz said, "we'll get someone here to move it."

Within hours after Nimitz had left the island, Buckner's

most immediate problem was solved—by the enemy. Concluding that their battered first line of defense could hardly hold out much longer, the Japanese withdrew southward to new positions. From there, on May 4, they launched the last thing in the world the Americans had expected: an all-out counteroffensive.

The extraordinary attack grew out of a stormy dispute on the night of May 2 in General Ushijima's headquarters beneath Shuri Castle. The occasion was a staff conference, well-lubricated with sake, and the antagonists were two very different personalities. Ushijima's chief of staff, Lieut. General Isamu Cho, was an extremist who had been a conspirator in the infamous Cherry Society plot to establish a military dictatorship in 1931, and who had issued the kill-all-prisoners order that preceded the rape of Nanking in 1937. Now, Cho's every instinct called for an aggressive move to smash the Americans.

Pitted against Cho was Ushijima's senior planning officer, Colonel Hiromichi Yahara, a cool and contemplative officer who thought banzai attacks were sheer stupidity. But Yahara stood alone in his arguments against an attack. Every other officer at the conference stood with Cho, and so in the end did Ushijima, who subsequently declared: "Each soldier will kill at least one American devil."

The results were calamitous. Japanese engineers, attempting to make amphibious landings behind the American troops on both the east and west coasts, were either blown out of the water or slaughtered when they reached the shore. Attacking by land, Japanese troops were caught in the open and mowed down. Although Ushijima and Cho kept trying, the failure was unmistakably clear by the afternoon of May 5. At 6 p.m. that day, Ushijima ordered all units to return to their preoffensive positions. Then he summoned Yahara to his headquarters and, with tears in his eyes, promised that henceforth he would abide by the colonel's advice. And Ushijima still proposed to make the Americans pay a fearsome price for Okinawa.

Despite the disaster of Cho's offensive, the struggle for Okinawa was far from over—and General Buckner knew it. "We will take our time and kill the Japanese gradually," he told correspondents as the Tenth Army prepared to assail Ushijima's new positions on the so-called Shuri Line, an eight-mile arc that ran from the Yonabaru area on the east coast, through the ancient town of Shuri in the center, to the port of Naha on the west coast.

For his general offensive, Buckner had available about 85,000 men, including those of the 1st and 6th Marine divisions, which had recently returned from their successful conquest of northern Okinawa.

Rumbling inland from their landing craft, U.S. tanks roam at will across the farmers' fields behind the invasion beaches. Japanese opposition to the Okinawa landing was so slight at first that a correspondent who came ashore with the Marine vanguard wrote, "It was almost as though we were the original explorers."

A 7th Division machine gunner scrambles for cover as Japanese defenders open fire on a ridge in southern Okinawa. It took the Americans four days to force the enemy from the ridge—and back to another defensive line.

Launching their effort on May 11, the Americans quickly discovered that the Shuri bastion was tougher than Ushijima's first defensive line, tougher even than Tarawa and Iwo Jima, tougher indeed than anything the Americans had faced in the Pacific war. Day after day, as the casualties mounted, they flung themselves at a grim succession of hills and ridges to which they gave fanciful names.

. . . . "Sugar Loaf Hill . . . Chocolate Drop . . . Strawberry Hill," . . . . gloated a propaganda broadcast from Tokyo. "Gee, these places sound wonderful! You can just see the candy houses with the white picket fences around them and the candy canes hanging from the trees, their red and white stripes glistening in the sun. But the only thing red about those places is the blood of Americans."

On May 21, after a terrible 10-day struggle, came the breakthrough Buckner had been waiting for: on the Tenth Army's left flank, the 96th Division opened an 800-yard corridor between Nakagusuku Bay and a defensive complex based on a 476-foot peak called Conical Hill. Only 1,000 yards to the south lay the town of Yonabaru and the road leading west to Naha, along which the Americans could complete the encirclement of the Japanese from the rear.

But Simon Bolivar Buckner Jr. was one of those hard-luck generals who are found in every war. Just as he was ready to exploit his opportunity, Okinawa's monsoon season drowned the front. Torrential downpours turned the roads into wheel-deep bogs and drenched all hope of any dramatic advance. Not until June 5 were offensive operations remotely feasible—and by then the Japanese had withdrawn to still another defensive line. "It was recognized that to stay would result in a quicker defeat," explained Colonel Yahara,

Deployed as skirmishers, infantrymen scramble up a devastated Okinawa ridge, still smoking from 35 minutes of fire from flame-throwing tanks. As two platoons of GIs neared the top of the ridge, Japanese hidden in caves hurled grenades and satchel charges to knock the Americans back down again.

Organizing a group of uprooted Okinawans, an American officer explains through an interpreter that they will be treated fairly and given food and shelter. The officer, a trained administrator of the U.S. Military Government, had been assigned to the invasion staff.

whose counsel was by now being heeded. "Consequently it was decided to retreat in accord with the Army policy of protracting the struggle as long as possible."

But there would be no more retreats. Beyond the Kiyamu Peninsula, where the latest defensive line cut across Okinawa's southern extremity, lay only the sea. To the remnants of his army, Ushijima issued a final general order: "The present position will be defended to the death, even to the last man."

That included Ushijima. Now, with the rains over, the Americans were coming hard, and the general awaited them in a roomy cave inside Hill 89, about 10 miles due south of Shuri. On June 12, the eastern sector of the Kiyamu line collapsed under pressure from the U.S. Army's 7th Infantry Division; by June 13, the 96th Division possessed Yaeju-dake, a series of hills and cliffs that dominated the center of the line; on June 18, Marines took Kunishi Ridge, the line's western anchor.

Two days later, with soldiers of the 7th Division standing atop Hill 89, a captured Japanese officer volunteered to take Ushijima a message offering him one last chance to surrender. But as the prisoner approached the command cave, a Japanese demolition crew inside blew it shut.

On the following night, as General Ushijima and General Cho prepared for the final act of hara-kiri, Colonel Yahara, the solemn strategist, asked for permission to join them in this final act. Ushijima refused, saying: "If you die there will be no one left who knows the truth about the battle of Okinawa. Bear the temporary shame but endure it. This is an order from your Army commander."

At 10 p.m. Ushijima and Cho sat down to an elaborate meal of rice, salmon, canned meats, potatoes, fried fish cakes, bean-curd soup, fresh cabbage, pineapples, tea and sake. Afterward, the generals and their staff exchanged numerous toasts with Scotch whisky, which Cho had carried from Shuri Castle. At 4 a.m., the last ceremony began, and a Japanese who had learned the details from witnesses to the event later described the scene: "The commanding general and the chief of staff sit down on the quilt, bow in reverence to the eastern sky, and Adjutant J respectfully presents the sword."

Ushijima and Cho each bared his stomach for disembowelment by a ceremonial knife, at the same time bowing his head for decapitation by an adjutant's drawn saber. According to the Japanese account, the end came quickly: "A simultaneous shout and a flash of a sword, then another repeated shout and a flash, and both generals had nobly accomplished their last duty to their Emperor."

That day—June 22, 1945—marked the end of organized Japanese resistance on Okinawa. Both sides had paid a ghastly price. The Japanese had lost about 110,000 killed and 10,755 taken prisoner during the bloodiest land battle of the Pacific war. Victory had cost the Americans 7,613 killed and missing, 31,807 wounded and 26,211 other casualties, most of them victims of combat fatigue.

Among the American dead was General Buckner, whose bad luck had held to the end. On June 18, he had climbed to an observation post to watch his troops seize the last of Okinawa's major ridgelines. As he gazed out over the battlefield, five enemy shells landed nearby in quick succession. Buckner fell, mortally wounded. Not one of the officers surrounding him was so much as scratched.

Preparing for a strike on April 13, 1945, that would destroy almost 11 square miles of Tokyo, an armorer checks the .50-caliber machine guns in the upper turret of a Superfortress; on the ground, ordnance men assemble clusters of incendiary bombs.

CHARIOTS OF DESTRUCTION

When they met in China in 1944, General Curtis E. LeMay and General Joseph W. "Vinegar Joe" Stilwell, the commander of the U.S. forces in the China-Burma-India theater, stayed up all night arguing about the value of strategic bombing. Nothing LeMay said would convince the old infantryman that strategic bombers could make much difference in the course of the War. But soon after the War ended, Stilwell made a special trip to

Planes from the 58th Bombardment Wing, which had flown under General Curtis LeMay's command in China and India, file along a taxiway in June 1945 at their new base on West Field, Tinian.

Guam to acknowledge his error. "You have done what you set out to do," he told LeMay. "I recognize now the terrible military virtues of strategic bombardment."

Without doubt, the B-29 campaign against Japan marked a turning point in the conduct of warfare. Because of the wholesale devastation the big bombers inflicted from long range, the importance of air power would never again be challenged. Indeed, the successful bombing of Japan—as well as Germany—contributed in 1947 to the creation of the U.S. Air Force, coequal with the Army and the Navy.

In LeMay, Air Commander General Wap Arnold had found a near-perfect instrument for bringing forth an independent air force. LeMay had commanded a heavy-bomber group in the campaign against Germany. He also relied on military intuition, which told him the decisive way to destroy Japan's ability to fight was a rain of fire. After the first fire bombings, Brigadier General Haywood S. Hansell Jr., who had preceded him as commander of the Marianas-based B-29s, conceded that, given the circumstances, LeMay's methods were infinitely

more effective than standard high-explosive bombing. "The tactical method selected by LeMay," said Hansell, "was a superb decision."

That decision caused immense loss of life and suffering among Japan's civilian population. But LeMay admitted having no regret. He later wrote, "I think it's more immoral to use less force that it is to use more." And to underscore the point, he cited the story of "a stupid man who was not basically cruel—just well-meaning." The man, he said, cut off his dog's tail an inch at a time "so that it wouldn't hurt so much."

A ROSTER OF TARGETS OBLITERATED

The ordnance loaded aboard a B-29 for an incendiary rain contained one of three combustibles: the bombers in the leading formations generally carried napalm, or jellied-gasoline bombs, which ignited small fires. A second wave of bombers usually dropped clusters of oil containers, which sprayed their contents over the napalm fires in showers, and the mixture ran though the streets in fiery streams. Magnesium thermite bombs, mixed with the oil and napalm, set fires of fierce intensity.

So loaded, the B-29s extracted a mind-numbing toll. By August 14, a total of 602 major Japanese war industries and military installations had been destroyed or severely damaged; inland shipping had been virtually eliminated; and nearly half of the aggregate area of 66 cities—178 square miles—had been razed.

Of the sectors within those cities that had been designed as targets, the Super-fortresses leveled an astonishing 92 per cent. And in one city, the chemical and textile manufacturing center of Toyama, the devastation was total.

The aerial photographs on these pages are representative entries in the B-29s' ledger of destruction; other entries include the cities of Sakai, 57 per cent destroyed, and Nagoya, which was 77 per cent destroyed. In each instance, the percentage given indicates the portion of the targeted area within each city or industrial complex destroyed by the War's end.

Tokyo: 86 per cent destroyed.

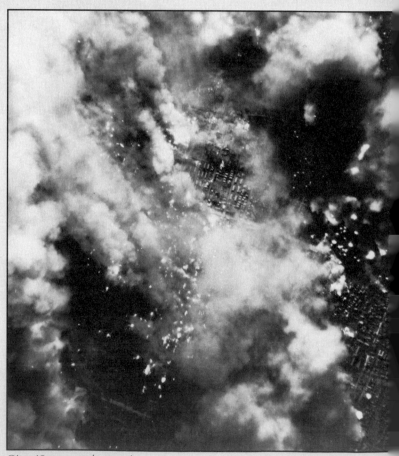

Oita: 40 per cent destroyed.

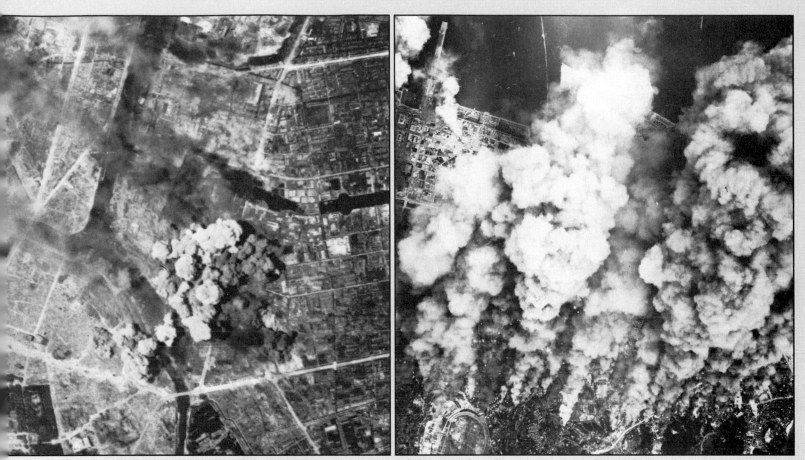

Atsuta aircraft plant: 65 per cent destroyed.

Yokohama naval installation: 100 per cent destroyed.

Otaki oil refinery: 45 per cent destroyed.

Kochi: 51 per cent destroyed.

TRIUMPH AND AFTERMATH

Celebrating V-J Day far from home, U.S. servicemen and servicewomen in Paris display copies of the newspaper Stars and Stripes proclaiming "Peace."

16

By the second week of April 1945, more than 6 million Soviet soldiers were deployed along the Eastern Front in positions that included a 27-mile-long bridgehead on the west bank of the Oder River, less than 40 miles from Berlin. At the same time the American vanguard of 3 million Allied troops stood on the Elbe River at a point just 53 miles southwest of the German capital. It was clear to all that Germany had irredeemably lost the War. As the European and American armies prepared for the last battles, one battle for life came to an end when on April 12, 1945, Franklin Delano Roosevelt, 32nd President of the United States, died of a cerebral hemorrhage in his tranquil haven at Warm Springs, Georgia.

Cloistered in the bowels of his underground bunker in the Reich Chancellery garden, Adolf Hitler was overjoyed upon hearing the news that his great American enemy was gone at last. Among the dictator's first acts, he summoned Minister of Armaments and War Production Albert Speer, who had fallen into disfavor for his defeatist talk. "Hitler hurried toward me with a degree of animation rare in him these days," Speer later recalled. "His words came in a great rush. 'Here we have the miracle I always predicted. Who was right? The war isn't lost. Roosevelt is dead!'"

But for Adolf Hitler, for his Germany and for his main surviving ally, Japan, there would be no miracle. In his hour of macabre celebration, the Führer himself was less than three weeks away from death by his own hand. Only eight days after that, the Third Reich would capitulate amid scenes of apocalyptic ruin. And less than five months in the future, the last of the Axis partners, stunned by the most destructive weapon ever unleashed upon humankind, would surrender aboard an American battleship anchored in Tokyo Bay.

Certainly one reason for Hitler's glee was his conviction that with Roosevelt's death, an end would come to the "unnatural coalition" between the Anglo-Americans and the Russians. In fact, that alliance had indeed frayed; but the quarrel was not so much between the Allied leaders and the Soviets. Rather, it pitted General Dwight Eisenhower against the British—specifically, Prime Minister Winston Churchill.

The quarrel stemmed from Eisenhower's decision to renounce Berlin as the final objective of the Allied armies. When on March 28, Eisenhower sent an announcement of his decision to Major General John R. Deane, head of the U.S. Military Mission in Moscow, for delivery by hand to Stalin, Churchill was furious. He wanted an Anglo-American capture of Berlin both as a matter of prestige and because he believed that possession of the city would give the Western Allies a post-war advantage over the Russians. Furthermore, Churchill protested that Eisenhower had overstepped himself by communicating directly with the political head of the Soviet state. However the U.S. Joint Chiefs-of-Staff backed Eisenhower to the hilt. Noting that Eisenhower was the European Supreme Allied Commander, they insisted that Stalin, as Supreme Commander of the Soviet armed forces, was his military counterpart. To be sure, President Roosevelt could have countermanded Eisenhower's decision, but in his dying days he lacked the strength to buck his military advisors—even had he wished to do so. The decision stood.

Eisenhower believed that Berlin, capital of a country already reeling toward collapse, no longer was of sufficient importance to warrant the heavy casualties that might be suffered in taking it. He wanted to finish off the enemy's war industries in central Germany. And he was preoccupied with

THE FINAL BATTLES

a rumored Alpine redoubt—the supposed lair where a large force of diehard Nazis would resist until the bitter end. The redoubt simply did not exist.

For his part, Stalin looked upon Eisenhower's rejection of Berlin with characteristic suspicion: he assumed that the American general intended just the opposite of what he said, and that Berlin would in fact be the next Anglo-American objective. That being the case, Stalin was in a hurry to beat his "little allies" to Berlin.

The generals who would lead the Soviet offensive were Marshal Georgy K. Zhukov, commanding the First Belorussian Army Front, and Marshal Ivan Konev at the head of the First Ukrainian Front. Relations between the two were poor, and Stalin had long played on their rivalry as a means of goading both generals to greater achievements. Now he was at it again.

As presented to Stalin, the Red Army plan called for Zhukov's armies to thrust straight westward toward Berlin. Konev's force, presently posted to the south of Zhukov, would drive west and northwest, then mount a secondary attack southwest toward Dresden; that attack would develop into an assault on Prague. Before approving the plan, however, Stalin drew a boundary line that blurred the distinction between the objectives of the competing commanders. Running west as well as to the south of Berlin, the line ostensibly gave the capital to Zhukov. But Stalin extended the boundary only as far as Lubben—45 miles southeast of Berlin—which Konev was supposed to reach on the third day of the offensive.

Both generals instantly realized that Stalin was challeng-

ing Konev to veer north from Lubben in an attempt to beat Zhukov into Berlin—and the race was on. From the Kremlin, the two marshals sped to Moscow Central Airport in order to return to their headquarters; they were in the air within two minutes of each other. Thereafter, said Konev, "We hardly had time to look for our hats and gloves."

As the Red Army hastily geared up for what would obviously be its last major onslaught, Hitler demanded that Berlin fight for its life with "fanaticism, imagination, every means of deception, cunning and deceit" from "every block, every house, every store, every hedge, every shell hole." Members of the *Volkssturm*, or home guard, were put to work along with women and children at digging antitank ditches and constructing other defenses in concentric belts surrounding the city. Within Berlin, overturned trucks, streetcars and railway cars weighted with bomb debris were to link jerry-built concrete walls, the shells of bombed buildings, trenches, and the natural barriers provided by rivers, lakes and canals.

But Major General Hellmuth Reymann, the city's commandant, realized that such preparations were mere illusion. He calculated that it would require at least 200,000 experienced troops to make a creditable last stand in Berlin. Instead, he had the youngsters of Hitler Youth and the old men of the *Volkssturm* to man his barricades. Many had no uniforms, a third were unarmed and the rest carried either one-shot grenade launchers, called *Panzerfaust*, or rifles for which there was frequently no ammunition. "It's madness!" exclaimed a German officer. "How are these people supposed to fight after they fire their single round? What does

Girding for the final defense of Berlin, a uniformed Hitler Youth learns how to fire the throwaway antitank weapon called Panzerfaust.

Headquarters expect them to do—use their empty weapons like billy clubs?"

In the foggy predawn darkness of April 16, 1945, Marshal Zhukov arrived at the command post of the Eighth Guards Army on the Oder River's west bank near the town of Küstrin. At exactly 5:00 a.m., Zhukov gave the signal to start his artillery bombardment. Nearly 17,000 field guns, mortars and multiple rocket launchers let loose with a salvo heard 40 miles away—in eastern Berlin. Half an hour later, the Eighth Guards Army and the Third and Fifth Shock armies surged from their starting points, launching the offensive that Zhukov expected to take his 750,000 men and 1,800 tanks to Berlin in very short order. He was soon disappointed. Across the broad Oder Valley, now waterlogged by spring rains, stood the Seelow Heights, a 28-mile stretch of fortified hills and bluffs that comprised the strongest sector of the 90-mile-long German defense system. The line was manned by troops of Army Group Vistula under General Gotthard Heinrici, a grim, gray and highly competent commander, who was respectfully described by his men as "our tough little bastard." Patiently waiting until the Soviets were well within range of the heights, the Germans opened up with everything they had—artillery, machine guns and submachine guns, rifles and *Panzerfaust*. Said the first report from the defenders: "The attack has been repulsed."

Never a man to suffer failure gladly, Georgy Zhukov exploded with what one of his staff members called "a stream of extremely forceful expressions." Again and again, his massed men and tanks assaulted the Seelow Heights; again and again they were driven back.

Pulling his Forty-seventh Army out of reserve, Zhukov hurled his soldiery at the heights throughout the next two days. "They keep coming at us in hordes, in wave after wave, with no regard for loss of life," reported a German officer. Yet the Seelow Heights still held—and Zhukov still raged. Said one of his generals: "We have a lion by the tail."

Zhukov's woes brought jubilation to Hitler and his fellow occupants of the *Führerbunker*, where, according to a Naval liaison officer, on April 18, the "voices of hope were loud." The voices of German hope were silenced on the following day, when Zhukov's forces finally broke through the Seelow Heights. By April 20, his Second Guards Tank Army had bludgeoned its way to Bernau, just 10 miles northeast of

Berlin, and was heading toward Oranienburg, 19 miles north of the capital. From there, Zhukov could sweep west around Berlin and join hands with Konev's tank units pushing up from the southeast.

And Konev was rolling. On April 16, with seven armies—500,000 men and 1,400 tanks—under his command, he had made a successful combat crossing of the swift, broad Neisse River and ripped an 18-mile hole in the German defenses. By mid-afternoon of the next day, advance elements of General Pavel S. Rybalko's Third Guards Tank Army and of General Dmitri D. Lelyushenko's Fourth Guards Tank Army were across the Spree River, with only a handful of defenders between them and the great city.

Presumably Konev's main mission was still to head for the Elbe, where his troops would meet American soldiers coming from the west. But the marshal had other ideas. "Things are going well with us," he told Stalin. "We have sufficient forces and are in a position to turn both our tank armies toward Berlin." At that, Stalin gave Konev the word: "Very good. I agree. Turn your tanks toward Berlin."

As Konev's armor swung north, the foot soldiers of his Thirteenth Army and Fifth Guards Army continued westward toward the Elbe and the tricky linkup with American forces. Farther south, the Fifty-second Army and the Polish Second Army swerved toward Dresden.

With Berlin as their goal, Konev's tanks moved at full throttle. In the next three days, Lelyushenko's army covered 87 miles, reaching the town of Luckenwalde, about 22 miles south of Berlin. Although Rybalko's army was only slightly slower—it made 79 miles during the same period—Konev showed his displeasure by radioing on April 19: "Comrade Rybalko, you are moving like a snail."

The next day, Rybalko made up for lost time by seizing Zossen, headquarters of the German General Staff, about 20 miles south of Berlin. His thrust, together with a southerly drive by one of Zhukov's armored columns, threatened to trap a major portion of Lieut. General Theodor Busse's German Ninth Army, which Hitler had obstinately kept in place to the east.

On that same day—April 21—Soviet units got their first distant sight of Berlin, wreathed in smoke from an American bombing raid the previous night. "Before us lay a huge city," wrote Sergeant Nikolai Vasilyev, a member of an artillery battery in the Fifth Shock Army. "A feeling of joy and exulta-

In a German propaganda photo, a troop of shovel-bearing civilians, many of them smiling young women, march off to dig antitank ditches and build fortifications for Berlin.

tion swept over us. This was the last enemy position, and the hour of retribution had come at last. We did not even notice a car draw up. Our army commander, General Berzarin, alighted from it. He issued an order to our commanding officer: 'Target: The Nazis in Berlin. Open fire!'"

The battery's rounds may have been the first to land in central Berlin, and among those who heard them was Adolf Hitler in the *Führerbunker*.

By then, it was clear even to Hitler that Roosevelt's death had worked no miracles—whereupon he determined to perform a few of his own. Among several crackpot schemes, the one the Führer most counted on was a counterattack north of Berlin by one of his pet soldiers, SS General Felix Steiner. There was, however, a major impediment to the plan: by the time Steiner received Hitler's order, his command had been stripped of units needed elsewhere. As Steiner later remarked, "I was a general without any troops."

No matter. Hitler airily assigned three widely scattered divisions, along with some other odds and ends, to Steiner, whom he informed: "You'll see, the Russians will yet suffer the bloodiest defeat in their history at the gates of Berlin."

Almost immediately, Hitler began bombarding his General Staff with questions about the progress of Steiner's attack. He got only evasive answers—until a memorable conference on the afternoon of April 22, when the recently installed Chief of Staff, General Hans Krebs, finally confessed that Steiner was still trying to cobble together a cohesive force and had not yet attacked at all.

With that, the Führer flew into a frenzy so violent that it shocked even the most hardened witnesses of Hitler's rages. Out of control, his eyes bulging, his face purple, Hitler screamed that all the world had betrayed and deserted him. "The war is lost!" he cried; it was the first time he had made such an unqualified admission.

After considerable comforting by the shocked officers, Hitler came out of his tantrum and the conference continued for three hours. To the generals, it was apparent that Hitler was washing his hands of all military decisions except those pertinent to the fight for Berlin. They implored him not to abandon Germany—and themselves. Who, someone asked, would give them their orders? Not I, Hitler replied, they should ask Reich Marshal Hermann Göring.

That petulant remark soon led to a melodramatic sequel. Upon leaving the conference in the *Führerbunker*, a Luftwaffe aide told Göring what Hitler had said. Thrilled at the prospect of becoming Germany's new Führer, Göring composed a telegram to Hitler, which included the following ill-considered question: "In view of your decision to remain in the fortress of Berlin, do you agree that I take over at once the total leadership of the Reich?"

When the message arrived at the *Führerbunker*, it fell into the hands of one of Göring's most dangerous enemies, Hitler's chief Nazi Party executive, the reptilian Martin Bormann. Easily convinced by Bormann that the Reich Marshal was trying to oust him as Führer, Hitler ordered Göring's arrest. And so, causing scarcely a ripple in the maelstrom of more significant events, fell Hermann Göring, once second only to Hitler in the Nazi regime hierarchy.

During the period that the Soviet armies were reaching for a stranglehold on Berlin, the Western Allies had been moving eastward across a broad front, their progress impeded only by sporadic opposition. Such was the condition of Germany's forces that Field Marshal Albert Kesselring, recently named to head a new southern command, would later recall with rueful pride. His troops, he said "marched, broke away, fought, were overrun, outflanked, battered and exhausted, only to regroup, fight and march again."

In the north, the Canadian First Army, part of Field Marshal Montgomery's Twenty-first Army Group, by April 20 had bisected the enemy's Netherlands command and trapped the Germans against the North Sea near Amsterdam. Four days later, the British Second Army XXX Corps fought its way into the battered port of Bremen, while two other corps closed to the Elbe along Montgomery's 90-mile front.

Far to the south, in mid-April, General Patton's Third Army reached its eastern stop-line, across a Mulde River tributary at Chemnitz. Like Montgomery, Patton was upset by Eisenhower's decision to leave Berlin to the Soviets. "Ike, I don't see how you figure that one," he had said. "We had better take Berlin and quick, and on to the Oder." Later during the discussion, Eisenhower remarked that he did not see why anyone would want to capture Berlin with all the prob-

As comrades look on, a Russian soldier kisses his rifle as part of an oath to avenge the city of Stalingrad and to fight to the death for the motherland. By April 15, 1945, no fewer than 1.3 million Red Army soldiers were poised along the rivers Oder and Neisse for the great assault on Berlin—the "final hour of vengeance," as Marshal Georgy K. Zhukov called it.

lems it entailed. At that, Patton put his hands on Eisenhower's shoulders and said, "I think history will answer that question for you."

Now, on April 19, Patton sent his tanks rumbling toward the southeast on a mission he could only have deemed of trifling importance: skirting Czechoslovakia's western border, he would aim at Linz, Austria. Along the way, he would also seek and destroy the Nazis' National Redoubt, rumored to be a fortified area in the mountains of southern Germany or western Austria. Patton was convinced that the National Redoubt was a hallucination; his present expedition would prove him correct.

At the same time, on the Allies' extreme right, General Jacob Devers' Sixth Army Group headed almost due south on a march perhaps hindered less by the Germans than by jurisdictional squabbles. Inspired by Charles de Gaulle's ardent desire to carve a place for France in the political settlements that would follow the War, General Jean de Lattre de Tassigny's First French Army constantly encroached on the objectives assigned to the U.S. Seventh Army, thereby interfering with the smooth flow of supplies. Nonetheless, with the French as uninvited but fighting guests, Lieut. General Alexander Patch's Seventh Army seized the Danube River city of Ulm on April 24.

Yet for all such successes in the north and south, the nervous attention of Allied commanders was focused on the center of the Western Front. There, Western and Soviet forces would presumably meet somewhere near the junction of the Elbe and the Mulde rivers. Fearful that an accidental clash might occur between Americans and Russians by now accustomed to shooting first and asking questions later, the U.S. First Army prohibited its patrols from probing more than five miles east of the Mulde.

But early on April 25, impatience got the better of Lieutenant Albert Kotzebue of the First Army's 69th Division. Determined to make the linkup himself, Kotzebue took a jeep patrol well beyond the five-mile limit, came upon a lone Soviet horseman and followed him to the town of Strehla on the Elbe. There, at 1:30 p.m., the Americans met Soviet soldiers of the Fifth Guards Army, which had branched off from the First Ukrainian Army Group when Konev turned his tanks toward Berlin. In reporting the encounter to his headquarters, however, Kotzebue gave the wrong map coordinates. By the time things got straightened out, official recognition for the U.S.-Soviet linkup had already gone to another group—a group that was not even looking for Russians.

Also on April 25, 2nd Lieutenant William D. Robertson, an intelligence officer of the same 69th Division, took three enlisted men on a patrol to search for Allied prisoners of war. Halfway between the Mulde and the Elbe, the little party ran into some released British POWs who said there were plenty of American and Russian prisoners in a camp near Torgau on the Elbe.

In mid-afternoon, Robertson and his men reached Torgau, where they heard small arms fire from across the river, pre-

Soviet tanks and guns jam the roadway near Berlin's Moltke Bridge on April 29, 1945. During the previous day, units of the Third Shock Army had stormed the

sumably from Soviet troops involved in some sort of fight. To identify themselves, the GIs stopped at a pharmacy, picked up colored inks, improvised an American flag and ran it up the turret of a riverside castle. The Russians paid no attention to the flag and even shot at Robertson. From the POW camp, Robertson's men fetched a Russian who shouted to his compatriots. The firing ceased and the Russians started over the river on the twisted girders of a wrecked bridge.

Robertson crawled onto the bridge and at mid-stream came face to face with the leading Russian. They grinned and pounded each other with a joy that needed no words.

Once the fact of a linkup had been officially established, both armies celebrated with toast after toast from an endless supply of Russian vodka. In all the fraternal hubbub, the faltering toast of a Soviet lieutenant perhaps best summed up the emotion on both sides: "You must pardon, I don't speak the right English, but we are very happy, so we drink a toast. My dear, quiet please. Today is the most happy day of our life. Long live our two great armies."

With Germany now severed at the waist, the Western Allies in both the north and the south moved swiftly to wind down their campaigns. While part of Montgomery's command sealed off the Jutland Peninsula in a move clearly calculated to block the Russians' land approaches to Denmark, other elements took Hamburg unopposed and, for all practical purposes, Allied operations on the northern flank ceased by the end of April.

The situation in the south was more complicated. There,

on April 30, with de Lattre's brave and bothersome French finally sidetracked, Devers' troops seized Munich, Germany's third largest city and the birthplace of the Nazi Party. Southward from Munich, the Americans paraded through toylike Bavarian towns where white sheets hung from countless windows in sign of surrender. Then at the end of their march, Devers' soldiers joined with Patton's in plugging the passes of the Austrian Alps, to prevent the escape from Italy of German troops fleeing from Field Marshal Sir Harold Alexander's successful spring offensive.

Since February, negotiations for the surrender of Italy had been going on between Allen Dulles, head of U.S. intelligence operations in Europe, and General Karl Wolff, the highest-ranking SS officer in Italy. Wolff, an unsavory character who had been involved in planning the death camps in Poland, was trying to save his own hide. Earlier in April, his connivings had stalled. Now, however, with German troops everywhere on the run, Wolff redoubled his efforts. With his help, Italy was formally surrendered on May 2, 1945.

By then, Berlin was in its final convulsions.

On the night of April 26, a slow Fieseler-Storch reconnaissance plane skimmed Berlin's treetops carrying two devoted Nazis. General Robert Ritter von Greim, the Luftwaffe commander in the Munich area, had been summoned to the *Führerbunker*, and he had brought along his friend Hanna Reitsch, a woman test pilot of international repute.

On the previous day, tanks of Konev's command had met

heavily defended bridge, the only one still intact over the Spree, and established a foothold just 600 yards from their ultimate goal—the Reichstag.

armored units belonging to Zhukov at Ketzin, on the Mittelland Canal, thereby completing Berlin's encirclement. Now, eight converging Soviet armies were pounding on Berlin's portals, and from Greim's low-flying plane the city looked like hell's anteroom.

Entire city blocks had been set afire by Soviet bombers and artillery. Here and there street fighting flared—a commotion of running men, white puffs of gun smoke and black sprays of rubble from erupting mortar shells or *Panzerfaust*. An artillery shell ripped open the underside of Greim's little plane and smashed the general's foot. Reitsch took the controls and landed safely near the Brandenburg Gate.

At the *Führerbunker*, Hitler declared that Greim had been called to replace that cowardly scoundrel Göring as commander-in-chief of the Luftwaffe. But for Greim and Reitsch, an even higher honor was in store: in response to their pleas, Hitler granted them permission to remain in the bunker and die with him.

Later that night, Hitler handed Reitsch two small blue ampules of potassium cyanide, one for herself and one for Greim. "I do not want any of us to fall to the Russians alive," Hitler said, "nor do I wish our bodies to be found by them. Each person is responsible for destroying his body so that nothing recognizable remains. Eva and I will have our bodies burned. You will devise your own method."

"My Führer," Reitsch sobbed, "why do you stay? Why do you deprive Germany of your life? Save yourself, my Führer; that is the wish of every German."

"No, Hanna," Hitler replied, "I must obey my own command and defend Berlin to the last."

At that moment, outside Hitler's concrete world, other Germans were fighting and dying. Amid the final twitches of Germany's once mighty war machine, only one movement held even the faintest hope of success. Out of the maniacal April 22 conference at which Hitler threw his famous fit had grown a scheme involving Lieut. General Walter Wenck's Twelfth Army. From its position facing the Americans on the Elbe, the Twelfth Army would turn and join General Busse's Ninth Army southeast of Berlin. After that, the combined force would attack toward Berlin and save the city.

Wenck, however, amended the plan. Realizing that Berlin was beyond rescue, he determined to wedge open a corridor to Busse's trapped army; then, rather than submit to the Russians' dubious mercies, the Ninth and Twelfth armies would head for the Elbe and surrender to the Americans.

Now, even as Hitler was passing out his lethal pills, part of Wenck's command, with no tanks and very little artillery, was inching eastward toward a road hub at Beelitz, a likely place for the projected linkup with the Ninth Army. Meanwhile, Busse and his men, surrounded since April 24

HITLER'S LAST REFUGE

On January 16, 1945, Hitler moved his headquarters from Bad Nauheim, west of Berlin, into a bunker that he had ordered constructed under the Reich Chancellery garden near the center of the capital city. Cramped and badly ventilated, its communication system consisting of one radio receiver, one radio telephone and one telephone switchboard, the *Führerbunker* seemed an absurd choice for the Reich's supreme headquarters. Yet Hitler preferred it to his generals' sophisticated OKW command bunker at Zossen, 20 miles away—a preference based, perhaps, on a mistrust of his generals following the attempt to assassinate him the previous summer.

Whatever its shortcomings, as a headquarters or home, the *Führerbunker* was virtually impregnable—both from Allied bombs and German plotters. The roof was 16 feet of concrete, the walls were six and a half feet thick, and the entire structure was buried six feet underground. Its main weakness was the marshy ground of Berlin, which had a high water table; if a large bomb had exploded close enough to the bunker to crack its walls, all the occupants of the structure might have drowned. Inside the bunker, the thunder of war was only a faint rumble—though after a near miss the structure would tremble and the overhead lamps would sway. All visitors, regardless of rank, were disarmed, searched and then required to show passes at SS checkpoints.

The bunker had 19 rooms. Besides Hitler, it housed a few guards, aides, personal servants and physicians. After mid-April, the residents included the Führer's mistress, Eva Braun, and Nazi propaganda chief Joseph Goebbels.

Though almost everyone else escaped the oppressive atmosphere of the bunker periodically, Hitler left very rarely and then for a few hours at most. The last formal occasion was April 20, to attend a celebration at the Reich in honor of his 56th birthday. Ten days later, back in the bunker, he took his own life, one of more than 50 million victims of the war he had started almost six years before.

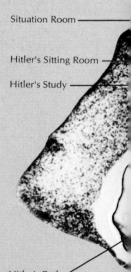

Hitler's Bedroom

Situation Room

Hitler's Sitting Room

Hitler's Study

Hitler's Bath and Dressing Rooms

Toilets

Eva Braun's Bed-Sitting-Room

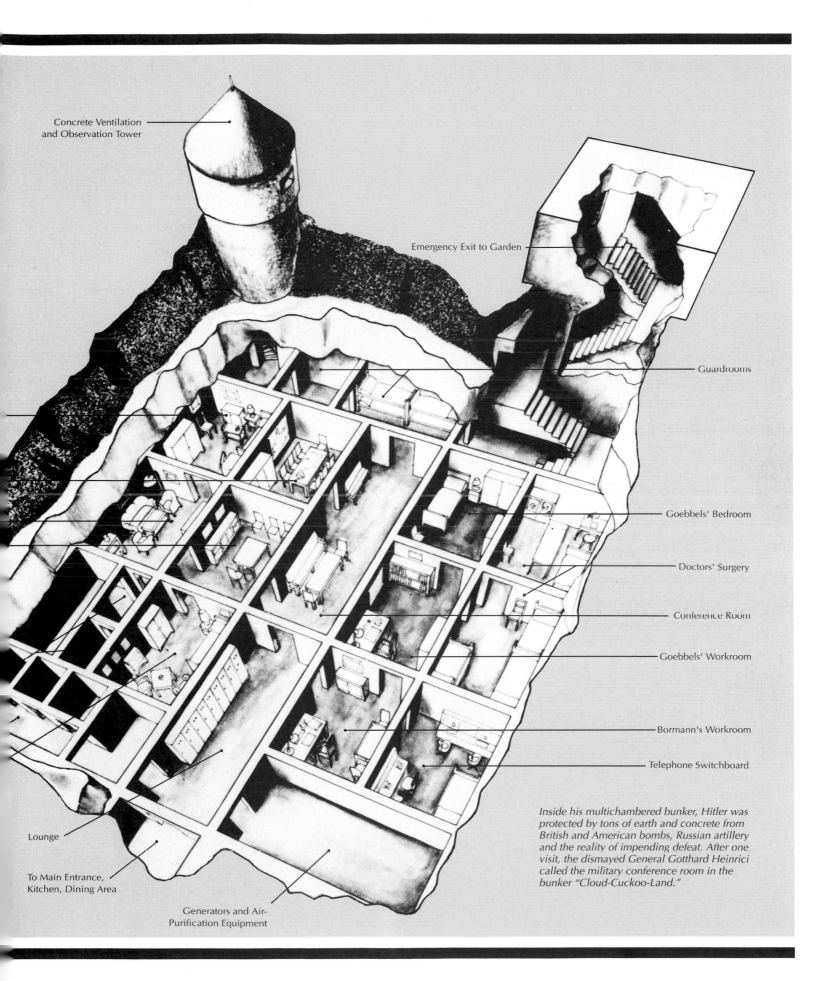

Concrete Ventilation
and Observation Tower

Emergency Exit to Garden

Guardrooms

Goebbels' Bedroom

Doctors' Surgery

Conference Room

Goebbels' Workroom

Bormann's Workroom

Telephone Switchboard

Lounge

To Main Entrance,
Kitchen, Dining Area

Generators and Air-
Purification Equipment

*Inside his multichambered bunker, Hitler was
protected by tons of earth and concrete from
British and American bombs, Russian artillery
and the reality of impending defeat. After one
visit, the dismayed General Gotthard Heinrici
called the military conference room in the
bunker "Cloud-Cuckoo-Land."*

and under attack by five Soviet armies, were struggling with pathetic bravery to reach their rescuers.

Already Busse's army had seized the Baruth-Zossen section of the highway between Berlin and Dresden—but only after some of the war's bloodiest fighting. As Marshal Konev wrote after revisiting Baruth nearly two decades later, "I still saw traces of the carnage. Rusty helmets and equipment were scattered in the woods, while the waters of one of the lakes, which had been filled with corpses during the fighting, could not yet be used."

On April 29, realizing that his men could go no farther, Wenck halted the Twelfth Army. But the Ninth Army continued to strive. On April 30, Busse's vanguard advanced to within one mile of Wenck's outposts at Beelitz. And the next morning Busse's very last tank broke through the Russians. Within hours, the pitiful remnants of the Ninth Army staggered into Wenck's lines. About one seventh of Busse's force—some 30,000 men—had survived. These troops, together with 70,000 of Wenck's, eventually managed to surrender to the U.S. Ninth Army.

In Berlin, flight was not an option: 75,000 German defenders trapped within the closing ring of Soviet steel could only fight, surrender or desert. On April 28, Zhukov's Eighth Guards Army, commanded by General Vasily I. Chuikov, the hero of Stalingrad's defense, started to storm the Landwehr Canal, south of the *Führerbunker*. Across the waterway, and only half a mile from Hitler's last lair, stood what little was left—about 3,500 men and 42 armored vehicles—of the Müncheberg Panzer Division, which had been beaten and battered all the way from the line of the Oder.

Still willing to fight, the Münchebergers set up their command post in a crowded subway tunnel under the Anhalter Railroad Station. "The station looks like an armed camp," one of the division's officers wrote in his diary. "Women and children huddling in niches and corners and listening for the sounds of battle. Suddenly water splashes into our command post. Screams, cries, curses in the tunnel. Water comes rushing through the tunnels. The crowds get panicky, stumble and fall over rails and ties. Children and wounded are deserted, people are trampled to death."

The flood had been caused by SS men who blew a hole in the wall between a subway tunnel and the Landwehr Canal to prevent the Russians from advancing through the underground passageways. They gave no thought to the countless civilians who used the subway as refuge.

For the Russians, the primary objective of the day was a symbolic prize: the immense, fire-gutted shell of the Reichstag, Germany's former legislative house. Not surprisingly, Stalin had awarded the honor of seizing the Reichstag to troops of his military favorite, Zhukov, and at 10:00 a.m.

three battalions of the 3rd Shock Army's 150th Division launched their assault. By mid-afternoon, they had broken into the cavernous structure.

At about that time, only a quarter of a mile to the south of the Reichstag, Adolf Hitler killed himself.

For Hitler, the final blow had involved the prim executioner, Reichsführer-SS Heinrich Himmler. For days, Himmler had been working behind Hitler's back to make a deal in which he would release a token number of Jews from the concentration camp at Ravensbruck as a prelude to negotiating a separate peace with the Western Allies. The Allies, of course, had no intention whatever of sitting down with the man who had cold-bloodedly sent millions of people to their deaths, and a desperate Himmler had been forced into the open.

Thus, on the night of April 28, Hitler received the shattering news that Himmler, in Lübeck, had made a formal offer of surrender to the West. Wallowing in what a member of his household staff described as "a helpless paroxysm of rage, full of hate and contempt," Hitler called Himmler's act "the most shameful betrayal in human history."

Still spewing vituperation, Hitler revoked the promise he had made to General Greim and Hanna Reitsch. Instead of dying with his Führer, Greim was ordered to fly out of Berlin to see that the traitorous Himmler received his just deserts. Greim hobbled off, managed to find a light observation plane and, with Reitsch at the controls, set forth on his mission. (In the event, Greim did confront Himmler, who later said the Luftwaffe commander had "reproved" him. About two weeks later, Greim made use of the cyanide capsule his Führer had given him. Reitsch survived to undergo capture and interrogation by American intelligence.)

Soon after the fliers departed, Hitler paid off his debt to the person he had prophesied would be the only one to remain perfectly loyal to him—Eva Braun. A minor city official named Walter Wagner, fighting in a home-guard unit, was pressed into service to preside at a wedding. With Joseph Goebbels and Martin Bormann as witnesses, Eva Braun and Adolf Hitler declared themselves man and wife. Wagner was then sent on his way—and died of gunshot wounds before he could return to his combat post.

Throughout the next day and far into the night, Hitler prepared to die. On April 30 he was up with the sullen sun. After a quiet morning with old associates, he joined his two secretaries and his cook for a vegetarian lunch of spaghetti and tossed salad. Eva spent the early afternoon cheerfully giving away her possessions to other inmates of the bunker.

Shortly before 3:30 p.m., the Hitlers shook hands all around and retired to the Führer's rooms. Others waited outside to hear the fatal pistol shot—but Hitler's suite was

Bearing their nation's flag, Russian foot soldiers pick their way through the last few yards to the Reichstag, its walls gaping with holes from Soviet shelling.

soundproof. Finally, Hitler's valet pushed open the door. The bitter-almond smell of cyanide and the cordite stink of gunpowder wafted out. Eva Braun was curled up on the sofa in a comfortable position, dead of cyanide poisoning. Hitler was slumped at the other end of the sofa: he had bitten into a cyanide capsule and in the next instant put a bullet through his brain.

The bodies were carried up the bunker's emergency stairway and deposited in a nearby shell hole in the garden. Cans of gasoline were poured into the crude grave. Two officers struck matches but a hot breeze blew them out. Finally, the valet ignited a twist of paper with his pocket lighter and handed it to Hitler's SS aide, who tossed it at the shell hole. The bodies of Adolf and Eva Hitler were enveloped in a sheet of flame.

But there was still more dying left to do. Sometime after 5:00 p.m., Magda Goebbels, wife of the fanatically faithful little Propaganda Minister, fed drugged candy to her six children, and while they slept she crushed cyanide capsules in their mouths. At about 8:30 p.m., Joseph Goebbels escorted Magda up the steps into the garden. They bit into cyanide capsules and died quickly. By arrangement, an SS aide fired shots into their heads for good measure, and the SS performed a perfunctory cremation.

Others chose to live by fleeing the bunker, but only a few made good their escapes. Although one of them may have been Martin Bormann, Arthur Axmann, chief of the Hitler Youth, later said he had seen Bormann's corpse near a bridge in western Berlin.

Not until next day did the Russians learn of Hitler's death, and when Zhukov informed Stalin by telephone, the Soviet dictator pronounced an epitaph—of sorts. "So that's the end of the bastard," said Stalin. "Too bad it was impossible to take him alive."

As one of his final acts in the *Führerbunker*, Hitler had dictated a will bequeathing the Third Reich to Grand Admiral Karl Dönitz, the ruthless, efficient commander-in-chief of the German Navy. One of Dönitz's first deeds was to dispel the pretensions of Heinrich Himmler, who was strutting around northern Germany as if he were the new Führer.

Summoning Himmler to his headquarters at Plön, Dönitz handed him the message of his own appointment as Hitler's successor. "He went very pale," recalled Dönitz. "Finally he stood up and bowed. 'Allow me,' he said, 'to become the second man in your state.' I told him it was out of the question."

For several days, Himmler drifted about northern Germany. Then he shaved off his mustache, donned an eye patch, adopted the pseudonym Heinrich Hitzinger and went into hiding. In mid-May a British dragnet caught up with him. When a doctor tried to investigate a little bulge in his cheek, Himmler bit down on a cyanide capsule and swiftly expired.

Meanwhile, Dönitz was aghast at what was happening to his people. In the Soviet drive west, Stalin's armies had

wreaked a terrible vengeance on soldier and civilian alike. Long, helpless lines of German refugees had been ground to pulp beneath the treads of Soviet tanks. Rape, murder and plunder were the order of the day. In the small town of Nemmersdorf, for just one instance, 72 women were later found raped and slaughtered, numbers of them nailed naked to the wheels of carts and the doors of barns. And now in Berlin, the victors visited upon the vanquished a plague of horrors unknown in modern warfare. Virtually the entire female population of Berlin came under savage assault; women of every age and condition were raped repeatedly, some of them two and three dozen times. According to a postwar study, more than 90,000 women sought some sort of medical assistance afterward. How many died or committed suicide will never be known. Nor will it be known how many men and boys were shot, bayoneted or clubbed to death.

There was nothing whatsoever that Dönitz could do about Germany's helpless civilians. But he could hope to maneuver his remaining combat forces so that they might surrender to the Western Allies instead of to the Russians. And to accomplish that he would have to play for time.

He was only partially successful: during the first few days of his regime, as many as 210,000 German troops evaded the Russians and streamed into American and British lines. But the escape of Germans from Yugoslavia, Austria, and especially Czechoslovakia had barely begun by the time Dönitz's delaying strategy began to unravel.

Confronted by an Eisenhower ultimatum that demanded both complete surrender in the West and simultaneous surrender to the Russians, Dönitz finally authorized General Alfred Jodl to journey to SHAEF's forward base in the French cathedral town of Rheims. Although he was under instructions to continue stalling, Jodl discovered soon after his arrival on the evening of May 6 that the Allies had wearied of the German waiting game.

Acting for Eisenhower, Lieut. General Walter Bedell Smith presented an instrument calling for the unconditional and simultaneous surrender at 11:01 p.m. on May 8 of all German land, sea and air forces on all fronts. Given a scant 30 minutes to make a decision, Jodl radioed Dönitz: "I see no alternative—chaos or signature."

Dönitz reluctantly agreed, and soon after midnight on April 7, representatives of the warring nations gathered in the SHAEF war room—a recreation hall in the red brick boys' school that served as headquarters—to sign the document of unconditional surrender. At precisely 2:41 a.m., Jodl was the first to affix his name, followed by General Smith for the Supreme Commander of the Allied Expeditionary Force and General Ivan Susloparov for the Soviet High Command.

Then, after receiving permission to speak, Jodl arose.

At Eisenhower's headquarters in Rheims, France, General Alfred Jodl stands to indicate his readiness to sign an unconditonal surrender covering all German forces. Jodl's aide, Major Wilhelm Oxenius, sits at left: at right is Admiral Hans-Georg von Friedeburg.

His child perched on his shoulder, a German soldier seeking a haven for his family trudges toward the British lines.

"With this signature," he said, "the German people and German armed forces are, for better or worse, delivered into the victor's hands. In this hour I can only express the hope that the victor will treat them with generosity."

From General Dwight Eisenhower came a message to the world: "The mission of this Allied force was fulfilled at 0241, local time, May 7, 1945."

Yet there was a hitch even then: six hours after the Rheims ceremony, Moscow claimed that General Susloparov had exceeded his authority and insisted that the official surrender document be signed in Berlin. And so, on May 8, 1945, it was.

Even though the war in Europe was officially over, the killing was not yet done. Indeed, even as the Germans were signing the surrender papers, some of the war's ugliest episodes were taking place in Prague, whose large population of resident Sudetan Germans was now swollen by German refugees from elsewhere in Czechoslovakia.

Frenzied by a need to avenge six years of suffering, the Czechs fell upon every German they could find, including their own Sudetan countrymen. German women were seized by maddened mobs, spat upon, shorn, painted with swastikas and publicly raped. Some were stripped and forced to work, nude, dismantling barricades. Some had their Achilles tendons cut, and crowds jeered as they screamed and flopped around on the ground. German children were thrown from windows and drowned in horse troughs.

Bound together with barbed wire, German men, women and children were rolled into the Vlatava River. In twos and threes, the dead floated downstream into the Elbe. Two weeks later—after the last of 30,000 German civilians had been killed in Prague—thousands of bodies were still being pulled from the river.

Neither did the German armed forces in Czechoslovakia escape the terror. Rushing westward to surrender to American forces, most were turned back at U.S. Third Army roadblocks drawn up by arrangement with the Soviets, just east of the towns of Karlsbad, Pilsen and Budweis. As a result, they suffered the fate they feared most: capture by Marshal Konev's First Ukrainian Army Group, whose two tank armies had rushed down from Berlin to seize Prague and occupy central and eastern Czechoslovakia.

From his precarious position at the head of the German government, Dönitz had been helpless to stem the violence against his countrymen in Czechoslovakia. Then, on May 23, he and Jodl were summoned by SHAEF authorities and ordered to consider themselves prisoners of war. The Third Reich, whose existence had been extended for a little more than three weeks after the death of its founder, was finally defunct.

Just five weeks after war in Europe had officially ended, the new President of the United States, Harry S Truman, landed in devastated Berlin for a summit meeting with Josef Stalin and Winston Churchill. At their sessions in suburban Potsdam, the Big Three planned to discuss how best to deal with a conquered Germany and a continent shattered by war. For Truman, however, Europe's future stood second to a more pressing American priority: victory over Japan.

On the day after his arrival, Truman toured the rubbled streets of the German capital, then returned to the "Little White House", a run-down villa that had belonged to a German movie producer. There, Secretary of War Henry Stimson handed him a cable from the U.S.: DIAGNOSIS NOT YET COMPLETE BUT RESULTS SEEM SATISFACTORY.

In its cryptic way, the message informed the President that a new day had dawned in the history of the human race: the U.S. had successfully tested an atomic bomb. For the Japanese, that awesome weapon would trigger a holocaustal nightmare of suffering and death. For the world, it would bring a kind of peace in a perilous postwar era called the Atomic Age.

The unparalleled technological achievement was the result of a supremely secret effort by hundreds of thousands of Americans, who had worked for the previous three years at far-flung installations under the aegis of an

A Czech partisan marches a German prisoner down a Prague street during the uprising of May 1945. The Czechs exacted a brutal vengeance for their years under the Nazi boot: in the course of three days, besides routing the few German troops and police left in the city, they killed 30,000 German civilian residents, mostly women and children.

President Harry S Truman, his back to the camera, turns toward Soviet Generalissimo Josef Stalin as the summit meeting at Potsdam begins on July 17, 1945. British Prime Minister Winston Churchill, at upper left, suggested that Truman lead the opening session of the conference, his first as a member of the Big Three.

obscure agency called the Manhattan Engineer District.

Their work had come to unearthly fruition on July 15, 1945 at the Army Air Force Alamagordo Bombing Range, about 200 miles south of Los Alamos. At 5:29 a.m. a bomb, incongruously named Fat Man, sent the fireball of the world's first atomic explosion boiling skyward. To one of those who were present, the New York Times' William Laurence, it was a moment in which "time stood still. Space contracted to a pin point. It was as though the earth had opened and the skies split. One felt as though he had been privileged to witness the birth of the world."

Upon receiving the news in Potsdam, Harry Truman was elated. To Truman, who had been given no inkling of the Manhattan Project while he was Roosevelt's Vice-President, the atomic bomb was "the greatest thing in history." Then and later, the President would find himself beset by advisors agonizing about the military necessity and the moral implications of the bomb. As far as Truman was concerned, the arguments were academic. "I regarded the bomb as a military weapon," he wrote later, "and never had any doubt that it should be used."

Behind that bare statement lay vital considerations. For one thing, by using the bomb the U.S. could avoid the appalling casualties—estimated at one million Americans—that would be suffered during an invasion of the Japanese home islands. For another, possession of the bomb meant that Soviet help against Japan was no longer required,

and the U.S. need make no more concessions to Stalin.

However, lest he later be accused of keeping his Soviet ally completely in the dark, Truman determined that he must give Stalin at least a hint of what had happened. Thus, just as a luncheon was breaking up on July 24, the American President walked nonchalantly up to Stalin's interpreter and asked him to "tell the Generalissimo that we have perfected a very powerful explosive which we are going to use against the Japanese and we think it will end the war." Stalin replied cooly, expressing a hope that the U.S. would "make good use of it against Japan."

Truman had not used the words "atomic" or "nuclear," and Stalin had asked no questions. In fact, he had need of none: Soviet intelligence had penetrated the Manhattan Project in 1943, and the U.S.S.R. was already working on its own nuclear weaponry. Its subsequent success would become a key ingredient in the peacetime struggle between East and West that soon became known as the Cold War.

Later that day, Truman approved an order to be issued by the Joint Chiefs-of-Staff. It began: "The Twentieth Air Force will deliver its first special bomb as soon as weather will permit visual bombing after about August 3, 1945, on one of these targets: Hiroshima, Kokura, Niigata or Nagasaki."

On July 26, half a world away from the Potsdam Conference, the heavy cruiser *Indianapolis* dropped anchor at Tinian in the Marianas. After a brief stay, the warship

departed for the Philippines. Three days out, the cruiser was sunk by torpedoes from the Japanese submarine *I-58*. Of the 1,200 men aboard, barely 300 would live to learn that the cargo they had left behind on Tinian contained the components of the first atomic bomb to be dropped on Japan.

When its assembly was completed under the direction of Navy Captain William Parsons, the Manhattan Project's chief ordnance officer, the bomb was 10 feet long, 28 inches thick and weighed about 9,000 pounds. To distinguish it from Fat Man, the spherical plutonium device tested at Alamagordo, the uranium bomb at Tinian was dubbed Little Boy.

In considering targets for Little Boy, a committee of scientists and military strategists had looked, according to General Groves, for places whose destruction "would most adversely affect the will of the Japanese to continue the war." The group had come up with a list of four cities, and now it was up to Major General Curtis E. LeMay, chief of staff of the Army's new Strategic Air Forces, Pacific, to make the final choice. On August 2, LeMay met on Guam with Colonel Paul W. Tibbets Jr., commander of the innocuously designated 509th Composite Group that was to drop the bomb. "Paul," said LeMay through a cloud of cigar smoke, "the primary's Hiroshima."

LeMay's selection of Hiroshima, on the main island of Honshu, was based on its twofold importance. In addition to serving as a major assembly point for convoys of the Japanese Navy, it was also the site of numerous war plants upon whose output the Japanese depended for the defense of their islands. To repel an invasion the Japanese fully expected to come from the sea, nearly 10,000 planes of all sorts were ready for employment as Kamikazes. Behind the suicide craft were nearly three million soldiers and 28 million civilians who were being trained to make a heroic last stand. Teenage girls were given long, sharp woodworking awls and told, "If you don't kill at least one enemy soldier, you don't deserve to die."

For the citizens of Hiroshima, all the feverish preparations were for nothing when doom struck from the sky.

At precisely 08:15:17 on August 6, 1945, Little Boy tumbled toward Hiroshima from a B-29 Superfortress named the Enola Gay. Forty-three seconds later, a pinkish, purplish flash appeared—and grew, and grew, and grew. From his tail gunner's seat, Sergeant George Caron spoke into a recorder and described the scene for posterity: "A column of smoke rising fast. It has a fiery red core. Here it comes, the mushroom shape that Captain Parsons spoke about. It's like a mass of bubbling molasses. It's nearly level with us and climbing. It's very black but there is a purplish tint to the cloud. The city must be below that."

So it was—what was left of it.

On the ground in Hiroshima, an unimaginable incandescence had swallowed the sky and outshone the sun. The heat in the fireball above the city was later calculated at 540,000 degrees F. At Ground Zero, directly below the fire-

In Japan, soldiers, farmers and women in traditional garb build a camouflaged gun emplacement as part of a defense network along Shibushi Bay on Kyushu.

THE CREATION OF THE BOMB

The chain of events that led to the creation of the bomb began with scientific experiments conducted during the 1930s. As physicists in the United States and on the Continent labored to discover how the atomic structure of matter might be transformed, uranium and plutonium seemed the most promising targets.

On December 9, 1938, two scientists in Berlin succeeded in accomplishing something extraordinary: they split the nucleus of an atom. By March 1939, refugee Hungarian physicist Leo Szilard produced a laboratory-scale chain reaction using uranium. This significant advance meant that nuclear power—and an atomic weapon—was indeed theoretically possible. "That night," said Szilard, "I knew the world was headed for sorrow."

As experiments continued to reveal the mysterious characteristics of uranium and plutonium, a burning moral question persisted: what should the scientists do with their potent new knowledge? Their answer to the question was dictated by concern that an enemy might develop the bomb first.

The scientists, albeit meeting with laboratory success, failed to spark governmental interest. They persuaded Albert Einstein, whose pioneering theory outlined the relationship between matter and energy, to sign a letter to President Roosevelt. The letter—which described the development of nuclear chain reactions that would generate vast amounts of power, and warned of the consequences—was received on October 11, 1939. The eventual result was presidential approval of a project named the Manhattan Engineer District (an obscurity intended to deflect attention from its real purpose), which in time, according to Hungarian scientist Edward Teller, turned "the whole of the United States" into a nuclear factory.

The so-called Manhattan Project, the most ambitious and costly scientific endeavor ever conceived by the mind of man, marshaled the genius of nuclear physicists, the resources of giant industry and the ingenuity of obscure craftsmen. At its peak, the project commanded the energies of more than 600,000 Americans, and all but a select few worked in ignorance of the common goal: the creation of an atomic bomb.

Finally, after three years of labor and more than 2 billion dollars spent, "Fat Man," the first atomic bomb, was created. But a monumental question remained: Would it work?

There was one way to find out; the site chosen for the July 16, 1945 test lay in the heart of the Army Air Forces' Alamogordo Bombing Range, about 200 miles south of Los Alamos, New Mexico. There, in the heat-seared, pitiless region known to early Spanish Explorers as *Jornada del Muerto* (Journey of Death), J. Robert Oppenheimer, the Manhattan Project's central laboratory scientific chief, clung to a post for support. As the bomb's fireball ascended over the desert, the stunned scientist thought of an ominous line from the Bhagavad-Gita, a sacred Hindu text: "I am become Death, the shatterer of worlds."

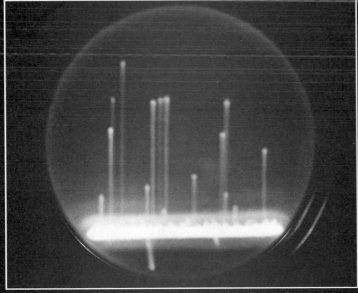

The vertical pulses on a voltage indicator record the bursts of energy released when U-235 (an isotope of natural uranium) atoms are split. By 1940, nuclear scientists possessed the raw materials and the crude process for creating the most powerful energy source ever conceived by mankind: U-235 plutonium set loose in an instantaneous chain reaction.

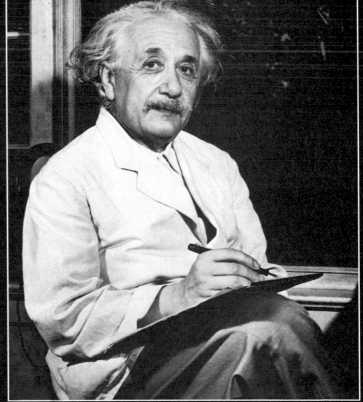

Albert Einstein makes notes in his study at Princeton University in 1943. It was Einstein's letter to President Franklin D. Roosevelt in 1939 that got the United States started on the Manhattan Project. The action ultimately taken, however, moved the gentle Einstein, years later, to remark: "I made one great mistake in my life, when I signed the letter to President Roosevelt."

"THE DAY THE SUN ROSE TWICE"

Then there was light brighter than any before it, light that would have outshone the noonday sun and been visible from Venus or Mars. It began as a brilliant, bleaching white, then deepened to yellow, peach and purple as the rolling fireball spiraled upward, spewing flame and trailing a skirt of molten sand. It lent to everything a preternatural clarity and suffused everything with a warmth derived from a core heat that was four times greater than that of the sun.

Among the observers, the response was awed silence. One scientist thought the air itself was on fire. Another, watching monitoring equipment, took the bomb for a dud until he noticed the light and realized that his needles had jumped off their scales. Men were knocked down when the shock wave hit seconds after the blast, and they were deafened by the roar that followed.

.006 second

.016 second

.034 second

2 seconds

4 seconds

6 seconds

Then came relief, even unscientific elation: The observers on one hill broke into a jig while others writhed in a snake dance through the south control center.

Agents in Albuquerque and Santa Fe saw the incredible light and wondered if anyone closer had survived. Hundreds of miles away, tremors were felt and windows rattled. Civilians thought an airborne bomber had exploded, or the Japanese had invaded, or a natural disaster had occurred—one variously suspected to be an earthquake, a meteor crash or an electrical storm. A woman on the Arizona border reported that the sun rose twice that day, once very quickly. Horses in stables whinnied hysterically, toads fell silent, dogs shivered all morning in the desert heat. A GI sleeping off a drunk at Trinity base camp leaped awake at the shock and was blinded by the light—something he took, during subsequent psychiatric treatment, to be God's punishment for drinking on the Sabbath.

A surging mass of boiling debris and gaseous flame, the nuclear blast (left) rumbles across the desert floor just one twentieth of a second after detonation. In the timed sequence below, the pictures taken during the first second (top row) were shot with a telephoto lens, the subsequent ones (bottom row) with a normal lens.

.072 second

.100 second

1 second

8 seconds

10 seconds

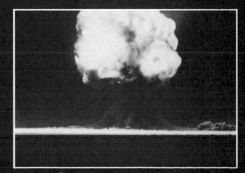
15 seconds

ball, the Shima Clinic, a private hospital, was virtually vaporized by heat of 11,000 degrees F and air pressure that reached eight tons per square yard.

As a gigantic hemisphere of superheated air rushed outward in every direction at 1,200 feet per second, clay roof tiles with a melting point of 2,300 degrees F. dissolved within 600 yards of Ground Zero; within 1,000 yards, the surface of granite building stones melted; two miles away, wooden buildings burst instantly into flame.

The bomb's frightful phenomena did not stop with the flash and the horrendous blast. At various times over different areas of the ruined city, rain fell. The huge drops were black, and they left on unburned skin gray stains that would not wash off. Those upon whom the rain fell had no way of knowing at the time that they were being pelted by drops polluted with lethal radioactivity.

Out of Hiroshima's turbulent gloom marched a stumbling, stunned parade of thousands—the naked, the blackened and the faceless—who had left their dead behind. Estimates would later put the death count as a direct result of the bomb at 140,000. But no one could predict the years and even decades in which the aftereffects of radiation would claim new victims.

In the U.S., President Truman issued a statement with a warning. "The force from which the sun draws its power has been loosed upon those who brought war to the Far East," it said. "If they do not now accept our terms they may expect a rain of ruin from the air, the like of which has never been seen on this earth."

There was no reply from Japan.

And now the Russian bear made known its intention to feast upon the stricken empire: in his Kremlin office on August 8, Foreign Minister Vyacheslav M. Molotov informed the Japanese Ambassador that a state of war existed between their nations. The next day at 5:00 p.m., 1.6 million Soviet troops crashed across the Manchurian border to assault Japan's Kwantung Army.

Still, Japan did not surrender, and on August 9, true to Truman's threat, another atomic bomb was dropped, this one on Nagasaki, a shipbuilding and torpedo-factory center on the southern island of Kyushu. In human terms, the Nagasaki plutonium bomb (its prototype was the original Fat Man) was somewhat less lethal than its Hiroshima predecessor: estimates later placed the death toll at 70,000.

With Nagasaki's cataclysm came Japan's capitulation. That night, after many tense hours of wrangling at an imperial conference, the shy marine biologist who was the 124th emperor in a line that went back to the seventh century A.D., at last stepped forth to lead his people in fact as well as in myth. "The time has come," said Emperor Hirohito, "when we must bear the unbearable."

By dawn on the morning of August 10, each Cabinet member had signed a statement accepting the surrender terms of the Potsdam Proclamation, on the condition that "the supreme power of the Emperor not be compromised." That was agreeable to the U.S., but only after some fancy diplomatic toe-dancing that enabled the Americans to meet the Japanese stipulation even while claiming that the surrender had been unconditional.

And so it was done.

Officers representing the Allied nations face the Japanese delegation across a table on the battleship Missouri on September 2, 1945. General MacArthur (at microphone) watches General Yoshijiro Umezu sign the surrender document.

At 8:55 o'clock on the morning of September 2, 1945, Japan's new Foreign Minister Mamoru Shigemitsu, who had years before lost his left leg to an assassin's bomb, painfully made his way up a gangway to the battleship *Missouri* in Tokyo Bay. Thousands of American sailors, soldiers and newsmen watched intently as General Douglas MacArthur took his place behind a mess table and faced the nine-member Japanese delegation. "It is my earnest hope," said MacArthur, his hands shaking visibly, "indeed the hope of all mankind, that from this solemn occasion a better world shall emerge out of the blood and carnage of the past."

After the peace treaty was signed, and as the Japanese were leaving, the sun came out for the first time that day, illuminating the peak of Mount Fuji and sparkling off the fusilages of 1,900 Allied planes that flew overhead in spectacular salute.

The greatest tragedy in mankind's history, one that had claimed 55 million military and civilian lives and consumed untold material wealth, was finally ended. After six years, the guns were silent.

SHATTERED WORLDS

A mushroom-shaped cloud boils up over Nagasaki as superheated air from the atomic fireball condenses in the cooler layers of the atmosphere. The pillar of steam, dust and ash rose more than 12 miles above the earth.

Government officials survey the rubble of Nagasaki 24 hours after the major industrial city was devastated by the second atomic bomb dropped on Japan.

AN UNIMAGINABLE FORCE

With a force beyond the previous comprehension of mankind, the atomic bombs of August 1945 reduced Hiroshima and Nagasaki from bustling centers of war industry to blackened wastelands. "It seemed impossible," said one eyewitness, "that such a scene could have been created by human means."

The bombs left thousands of victims to die slow, agonizing deaths. For thousands more, it had been more merciful; they had died in the blinking of an eye—so quickly that perhaps they had been unaware of dying.

In an effort to calculate the dimensions of the bombs' power, a group of Japanese scientists probed through the ruins for days afterward. They discovered that the air bursts had produced pressures that matched the sustained thrust a tidal wave, knocking down all but the strongest buildings of concrete and steel. Heat, measured in thousands of degrees Fahrenheit and traveling at the speed of light, had set fire to wooden structures that were more than a mile from Ground Zero, the hypocenter above which each bomb exploded. At twice that distance, infrared rays had charred telephone poles and burned human skin.

In Hiroshima, a thermal wave swept out over the city, setting alight the homes in its path. Into the vacuum created by its passing roared hurricane-like winds, fanning a fire storm that raged for hours. In all, 62,000 of Hiroshima's 90,000 buildings were destroyed.

In Nagasaki, hills separating its industrial quarter from the rest of the city blocked the thermal wave, and no fire storm followed. Even so, the wave of heat instantly ignited wooden buildings within two miles of the hypocenter, and 11,500 of the city's 52,000 residences burned to the ground.

Exactly how many people died in Hiroshima as a direct result of the atomic bomb has never been determined with strict accuracy. Initial figures placed the dead at 68,670 and the wounded at 72,880. Later estimates raised the death count to 140,000. At Nagasaki, the plutonium bomb proved to be a reaper not so lethal as its Hiroshima predecessor: 37,507 dead, 26,709 wounded. By December 1945, the death count was raised to 70,000.

But the horror of the bombs extended well beyond the casualty lists of the times. In the years and even decades that followed the appearance of the mushroom clouds, latent radiation chose new victims at random and with little warning. Indeed for a time, there was a rumor that the Americans had seeded their devilish bombs with some virulent germ or lingering poison gas. As hundreds of seemingly healthy people became ill and died with symptoms of radiation sickness, or from illnesses thought to be spawned by radiation, the people of Hiroshima and Nagasaki came to realize that none among them could be absolutely sure of having escaped the wrath of the nuclear explosions. Thus to the list of terrors introduced by the atomic bomb was added another: the terror of the unknown.

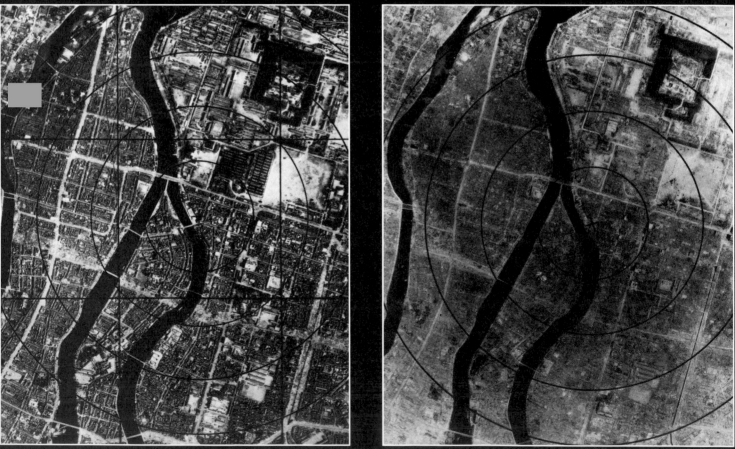

Aerial photographs of Hiroshima before and after August 6 attest to the bomb's devastating effect. An X marks the approximate drop point, or Ground Zero; the circles indicate 1,000-foot intervals. The intended aiming point was the T-shaped Aioi Bridge, visible at the upper left of the inner circle.

On the day after the atomic bomb was dropped on Nagasaki, a wounded woman sips water from a canteen while her moribund companions sit or sprawl lethargically amidst the ruins of the city.

Shadows burned into a wooden observation tower and outlined in chalk by investigators record a Nagasaki air-raid observer's last moments. After descending from his post by laddor (left), the observer hung up his sword belt (right) and was unbuttoning his jacket when the bomb exploded.

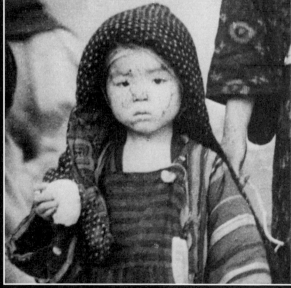

His face still blank from the horror and shock almost 24 hours after the bomb blast, a bandaged child clutches his emergency ration—a ball of boiled rice distributed by a relief party.

435

SCENES OF HORROR THAT SEARED THE SOUL

Pika-don was the name the Japanese invented to describe the incredibly powerful weapons that exploded over Hiroshima on August 6, 1945, and over Nagasaki three days later. The term combines the word for "lightning flash" with the sound of an explosion; its syllables faintly imitate a sky-splitting crackle followed by a thunderclap. What happened next remained stamped forever in the minds of those who witnessed the calamity and lived to tell about it.

There were almost no survivors within a 500-yard radius of Ground Zero. Those beyond that lethal range recalled seeing in the first seconds a brilliant blue-white flash that became a burgeoning orange ball, emitting unbearable heat. Almost at once a violent blast of air shredded buildings, clothes and flesh, and everything combustible seemed to take fire.

The appalling hours that followed are illustrated on these two pages by eyewitnesses who almost 30 years

later were inspired by a Japanese television documentary to turn to art as a forum for recording—and exorcising—their memories of the awful event. Using pencils, crayons, paints or marking pens, more than 1,000 ordinary citizens of Hiroshima and Nagasaki called upon their nightmarish recollections to create these extraordinarily vivid images. The Japan Broadcasting Corporation assembled the drawings for public exhibition, and selections were later featured in a book entitled *Unforgettable Fire*.

The artists felt compelled to pass on their memories to a generation they fervently hoped would thereby sense the horror of war without experiencing it firsthand. "I still cannot erase the scene from my memory," said one aged survivor. "Before I died, I had to draw it and leave it for others."

Many were frustrated by the impossibility of fully conveying what they remembered. One elderly woman made sketch after sketch, then exclaimed bitterly: "Even if I drew a hundred pictures, they could not tell you of my experiences."

In artist Kishiro Nagara's picture, ash-blackened radioactive rain falls on a group of scorched-naked schoolgirls and two straggling boys (right) following a teacher seeking shelter.

In Kizo Kawakami's vivid recollection of an outdoor aid station in Hiroshima, a mother, with dressings on her burns, nurses her child while an attendant peels charred clothing from a woman's wounds.

The body of a little girl is huddled against the stone embankment of the Enko River, where she died nursing her wounds. Masato Yamashita remembered finding her there three days after the Hiroshima bombing.

THE AFTERMATH: EUROPE

A young Polish girl surveys the ruins of the Warsaw ghetto in April 1946. More than 50,000 bodies lay buried beneath the rubble

THE POLITICAL FACE OF POSTWAR EUROPE

The redrawn map of Europe that emerged from World War II ref█████ one immense change: the westward spread of Communism through both the expansion of the Soviet Union and the imposition of Communist governments upon land █e Red Army had occupied.

With modest adjustments, Western Europe reverted to its prewar boundaries. But not so the East. From Finland southward to Rumania, the border of the Soviet Union was extended westward. On the Baltic Sea, Estonia, Latvia and Lithuania no longer existed, except as provincial "republics" within the U.S.S.R. East Prussia—a former German territory just southwest of Lithuania—was divided between Poland and the Soviet Union. Poland, which had been carved in two by Germany and the Soviet Union at the beginning of the War, now gained territory in the West from Germany; German occupants of the area were forcibly displaced. On the other hand, a large eastern section of Poland—which had been occupied by the Red Army in 1939, was lost to the U.S.S.R. And truncated Germany was divided, east from west, into two eventually independent states.

Not long after the War's end, all the nations of Eastern Europe except Greece and Turkey had Communist govern-ment█ █████inated by the Soviet Union. Although not occu-pied █y the Red Army, Yugoslavia and Albania, where Communists had led the resistance against German occupation, were governed by their own Communist regimes.

POSTWAR BOUNDARIES ———————

PREWAR BOUNDARIES – – – – –

SOVIET-IMPOSED COMMUNISM

INDIGENOUS COMMUNISM

TERRITORY GAINED BY THE SOVIET UNION

TERRITORY LOST BY GERMANY

0   100   200   300   400
SCALE OF MILES

Reykjavik
Iceland

Norwegian Sea

North Atlantic Ocean

North Sea

Dublin
Ireland

United Kingdom

London   Amsterdam

Brussels
Belgium —

Paris
Luxembourg

France

Bern
Switzerland —

Portugal
Lisbon

Madrid
Spain

Beneath a newly designed emblem of a world framed by olive branches, symbols of peace, the General Assembly of the United Nations convenes in London in 1946.

A UNITED FRONT AGAINST FUTURE WARS

In a great London hall on January 10, 1946, Acting President Zuleta Angel, a Colombian, solemnly convened the first general session of the United Nations by quoting from its Charter: "Determined to save succeeding generations from the scourge of war," he said simply, "we have come."

The U.N., like its failed predecessor the League of Nations, had been conceived in the heat of war as a mechanism for avoiding future conflicts. President Roosevelt was one of its earliest advocates; Prime Minister Churchill had passionately declared that "Twice in a single generation the catastrophe of world war has fallen upon us. Do we not owe it to ourselves, to our children, to mankind tormented to make sure that these catastrophes shall not engulf us for the third time?"

Early in 1945, envoys of the Allied governments met in San Francisco and wrote a charter for a United Nations Organization that was subsequently signed by 51 countries. The Charter not only established principles of peaceful coexistence among nations but also promised individuals the right to basic human freedoms.

The U.N. organized itself into six units: the Economic and Social Council to improve world living standards; the Trusteeship Council to protect the interests of those living in trust territories; the International Court of Justice; an administrative Secretariat; and, most visibly, two deliberative bodies, the General Assembly and the Security Council.

The General Assembly gave every nation the chance to be heard on the world stage. The smaller Security Council was empowered to make decisions on matters of international peace and security. It originally had five permanent seats, held by the major wartime Allies (China, France, the U.S.S.R., the United Kingdom and the U.S.), and six rotating seats filled by nations elected for two-year terms.

However ideally conceived, no world body can be more potent than its sovereign parts allow, and the U.N. proved no exception. Seven votes were needed to pass a resolution in the Security Council, and a single "no" from a permanent member could defeat it. In February 1946, the Soviet Union became the first to use the veto: it killed a resolution urging the withdrawal of French and British troops from newly independent Syria and Lebanon.

Eventually the diverging interests of the Communist and non-Communist worlds, as well as such volatile issues as independence for Indonesia and the partition of Palestine, ended the U.N.'s honeymoon phase.

Nevertheless, the United Nations survived, finding a permanent home in New York City in 1951, and there were those who continued to share President Harry Truman's spirited mandate to the 1945 San Francisco planning conference: "You are to be the architects of a better world. In your hands rests our future."

A trio of world leaders, British Prime Minister Clement Attlee, U.S. President Harry S Truman and Soviet dictator Josef Stalin put on a show of harmony during the Potsdam Conference in July 1945. One intention of the conference—to continue in peacetime the Grand Alliance that had won the War—lived on in spirit with the conception of the United Nations.

A MERCILESS WAR'S HORRENDOUS PRICE

Often called the greatest tragedy in mankind's history, World War II exacted a fearful price in death and destruction. From London to the gates of Moscow, from Finland to Greece, much of Europe lay in ruins, and the death toll was so huge that it beggared ordinary grief. More than 33 million Europeans are known to have lost their lives and the actual number was probably closer to 40 million. Ironically, battle deaths—except on the ferocious slaughterhouse of the Russian front—were light compared to the wholesale carnage among Europe's civil populations; less than one million uniformed combatants were killed on the various western fronts from Norway to North Africa, and from Normandy to the Rhine.

Eastern Europe had suffered the most, both in actual numbers and percentage of population killed. Partly in combat, but in the majority of cases through cold-blooded murder, Poland had lost more than one sixth of its pre-war population of 32 million. Some 20 million Russians had perished, or one tenth of the nation's population. Moreover, an estimated 6,500,000 Jews, Gypsies and others deemed "undesirable" by Hitler's murderous minions had been liquidated.

The material destruction in Europe was as appalling as the human slaughter. Hundreds upon hundreds of cities suffered major damage from air raids, shellfire, street fighting and the scorched-earth policies of both Germans and Russians. The Polish capital of Warsaw had almost been wiped from the face of the earth. Ancient and beautiful German cities like Hamburg and Dresden had been incinerated by fire storms ignited by incendiary bombs. Berlin was so bat-tered that engineers estimated it would take 15 years to clear the rubble. The Austrian town of Wiener Neustadt, for example, had been virtually obliterated by air raids followed by street battles, and its population was reduced from a pre-war 45,000 to a meager 860. "What is Europe now?" wrote Winston Churchill in 1947. "A rubble heap, a charnel house, a breeding ground of pestilence and hate."

Across this ravaged landscape wandered millions of displaced persons, trying first of all to find something to eat, then to make their way home. Hunger was everywhere as Europe's fields lay fallow, and the little that was grown could not be distributed by the Continent's ruined transportation systems. Somehow many survived and managed to get home alive if not intact. But for many others the road would prove too long, and they joined the legions of the dead in the mass grave that Europe had become.

After returning by train from a Russian POW camp in September 1945, two former German soldiers enter occupied Berlin on one pair of feet. By then, Germany was a nation in purgatory.

In a Sicily ravaged by war, two ragged and barefooted children hungrily watch a man finish a bowl of gruel in a Palermo d...

GERMANY'S BITTER HARVEST

Nowhere was the physical devastation more numbing than in Germany. Bombed around the clock for months, invaded by armies from both east and west, the nation that had begun the conflict ended up half junkyard, half graveyard. His first sight of █████in, where 95 per cent of the central city was in ruins, appalled Lieut. General Lucius D. Clay, the brilliant United States officer assigned to be military governor of the American-occupied sectors of Germany. "Wherever we looked we saw desolation," Clay wrote. "It was like a city of the dead." And later he added: "Suffering and shock were visible in every face. Dead bodies still remained in canals and lakes and were being dug out from under bomb debris."

And many thousands more would die, as famine and disease spread through Berlin and Germany's other towns and cities. No less than 4,000 Berliners died each day during August 1945, and fully half of all babies born that month failed to survive. Only large imports of food into the British and American zones during the first post-war winter kept the average German ration at a bare 1500 calories or so per day, and the spring of 1946 was worse as grain shortages halted shipments. More and more Germans lived on a single daily meal of watery soup with perhaps one marble-sized meatball. People often collapsed at work or in the streets; untold thousands died of malnutrition. Most children went without shoes, and many people lacked winter coats.

In the major urban centers, housing was virtually nonexistent. The fortunate found some shelter in ruined houses or apartments; many █████in caves that had been dug beneath the

In bombed-out Hamburg, a couple hangs up laundry in an apartment without walls.

A Dresden couple in their seventies labor patiently in the rubble of their fire-bombed city, sorting out reusable bricks and stone. Organized into groups, thousands of Germans devoted their Sundays and whatever free time they had to the massive job of salvaging the cities.

rubble. In the city of Dusseldorf, where 95 per cent of the residential structures were uninhabitable, the average living space was reduced to only four square yards per person.

There were few if any jobs. Industry was at a standstill even where factories and power plants were not being dismantled by the Russians and shipped to the Soviet Union as war reparations. Those able to work were lucky to earn one hot meal a day laboring in rubble-clearing crews and at similar menial tasks.

What kept many urban Germans alive was the black market. Trading their precious remaining possessions—Leica cameras, Zeiss binoculars, objets d'art—they obtained sugar and canned rations from the occupying troops who had access to well-stocked post exchanges.

The more enterprising city dwellers had yet another strategy for survival: they took trains—the few that were running—into the countryside, selling their valuables to farmers for potatoes, eggs and poultry. They also bartered for post exchange cigarettes, which became, with the collapse of the German currency, a substitute medium of exchange. Many Allied soldiers profited hugely from this black market system; the German townspeople managed barely to survive.

Hope of surcease from the agony came in late 1946 when the U.S. promised to aid the Germans in rebuilding their shattered economy. Still, it would be two more years before the ingredients of real change—larger imports of food and raw materials—began to have a significant impact on everyday life.

A member of the vast army of German unemployed wears a sign pleading, "I am looking for work. I will do anything!"

NAZISM ON TRIAL

No legal proceeding like it had ever been seen before—the trial of a nation's leaders for their so-called "crimes against humanity" and for waging aggressive war. "This trial is unique in the history of jurisprudence," proclaimed Britain's Lord Justice Geoffrey Lawrence, chief of the four judges representing the Allies. Civilization itself, said the U.S. prosecutor Robert H. Jackson, "was the real complaining party."

The trial, held in Nuremberg where the Nazi Party had once staged its huge annual rallies, took 216 days; the full transcript ran to 10 million words. The testimonies of streams of witnesses, backed by documents, photographs and newsreels, revealed crimes of unspeakable magnitude and horror: the extermination of 11 million Jews, Gypsies, Slavs, prisoners of war and other captives in hideous circumstances and nauseating quantities; the wholesale use of torture and murder by the Gestapo, SS and other Nazi police agencies; mass deportations and use of slave labor; sadistic medical experiments—an almost limitless inventory of infamy.

Facing these ghastly charges were Reich Marshal Hermann Göring and Germany's ranking officers. Not all the top leaders could be tried, of course: Adolph Hitler, SS chief Heinrich Himmler and propaganda head Joseph Goebbels had committed suicide. But the worst of their vile henchmen were there. Eleven were sentenced to death, three acquitted and seven given prison terms ranging up to life behind bars. Only one acknowledged the justice of his punishment. "A thousand years will pass," said Hans Frank, the brutal Nazi Governor-General of Poland, "and still this guilt of Germany will not have been erased."

In the crowded courtroom at Nuremberg, the U.S. prosecutor Robert H. Jackson, standing at center, examines a witness (top) while 21 Nazis sit in the dock at far left. In a uniform stripped of all but buttons, Hermann Göring (inset) arrives in court on November 26, 1945, one of the 21 leading Nazis on trial

JUSTICE AT NUREMBERG

Security was extraordinarily strict in the courtroom and nearby prison block at Nuremberg, to keep diehard Nazis from trying to free the prisoners and disrupt the trial, and to prevent suicide among the prisoners. Even so, Labor dictator Robert Ley did manage to hang himself in his cell; thereafter, the security became even more rigorous. Shifts of alert MPs stood guard day and night outside each cell, keeping constant watch on the prisoners, who were ordered to keep faces and hands visible even while they slept.

The Nazis reacted in different ways to their imprisonment and trial. Foreign Minister Joachim von Ribbentrop became slovenly, while General Alfred Jodl maintained his cell, uniform and person in perpetual inspection order. Onetime Deputy Führer Rudolf Hess goose-stepped around the exercise yard; and Julius Streicher, editor of the strident *Der Stümer,* was reduced to faking nightmares to get attention. Hermann Göring, on a prison diet and off morphine, became a mere shadow of his former self while losing 120 pounds.

When the verdicts were rendered, the eleven death sentences by hanging were carried out in the prison gymnasium in the early hours of October 16, 1946. An unrepentant Streicher screamed "Heil Hitler!" just before the gallows trap was sprung. Ribbentrop murmured "peace to the world" as he left it. The only one to cheat the noose was Göring, who had managed somehow to obtain and take cyanide just a few hours before the execution. His body, like the others, was taken to Dachau where the concentration camp's death ovens were relighted. All the cremated remains were scattered in the Isar River, leaving no relics and no graves to inspire any future Nazis.

Inside the prison at Nuremberg, American MPs—one per cell—keep watch during their three-hour shift.

The guards used the hand lamps by the cell doors to check the prisoners at night. Wire mesh was hung on the walkways above to prevent suicide attempts.

ARMIES OF WANDERERS

With the end of World War II began the greatest and most agonizing cross-migration in human history. Some 50 million people had been uprooted by the conflict, and the survivors among them all seemed to be moving at once. People of every European nationality were struggling to return home or reach some other secure haven. Among them were slave laborers, concentration-camp inmates, prisoners of war, civilians who had fled bombardment, and countless others who had been caught up in the maelstrom of battle.

Among the more forlorn refugees wandering the devastated landscape were millions of displaced Germans. Some had been sent by Hitler during the War to colonize conquered lands, others had lost their homes when the postwar agreements moved the Polish border well into eastern Germany. Waves of these Germans had already fled westward before the advancing Red Army and now at least 6 million more were forcibly expelled from their homes and sent hurrying west. In their journey to food-scarce Germany, nearly 2 million perished.

The roads of Europe were jammed with columns of people, some plodding on foot, others on bicycles and in horse-drawn carts. Trains and trucks that had carried troops to war and Jews to slaughter now hauled an army of what one American observer called "compass-point citizens" north, south, east and west across the ravaged face of Europe. For some, the peace brought joyous reunion with lost loved ones. But for most, the struggle went unrelieved.

Searching for news of loved ones, German displaced persons scan a public bulletin board where members of separated families posted notices in hopes of tracing wives, husbands and children.

Weeping with joy, a Viennese mother welcomes her son in 1945. Thousands of such meetings took place as men from various countries, drafted as soldiers or laborers by the Germans, trekked home from distant factories or fighting fronts, seeking out their lost families.

A tragic sequence of photographs in October 1945 shows a group of German mothers and children, evicted from Poland, trudging into a Berlin rail yard (top). There, one mother clasps her son tighter for warmth (middle), then realizes he has died and grieves over his body (bottom).

An ill-fated immigrant ship, Exodus 1947, wallows in Haifa harbor, its side stove in by a blockading British destroyer. Most of the Jews aboard were transferred

to prison ships and taken to DP camps near Hamburg, Germany.

AN AGONIZING EXODUS

Swelling the ranks of displaced persons, or DPs, were hundreds of thousands of the 3 million European Jews who had somehow escaped death in the Nazi gas chambers. For many, whose homes and families were gone, Europe no longer seemed a viable place to live. They were determined instead to rebuild their lives in a new Jewish homeland in Palestine, the Biblical land "of milk and honey" inhabited by their distant ancestors.

The trouble was that the British, who governed Palestine under mandate from the old League of Nations, were determined to limit Jewish immigration. They feared—rightly—that a large influx of Jews would stir Palestine's Arab majority to violence. Since the British quota allowed but 1,500 Jews to enter Palestine each month, the only recourse for many was to slip into the Promised Land clandestinely.

They were helped by the Haganah, the Jewish national defense movement in Palestine, whose agents bribed border guards, arranged truck and train transportation and chartered ships to carry groups of immigrants across the Mediterranean to Palestine from small French and Italian ports.

For all of the Haganah's help, the exodus was long, and agonizingly difficult—often crowned with bitter disappointment. Some ships secretly unloaded their packed human cargoes, and the British allowed some illegals to stay. But other ships were intercepted and the immigrants roughly turned back. Many were interned on the island of Cyprus; some were sent all the way to Europe. Still, dozens of crowded, rickety ships continued to risk the British blockade. In all, 70,000 Jews set out for Palestine between the end of the War and the creation of the State of Israel in 1948.

ISRAEL: A NATION BORN IN VIOLENCE

Jewish survivors of the Holocaust were determined to enforce the long-standing claim of Jews everywhere to a homeland. But the Arabs of Palestine bitterly resented any influx of Jews, demanding to know why they should pay with their land for Hitler's crimes. As more and more Jews arrived, vicious fighting erupted, and both groups vented their rage on Palestine's British governors. The obvious solution was to share the tiny patch of land on the shore of the Mediterranean. But ethnic hatreds ran too deep and Jewish and Arab extremists resorted to any tactics to enlarge their portion.

On the Jewish side there was the Haganah, an increasingly well-equipped underground army, and two extremist groups, the Irgun and the Stern Gang, both dedicated to driving the British from Palestine through terrorist activities. The earliest raids, directed by the Haganah, were meant to help illegal immigrants reach Palestine. Haganah raiders sank British patrol boats, attacked coastal radar stations and freed immigrants penned up for deportation.

Jewish activists soon expanded their attacks, mining roads, blowing up bridges, troop trains and RAF airfields, bombing oil refineries and cutting oil pipelines. Meanwhile, the Irgun and the Stern Gang turned to guerrilla warfare of the most radical sort, tossing hand grenades into police stations, planting bombs and mines inside army posts, train stations, tax offices and banks. Stern Gang members machine-gunned policemen from rooftops and robbed banks and armored cars as a means of financing their terrorist operations. By the end of 1946, Jewish assassins had claimed 373 victims.

A United Nations decision in 1947 to partition Palestine into Arab and Jewish sectors—which led the next year to an independent Israel—did nothing to allay the violence. The morning after partition was announced, seven Jews died in random killings throughout Palestine. Two days later, an Arab mob rioted in Jerusalem, stabbing and stoning Jews, looting and burning Jewish shops. Jews hit back, burning an Arab theater and other establishments.

Despite the best efforts of the British, the fighting continued to flare sporadically. In the month after partition was announced, 489 people of all faiths died in the violence.

"This Christmas week in the Holy Land," wrote an American journalist, "shepherds went armed, travelers to Bethlehem were shot at, and wise men stayed indoors."

As 1948 began, Palestine's strife escalated into civil war. The Haganah stepped up recruiting, while Arab youths crossed into Syria for training with the Syrian army, and Syrian and Lebanese guerrillas entered Palestine to raid Jewish settlements. As the time approached for the British to depart, both sides feverishly bought and stockpiled arms. Arabs throughout the Middle East called for a *jihad*, or holy war, against the Jews. The initial effort to throw the Jews and their new state of Israel into the sea was blunted by disharmony among Arab leaders.

The Israeli state was officially proclaimed on May 14, 1948. It was immediately recognized and given international status by the United States government, and soon by other nations as well. Even so, the battles with Arabs living inside and outside Israel's borders continued, interrupted only by brief and ineffective ceasefires arranged by the United Nations.

Yet for all its enemies and despite a 1948 population of only about 720,000, the new nation managed to survive until, strengthened by more than a million new immigrants in the next dozen years, it became more firmly established—the first independent Jewish homeland in more than 1,800 years.

A Jewish-owned taxi burns in front of Jerusalem's Damascus Gate, the entrance to the Arab section of the city. The vehicle was seized and set afire in retaliation for a raid in which taxiborne Jewish terrorists killed 15 people in the Arab market.

Veteran fighters in the Haganah, the Jewish underground army, stand at attention as the new Israeli flag is raised on the afternoon of May 14, 1948 (below). Groups such as the Haganah and Jewish terrorist organizations provided the backbone for the new state's efficient, hard-striking army.

An Orthodox Jew (above) is searched before entering a British compound for questioning after the bombing of a British officers' club by terrorists in Jerusalem. The bombing was one of 16 attacks on British targets on a single day—March 1, 1947—that killed 22 people.

Standing above Communist rebel dead, Greek officers and Lieut. General James A. Van Fleet (right), chief U.S. military representative in Greece, study the scene of a guerrilla defeat as the terrible civil war neared its end in May of 1949.

THE POLITICS OF CONFRONTATION

The overriding fact of political life all across Europe after World War II was a massive shift to the left. Disillusioned with the old-line conservative politics and politicians they blamed for the conflict, millions of Europeans embraced Communist and Socialist promises of change.

Communist parties became especially strong in France and Italy where urban workers had long been drawn toward Marxism. In fact, as early as the first postwar election, leftist governments that included Communists came to power in both countries; almost a third of the seats in France's legislature were held by Communist deputies. For some time thereafter, the two nations seemed on the brink of Communist takeover.

France's economy was in perilous shape; food and jobs were scarce while prices skyrocketed. The Communist party, playing on the people's anger and uncertainty, soon had a dues-paying membership of 900,000 and an even larger army of sympathizers. But in 1948 the French Communists overplayed their hand. Urged by Moscow to foment more

Parisian leftists hurl café chairs at retreating police during an Armistice Day riot on November 11, 1948. The violence began when left-wing veterans and Resistance groups, who had decided to boycott the official celebration, attacked police lines along the Champs Élysées.

unrest and so speed their takeover bid, party leaders called for a general strike designed to paralyze industry and communications. Industrial sabotage, train derailments and violent battles occurred in a number of cities.

In response, the French government called out 80,000 troops and took other emergency measures. More important, many Frenchmen perceived that the Communists were crippling the nation in order to serve their own interests and Moscow's. In a stunning backlash, voters gave a new anti-Communist political party headed by Charles de Gaulle an overwhelming electoral victory in late 1948. Although street riots continued to flare, Communist party membership and power declined steadily, especially after the economy gained momentum with Marshall Plan aid.

The Italian Communist party followed much the same trajectory. Gaining 19 per cent of the vote in the first postwar election of 1946 and quickly picking up additional strength, the Communists seemed likely to seize power by peaceful means. But then, as in France, they tried to hurry the process through violent strikes and street battles, even employing squads of gunmen to assassinate well-known anti-Communists and other enemies.

Deeply alarmed, the centrist Christian Democrats, backed by the Catholic Church and campaign funds channeled from the U.S., waged a full-bore campaign as the 1948 elections approached—and won a landslide victory. More post-election violence earned the Communists only further distrust and the party's drive for power guttered out.

Across the Ionian Sea from Italy's toe, Communism was waging a different kind of battle: a murderous civil war in Greece. There as elsewhere, some of the staunchest wartime resistance to the German occupation had been Communist-led. After the German defeat, the Greek Communist guerrillas tried to take over the country. They were not defeated until 1949, after four years of fighting that killed almost 160,000 soldiers and civilians. According to counterinsurgency experts who studied that war, the bitter experiences of Greece—like those of France and Italy—had important implications for Communism: it could not come to power in a nation where it had not won the population to its cause.

In a poster designed to rally the Italian anti-Communist vote, a ballot falls like a sharp wedge, chopping off the burning fuse of Communist revolution before it destroys Italy. "Save yourself!" the legend reads; "Vote!"

Fleeing from the horrors of imprisonment in Russia, a terror-stricken Italian POW calls out to Italians at home, "Listen to me! Vote for Italy, not the Popular Front."

AN IRON CURTAIN DESCENDS

"From Stettin in the Baltic to Trieste in the Adriatic, an iron curtain has descended across the Continent," declared former British Prime Minister Winston Churchill in March 1946. "Behind that line lie all the capitals of the ancient states of Central and Eastern Europe. Warsaw, Berlin, Prague, Vienna, Budapest, Belgrade, Bucharest and Sofia—all these famous cities and the populations around them lie in what I must call the Soviet sphere. This is certainly not the liberated Europe we fought to build up. Nor is it one which contains the essentials of permanent peace."

Churchill's famous 1946 iron curtain speech, delivered at a college in Missouri, shocked Americans by publicly stating for the first time that the Soviet Union, a great ally in the fight against Nazi Germany, showed signs of becoming a dangerous adversary. In defiance of wartime agreements that nations liberated from Nazi rule should be free and independent, Stalin's Russia was imposing repressive Communist regimes on half a dozen countries—and seemed ready to subvert even more.

Among the nations already in the Soviet orbit was Poland. There the Russians had quickly undermined the legitimate government, which had spent the war years in exile in London. Then, in an adroitly rigged election, a Communist coalition gained 394 of the Polish parliament's 444 seats, completing the takeover.

Hungary went much the same way. First "people's courts" purged influential Hungarians likely to oppose Communist rule. Shortly thereafter the police and gangs of toughs cooperated to force opposing political parties out of business. By 1948, the Communists were firmly in control and all opposition had vanished.

Rumania was taken over through blatant threats. In 1945, Moscow ordered King Michael to appoint a government run by the Rumanian Communist party, the National Democratic Front—or else find his nation invaded by the Red Army. The King gave in and by 1948, after a couple of staged elections, Rumania was a People's Republic in name as well as fact. Bulgaria fell under Soviet-dominated Communist rule with equal speed.

Albania also became a Communist state, and a home-grown Communist government under Marshal Tito took control of Yugoslavia.

More shocking still to the West was the Communist takeover of Czechoslovakia, before the War a prosperous, progressive democratic state. There, a postwar election had given the local Communists a dozen posts in the 26-seat cabinet. But little untoward happened until 1948. Then the Communist interior minister suddenly

A Czech Workers' Militia squad, used to terrorize non-Communist opposition, parades through the Old Town Square of Prague to celebrate the 1948 Red victory.

began firing the country's non-Communist police chiefs and replacing them with party members. This ominous, high-handed move caused a number of other cabinet members to resign—and also brought out armed bands of Communist People's Militia that rampaged through the streets. Faced with this internal violence coupled with a Soviet threat to send in the Red Army to "safeguard Czechoslovakia's independence," the nation's president, Eduard Beneš, fell and the Communists took over.

With Czechoslovakia now in the Soviet orbit, Stalin's array of satellite states buffering Russia from the West was complete. The West was growing anxious. Searching for a policy to deal with the Soviet Union's aggressive moves, the wartime allies developed a program that came to be called containment—making it clear to Stalin that any further Soviet expansionism would be met by strong countermeasures.

To back up this policy, President Truman announced in early 1947 that the U.S. would thenceforth give aid to any country in the world threatened by Communist subversion or invasion. The "Truman Doctrine" was aimed specifically at the Red guerrillas trying to conquer Greece, but it clearly included the rest of Europe.

Giving containment more muscle was the 1949 formation of the North Atlantic Treaty Organization—NATO for short—that leagued the armed forces of the U.S., Britain, France, Belgium, the Netherlands and Luxembourg under a joint command and committed them to resist Soviet aggression in Europe. The Marshall Plan of massive economic aid to the nations of Western Europe was also designed in part to buttress them against Communist subversion and pressure. So were some economic moves ostensibly aimed at revitalizing Germany's ravaged economy.

The Kremlin responded with anger and alarm to this new, tougher policy—and Stalin thought he saw the spot where he could counterstrike at the Western allies.

The spot was Berlin—in a postwar Germany divided into two zones, one controlled by the Russians, the western portion by Britain, the U.S. and France. Although Berlin was deep within the Soviet zone, it was similarly divided by postwar agreement. The Allied occupation forces there, as well as Berliners living in Allied sectors, were clearly out on a limb, isolated 200 miles inside the Soviet zone, and dependent for supplies on roads and rails running through Russian-controlled areas. Stalin began to strike at these links in the spring of 1948, obstructing roads and turning back trainloads of food and fuel. The Allied response was perhaps the most dramatic episode of the immediate postwar era—the huge Berlin Airlift to supply the city by flying over the heads of the blockading Russians.

A burned-out bus functions as a Red Army roadblock on a main road leading to beleaguered Berlin from the British-controlled zone of Germany.

461

THE BERLIN AIRLIFT

The Soviets began seriously challenging the Western powers' routes through Germany's Russian zone and into Berlin on April 1, 1948, by turning back two incoming trainloads of supplies. To this initial provocation, Lieut. General Lucius Clay mounted an immediate response: he ordered the United States Air Force to make 30 cargo flights the next day into Berlin's Tempelhof airfield. The idea of bringing in supplies by air was born.

Soviet harassment intensified through April and May. Mail was stopped, water supplies were cut because of "technical difficulties," roads were closed for "repairs." Then on June 23 came a loud thunderclap: a blunt Soviet-style dispatch announced that all traffic in and out of West Berlin would be suspended as of the next morning. The blockade would be total—no coal shipments and no food for the two million inhabitants of the Allied sectors of the city.

The Western powers had two alternatives. They could give up their occupation rights and abandon Berlin, or they could force the issue and risk war. General Clay was for persevering. "When Berlin falls, West Germany will be next," he warned,

and the rest of Europe might then fall to the Soviets as well. Agreeing fully, President Truman declared: "We are going to stay, period."

Clay, thinking the Russians were probably bluffing, at first favored sending through an armored column to break the blockade. But the idea of a less risky airlift quickly won out. Within a day, cargo planes were winging into Berlin; planning had begun for a huge effort of indefinite duration. Hundreds of U.S. Air Force and RAF transport aircraft arrived at West German fields from all over the globe and were integrated into a round-the-clock shuttle.

By July, Allied planes were carrying as much as 1,500 tons of food and fuel a day—however still far short of the 4,500 tons that the city needed to survive. Clearly the airlift's capacity, for coal in particular, had to be improved before winter. In response, the U.S. Air Force brought in 180 C-54s, big, four-engined craft whose cargo capacity of nine tons was three times that of the original twin-engined C-47s. Major General William Tunner, who during the War had masterminded the Allied air-supply operation over "the Hump" from India to China, was named to command the airlift.

Tunner ordered aircrews to stay in

their planes between landing and takeoff, both at Berlin and while loading at West German airfields. Food was sent out to the fliers and weathermen came on board to brief them, mechanics serviced the planes while cargoes were being stowed. Tunner's methods and the additional aircraft paid off. By October, the average turnaround time had been cut to 30 minutes and one million sacks of coal had been delivered.

The airlift flew in everything Berliners asked for, from Volkswagens for the police to two million seedlings to replace trees cut for fuel. When Tempelhof field in the U.S. sector and Gatow in the British zone became too crowded, the planes flew in machinery to build a third field, Tegel, in the French sector.

By the spring of 1949, 400 aircraft were in service, carrying an average of 8,000 tons of cargo a day. Generals took the places of weary co-pilots; the drone of aircraft over Berlin never ceased. To hammer home to the Soviets that their blockade was not working, the airlift commanders decided on April 16 to flex their muscles. On that day 1,398 flights lifted an astonishing 12,994 tons of supplies into West Berlin. Four weeks later, on May 12, the Russians agreed to reopen roads and rail lines into the besieged city.

All over West Berlin, Germans, Americans, Britons and Frenchmen celebrated the end of the blockade and the accomplishment of a staggering logistical feat. During a period of 11 months, 1,592,287 tons of goods had been delivered by air to keep the city alive. West Berliners in particular celebrated what they recognized as the end of a Soviet threat and the beginning of their readmission to the world community. General Clay later declared, "I saw the spirit and soul of a people reborn."

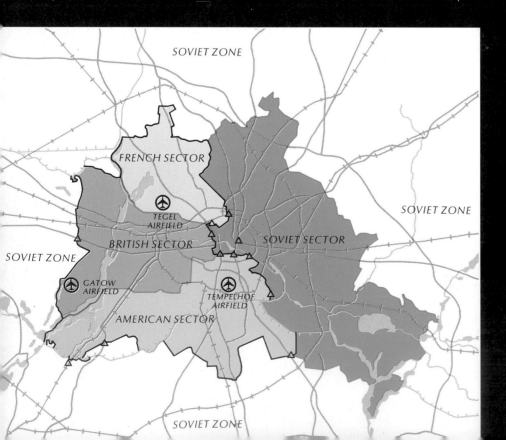

SOVIET ZONE

FRENCH SECTOR

TEGEL
AIRFIELD

BRITISH SECTOR

SOVIET ZONE

SOVIET SECTOR

SOVIET ZONE

GATOW
AIRFIELD

TEMPELHOF
AIRFIELD

AMERICAN SECTOR

SOVIET ZONE

Surrounded by the Soviet-run zone of Germany, Berlin was divided internally into Soviet, British, French and U.S. sectors. The map at left shows the network of roads, railways and canals that served the city, and the three airports in the allied sectors that were used by the airlift during the 1948-1949 Soviet blockade.

Citizens of rubble-strewn West Berlin watch as a supply-laden C-47 lands. "The sound of the engines," wrote one Berliner, "is beautiful music to our ears."

EUROPE'S CLIMB UP A LIFELINE OF HOPE

Secretary of State George C. Marshall's speech was so short, simple and understated that few of those who heard it at Harvard University's 1947 graduation exercises understood what a monumental commitment Marshall was proposing. "The United States," he said quietly, "should do whatever it is able to do to assist in the return of normal economic health in the world, without which there can be no political stability and no assured peace."

What the calm words meant was that the U.S. should—and with Congress' approval would—send billions of dollars to Europe, to jump start the war-ravaged economy of any nation that asked for aid, including former enemies Italy and Germany. The Marshall Plan, of course, included benefits for the U.S. A more prosperous Europe would be better able to resist Communist encroachment, and having healthy economies across the Atlantic would benefit American trade. But it was also a product of the sympathy Americans and their leaders such as Marshall, President Truman and Former Secretary of State James F. Byrnes felt for people suffering from hunger and despair. "It was a lifeline to sinking men," said British Foreign Minister Ernest Bevin. "We grabbed the lifeline with both hands."

What the plan did, in essence, was help the Europeans help themselves, by supplying food for workers and the materials for them to work on. "The worst of the many vicious cycles that beset the European peoples," Marshall explained, was "the inability of the European workshop to get food and raw materials required to produce the exports necessary to get the purchasing power for food and raw materials." So what went abroad was not necessarily dollars per se, but wheat for hungry workmen, then livestock and fertilizer to help Europe's farmers produce more food on their own.

Marshall Plan money also helped moribund industries. For example, it retooled automotive plants in France, England, Italy and West Germany and paid for imports of such raw materials as copper for electrical wire, nickel for hardening steel and zinc for die-casting. By 1952, Europe was producing nearly twice as many motor vehi-

Trucks take shape on a production line at Italy's Alfa Romeo auto works (above). To help speed assembly, Marshall Plan officials arranged for advice from Detroit experts. At right, soldier-statesman George C. Marshall pleads for his plan at a Congressional hearing.

cles as it had before the War. As for housing, Marshall Plan dollars, by revitalizing the steel and cement industries, spawned an amazing burst of new construction, and the rebuilding of bomb-blasted structures.

Congress put strict limits on the program's dimensions: $17 billion to be spent over four years. As it turned out, the limits were unnecessary: in half the time and at far smaller cost, the benefits of Marshall's scheme were evident in all 16 nations that subscribed to the Plan. The economics of capitalism and the Europeans' hard work multiplied every Marshall Plan dollar into six dollars' worth of goods, services and capital equipment.

By the time the Plan formally ended in 1952, a new Europe—more united and prosperous than the old one—was rising from the ashes of the War. Marshall's program, declared the Foreign Minister of France, "will be reckoned among the most decisive events in the history of the Western world." And the London *Economist* praised the Marshall Plan as "the most straightforward, generous thing that any country has ever done for others."

Port workers in Marseilles stack sacks of grain rushed to France in 1948.

An apartment block in Hamburg, Germany (left), is a ruined shell after Allied air raids in 1943. The same apartments (right), now restored with a combination of United States aid and German energy, accept new tenants in 1951.

AFTERMATH: ASIA

Like a phoenix arising from the ashes, Hiroshima, the symbol of atomic devastation, had by 1952 returned to its status as a vibrant commercial and industrial metropolis.

ASIA FOR THE ASIANS

World War II had unleashed forces that would permanently change the political complexion of the Asian continent. In areas that had long lived under colonial domination, the Japanese propaganda message—Asia for Asians—had sunk in. Wielded by Japanese power had indeed driven Occidentals out of one colonial enclave after another.

As colonialism was seeing its last days, the transitions were everywhere marked by violence, some anticolonialist in origin, some religious, and some fomented by Communists who had fought against the Japanese and were now themselves lunging for power.

European colonialists who in 1945 expected to resume control of their Asian possessions shared a common error: scant respect for the Asians' ability to fight for independence. Said one Frenchman in Saigon of the growing Vietnamese insurgency: "Nothing—some agitators bought by the Japanese. We'll kill them off. It won't take long."

Such monumental arrogance led to some mighty falls. The French in Indochina and the Dutch in Indonesia repeatedly misjudged their own weaknesses and their adversaries' strengths. The results were years of stalemate and eventual defeat. In Burma, independence finally came in January 1948, but only after the British realized that they lacked the means to enforce continued colonial rule.

Even where local conditions were interpreted correctly, bloodshed followed. In Malaya, the British, although willing to relinquish power by 1948, ended up staying on another nine years spearheading a counterinsurgency operation against Communists. In the Philippines, the U.S., true to its promise, hauled down the stars and stripes on July 4, 1946—before Philippine Communists could marshal their forces. But it was not long before the fledgling Philippine government, in its turn, was quelling a bitter Communist uprising. In India, scarcely had the British raj fulfilled its promise of independence when the country faced partition and savage communal riots.

Perhaps the bloodiest struggle of all took place in a land that had never been under colonial rule. China, however, had been engaged in a bitter civil war for many years, and the combatants had often set aside their hatreds to present a common front against the Japanese. That war now resumed with full fury, and when it ended in 1949 with millions dead, Chiang Kai-shek's Nationalists had fled to Taiwan leaving Mao Tse-tung's communists in command of the world's most populous country.

Only Japan escaped violent confrontation. The Japanese had lost almost two million people during the War; their land, in ruins, was occupied by 450,000 American troops, who would help ensure a peaceful transition.

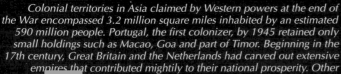

Colonial territories in Asia claimed by Western powers at the end of the War encompassed 3.2 million square miles inhabited by an estimated 590 million people. Portugal, the first colonizer, by 1945 retained only small holdings such as Macao, Goa and part of Timor. Beginning in the 17th century, Great Britain and the Netherlands had carved out extensive empires that contributed mightily to their national prosperity. Other Western holdings in Asia—primarily French Indochina, the American Philippines and the Australian Trust Territory of New Guinea—were less profitable but prized for reasons of national prestige or military strategy.

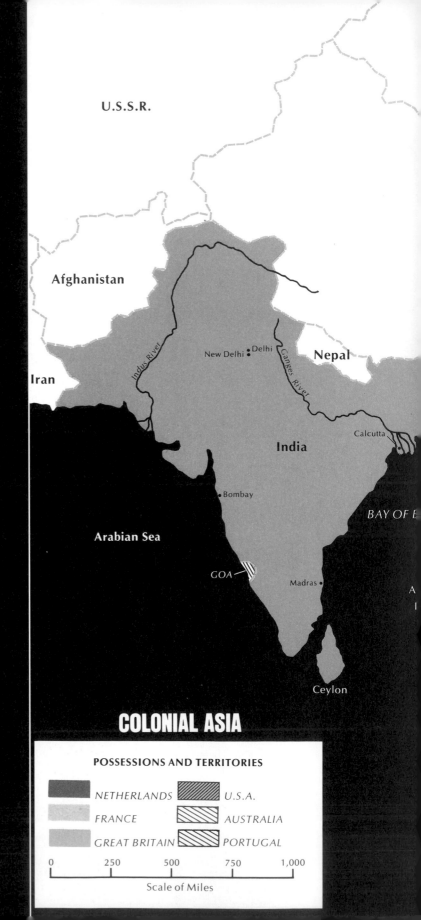

COLONIAL ASIA

POSSESSIONS AND TERRITORIES

NETHERLANDS	U.S.A.
FRANCE	AUSTRALIA
GREAT BRITAIN	PORTUGAL

Scale of Miles: 0 — 250 — 500 — 750 — 1,000

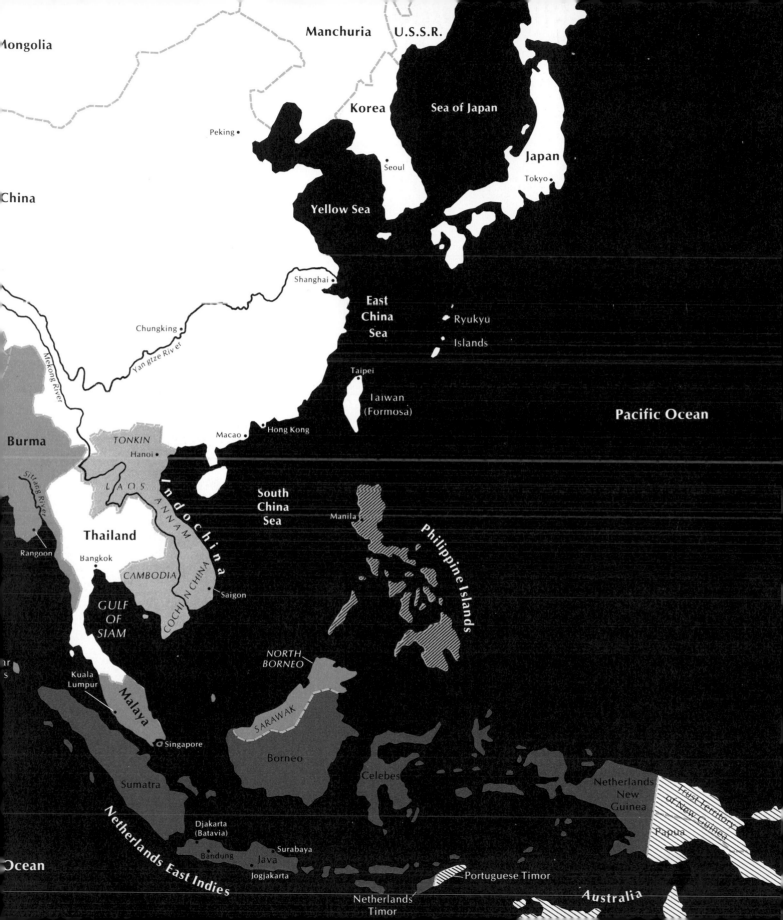

Mongolia

Manchuria

U.S.S.R.

Korea

Sea of Japan

Japan

China

Peking •

Seoul •

Tokyo •

Yellow Sea

Shanghai •

East
China
Sea

Ryukyu

Chungking •

Yangtze River

Islands

Taipei •

Taiwan
(Formosa)

Pacific Ocean

Mekong River

TONKIN

Macao •

Hong Kong •

Burma

Hanoi •

Sittang River

LAOS

ANNAM

South
China
Sea

Manila •

Philippine Islands

Thailand

Rangoon •

Bangkok •

CAMBODIA

COCHIN CHINA

Saigon •

Indochina

*GULF
OF
SIAM*

*NORTH
BORNEO*

Kuala
Lumpur •

SARAWAK

Malaya

Singapore ⊙

Borneo

Celebes

Netherlands
New
Guinea

*Trust Territory
or New Guinea*

Sumatra

Papua

Netherlands East Indies

Djakarta
(Batavia) •

Surabaya •

Bandung •

Java

Portuguese Timor

Ocean

Jogjakarta •

Netherlands
Timor

Australia

BENIGN OCCUPATION OF JAPAN

In contrast to the rules established for Allied soldiers occupying Germany, GIs in Japan were allowed to mingle with the local civilians. General Douglas MacArthur, Supreme Commander of the occupation forces, felt that orders against fraternizing were unenforceable. "My father told me never to give an order unless I was certain it would be carried out."

In the early days of the Occupation the Japanese lived in fear of being brutally treated. However, MacArthur decreed that a GI who so much as slapped a Japanese would get five years in prison—rapists faced the death penalty—and American restraint helped calm Japanese fears.

Japanese behavior toward the occupiers was courteous and respectful. Still, despite the best of intentions, cultural misunderstandings were inevitable. On one occasion Japanese soldiers stood in apparent disdain with their backs toward a passing motorcade bearing MacArthur. Only later was it learned that the soldiers were actually honoring the Supreme Commander as they would the person of their own Emperor. But victors and vanquished quickly found that they shared a common passion: baseball. The Japanese had been playing baseball since the 1870s, almost as long as the Americans, and soon teams of GIs vied with local clubs throughout Japan in friendly competition.

If the Japanese seemed fascinated by their American conquerors, the Americans in turn were captivated by Japan and its people. Armed only with cameras, many GIs toured the island nation, staying in country inns, soaking in communal hot tubs, and learning to eat raw fish. And 6,000 took home Japanese brides.

As the Occupation begins, U.S. Marines in amphibious vehicles look over a rainy street scene at a staging depot in Saga, a port in southern Japan. Inset: General MacArthur poses with Emperor Hirohito (inset). By tradition a distant, godlike figure, the Emperor renounced his "divine" status on January 1, 1946. The formerly aloof Son of Heaven began to mingle with the people, a clear harbinger of democracy. Meanwhile, MacArthur himself took on demigod-like status as he helped the Japanese achieve constitutional and economic rebirth.

AN ECONOMY REBORN

Prewar Japan had been Asia's premier industria▮ nation, and as a trader it had ▮▮ked fifth in the world. But in 194▮, Japan's economy lay shattered: relentless U.S. bombing had leveled its cities, wrecked much of the coastal transport system and destroyed manufacturing capability.

Simple sustenance was the first goal of the Japanese—and also of their American occupiers, who began pouring relief aid into Japan at a rate that reached $400 million per year. If Japan was to support itself once again, its industrial base must be rebuilt. Late in 1948, a group of American planners, including executives recruited from private business, charted an ambitious new economic course for Japan▮ The goal was the country's self-sufficiency within five years.

Triggering such a recovery required additional American outlays: $74 million in 1949 and $165 million in 1950, mainly to import raw materials—the stimulus the Japanese needed to launch what was to become a miraculous economic revival. The comeback was accelerated in 1950 by the onset of the Korean War, during which Japan became a base for supply, staging and repair base for United Nations combat forces.

American projections called for a fivefold increase in Japanese exports, from $259 million in 1948 to $1.3 billion in 1953. Working with American production experts, the Japanese fulfilled this tall order. A balanced government budget and higher taxes helped curb runaway inflation.

The textile industry had accounted for almost half of Japan's prewar export income, and with U.S. aid, it became one of the first to revive. By 1951 Japan was exporting one billion square yards of cotton cloth—more than any other nation. By that same year, coal, iron and steel production had reached almost 80 per cent of wartime peaks.

American-supported changes in the industrial milieu were accompanied by vital shifts in the agricultural sector. Until 1945, almost half of Japan's farmland was worked by sharecroppers, who had to hand over roughly 50 per cent of each harvest to their landlords. In 1946, with fir▮ guidance from General Douglas M▮Arthur's staff, the Japanese Die▮ ▮sed the Farm Land Reform Ac▮ ▮hich ▮▮ effect turned over the la▮d to those who farmed it.

American Occupation policy also encouraged Japanese labo▮ to organize. But for many worker▮ ▮▮t to bargain collectively wa▮ ▮ershadowed by the almost fami▮▮ relationship between the Japanese worker and his employer: unions did not have to fight for job security, be▮ use most companies felt an obligation to keep their employees on the payroll even when there was no work for them.

It was in some relatively new areas, however, that Japan's recovery ▮▮ really about to take wing. ▮n Ju▮ 1950, the four-year-old Tokyo Communications Engineeri▮▮ Corporation, later renamed Sony, marketed Japan's first magnetic tap▮ recorde▮ ▮n 1952 Japan's automot▮▮ ▮ctories exported their first 1,000 c▮▮ ▮he next year, with help from su▮▮ ▮merican firms as RCA, the fledgling Japanese television industry produ▮▮▮ ▮▮ sold its first 14,000 TV sets.

By 1954, no furt▮▮▮ ▮ was required from the U▮▮▮ States. Japan's gross national pro▮▮ ▮ and the personal income of i▮s people matched prewar peak figures and would continue to rise. In the rebuilt cities, shops bulged with consumer goods, new cars jammed the streets and, in the words of a contemporary newspaper editor, "smart ▮▮▮▮ people were working and p▮ying in an almost carnival atmosphere of buoyancy and vitality."

Visitors to the Japan Broadcasting Company in 1948 watch a demonstration of television on a cumbersome experimental console. The screen itself—seen reflected by a mirror set into the lifted top—measured only 8 by 10 inches.

The 1948 Datsun two-door sedan, a prototype designed for eventual export, had a top speed of 35 miles per hour. By 1952, Japan's automotive factories were exporting these small vehicles in the first wave of a major trade campaign.

In the first transaction under Japan's 1946 land reform law, a government official (below, left) hands a former tenant the deed to his rice field near Yokohama. The parcels tenants could buy were small—the average size being only 2.5 acres. Yet many farmers were able to double their previous incomes, and the social benefits were enormous. Two million hitherto landless tenants and their families were now property owners, with an entrepeneur's vested interest in the future of the new Japan.

A LAND DIVIDED AGAINST ITSELF

At midnight on August 14, 1947, India's first Prime Minister, Jawaharlal Nehru, formally proclaimed his nation's independence from Great Britain. To Nehru and his mentor Mohandas Gandhi, both of whom had sought self-rule through nonviolence for many prewar years, the moment represented "a tryst with destiny."

Even as the celebratory fireworks began, so did the rioting and bloodshed. India would see all hopes for a great and unified nation doomed by an implacable three-way strife among the land's 250 million Hindus, 90 million Muslims and 6 million Sikhs.

The catalyst for catastrophe had been the insistence of Muslim leader Mohammad Ali Jinnah for a separate Muslim state to be sliced off the body of India and called Pakistan. To India's Hindu majority, led by Nehru, mutilation of their homeland was sacrilege. Their charismatic spiritual guide Gandhi—revered as the Mahatma, or Great Soul—declaimed repeatedly: "You shall have to divide my body before you divide India." Jinnah, possessed by his own dream, replied with equal passion: "No power on earth can prevent Pakistan."

Spurred on by Jinnah, masses of Calcutta Muslims turned out on Direct Action Day—August 16, 1946—to demonstrate their support for partition. Marches and rallies swelled into a four-day orgy of Muslims slaughtering Hindus and being slaughtered in turn by vengeful Hindus and Sikhs.

Reluctantly, Nehru and the departing British concluded that partition was preferable to unending chaos. Under a hastily drawn-up compromise plan, British India was chopped into two independent states. Areas with a Hindu majority would form the new India, and areas with a Muslim majority would become the state of Pakistan—which would occupy two enclaves one thousand miles apart. Bengal and the Punjab, areas of mixed populations, were to be arbitrarily divided between Pakistan and India.

The result, as independence dawned, was a bloody cross-migration as Hindus and Moslems sought safety in areas dominated by their respective coreligionists. By the time the brutal trek was over in the spring of 1948, between 10 and 16 million people had been transplanted and hundreds of thousands were dead.

Jawaharlal Nehru, Mohandas Gandhi's protégé and future prime minister of India, listens intently to his mentor at a meeting of the Congress Party in 1946.

Stumbling wearily toward Pakistan, a caravan of Muslim refugees from Hindu India follows a trail in the Punjab past the remains of a group attacked earlier by Sikhs.

MERDEKA!

On August 17, 1945, while Japanese troops still occupied the capital city of Djakarta, Indonesian nationalist leader "Bung" ("brother") Sukarno stepped up to a stolen Japanese microphone and announced simply: "We the people of Indonesia hereby declare Indonesia's independence." To rally the masses behind the new Republic, Sukarno decreed a powerful new symbol: "*Merdeka*" ("Freedom"), spoken as a greet with one hand raised, its fingers spread apart. The word was soon heard everywhere.

The Dutch, who for more than 300 years had controlled much of the profitable archipelago they called the Netherlands East Indies, dismissed the new republic as a puppet regime established by the Japanese. Weeks later, when the War formally ended for Japan, the Dutch assumed that their control of the Indies would be reinstated. Accordingly, they persuaded the British to maintain European authority until Dutch military forces could be organized for reoccupation.

Sukarno and his colleagues now realized that they were on center stage before the world. In order to win support, they would have to prove their government legitimate. Their mandate became a twofold one: maintaining calm among the various dissident groups, some of which favored armed struggle, while keeping peace with the interim British forces and arriving contingents of Dutch troops.

Despite Sukarno's attempts to maintain order, anti-colonial feeling finally erupted in a ferocious climax at the battle of Surabaya in November 1945, during which it took the British three weeks of hard fighting to conquer the city. Stunned by the Indonesians' zealous resistance, the British pressured the Dutch to negotiate with the Republic. World opinion began to swing against the Netherlands—but still the Dutch fought on stubbornly.

It took four more years of resistance, further complicated by internal struggles against local Communist insurgencies, for the Indonesian nationalists to triumph. Finally, on December 27, 1949, the Dutch transferred full sovereignty to the new federation, the Republic of the United States of Indonesia.

The next day, Sukarno was greeted in Djakarta by a sea of rejoicing people. The man Indonesians called "brother" now exclaimed to the crowd, "Thank God. We are free."

Dutch troops, moving back into Indonesia to replace the interim British occupation force early in 1946, frisk Indonesian civilians at a street checkpoint in Djakarta. The Dutch badly wanted the Indies back as a primary element in rebuilding their war-shattered economy.

While Japanese forces still hold power in Djarkata, nationalist leader Sukarno declares Indonesian independence on August 17, 1945. Although he was the symbol of the struggle for freedom, his own government would later become increasingly dictatorial.

Indonesian nationalists in a motley array of uniforms wave their weapons in triumph after capturing a town—and the hardware of some of its defenders. Though the Dutch held the major cities, the guerrilla army prevented them from ever establishing complete control over their former domain.

MALAYA: INDEPENDENCE DELAYED

When the Japanese began their wartime sweep through Asia, no independence movement had yet existed in Malaya. Indeed, Malaya had no history as a country: stretching 450 miles south of Thailand on the Malay peninsula, it was a loose coalition of 12 states, each governed by a sultan (a spiritual leader of the moslem Malays), who was advised by a British Resident responsible to the High Commissioner in Singapore.

Three ethnic communities—Malay, Chinese and Indian—coexisted uneasily in the Malayan states. Divided on racial, religious and cultural grounds, they shared no concept of self-government or dream of nationhood.

When the British returned to Malaya in September 1945, they planned to unify all the states in a Malayan Union, creating a central colonial government in Kuala Lumpur and stripping the sultans of their powers. The Malays were outraged and a spirit of nationalism was born. So fierce were the protests, in fact, that the British backed down, agreeing to establish the more acceptable Federation of Malaya, under which the sultans retained their old powers.

Meanwhile Communists, many of whom were Chinese Malays trained by the British to harass the Japanese—now had their own agenda: the destruction of Malaya's economy. Using weapons hidden in the jungle since 1945, they launched a long campaign of savage assaults on the country's tin mines and rubber plantations. In June the new federal government declared a state of emergency and embarked on a long anti-terrorist campaign that delayed independence until 1957, the year when Malaya became independent within the British Commonwealth.

Safely indoors after a day's work, a planter relaxes at home with a newspaper—keeping a loaded Bren gun and extra ammunition within reach. British planters were among the prime targets of the Communist uprising that erupted in Malaya in 1948, and continued until after Malaya became independent in 1957.

Searching for Communist guerrillas in 1949, a team from a Malay-British police task force checks the identity of a farmer in Malaya's interior. Special measures, such as resettlement of people from the countryside into new fortified villages, helped break up the terrorists' supply and support system.

A group of captured guerrillas—including three women—are guarded by a British soldier after a fight in which their leader (right) was killed. Most insurgents were Chinese but some, like those seen here, were Malay Communists.

VIETNAM: 1945-1954

In July of 1945, a group of American Office of Strategic Services (OSS) agents parachuted into northern Vietnam to help coordinate guerrilla action against the Japanese. The Americans came away impressed by the guerrilla chieftain—a slight, middle-aged Vietnamese with a high forehead and a wispy goatee. The OSS leader described him as "a brilliant and capable man"; the man's followers called him Ho Chi Minh ("He who enlightens"). Just how brilliant and capable he was would soon be seen by the rest of the world.

For almost a century, Indochina had been a colony of France, and the French, like the Dutch, were eager to reassert their rule. But they now faced an independence movement dominated by home-grown Communists led by Ho Chi Minh. By the time of Japan's surrender, Ho and his Vietminh forces had already won control

In La Pagode, a café in Saigon, two overly indulgent young Frenchwomen pamper their pet dogs. When the French returned to Indochina in 1945, many shrugged off the danger and clung determinedly to the old ways. They were eventually forced, however, to acknowledge that times had changed.

of North Vietnam and had established a provisional government in Hanoi, the former French colonial capital.

The French Army, under orders to restore control at whatever cost, fully expected to sweep all opposition aside, and for a time it seemed that they would succeed. Though Ho had command of the north, the French easily gained control of the south.

And yet, by early 1946, neither the French nor Ho's Vietminh was committed to an all-out war. Conferences in Hanoi between Ho and French negotiator Jean Sainteny produced an accord: France would recognize Ho's Hanoi regime as a Free State to be part of the French Union—an association similar to the British Commonwealth.

But the agreement fell apart in October 1946 when France adopted a new constitution that made no provision for truly independent nations within the French Union. Tension heightened between the 60,000 intensively trained but ill-equipped Vietminh guerrillas and the 50,000 well-equipped French troops.

On November 20, the captain of a French gunboat in Haiphong Harbor, apparently mistaking a throng of refugees for a hostile force, shelled the city; 6,000 civilians were killed. The Vietminh retaliated with massive

assaults on French garrisons throughout Vietnam and attacks on French civilians in their homes. A war was on.

Although the French counted on their superiority in tanks, artillery and naval units to achieve rapid victory, neither their heavy equipment nor conventional fighting skill could prevail against the guerrilla tactics of the Vietminh. Setting up a puppet state in the south with Saigon as its capital only succeeded in dividing Vietnam in two. The Vietminh were determined and elusive, and even American military aid proved futile for the French cause.

In 1954, the French suffered a humiliating defeat at the valley fortress of Dienbienphu. Cut off and besieged, almost 11,000 French Union soldiers surrendered to guerrilla forces. The struggle was over for the French, their colony was lost, and so were 600,000 Vietnamese and French lives.

Yet peace still did not come. Ho Chi Minh was secure in the north—but the French legacy in the south was a rival government, supported now by the United States, which had decided to keep at least that portion of Vietnam free of Communist rule. It would be almost two decades before the Americans would be forced to retreat and allow Asians to decide for Asia.

Between bargaining talks with the despised French in 1946, Ho Chi Minh shares a plane with key French negotiator Jean Sainteny—who later said that Ho "had the look of a hunted animal ready to spring."

Their weapons slung from bamboo poles, members of a Vietminh light artillery unit make their way along a hidden trail. The guerrillas were at home in the jungle and bush, which offered an ideal environment with ample cover and an abundant supply of the bamboo stalks needed to fashion the poisoned shafts called punji sticks.

CHINA'S WAR WITHIN

During the eight years of Japan's war with China—1937 to 1945—the Japanese had ravaged the giant country, devastating cities, transportation systems and vast tracts of cropland. An estimated 15 million Chinese had died, and starvation and pestilence threatened the living. Eighteen years of intermittent internal struggles between the Nationalist government of Chiang Kai-shek and China's Communists led by Mao Tse-tung had compounded the destruction.

And now, at War's end, a nation already plunged into anarchy concentrated all energies on unrelenting civil war. From 1945 to 1949, the fighting seesawed back and forth, as the Communists drew their strength from the countryside and the Nationalists concentrated their power in the cities. Both the U.S. and the Soviet Union urged reconciliation, yet rarely did the Chinese parties vying for mastery bend to the wishes of outsiders. Mao, staunch revolutionary and believer in class struggle, and Chiang, stern traditionalist intent on reviving the values of old China, marched to their own martial hymns.

Postwar truce agreements were made and broken; hostilities were renewed and intensified. The Red Army, once masters of the hit-and-run guerrilla operation, also became adept at fighting, and surviving, major confrontations. The army's policy of treating civilians with great respect—in contrast to the Nationalist Army's often exploitative behavior—won it popular support, even from Chiang's forces. "The Red Army," declared Mao, "lives among the people as the fish dwells in the water."

Slowly, inexorably, Nationalist forces retreated, surrendering the two Chinese capitals of Peking and Nanking early in 1949. By the end of that year, it was all over and Chiang Kai-shek and his Nationalists had fled to the island bastion of Taiwan. On October 1, 1949, Mao Tse-tung appeared in the vast T'ien An Men Square outside the walls of Peking's historic Forbidden City and formally declared the world's second most powerful communist state: The People's Republic of China.

Though implacable foes, Mao Tse-tung and Chiang Kai-shek manage to force smiles as they toast each other during reconciliation talks convened in Chungking in August and September of 1945 at the urging of the United States. It was the first time the two enemies had met since 1927, and it would be the last.

A triumphant Communist Army unit parades through Peking on February 3, 1949, their trucks adorned with propaganda posters depicting Chinese Nationalists in craven flight from the Red Army. Many vehicles in the procession had been intercepted by the Communists from trainloads of supplies intended by the United States for delivery to the Nationalist forces.

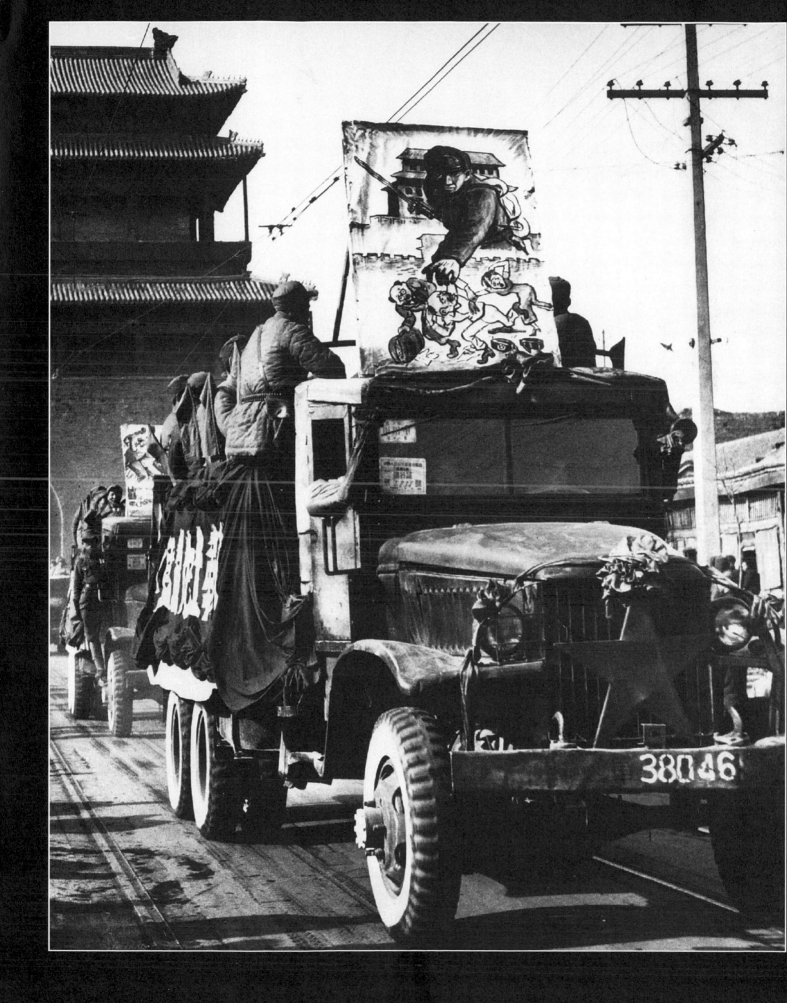

THE KOREAN WAR

By 1945, the Japanese had occupied Korea and dominated its people for 40 years. During the War they had used the country as a source of raw materials, heavy equipment and labor; at war's end they left a country in a state of economic chaos and a people altogether lacking experience in self-rule—but not without dreams of independence.

As a result of agreements made at the Potsdam Conference in July 1945, the Korean peninsula was divided along the 38th parallel—into a Soviet sphere of influence in the north and a U.S. sphere in the south. Intended as no more than a temporary expedient, the 38th parallel became a hostile boundary bristling with checkpoints and bunkers as relations between the Soviets and the Americans soured.

A sign near an American outpost warns travelers that they are approaching the border separating South and North Korea. The impractical line not only cut across countryside and mountain ranges but bisected several towns and villages.

From their observation post on a mountain ridge, South Korean guards keep watch along the border. To the right and rear is Communist territory.

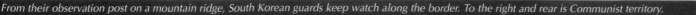

The Russians took firm hold of the north, freezing the 38th parallel as a permanent border between the two military control zones, and denying outsiders entry to North Korea. They also blocked the transit of goods and services flowing between north to south, effectively disrupting the remnants of Korea's political and economic unity.

For a time thereafter, 120,000 Soviet troops occupied North Korea, while 50,000 U.S. troops were garrisoned in the south. These American troops struggled to maintain peace while U.N.-sponsored elections produced, in August 1948, the formal proclamation of the Republic of Korea headed by a 70-year-old zealot named Syngman Rhee. A month later, the Russian occupiers of the north responded by proclaiming their own new nation: the Democratic People's Republic of Korea, under a one-time Communist guerrilla named Kim Il-sung.

Shortly thereafter, both occupation forces pulled out. But the odds remaining were far from even. The Red Army left a strong and well-equipped North Korean Army in its place; by contrast, the Americans left a small and lightly equipped force.

In a drenching, predawn rain on June 25, 1950, the North Korean army hurled itself across the 38th parallel. Invading tanks rolled forward unchecked, and Russian-built Yak fighter-bombers began bombing and strafing Rhee's capital, Seoul. The United Nations Security Council immediately condemned the blatant aggression; President Truman committed the U.S. to South Korea's defense. American troops, commanded by General Douglas MacArthur began arriving from Japan on July 4, and were thrown piecemeal into battle. Within a few weeks they had suffered 6,000 casualties, including 1,884 dead; the South Koreans had lost 50 percent of their army.

By August 4, the remaining 45,000 South Korean troops with American reinforcements were defending a perimeter only 50 miles wide and 80 miles deep centered on the port of Pusan at the tip of the Korean peninsula. And there, with the aid of air power, they held fast.

The fighting went on for three years, and eventually ended back at the 38th parallel. But the nation that had once been whole was still divided. The conflict in Korea and its deadlocked conclusion reflected a pattern of international confrontation that was perhaps the saddest and most perilous legacy of World War II.

Gesturing in the direction of Communist positions, a South Korean general explains the tactical situation to U.S. envoy John Foster Dulles, who visited the 38th parallel in mid-June of 1950. When the North Koreans struck across the parallel a few days later, Dulles urged President Truman to commit American troops and matériel to stem the invasion.

INDEX

Numerals in *italics* indicate an illustration of the subject mentioned.

Juichin, 27
Juno Beach, 289, 295-296
Jutland Peninsula, 417

K

Kaga (aircraft carrier), 258
Kagoshima, 161
Kahuku Point, 162
Kaiser, Henry J., *118*
Kakazu Ridge, 402. *See also* Okinawa
Kaku, Tomeo, 259
Kalach: and Paulus, 193, 199; and Red Army, 193; and
    Timoshenko, 193
Kamikaze, 173, 389, *390-391*, 426
Kaminski, Mieczyslaw, 378
Kaneohe, 166
Kasserine Pass, 224
Katyusha (rocket launcher), *196-197*
Keitel, Wilhelm: and Hitler, 316; and Rundstedt, 301
Kempf, Werner, 366
Kenney, George C., 264
Kerch Peninsula, 186
Kesselring, Albert: and Gothic Line, 237; and Hitler,
    230; and Rome, 230; and Rommel, 224; and
    Rundstedt, 339; and Salerno, 228; surrender of,
    237-239
Kharkov, 366-367; and Timoshenko, 185
Khrushchev, Nikita S., *199*
Kim Il-sung, 485
King, Edward, 168
King, Ernest J., 396, 397
Kingman, Howard F., 268
Kinkaid, Thomas C., 387
Kinnard, Harry, 327
Kirby, Bill, 232
Kirk Sound, 100
Kirponos, M. P., 130
Kisaragi (destroyer), 167
Klaipeda, *375*
Kleist, Ewald von: and Donets River, 185; and Hitler,
    193; and Red Army, 186; and Rostov, 193; and
    Soviet Union, 185; and Ukraine, 130
Kluge, Günther von: and Hitler, 303, 306-307, 308;
    replacement of, 308; suicide of, 308
Knox, Frank, 263
Koba. *See* Stalin, Josef
Kokoda Track: and Australia, army of, *261*-262; and
    Imperial Army, 261; and MacArthur, 262
Kokott, Heinz, 326, 328
Kolchak, Alexander, 16
Komorowski, Tadeusz, 378
Konev, Ivan: and Berlin, 413; and Breslau, 379; and
    Cherkassy, 369-370; and Czechoslovakia, 424; and
    Kursk, 364; and Stalin, 414; and Ukraine, 369, 372;
    and Zhukov, 413
Konoye, Fumimaro, 160
Kopets, I. I., 123
Korea, *484-485*
Korean War, 485
Kota Bharu, 170
Kotzebue, Albert, 416
Kovpak, Sidor A., *210*
Kra Isthmus, 170
Kravchenko, A. G., 368
Krebs, Hans, 415
Kristallnacht, 48
Krueger, Walter: and Corregidor, 392; and Dulag, 387;
    and MacArthur, 389; and Ormoc, 388; and
    Tacloban, 387
Kuantan, 170
Kumusi River, and Australia, army of, *261*, 262
Kunkel, John, 350
Kurai tanima, 158
Kuribayashi, Tadamichi, and Iwo Jima, 397-399, 400
Kurita, Takeo: and Leyte, 384, 386; and Sprague, 386,
    387

364; and Model, 362-363, 364-365; and Red Army,
    363; and Rokossovsky, 363, 364, 365; and
    Rotmistrov, 365; and Vatutin, 363
Kutuzov, Mikhail, 182
Kutuzov (operation), 366
Kwai Noi River, 175
Kwajalein, 166; surrender of, 270
Kyle, Duncan, 308

L

Lamon Bay, 168
Landing craft, vehicle and personnel. *See* Higgins boats
Landing craft infantry, *293*
Landing craft infantry (rocket), *275*
Landing craft tank, *293*
Landing vehicle, tracked, 268
Lang, Anton, 5
Lanphier, Thomas, *263*
Lanzerath, 318
Larkin, John, 222
Lauer, Walter E., 320
Laurence, William, 425
Laval, Pierre, *29*; and Hoare, 30; resignation of, 30
Lawrence, Geoffrey, 448
LCI, *293*
LCI (R), *275*
LCTs, *293*
LCVPs. *See* Higgins boats
Lea, Tom, painting by, *276-277*
Leach, John, 171
League of German Girls, *40-41*
League of Nations, *29*; covenant of, 13, 15; demise of,
    24, 28; and Franco, 32-33; and Hoare, 28; and Italy,
    29, 31; and Manchuria, 24; purposes of, 13; and
    Rhineland, 46; and Selassie, 31; and Wilson, 12, 13,
    14, 15-18
Leahy, William D., 381
Leathers, Frederick J., *380-381*
Lebensraum, defined, 48
Leclerc, Jacques, 311
Ledo-Burma Road, 272, *273*
Lee, Willis, 387
Leeb, Wilhelm Ritter von, 79, 123
Leigh-Mallory, Trafford, *286-287*; and D-Day, 287; and
    glider pilots, 290; and Montgomery, 304
Lelyushenko, Dmitri D., 414
LeMay, Curtis E.: and atomic bomb, 426; and Stilwell,
    406
Lenin, V. I., *12*; death of, 126; and Stalin, 126
Leningrad, *map* 129; and Hitler, 128; and Hoth, 125;
    and Luftwaffe, 128; and Red Army, 369; siege of,
    128-130; starvation in, 128-130
Léopold (king of Belgium), 69, 74
Lexington (aircraft carrier), 177, *178*, 252
Ley, Robert, 450
Leyte, *385*; and Halsey, 382; and Kurita, 384, 386; and
    MacArthur, 382, *392*; and Nishimura, 384; and
    Ozawa, 384; and Yamashita, 387
Liberty ships, *118-119*
"Lili Marlene" (song), 219
Lille, 69
Lindemann, Ernst, 109
Liners. *See specific liners*
List, Siegmund, 193
Lithuania, 62
Little Boy, 426. *See also* Atomic bomb
Littorio (battleship), *246*
Ljubljana Gap, 309
Lloyd George, David, *13*; and Paris Peace Conference,
    14, 15; and Wilson, 13
Locarno Pact (1925), 46
London, *90. See also* Blitz
London Submarine Protocol of 1936, 102
Long March, 26, *map* 27
Lopatin, Aleksandr I., 199
"Lost Battalion", 307
Lotta di Classe, La (newspaper), 19
Louisville (cruiser), 389

Loyalists, 32-33
LSTs, *387*
Lübbe, Marinus van der, 23
Lublin Committee, 376
Lucas, John P.: and Anzio, 233, 236; and Churchill,
    234; replacement of, 234; and Truscott, 234
Lucy (spy), 363
Ludendorff, Erich, 22
Ludendorff Bridge, *338-339*
Luftwaffe, *90*; background of, 47; and Bastogne, 328;
    and Bristol, 94; and Britain, Battle of, 81, 88-92, 94;
    and Cardiff, 94; and Coventry, 94; formations of, 85;
    and Göring, 189; and Harstad, *64-65*; and
    Leningrad, 128; and Malta, 220, 249; and Paris, 79;
    and Plymouth, 94; and Poland, air force of, 84; and
    Portsmouth, 94; and Rotterdam, 72; Royal Air Force
    compared to, 84, 85; and Salerno, 229; size of, 84;
    and Soviet Union, 123; and Stalingrad, 199, *203*,
    206; and tactical air power, 340; and Tobruk, 218;
    and Warsaw, *61*; weaknesses of, 46, 188-189
Lumberjack (operation): and Bradley, 333, 338; and
    Hodges, 333; and Patton, 333
Lunga Point airfield, 261
Luttwitz, Heinrich von, 306
Lutze, Victor, *38-39*
Luxembourg, 312
Luzon, *maps* 167, 389; invasion of, 167-168; and
    MacArthur, 388; and United States, air force of, 167;
    and Yamashita, 388-389, 394
LVTs, 268
Lyutezh, 368

M

MacArthur, Douglas, *470*; and Australia, 168; and
    Bataan, 168; and Buna, 262, 264; and Corregidor,
    392; and Eichelberger, 262; and Fertig, 396; and
    Hollandia, 270; and Japan, 471; and Japan, surren-
    der of, *430-431*; and Kokoda Track, 262; and
    Korean War, 485; and Krueger, 389; and Leyte, 382,
    392; and Luzon, 388; and Madung, 270; and
    Manila, 389, 394; and Milne Bay, 262; and
    Mindanao, 168; and Morotai Island, 270; and
    Ormoc, 388; and Philippines, 267, 275, 382, 394;
    and Port Moresby, 262; and Quezon, *166*; and
    Roosevelt, 168; and Saidor, 270; and Sio, 270; and
    Solomon Islands, 264; unpopularity of, 168; and
    Wainwright, 168, 170
McAuliffe, Anthony C.: and Bastogne, 326; and
    Middleton, 325; and Moore, 326
MacDonald, Ramsay, 47
Macintyre, Donald G. F., *113*
McMillin, George, 166
McNair, Lesley J., 305
Madung, 270
Magic (code intercepts), 160
Maginot, André, 63
Maginot Line, *63*, 64; irrelevancy of, 76; piercing of, 79
Magnitogorsk, 189, 190
Majdanek concentration camp, *154*
Makin, 267
Malaya, *map* 170; and Churchill, 171; Communism in,
    479; Japanese invasion of, 170, 171; and Phillips,
    170, 171; surrender of, 170; and Wavell, 171; and
    Yamashita, 170, 171. *See also specific battles*
Malenkov, Georgy M., 375
Malinovsky, Rodion, 372
Malinta Hill, 392-393. *See also* Corregidor
Malinta Tunnel, *167, 169*; and Wainwright, 168
Malmédy, 324
Malmédy Massacre, 318-319
Malta, *250-251*; and Luftwaffe, 220, 249
Mamayev Hill, 200. *See also* Stalingrad
Manchester (cruiser), *240-241*
Manchuria: and Imperial Army, 24, 27; and League of
    Nations, 24
Manhattan Project, 427. *See also* Atomic bomb
Manila, *393*; and Eichelberger, 392; and Iwabuchi,
    392, 393-394; Japanese occupation of, 168; and

PICTURE CREDITS

Credits are read from left to right, from top to bottom by semicolons.

London. **301** Wide World; UPI. **302** U.S. Army. **303** Frank Scherschel for LIFE. **304** Map by Elie Sabban. **305** Ullstein Bilderdienst, Berlin; UPI. **306** Map by Elie Sabban. **307** U.S. Army; map by Elie Sabban. **308** UPI. **310** UPI. **312** Rapho, Paris. **313** Map by Elie Sabban. **314** Bundersarchiv, Koblenz; Imperial War Museum, London. **315** Imperial War Museum, London. **317** U.S. Army. **320** U.S. Army. **321** Imperial War Museum, London. **322** U.S. Army. **323** U.S. Army. **324** U.S. Army. **325** U.S. Army. **327** U.S. Army. **328** U.S. Army. **328, 329** UPI. **330** Elie Sabban. **331** George Silk for LIFE. **332** Ullstein Bilderdient, Berlin (West). **334, 335** Map by Tarijy Elsab. **336** George Silk for LIFE. **338** Wide World. **339** U.S. Army; UPI. **340** U.S. Air Force. **341** Imperial War Museum; U.S. Army. **342** Robert Capa from Magnum for LIFE (2). **343** Robert Capa from Magnum for LIFE. **344, 345** U.S. Army. (2) William Vandivert for LIFE. **346** Keystone Press Agency Ltd., London. **347, 349** U.S. Army. **350** Margaret Bourke-White for LIFE. **351** Bildarchiv Preussischer, Kulturbesitz, Berlin (West); George Rodger for LIFE; Wide World. **352** Johnny Florea for LIFE. **353** U.S. Army. **354, 355** Harry V. Hofmann Verlag, Hamburg. **356** U.S. Air Force. **357** © Dr. Wolf Strache, Stuttgart. **358** Ullstein Bilderdient, Berlin (West) (2); Ullstein/Photoreporters. **359** Landesbildstelle, Berlin (West); Suddeutscher Verlag, Bilderdienst, Munich. **360** Fisher-Foto, Cologne; Bildarchiv Preussischer Kulturbesitz, Berlin (West). **361** Ullstein Bilderdienst, Berlin (West). **363** Yakov Ryumkin, Moscow. **364** Map by Tarijy Elsab. **365** Novosti Press Agency, London. **366** Bundersarchiv, Koblenz. **367** Fotokhronika-TASS, Moscow. **368** From *Der Russlandkrieg* by Paul Carell, © 1967, Verlag Ullstein GmbH, Frankfurt/M-Berlin; ADN Zentralbild, Berlin. **370** Novosti Press Agency, Rome. **371** Sovfoto. **373** Novosti, Rome. **375** Sovfoto. **376** BBC Hulton Picture Library; Sovfoto. **379** Wide World; Jerzy Tomaszewski. **379** Dmitri Baltermants, Moscow. **380, 381** National Archives. **383** Carl Mydans for LIFE. **384** Naval Historical Center. **385** U.S. Navy, National Archives. **386** U.S. Navy. **388** Map by Elie Sabban. **390** U.S. Navy, National Archives; Nihon Hoso, Kyokai, Japan. **391** U.S. Navy, National Archives. **393** U.S. Navy, National Archives. **394, 395** U.S. Navy, National Archives. **396** Map by Elie Sabban. **397** U.S. Coast Guard, National Archives. **399** Defense Intelligence Agency. **400** Lou Lowery; U.S. Marine Corps. **401** Map by Elie

Sabban. **402** U.S. Navy, National Archives. **403, 404** W. Eugene Smith for LIFE. **405** J.R. Eyerman for LIFE. **406** U.S. Air Force. **407, 408** J.R. Eyerman for LIFE; **408, 409** U.S. Air Force. **410, 411** U.S. Army. **413** Bildarchiv Preussischer Kulturbesitz, Berlin (West); ADN Zentralbild, Berlin. **415** Mikhail Markov, Moscow. **416, 417** Sovfoto. **418, 419** Drawing by Hanno Engler, courtesy Bildarchiv Preussischer Kulturbesitz, Berlin (West). **421** Ivan Shagin, TASS from Sovfoto. **422** The Bettman Archives. **423** Imperial War Museum. **424** Jiri Janovsky, courtesy Vladimir Remes, Prague. **425** UPI. **426** Shunkichi Kichuchi. **427** Fritz Goro for LIFE; Goro from Black Star; UPI. **428, 429** Los Alamos National Laboratory. **430, 431** Carl Mydans for LIFE. **432, 433** Yosuke Yamabata; (inset) Wide World. **434** U.S. Air Force. **435** Eiichi Matsumoto; Yosuke Yamabata (2). **436** Painting by Masao Kobayashi. **437** Painting by Masaki Yamashita, painting by Tomiko Ikeshoji. **438** UPI. **440, 441** Map by Bill Hezlep. **442** David E. Scherman for LIFE. **443** U.S. Army. **444** Leonard McCombe. **445** Ernst Haas from Magnum from *Ende und Anfang*, by Zsolnay Verlag, Vienna. **446** Imperial War Museum, London. **447** Suddeutscher Verlag, Bilderdienst, Munich; Keystone, Hamburg. **448, 449** Courtesy Time Inc. Picture Collection. **449** U.S. Army. **450, 451** U.S. Army. **452** Edward Clark International (3); BBC Hulton Picture Library. **453** Frederico Patellani, Milan. **454, 455** Wide World. **456** Wide World. **457** David D. Duncan for LIFE. **458** David D. Duncan for LIFE; Interpress. **459** Rizzoli, Milan; Museo Civico L. Bailo, Treviso, Italy. **460** Walter Sanders for LIFE. **461** Keystone, Hamburg. **462** Map by Bill Hezlep. **463** Walter Sanders for LIFE. **464** Dmitri Kessel for LIFE; Francis Miller for LIFE. **465** Ernst Haas from Magnum, courtesy George C. Marshall Research Foundation; National Archives (2). **466, 467** Wide World. **468, 469** Map by Leonard Vigliarolo and Diana Raquel Vazquez. **470** U.S. Army. **470, 471** U.S. Marine Corps. **472** Wide World. **473** Wide World (2). **474** UPI. **475** Margaret Bourke-White for LIFE. **476** Dutch Institute for Military History, The Hague. **477** Information Section, Consulate General of Indonesia, National Archives. **478** BBC Hulton Picture Library (2). **479** Jack Birns for LIFE. **480** Jack Birns for LIFE. **481** Jean-Loup Charmet, Private Collection, Paris; Sovfoto. **482** UPI. **483** Jim Burke for LIFE. **484** U.S. Army; Wide World. **485** U.S. Army.

ACKNOWLEDGEMENTS

For help given in the preparation of this book, the editors wish to thank the following:

Trygve Bratteteig; Maurice Gagnon; Ebenezer George; Daniel German; Jane MacGregor; Nancy McClary; Jennifer Meltzer; Kelly Mulcair; Solange Pelland; Larry Pogue; Line Roberge; Brenda Rolfe; David Schulze; Odette Sévigny; Natalie Watanabe; Baltimore County Public Library, Towson, Maryland; Cedarbrae District Library, Scarborough; Côte Saint-Luc Municipal Library; Concordia University, Norris Library; Etobicoke Public Library, Richview Branch; Ottawa Public Library.

CONTENTS

IT IS FIFTY YEARS NOW, and the faces, the scenes and sounds and some of the feelings come back, again and again. There is no human experience like war, especially great and extended war, a war that involves whole nations and whole families. World War II was total war. It bore little relationship to Korea or Vietnam. Psychologically, America was almost ready for World War II when it began, as it was not ready years later for Vietnam and Korea. By the time we entered World War II, we had had the national argument before national action was required.

The invasion of Poland, after all, was more than two years before Pearl Harbor. On that September 3, 1939, I stood, a healthy, twenty-six-year-old, safely neutral American, at a radio station window in Paris. I knew what was happening; a piece of paper in my hand told me that France would be at war in six short hours, at 5 p.m. I was sud-

Eric Sevareid at his cabin in the foothills of the Blue Ridge Mountains of Virginia.

denly the audience, and all around me was the play. The hawker of shoelaces in the street hawked away, his cadences unaltered. The girl in the beauty shop went on polishing the metal hoods for her lady customers. The sanitation worker opened the hydrant on the corner and the Seine's water gurgled down the gutter as always. History was about to round the corner and hit them all like a runaway lorry, and they did not know.

In the early morning we stood in the Gare de l'Est. Here, in 1914, the young Frenchmen had assembled, scrambling, scuffling, shouting, singing songs about the glories of war and victory. It dawned on me that many before me now, the older ones, were the very same men, those who had survived the trenches. They shuffled this time, their wives, hair pinned carelessly in place, bedroom slippers on their feet, clinging to their arms, eyes glazed from all-night weeping. From the train, as far as one could see down the line of cars, the faces looked back from the windows. Another American witness, the columnist Dorothy Thompson, said, "Not one replaceable face." These were not like men at the start of a war; they were like tired men at the end of a war. They had never recovered from the First One. France had never recovered, and it was sending the walking wounded to fight again.

FOREWORD

This was all too soon and France was too civilized and too close to Germany. As were Poland, Belgium, Holland, Denmark, Norway and, for that matter, the putative enemy, Italy. Germany was different. There, the underworld had risen. The basis of Nazism was hate. I had been in Germany a year before and I could feel it everywhere, from the snickers of the bulky German women as they pointed to my young wife's saucy little hat, to the startling black-and-red signs proclaiming "Jews Unwanted," posted even in the little shop of Anton Lang who had played the Christ at Oberammergau.

They were on the march now, the glorified gangsters of Germany, Italy and Japan. A true world conspiracy. The forces behind World War I had been, I have come to believe, more psychological than anything else—fear and boredom. But this time the prime force was plain and simple aggression. It had to be resisted. Not so many years ago Justice Hugo Black said to me that he was convinced World War II was the only American war, besides the American Revolution, that was justified.

As a young American from the isolated and isolationist Midwest, I thought, in that autumn of 1939, that America could and should avoid this war, too. But I changed, as reporting war became my way of life over the next five and a half years. I was involved in the fall of Paris, the great city like a beautiful woman in a coma, its lifeblood ebbing away through every vein. In the fall of France. In the first Battle of Britain. In Washington and Roosevelt's political battle to make America ready for what he knew was coming. In resentful India, looking to independence more than to any military victory. In Chiang's disorganized, disinterested China, more apprehensive of the Chinese Communists than of the Japanese invaders. Then the long, miserable push over the mountain ridges of Italy, the not very difficult invasion of France from the south and then the last Battle of Britain under the V2s, which gave no warning at all. And finally, the breaching of Hitler's moat, the crossing of the Rhine into his dirty, desolate castle.

There, hundreds of Italian and other slave-laborers, eyes blood-shot, hair matted, trudged by, some on footgear of bloodied rags. German civilians regarded them from the sidewalks, unseeing. They regarded us, their conquerors, in sullen silence. They felt nothing toward us, save resentment, and I realized I felt nothing toward them. Nothing. Years of war can drain away something of

what makes one human, even for observers, like me. I did not go farther into Germany, to the death camps. I am rather glad that I did not. I have memories enough.

I had lost something of my being, yes, but I had not been brutalized by war. The journalist, the observer, is too privileged for that to happen. Thirty-five American war reporters were killed in that war, many injured or invaded by war-time diseases that plagued them for years. And the chroniclers of the war had to put themselves in harm's way by an exercise of their own will, not by the unanswerable command of a superior. But they possessed the vast advantage of being essentially free, while the men in uniform were essentially slaves. That was the chasm between us. Toward the end of the fighting I realized the chasm could never be closed, that I would never enter the realm of their spirits, feel their fears, exult in their victories, dream their dreams or awake from their nightmares. I could watch these Americans abroad as conquerors, a role they played with awkwardness. (They did not want to rule foreign lands; they just wanted to get home to their own.) I could see that some had been brutalized, others ennobled by the fighting and suffering. I sensed that they and their families at home would be, in a certain sense, forever strangers.

Eric Sevareid (right) with John Davies, General Joseph W. Stillwell's political officer, in Chabua, India the day they emerged from the Naga Hills. While flying the treacherous Hump route from India to China in 1943, the C-46 in which they were flying crashed. Of the 20 passengers aboard, only the copilot died; the others bailed out in the biggest mass amateur parachute jump ever made. It took them, however, a full month to make their way out of the hills to Chabua.

We chroniclers did our imperfect best to bring about what General George C. Marshall, the hulking, homely man of greatness, had told some of us he wanted to see: the truth of the war as it unfolded. Short of breaches of security, he wanted us to tell it all, including the failures, the stupidities, the horrors. He did not want to see a repetition of World War I, after which the civilian populations of the Allied countries awoke from the sleep of censorship to read the truth of the terrible trench warfare. The result was a wave of pacifism, of anti-militarism that obsessed a whole generation of the educated young (including me) and left civilized nations intellectually naked as the warlords gathered their armor.

This did not happen after World War II, because its causes were clear, its necessity absolute, its management generally sensible, its ending final. And because this war was reported as it unfolded, in spite of endless conflicts between reporters and censors. Not totally, not always accurately, but General Marshall's mandate to us was essentially fulfilled. This time, sound was added to words, with the broadcasts, and this time the role of pictures was enormously expanded in their undeniability, as this book so brilliantly shows. No, the "revisionist," post-Vietnam historians who describe the World War II journalists as uncritical handmaidens to government and military do not understand total war or what really happened in the field.

The fire that flared up that first day of September a half century ago consumed some tens of millions of men, women and children all over the world. Nothing can truly compensate for that. Yet, while the war period left us with certain potential terrors, nuclear and chemical, it also helped to produce in our present time a worldwide yearning for personal freedoms and peace between nations. We are seeing an enormous increase in material well-being, in the northern hemisphere at least. We see an integrated world economy developing and a thousand groups and procedures for international cooperation.

In so many ways, the West has won the world; even the leaders of Russia and China admit it. America went into the great War the world's hope, and came out of it the world's necessity. By and large we lived up to that prodigious role that history assigned us.

We may all of us remain "trapped between earth and a glimpse of heaven," but even after the frightful test of World War II the signs are that men everywhere are refusing to abandon the glimpse.

ERIC SEVAREID
Washington, D.C.

THE YEARS BETWEEN THE WARS

Ingenious French peasants use an abandoned tank as a tractor to help a team of horses, in preparation for the first post-war planting of their fields.

1

World War I had bled Europe for more than four agonizing years. For the first time in history, men had fought one another not only on land and sea but in the air. They had employed implements whose ferocity few had foreseen: planes dropping bombs, submarines firing torpedoes, giant cannon hurling tons of steel, poison gas spreading deadly fumes. Soldiers had endured intolerable conditions dictated by a new military concept, trench warfare. France counted 1.4 million dead, Germany 1.8 million, the British Empire 900,000, and Italy 650,000. In still-bleeding Russia, it was impossible even to make an estimate of the lives lost. The long war and its dénouement had brought chaos, hunger and despair to millions of people. Yet, there was, on Armistice Day, a great surge of hope and an expectation that mankind was on the threshold of a new era.

At 7 a.m, the train crept to a stop deep in the forest of Compiègne. Mist shrouded the trees around the clearing. It was November 8, 1918. World War I was ending and World War II was beginning—though scarcely anyone could imagine it at the time.

From the train's rear car, the passengers could see another car on the siding. They did not know where they were but they knew this was the end of a nightmare journey—a journey they hoped would end the fighting.

A French Army officer appeared to inform the six German passengers that Marshal Ferdinand Foch, Supreme Commander of the Allied Forces, would receive them at 9 a.m. Matthias Erzberger, the spokesman of the group and a leader in Germany's Catholic Center Party, reflected that seeking an armistice was a strange mission for a civilian. But the new parliamentary government in Berlin did not altogether trust the military, and the High Command was only too happy to avoid the onus of bearing the white flag. Erzberger recalled Field Marshal Paul von Hindenburg's last words to him: "God go with you, and try to get the best you can for our country."

A few minutes before nine that morning, the Germans entered Foch's sleeping car headquarters. Then, ramrod-straight at age 67, Foch appeared. "What brings these gentlemen here?" he asked. Erzberger said they had come to receive the Allied proposals for an armistice.

"I have no proposals to make," said Foch.

A moment of consternation followed; one of the Germans asked how he wanted them to express themselves.

"Do you ask for an armistice?" replied Foch, icily formal. "If you do, I can acquaint you with the conditions under which it can be obtained." They asked for an armistice.

There was complete silence as an aide read out 34 terms. For the first time, the Germans comprehended the magnitude of their defeat. Germany was to evacuate all captured territory it now held—most of Belgium and Luxembourg and a sixth of France—plus Alsace and Lorraine, the provinces it had annexed from France after the war of 1870-1871. Allied forces would move into Germany to occupy the Rhine's left bank and the three bridgeheads on the right. The German fleet was to steam to the British naval base at Scapa Flow in Scotland for internment. Germany would turn over 150,000 freight cars, 5,000 locomotives and 5,000 trucks. War materials to be surrendered included 1,700 aircraft, 5,000 artillery pieces and 25,000 machine guns.

When the reading ended, Erzberger asked for an immediate cease-fire. Foch refused; there would be no cease-fire until the Germans accepted all 34 terms. They had 72 hours in which to decide. Three days later in Foch's railcar at Compiègne, Erzberger signed the armistice.

"A PEACE RESTING ON QUICKSAND"

The cease-fire took effect at 11 a.m. on November 11, 1918. An eerie silence fell along the battle lines. "Peace came so suddenly we were stunned," wrote a French officer. "Walking along our trenches some hours after, I was surprised to see all our soldiers at listening posts or in shelters as if the war were still on."

In contrast was the scene in the cities. London throbbed with wild celebrations. "Total strangers copulated in doorways and on pavements," wrote British historian A.J.P. Taylor. "They were asserting the triumph of life over death." Prime Minister David Lloyd George, too exuberant to wait for formalities, came out of his 10 Downing Street residence at 10:55 a.m. and kept shouting to startled onlookers: "At 11 o'clock this morning the War will be over!"

In Paris, 20,000 people massed in front of the brilliantly lit Opéra and joyously sang the *Marseillaise*. Georges Clemenceau, the 77-year-old premier, reported the Armistice terms to an assemblage of the Chamber of Deputies and Senate, wiped his eyes, and hurried away to spend the afternoon alone, walking in his garden. In Milan the editor of the daily *Il Popolo*, Benito Mussolini—veteran of a short and undistinguished tour on the Italian front against the Germans chief allies, the Austrians—held court for some admirers dressed in swaggering black uniforms.

In the United States, shrieking factory whistles added to the clamor of jubilant crowds, and in Washington President Woodrow Wilson wrote out a statement pledging Americans to assist in establishing "a just democracy

The victors of World War I redrew the map of Europe, leaving the continent more bitterly divided than ever. Within 15 years of the peace talks at Paris, the redrawn map would clearly be seen as a blueprint for another war.

throughout the world." But in Russia the day passed virtually without notice. Having made a separate peace with Germany eight months earlier, the country was now in the throes of civil war between counter-revolutionary White forces and Red armies committed to the Bolshevik cause of Vladimir Ilyich Ulyanov, better known as Lenin.

Nowhere did word of the Armistice prove more shattering than at a military hospital in the small German town of Pasewalk. Among the soldiers who heard the news from a sobbing pastor was an obscure corporal, Adolf Hitler, still half blinded as a result of a British gas attack on the Belgian Front. As he later described his reaction: "I tottered and groped my way back to the ward, threw myself on my bunk, and dug my burning head into my blanket and pillow. So it had all been in vain. In vain all the sacrifices and privations." The Armistice, he raged, was "the greatest villainy of the century."

In the wake of four years of unprecedented destruction in Europe, farmers returned to their fields; refugees and soldiers trudged home. By Armistice Day the treasuries of the combatants were depleted. Although hostilities were over, the Allies continued their wartime blockade of food shipments bound for German ports. Malnutrition was now widespread in Germany; populations in lands farther east faced more acute famine. Yet despite the carnage and grief, there was, on November 11, a hope that another such holocaust would be made impossible.

This hope fed two messianic visions. One came out of Russia, where Lenin was calling for a world revolution that, under Communism, would sweep away old notions of private property and class distinctions, and unite the human race. The other came from the U.S., where President Woodrow Wilson had captured the imagination of people everywhere by proclaiming the principles he believed essential for establishing a just and lasting peace.

Wilson had first enumerated his aims in 14 points to Congress in January 1918. In place of secret agreements, he said, there would be "open covenants of peace, openly arrived at." Armaments would be reduced "to the lowest

point consistent with domestic safety." All barriers to trade would be removed. There would be no annexations and no "punitive damages." One proposal above all engrossed Wilson: a league of nations was to be formed, charged with keeping the peace and guaranteeing the independence and security of "great and small states alike."

It was on the basis of these declarations that the Germans had turned to Wilson, not to the leaders of Britain or France, when they decided to seek an armistice. It was from Wilson, after a series of rigidly polite exchanges by transatlantic wireless, that they had learned that Marshal Foch would receive them.

Of all the world leaders, none seemed to hold a stronger hand than the American President. The United States, which had not entered the war until April 1917, almost three years after it began, was now the most powerful nation on earth. The arrival in France of 1.7 million fresh U.S. troops had turned the tide against Germany in the summer of 1918. Shielded by the broad Atlantic, the U.S. itself had been spared physical destruction of any sort. Its great economic strength was Wilson's to command for postwar healing.

The President, a man of vision and high ideals, was also an extraordinarily complicated personality. A scholar turned politician, he intimidated many by the force of his intellect, and his glacial formality kept associates at a distance. Although no previous President had ever left the country while in office, Wilson was determined to head the American delegation to the peace conference in Paris in January 1919. He rejected all arguments: he had sent young men overseas to die and he must see that "others shall not be called upon to make that sacrifice again."

Arriving at the French harbor of Brest, Wilson was given a reception never before or since accorded a visiting statesman. An almost religious fervor greeted him on his visits to England and Italy before the conference opened. Children strewed flowers in his path; immense crowds cheered themselves hoarse. Watching them, Herbert Hoover, chosen by Wilson to set up the machinery for postwar relief and reconstruction, later observed that to these people "no such evangel of peace had appeared since Christ preached the Sermon on the Mount."

The Paris Peace Conference opened on January 18, 1919, in the massive stone pile of the French Ministry of Foreign Affairs on the Quai d'Orsay, on the left bank of the Seine. The sheer immensity of the task was appalling. The conference was charged with settling the future of 400 million Europeans, 10 million former subjects of the Ottoman Turks in the Middle East, and some 12 million people in the colonies Germany had held in Africa and the Pacific.

Russia was not represented at the peace conference. The

On October 25, 1917, the day of the Bolshevik takeover, Lenin proclaims the new Soviet government to an ecstatic throng gathered in the Smolny Institute in Petrograd. Standing behind him is Stalin, whose role in these events was actually minor, but who would seize power after Lenin's death.

outcome of its civil war was still in doubt, and the Western powers refused to recognize the Bolshevik government as long as a final White victory appeared possible. Germany and its wartime allies—now the states of Austria, Hungary, Bulgaria and Turkey—were barred from a place at the peace table. The peace terms were to be hammered out by 32 nations, large and small, that had either been at war with or had severed relations with Germany.

From the start it was clear that the conference was too big for Wilson's dream of "open covenants . . . openly arrived at." Soon such prickly problems as territorial boundaries were passed to special commissions. A Council of Ten, with two members from each principal Allied power—Britain, France, the United States, Italy and Japan—was set up as the ruling body. But the crucial decisions fell to the so-called Big Four: Clemenceau, Lloyd George, Wilson and Premier Vittorio Orlando of Italy.

The Big Four could not have been more unlike in background, temperament and their views on what the peace should mean to their own countries. Clemenceau—fondly called the Tiger by his countrymen—was chairman of the conference and a formidable figure across any table. He habitually wore a skullcap, gloves to hide the eczema on his hands, and a sardonic air. A radical in his youth, long since grown cynical, he remarked when he first heard of Wilson's Fourteen points: "God gave us the Ten Commandments and we broke them. Wilson gave us his Fourteen Points and we shall see." He was willing to indulge Wilson's lofty generalities as long as he got what he wanted—a Germany that would never again be in a position to invade France, as it had twice in the past 50 years. The Tiger wanted France's tricolor planted on the Rhine or, failing that, a separate Rhineland as a buffer state.

Lloyd George, at age 56, was a Welshman with a shock of white hair, a quick tongue, and a cheerful mien that masked a flair for adroit political maneuvering. He had battled his way to the top by denouncing the aristocratic establishment and fighting for such radical social reforms as old-age pensions. He was now a thorough pragmatist. He and his Liberal Party had just won a new vote of confidence in a post-Armistice election based on a pugnacious campaign pledge to "Squeeze the German orange until the pips squeak." In Paris, he intended to preserve Britain's supremacy of the seas and to restore its prewar trading advantages. Orlando, a gentle and learned man, was there to see that Italy received the territories it had been secretly promised in 1915 by Britain and France as a reward for joining the War on the Allied side.

At Wilson's insistence the conference dealt first with the Covenant—the constitution of the League of Nations. The word "covenant" was Wilson's choice, an echo of his Presbyterian boyhood. He devoutly believed the League would be the instrument by which future wars would be prevented. But the specifics posed complications. To placate critics back home who were fearful of yielding up United States sovereignty, Wilson had to insist that the Covenant include a phrase stating that the League did not supersede "regional understandings like the Monroe Doctrine." The Japanese raised an embarrassing point when they urged that the Covenant affirm the principle of racial equality. This was traded off by an amendment requiring all decisions made at League meetings be unanimously approved—thus giving veto power to any one member.

The President compromised on other issues in the hope that the League would later put things right. Two cases arose regarding Italy and Japan. By the secret Treaty of London in

WILSON LLOYD GEORGE ORLANDO CLEMENCEAU

The Big Four at the 1919 Paris Peace Conference, the United States's Woodrow Wilson, Britain's David Lloyd George, Italy's Vittorio Orlando and France's Georges Clemenceau, comprised a quartet of discordant personalities. Lloyd George derided Wilson as a combination of "the unscrupulous partisan, the exalted idealist and the man of rather petty and personal rancors." Ironically, although each leader achieved some of his aims, within two years all four had been politically repudiated on their own home grounds by countrymen who felt that their nations had been duped or shortchanged in the peace settlement.

1915, Italy had been promised the South Tyrol and the region of Trieste—both then belonging to Austria-Hungary—and a slice of the Dalmatian coast, now part of the new kingdom of Yugoslavia. Wilson went along with the Tyrolean deal, though it meant putting a quarter million Austrians under Italian rule, but he balked at other demands. When he went over Orlando's head and issued a manifesto to the people of Italy urging them to place world peace above national interest, Orlando quit the conference and left for home. "The Italians must choose between Wilson and me," asserted Orlando; he was later to return to sign the peace treaty.

Japan claimed what it had been promised in a secret pact with the Allies in 1917: a takeover of Germany's concessions—in effect, control over important industries in China's Shantung Province. Though China, too, was an ally, with 175,000 men serving as behind-the-lines laborers in Europe, Africa and the Middle East at the War's end, Wilson acquiesced to Japan's demand. When his press secretary protested that this went counter to American and world opinion, Wilson said wearily: "I know that, but if the Italians remain away and the Japanese go home, what becomes of the League of Nations?"

By April the ceremonial air of January was long since gone, and the tempers of the remaining Big Three were fraying. At one point or another each man threatened to quit. The most bitter disputes came over Germany. Clemenceau wanted it permanently weakened. Wilson and Lloyd George were more lenient. Britain did not relish the prospect of a too-powerful France in postwar Europe; moreover, the British thought a revived Germany would serve Britain well as a trading partner. At one snappish session Clemenceau accused Lloyd George of being an enemy of France. "Surely," was the cool reply. "That is our traditional policy."

Against Clemenceau's demand for a separate Rhineland as a buffer state, his colleagues stood adamant. They did,

however, agree that the region should be demilitarized. There were other satisfactions for Clemenceau. Alsace and Lorraine would be returned to France. Germany's Army would number no more than 100,000 men. There was to be no German air force at all. The production of planes and submarines was forbidden and the manufacture of war materials strictly limited. All German colonies were to be surrendered. Large areas of Germany itself, to the east, were to go to the newly independent Poland.

The issue of reparations to be paid by Germany proved an unchewable bone, and the problem was deferred to a special commission. Meanwhile, Germany was to pay five billion dollars in gold or its equivalent, beginning in May 1921. One other obligation—later known as Article 231—was to infuriate the Germans and rankle long and dangerously. Germany was to accept "the responsibility for causing all the loss and damage" sustained by the Allies as a consequence of a war "imposed" upon them by the "aggression" of Germany and its partners. As the Germans read it, Article 231 was a verdict of war guilt.

The closing weeks of the peace conference, a British diplomatic aide wrote, "flew past us in a hysterical nightmare." Among other things that were left undone was the convening of a congress—intended as a follow-up to the conference—to which Germany was to have been invited to discuss the Allied peace terms. Some items, such as German disarmament and territorial concessions, were to be nonnegotiable. Others, including economic matters, were to be open to argument and possible change.

In the six months since the Armistice, the German people had suffered the trauma of defeat. Many had known starvation; the Allied blockade—not lifted till March 1919—had closed off food from abroad, and German farmers either hoarded their produce or bootlegged it to those who could pay. Revolutionary uprisings in a number of cities had ousted local officials and replaced them with Soviet-style councils of soldiers and workers. In once-orderly Germany, savage street fighting between factions of the Left and Right became common.

Yet in the face of Germany's turmoil, a republic had been proclaimed, a representative assembly elected, and the seat of government moved from Berlin to the town of Weimar. Guiding the new republic was Chancellor Friedrich Ebert, leader of the Social Democrats.

The Germans had managed to survive as a nation, but they had also been living on rash expectations. They did not sense the hatred they had engendered, and they had little feeling of war guilt. Having sued for the Armistice on the basis of Wilson's Fourteen Points, they were not prepared for the severity of the terms presented to them at Versailles.

Reprieved by defeat and lucky to be alive—the War had cost Germany 1.8 million men—this teenage German soldier was typical of those surviving.

Military aides of the Allied peacemakers climb up on tables, footstools and sofas for a peek into the main conference room in the Trianon Palace at Versailles on the fateful day of May 7, 1919. At the moment this picture was taken, the humiliating peace terms on which the Allies had agreed were being handed to a stunned, deeply angry German delegation.

Heading the German delegation summoned to the conference was Count Ulrich von Brockdorff-Rantzau, Germany's new Foreign Minister. This proud nobleman was shocked to be received like a criminal before the bar of justice. Clemenceau stiffly presented the treaty and said no discussion of its terms was permitted. German objections must be presented in writing.

Clemenceau had risen to make his remarks. The Count replied sitting down. Later he was to say that he feared he might break down if he stood up, but others at the scene saw the gesture as calculated insolence. Clemenceau purpled. Lloyd George vented his feelings by snapping a letter opener in two. Wilson murmured: "Isn't it just like them?"

The Count did not hide his anger. Bitterly he said: "It is demanded that we confess ourselves guilty. Such a confession in my mouth would be a lie." Hundreds of thousands of noncombatants, he asserted, had perished because of the Allied food blockade. "Think of that when you speak of guilt and punishment."

The Germans back home reacted with outrage and a sense of betrayal. Ebert, now President, called the terms "unrealizable and unbearable." The Count resigned rather than sign the treaty. Mass protests were held throughout the country, and there was even furious talk of resuming the war. In the end, the Germans filed 443 pages of objections to the 230-page treaty but won only slight mitigation of the terms.

The signing ceremony took place June 28 in the Palace of Versailles in the Hall of Mirrors, the same resplendent room where half a century earlier Otto von Bismarck had proclaimed a new German empire after defeating France in the Franco-Prussian war. As the ceremony proceeded, guns began to boom outside and the sumptuous fountains of Versailles played for the first time since the War began.

In July, Wilson returned to Washington, directly to the Senate to urge the treaty's ratification. The President was pale and tense, fully aware of the mounting opposition to the proposed League of Nations. Above all was a distrust of the Covenant of the League of Nations, which had been incorporated in the treaty. Many Americans feared Article X of the Covenant, which provided for preserving the territorial integrity of League members. The Article would, it was argued, suck the United States into all sorts of little wars in Europe.

Determined that the Senate should accept or reject the treaty in its entirety, Wilson decided to appeal directly to his countrymen. Though exhausted and suffering the aftereffects of a severe infection, he undertook a cross-country speaking tour. His wife pleaded against it in vain. When his physician warned him to conserve his strength, Wilson brusquely cut him off: "I cannot put my personal safety, my health in balance against my duty."

Wilson planned 26 major speeches, but in Pueblo, Colorado, he suffered a stroke. The presidential train roared back to Washington with the tracks cleared and the blinds drawn. For two months Wilson remained in critical condition. When the President was able again to face affairs of

KILLING GROUND IN RUSSIA

In the five years following the first rattle of gunfire in the Bolshevik uprising in 1917, life became Russia's cheapest commodity. Czarist troops mutinied, murdering their officers. Cities seethed with mobs of rampaging soldiers and sailors, whose numbers swelled when a quickly concluded peace with Germany released millions of men from the front. This was a golden chance to settle grudges, political or personal. Thousands did; but soon this random killing grew into the more methodical death dance of a civil war.

The Red armies of the Bolsheviks battled the White forces of the counter-revolutionaries all around the edges of the former Russian Empire. Guerrillas harried both sides, and few opportunities for slaughter were missed, on the battlefield or elsewhere. At Stavrapol in southern Russia, White General Peter Wrangel captured 3,000 Red soldiers and—to induce the rank and file to join his forces—shot all 370 of their officers and noncoms. At Nikolaevsk, one Siberian partisan band massacred 6,000 Russian men, women and children, along with a Japanese garrison. Red sailors at Sevastopol slaughtered hundreds of men, women and children. Siberian forces under the White commander Alexander Kolchak executed 1,500 captives at Omsk. White Cossacks dragged in prisoners at the ends of lariats; Reds nailed the epaulettes of captured White officers to their shoulders. A troublesome Red guerrilla who fell into White hands was roasted alive in the firebox of a locomotive.

Horrifying though these military killings were, what happened to civilians was, if anything, worse. White pogroms in southern Russia alone killed some 100,000 Jews. The Cheka, or Red secret police, executed scores of thousands—including 500 luckless victims in Petrograd slain in retaliation for the assassination of the local Cheka boss. Disease and hunger, sweeping the land in the wake of national chaos, took 3.5 million Russians from typhus and another two million or more from starvation. Altogether, those five ghastly years of civil war, accompanied by the famine and pestilence, killed up to 15 million Russians—6.5 million more than the combined total deaths on all fronts during World War I.

Mutinous machine gunners roll through Petrograd in June 1917 to protest sending more men to the front in the final days of the war with Germany.

Soldiers of one of the many White Armies that fought in Russia's three-year civil war survey a heap of Bolshevik corpses. At first the White Armies easily routed the undisciplined Reds. But from 1918 on, War Commissar Leon Trotsky, rushing from one battlefront to another in his armored train, reorganized the Red Armies and went on the offensive. Among Trotsky's conducive disciplinary measures were firing squads for laggards and turncoats.

state, his wife, among others, urged him to consider a compromise that might save the League. "Little girl, don't you desert me; that I cannot stand," he replied. "Better to go down fighting than to dip your colors to dishonorable compromise." To the end, with Wilson, it was all or nothing. The United States did not ratify the treaty; it signed a separate peace with Germany in 1921.

The Treaty of Versailles brought no peace; rather, it led to 20 years of recurring crises that culminated in World War II. The redrawn map of Europe provided boundaries for the new states of Poland, Czechoslovakia, Rumania and Yugoslavia. Yet those new boundaries placed in close proximity many ethnic minorities who were mutually and traditionally antagonistic. And on the Chinese mainland Japan now had a strong physical presence.

Instead of reconciliation, the treaty left a legacy of frustration and hatred. The French felt deprived of the full fruits of victory. The Italians felt cheated of their territorial ambitions. The Germans felt utterly betrayed by the peacemakers. The Russians, having had no voice at the conference, felt no need to abide by its decisions. The United States, having kept itself apart from the League, retreated into isolationism.

Woodrow Wilson had made a bleak prophesy in January 1917. A punitive peace, he warned, would "leave a sting, a resentment, a bitter memory upon which the terms of peace would rest, not permanently, but only as upon quicksand." By 1919 the prophesy was beginning to come true.

The stable world order envisioned by some signers of the World War I treaties perished in violence almost before the negotiators got home. Starting with Russia, one nation after another exchanged the evils of war for those of revolution and counter-revolution. The counter-revolutionaries usually won; Red uprisings in Hungary and in parts of Germany soon were crushed. In these and other countries where peace alone had proved no cure for misery, people erupted in frantic epidemics of strikes and street fighting.

Underdogs everywhere were becoming more militant. Black American soldiers arrived home from combat with a new self-assurance that irked many whites, and the resulting friction exploded into race riots. In Britain, miners triggered an unprecedented general strike. In British outposts, authorities jailed, flogged and shot Indians clamoring for more self-determination, but in so doing merely swelled the followings of nationalist leaders like Mohandas K. Gandhi. Elsewhere, nationalists declared open season on the minorities that had been marooned by new treaty boundaries or by rampaging armies. Resurgent Turks first defeated an armed Greek incursion, then started expanding themselves, in the course of which they slaughtered hundreds of thousands of Greek and Armenian civilians trapped behind the new Turkish borders.

Underlying all these disruptive forces was economic disarray. The war left millions struggling to survive amid shortages of everything—except, in places, paper money. Successive German governments fell when the economy could not support their flimsy currencies. And as one European regime after another failed to assure its citizens of enough food, clothing, shelter or safety, discouraged masses hearkened increasingly to demagogues who offered to lead them in a march back to some long-lost glory.

As Communism entrenched itself in Russia, a rival ideology rose to the challenge in Europe. It first appeared as Fascism in Italy, then took on a more demonic form as Nazism in Germany. This new totalitarianism was largely the creation of two men—Benito Mussolini and Adolf Hitler. Playing on the fears and frustrations of their time, they exploited the mystique of national pride and the spirit of violence unleashed by World War I in pursuit of power. They succeeded beyond all imagining. Benito Mussolini ruled as Italy's dictator, the Duce, for 21 years; Adolf Hitler, the Führer, was Germany's undisputed master for 12 years.

Italy's leader was born in 1883 in Romagna, the son of a blacksmith and an anarchist who named his firstborn after the Mexican revolutionary, Benito Juárez. Even as a boy

A German housewife lights her breakfast fire with worthless currency. The value of the mark declined steadily after Germany's World War I defeat until, in the early 1920s, it plummeted out of control.

Mussolini was a hellion, with a record of knifing at least three people and expulsion from school. When compulsory military duty impended, Mussolini decamped for Switzerland. There he met Angelica Balabanoff, a Russian expatriate who became his mentor in Marxism and encouraged his ambitions as a writer; this relationship transformed his life. He began contributing articles to Socialist newspapers and, back in Italy in 1904 under amnesty for deserters, he extolled his extremist views in a weekly paper *La Lotta di Classe* (The Class Struggle).

Mussolini's newfound appetite for politics and print grew. He led antiwar riots and publicly declared that "the national flag is a rag to be planted on a dunghill." Tried for subver-

sion, he went to prison for five months. On his release, the Socialists hailed him as a coming leader and named him editor of their national daily, *Avanti!* (Forward!). He had become a public figure.

When World War I broke out in 1914, *Avanti!*'s anti-neutrality position enraged the Socialists; they expelled the editor from the party and the paper. Mussolini now bought his own paper, *Il Popolo d'Italia* (The People of Italy), which denounced pacifism. When Italy joined the Allies in 1915, he enlisted in the Army and served on the Alpine front; he never rose above the rank of sergeant.

Three years later, in 1917, world peace found Mussolini with a newspaper but without a party. Italy was in a sorry

Banner-waving Fascist Black Shirts swagger in Rome after a coup that helped bring to dictatorial power a self-assured newspaper editor named Benito Mussolini.

state. The war had cost the country 138 billion lire; millions of demobilized soldiers were now jobless and hungry. Amid inflation, strikes, and pillaging of food shops, some talked of violent redress against an ungrateful country. Mussolini watched these events and planned his strategy accordingly. In March 1919, *Il Popolo* ran a series of notices about a group forming to fight "against the forces dissolving victory and the nation." A meeting was scheduled—attended by 145 men, among them veterans of the *Arditi*, Italy's cocky, black-clad shock troops.

Mussolini proposed a *fascio di combattimento*—a combat group—with a threefold mission: to uphold "the material and moral claims" of veterans; to oppose "the imperialism of any countries damaging to Italy"; and, most urgent in view of an upcoming election, "to fight with all their means the candidates that were milk-and-water Italians." From this meager start Fascism was to emerge and flourish.

Before long, Mussolini's new *fascio* (from the Latin *fasces*, the tight bundle of rods carried in ancient Rome as a symbol of authority) had adopted a dramatic all-black uniform. Its members would later be known as the Black Shirts.

By the following year, Mussolini was head of a movement of 2,200 local *fasci* groups with 320,000 members. In a May 1921 election, the Fascists, backed by industrialists, won 35 seats in the Chamber of Deputies, Mussolini himself polling 125,000 votes as opposed to the 4,000 that he had garnered only two years earlier. But he was having trouble with his party; Fascism had not yet become a one-man show.

Much of the power still lay with the fire-eating local Fascist bosses who called themselves Ras, after the feudal chieftains of Ethiopia. In May 1922, the Ras launched an assault on government authority, taking over the town hall of Ferrara and demanding that the mayor start a program of public works for the unemployed. They repeated the maneu-ver in Bologna, Ravenna and Parma, and success moved them to plan a government takeover.

Mussolini, now in step with his followers, electrified a rally at Naples on October 24 by shouting: "Either the government will be given to us or we will seize it by marching on Rome!" The crowd roared: "A Roma! A Roma! A Roma!"

Three days later, 14,000 Fascists converged on the outskirts of Rome. Italy's premier, Luigi Facta, tried to dicker with Mussolini, offering him a Cabinet post. When Mussolini refused, Facta urged the King to declare a state of siege. Instead the King invited Mussolini to form a government.

At 39, Mussolini was the youngest leader in Italy's history. In his first address to Parliament, he made his contempt for that body eminently clear: "I could have transformed this gray hall into an armed camp of Black Shirts, a bivouac for corpses." The cowed deputies voted him emergency authority to rule without them for the next 12 months.

Italy at first responded almost magically to his leadership. The strikers went back to work, the students to their books—and Mussolini tightened his grip. In an April 1924 election, the Fascists polled 65 per cent of the votes. When the new parliament assembled in May, Giacomo Matteotti, a moderate Socialist, accused the Fascists of widespread fraud. The Fascist majority in the Chamber howled for his blood. Mussolini turned to a henchman and said: "This man, after this speech, must not be allowed to go around."

Ten days later Matteotti disappeared. Shortly after, his battered body was found in a shallow grave near Rome. Blazing headlines in the non-Fascist press blamed Mussolini. An outraged opposition withdrew from Parliament, hoping to force the King to ask for Mussolini's resignation. The King refused to intervene.

On January 3, 1925, the Duce addressed Parliament: "Italy wants peace, work and calm," he said. "I will give these things with love if possible, with force if necessary." With these words, civil liberties ceased to exist for the Italians. So did freedom of the press. Thereafter Mussolini conducted himself as the sole government, subject only nominally to the King.

In 1919, while Mussolini had been forming his Fascist party, Adolf Hitler was a 30-year-old nonentity living in the Munich barracks of his old regiment. He had no other home and wanted none. He revered the military and anything else that summoned up Germany's former glory. His passion for Germany was odd, since it was not his native land. He was an Austrian, the son of a customs official with a salary sufficient to provide a good schooling for his family.

As a child, Hitler had detested school. But one of his few "satisfactory" grades was drawing—and so a dream took shape: He would become an artist or architect. He spent

Mussolini's blatant egotism came across most clearly in a life style of the classic aspirer, with palatial working quarters and a prodigal supply of flashy uniforms.

hours sketching grandiose imaginary mansions, and at 16 headed for Vienna to apply for admission to the prestigious Academy of Fine Arts. He was rejected, his trial sketches judged "without sufficient merit."

When his parents died, Hitler lived on a small government grant until reaching adulthood. Thereafter, he eked out a living selling an occasional watercolor, and produced posters advertising soap and antiperspirant powder. A men's hostel in Vienna for down-and-outers provided a roof overhead, and living was cheap; Hitler was a nonsmoker, nondrinker and a vegetarian.

The cosmopolitan capital of Vienna had attracted people from all over the Habsburg empire—Czechs, Serbs, Croats, Poles, Hungarians, Rumanians. Pamphleteers railed against this polyglot influx, spewing a special hatred for the immigrants who were Jews. The Germanic strain, they warned, represented a master race that must not be defiled—a doctrine Hitler embraced completely.

In 1913 he moved to Munich and when war came enlisted in a Bavarian infantry regiment. His bravery on the western Front won him the Iron Cross, First Class—a rare honor for a corporal. Except for a gas attack that temporarily blinded him in 1918, his only injury after four years under fire was a leg wound. Hitler came out of the war convinced he had been spared for some special mission in life.

An inkling of the form that mission would take emerged soon after he returned to Munich in early 1919. Political turmoil threatened to tear Germany apart. The new Republic commanded little respect; its middle-of-the-road leaders bore the stigma of having signed the hated Armistice. On the Left, the Socialists and the Communists still hoped for a revolution; Munich itself had a brief taste of a Red regime. On the Right, determined to prevent a recurrence of such episodes, stood the nobility, the upper middle class and the Army. Reservist Hitler was delighted to be given a berth in the district command's political department. He was assigned to check up on a tiny, possibly subversive, group calling itself the German Workers Party.

To his pleasant surprise the party turned out to be fervently nationalist and patriotic. Intrigued, Hitler became a member, and revealed an unexpected gift for propaganda and organization. He soon began to mold the party to his own ends. He changed its name to National Socialist German Workers Party (Nationalsozialistische Deutsche Arbeiterspartei—Nazi for short), adopted a striking party emblem, the swastika, and insisted on "Heil" as an obligatory greeting between party members meaning "Hail."

In addition, he issued a manifesto demanding abrogation of the Versailles Treaty, denial of German citizenship to Jews, confiscation of war profits, and profit sharing in industry. For

party rallies—where Hitler discovered he had an ability to work up an audience to a frenzy—he recruited burly veterans to put down hecklers. Uniformed in brown shirts, dark trousers and high black boots, they became known as Storm Troopers and, like Mussolini's Black Shirts, relished brawling in the streets with toughs of the Left.

In 1923 the French army occupied the Ruhr, Germany's industrial heart, claiming that Germany had defaulted on reparations. Outraged, the government ordered passive resistance and workers everywhere walked off their jobs. Giving the workers financial support, the government began printing millions, then billions and finally trillions of marks. The mark's value plummeted by November to four billion to the dollar. Scenes of Germans pushing barrows heaped with marks to buy a bag of potatoes became common. The government moved to stop the drain on the economy: it called off the resistance and resumed reparations. But it was also forced to place the country under a state of emergency.

During this crisis, Hitler seized an opportunity in Bavaria, which had long been separatist in sentiment. Suspecting the Bavarian government might use the crisis to break with Berlin, Hitler staged a Nazi takeover. The chance presented itself when the government held a meeting for civil servants in a large Munich beer hall. Hitler burst in, accompanied by former World War I ace Hermann Göring and a bodyguard of Storm Troopers. As they set up a machine gun, Hitler leaped onto a table and fired a revolver shot into the ceiling.

"The national revolution has begun," he shouted. "This hall has been surrounded by 600 heavily armed men. The Bavarian and National governments have been removed and a provisional government formed. The army and the police barracks have been occupied; troops and police are marching on the city under the swastika banner."

Although Hitler assumed a baleful air on the public platform, his manner in Munich's salons could charm and disarm. In the short span of two years, he moved from anonymity to celebrity in Munich.

The astounded audience did not know it, but this was pure bluff. Waving his revolver, Hitler forced the government officials into a nearby room, while Göring took over the crowd, shouting, "You have your beer, keep drinking! You have nothing to worry about." Meanwhile an envoy had been sent to General Erich Ludendorff—the famed First Quartermaster General of Germany's wartime armies and a dabbler in rascist and nationalistic theories—to persuade him to join the *putsch*, or attempted coup d'état.

When the General entered the beerhall, the Bavarian officials agreed to appear with him and Hitler in a show of unity. The crowd cheered and the officials left, presumably to order the police and troops to join the uprising. Instead one official ordered local radio stations to broadcast that the state had repudiated the *putsch*.

The next morning, Hitler and Ludendorff marched through Munich, followed by 2,000 cheering Storm Troopers and sympathizers. A skirmish with police ensued; Hitler was arrested and tried for treason. At the trial, in a single sentence, he touched a painful chord in German memories as he declared, "There can be no question of treason that aims to undo the betrayal of a country." The trial took 24 days, and all Germany's attention was riveted on it. Hitler later described the failure of the *putsch* as "the greatest stroke of luck in my life."

Imprisoned in Landsberg Fortress, Hitler served only nine months of a five-year sentence, and there wrote *Mein Kampf* (My Struggle), in part a blueprint of his future plans. It was to serve as the Nazis' bible. Eight more years would elapse before Hitler became dictator of Germany.

After his parole from prison in December 1924, he set himself two goals: to strengthen his party and to attain power by legal means. Both took longer than he expected. For five years Germany enjoyed a period of prosperity, thanks in part to large loans from foreign banks and an easing of reparations. The election of the highly respected Field Marshal Paul von Hindenburg as President added to the country's stability.

In September 1930, the Nazis won 107 seats in the Reichstag, Germany's parliament, a block second only to the leading Social Democrats. The world was by now in the grip of depression. The United States, still reeling from the effects of the 1929 stock market crash, no longer had bank loans to offer. Germany was hit hard. By 1932, many businesses were in ruins, more than 6,000,000 Germans were unemployed, and farmers were losing their lands in forced sales. As social tensions rose, the Nazis and Communists gained at the expense of the moderate center.

In the July 1932 election Hitler scored his greatest elec-

High above the crowd, standing apart even from aides and officials, Adolf Hitler (left) and Benito Mussolini gaze down upon a 1938 Fascist rally in Rome. Both men were magnetic leaders, and instinctive politicians, operating from a foundation of masterful contrivance and studied manipulation.

22

toral victory to date. The National Socialists won 230 seats out of 608—the largest block, though not a majority. But Hitler was in desperate straits. His campaigns had all but bankrupted his party. At this juncture, a group of big industrialists, alarmed at the deteriorating political situation, offered to pay the Nazis' debts—in return for Hitler's promise to keep his hands off industry once in power. Pressure was then put on Hindenburg to make Hitler Chancellor. "The Bavarian corporal"—as Hindenburg contemptuously called Hitler—accepted. But Hitler demanded a new election, calculating that with his new prestige as Chancellor the Nazis would win a majority.

In February 1933, as the new campaign got underway, the Reichstag building was set on fire. A feeble-minded Dutch Communist, Marinus van der Lübbe, was caught at the scene, confessed to arson and was later beheaded. Hitler exploited the incident with diabolical brilliance. Claiming the fire was a signal for a Communist uprising, he persuaded Hindenburg to issue an emergency decree annulling all civil rights. Hermann Göring, now the Prussian Minister of the Interior, rounded up 4,000 Communists, using Storm Troopers deputized as auxiliary police.

Despite the recourse to terror, the Nazi party still failed to win a majority, though its seats were increased to 288. Hitler proclaimed a Nazi victory, and two days later rose in the Reichstag to demand immediate passage of an act that would enable him to rule by decree for four years. It was approved with 94 Social Democrats dissenting—24 of whom were subsequently murdered. Three months later the opposing party was banned, and its seats in the Reichstag vacated. By summer 1933, all other parties were outlawed and most of Hitler's opponents were in jail, exile or concentration camps.

All over Germany, Hitler paid off old scores. Ernst Röhm, for example—Hitler's old Munich comrade and the ambitious leader of the powerful Storm Troopers—had been incautious about his ambition. His aim was to merge the Storm Troopers with the regular army, with the whole under his command. On June 30, 1934, Röhm was shot by the black-coated *Schutzstaffel* (protection squad), whose members were bound by a personal oath of loyalty to Hitler.

Meanwhile, Hitler's blood purge continued. Officially it was announced that 74 enemies of the state had been executed and three forced to commit suicide for plotting mutiny and rebellion. Later evidence put the toll much higher.

The effect was to shock the German people into total obedience. On August 2, Hindenburg died. Hitler, now 45, was proclaimed President. In a subsequent plebiscite 38,360,000 Germans voted to ratify his assumption of power. The Nazi reign was under way.

2

Turning points in world history are seldom recognized except in retrospect. The 1930s were marked by several such historical watersheds. The decisions taken—or left untaken—during those years by the League of Nations so weakened its moral authority that its demise was inevitable. And with its death would die, for that era at least, the hope that the rule of law would prevail in international affairs. As one disillusioned critic suggested in 1935, a new sign should have been erected over the portals of the League: "Abandon half, all ye who enter here—half your territory, half your prestige."

The incident had been contrived with some care. On the night of September 18, 1931, a small charge of dynamite exploded in the marshaling yards of the Japanese-owned south Manchurian Railroad just outside of Mukden, the capital of Manchuria. Ostensibly aimed at damaging a Japanese troop train, the bomb did little damage, for a train soon passed over the tracks. But the explosion, set off by Manchurian agents of the Japanese, served its purpose. It offered an excuse for feigned outrage—and for the Japanese army that was protecting Imperial interests in Manchuria to swarm over the country.

Lying between Siberia and Korea, Manchuria was a land of great riches, with vast deposits of iron and coal among other treasures. Although part of China, the territory had long been coveted by Russia and Japan, and both countries held zones of special interest there. But the Japanese wanted more. Overcrowded on their home islands, short of farmland and natural resources, they planned to seize all of Manchuria, turn it into a buffer state between Russia and their Korean holdings, and unlock its riches for themselves.

When the Japanese struck southern Manchuria, seizing towns and communications centers immediately after the Mukden incident, Chiang Kai-shek, Generalissimo of all China, at first counseled a policy of no resistance. He announced that China would take its case to the League of Nations. It was a policy that might have restrained the Japanese if any one of the major powers had been prepared to espouse China's rights. Unfortunately, none was. At the League's faraway headquarters in Geneva, the Japanese representatives insisted that they had acted only to restore order, that they had no territorial ambitions and that they would most certainly withdraw once safety of life and property had been assured. In February, however, Manchuria was proclaimed a separate nation under the protection of Japan.

The League appointed a commission to investigate the affair. When the commission finally reported in 1932, it flatly condemned Japanese aggression. Japan, however, had no intention of apologizing or surrendering what it had gained. When the other nations at Geneva accepted the report, the Japanese walked out and quit the League, then boldly began pushing their Manchurian invasion farther into the interior toward the Chinese provinces of Jehol and Chahar.

Chiang was stunned by the League's impotence, and he quickly concluded that only a China unified under his command could hope to expel the Japanese invaders. The idea of one China with himself as its leader was nothing new for Chiang; it had long been his most ardent goal. As chief of the Nationalist Party, he had for years been fighting to suppress the Chinese Communists, who fiercely rejected his

A WORLD IN TURMOIL

Launching their campaign against China, Japanese scramble up the Great Wall, built in the Third Century B.C. to ward off marauding northern tribes.

rule. But Chiang had suspended his anti-Communist campaigns when the Japanese invaded Manchuria and he had appealed to the League. Now, he resumed the offensive with particular zeal.

Communist-held areas were encircled by fortified lines of pillboxes and machine guns; a blockade was established to cut off all shipments and communications between the interior and the coast. Within their tightening perimeter at the city of Juichin, one group of Communists held on under the leadership of a professional soldier named Chu Teh and a rising young intellectual known as Mao Tse-tung. They were joined there by another senior member of the so-called All-China Soviet, Chou En-lai.

Chiang's full-scale campaign squeezed the Communists harder than ever before—one estimate places the number of soldiers and civilians killed or starved to death at the astounding total of one million. By mid-1934, they were forced to a painful decision: try to break out of the Nationalists' fortified ring at the cost of heavy casualties or remain and face a slower but more certain death.

In October of that year 100,000 men and 35 women, led by Mao, Chou and various Communist generals, packed their belongings and set off on what became known as the Long March—a military exploit that made Hannibal's march over the Alps, as one observer put it, look like a holiday excursion. They traveled well over 6,000 miles in 368 days on foot, crossing 18 mountain ranges and 24 rivers, breaking through the enveloping armies sent after them by Chiang. They found the sanctuary they were seeking in the fastness of Shensi Province in central China. Their success, however, was bought at a terrible price: of the roughly 100,000 who began the march, fewer than 20,000 finished it. The

survivors, moreover, found themselves in a new home as remote, as primitive and as poor as any in all China. Here, hopefully awaiting other bands of Communist survivors, they settled down to begin once more the rebuilding of the Chinese Soviet state.

The Communists might not have been able to survive in their new base, remote as it was, except for significant changes that were taking place elsewhere. Each new Japanese advance in the north brought a renewed hatred of Japan, and Chiang's countrymen increasingly questioned why Chinese should be killing Chinese while the Imperial emissaries of the Rising Sun—Japan—were biting into their country and swallowing it piece by piece.

The controversy culminated in a bold strike by Marshal Chang Hsueh-liang, commander of the Nationalist legions, who strongly protested orders to attack the Communists. The Marshal and his colleagues kidnapped Chiang in order to reason with him from a position of strength. The result was an agreement in December 1936: Chinese Nationalists and Communists would negotiate to end the civil war, and make preparations for a joint armed struggle against Japan.

The agreement did not produce a signed declaration of war against Japan, but the Japanese read the portents quickly and accurately enough. The general of Japan's Manchurian army warned that if Nationalist China did not join his country in opposing Communism he would take "all the steps necessary to assure peace." By then, however, the Nationalist and Communists, much as they distrusted each other, had begun negotiations to end the civil war and make preparations for a joint campaign against the Japanese.

Those hostilities broke out in a matter of months—on July 7, 1937. A Japanese company on a training exercise near the Marco Polo bridge at the walled town of Wanping outside Peking attempted to search the town for a missing company member. The Chinese garrison refused entry, and the Japanese opened fire. Soon a minor battle was on. At first the fight seemed a containable scuffle, but it soon blazed into a full-scale war.

Using the skirmish as an excuse, the North China Japanese Command sent a punitive expedition to attack Peking. Waves of aircraft droned over North China, bombing and strafing everything that moved on the roads. Columns of infantry led by tanks rumbled across the plains, seized Peking and Tientsin, breached the strategic Nankow Pass and the Great Wall of China, and fanned out south down rail and highway routes to the Yellow River. The Chinese troops, long on manpower but still short on coordination, tactics and modern weapons, turned to the Soviet Union for help. Within weeks, China signed a nonagression pact with its

China's leader, Chiang Kai-shek (standing) was a former protégé of the great Nationalist revolutionary, Sun Yat-sen (seated); the close relationship between the two is suggested in this 1924 portrait. The son of a middle-class salt merchant, Chiang had risen to the top of the Nationalist military establishment and assumed control of the Kuomintang, as the Nationalist Party was called. When Sun Yat-sen died in 1925, Chiang came to power.

DISMEMBERMENT OF THE MIDDLE KINGDOM

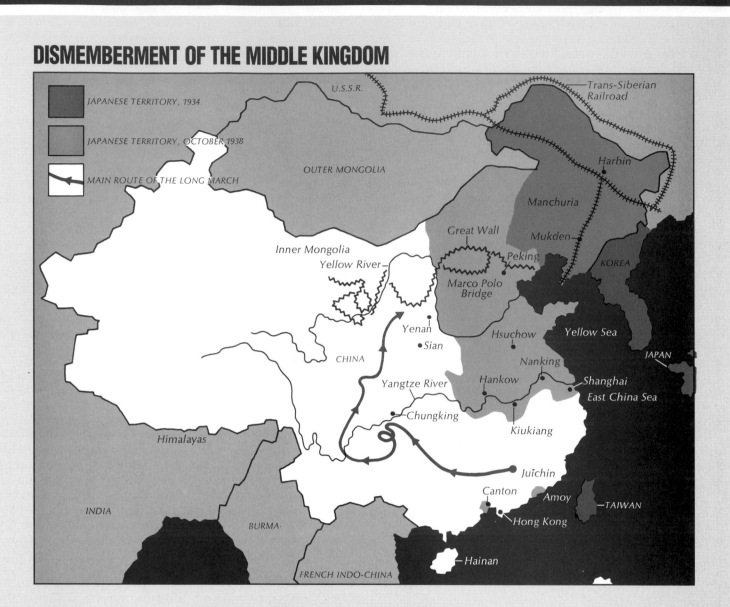

China in the 1930s was a wounded giant, torn by a civil war and a foreign invasion that engulfed the populous central, southern and eastern areas of the country, traditionally called the Middle Kingdom by the Chinese.

When the decade began, Chinese were already fighting Chinese. Communist rebel troops had stopped Nationalist government offensives led by Generalissimo Chiang Kai-shek. But in 1934 Chiang's forces trapped the Red Armies in the southeastern city of Juichin. The Communists broke out and, to escape annihilation, set off in an epic retreat called the Long March. This desperate journey

began in October, and covered a serpentine track of 6,000 miles through central China. The march ended a year later with the establishment of Red strongholds outside Yenan near a section of the Great Wall (serrated line).

Meanwhile, the Japanese, who had ruled Korea and Taiwan (dark red) since 1895 and had an army strung out along the rail line running south from Harbin, began to move. In 1931 its army, virtually unopposed by the Chinese, who were busy fighting each other, occupied all of Manchuria. The Japanese moved again in July 1937. This time, the invasion, which started with a firefight at the ancient

Marco Polo Bridge near Peking, turned into a full-scale war, a Far Eastern preview of Hitler's blitzkrieg.

In the first six months, Japanese troops pouring across the Great Wall captured Peking and sacked Shanghai and the Nationalist capital at Nanking. The Japanese went on to take the ports of Amoy and Canton and a second Nationalist capital at Hankow. By the decade's end, the Nationalists had retreated up the Yangtze Valley to the city of Chungking, leaving in Japanese hands a swath of newly conquered territory (light red) larger than France, Germany, Spain and Italy combined.

Communist neighbor, complete with secret clauses promising China airplanes, munitions and other aid.

For Japan, early hopes of forcing surrender by a single overwhelming strike vanished. Although one after another of the cities fell and Chinese armies suffered casualties running in the hundreds of thousands, the forces kept fighting, falling back and fighting again.

Chiang's withdrawal kept his battered army reasonably intact. But it also left a large part of the nation naked in the face of an increasingly ruthless foe. In December, the Japanese marched into the virtually defenseless city of Nanking and reduced it in sadistic fashion. For sheer butchery, the rape of Nanking ranks among the most appalling outrages in history. Twenty thousand Chinese men of military age were marched out of the city and used for bayonet practice, machine-gunned or doused with gasoline and set on fire. Perhaps 20,000 women and girls were raped, killed or mutilated. By the time it was over, more than 40,000 unarmed Chinese had been slaughtered.

The Japanese officers, who talked of bringing a Japanese-inspired "renaissance" to Asia, had intended the massacre to terrify the Chinese into making peace. The plan failed; Chiang spurned negotiations with Tokyo. As the months passed, it became obvious that he intended to retreat and defend until the Japanese, overextended and exhausted, defeated themselves—or until the United States, Britain or other powers could be drawn into war on his side. But despite lobbying, the United States' fear of involvement in a foreign war proved too strong: the most that could be mustered officially was a token loan of $25 million.

The Japanese tried to pursue and destroy Chiang's forces. But the enormous expanse of China, served by only a threading of dirt roads, swallowed up the advancing Japanese troops. China became a quagmire for the Imperial Army. The more deeply Japan became involved in China, the more sharply Tokyo found itself in collision with the West—especially with the United States, which had long nurtured a special fondness for China.

Although frustrated by a costly stalemate in a land of over 400 million people that bent and bled and burned but would not break, the island-born Japanese hung on too. Yet at last they began to turn their eyes to the easier and more alluring prizes that lay far to the southeast.

The failure of the League of Nations to fulfill its mandate as a just and powerful arbiter had cost China 2 million casualties. Many League members began to wonder which country would next pay the price. Even in Geneva, the home of the League, the organization was viewed by many as a futile debating society.

There was, however, on September 11, 1935, in Geneva, at least one League representative who still believed that it might be possible to inject some new life into its crippled body. When Sir Samuel Hoare, Britain's Foreign Secretary, spoke before the League, representatives of 54 member nations listened in growing surprise. In a flat, matter-of-fact voice, all the more impressive for its tonelessness, Hoare summoned the League to live up to what Woodrow Wilson had envisioned for it—a group of nations that would act in concert to deter and, if necessary, punish aggression. Hoare brought his hand down sharply on the podium as he asserted: "Britain stands for steady and collective resistance to all acts of unprovoked aggression!"

In the thunderous applause that followed that pledge, only Italy's envoy, Baron Pompeo Aloisi, sat silent. Though Hoare had not identified the aggressor in his speech, there was no question in anyone's mind which nation he meant: Benito Mussolini's Italy.

In fact, Benito Mussolini had not bothered to conceal his designs on Africa's major independent country, Ethiopia. Despite Italian sacrifices in World War I, at the peace table Italy had been "left only the crumbs from the sumptuous colonial booty of others," as the Duce saw it. That wrong, Italy's dictator determined, would be righted—and Ethiopia would be his test case. Even as Hoare spoke, 300,000 of the Duce's soldiers stood ready to move in as soon as the June-to-September rainy season ended.

The members of the League were well aware of Mussolini's ambitions, yet they drew new hope from the Foreign Secretary's words. Most delegates agreed with the Belgian representative that there could be but one interpretation of Hoare's remarks: The British have decided to stop Mussolini, even if that means using force. Even the representative of the Soviet Union—which had joined the

The machinations of three men helped weaken the League of Nations, shown here in session. France's Premier Pierre Laval (center) and Britain's Foreign Secretary Sir Samuel Hoare (right) sought to deter the Duce from further aggression by confiding to Italy's League representative Baron Pompeo Aloisi (left) a secret plan for carving up Ethiopia and giving Italy a conquest without added bloodshed. It was an arrangement nobody really liked: Mussolini felt Italy needed a war to gain world respect; and when the scheme leaked, Laval had to step down, as did Hoare. The British cabinet member was widely criticized in England; his countrymen called him, among other things, "Slippery Sam."

The Japanese generals who took time out to toast the early success of their China campaign in 1937-1938 drew their jubilation not only from the quick rout of a numerically superior enemy, but from deep cultural roots. By the very act of fighting they were fulfilling the ancient role of samurai.

League only the year before—proved less wary than usual. "This assembly," he ventured to predict, "may become a landmark in the new history of the League." Yet even while the representatives discussed the day with optimism, Hoare sat in his hotel suite, reading and rereading his speech, puzzling over why it had evoked so fervent a response. By his own later account, all he had meant to do at the League was to bluff Mussolini into calling off his war; Britain had no intention of resorting to arms. The bluff turned out to be one of diplomacy's more dismal failures. Within three weeks, Mussolini's legions would advance into Ethiopia.

At dawn on October 3 the Duce's forces, striking south from Eritrea, moved into Ethiopia. Banners and blaring trumpets gave the expedition a festive air. On the eve of the invasion, Mussolini had addressed a cheering multitude in Rome: "Not only is an army marching, but forty million Italians are marching in unison." Should the League take action against Italy, he was prepared. "To sanctions of an economic nature we will reply with discipline, with sobriety and a spirit of sacrifice," he shouted. "To sanctions of a military nature we will reply with war."

The League's response was uncharacteristically fast and firm. By an overwhelming vote a week later, it branded Italy an aggressor—the first such action in League history. At first glance, the recommended sanctions seemed properly punitive. League members were to halt all arms exports to Italy, cancel all financial transactions and stop buying Italian goods. But the sanctions did not include closing the Suez canal, which would have stopped the venture cold, since

Italy's primary access to Ethiopia lay through the waterway. Moreover, the list of trade items to be denied Italy were ludicrous in some respects: camels, mules, donkeys and aluminum, a metal Italy produced in abundance. Yet there was no embargo on such fundamental materials of war as coal, iron, steel and, above all, oil.

As finally approved, the sanctions represented little more than a slap on the wrist. But Mussolini seized upon them to spur his people to greater effort. He invited voluntary contributions of gold; in nationwide ceremonies, Italians exchanged gold wedding rings for bands of steel.

The Duce had even further cause to be gratified. The opening months of the Ethiopian campaign had gone exceedingly well. Just before the war's outbreak, Emperor Haile Selassie had pulled out all his border forces in hope of avoiding provocations. Italian columns had easily taken objective after objective. One victory was especially gratifying to the invaders. At Adowa, in 1896, another Ethiopian emperor had inflicted a stunning defeat upon another Italian force bent on conquest. The "shame of Adowa," as it came to be called in Italy, was erased only three days after the war began. The town yielded under an onslaught it had no way of stopping: bombing from the air. By early December Italian columns were 80 miles inside Ethiopia, albeit temporarily halted. To reach the capital, Addis Ababa, roads needed to be built to accommodate the heavy artillery and mechanized equipment of warfare.

The diplomats, meanwhile, were not idle. Perhaps, they thought, Mussolini might be amenable to ending the war

BARON POMPEO ALOISI   PIERRE LAVAL   SIR SAMUEL HOARE

now—provided the terms of a settlement appeared attractive enough. On Saturday, December 7, Hoare, on his way to a holiday in Switzerland, visited France's Premier Pierre Laval. By the time they parted on Sunday evening, a plan had been hatched to persuade Mussolini to cut short his Ethiopian venture. They were confident of success; private talks with Baron Aloisi, the Duce's representative at Geneva, had given them grounds for optimism.

Under the proposal, 60,000 square miles of Ethiopia would be ceded to Italy outright. Another 160,000 square miles, virtually the southern half of the country, were to be "reserved" as an Italian "zone of economic expansion and settlement." Ethiopia would get an outlet to the Red Sea—and if Mussolini balked at having this corridor carved out of his new holdings, either Britain or France would allow it to run through their own neighboring colonies.

The plan was meant to be kept secret until approved by the French and British governments, the belligerents and the League. But alert French journalists got wind of it, and by Monday it was making headlines around the world. Word of the scandalized reaction reached Hoare in Switzerland. Gliding around an ice rink, he fell and broke his nose. "Too bad it wasn't his neck," one former admirer remarked.

For the plan's coauthors, the reckoning came quickly. Both men had to resign their posts. Hoare surrendered the seals of his office to King George V—only to receive the unkindest cut of all, in the form of a royal joke. "You know what they're all saying," the King told him. "No more coals to Newcastle, no more Hoares to Paris."

The odds against Ethiopia in a war were evident from the start. To counter Italy's planes, tanks and enormously superior firepower, Ethiopia's major weapon was manpower—mostly untrained. Emperor Haile Selassie's mobilization order read: "Everyone will now be mobilized, and all boys old enough to carry a spear will be sent to Addis Ababa. Married men will take their wives to carry food and cook. Those without wives will take any woman without a husband." To those who disobeyed, there was a dire warning: "Anyone found at home after receipt of this order will be hanged."

In mid-January of 1936, after two months of road-building, the Italian forces resumed their advance on Addis Ababa. As the fighting heated up, the League was deluged with complaints of violations of the "rules of war." The Italians accused the Ethiopians of mutilating and decapitating the soldiers they killed, and of firing prohibited dum-dums—bullets that expanded on impact with shattering effect. The Ethiopians accused the Italians of using poisonous mustard gas, sprayed over the ground or dropped

Self-assured Italian infantrymen armed with rifles and carrying ammunition, dismounted machine gun barrels and tripods, march up an Ethiopian hill.

in bombs. But a League investigation became moot in early March, when Ethiopian resistance suddenly crumbled and the war came to an end.

On June 30 Emperor Haile Selassie appeared in Geneva at a special session of the League Assembly convened at his request. He had managed to get safely out of Ethiopia three days before the fall of Addis Ababa in May. Small and thin, a black cloak around his shoulders, he looked too frail to bear the weight of his array of titles: Conquering Lion of the Tribe of Judah, Elect of God, King of Kings, Emperor of Ethiopia. He spoke in Amharic. Almost at once a group of Italian journalists in the visitors' gallery rose to jeer and whistle him down—as the Duce had instructed them to do. Amid the tasteless furor, the Rumanian delegate demanded, "throw the savages out." Haile Selassie remained silent and motionless while this was done. He then resumed his speech.

He spoke for 45 minutes, combining a detailed review of the war and an impassioned appeal for justice. It was destined to go unheeded. Two weeks later the League called off sanctions against Italy.

But Haile Selassie's words remained to haunt League members. What was now essentially at stake, he said, was international morality, the confidence that any nation could place in any treaties, the value that small states, in particular, could attach to promises that their integrity and independence would be respected and ensured.

"It is us today," he said. "It will be you tomorrow."

Less than a month after Haile Selassie's portentous speech before the League in Geneva, still another event took place that was to bring Europe one step closer to world war. General Francisco Franco landed in Spanish Morocco to command 24,000 rebel troops in an uprising against the left-wing government of the five-year-old Republic of Spain.

Although fought on the battlefields of Spain, the Spanish Civil War was to offer a dress rehearsal not only for new weaponry and tactics, but for combat by some of the major actors in the global catastrophe to come.

In faction-ridden Spain, violence and injustice had long been facts of life. As the 1930s began, 7,000 absentee landlords in one large rural part of Spain controlled 60 per cent of all arable land, while millions of landless peasants barely subsisted. Faced with a potential uprising, King Alfonso XIII's regime agreed to general elections in 1931. As a result, a so-called Republican government came to power with a mandate to sweep out the monarchy.

Neither factionalism nor violence died with the advent of the Republic. Within four years, Spain was completely split. On the Left, the Republicans had the backing of socialists, trade-unionists, Communists and various liberal splinter groups; on the Right were Army leaders, die-hard monarchists, Falangists (a right-wing movement resembling Italian Fascism), landowners and Roman Catholic parties.

Under parliamentary pressure, the government held general elections in February of 1936, and the Left was returned to power. But a round of political assassinations soon followed. When on July 13, José Calvo Sotelo, parliamentary leader of the Right, was murdered, his supporters urged the military to overthrow the Republic. In fact, the generals were nearly ready.

Among the leading plotters in the military, General Francisco Franco was a man with a chilling reputation. As commander of the Spanish Foreign Legion in the 1920s he had seemed a living embodiment of the Legion's motto: "Down with Intelligence! Long live Death!" Now in the uproar over the murder of Sotelo, he called for the defense of the "Unity of the Motherland" and flew to Spanish Morocco to assume command of the Army of Africa.

The rebels' plan called for Franco's fellow conspirator in the north of Spain, General Emilio Mola, to dispatch his men south toward Madrid. Franco himself would lead his forces across the Mediterranean and enter Spain from the south, where key cities in the southwest and parts of western Spain were already sympathetic to the rebellion. The two armies would close in on either side of the capital. If Madrid fell early, Republican resistance everywhere would be crushed, ending the war. But as Franco cautiously predicted, the conflict was to be "difficult, bloody and last a long time."

Of the 165,000 men in the Spanish Army, approximately 30 per cent—mostly of lower rank—remained loyal to the government; and when the enlisted men of Spain's Navy were ordered to take up arms against the Republic, they refused. Two days after the first shots of war were fired, 98 per cent of the officers on all ships at sea were dead. The Navy, now commanded by committees of crewmen, clamped a blockade on the Army of Africa.

With Franco's Army of Africa trapped in Morocco, the rebels—or Nationalists as they were now called—could make no significant march through Spain. Franco appealed to Mussolini and Hitler for help, and was amply supported by both men. For example, by August, 30 German transport planes were airborne for Morocco, followed by six fighter aircaft—the nucleus of the so-called Condor Legion, an air and ground force composed entirely of Germans. Soon large numbers of German technicians and flyers arrived in Spain wearing civilian clothes and carrying tourist passports to get

Defiance burns in the eyes of this exhausted Ethiopian prisoner, a member of Haile Selassie's elite Imperial Guard. Marshal Pietro Badoglio, the Italian commander, gave these troops credit for "a remarkable degree of training combined with a superb contempt for danger."

them through Loyalist territories and into areas under Nationalist control.

The Loyalists—as those loyal to the Republic were called—also sought foreign aid. France, in an early, but short-lived, burst of support, supplied 200 planes and some ground weapons. The United States and Britain contributed only relief food and clothing. Russia sent the Loyalists 550 men and at least 240 planes, 1,200 guns and 700 tanks. In return Madrid shipped its gold reserve, more than $315 million, to Odessa.

In addition, a surge of Loyalist foreign volunteers arrived as part of a combined force called the International Brigades. These were made up of men recruited throughout Europe, the United States and Canada, with most of the organization coming from Communists who furnished the Brigades with the bulk of their senior officers. Eventually 40,000 people bore arms in the Brigades, including 3,000 Americans of the Abraham Lincoln Brigade.

In late September of 1936, bolstered by German and Italian airpower, Franco was able to ship his Army of Africa into southern Spain. He was sworn in as Nationalist head of state on October 1, and signs appeared immediately at Nationalist outposts: "One State. One Country. One Chief." Firmly in power, Franco began moving his Army toward Madrid. In the city itself, frightening posters went up: "At Badajoz the Fascists shot two thousand. If Madrid falls, they will shoot half the city."

General Miaja, the commander in defense of Madrid, spoke bluntly to his deputies: "Madrid is at the mercy of the enemy. The moment has come in which you must act as men! *Machos!* I want those who stay with me to know how to die." As the Nationalists launched their assault, Miaja's orders reached the streets: no retreat except to the cemetery.

For one critical day, Miaja was able to hold off the enemy. Then on November 8, reinforcements from the International Brigades entered the city and the resistance hardened. As Franco's troops struck on the ground, Hitler's bombers assaulted from the air. But the German bombs had the effect on Madrid that they would have later on other European cities; they stiffened rather than broke morale. *¡No pasaran!*—They shall not pass!—became the Loyalist slogan.

At the end of March 1937, Franco acceded to the stubbornness of Madrid and called off the attack. For nearly two years he would keep the city under attack. But he acknowledged that his efforts for a quick knockout had been thwarted—and that he needed a new plan to win the war. The strategy he chose was attrition—to swallow up territory until virtually all Spain was under his rule; he could then overwhelm remaining Loyalist territory with siege and concentrated attack.

In April, as the Nationalists moved north, the Condor Legion began using the Basque country as a testing ground for such new techniques as the combined use of incendiary and high-explosive bombs. Bilbao and Durango were hit first, but the nearby town of Guernica became the most celebrated bombing target—and a symbol of total war.

Guernica, a town of about 7,000 people, had two small munitions plants. At 4 p.m. on April 26, two nuns rang a warning bell and called, "*¡Aviones! ¡Aviones!*" (Planes! Planes!) Above was a group of Heinkel bombers, one of which dropped 550-pound bombs into a crowded plaza. "A group of women and children," according to one survivor, "were lifted high into the air, maybe twenty feet or so, and they started to break up. Legs, arms, heads and bits and pieces flying everywhere."

Eight more waves of planes came over the town before dark. Although 1,600 people were killed and 900 wounded, neither munitions plant was hit by the German bombers, whose equipment was too primitive to permit accuracy. Sympathizers outside Spain, shocked by news stories of mass civilian deaths, brought charges of indiscriminate destruction. Berlin sent strict orders to the Condor Legion "to 'hush up' about the raid." Propagandists for Franco hinted that the town had been leveled by Basque dynamiters. In Paris, Pablo Picasso began work on the classic painting, *Guernica,* which was destined to become a talisman for the adherents of Republican Spain.

There followed months of bitter fighting as the Nationalists continued to gain the advantage. In the early spring of 1938, the Germans were persuaded to get more involved in the Franco army's strategy and tactics. They decided to experiment with a coordinated tank and aerial assault, and to throw their tanks in as a unit instead of being split up among infantry divisions according to old-fashioned military doctrine.

Attacking east from Teruel, recently recaptured from the Loyalists, the German panzers tore through Republican lines. The German 88mm gun, which was to earn a reputation as perhaps the most effective field weapon of World War II, made its debut; in one encounter it knocked out three Republican tanks in three minutes. On April 15, the Nationalist troops reached the sea at Vinaroz, splitting Republican Spain into two isolated wedges of land.

As their holdings diminished, the Loyalists tried one more offensive in July, attacking south across the Ebro River. The assault failed, leaving 70,000 Loyalists killed, wounded or captured. In besieged Madrid, the daily food ration was now two ounces of lentils, beans or rice per person. Realizing the futility of further fighting, the Loyalist government announced on September 21 that it was willing to withdraw

Staring eyes and gaping mouths of Spanish children who were killed during a bombing raid on the city of Madrid lend a terrible reality to this Republican poster that says: "Murderers! Who upon seeing this would not take up arms to annihilate Fascism?" Atrocity scenes were also used as propaganda by Franco's Nationalists—who, for example, printed posters that showed priests and nuns being beaten by Republican thugs.

1943 *(continued from inside front cover)*

JUNE

13 – Axis forces defeated in Tunisia; African campaign concluded

22 – German U-boats withdrawn from North Atlantic; Battle of Atlantic won by Allies

30 – U.S. retakes Attu

JULY

5-17 – Huge tank battle at Kursk on Eastern Front

9 – Allied invasion of Sicily

24 – Allies bomb German installations in Norway; Allies begin saturation bombing of Hamburg

25 – Mussolini overthrown and arrested, succeeded by Pietro Badoglio

AUGUST

5 – Soviets recapture Orel and Belgorod, in drive to Dnieper River, last major German defensive line in Soviet territory

6 – Japanese defeated in naval battle of Vella Gulf, Solomon Islands

14-24 – Roosevelt and Churchill meet in Quebec City for Allied Quadrant Conference

17 – Allies complete conquest of Sicily

23 – Soviets retake Kharkov

SEPTEMBER

3 – Allies land on Italian mainland across Strait of Messina

8 – Italy makes peace with Allies

9 – Allied landings at Salerno, Italy

10 – German forces occupy Rome

12 – Mussolini freed by S.S. Captain Skorzeny and taken to Germany

17 – Germans withdraw from Salerno

22 – Soviet secure first bridgehead across Dnieper

24 – Germans retreat from Smolensk on Eastern Front

OCTOBER

1 – Allies capture Naples

4 – Allies gain control of Corsica

13 – Italy declares war on Germany

14 – Canadian forces take Campobasso

18 – U.S., British and Soviet Foreign Ministers meet in Moscow

NOVEMBER

1 – U.S. forces invade Bougainville in Solomon Islands

7 – Kiev liberated; German defenses on Dnieper begin to crumble

20 – Allies attack across Sangro River in Italy

21 – U.S. troops land on Makin and Tarawa in Gilbert Islands

22-26 – Roosevelt, Churchill and Chiang Kai-shek meet in Cairo to plan Allied operations in Asia

28-**DECEMBER 1** – Roosevelt, Churchill and Stalin meet in Tehran to plan invasion of France

DECEMBER

3-7 – Roosevelt, Churchill and Chiang Kai-shek resume meeting in Cairo

24 – Eisenhower named to direct invasion of Europe

26 – U.S. forces land at Cape Gloucester in Solomon Islands

1944

JANUARY

16 – Eisenhower appointed Supreme Commander of Allied forces in Europe

22 – Allies establish beachhead at Anzio, Italy

25 – Chinese forces begin counteroffensive in Burma

27 – Soviets defeat Germans at Leningrad

29 – U.S. landings on Admiralty Islands

31 – U.S. landings on Marshall Islands

FEBRUARY

3 – Allied offensive in Italy stalls at Cassino

7 – U.S. forces take Kwajalein in Marshall Islands

15 – Allied bombing of Monte Cassino; Soviets reenter Estonia

18 – U.S. naval air forces cripple Japanese installations on Truk Island, in Caroline Islands

MARCH

8 – Japan launches major offensive in Burma

15 – Japan invades India

30 – RAF air raid on Nuremberg

APRIL

10 – Soviets recapture Odessa in Ukraine

15 – Soviets take Tarnopol in Ukraine

22 – U.S. forces land on Hollandia, Dutch New Guinea

MAY

9 – Soviets recapture Sevastopol

18 – Germans withdraw from Monte Cassino

23 – Allies break out of Anzio beachhead

JUNE

4 – Allies enter Rome

6 – D-Day, Allied landings in Normandy

9 – Soviet forces attack Finland

15 – U.S. bombs Tokyo; U.S. troops land on Saipan in Mariana Islands

19-20 – Japanese fleet defeated in Battle of the Philippine Sea

22 – Soviet offensive in Belorussia begins; Japanese retreat from India

27 – Allies liberate Cherbourg, France

JULY

9 – British enter Caen, France; U.S. forces complete capture of Saipan

18 – U.S. troops liberate St-Lô, France

19 – Tojo Cabinet resigns

20 – Attempt on Hitler's life fails

21 – U.S. invades Guam in Mariana Islands

25 – Allies begin breakout of Normandy

28 – Soviets retake Brest-Litovsk, Belorussia

29 – Soviets reach Gulf of Riga in Latvia

AUGUST

1 – Polish patriots revolt in Warsaw as Soviet armies approach city

10 – U.S. forces complete occupation of Guam

11 – Germans withdraw from Florence

15 – Allied landings in southern France

16 – Allies liberate Falaise in northern France

21 – 60,000 Germans trapped by Allies in Argentan-Falaise pocket

22 – Japanese complete withdrawal from India

23 – Rumania surrenders to Soviets

25 – Paris liberated; Allied troops begin attack on Gothic Line in Italy

SEPTEMBER

1 – Dieppe liberated

3 – Brussels liberated

4 – Antwerp liberated

5 – Soviet Union declares war on Bulgaria

8 – Armistice between Soviet Union and Bulgaria; Bulgaria declares war on Germany

12 – Rumania signs armistice with Allies

17-26 – Disastrous Allied airborne operation to seize control of river crossings in Holland and across Lower Rhine

19 – Armistice between Finland and Allies

25 – Allies break through Gothic Line in Italy

OCTOBER

2 – Germans crush revolt in Warsaw while Soviet armies pause and refit a few miles away; Allies penetrate West Wall into Germany

5 – British land in Greece

14 – British enter Athens; Rommel commits suicide

20 – U.S. landings on Leyte in Philippines; Belgrade taken by Soviet forces and Yugoslav partisans

23 – Allies recognize de Gaulle as temporary head of provisional French government

23-26 – U.S. naval forces inflict calamitous losses on Japanese navy in Battle of Leyte Gulf

NOVEMBER

7 – Roosevelt wins fourth term as U.S. president

28 – Antwerp opened to supply ships